Database Management
Theory and Application

Database Management
Theory and Application

John C. Shepherd
Duquesne University

IRWIN

Homewood, IL 60430
Boston, MA 02116

We recognize that certain terms in this book are trademarks, and we have made every effort to print these throughout the text with the capitalization and punctuation used by the holder of the trademark.

© RICHARD D. IRWIN, INC., 1990

Senior sponsoring editor: *Lawrence E. Alexander*
Developmental editor: *Rebecca J. Johnson*
Project editor: *Waivah Clement*
Production manager: *Carma W. Fazio*
Designer: *Image House*
Artist: *Benoit Design*
Compositor: *J.M. Post Graphics, Corp.*
Typeface: *10/12 Palatino*
Printer: *R.R. Donnelley & Sons Company*

Library of Congress Cataloging-in-Publication Data

Shepherd, John C.
    Database management : theory and application / John C. Shepherd.
      p.   cm.
    ISBN 0-256-07829-7
    1. Data base management.   I. Title
    QA76.9.D3S534 1990
    005.74—dc20
                                       8927933
                                         CIP

Printed in the United States of America
1 2 3 4 5 6 7 8 9 0 DO 7 6 5 4 3 2 1 0

PREFACE

INTENDED AUDIENCE FOR THIS BOOK

Database Management: *Theory and Application* is appropriate for an applied programmer/analyst–oriented course in database management. It is recommended that students have had at least one COBOL course, as this is the language used in the examples. It is also beneficial if students have already developed sequential and random access programs, which provide a basis for comparing the traditional file-processing methods with the database approach.

This book is best suited to those courses emphasizing database application programming from an applied but thorough approach. It covers each of the three data models (relational, network, and hierarchical) in great detail and describes the theoretical basis for each.

For those courses that take a more managerial, database administration approach, Parts I, II, and VI, which deal with database and design concepts, will be of most benefit. Parts III, IV, and V discuss the data models, beginning with the theoretical foundation of each model, and contain numerous programming examples.

PURPOSE OF THIS BOOK

Today's database environment is changing. For the first time, there is a preferred database methodology and language: the relational approach and Structured Query Language (SQL). However, as recently as early 1989, there were more than three times as many commercial sales of network and hierarchical database packages. Some current texts ignore these models or cover them in just a single chapter. Thus, students may not learn how to develop applications with the network and hierarchical database products used by more than 15,000 organizations.

Using many years of experience as a DBA and many more as a programmer using a database management system (DBMS), I provide intensive coverage of actual commercial packages so that students can use the text as a reference after graduation. For example, instead of merely saying that a program should check for error codes after invoking the DBMS, I provide actual values to be checked. When I worked in this field prior to entering the teaching profession, no books on the market offered appropriate coverage of commercial packages. When faced with the task of developing a program that used a DBMS, students either had to read vendors' reference manuals or attend training sessions in order to gain even a rudimentary knowledge about how to write such programs. This book attempts to fill that vacuum.

FEATURES

Specific features of this text include:

- *A carefully constructed foundation for each of the three data models.* Part I, which discusses the theory behind database management, builds a foundation for the three parts devoted to the data models. Chapter 3 on data structures is particularly complete. All of the database management systems discussed in this book use a data structure for their implementation. By studying data structures, students are better prepared to understand how the packages work, how they are implemented, and why they must be used in the manner described.

- *At least two chapters devoted to each model.* The first chapter opening each model-related part introduces the concepts behind the model and how to define the database. The second chapter shows how to manipulate the resulting database. The relational model will eventually be so dominant that current texts might be able to successfully get away with eliminating a discussion of the network and hierarchical models. The early-1990 reality, however, is that thousands of organizations are still using applications written to take advantage of database systems built on these two models. Parts IV and V provide thorough coverage of the CODASYL network and hierarchical models.

- *Pedagogical symmetry for each data model.* In addition to the traditional sections on data storage and retrieval, the chapters devoted to each model contain sections on data integrity, data backup and recovery, and transaction processing. This enables students to compare and contrast all three models.

- *Integrated microcomputer coverage.* The hierarchical and network parts contain an integrated section, while micro-based versions of relational packages are discussed in Chapter 14.

- *Skills-oriented approach.* This book includes more programming examples for each model than any current text. Whenever possible, I have tried to illustrate more than just a few lines of code. It is vital that students be able to use a DBMS after they graduate. Only by seeing many complete examples can this be accomplished.

- *Fourth-generation language coverage.* One of the database trends I have observed from my consulting work is the tendency of organizations and software developers to use SQL in concert with a fourth-generation language (4GL). Chapter 8 on embedded SQL and Chapter 14 on data efficiencies discuss how SQL can be used in such an environment. While most database applications are written in COBOL, the relational approach requires new languages to fully exploit its power.

- *Managerial coverage.* The human element in database management cannot be ignored. The roles of the database administrator (DBA), programmer, analyst, and end user are clearly defined throughout the text. For example, Part II is oriented toward the database administration function, and Part VI discusses where the database market is headed. Finally, each of the three data model–related parts includes thorough coverage of the model's concepts in a program-free context.

- *Up-to-date information.* Writing a text about a topic as dynamic as database is quite a task. Over the course of a couple of years, a text goes through several drafts. In many subject areas, changes to texts from draft to draft are often aimed at correcting grammatical, organizational, and conceptual errors. This wasn't the case with this book. Each new draft had to be updated to include new topics. For example, the DB2 coverage was updated for the final time less than one month after the most recent IBM version was released, and the discussions about database machines, distributed databases, and 4GLs reflect research and developments that were less than a month old when I wrote the last draft.

- *Chapter-opening cases.* Many chapter-opening cases illustrate what *not* to do or how the concepts discussed in the chapter could have been used to avoid the problem presented in the case. In this text, each case includes a series of discussion questions to help prepare students for the chapter that follows. Two of the cases are integrated throughout the text so that students can compare problem solutions using a package from each data model.

- *Chapter objectives.* After each opening case, the chapter proceeds with behavioral objectives that students should be able to achieve after reading the chapter. Very few texts in this market provide chapter objectives for students to test themselves.

- *An integrated case.* Based on over seven years of consulting in the hospital industry, I developed an integrated case study, Community Hospital, which demonstrates how to implement concepts discussed in the particular chapter. Several of the case episodes demonstrate a complete COBOL program that illustrates how a DBMS is used. By placing this material in a case format, I could illustrate all the "messy" details without getting bogged down in the chapters. The case approach also offered a unique opportunity to show how an application might look if programmed using a package from each data model.

- *Solved problems.* Most chapters contain numerous problems and accompanying solutions. This technique has proven an effective learning device, as it lets students see how to apply a concept to solve an actual problem. In many cases, the same problems are used in different chapters so that students can see how the problem is solved for each model.

- *Annotated bibliography.* The bibliography at the end of the text contains many references, several of them annotated.

ORGANIZATION

Part I introduces students to the database approach, data, data relationships, and data structures—the mechanisms for implementing data relationships. Because the structures are stored on disk drives, instructors might find it useful to supplement Part I with Appendixes A and B.

Part II covers the design of a database. Chapter 4 presents an approach for developing the conceptual design, a model of the organizations' entities and the relationships among them. The major thrust of this chapter is a discussion of normalization, a technique originally designed for the relational approach that is applied to all of the data models. This approach has seldom been taken, but it makes the chapter applicable regardless of the data model being covered in class. Chapter 5 shows students how to map the conceptual model to one compatible with the organization's DBMS and how to physically implement the transformed design using a data structure.

Part III covers the relational model, probably the most important model in this book. Chapter 6 discusses relational algebra. This method for manipulating relational databases has proven an effective way for students to grasp the concept of set-at-a-time versus the more conventional record-at-a-time processing to which they have become accustomed. This chapter also includes a highly comprehensive discussion of Query-By-Example, an IBM-developed approach that lets end users easily manipulate a relational database. Chapters 7 and 8 discuss Structured Query Language, first in an interactive mode and then embedded in COBOL and 4GL programs. Learning SQL before studying other database management languages can be somewhat misleading. What SQL can do in one statement, the network and hierarchical models would require more than twenty. It may be beneficial to assign the parts out of sequence, saving the easiest for last, so that students can better appreciate the power and benefits of the relational approach.

Parts IV and V discuss the network and hierarchical models, respectively. Both models had their origins in the 1960s and are significantly more complex than the relational approach. Part IV uses the industry standard DBMS developed by CODASYL as the basis for the discussion. The Community Hospital continuing case shows how Cullinet's IDMS/R package, the market leader for the network model, differs from the standard.

Part V discusses IBM's hierarchical package, IMS. As of early 1989, there were still more than twice as many IMS installations as relational ones, so these chapters are particularly important.

Part VI is devoted to management of the database. Chapter 13 discusses the duties and responsibilities of the database administrator (DBA), the individual usually responsible for database management. This chapter also returns to some topics addressed in Chapter 1: concurrency control and backup and recovery. Chapter 14 illustrates some of the current trends in database management, including how organizations are organizing their data for more efficient access.

By distributing the data to the end users, data communications costs as well as response time can be reduced. Another way to gain efficiency is to use a dedicated machine that performs the data access operations, a device usually referred to as a *database machine.* The final technique for improving the efficiency of data retrieval is the use of a 4GL. Two such packages are discussed in the chapter.

ACKNOWLEDGMENTS

I wish to acknowledge the assistance given to me by Cullinet and IBM, both of which provided me with reference materials and answered my questions relating to their database packages. I also want to thank ALCOA for assisting me with the IMS portion of the text. Finally, I wish to express my gratitude to the dedicated reviewers of this text, without whom this book would not have been possible:

James Benjamin
Southern Illinois University
at Edwardsville

Ralph Bisland
University of Southern Mississippi

Norman Brammer
Colorado State University

Helen Casey
Sam Houston State University

William Cornette
Southwest Missouri State

Ralph Duffy
North Seattle Community College

Carl Friedman
University of the District of Columbia

Alden Lorents
Northern Arizona University

Laurie MacDonald
Bryant College

Don Musselman
James Madison University

Richard Ramirez
Arizona State University

Shannon Scanlon
Henry Ford Community College

Steven Schindler
Kent State University

Glenn Smith
James Madison University

Marguerite Summers
Murray State University

Elizabeth Unger
Kansas State University

Susan White
Catonsville Community College

Peggy Wingo
Richland College

John C. Shepherd

C O N T E N T S

PART

I

Database Fundamentals

Part I of this text builds on database fundamentals. In Chapter 1, we first look at what constitutes a database system. Then we examine the primary characteristics of the database approach, along with the tools, techniques, and procedures for developing information systems. Next, we discuss the differences between the traditional, nondatabase approach to information system design and the database approach. We illustrate the problems that arise with the traditional approach and then show how the database approach alleviates most of them. As we step from problem to problem, we build a list of database advantages and disadvantages. Finally, we look at the role of each component of the database system. Probably the most important component is the software that manages the database: the database management system (DBMS). The remainder of the chapter summarizes the subsystems of a DBMS.

The first episode in the continuing case study of Community Hospital follows Chapter 1. You will find these episodes periodically throughout the text, placed after specific chapters to reinforce the main points of that chap-

ter. Episode 1 introduces us to the organization of the hospital and to a new request for information made by the board of directors.

Chapter 2 looks at the characteristics of data, the object that a DBMS manages. First, we examine the concepts of entities and their relationships. Next, we look at data integrity, security, independence, and the three major data models: relational, network, and hierarchical.

Episode 2 of the continuing case follows. The dominant theme is how the hospital adopted the database approach and developed a list of entities and their relationships.

In contrast to Chapter 2, which is concerned with the logical relationships among objects, Chapter 3 examines how those relationships can be physically implemented. First, we look at pointers—mechanisms for relating data to other data. Then we examine eight data structures—the actual relationships—and see how to use and produce them. This is an important chapter, because both the network and hierarchical models make substantial use of data structures; the relational model's reliance on the structures discussed in Chapter 3 is minimal.

1

1

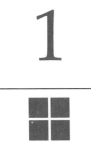

Database Overview

MINICASE Hi-Teck Information Systems

Hi-Teck Information Systems, a contract programming organization, has been using its accounts payable system for three years. Megan and Christopher are programmers and have just been called to a meeting by their project manager, Michelle, to discuss problems Hi-Teck is experiencing with the system. Michelle wants to tell them about the new hardware about to be installed.

Michelle opened the meeting: "Thanks for coming. I'd like to start by describing the new disk drives we're about to install and the changes we need to make to the accounts payable system."

As Michelle began describing the new drives, Megan's mind wandered back to the last time Hi-Teck had installed new drives. Because the drives had a higher track capacity and more tracks per cylinder than the previous ones, she had to change every one of her programs that used random access. It took her three months, and she ended up having to make changes to programs that weren't even hers! The problems caused by

upgrading still plagued her. Just last week, she had been called in because the end-of-year routines had abnormally ended (ABENDed). She hoped the new upgrade wouldn't cause such problems.

Michelle continued, "Another problem is that John Reese [accounts payable manager] has been bugging me for over three months to add four new columns to his accounts payable aging report. I stalled him as long as I could until you two finished up that payroll system. Megan, I want you to find out which programs use the VENDOR master file, because that's the file we will have to add the new fields to. Don't limit your search to just the payables system, though. I know other systems probably use the file too."

Michelle then turned to Christopher. "Chris, John also wants a new report by Friday. I want you to create a new file. Extract most of the fields from the VENDOR, APOPEN, and INVENTORY files. Then add new fields for period-to-date units used and dollars used. Since he wants the new report every month, create a new program that dynamically extracts the data from the existing files I just mentioned, adds the new ones, and then generates the new file. That way, every month the new file will automatically be updated as part of the monthly processing."

Michelle concluded the meeting by telling Megan and Chris to plan on another meeting to discuss their progress on Tuesday at 9:00 A.M.

Discussion

1. Where might Megan look to determine which programs use the VENDOR file?

2. What's wrong with Megan's thinking that the VENDOR file belongs to her and with Michelle's saying that the accounts payable system belongs to John?

3. What kinds of changes might Megan have had to make to her programs when the disk drives were last upgraded?

4. What are the disadvantages of creating a redundant file as Michelle is suggesting to Chris?

5. Give some alternatives to the redundant-file approach.

As we progress through Chapter 1, we will see that Megan's problems are due largely to the fact that Hi-Teck doesn't use a database system for its information processing. More specifically, her problems are due to two of the major problems associated with the more conventional information systems (IS) processing methods: several kinds of redundancy and a lack of data independence.

At the conclusion of the chapter, you will be able to:

- Describe the database approach to data and information management and control.
- Recognize the problems that arise from the nondatabase environment.
- Discuss how the database approach solves these problems.
- Explain the objectives of the database approach.
- Discuss the advantages and disadvantages of the database approach.
- Describe the responsibilities of programmers, analysts, database administrators, users, and the database management system with respect to the database approach.

1.1 DATABASE SYSTEMS

This text explores **database systems**—cost-effective methods for storing, organizing, retrieving, and managing data. Conventional methods have proven costly, error prone, inflexible, and susceptible to security invasions, but the results of using a database system have been just the opposite. A database system is cost effective in the long run, possesses inherent data error elimination methods, provides great flexibility, and has mechanisms that ensure a sound security environment even when many users simultaneously share the same data.

Figure 1.1 shows that a database system is composed of six subsystems:

- Database
- Database administrator
- Database management system
- Application programs
- Users
- Hardware

Once the enterprise makes a total commitment to using a database system, it usually hires a **database administrator (DBA)**. Through policies and procedures created by the DBA, information systems management, internal auditors, and end users, the DBA receives the responsibility and authority for managing all of the organization's data. More specific duties include ensuring the security and integrity of data, installing and maintaining software known as the **DataBase Management System (DBMS)**, educating programmers, analysts and end users concerning use of the DBMS, and resolving conflicts that arise due to data sharing.

One of the arrows in Figure 1.1 shows the DBA entering commands to help manage the database. These commands are interpreted by database utility programs. Typical tasks of such programs are reorganizing the database, fixing damaged records, and optimizing the database for better performance.

The **database** is a collection of related records stored with a minimum of redundancy that many users can share simultaneously. The records contain data about entities, items in the organization's environments, and are stored on a disk drive, sometimes called a **direct access storage device (DASD)**, and controlled by the DBMS, which in turn is managed by the database administrator.

Over the last 20 years, three distinct data models have evolved. For our purposes, a **data model** consists of the permissible relationships among different types of records within the database, as well as a set of tools for operating on the records. The models are known as the **relational**, the **network**, and the **hierarchical** (or *tree*). There is also a minor database management model known as the **inverted** family.

Certainly the DBMS is one of the most important database subsystems. A DBMS has at least two components: a **data description language (DDL)**, which defines fields, records, and relationships among the different types of records, and a **data manipulation language (DML)**, which application programs use to store and retrieve data in the database. Many DBMSs include a third component: the **data control language (DCL)**, which is responsible for data security. The organization can also acquire optional utilities for improving database performance and repairing damaged databases, report and query generators for ad

FIGURE 1.1   **A Model of a Database System**

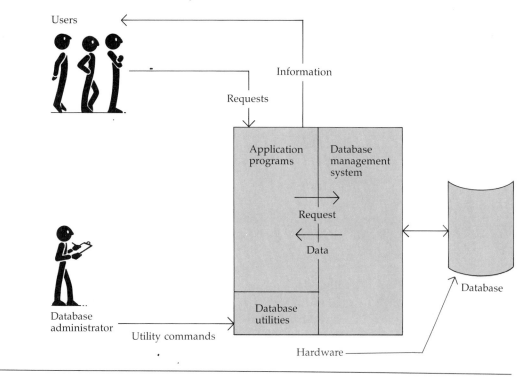

hoc reporting needs, and a **data dictionary**—a program that cross-references items such as fields, records, files, programs, and information systems.

An application program that accesses the database through calls to the DBMS is called a **host program**. There are at least three categories of host languages. The first is **third-generation**, or **procedural**, **languages** such as COBOL. The second is **fourth-generation**, or **nonprocedural**, **languages** (4GLs) which allow end users to specify *which* data they want without having to specify *how* to retrieve it. The third is **query languages**, which are similar to 4GLs but are limited in their hard copy reporting capabilities and usually require some programming skills to use them. Despite the hype over 4GLs, most of today's application programs are still written by programmer/analysts using the third-generation languages. This text is concerned mainly with how to develop information systems using the third-generation language COBOL.

In this chapter, we will first consider what the database approach is and its advantages and disadvantages. Next, we will examine some of the problems that arise from using the conventional application-specific, file-oriented information systems development techniques and see how the database approach attempts to remedy them. We will also consider some of the problems that can arise even after adopting the database approach. Then we will examine the roles of the DBA, analysts, programmers, end users, and the DBMS in solving these problems.

The next section describes the database approach to information systems development, focusing on the sharing of a centralized database among all end users throughout the organization.

1.2   THE DATABASE APPROACH: SHAREABILITY AND COOPERATION

Three distinct features characterize the database approach to information and data processing:

- Shareability of data
- Centralized data management and control
- Adaptability

Shareability of Data

Probably the most important characteristic of the database approach is the storage of data in a centralized repository—a database—to which all potential users are permitted access. Sharing of data enables employees to exchange ideas and work toward common organizationwide goals and objectives. This feature reduces the tendency for users and user groups to become "islands of information"—separate self-sufficient entities who are often unwilling or unable to share data with one another.

Shareability means that end users must adopt an attitude of cooperation. Unless they are willing to cooperate in the process of sharing data for the good of the organization, the approach is doomed to failure. Unfortunately, most end users, and even many IS professionals, feel that data belongs solely to them and no one else should have access to it. We saw this attitude in the minicase, in which Megan thought of the VENDOR file as hers. Such an attitude must change if the database approach is to succeed. The database approach, therefore, attempts to foster an attitude of sharing and cooperation, rather than the self-centered view that often results from conventional data management techniques.

Centralized Data Management and Control

All users—including programmers and analysts, in addition to the end users of data within the functional organizational units—must be willing to accept centralized management and control of data. The organizational unit having this control is the **database administration** function and is usually managed by the

DBA. Although it often is difficult for users and IS employees to relinquish this control, the database approach requires that the database administration unit be the custodian of the database or databases. Disputes can and will occur as more and more users share the same pool of data. However, centralization enables the DBA to be impartial toward individual departments' needs and to make decisions that are in the best interests of the entire organization.

Adaptability

Finally, the database approach is adaptable to change because it allows users to easily relate existing data items to other data items as quickly as they change their minds. Much of its flexibility comes from the fact that the database approach forces us to look at the data needs of the overall organization, rather than at the reporting needs of individual applications. The DBA—or another employee, the *data modeler*—attempts to model the relationships of all, or most, of the entities within the organization, even before anyone requests reports from the data. This is in direct contrast to the traditional approach, in which analysts first focus on the reporting needs of particular user groups or applications and then develop the information systems around those needs.

Refer back to Chris's problem in the minicase. He needs to produce a report in less than a week. The report requires the extraction of existing fields from several files and the addition of some new ones. The problem is that the designer of the existing system didn't foresee the new report; hence, the data was spread across several files and, in some cases, didn't exist at all. However, if the database approach were followed, all the necessary data would already be stored and readily accessible.

Because the central database is shared and data can easily be related to other data, new requests are readily assimilated into the existing database. As the database grows, new requests become even easier to accommodate because more data already exists within the database.

1.3   FILE PROCESSING VERSUS THE DATABASE APPROACH

File processing is the term associated with data management techniques that focus on the informational needs of individual applications and make little or no attempt to relate files or records to one another except as specific applications require. Organizations that use this approach to develop information systems are likely to encounter several problems, some of which are presented in Figure 1.2. We will now discuss these problems and how the database approach attempts to solve them.

FIGURE 1.2   Problems Associated with Using Traditional Data and Information Processing Techniques

1. Distributed ownership
2. Redundancy
3. Inability to easily respond to ad hoc reporting needs
4. No data independence
5. Excessive costs

Problem 1: Distributed Ownership

Distributed ownership, also called the **"my-file" attitude**, refers to the belief that individual files belong to a specific application, department, or user. We saw this attitude in the minicase, where Megan viewed the programs she was asked to change as belonging to her. Such an attitude can lead to at least two detrimental side effects: redundancy and islands of information.

Redundancy. When file processing techniques focus on data specific to individual applications, it is only natural for end users and IS employees to feel that data belongs to the department for which it is collected, entered, and processed. Thus, when a new application is being developed, programmers and analysts, like Michelle in the minicase, frequently create completely new files and programs even if both are readily available in other applications.

Islands of Information. A second and perhaps even more troublesome problem is the fact that user groups develop their own data environments, which are independently maintained. Like an island, the users often become self-sufficient and cut off from others, willing to neither share nor receive information. The organization suffers because information is not disseminated and faulty decisions are made. Only by sharing data can employees cooperate in accomplishing organization goals.

Database Solutions. Whereas advocates of distributed ownership view data as belonging to an individual application or department, supporters of the database approach consider data an organizational asset and believe that any disputes about usage and ownership should be resolved by the manager of that data: the DBA.

> Database Advantage 1: Shared data

If the organization has a single individual with sufficient authority and responsibility to manage its data, departmental disputes over ownership should not arise. When questions about departmental data collection, processing, or sharing arise, the DBA will resolve them in the best interests of the organization, rather than for a single department, regardless of corporate politics.

> Database Advantage 2: Centralized control

Problem 2: Redundancy

Redundancy is the duplication of fields and files, especially across applications. Such duplication causes many problems. Consider those which Chris faces in the minicase when he is asked to create a new file that is to contain many of the fields from existing files as well as several new ones. He has only two choices.

The first is to add the new fields to the existing files and then use the updated files for both the current and new applications. While this approach will control redundancy, it also requires that Chris be sure that the old reports will continue to be correct and that all other systems using the original files will also be changed to accommodate those files' new structure.

The second choice is to extract the desired fields from the old files and integrate them with the two additional period-to-date fields into a clearly redundant file that will conform only to the needs of the new application. Unfortunately, most programmers choose the second alternative, and that leads to the proliferation of redundancy.

Costs of Redundancy. One problem with redundancy is that it wastes disk space because the same field is carried multiple times. Furthermore, each occurrence of the field means that an analyst, a programmer, a data entry clerk, and a computer are all involved in getting that data to the disk. Each additional time the data is processed, the monetary costs associated with these resources will increase.

Another major problem with redundancy is the possibility of *"multiple versions of the truth,"* a term meaning that inconsistent data exists. If decisions are made based on such data, they may be costly—and often incorrect. For instance, consider the accounts payable system mentioned in the Hi-Teck minicase. Assume the system contains a VENDOR master file that carries a vendor number, name, address, and phone number and an APOPEN (Accounts Payable Open) file that carries an invoice number, invoice date, terms, vendor number, and number of items. Notice that the vendor number appears in both files. Now the purchasing department calls to inform accounts payable that a wrong vendor number was assigned to a vendor and provides the correct value. A clerk immediately changes the vendor number in the VENDOR master file but fails to do so for all the matching APOPEN records. Both files now contain a different vendor code value for the "same" vendor; both "think" they have the correct value, but invoices paid based on the incorrect vendor number can result in the proper vendor not being paid or a vendor receiving payment to which it isn't entitled.

Database solutions. The database approach to redundancy is quite simple: It eliminates it or at least *controls* it. The best way to control redundancy is to start the database development process with a conceptual design that will reduce redundancy to the lowest possible level.

First, rather than focusing on the reporting needs of a single application, the database approach takes a broader view that considers the enterprise's *entities*: things, events, and people within the organization. For Hi-Teck, the entities might be vendors, invoices, due dates, and employees. Characteristics of entities are called *attributes*; for example, the attributes of a vendor might include number, name, phone number, and so on.

Next, each entity is transformed into a record and each attribute into a field. Notice that fields are thus independent of specific applications, as they are assigned based on the DBA's understanding of which characteristics define an entity.

The next step is normalization, which is a design procedure that not only helps reduce redundancy, but also the likelihood of the occurrence of some specific data-related problems, called **anomalies.** As part of the normalization procedure, new records can evolve and fields may be transferred from existing records to the new ones. When we discuss normalization in Chapter 4, you will see that redundancy isn't eliminated, but it is controlled.

> Database Advantage 3: Redundancy control

Once the physical database is in full use, data items will be stored a minimum number of times—ideally once. The fewer the number of replications of data, the more likely it is that the data will be correct. Along with a reduction in costs, redundancy control results in improved consistency, accuracy, and reliability of data—all characteristics of **data integrity**.

> Database Advantage 4: Improved data integrity

In addition to controlling redundancy to help eliminate data integrity problems, the organization may use **referential integrity constraints**. Such constraints might instruct the DBMS to not permit the altering of the vendor code of a record in the VENDOR master file if there are any related records in the APOPEN file or, if the vendor code in the VENDOR file is changed, to automatically update the vendor code value for the related APOPEN records.

One reason redundancy occurs is users' fear that sharing data will make security breaches more likely. This is a reasonable fear with conventional file processing methods, which contain no inherent security mechanisms. As a result, users want to retain data ownership, forcing new applications to develop redundant files. However, most DBMS packages provide for passwords that can be applied to fields, combinations of fields, conceptual files, DML commands, and even complete databases. These passwords make it impossible for unauthorized users to access the database.

> Database Advantage 5: Improved data security

Problem 3: Inability to Respond to Ad Hoc Reports

The next difficulty in using traditional, file-oriented processing methods is the inability to quickly respond to unplanned-for reports. With the traditional approach, analysts usually begin their projects by focusing on the end user's reporting requirements. Next, they design the inputs necessary to generate the data to be printed. Finally, they design the programs. This approach severely limits the flexibility of the resulting systems in general and of the files in particular.

Files designed this way meet very specific reporting needs, rather than simply modeling the organization's entity relationships. As we saw earlier, entities are elements in the organization's environment. *Relationships* are associations among these entities. For example, among the entities vendor, invoice, and due date, we can say that vendors send invoices and invoices are due on specific due dates.

Figure 1.3 shows one way to model these relationships. The rectangles are called **conceptual files**, and the lines represent the relationships. In the figure,

---

FIGURE 1.3   **An Example of How to Model Relationships among Conceptual Files**

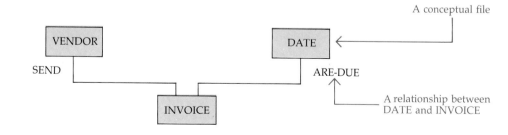

A VENDOR can SEND many INVOICEs, and on a given DATE many INVOICEs ARE-DUE.

---

all relationships are one-to-many; for example, one VENDOR can send many INVOICEs, and an INVOICE is related to no more than one VENDOR.

Database Solutions. The database approach begins by developing a **conceptual database**—a diagram that accurately describes the organization's entities and the relationships among them. Sometimes the conceptual database is called a **schema**. It is important that this database be developed independently of the reporting needs, the DBMS, and the hardware. To accomplish this, the DBA considers every possible entity within the organization and then indicates how each entity relates to the others.

The result of this process is a diagram like that in Figure 1.3, but much more complicated, which models all the data requirements within the organization and eventually is converted into a physical database by the DBA through the DDL portion of the DBMS. Hopefully, by following this approach, the DBA will create a thorough conceptual database that will quickly and easily respond to any reporting needs that arise.

> Database Advantage 6: Flexible conceptual design

In practice, developing a conceptual database for the entire organization is usually too complicated. As a result, most organizations have resigned themselves to the fact that several databases will exist. Some organizations design the conceptual databases around applications, but this has the same limitations as the conventional application-oriented approach. The best alternative may be to have the DBA develop functional databases; for example, there might be a financial database, a marketing database, and so on. Yet another approach is to start with a conceptual database for the organization and simply divide the conceptual database into smaller parts.

> Database Disadvantage 1: Complex conceptual design process

Regardless of the approach used, the resulting database (or databases) is designed around the organization rather than around specific applications. Fortunately, end users can view just the portions of the conceptual database that they need. These views are called **subschemas**, **external databases**, or **user views**. Because individual users may not want all the record types, fields, or relationships found in the conceptual database, applications should allow them to choose only those items they need. These individual user views of the data may differ not only from one program to the next, but also from the conceptual database's view.

External databases are defined on the conceptual database, and they can be

FIGURE 1.4   **Two Possible User Views of Figure 1.3**

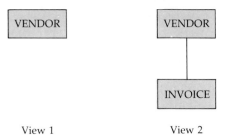

View 1   View 2

View 1 makes available only the records in the VENDOR file, while view 2 grants access to both VENDORs and INVOICEs and also relates the two conceptual files.

unlimited in number. This means that each end user is free to choose just those portions of the overall database important to him or her, provided the selected components (record types, fields, and relationships) are part of the conceptual database. This provides an extremely flexible way to adapt the existing data to the varying needs of users.

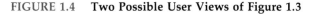

Database Advantage 7: Multiple external databases

Figure 1.4 shows two user views based on the conceptual database from Figure 1.3. Users of the first view can access only VENDOR records, while those using the second view can access records from both the VENDOR and INVOICE files.

Since the conceptual database models the actual data and its relationships in the organization, it should be able to respond to any reporting needs that arise because reports are nothing more than hard-copy (or displayed) representations of data and their relationships. By allowing end users to choose just the data and relationships they need, the database can meet the reporting needs of any situation.

Problem 4: Lack of Data Independence

The next negative characteristic of traditional file processing is the lack of data independence. The term **data independence** encompasses two ideas:

1. Fields can be added or deleted or their names or specifications changed without having to recompile existing programs. This feature is called **logical data independence**.

2. Changes can be made to the physical characteristics of the data, such as moving the data to a new disk volume or changing an indexed or keyed field, without affecting existing programs. This property is called **physical data independence**.

Logical data independence means that new fields can be added or existing ones deleted or rearranged without affecting existing programs. Naturally, this assumes that the programs don't reference the items that are deleted. Physical data independence permits a new index to be added or an existing one deleted, the access method for a file to be switched, a new disk drive to be acquired, or any other kind of change that affects the storage of the data to be made, all without affecting existing programs. Users should not need to know the underlying structure of the data.

Because data independence greatly reduces the need to make changes to existing code, it is often thought to protect the programming investment. As Megan found out, without data independence, when existing disk drives are replaced with ones having a different number of tracks per surface, number of tracks per cylinder, or a new recording density, it may be necessary to change a COBOL program's SELECT statements, JCL statements, and, most important, hashing routines used in a PROCEDURE DIVISION to locate records on the disk.

Database Solutions. One way the database approach shields programs from changes to data is to have all file and record definitions defined outside the application program. These definitions are coded by the DBA using the DDL portion of the database management system and become part of the data dictionary. As Figure 1.5 shows, the file and record definitions are compiled and converted into object modules by the DBA. Application programs must then include these object modules with the remainder of their code at link-edit time. After the programs are link-edited, they will contain the externally defined data descriptions.

The output of the DDL translation is a machine language module that defines all the records and the relationships among them. For instance, if the DBA changes a field's specification from PIC 9(4) to PIC 9(5), he or she will have to retranslate the DDL to create a new library member; then each application using the definition may have to be relinked. However, there would be no need to recompile any programs.

Another mechanism for enhancing data independence is the usage of external databases, or views. Recall that a view is a subset of a conceptual database and that it contains conceptual files. The fields in a view can be defined as subsets of the fields from the file or files on which the view is defined. For example, assume that a file in a conceptual database contains five fields, F1 through F5, and that the DBA has defined a view that is based on the file but contains only

---

FIGURE 1.5   Dynamically Including Data Descriptions in Application Programs

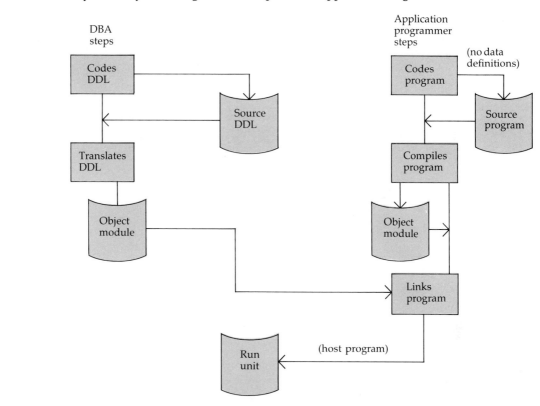

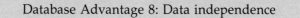

fields F1 and F3. If someone deletes field F2 from the original file definition, there will be no impact at all on programs using that view.

Database Advantage 8: Data independence

Problem 5: Excessive Costs

It has been estimated that 70 to 90 percent of the work in an IS department is expended on maintaining existing systems. This severely limits the amount of new development the department can do, causing large backlogs of projects waiting to be started. The database approach can relieve this backlog by reducing the amount of time spent on maintaining existing systems.

As we have seen, the traditional approach is characterized by redundant data and programs, programs and files that are not independent of the data's storage characteristics, and a certain amount of confusion among programmers as they attempt to adapt new reporting requirements to the old file structures. Compounding the confusion is a lack of adequate, up-to-date documentation that can cross-reference fields, files, and programs to one another. All of these factors lead to increased IS departmental budgets.

Database Solutions. We already covered the ways the database approach controls redundancy, how it provides data independence, and why it is adaptable to new requirements. All these features lead to substantial cost reductions.

> Database Advantage 9: Reduced overall monetary costs

However, the database approach brings some costs of its own. Some of these expenses are:

- DBA and staff
- Planning time
- DBMS acquisition
- Hardware
- More complex programming
- Potentially longer-running application
- Conversion
- Operations

First, the organization must hire a DBA and staff. Next, the DBA must design the conceptual database and plan how to implement it. This will require many hundreds of hours for both the DBA and users who participate in the process.

> Database Disadvantage 2: Need to hire database-related employees

Then the DBMS must be acquired. Mainframe versions of these packages range from $15,000 to over $100,000. In addition, there are hidden hardware costs; for example, extra main and secondary memory will be needed to accommodate the DBMS and resulting databases.

Next, programmers, analysts, and users must be trained to use the DBMS. Training costs are extremely high. To send an employee to a three- or four-day training course will cost at least $600 to $900 for the course plus $100 to $200 per day for lodging and meal expenses, not to mention the opportunity cost of lost work while undergoing training. An alternative is in-house training, but that too is expensive.

> **Database Disadvantage 3: High DBMS acquisition costs**

The DBMS also makes the testing step in the systems development life cycle (SDLC) more complex. Organizations cannot test programs and systems against the production database because of possible bugs within the programs. Instead, organizations maintain test databases for this purpose. **Test databases** contain either test data or a duplicate set of data from the live database. If the latter option is chosen, the test database must be altered as the live database is changed (new files added, field specifications changed, etc.).

> **Database Disadvantage 4: More complex programmer environment**

Once tested, the new application is allowed to access the production database. Unfortunately, there probably will still be bugs in the new application, even after thorough testing. Many logic errors can bring down the entire database and, along with it, all users accessing that database. With traditional methods, only one application is halted when a file's integrity is impaired. When a database fails due to a hardware or software error, instead of a single application being affected, all applications utilizing the database must be halted until the error is corrected—usually by the DBA.

This means that the database approach requires taking extra precautions when designing applications to ensure that programs are bug free. In the event the database is rendered unusable, the DBA will have to restore the database from a backup copy.

> **Database Disadvantage 5: Potentially catastrophic program failures**

As a program's complexity increases, so does the amount of time necessary to run the program. As a result, organizations often find that when applications are rewritten to use a DBMS, they take longer to execute. Because of this, they must acquire faster CPUs or disk drives. Also, because the DBMS is almost always memory resident, more memory might be necessary.

> **Database Disadvantage 6: Longer running time for individual applications**

Undoubtedly, as applications are converted to a new DBMS, there will be additional costs as data is extracted from conventional files and programs are changed to interface with the DBMS. These costs are also quite high and effectively tie up programmers who normally would be working on new systems.

> Database Disadvantage 7: High DBMS operations

As you can see, both cost savings and cost increases accompany the database approach. Many companies have adopted the database approach not because the quantifiable savings exceed the quantifiable costs but because they feel the unquantifiable benefits derived from more accurate, consistent, timely, and shared data far outweigh any costs. The trend today is for companies to become more dependent on the approach, not less.

Database Approach Summary

This section has described several characteristics of the database approach to information processing:

Data is an organizational asset managed by a database administrator.

The database approach controls redundancy.

Use of a data dictionary ensures consistent, accurate documentation and centralized data control.

The database approach permits shared access to data.

External data definitions and user views provide data independence.

The database approach brings a new way of thinking and some new tools that permit the control of redundancy, build flexibility into the data design, and centralize the control of data with a database administrator.

1.4   ROLES

At the beginning of the chapter, we outlined several subsystems that make up a database system. We will now focus on the functions of some of those subsystems.

Database Administrator

The database administrator is the person responsible for managing the organization's data. Although much of the actual data maintenance is done through applications, the DBA has the ultimate authority and responsibility for ensuring that the data is secure, accurate, and timely.

Specific responsibilities include building and maintaining the data dictionary, resolving disputes concerning data usage and control, training users, programmers, and analysts about database concepts, and designing and maintaining the conceptual and physical databases. In addition, the DBA monitors the performance of the database using utility packages and, based on the results of the monitoring, "tunes" the database for higher performance. Still another DBA responsibility is performing database backup and recovery operations.

Systems Analyst

The systems analyst must learn the new approach and adjust the way he or she customarily designs systems. After determining the user's informational needs, the analyst meets with the DBA to see if those needs can be satisfied using existing data relationships in the conceptual database or whether new data and relationships are necessary. The basis for this meeting will be the user's conceptual view that the systems analyst may have to design.

The DBA decides whether the user's view should be included in the conceptual database, or whether the proposed system will be better designed using traditional file processing techniques. If the DBA chooses the latter option, the analyst will resort to the conventional steps in the SDLC. If the DBA selects the former path, the analyst and the DBA will work together to assimilate the new entities and relationships into the existing database.

In addition to understanding topics such as report design, input design, and file design, the analyst must understand how to design the new system around the existing database and how to use user-oriented, report generation packages. But the analyst need not scrap all that he or she has learned about traditional file design, because not all new systems should be included in the database. Some systems will be of a one-time nature or just will not fit in with the IS department's objectives in some way and thus will not be included in the conceptual design. Such systems will be developed in the traditional ways.

Programmers

Programmers face the difficult task of writing the source code to actually interface with the database through the DML. This means that programmers must first learn the DML for the DBMS chosen by the organization. Using a DML requires that programmers be willing to learn and implement some new programming techniques. Also, while IS employees are fond of criticizing users who resist change, many of them balk at internal changes within the IS department. Therefore, the organization can expect some difficulties as they introduce these new techniques.

Using the DBMS also means programmers must go to the DBA for field names and specifications, be willing to strictly adhere to standards (something few people like to do), suppress creativity in writing file-handling procedures, and learn how to debug programs that access the DBMS when they end prematurely.

When a conventional program terminates unexpectedly, it is difficult to locate the exact instruction causing the problem because many languages do not specifically show the source statement that created it. Instead, the programmer must perform hexadecimal or octal arithmetic as he or she pours through a very large memory dump that shows the contents of virtually every byte in the program's memory partition. This is complicated enough, but when the program branches off into code written by the vendor of the DBMS, the process becomes even more cumbersome.

Users

Users provide the initial information the DBA uses to design the conceptual database. Because the database approach treats all users as equals, individual users often fear their own interests are not being served and hence refuse to cooperate. Users must agree to cooperate not only with one another, but with the systems analyst, programmers, and the DBA as well. As we saw earlier, unless this cooperation is guaranteed, the entire approach may be jeopardized.

User cooperation must be active rather than passive. Users must play an active role in designing their views, or the systems analyst or DBA will decide the entities and relationships for them—a situation that more often than not results in failure. It is very important that users be involved in the design of their databases just as they are in most of the other steps in the SDLC.

Users may also be responsible for learning a 4GL that will allow them to easily extract data. This may seem trivial, but getting users to take time away from their busy schedules to learn how to write programs is not an easy task.

The Database Management System (DBMS)

Throughout this chapter, we have frequently mentioned a DBMS that permits an organization to solve the problems associated with using traditional file processing methods. The database management system is a software package that allows users to define, maintain, and manipulate data stored within the database.

DBMS Components. DBMS packages have at least two major components: a DDL to define fields, records, and relationships among the records and a DML to manipulate the data. As we saw earlier, there may be a third component, which is responsible for data security: the DCL. Other optional components include query languages, utilities, and a data dictionary.

Data Description Language (DDL). The data description language defines the conceptual database and turns it into a physical database. Specifically it defines:

- All data items (type, specification, etc.)
- All record types (tables in the relational model)

- The relationships among record types (not in the relational model)
- User views, or subschemas

The DDL module is usually controlled by the DBA, but it may be the programmer/analyst's responsibility to develop the users' views.

Data Manipulation Language (DML). The data manipulation language consists of commands used by a host program to store, update, retrieve, or delete records from the database. As Figure 1.6 shows, the success or failure of a DML call is returned to the application in the form of an error status variable. Every time a host program calls the DBMS, it must check the value of the error status variable and take appropriate actions depending on its value.

Data Control Language (DCL). The data control language is used to grant rights to individuals as well as revoke them. A **right** is the individual or group privilege to perform a data manipulation operation. For example, through the DCL, the DBA might grant a clerk the right to access and delete INVENTORY records but not to change them. Should the clerk abuse the deletion (or any other) right, the right can be revoked.

Not all DBMS packages refer to these three components by these terms, and many combine the DML and DCL into a single DML. However, all DBMSs must be able to perform the same basic functions.

There are other DBMS subsystems that play a lesser role: query languages, utilities, and a data dictionary.

FIGURE 1.6   **Application/DBMS Interfacing**

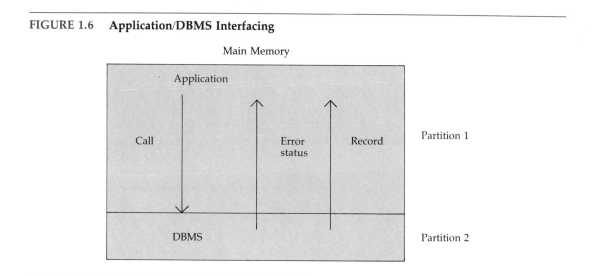

Query Languages. Query languages are usually extra-cost options that allow end users to produce simple on-line or batch reports with a minimum of interaction with the IS department. Unfortunately, the resulting programs often are inefficient and possess limited capabilities. Chapter 13 discusses the most popular query languages in greater detail.

Utilities. Utilities are special-purpose programs the DBA uses to:

- Assign passwords and security levels
- Backup the database
- Restore the database
- Monitor database usage and performance
- Tune the database

Chapter 13 discusses these features in detail.

Data Dictionary. Still another DBMS component is the data dictionary. Some vendors include this software package, while others charge extra for it. At a minimum, the DDL portion of the DBMS can be considered a skeleton data dictionary. Like the English dictionary that alphabetizes words, a data dictionary alphabetizes field names. Each file and field must be precisely defined, because all applications using the DBMS must use the correct names. Without such a dictionary, it would be impossible to write programs to process the data in the database.

The data dictionary also provides file information about items such as aliases, descriptions, volume of records, security needs, and names of the fields in the records. Field specifications might include type, length, editing criteria, and so on. Variations of the dictionary provide cross-references between fields and programs, programs and systems, records and programs, and programs and procedures. An excellent first project for IS departments that have just acquired a DBMS without a data dictionary is to develop a dictionary using the new software.

Figure 1.7 illustrates portions of various data dictionary components. Figure 1.7(a) shows an alphabetical listing of each field the DBA has defined. Programmers use this listing when coding their programs. Figure 1.7(b) shows a cross-reference listing of each field against the programs accessing it. Using this listing, a programmer can easily determine which programs must be changed when a particular field specification is altered.

Figure 1.7(c) illustrates a cross-reference between record names and programs. In the minicase that opens this chapter, had Hi-Teck used such a dictionary system, Megan would have little trouble finding every program using the VENDOR file Michelle has asked her to change.

The data dictionary often accompanies the DBMS when the system is initially purchased or leased. If not, a data dictionary must be acquired or developed at

FIGURE 1.7   **Sample Data Dictionary Functions**

(a) Field Definition Component of a Data Dictionary

Field	Description	PIC	Edit
C-ID	Customer number	X(10)	Check digit
C-PHONE	Customer phone number	X(10)	Bytes 1–3 = area code Bytes 4–6 = trunk number Bytes 7–10 = individual number
SS-NO	Social security number	X(9)	No hyphens

(b) Field/Program Cross-Reference Portion of a Data Dictionary

Field	Program	Program Description
C-ID	AR1004 AR1008 OM10 OM100	A/R edit A/R update Order entry Order edit
C-PHONE	AR1004 AR1008 AR1222 OM100	A/R edit A/R update Print statements Order edit

(c) Record/Program Cross-Reference Portion of a Data Dictionary

Record	Program	Program Description
CUST-REC	AR1004 AR1008 AR1222 OM10 OM100	A/R edit A/R update Print statements Order entry Order edit
ORDER-REC	OM10 OM100	Order entry Order edit

extra cost. Commercial data dictionaries range from $6,000 to $40,000. As you can see, they are not inexpensive; however, they are indispensable.

DBMS Features. DBMS packages contain some fairly standard features that enable users to describe the data relationships making up the database, store data in the database, and update and retrieve existing data.

High-Level Language Interfaces. Programmers usually process the data in the database via the standard high-level, third-generation languages with which they are already familiar: COBOL, FORTRAN, etc. The disk input/output operations are delegated to the DBMS through "calls" to machine language or assembler routines that are co-resident portions of the DBMS that share main memory with the application program (see Figure 1.6).

Another option is to embed the DBMS calls into a 4GL. Most vendors of relational DBMS products, such as Ingres, Informix, and Oracle, include a 4GL with their packages. Studies have shown that application development done using a 4GL results in an operative system 10 to 20 times faster than is possible using a 3GL. The trade-off is usually speed of execution: 4GLs typically run slower than their 3GL counterparts.

External Data and File Definitions. Data and "file" descriptions are done outside of the application through the DDL. This is accomplished by coding the descriptions and then translating them into machine language instructions by a series of short Job Control Language (JCL) statements, as we saw in the section on data independence.

Shared Access. In the ideal database environment, there is only one file: the database. Many users must be able to simultaneously share the data in the database without incurring any of the problems that are associated with multiuser access.

Most file processing systems do not permit multiple users to simultaneously use the same files. This is necessary to avoid **interleaved**, or **concurrent**, **updating**. Consider the inventory application in Figure 1.8. There are two on-line terminals, each being used by a clerk. Both clerks simultaneously retrieve Widget. Each screen shows 10 units on hand. Clerk 1 sells three units and rewrites the record to the disk. The stored inventory record now indicates seven units on hand. Clerk 2's terminal still shows 10 units on hand, the amount available when

---

FIGURE 1.8   **An Example of Interleaved Updating**

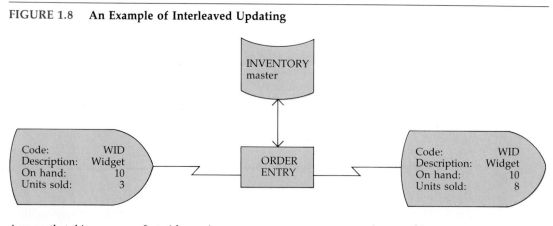

Assume that this user saves first. After saving the data on the screen, units on hand will equal 7.

Assume this user saves next. Units on hand will equal 2 instead of –1.

Instead of showing a stockout, the INVENTORY master file will indicate two units on hand.

FIGURE 1.9   **How a Deadly Embrace Occurs**

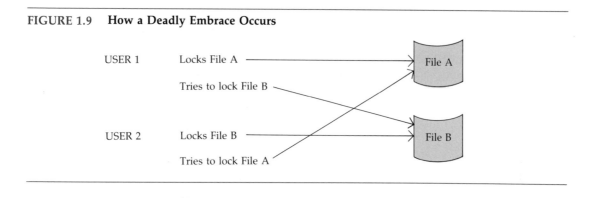

the record originally was retrieved. This user now sells eight units and rewrites the record. Rather than indicating a "stockout," the disk record will show two units on hand.

Database systems must permit multiple users to access records while controlling the problem of interleaved updating. The most common way to accomplish this is to use a **lock**, a mechanism that limits access to system resources, including records and files, to one user at a time. Once a lock is set, any attempt by another user to use the locked resource will result in the operating system or DBMS returning an error status. Data locks are usually imposed on either the file or the record level. The level of the lock is called the lock's **granularity**.

No matter which granularity is selected, it can lead to yet another problem known as a **deadlock**, or **deadly embrace**. This can occur when two or more applications are simultaneously using locks while attempting to use the same set of records or files.

Let's look briefly at how file locking can produce this problem. Suppose there are two files, A and B, as in Figure 1.9. User 1's application has opened and locked file A, thus denying user 2 access to it. At the same time, user 2's application has opened and locked file B, denying access by user 1. User 1 now attempts to open file B but finds it is locked. Then the application program executes a looping procedure, which waits a designated number of seconds and then again attempts to open the file. At the same time, user 2 tries to use file A and finds it is locked. User 2's program also goes into a "wait" loop, doing nothing but wait for the locked file to be released. Both programs are hopelessly locked, with each attempting to access a file held by the other. Neither program can continue without an external interrupt by an operator or user.

Ability to Have Different User Views. Recall that user views, also called *sub-schemas* or *external databases*, represent how the users or applications perceive the data as related to one another. This ability permits the programmer to quickly respond to ad hoc reporting needs and helps secure the data from unauthorized access.

Improved Data Accessibility. With conventional file processing techniques, a given file will probably have one, or at most two, **access paths**—fields used as a basis for retrieval of records. For example, using traditional file processing techniques, an application might be able to retrieve STUDENT master file records based on STUDENTID and STUDENTNAME only. With a DBMS, in contrast, the number of access paths is virtually unlimited. For example, users could access STUDENTs based on MAJOR, STATE, DORMCODE, or any of the other fields located in a STUDENT record or even on fields not stored there!

Enforcement of Standards. Because management of the organization's data is now assigned to the DBA, there can be centralized control over things such as data item, record and file names, data specifications and usage, and security procedures.

Improved Data Security. Data security has several aspects, but two of the most important are (1) securing the data from unauthorized access and (2) providing protection against disasters, such as hardware failure, fire, or incorrect posting of data.

Guarding against unauthorized access usually is done by using passwords on complete databases, views, records, fields, combinations of fields, and/or DML commands. Only after providing the correct password does a user receive access to the requested data. A second technique is to encrypt the stored data so that it will be unreadable unless unencrypted by means of a program. Thus, if anyone attempts to bypass the applications that call upon the unencryption routines to read and write this data and instead use a disk utility to look at the data directly, he or she will see nothing but gibberish.

To be able to recover from catastrophes such as hardware failure, floods, fire, application of incorrect data, and so on, the DBMS usually maintains a **journal**, or **log, file**. A journal file may store record images before they are updated (**before image**) and after they are updated (**after image**), as well as the transaction. For example, assume the current street address for employee number 1234 is being changed from "123 Main St." to "456 Oak St." Three records will be created on the journal file: "123 Main St." (the before image), "456 Oak St." (the after image), and "456 Oak St." (the transaction).

In order to be able to recover the data, there must also be a complete backup of the database that was created at the same time the current journal file was begun. Then, if a disaster occurs, the original database can be restored from the backup file and all the transactions up to the one just prior to the disaster can be reprocessed.

"Reapplying" transactions is known as **rollforward**. For example, assume a disaster occurs at 2:00 P.M. First, the most recent backup will be restored; then all transactions prior to 2:00 P.M. can be read from the journal file and reapplied to the database.

A technique that is useful when the exact time of the disaster is unknown,

FIGURE 1.10   **A Typical Annual Total Cost Curve Associated with Using the Database Approach**

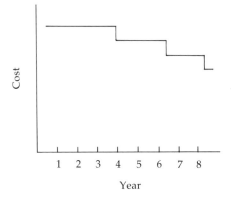

but its cause is suspected to be incorrect input, consists of reading the journal file backward to a point near where the disaster occurred. As each triplet of records is read from the journal file, the before image can be restored, thus removing the effects of the transaction. This process of removing transactions is known as **rollback**.

Ensuring data security is a major worry of end users. The database approach usually includes provisions for the DBA to guarantee protection of data against unauthorized users and natural disasters.

Lower Costs. When a company first decides to use a database system, it initially incurs many fixed costs: the hiring of the DBA, the acquisition of the DBMS, programmer and analyst training, and perhaps a lengthening of the system life cycle as unfamiliar concepts are used for the first time. Figure 1.10 shows that initially the total cost due to using a DBMS is considerable. As more applications are brought under the DBMS umbrella, however, the costs associated with redundancy and changes in hardware or data specifications will begin to decrease. In time, the variable cost savings should equal and surpass the additional startup costs. Unfortunately, many companies give up trying to use a DBMS after a year or so when they see an increase in costs rather than waiting to realize the benefits in subsequent years.

1.5 SUMMARY

Databases are collections of related records that are stored with a minimum of redundancy and are shareable among several users simultaneously. They are accessed by high-level languages or through query languages or 4GLs that invoke a DBMS whenever data must be stored or retrieved. Most DBMSs have three functional parts: a DDL to define records, fields, and relationships among records, a DML to allow the application program to manipulate the database, and a DCL for security purposes.

Using a DBMS in an IS department results in a shift in philosophy. The new ideals embody the following:

- Data is an organizational shared resource.
- There must be a single manager of the data.
- Data must be secured against unauthorized use.
- Redundancy must be controlled.
- Records should be relatable to one another.
- Changing data specifications should not necessitate making program changes.
- A software package known as a *database management system* is used to describe and manipulate the data.

The database approach tries to overcome many problems inherent in a non-database environment. By using a DBMS, information systems departments can expect to save money while controlling redundancy, increasing their ability to respond to ad hoc reporting needs, and reducing the time spent on maintaining data and programs. Further, a DBMS will protect existing programs, because hardware and data changes will not result in having to recompile existing programs.

The employee responsible for creating and maintaining the database is the database administrator. Among the duties of this employee discussed in this chapter are:

- Planning the database
- Creating the conceptual database
- Defining fields and records
- Translating the schema via the DDL
- Maintaining the data dictionary
- Assigning passwords
- Helping programmers and analysts interface with the DBMS

REVIEW QUESTIONS

1. Discuss three problems associated with the nondatabase approach, and explain how the database approach solves them.
2. What is the "my-file" concept, and what is wrong with it?
3. What is interleaved updating, and how do we overcome it?
4. What is redundancy? Why is it costly, and how can we control it?
5. What is meant by "island of information," and why is it undesirable?

6. Explain how a deadly embrace can occur while using record locking.

7. Distinguish between a schema and a subschema.

8. Describe five DBA functions.

9. What are the two functional parts of any DBMS?

10. Describe four DBMS features.

11. Describe three problems that can result from the database approach.

12. Who would make a better DBA, a strong technical person or a "people-oriented" employee?

13. Explain the difference between rollforward and rollback.

14. Under what circumstances might a database management system be inadvisable?

15. We have assumed that the DBA function is a centralized one. How would this assumption affect a decentralized organization in which data is physically distributed to different locations?

▟ EPISODE 1

Community Hospital: Background Information

The first episode of our continuing case provides background information about Community Hospital, the information systems (IS) staff, and a request from the hospital's board of directors to the IS department to provide some new information and to improve some of the current information.

Community Hospital has a 300-bed capacity and thus is considered a medium-size hospital. Last year, the board of directors eliminated the pediatric and maternity units, leaving 11 patient care nursing units. Eight of the units have designations such as 1E, 2W, and so on. The first character in the nursing unit code designates the floor number (the hospital has two floors); the second character specifies the quadrant of (location on) the floor. The other three units are the Cardiac Care Unit (CCU), the Intermediate Care Unit (ICU), and the Critical Care Unit (CU).

Functionally, the hospital is organized into the seven departments shown in Exhibit 1. Exhibit 2 shows how the information systems department is organized.

Bill Moore has been with the hospital for 17 years and is known as a progressive manager, one who is willing to try new ideas. When Barb Scholl was hired 18 months ago to begin the new database administration function, she immediately asked two of Community Hospital's best programmers to join her. Alan Jones came from systems programming, while Kevin Vance was one of the top application programmers. Robin Kennedy's group is responsible both for new-systems development and for maintaining existing systems. Frank Young's operations department is responsible for computer operations, data entry, and systems programming.

One month ago, Mary Winters, chief hospital administrator, called Bill into a meeting, where she told him about a recent decision of the board of directors.

EXHIBIT 1   Community Hospital Organization Chart

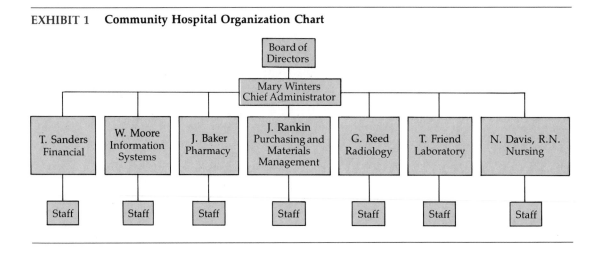

EXHIBIT 2   Organization of the Community Hospital Information Systems Department

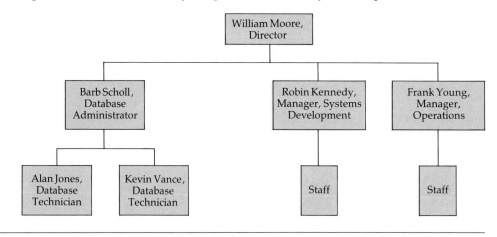

The board felt the hospital was losing money because of lost patient charges and was unable to categorize and account for charges related to particular illnesses.

Mary also explained that in the mid-1980s, medicare had begun reimbursing all hospitals based not on actual costs incurred but on a patient's diagnosis-related group (DRG). For example, there is a flat fee paid for patients with pneumonia, another for those having a broken fibula, and so on. Suddenly, hospitals had to know exactly what it would cost to treat patients within each DRG so they could determine for which illnesses they were overspending. Community Hospital currently had no such system.

Because of these problems, the board

had ordered Mary to instruct the IS department to design a plan for implementing a new patient care information system. At the conclusion of their meeting, Mary passed the responsibility to Bill. She told him his plan had to be presented to her in six months, one month before the next board meeting.

Bill Moore left the meeting with mixed emotions. Although the mandate from the board meant he had almost free reign to redesign an aging collection of systems, it wasn't sufficiently broad to allow him to totally implement an entirely new set of systems. He felt that even though the patient-related portions of the information systems represented most of the existing work of his department, simply revising them now meant that in a year or two he would be asked to redo them. With these thoughts in mind, he called a meeting with Barb Scholl and Robin Kennedy.

Bill began, "Thanks for being on time. You've probably heard rumors of the request made by the board." He proceeded to describe the board's request. As he finished discussing the specific objectives, he added, "I might be going out on a limb, but I want you two to give me a plan that will not only facilitate patient information processing but enable the entire hospital to better respond to the ever-changing needs of government, the board of directors, and the end users within the hospital. There must be a way we can adapt to change without having to spend several months developing the code each time. I'm tired of patching programs that were written 5 or 10 years ago and have been repeatedly changed as new information was requested. Our disk storage

needs have grown by 10 to 15 percent every year, as has our staff size and budget. So I want you expand the request made by the board to include the needs of the entire hospital."

Barb replied, "Bill, I'm sorry but because I'm fairly new here, could you review for me the various ways we generate a patient charge?"

Bill said, "Let me see . . . pharmacy is the biggest generator of patient charges because each medicine must be billed and most patients receive anywhere from 5 to 10 meds [medications] three or four times a day. Of course, this includes intravenous [IVs] and all other forms of medicine. Another problem is materials management. Patients receiving things like gauze, braces, catheters, and so on also have to be billed. The paperwork for this is quite a job. The other major billing area is the labs. Each test must be billed and the results cataloged. We don't have to worry about physician charges, because their private practices bill the patients directly. Nor do we have to worry about dietary, because their charges are reflected in the daily room charge."

As the meeting broke up, Bill summarized, "OK. Let's meet in a month. At that meeting, I want you both to present an overall plan that addresses the informational needs of the entire hospital. The plan must take into account my desire for adaptability, reduced disk storage, and maintenance costs and must concentrate, at least initially, on the patient processing components. Any questions?"

Despite their confusion and doubt, Barb and Robin shrugged their shoulders and shook their heads, indicating they had no questions.

2

Data
The Foundation of the Database

MINICASE Suburban Hospital

Suburban Hospital's pharmacy director, Ann, has asked John, a systems analyst, to meet her to discuss the development of a system for managing the dispensing of medicines to patients.

Ann Thanks for coming. I really need help.

John What's the problem?

Ann Well, I'm having trouble keeping track of my drug inventory, which patients get which medications when, and getting the billing done on time. Accounts receivable insists that we bill every day, and it's just too time consuming for me to get the billing done and also manage the pharmacy. It's even worse when a patient is discharged, because we have to provide a complete billing summary.

John Tell me what your department does in a typical day.

Ann Let's see. Throughout the day, we get new physician orders specifying which medications to administer to which patients and when. Of course, reading the physician or-

ders can be almost impossible! Anyway, we add the new orders to the SHO337 . . .

John Whoa! What's a SHO337?

Ann That's the form number assigned to our profile forms. A profile is a card with patient information at the top and a list of medications for that patient on the bottom.

John What type of information does the card have?

Ann Here's a sample. (See next page.)

John There's the patient's number, name, room number, a spot for diagnoses, physician name, billing number, admission date, discharge date, sex, and room for three allergies at the top. The bottom has each medication's name, the amount to dispense, the dosage schedule, the units actually dispensed each day, and the initials of the pharmacist who set out the medications.

Let me see, I guess that there's a one-to-many relationship between a patient and his orders, right?

Sample Patient Profile Card for Suburban Hospital

| Patient Number: 10113 | | | Billing Number: 12X | |
| Name: Smith, Ann | | | Room: 1A-102-2 | |

Primary Physician: Lundberg
Diagnoses: 1. <u>Angina</u>   2._____   3._____
Admission Date: 12/15/XX   Discharge Date:
Sex: F
Allergies: 1._____   2._____   3._____

Medication Name	Units	Dosage	Schedule	Units Dispensed
Penicillin	2	100mg	TID	30
Aspirin	2	250mg	QID	75

Form #SHO337

Ann Huh?

John Sorry. I mean each patient is associated with many orders, right?

Ann Yes. Also, each order is for a single drug.

John I don't see any billing information.

Ann Our billing clerk uses a formulary master book to match the drug on the profile to a corresponding item in the master book.

John Wait a minute. What's a formulary?

Ann That's what most people call an inventory.

John Oh, OK.

Ann Anyway, the clerk matches the drug on the profile to one of the formulary items to pick up the charge per dose. Then she multiplies the unit charge by the units dispensed to arrive at a billing amount. This is transferred to the billing input sheet and sent to data processing by noon each day.

John How do you know how many units to charge for each day?

Ann Each day we fill a cart that goes to each nursing unit. In the cart is a drawer for each patient. In the drawers are the individual medicines for that patient for the entire day; that's the amount that is put on the profile card in the "units dispensed" area.

John It must be tough to tell in advance exactly how many units of each drug each patient will get.

Ann You're not kidding! A major problem is keeping track of which patient gets which drugs at which time.

John OK, I think I'll set up a patient file, a medication file, an order file, and a physician file. The patient file will have fields for most of the stuff you keep on the top of your profile, plus a switch for active or discharged. The medication file will have fields for . . .

Ann What are you talking about?

Discussion

1. Why do John and Ann have difficulty communicating?

2. What steps should John follow to create his record descriptions if he is following traditional (structured) systems analysis techniques?

3. About which items will John need to collect data?

4. Are there any interrelationships among the items?

In this chapter, we will learn about data, the base on which the database system is built. Users and programmer/analysts use different vocabularies when talking about data, and this can cause a communication problem. Further, programmers use one set of terms for defining the data in the data dictionary and another set when describing the data to the computer in their programs. As you will see, data has many characteristics and much associated terminology.

At the conclusion of this chapter, you will be able to:

- Define the three data realms and the relevant terminology for each.
- Discuss the characteristics of data.
- Diagram record relationships.
- Understand the importance of the diagramming tools.
- Define the three primary data models and name a representative DBMS package from each.

2.1 DATA VERSUS INFORMATION

Webster defines data as "facts used as a basis for reasoning." (Originally a plural word, it is now acceptable to also use it in a singular sense.) Only when data is processed can information result. This transformation is usually the responsibility of the application programs, such as the accounts payable, accounts receivable, and payroll systems. This text is mostly concerned not about how to write application programs but about data: how to store it and retrieve it in a timely, accurate, and cost-efficient way using the database approach.

2.2 THE REAL WORLD VERSUS THE ABSTRACT WORLD

In the minicase that opens this chapter, John and Ann have difficulty communicating because John's job requires him to take real-world concepts and translate them into requirements that ultimately can be implemented on the computer in the form of a database. In so doing, he thinks in terms of the

---

FIGURE 2.1   The Three Data Realms and Their Associated Terminology

Logical Realm	Programmer Realm	Storage Realm
Attribute	Data item, field	
Atomic attribute	Data element	
Composite attribute	Element group, group data item	
Attribute value	Data value, data element value	Bytes, characters
Entity	Record	
Entity class	Record type, file	Data set, file
Entity occurrence	Record occurrence, record instance	Physical record, data subblock, area, extent
Identifier	Primary key	Key subblock value
Multivalued attribute	Variable-length data item	Variable-length data subblock

---

abstract world of information systems, while Ann thinks in terms of words peculiar to her profession.

Databases attempt to abstractly model certain real-world elements in the organization's environment. This modeling process requires interaction among three levels, or realms, of abstraction: logical (real), programmer, and storage. Ann deals with data and information in the logical world, while John must translate her requirements into an abstraction understandable first by a programming language and then by the access method for storage on a disk drive.

Each of the three realms has its own vocabulary, which is summarized in Figure 2.1. In the remainder of this section, we will discuss the terminology unique to each realm.

The User's Logical World

In the logical world, we are not concerned with how data will be represented on the disk drives or with how to specify it to the access methods. Rather, we need to understand which data is important to the user, what the characteristics of the data are, and how the data relates to other data.

Organizations make decisions based on information about **entities**: people, events, or things in their environments. Among Suburban Hospital's entities are Patients, Physicians, Medications, and Patient Orders. Each entity belongs to exactly one **entity class**, also called an **entity type** or **entity set**. All of the entities in a given class have exactly the same characteristics; for example, they are all patients or all physicians. These classes have been chosen so that information can be presented in a more meaningful way.

As John began his project, he decided to group patients into a Patient entity class, orders into an Order class, and so on. Rather than having one Patient entity class, he first thought about grouping patients into two classes: Active Patients and Discharged Patients. He finally decided it would be more efficient to have just one class and to carry a data item that would indicate patient status: active or discharged. Grouping entities into correct classes is somewhat arbitrary, but choosing the correct classes is an important step in designing a database. Figure 2.2 shows the entity classes John set up for Suburban's pharmacy.

Entity classes are usually related to, or associated with, other entity classes. For example, there is an association between Patient and Order and between

---

FIGURE 2.2   **Suburban Hospital's Pharmacy Entity Classes and Their Attributes**

Entity class: Patient

Attributes:
  Patient Number
  Billing Number
  Name
  Sex
  Admit Date
  Discharge Date
  Location
    Nursing Unit
    Room
    Bed
  Physician Code
  Diagnoses
  Allergy
    Type
    Severity Level
  Status

Entity class: Medication

Attributes:
  Code
  Description
  On Hand
  On Order
  Type
  Cost per Unit
  Charge per Unit
  Units Used This Month
  Units Used Year to Date

Entity class: Physician

Attributes:
  Physician code
  Name
  Extension
  Secretary Code

Entity class: Order

Attributes:
  Order Number
  Status
  Patient Number
  Medication Code
  Date Entered
  Pharmacist Initials
  Date Last Changed
  Schedule Code
  Units to Dispense
  Billing Units Dispensed
  Total Units Dispensed

Entity class: Schedule

Attributes:
  Code
  Drug Due Times

Entity class: Allergy

Attributes:
  Allergy Code
  Allergy Description

Entity class: Diagnosis

Attributes:
  Illness Code
  Illness Description

Entity class: Secretary

Attributes:
  Secretary Code
  Secretary Name
  Secretary Phone
  Secretary Address
  Secretary Street
  Secretary City
  Secretary State
  Secretary Zip

Entity class: Medication Type

Attributes:
  Type Code
  Type Description

Physician and Patient. Studying these relationships among entity classes is a very important step in the DBA's design of the database and is the subject of Section 2.5.

Specific patients, orders, medications, and so on are examples of **entity occurrences,** or **entity instances.** Figure 2.3 shows two Patient occurrences.

Entity occurrences are distinguished from one another on the basis of one of the data items called an **identifier.** Since each patient has a different patient number, John has used that number as the Patient identifier. An identifier is merely one of several characteristics associated with each entity. When discussing entities, we will use the term **attribute** to describe their characteristics rather than the programmer term, **data item.** In Figure 2.2, each patient entity has 16 attributes. Two ways to categorize attributes are (1) atomic versus composite and (2) single valued versus multivalued.

An **atomic attribute** consists of a single item, while a **composite attribute,** or **aggregate attribute,** contains several. Patient Number is an example of an atomic attribute. Location is a composite attribute containing Nursing Unit, Room, and Bed. For the Patient entity in Figure 2.2, there are 14 atomic and 2 composite attributes. (Both Location and Allergy are composite, with each containing two or more atomic attributes.)

FIGURE 2.3   **Some Suburban Hospital Patient Occurrences**

Entity: Patient

Entity class: Patients

Entity occurrences: **Values**

Attributes		
Patient Number	001	123
Billing Number	3434345	3456566
Name	Adams, Bruce	Collins, Frank
Sex	Male	Male
Admit Date	01/01/XX	01/15/XX
Discharge Date	NULL	NULL
Location		
Nursing Unit	1A	1A
Room	101	101
Bed	B	A
Physician Code	1001	1001
Diagnoses	Angina	Hypertension
	Laryngitis	Laryngitis
Allergy		
Type	Penicillin	None
Severity Level	Mild	
Type	Bee stings	
Severity Level	Severe	
Status	A	A

Attributes associated with a particular entity occurrence can also be single valued or multivalued. Patient Number is **single valued,** because a particular patient can have only one such number. However, Diagnoses is **multivalued,** because a patient can have many illnesses.

Multivalued composite attributes, such as Allergy in Figures 2.2 and 2.3, are called **repeating aggregates.** Allergy itself is an aggregate consisting of Type and Severity Level. Because every patient can have up to three allergies, the entire aggregate can repeat up to three times. Thus, for a given patient the entire aggregate can take on three different sets of values.

The set of possible values an attribute can have is called its **domain.** For example, the domain of "Sex" might be "Male," "Female," or "M," "F." Often it is only by knowing the **semantics** of the data—the rules and meanings concerning the data—that we can correctly define the domain. Later in this chapter, we will look at the two ways to describe domains: explicitly and implicitly.

The Programmer's Data World: The Data Dictionary

After collecting information about entities, attributes, and relationships, programmer/analysts or DBAs usually document their findings in a data dictionary of the type we saw in Chapter 1. Data about data is sometimes called **meta-data.** Thus, the programmer realm is sometimes referred to as the *meta-data realm.*

Programmers and analysts refer to entity classes as **record types** or **data stores,** and to specific entities as **record occurrences** or **record instances,** and to attributes as **data elements** or **data items.** The identifier attribute is called either the **identifier** or the **primary key.**

In Suburban Hospital's data dictionary, the aggregate attribute Location would become an **element group.** Similarly, when adding to the data dictionary, John converted the multivalued attribute, Diagnoses, into the **repeating element,** ILLNESS__CODE, and the repeating aggregate, Allergy, into the **repeating group,** Allergy. Notice that the programmer's group data item corresponds to the real-world composite attribute and a repeating group to a repeating aggregate.

Sometimes files must be represented in a language-free, DBMS-free environment. Such files are called **conceptual files,** meaning they may not exist as the user perceives them. The record that is actually passed to the FD in a COBOL program is a **logical record,** and the collection of all such records is a **logical file.** Such logical files are what programmers usually think of when they refer to a "file."

A conceptual record can consist of portions of one or more logical records. The logical records, in turn, are extracted from physical records found in the **physical file,** which is stored on a disk. The physical file also contains overhead that is not passed to the program. Thus, a logical record is a subset of a physical record. Much of the time the conceptual and logical files will be the same, and

---

FIGURE 2.4   Conceptual File Definitions for Suburban Hospital

PATIENT (PATIENT_NO, BILLING_NO, PATIENT_NAME, SEX, ADMIT_DATE,

DISCHARGE_DATE, NURSING_UNIT, ROOM, BED, PHYSICIAN_CODE, STATUS,

ILLNESS_CODE, ALLERGY)

PATIENT_ILLNESS (PATIENT_NO, ILLNESS_CODE)

PATIENT_ALLERGIES (PATIENT_NO, ALLERGY_CODE, LEVEL)

PHYSICIAN (PHYSICIAN_NO, PHYSICIAN_NAME, EXTENSION)

ORDER (ORDER_NUMBER, STATUS, PATIENT_NO, MEDICATION_CODE,

DATE_ENTERED, INITIALS, CHANGE_DATE, SCHEDULE, UNITS,

BILLING_UNITS)

MEDICATION (MEDICATION_CODE, DESCRIPTION, ON_HAND, ON_ORDER, TYPE,

COST, CHARGE, UNITS_MTD, UNITS_YTD)

MEDICATION_TYPE (TYPE_CODE, TYPE_DESCRIPTION)

SCHEDULE (CODE, TIME)

ILLNESS (CODE, DESCRIPTION)

TREATS (PHYSICIAN_NO, PATIENT_NO)

ALLERGY (CODE, DESCRIPTION)

---

we won't differentiate between them. Only when the conceptual file is a composite of several different types of records or a subset of one or more logical files will the conceptual file be different from the logical one.

Conceptual files are sometimes represented like those shown in Figure 2.4. The name of the file is listed first, the fields are listed inside the parentheses, and the primary key(s) is underlined. Some people prefer to append the primary key names after the file name and fields, for example, ILLNESS (CODE, DESCRIPTION) Keys: CODE.

Notice that ILLNESS_CODE and ALLERGY have a line over them. This indicates a repeating item or group. Based on the semantics described earlier, we know that ILLNESS is a single data item and ALLERGY is a repeating group, with each occurrence containing a code and a severity level.

Some files can be represented as two-dimensional tables, called **flat files** or **tables.** A flat-file representation consists of columns that represent fields and rows that represent records. Figure 2.5 shows examples of flat-file occurrences for most of the Suburban Hospital files from Figure 2.4.

FIGURE 2.5 Portions of Several Suburban Hospital Files, Shown as Flat-File Occurrences

File: PHYSICIAN

PHYSICIAN_NO	PHYSICIAN_NAME	EXTENSION
1000	STARZL, THOMAS	2929
1001	SMITH, JOHN	3478
1005	STYLES, ROBERT	3566
900	BULL, MARY	2222

File: TREATS

PHYSICIAN_NO	PATIENT_NO
1000	123
1001	3434
1001	1
1000	1

File: ORDER

ORDER_NUMBER	STATUS	PATIENT_NO	MEDICATION_CODE	DATE_ENTERED	INITIALS	CHANGE_DATE	SCHEDULE	UNITS	BILLING_UNITS
1	A	1	PCN	01/02/XX	AGS		TID	3	21
2	A	1	TAG	01/02/XX	BAS	01/04/XX	QID	2	12
7	I	1	ASP	01/01/XX	AGS	01/01/XX	TID	2	0
10	A	123	PCN	01/15/XX	BAS		TID	1	2

File: MEDICATION

MEDICATION_CODE	DESCRIPTION	ON_HAND	ON_ORDER	TYPE	COST	CHARGE	UNITS_MTD	UNITS_YTD
PCNL	Penicillin Liquid	1L		2	.50	2.50	100	750
PCNS	Penicillin Solid	1000		1	.25	2.00	350	1250
TAG	Tagamet	1500	500	1	1.00	10.00	98	200
ASPS	Aspirin Solid	12000		1	.02	.75	1200	9875

File: SCHEDULE

CODE	TIME
QID	0600
QID	1200
QID	1800
QID	2400
TID	0800
TID	1600
TID	2400

File: ILLNESS

CODE	DESCRIPTION
1	Angina
2	Broken Bone
3	Pneumonia
4	Cardiac Arrest
5	Chest Pain
6	Arthroscopy

File: MEDICATION TYPE

TYPE_CODE	TYPE_DESCRIPTION
1	Oral Solid
2	Oral Liquid
3	Injectable
4	Topical Ointment

File: ALLERGY

CODE	DESCRIPTION
1	Penicillin
2	Bee Stings

FIGURE 2.6 Decomposing the PATIENT File into Several Flat Files

Beneath each file occurrence is the corresponding conceptual file definition

File: PATIENT

PATIENT_NO	BILLING_NO	PATIENT_NAME	SEX	ADMIT_DATE	DISCHARGE_DATE	LOCATION	PHYSICIAN_CODE	STATUS
1	345345	Smith, Robin	F	01/01/XX		1A 102 B	1001	A
123	456456	Baker, Megan	F	01/13/XX		1A 102 A	1000	A
3434	333333	Adams, Sam	M	01/15/XX	02/15/XX		1000	D

PATIENT (PATIENT_NO, BILLING_NO, PATIENT_NAME, SEX, ADMIT_DATE, DISCHARGE_DATE, LOCATION, PHYSICIAN_CODE, STATUS)

File: PATIENT_ILLNESS

PATIENT_NO	ILLNESS_CODE
1	01
1	03
1	07
123	01
3434	03

File: PATIENT_ALLERGY

PATIENT_NO	ALLERGY_CODE	LEVEL
1	1	7
1	5	9

PATIENT_ILLNESS (PATIENT_NO, ILLNESS_CODE) PATIENT_ALLERGY (PATIENT_NO, ALLERGY_CODE, LEVEL)

The original PATIENT file cannot be represented as a flat file, because a flat file cannot contain repeating elements. The process of ensuring that files can be properly defined as flat files, together with choosing the proper data elements to store in each table, is called **normalization.** Look again at the PATIENT file in Figure 2.4. ILLNESS__CODE is a repeating element and ALLERGY a repeating group. To store PATIENT as a flat file, we must remove all repeating elements and groups and place them into separate but related files. To do this, we set up a new flat file consisting of the repeating attribute and the primary key from the original file as in Figure 2.6.

Figure 2.6 shows that we have decomposed the original PATIENT file into three flat files: a modified PATIENT file and two new ones—PATIENT__ILL-NESS and PATIENT__ALLERGY. The PATIENT__ILLNESS file contains PATIENT__NO (the primary key for PATIENT) and ILLNESS__CODE (the re-peating element), while the PATIENT__ALLERGY file carries PATIENT__NO, ALLERGY__CODE, and LEVEL. The modified PATIENT file contains the re-maining fields originally found in Figure 2.4. The PATIENT__NO field in each of the two new files relates their records to the corresponding Patient entry in the PATIENT file. Without this element, there would be no way to determine, say, to which patient a PATIENT__ILLNESS record occurrence pertains. Again, this topic of design will be more fully developed in Chapter 3.

The primary key for each of the new files must be composite: PATIENT__ NO + ILLNESS__CODE for the first file and PATIENT__NO + ALLERGY__ CODE for the second. (A comma is sometimes used instead of the + to indicate a composite key.)PATIENT__NO by itself is not unique, as we can see by looking at the data for the PATIENT__ILLNESS file in Figure 2.6. Three of the occurrences in the file have the PATIENT__NO value 1, which verifies the fact that PATIENT__CODE does not uniquely identify an occurrence of PATIENT__ILL-NESS and thus cannot by itself be a primary key field.

The Physical Stored Data World: Data as Seen by Programs and Disk Drives

Because in this text we consider disk drives as being the only secondary storage device suitable for storing the database, all data elements eventually must be stored as bytes on a disk. To accomplish this, the programmer/analyst first converts the data element entries in the data dictionary into **fields,** which are defined within the application program. Single-valued data elements become fields, multivalued elements such as illness become COBOL **tables,** and re-peating groups are now called **multipart tables.** When the program is finally executed, the field-defined data is converted into bytes, which are grouped into physical records and then stored by the access method and disk controller. The named collection of record occurrences for a particular record type is a **file.**

2.3   DATA ELEMENT AND FIELD CHARACTERISTICS

Data elements are the data dictionary representation of the real-world attributes, while fields are the programmer/analyst's way of describing the data elements to the chosen programming language. For the most part, we will use the terms interchangeably in this section. Both have important characteristics that must be either carefully defined by the programmer/analyst or preserved by the resulting application program. Among these characteristics are:

- Name
- Type
- Representation
- Length
- Origin
- Domain
- Value
- Data independence
- Key versus nonkey
- Data integrity
- Data security

Name

Data elements and fields must have names. Because they can be qualified, their names need not be unique. We can have NAME as a field in the PATIENT file as well as in the MEDICATION one. To refer to the PATIENT name, we would use PATIENT.NAME. The MEDICATION name field will thus be specified as MEDICATION.NAME.

In situations independent of language, we use the underline character to separate portions of a field name to reduce confusion. For example, would DOLLAR-COST mean "subtract COST from DOLLAR," or is it a field name? Because a database must be independent of language, use of the underline character will prevent confusion about whether or not a subtracting operation was intended. Thus, we use PATIENT__NAME, and MEDICATION__COST as field names rather than PATIENT-NAME and MEDICATION-NAME. However, when a specific language is specified, we use the naming conventions for that language.

To avoid possible confusion about whether we are discussing attributes, data elements, or fields, we will use the following conventions:

- The first letters of attribute names will be capitalized.
- Data element and field names will be in capital letters.

- Field names will contain no embedded blanks. When we intend a specific COBOL field, we will follow the COBOL naming convention. When we intend a more general field name, we will use the underline character to separate the portions of the name. Thus, PATIENT NUMBER is a data element found in a data dictionary, PATIENT_NUMBER is a field name that is independent of language, and PATIENT-NUMBER is a COBOL field name.
- When we are discussing the name of an entity class, the first letter of the name will be capitalized. When we are using a file name, the name will be in capital letters.

Type

Fields and data elements usually are designated as either numeric or alphanumeric. Numeric data elements and fields can be further classified as integer or decimal. Some database management systems have other field types, including money, date, time, time-stamp (the exact time a record was created), memo (a free-form annotation attached to a record), and graphic.

Representation

Fields must be converted to bytes and then stored on a secondary storage device such as a disk drive. The *representation* of the field refers to how the field is represented by the computer and stored both in main memory and on the disk.

Length

The field's *length* refers to the number of characters or digits used to define the field. This number can differ from the actual number of bytes necessary to physically store it.

Origin: Real versus Virtual

Real fields exist in a file; virtual fields do not. For instance, PATIENT_CHARGE might be calculated when needed as ORDER.BILLING_UNITS * MEDICATION.UNIT_PRICE. Rather than storing the PATIENT_CHARGE and using up disk storage, we can compute its value whenever necessary.

Domain

The *domain* of a field or data element is the set of allowable values it may take on. Domains can be implicitly or explicitly defined.

Implicit Domains. Domains are **implicitly defined** by providing both the type and the range of a data element or field. The domain for PATIENT__NO could be implicitly defined as "integer with a range of 1-999999999."

Explicit Domains. Domains are **explicitly defined** by listing all the possible values the item can have. The domain of the STATUS data item might be stated as A, D. Similarly, the domain of SEX is probably best explicitly specified as Male, Female. As we saw earlier in this chapter, an alternative domain might be M, F; only by knowing the semantics can we be sure the domain is defined properly.

Provided the database management system has the feature, domains can be used to help make the stored data more accurate by enforcing domain checks as records are stored. This idea is more fully discussed in the section on data integrity.

Value

Stored data consists of specific values taken from each field's domain. Many of the remaining characteristics discussed in this section concern preserving the quality of these data values.

When we don't know a field's value, we want to be able to use the special word NULL to indicate this. **NULL** has a meaning different from that of blank or zero; it means the value of the field is unknown. For example, when a patient is admitted to Suburban Hospital and his or her physician is not known, the PHYSICIAN__CODE value will be NULL. Unfortunately, not all languages support the NULL data value concept.

Data Independence

Data independence refers to the insulation of a program or user from the data's logical and physical organization. We introduced you to this concept in Section 1.4 of Chapter 1, where we saw that there are two kinds of data independence: logical and physical.

Logical Data Independence. *Logical data independence* means that changes to the way the fields are arranged within the record do not affect how the programmer or user accesses or views the record. If a new field can be added or existing fields rearranged or deleted without affecting the existing users of that record, we have logical data independence. This precludes the situation where a user references an item that has been deleted.

Physical Data Independence. *Physical data independence* refers to the ability to shield users and programs from access strategies, data storage characteristics, and the location of the data. If any of these items change and no user is affected, we have physical data independence. An **access strategy** consists of the access method plus relevant data such as the primary key or indexed field name. *Data storage characteristics* refer to the data's type and representation. The *location* of the data refers to where the data resides: the device type and location of the records on the device.

To illustrate, John started to change the primary key for the PATIENT file from PATIENT_NO to LOCATION. After thinking about the contemplated change, he realized he would have to recompile every program that used the PATIENT file. The SELECT statements would require changing to accommodate the new primary key, and several PROCEDURE DIVISION statements would require changes reflecting the need to MOVE values to the new key. In other words, John's programs were not independent of access strategy.

Other changes John considered were making the PATIENT_NO field COMP-3, and changing the location of the records from cylinders 10-20 to 30-40. After consulting with the DBA, John was informed that these changes would require a comprehensive changing of existing programs and JCL. John decided not to go ahead with his planned changes. He correctly concluded that the basic access methods and COBOL would not provide the desired physical and logical data independence.

Key versus Nonkey

Key fields are used to access or sequence stored records. There are six key types:

- Primary
- Candidate (alternate)
- Composite (concatenate)
- Secondary
- Sort (control)
- Foreign

Primary Keys. As you read this section, you may find it useful to refer to Figure 2.4. A **primary key** uniquely distinguishes one record occurrence from all others; no two occurrences can have the same primary key value. The primary key for PATIENT would be PATIENT_NO, since no two patients in the PATIENT file can have the same number. This is indicated by the underlining of the PATIENT_NO field in Figure 2.4.

Composite Keys. Primary keys can be atomic or composite. **Composite keys,** also called **concatenated keys,** consist of two or more data elements. The PATIENT_NO key just mentioned is an atomic one. Had John chosen to use LOCATION, which consists of NURSING_UNIT + ROOM + BED, plus STATUS as the primary key (it is unique), we would have an example of a composite primary key. John would need STATUS as part of the key because there could be a discharged patient in the system who had been assigned to the same room and bed as a currently active patient. The components of such composite primary keys are called **subkeys.**

Candidate Keys. Sometimes it is unclear which field to select as the primary key because of **candidate,** or **alternate, keys.** These are additional fields that also have the uniqueness property. For example, patients at Suburban can be uniquely identified using either the PATIENT__NO or LOCATION + STATUS elements. Both the atomic and the composite key have the required uniqueness property; hence, either could be chosen as the primary key, which makes them both candidate keys.

In addition to the uniqueness requirement, candidate keys must possess (1) time invariant uniqueness and (2) parsimony. Being **time invariant unique** means that over time no two records will ever have the same value for the chosen primary key field. For instance, at the present time there are no two Suburban patients with the same value of PATIENT__NAME. However, because there might be two such patients in the future, John did not consider PATIENT__ NAME a candidate key.

Parsimonious means being as short as possible. Because the candidate key LOCATION is unique, adding PATIENT__NAME to it would also result in a suitable primary key; no two patients would ever have a duplicate value of NURSING__UNIT + ROOM + BED + PATIENT__NAME. However, this would violate the parsimony requirement.

Secondary Keys. A **secondary key** is a nonunique field that is used as an alternative search path. For example, two PATIENT records in Figure 2.6 have a PHYSICIAN__CODE value of 1000. If that physician leaves the hospital, it is likely that an administrator would want to know all the patients treated by the physician so that a new one could be assigned. This means that PHYSICIAN __CODE is a secondary PATIENT key.

Sort Keys. A **sort key,** also called a **control key,** is used to physically sequence sequentially organized files. The user's perceived ordering of the records is called the **logical sequence.** Choosing a different sort key and then actually sorting the sequential file based on the new key will result in a new file that is physically and logically in the new order. Each new reporting sequence will require a new sort.

Foreign Keys. A **foreign key** is a field in a file whose values must either be NULL or match a primary key value for a record in another file. It is one way to relate records of one type to records of another. The file in which the foreign key is found is often called the **dependent file** and the file to which it refers is the **parent file.** For example, one of the fields in the conceptual PATIENT file

FIGURE 2.7   Example of a Foreign Key

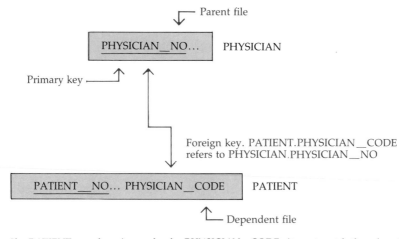

If a PATIENT record carries a value for PHYSICIAN__CODE, it must match the value of some occurrence of PHYSICIAN__NO, the primary key for PHYSICIAN, the parent file.

in Figure 2.6 is PHYSICIAN__CODE. If the patient's physician code is un-known, we store the value NULL to so designate it. But if the code is known, we want to constrain it such that it will match a primary key value (PHYSICIAN.PHYSICIAN__NO) for one of the physicians in the PHYSICIAN file. This makes PATIENT.PHYSICIAN__CODE a foreign key. If this foreign key constraint is enforced, there can never be a PATIENT record that contains a PHYSICIAN__CODE value that doesn't refer to a record in the PHYSICIAN file, which certainly enhances the integrity of the data. The enforcement of such foreign key rules is called **referential integrity,** a subject discussed in the next section.

Figure 2.7 shows this conceptually. PATIENT is the dependent file and PHY-SICIAN the parent. When a PATIENT record is stored with a value for PHYSICIAN__CODE, that value, if not NULL, must match a value of PHYSICIAN__NO in the PHYSICIAN file. For example, if a patient is admitted with a PHYSICIAN__CODE value of 101, there must be a record in the PHY-SICIAN file with a matching PHYSICIAN__NO value.

Data Integrity

Data integrity refers to the data's accuracy, completeness, timeliness, and re-liability. Usually it is up to programmers to maintain data integrity by imposing edit checks on the fields before they are actually stored. Among the techniques the DBMS can use to help guard the integrity of data are:

- Domain constraints
- Referential integrity constraints
- Entity integrity
- Concurrency control
- Use of a commitment policy
- Use of journal files and backups

First, let's review the concept of domain enforcement. When a PATIENT is being stored, the value of the PATIENT__NO field should automatically be compared to its domain. If the observed value is outside the domain, the record should be rejected. This is an example of a domain constraint, which helps ensure that the data is accurate. Another way to help guarantee data integrity is through the enforcement of foreign keys.

As we saw above, one of the PATIENT's foreign keys, PHYSICIAN__CODE, must always have a value that matches that of PHYSICIAN__NO for some record in the PHYSICIAN file. This rule enforcement is usually called **referential integrity** and is the subject of much discussion with respect to DBMSs, because while everyone agrees that it is necessary, few languages or DBMSs support it. Usually, the programmer must supply the necessary coding using conventional statements from the chosen language.

There are three kinds of referential integrity: insertion, deletion, and update.

Insertion integrity means that when a dependent record is stored, the DBMS automatically enforces the foreign key constraint. If no parent occurrence that matches the foreign value is found, the storage attempt is rejected and a suitable error message is returned to the host program. We saw an example of this earlier.

Deletion integrity is a bit more complicated. It refers to the action to be taken with regard to the dependent records when a parent is deleted. For example, suppose a physician leaves Suburban Hospital and there are many PATIENT records related to that physician through the PHYSICIAN__CODE foreign key value. There are three possible rules to use:

- Cascade
- Set to NULL
- Restrict

The **cascade rule** means that when a parent is deleted, so are all its dependents. In our PHYSICIAN/PATIENT example, the cascade deletion of a PHYSICIAN record would result in the deletion of all the related PATIENT records— not a wise choice. The **set-to-NULL rule** results in the severing of relationships by setting the foreign key value to NULL. Here the PHYSICIAN__CODE value for all the PATIENT records related to the departed physician would be set to NULL. In effect, this choice would remove the dependency. Finally, the **restrict rule** means that if a parent record has one or more dependents, the parent cannot be deleted. A good example would be the foreign key MEDICATION __CODE found in the ORDER file, which contains an occurrence for every prescribed medication. Among its other fields (see Figure 2.5) are PATIENT __NO, DATE__ENTERED, MEDICATION__CODE, and so on. Whenever an occurrence of ORDER is stored, we must be sure that the prescribed medication is in the MEDICATION file. Thus, ORDER.MEDICATION__CODE refers to the MEDICATION file and is a foreign key. Now assume that 10 patients are on a particular drug and the director of the pharmacy decides to delete that drug from the MEDICATION file. Because there are patients receiving the medication, we can't permit this to occur; if we do, we won't be able to find the drug in the MEDICATION file whenever a bill or a list of drugs to be dispensed is required. By specifying restrict for deletions of MEDICATION records, this cannot occur.

Update integrity means that when a parent's primary key value changes (something we probably should not permit), the foreign key values for all dependents should be changed to the same value. For example, a physician's PHYSICIAN__NO value is changed from P102 to PH122. With update integrity, all PATIENT records related to that physician through the PHYSICIAN__CODE field in the PATIENT file would automatically be changed to the new value.

Referential integrity helps guarantee data consistency so that we don't end up with "multiple versions of the truth." When a relationship exists between two files, we must make sure that the fields that relate them are consistent. Ideally, we want the DBMS to automatically enforce all such relationships rather than force programmers to do so. Whenever the relating values differ, the integrity of the data is threatened.

The third way to help ensure data integrity is to establish **entity integrity.** This means that no field participating as a primary key can ever have a null value. Assume that LOCATION, a composite field consisting of NURSING__ UNIT, ROOM, and BED, is chosen as the primary PATIENT key. With entity integrity, the DBMS could ensure that no patient could ever have a null value for BED, or for either of the other two fields.

Failure to enforce domain constraints, referential integrity, and entity integrity can destroy the integrity of the stored data. However, there are at least two more ways for this to occur: concurrent updating problems and program abnormal endings (ABENDs).

As we saw in Chapter 1, concurrent updating problems can occur when two or more users try to update the same record at the same time. Such problems occur only with on-line systems having several users or with batch systems in which multiple programs are being concurrently processed.

Program abnormal endings (ABEND) can occur from programming errors or from hardware failures. For example, assume John is updating the ORDER file. A particular patient order is being filled; it calls for one dose of penicillin three times a day. The ORDER record is properly updated to indicate that the daily doses have been dispensed, but when the Penicillin record in the MEDICATION file is about to be changed to reflect the new usage figures, a lightning strike occurs and the system fails. Only part of the update is complete, and the integrity of the MEDICATION data is in jeopardy.

The most common way to prevent incomplete processing from threatening the integrity of data is to use a **commitment** policy. This means that transactions are not immediately posted to files but are kept in memory or in temporary files until the application issues a COMMIT command. At that time, all transactions since the last COMMIT are posted to the appropriate files. If an ABEND occurs, the COMMIT won't be issued; therefore, none of the data will be posted, which will eliminate the partial-update problem. Although COBOL does not support the commitment concept, this feature is available with most DBMSs.

Suburban Hospital also uses log files and backup tapes to help ensure data is accurate. As discussed in Section 1.4 in Chapter 1, a *log file,* also called a *journal file,* is usually kept on tape and records before images, after images, and transactions. In addition, Suburban operations staff employees make a complete tape backup of every disk drive every day (at midnight). Using their log files, Suburban therefore can do a rollforward or rollback to restore a file to a prior state or undo a transaction, respectively. For example, if a disk head crashes, the backup tape can be used to restore the files as of the last backup time (midnight). Then every transaction record from midnight to the time of the disk failure can be read from the log file and reapplied to restore the disk to its last correct state. This is the **rollforward** process. When an invalid transaction is incorrectly posted to a file, the effect can be removed by finding the bad transaction in the log file and then applying the corresponding before-image to the file. This is an example of a **rollback.**

Data Security

Secure data can be accessed only by authorized users. Data security can be ensured through several means, including physical controls, departmental policies, operating system controls, and controls on the data itself. Because this text focuses on data, we will discuss data control techniques.

There are at least four ways to use data controls to ensure data security:

- Assign passwords
- Assign rights
- Use views
- Use encryption

Passwords can be applied to fields, to combinations of fields, to files, or to DML commands. Some operating systems and/or DBMS software also provide for rights, which, as we saw in Section 1.4 of Chapter 1, grant individuals certain DML privileges. A data view can serve either as a filter, keeping unauthorized employees from seeing complete records, or as a combiner of fields, extracting fields from several records.

Assigning Passwords. John decided to use passwords for the PATIENT and ORDER files. Anyone accessing a PATIENT record would be asked for the password DELTA, and accessing ORDER records would require the user to know the password WATSON. These are examples of passwords used at the file level.

Some DBMS languages allow passwords to be assigned at the field or combination-of-fields level or even at the command level. A delete operation might require a different password than an add operation.

Assigning Rights. Another way to ensure data security is to assign passwords to individuals rather than assigning passwords to the data. Through their passwords, the individuals receive access rights to different files or fields. For example, one individual may have "read" rights but not "write" rights to the ORDER file. Another may have "add" rights but not "delete" rights. The language or operating system matches the user-supplied password to the rights granted to that user. Users who attempt to perform unauthorized actions will be stopped, because the application will refuse to complete the transaction.

Figure 2.8 shows the rights associated with four of the passwords for the Suburban pharmacy system. Ann has chosen the password: BOSS. She is given all rights. In fact, anyone logging into the pharmacy system with that password has all rights to all files. We must take special care to prevent passwords from being discovered by unauthorized users. One way to accomplish this is to not show passwords as they are being entered via visual display devices.

John has chosen to use his name as his password, but this is a poor security choice. He also has all rights. The billing clerk has chosen XHY as her password, a much better choice than John's. She cannot access PATIENT records, only read ORDER records; but because she works with the billing process, she has all rights to the MEDICATION file. The user of password A12 can read, write, and print PATIENT records. While not all operating systems support the rights concept, those that do provide a sound mechanism for ensuring security.

FIGURE 2.8   **Suburban Hospital File Rights**

Password	BOSS	John	XHY	A12
PATIENTS	A	A	N	R,W,P
ORDER	A	A	R	A
MEDICATIONS	A	A	A	A
PHYSICIANS	A	A	R,W	R,P
SCHEDULE	A	A	R,W	A
ALLERGIES	A	A	R,W	A
DIAGNOSES	A	A	R,W	A

A = All   N = None   P = Print   R = Read   W = Write

FIGURE 2.9   **Two Different Views Based on the Conceptual File ORDER**

Password: CLERK
CLERK__ORDER (PATIENT__NO, MEDICATION__CODE, BILLING__UNITS)

Password: BOSS
BOSS__ORDER: All fields

Using Views. Another way to strengthen security is to restrict users to certain combinations of fields, a concept known as an **external view.** Figure 2.9 shows how Ann's view of an ORDER record could be made substantially broader than that of the pharmacy clerk. The clerk can see only PATIENT__NO, MEDICATION__CODE, and BILLING__UNITS. Ann's view includes the entire record.

As far as end users are concerned, views are the same as files. With few exceptions, they can be updated just like the files on which they are based. The underlying files from which the views are created are sometimes called **base files.**

Encryption. As described in Chapter 1, by transforming stored data into bit combinations that don't conform to EBCDIC or ASCII standards or by substituting one binary code for another, data will be unable to be displayed or read into applications unless it is first unencrypted. Many commercial DBMSs offer encryption/unencryption capability.

2.4   RELATIONSHIPS AND ASSOCIATIONS: RELATING ENTITIES

A *relationship* is an association between attributes (hence data elements and fields) or between entity classes (thus record types). Attributes are related to other attributes and entity classes to other entity classes in the real world and must be similarly related in the database model of the real world. Before we can define these relationships for the DBMS, we must understand them. One way to do this is to conceptually model the relationships using one or more diagramming techniques. In this section, we look at the kinds of relationships we expect to find, the benefits of studying the relationships, and how to diagram them.

Attributes are related to attributes and entity classes to entity classes according to one of four **association types:** 1:1 (one-to-one), 1:M (one-to-many), M:N (many-to-many), or not at all. There is also a relationship called a **loop,** or **recursive, relationship.** As usual, we will use the words *entity class, record type,* and *conceptual file* interchangeably in this discussion. All relationships are *bidirectional;* that is, if A is related to B, B is related to A. Determining the semantics of the relationship types can be done after the DBA or systems analyst has discovered and analyzed the organization's rules, or constraints, concerning the attributes and entity classes. Like other desired system information, these rules are discovered through the normal data-collecting techniques—interviews, questionnaires, studying the present system, and so on—and are statements about attribute domains and attribute and entity relationships.

In addition to being grouped into one of four association types, entities can be categorized as having one of two possible **membership classes:** required or optional. Either an entity is required to participate in a relationship, or its membership can be optional.

One-to-One Relationships

A **one-to-one relationship (1:1)** between two entity classes or record types means that one entity occurrence of the first entity class is associated with at most one entity occurrence of the second. Also, one occurrence of the second class is related to at most one occurrence of the first. We should point out that such association types are rare.

At Suburban Hospital, Physician and Secretary are two entity classes: A particular physician is assigned at most one secretary, and each secretary works for no more than one physician. Furthermore, some physicians do not have secretaries, and some secretaries don't work for physicians. This suggests a 1:1 association between Physician and Secretary.

Figure 2.10 shows one way to conceptually model a one-to-one record type or entity class association. It is known as a **data structure diagram (DSD)** or **Bachman diagram,** the latter so named to honor its creator, Charles Bachman. The rectangles represent the entity classes, or record types; the data elements, or fields, are sometimes written inside the rectangle; the primary key is underlined. Because we often need to refer to items like those in the rectangles, because they can be referred to as entities, files, record types, and so forth, and because they pertain to our conceptualization of such things, we will use the more general term *conceptual file* when we wish to refer to the class of all these related terms. The bidirectional arrow in Figure 2.10 indicates the 1:1 relationship between the entity classes Physician and Secretary.

When Bachman developed the data structure diagramming technique, he did not provide for membership rules, so we must adapt his idea when we need to show them. Optional membership in a relationship is indicated by a small circle on the DSD, while mandatory membership is indicated by a small line. Sometimes we will show only the entity's name and leave out those of the attributes; at other times, we won't show the membership rules. However, Figure 2.10 shows everything. There, both entity classes have optional membership in the relationship because it is possible for a Secretary not to be assigned to a Physician and for a Physician not to have a Secretary.

FIGURE 2.10   A 1:1 Relationship between Two Entities

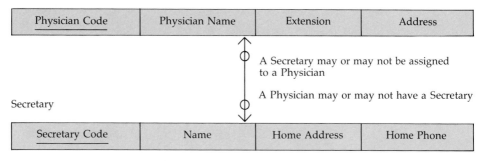

Physician

Physician Code	Physician Name	Extension	Address

A Secretary may or may not be assigned to a Physician

A Physician may or may not have a Secretary

Secretary

Secretary Code	Name	Home Address	Home Phone

Each Physician is associated with at most one Secretary, and each Secretary is associated with at most one Physician.

One-to-Many Relationships

Most associations between entity classes are **one-to-many (1:M) relationships.** This means that one entity occurrence of the first entity class is associated with zero, one, or many occurrences of the second. Conversely, each occurrence of the second entity class is associated with up to one occurrence of the first.

A 1:M relationship exists between the PATIENT and ORDER conceptual files (as we indicated we might, we have switched from entity to file). A given PATIENT occurrence can be related to several pharmacy ORDERs. Look at the ORDER occurrences for patient number 1 in Figure 2.5. There are three; thus, a 1:3 relationship exists between this patient and his orders. On the other hand, order number 1 is associated only with patient number 1; hence, a 1:1 relationship in this direction.

This association is conceptually diagrammed as a DSD in Figure 2.11. The double arrowhead from PATIENT to ORDER represents the 1:M relationship between the two conceptual files.

To completely describe the relationship between PATIENT and ORDER, we must decide on their membership rules vis-à-vis their relationship. First, consider the PATIENT-to-ORDER association. Since a patient may or may not have a pharmacy order, there can be a PATIENT occurrence without a corresponding ORDER occurrence; thus, Figure 2.11 shows a circle near the ORDER record type. On the other hand, there cannot be an ORDER occurrence without a corresponding PATIENT occurrence; hence, Figure 2.11 shows a small line just below the PATIENT record type to designate required membership. Note the similarity of this example to the concept of a foreign key. We could have said there cannot be a PATIENT__NO value in any ORDER occurrence that doesn't

---

FIGURE 2.11   Using a DSD to Model a 1:M Relationship between Two Conceptual Files

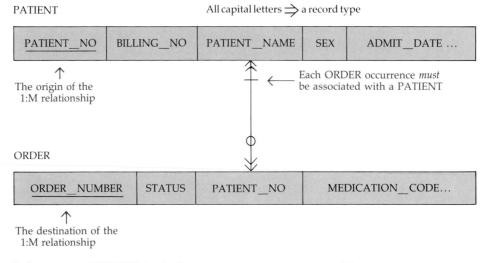

PATIENT   All capital letters $\Rightarrow$ a record type

The origin of the
1:M relationship

Each ORDER occurrence *must*
be associated with a PATIENT

ORDER

The destination of the
1:M relationship

Each occurrence of PATIENT is related to zero, one, or more occurrences of ORDER. Also, each ORDER occurrence is related to exactly one PATIENT.

---

match some PATIENT__NO value in the PATIENT file. A foreign key enforcement policy is one way to implement a required-membership constraint.

One-to-many associations play a very important role in database design, and it is convenient to be able to generally discuss the two conceptual files that participate in the 1:M association. With that objective in mind, we will call the conceptual file where the arrow begins the **source,** or **origin,** and the other file (on the "many" side) the **destination,** or, as we saw earlier in the section on foreign keys, the **dependent.**

An occurrence of a data structure diagram consists of occurrences of the conceptual files shown in the diagram. Starting with a designated conceptual file, we show an occurrence of it and all the related occurrences of the other conceptual files. Figure 2.12 shows an occurrence of the DSD in Figure 2.11.

The conceptual file at the top of Figure 2.11 is PATIENT; the occurrence of the DSD in Figure 2.12 therefore begins with a specific PATIENT occurrence—patient number 1. The next conceptual file in Figure 2.11 is ORDER; hence, the next collection of occurrences must be from the ORDER file and must be related to the chosen patient. Since patient number 1 has three orders associated with him, we have shown three occurrences of the ORDER file. The arrows connecting the ORDER occurrences merely depict the continuing logical relationship of the PATIENT record occurrence to the associated ORDER record occurrences. We say *logical* because the diagram is free from hardware considerations and reflects the sequencing of records from the user's perspective.

FIGURE 2.12   An Occurrence of a 1:M Relationship from a DSD

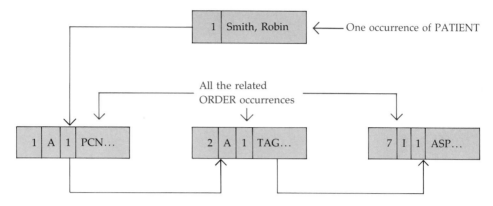

This diagram shows an occurrence of the origin and all the related destination occurrences.

Many-to-Many Relationships

A **many-to-many (M:N) association** between entity classes means that one occurrence of the first entity class is associated with zero, one, or many occurrences of the second. Also, each occurrence of the second entity class is associated with zero, one, or several occurrences of the first. This association type is also called a **complex relationship.**

As an example of this, assume that Patients can have several Physicians and each Physician can treat many Patients. This means that there is a M:N relationship between PHYSICIAN and PATIENT. Part (a) of Figure 2.13 shows how to diagram this using a DSD. The double arrowhead in each direction shows the M:N nature of the relationship. It means that at least one PHYSICIAN occurrence can be associated with many PATIENT occurrences and a given PATIENT occurrence can be associated with many PHYSICIAN occurrences. Part (b) of the figure shows some data values associated with the M:N relationship. Notice that patient 101 is associated with two physicians (a 1:2 relationship between PATIENT and PHYSICIAN) and the physician with code AKL is treating three patients (a 1:3 relationship between PHYSICIAN and PATIENT).

Suburban Hospital permits physicians to be on its research staff. In our example, this means that some physicians might not treat patients. Thus, there can be a PHYSICIAN occurrence with no related PATIENT occurrences, indicating an optional relationship from PHYSICIAN to PATIENT. On the other hand, every patient at Suburban is assigned to a PHYSICIAN, so this association is required.

With few exceptions, DBMSs cannot handle complex relationships. In Chapter 4, we will see how to reduce a complex relationship into a pair of simple (1:M) relationships.

FIGURE 2.13   An Example of a Complex Relationship

(a) A DSD showing a M:N relationship between two record types PATIENT and PHYSICIAN

PATIENT

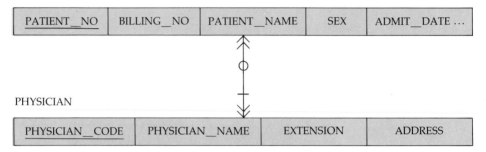

PHYSICIAN

Each patient can be treated by several physicians, and each physician can treat many patients.

(b) An occurrence of the complex relationship from part (a)

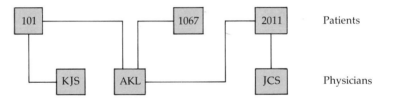

There are three patients and three physicians. Patient 101 is treated by two physicians, and physician AKL treats three patients.

Cycles

A **cycle** is a path that begins at an occurrence of a given type and proceeds through a set of related occurrences of different types, and eventually leads back to the original starting type, although not necessarily to the same occurrence. To illustrate, suppose physicians can be assigned to one of several hospital departments such as Surgical, Acute Care, Out-Patient, and so on, and that patients are also assigned to such departments. Figure 2.14 shows two new conceptual files: PHYSICIAN_DEPARTMENT_ASSIGNMENTS and PATIENT_DEPT_ASSIGNMENTS. The first shows to which department a physician is assigned; the second represents the department to which a patient is admitted. We will use data from these files as we examine the example of a cycle that follows.

Figure 2.15 shows a DSD with entities and its occurrence, both of which we will use to illustrate the cycle. The DSD shows that Department is related to

FIGURE 2.14   **Some Additional Suburban Hospital Files**

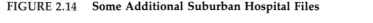

PHYSICIAN__DEPARTMENT__ASSIGNMENTS

DEPT	PHYSICIAN
SURGICAL	1000
SURGICAL	900
OUT-PATIENT	1001
ACUTE CARE	1005

PATIENT__DEPT__ASSIGNMENTS

PATIENT__NO	DEPT
123	OUT-PATIENT
1	SURGICAL
3434	SURGICAL

FIGURE 2.15   **An Example of a Cycle**

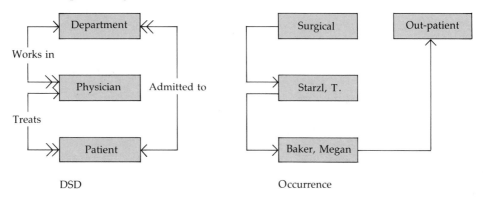

DSD   Occurrence

This DSD shows that the PHYSICIANs work in a DEPARTMENT and treat PATIENTs who are admitted to DEPARTMENTs for treatment. Dr. Starzl works in the surgical department and treats Megan. However, Megan was admitted as an out-patient. By following the path through the occurrence, we begin at an occurrence of DEPARTMENT and end there, although not at the same occurrence.

Physician, Physician to Patient, and Patient to Department; the end and beginning points are the same. Looking at this from an occurrence viewpoint, starting at the Surgical Department occurrence, we find that one of the related occurrences of Physician is Starzl (PHYSICIAN__CODE = 1000 in Figure 2.14). From that Physician occurrence, we proceed to the first Patient treated by Starzl. According to Figure 2.15, that would be Patient 123 (Megan Baker). Thus far, our navigation of the DSD has led us from Department to Physician, then to Patient. After retrieving the Baker occurrence of Patient, we follow the DSD occurrence back to the Department into which Megan was admitted. According to Figure 2.14, she is assigned to the Out-Patient Department, not the Surgical one. Although we have completed the cycle (we ended up at the entity from which we began), the specific occurrence of the ending point differs.

Note that not all cycles end up at an occurrence other than the starting point. Furthermore, some DBMS packages can deal with cycles, others cannot.

FIGURE 2.16   **A Loop**

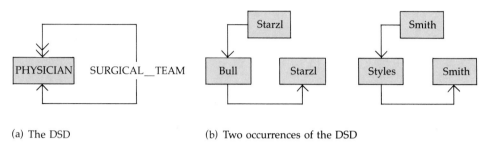

(a) The DSD   (b) Two occurrences of the DSD

A PHYSICIAN is assigned to a SURGICAL TEAM consisting of many PHYSICIANs. Thus, PHYSICIANs are related to PHYSICIANs.

Loops

Loops, also called **recursive relationships,** are 1:M relationships among occurrences of the same type. Suppose that physicians are assigned to surgical teams. This means that we can create a conceptual association among the PHYSICIAN occurrences as shown in Figure 2.16(a). The occurrence of the association, shown as Figure 2.16(b), indicates that Drs. Starzl and Bull are on a team headed by Dr. Starzl. In other words, PHYSICIANs are related to PHYSICIANs; we have a loop. Such intrarecord relationships should be avoided, although some DBMS packages can handle them effectively.

Modeling Record/Entity Relationships

There are two commonly used tools for modeling relationships among record types: data structure diagrams (DSDs) and entity-relationship diagrams (ERDs).

Data Structure Diagrams. We already have discussed the data structure diagramming technique. Figure 2.17 shows a much more complete data structure diagram for the Suburban Hospital example. Recall that a single arrowhead in both directions indicates a 1:1 relationship, a single arrowhead in one direction and a double one in the other represents a 1:M association, and a double arrowhead in both directions depicts a M:N association. We have intentionally left out the membership rules so that you can insert them as an exercise at the end of the chapter.

In Figure 2.17, there is a 1:1 relationship between Bed and Patient. (Despite a relaxing of rules at Suburban, there is still only one patient allowed per bed, and each bed has zero or one patients in it.) The association between Illness

FIGURE 2.17   **The Complete DSD for Suburban Hospital's Pharmacy**

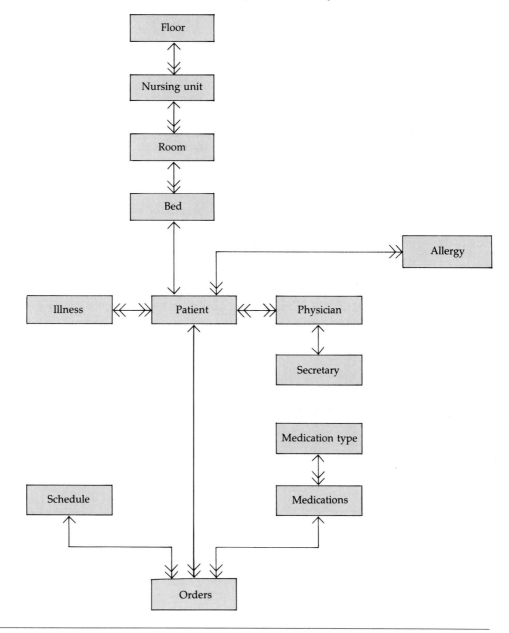

and Patient is M:N, and so is the one between Allergy and Patient. Finally, the relationship between Patient and Order is 1:M; each Patient at Suburban has zero or more pharmacy Orders, but each Order is associated with only one Patient.

Entity-Relationship Diagramming. The **entity-relationship (E-R) diagram** technique puts more emphasis on the relationship between entities than does the DSD method. Figure 2.18 shows a fairly simple E-R diagram. The rectangles refer to the entity classes Physician and Patient, and the diamond to the relationship between them. The small bullet inside the Patient entity means that Patient has a required membership in the Treats relationship; the bullet outside the Physician entity means that Physician has an optional membership in the relationship. The 1 and M refer to the type of relationship (1:M). The relationship has been given the name "Treats."

Naming relationships can be troublesome. In this case, do Physicians "treat" Patients or are Patients "treated" by Physicians? There is no one solution to the problem. The important point is that the E-R diagramming technique forces us to think carefully about the nature of the relationship.

After checking Suburban's rules regarding the relationship between Physicians and Patients, John realized he had made a mistake: Physicians could treat many Patients, and each Patient could be treated by several Physicians. Figure 2.19 shows the correct E-R diagram for this M:N association. Each Physician can treat many Patients, and each Patient can be treated by several Physicians. This

---

FIGURE 2.18   An Example of an Entity-Relationship (E-R) Diagram

This E-R diagram states that one Physician Treats many Patients and that a Single Patient can be associated with only one Physician.

FIGURE 2.19   A M:N Relationship Represented as an E-R Diagram

FIGURE 2.20   **How to Use an E-R Diagram to Conceptually Show a Complex (M:N) Relationship**

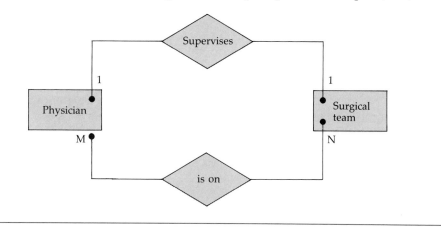

figure represents a single relationship between two entities, but E-R diagrams can also represent multiple relationships.

As we saw earlier, a surgical team at Suburban is composed of many physicians, and one physician is assigned as the head of the team. Figure 2.20 diagrams these relationships. Each Physician can be on several teams, and each team must consist of several Physicians. In addition, one Physician must be assigned as the Supervisor of a team, and each team must have a Supervisor.

Modeling Summary. In this section, we presented two tools that can be used to model entities and their relationships to other entities. The remainder of the text uses the DSD technique, although the trend in many organizations is to use the E-R technique. Both of these tools are used to describe the conceptual and external databases, discussed in the section.

2.5   DATA VIEWS OR PERSPECTIVES: A TAXONOMY OF DATABASE TYPES

The database environment should try to provide as many of the desirable data characteristics discussed in Section 2.3 as possible. By using different perspectives of the data, we can ensure data integrity, security, independence, and privacy. This entails three perspectives, or views (not to be confused with the term *user view*):

- The conceptual
- The external
- The physical

The **conceptual perspective,** also known as the **conceptual database,** or **schema,** is independent of hardware and represents the organization's overall global view of the entities and their interrelationships. Either the E-R diagram or the DSD technique can be used to depict the conceptual database.

The **external perspective,** or **external database,** or **subschema** (which we have been calling the *user view*), is the perspective of a user or group of users. This concept was illustrated in the section on data security, in the example in which the clerk's view of the data substantially differed from the pharmacy director's. There can be many external views of the conceptual database.

The **physical perspective,** or **physical database,** pertains to how the conceptual and external views are physically implemented on the disk. It involves such things as access strategies, pointers, physical location on the drives, and so on.

Historical Perspective

The development of the three views of data can be traced to ANSI (American National Standards Institute). ANSI is divided into many committees. One, known as the X3 Committee, is devoted to computers and information processing. Figure 2.21 depicts its structure.

X3 has two subcommittees responsible for developing database standards: SPARC (Standards Planning and Requirements Committee) and H2 (Database Languages). One of the standards ANSI/X3/SPARC has endorsed is a **database framework** for implementing DBMS software consisting of the three perspectives just discussed. In this section, we will elaborate on these views.

The Conceptual View

At the conceptual level, the DBA is concerned with entities, attributes, and relationships for the entire organization. The conceptual data view is totally independent of both the hardware and specific users' views. Assuming that Suburban Hospital decided to take the database design approach in which a database is designed for each user area within the organization, Figure 2.17 could be considered a conceptual database.

Depending on which commercial DBMS a company uses, the conceptual database might need to be adapted to fit the data model the package requires. As we saw in Chapter 1, there are three important data models: relational, hierarchical, and network. These are a collection of tools and techniques for describing data (through a module called the *data description language,* or *DDL*); for manipulating the data in the database (via the *data manipulation language,* or *DML,* module); and an inherent **data structure**—a term meaning the relationships among records. Section 2.6 provides an overview of the three data models. Data structures are discussed in Chapter 4.

FIGURE 2.21   The Computer-Related Structure of the American National Standards Institute

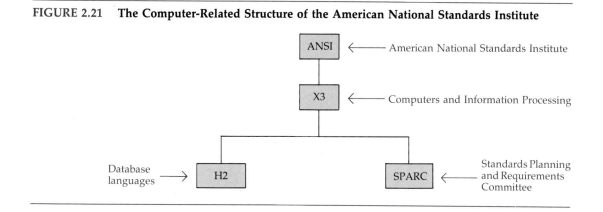

The External View

External views are those of specific users. These views are also logical in that they are independent of hardware and application programming and represent the data view from the user's perspective. Often external views are called *sub-schemas, user schemas,* or *user views.* Each user is able to define the entities, attributes, and relationships he or she requires. External perspectives are based on the conceptual perspective, but they can be any subset of it. Typically, these views are also modeled using either the DSD or E-R diagramming tools outlined earlier. It is through these views that we help guarantee data privacy, integrity, and security.

The Physical View

The physical view of the data consists of the world of access strategies, pointers, cylinders, tracks, and so on. **Pointers** are fields attached to record occurrences that lead from the current record to the next related one. By using pointers, the network and hierarchical data models are able to relate record occurrences to each other. The relational model makes heavy use of indexes to physically assist with relating records. An **index** is a file containing field values and associated record locations and is often used to aid with direct access.

2.6   DATA MODELS

Each of the three main data models has been implemented by one or more vendors and is currently being marketed as a DBMS package. This section will introduce you to these models and to some representative software. Remember that a data model consists of a data structure and methods of operating on it.

The Relational Data Model

The **relational data model** is the basis for virtually every new mainframe-oriented (and also most microcomputer-oriented) DBMS package commercially released over the past four to five years. It is the most flexible and easiest to understand of the three models. Furthermore, it is the model recently accepted by ANSI as its standard. Unfortunately, it is usually the least efficient. However, its merits—flexibility and appeal to end users—far outweigh its faults.

Representative Commercial Packages. In 1984, ANSI/X3/H2 wrote a draft proposal calling for a standard Relational Database Language (RDL) based on IBM's Structured Query Language (SQL, pronounced "sequel"). One version of SQL is an IBM package called SQL/DS (Structured Query Language/Data System), which runs on mainframes using the DOS/VSE or DOS/CMS operating systems. An almost identical IBM package for its MVS and MVS/XA operating systems is Database 2 (DB2). A third version, OS/2 Extended Edition, is included with IBM's microcomputer operating system. Other companies produce their own SQL-based packages. These include IDMS/R by Cullinet, Model 204 by Computer Company of America, ORACLE by Oracle Corporation, INGRES-SQL by INGRES, and INFORMIX-SQL by Relational Database Systems (RDS). The last three are available on micro- and minicomputers, as well as on mainframes.

Data Structure. The relational data model represents entities and their attributes as tables, or flat files. Only files that can be so represented can be stored and manipulated by a relational DBMS.

The relational terms are adapted from the mathematical theories of set theory and logic that were first applied to computer files by an IBM employee, Dr. E. F. Codd, in a 1970 article. As we saw earlier in the chapter, conceptual files are called *relations*, but when referring to a DBMS implementation of the relational approach, such as with IBM's DB2, we refer to them as *tables*. Also, at the conceptual level, records are known as *tuples* while most practitioners call them *rows*. Finally, fields are called *attributes* at the conceptual level and *columns* of a table by practitioners. A database is a collection of related tables, and many databases may exist. An external data view (remember, this is a user's perspective of the data) is called a *view*. Figure 2.22 lists these terms and their COBOL counterparts.

FIGURE 2.22   Relational and COBOL Terminology

Relational Term	COBOL Term
Attribute, column	Field
Tuple, row	Record
Relation, table	File

FIGURE 2.23   Occurrence of the PHYSICIAN Table with Some Associated Relational Terms

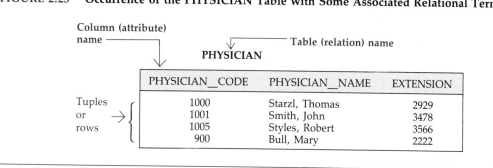

Figure 2.23 reproduces the PHYSICIAN table occurrence from Figure 2.5 using the relational terminology. As you can see, there are three columns (attributes) and four rows (tuples) in the table occurrence. Using COBOL terminology, we could say that the PHYSICIAN file has three fields and four records.

DML. Manipulation of tables is usually done via SQL DML commands or by using a graphical approach called **Query By Example (QBE).** When SQL is used, it can be invoked at a terminal in an interactive mode or embedded in third- or fourth-generation languages.

These packages are so easy to use that IBM suggests allowing users to utilize them to do much of their own ad hoc reporting. This strategy is part of IBM's Information Center concept that is becoming increasingly popular.

An Information Center is supposed to eliminate much of the "red tape" that lengthens project cycles to often absurd levels. Each user group is assigned to a programmer or systems analyst. Rather than having to fill in the usual request forms for an IS project, the users in the group can go directly to the assigned analyst or even develop their own programs using the interactive form of SQL. Only when their requests are too complicated for them to resolve on their own will they ask the analyst for assistance. If the analyst believes a request is larger than is acceptable under the Information Center guidelines, he or she will order the user to submit a request for IS services through more conventional means.

The Hierarchical Data Model

The **hierarchical data model** was developed in the early 1960s by IBM and two of its customers, Rockwell and Caterpillar. Both of these companies needed a bill of materials processor (BOMP) that would print out the total number of each component necessary to meet a given production schedule for a particular product. A bill of materials is nothing more than a sequence of 1:M relationships between the subassemblies necessary for producing an item. This very narrow problem required a specific solution. Solving the problem led IBM to market a DBMS that could solve the bill-of-materials problem very well but was somewhat limited in its flexibility.

Representative Commercial Package. The most significant software package in this family is IBM's IMS (Information Management System). This package has been marketed since 1969 and as recently as 1988 had sold more copies than any other mainframe DBMS software.

Data Structure. The hierarchical data model is sometimes called the *tree data model*, because it can implement only those databases in which the DSDs resemble upside-down trees (the root at the top, the branches at the bottom). In addition, the hierarchical model cannot permit a conceptual file to be the destination for more than one 1:M relationship and, like all the data models, allows no M:N relationships.

In Figure 2.24, no conceptual file is the destination of more than one relationship. Conceptual file C is the destination of a single 1:M relationship between A and itself. In fact, no conceptual file in the diagram is the destination of more than one such relationship. There is no such restriction regarding being the source of a 1:M relationship. For example, conceptual file A is the source of two 1:M relationships: one to B and one to C. Notice that conceptual files D and E

FIGURE 2.24   A Typical Hierarchical DSD

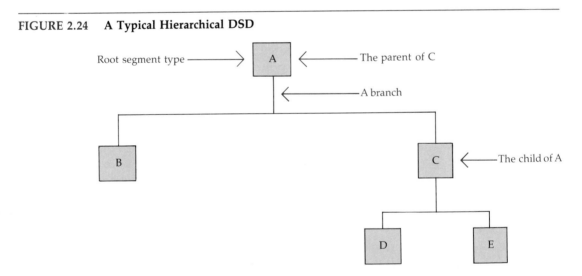

Note that no node is the destination for more than one 1:M relationship. To use hierarchical terminology, no child has more than one parent.

FIGURE 2.25   A Nonhierarchical DSD

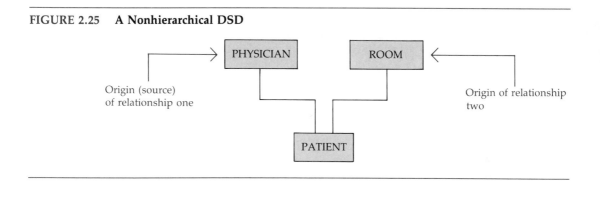

FIGURE 2.26   Hierarchical and COBOL Terminology

Hierarchical Term	COBOL Term
Node, segment type	File
Node, segment occurrence	Record
Field, data item	Field

are not a source of any 1:M relationships. Finally, note that there are no arrowheads on the diagram. Proponents of the hierarchical approach don't use them, as they assume that all relationships are 1:M. If a relationship is 1:1, a simple note is usually made on the diagram.

Contrast Figure 2.24 to Figure 2.25, where PATIENT is the destination of two 1:M relationships. Figure 2.24 is an acceptable hierarchical data structure, but Figure 2.25 is not.

With the hierarchical model, conceptual files are called **segment types** or **nodes** and occurrences **segment occurrences** or **segment instances.** Fields may be called **fields** or **data items.** Relationships between segments are called **parent-child relationships.** In a 1:M relationship, the segment occurring once—the origin— is the parent, while the other one is the child segment type. Because there are many Orders for a given Patient, the association between the two segment types is 1:M. This makes PATIENT the parent segment type and ORDER the child. Figure 2.26 summarizes these terms and compares them to some familiar COBOL terminology.

While a segment may be the parent of many 1:M relationships, it can be the child of only one. In fact, every segment except the one at the top, called the **root segment type,** must have exactly one parent. Databases are defined as collections of tree occurrences and called **physical databases.** External data views are known as **logical databases.**

DML. IMS has a name for its DML: Data Language I (DL/I). The language must be called from a host program, and its syntax is quite rigid. The DL/I calls allow users to retrieve child segments sequentially. Unfortunately, unless a user knows these parent-child relationships in advance, the records cannot be so processed. DL/I also allows indexed or hashed access to root segment occurrences.

The Network Data Model

The **network data model** originated from CODASYL, another group interested in promoting data processing standards. In April 1971, CODASYL released a document produced by one of its subcommittees known as the Database Task Group (DBTG). This document became the cornerstone for the network model.

Representative Commercial Packages. The best-selling CODASYL DBMS is Cullinet's IDMS/R. Most of the major mainframe hardware vendors (except IBM) also market network-based DBMSs.

Data Structure. First, the network model uses the term **record type** instead of *conceptual file* and **set type** to refer to 1:M relationships. Like record types, set types are assigned names. Next, the data relationships that can be implemented under this model are much more flexible than those permitted by the hierarchical model. Whereas with the hierarchical data model no more than one segment

---

FIGURE 2.27   A Network DSD

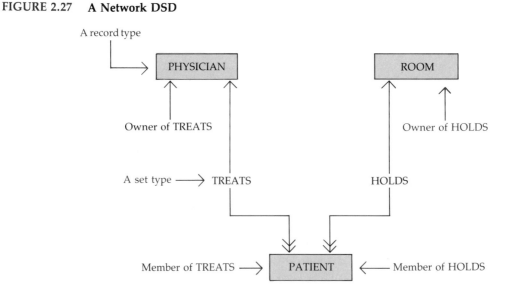

FIGURE 2.28   **Network and COBOL Terminology**

Network Term	COBOL Term
Record, type	File
Record occurrence	Record
Field, data item	Field

---

type can serve as a destination for multiple 1:M relationships, no such restriction is necessary for the network model. Unfortunately, the network model, like the others, permits no M:N relationships.

Figure 2.27 shows a typical network data structure. There are two 1:M relationships (set types) having PATIENT as their destination: TREATS and HOLDS.

In hierarchical terminology, PATIENT has two parents: PHYSICIAN and ROOM; conversely, PATIENT is a child of both PHYSICIAN and ROOM. Network terminology for a parent is **owner of the set type** (**owner** for short); the corresponding network term for child is **member of the set type** (or simply **member**). Thus, we would say that PHYSICIAN is the owner of the TREATS set type and PATIENT is the member of the HOLDS set type. This model calls the conceptual database the *schema*, while external databases are *subschemas*. Figure 2.28 summarizes these terms and their COBOL equivalents.

DML. As with the other models, the DML in a network model is invoked via calls to the DBMS from the host language. As with the hierarchical model, the structure is quite rigid and requires intimate knowledge of record names, field names, and set names.

2.7 SUMMARY

This chapter looked at data, the base on which a database is built. Data has many characteristics, some of which may be called by different names by members of each of the three data realms we discussed in Section 2.2. The data characteristics discussed were name, type, representation, length, real versus virtual, domain, value, data independence, key versus nonkey, integrity, security, and privacy.

Fields are related to other fields and records to other records in one of four ways: 1:1, 1:M, M:N, or not at all. We can explicitly show interrecord relationships using the tools of data structure diagrams and entity-relationship diagrams. By studying the nature of the relationships among the record types, we can determine whether we need to use a flexible but complicated network model or a simpler but more rigid hierarchical one. The relational data model, like the network model, is very flexible and much easier to use. This is the model from which almost all new DBMS software is built.

REVIEW QUESTIONS

1. What can programmers and analysts do to help clarify terminology used in discussions with users?
2. Why is data independence important?
3. Should a data dictionary be on-line or kept in hard-copy form?
4. Discuss how domain and foreign key constraints can improve data integrity.
5. Explain what is meant by a candidate key, and give an example that relates to your university.
6. Give an example of a view.
7. Distinguish between data and information.
8. Define *entity*, *entity class*, and *attribute*, and give an example of each.
9. Distinguish among an attribute, a data element, and a field.
10. What is a repeating element? A repeating group?
11. What is the physical-world term for a multivalued attribute?
12. Explain the characteristics of a flat file.
13. How do we differentiate between attribute names that are the same but pertain to different entity classes?
14. Give an example of a virtual field that might be carried in a STUDENT file.
15. What is the primary advantage and disadvantage of virtual fields?
16. Give an implicitly enumerated domain for social security number.
17. List the six key types, and give an example of each for a STUDENT file.
18. What are the characteristics of a primary key?
19. Assume your university has an advising system that has a master file containing student numbers, names, family data such as parent name, address, and so on, as well as every course taken by the student, together with the grade. Describe what kinds of security measures could be used that would permit a student access, but only to the records pertaining to that student.
20. Explain encryption and how we might implement it.
21. Draw a data structure diagram for the following scenario. Vendors send us invoices that contain several line items. Each line item contains item code, item description, units sent, and unit price. (Hint: First list the entities, then the attributes for each entity, and then the relationships among the entities.)
22. Draw an E-R diagram for Question 21.
23. What are the two components of a data model?
24. Describe the three main data models and a representative software package from each.
25. Use the section on data integrity to decide which of the three options should be applied to:

    a. A Purchase Order/Line Item relationship.

b. An Inventory/Line Item relationship.

c. A Vendor/Purchase Order relationship.

For all three parts, assume the parent is being deleted. Justify your answers.

▪▪ EPISODE 2

Community Hospital Adopts the Database Approach

In Episode 1, the IS staff of Community Hospital was beginning to realize the inadequacies of their current information systems. Bill Moore assigned Barb Scholl and Robin Kennedy the responsibility of creating a plan and/or an approach to help make the ever-changing hospital environment easier to cope with. This episode looks at their results.

The members of the project team decided to adopt the database approach. They felt that by using this methodology, all of Bill's objectives could be met. The first thing they did was decide on the hospital's entities and the relationships among them. Exhibit 1 shows the results of their study.

The team decided that the 14 entity classes shown in Exhibit 1 might have to be further divided at a later date but represented a good starting point for their database design. After drawing the data structure chart in Exhibit 1, they attached attributes to each entity class as shown in Exhibit 2.

At their next meeting, Barb and Robin presented the results of their analysis to Bill. They began by pointing out some of the relationships on their DSD. Barb went first.

"There is a many-to-many relationship between Physician and Patient, because admissions said they assign up to three physicians to a single patient and, obviously, each physician treats many pa-

tients. We finally decided to make the relationship between Invoice and Purchase Order one-to-many, because an invoice usually covers several of our purchase orders.

"Notice that while the Lab Results to PatBill relationship is 1:1, the other three relationships involving the PatBill entity class are 1:M. Each Pharmacy Order can generate several billing entries, because a particular order is filled several times a day, but each billing entry can be related only to a single Pharmacy Order. The same is true for Supplies Used. A patient can receive the same supply item several times a day, so there could be many billing entries for each item used. The Lab Results to PatBill relationship is one-to-one, because each lab test generates exactly one patient charge. Any questions, Bill?"

Bill responded, "Yes. Explain why the relationship between Insurance Co. and Patient is many to many."

Robin interjected, "That was my doing. I figured that each patient could have several insurance companies, and certainly each company could insure several of our patients."

Bill continued, "Did you check with admissions for the correct policy?"

Robin replied, "No, but I will before the next meeting. OK?"

Because Bill wanted to be sure his team understood the importance of deter-

EXHIBIT 1   Initial Database Design for Community Hospital

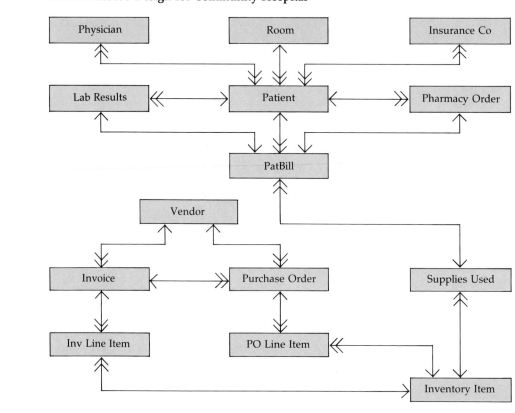

mining the organizational "rules" that applied to each relationship, he gave Robin a long lecture on the importance of determining rules and the part rules play in determining the relationships among entity classes. He finished by agreeing to allow Robin to respond to his question at the next meeting provided she re-examined all the rules pertaining to the relationships presented in Exhibit 1.

Bill decided that the initial design was only partially finished. He noticed several problems, including repeating fields, attributes associated with incorrect entities, and some entities that seemed to be missing attributes. As examples of these problems, he pointed out to the other two team members: Why carry the charge in each lab test? It seemed to make more sense to set up an entity class called Test containing an attribute for Charge. He pointed out the same kind of problem with the Pharmacy Order entity: Why carry Charge in there when the charge could be associated with a particular medicine?

Other problems he indicated were: Where would they get information about the medications in each Pharmacy Order? Should the medications be considered occurrences of Inventory Items, or should a special entity class called Formulary be

EXHIBIT 2   Tentative Attributes Associated with the Entity Classes for Community Hospital

Room

Nursing Unit
Room No
Bed
Patient No

Patient

Number
Name
Admit Date
DRG
Discharge Date
Nursing Unit
Room
Bed
Physician Code 1
Physician Code 2
Physician Code 3
Allergy Code 1
Allergy Code 2
Allergy Code 3
Insurance Co 1
Insurance Co 2
Height
Weight
Sex
Religion

Insurance Co

Code
Name
Address
Phone
Contact

Lab Results

Test Type
Date
Patient Code
Results
Charge

Physician

Code
Name
Extension
Home Phone
Medicare No

Vendor

Code
Address
Phone
Contact
To Date $

Purchase Order

Number
Vendor Code
Date
Total Amt
Tax

Invoice

Vendor Number
Voucher Number
Date
Total Amt
PO No 1
PO No 2
PO No 3
PO No 4

Inventory Item

Item Code
Description
Vendor 1
Vendor 2
Avg Cost
Charge
$ Usage TD
Units Used TD

PO Line Item

PO No
Item Code
Units Ordered
Item Price

Inv Line Item

Invoice No
Item Code
Units Received
Charge per Item

Supplies Used

Patient No
Item Code
Units Charged

Pharmacy Orders

Patient No
Medicine Code
Quantity Dispensed
Schedule
Charge per Dose
Quantity to Be Billed

PatBill

Patient No
Department Code
Total Charge
Units Billed

set up? How could they tie Physicians to Patients and Patients to Physicians? Perhaps a new entity class called Is Treated By was needed. How should they bill for pharmacy's charges? Was it better to update the PatBill entity class just as an order was filled, or should the charge be considered an attribute of the Pharmacy Order class as indicated by the Quantity to Be Billed attribute in Exhibit 2? Barb and Robin had assumed that the Quantity to Be Billed attribute could be used to do a batch update of the PatBill entity class. Why should they carry the Patient "No" in the Room entity when the patient's location was an attribute of Patient? Finally, where would they get the department descriptions to match against the department code in the PatBill entity class?

Bill told his staff to redo their design and report back in three weeks. After we look at designing a database in more detail, we'll see how the team changed the design.

CHAPTER

3

Database Structures

Implementing Relationships

MINICASE ICU Library

This minicase isn't intended to be realistic. However, the manner in which the books are organized for the fictitious university library accurately demonstrates how link lists, the basis for most of this chapter, can be used to accomplish a sequential organization and access of objects.

ICU is a small university located in the foothills of the Greenridge Mountains. Its librarian, J. C. Antiquarian, has just started a database section in the library. In the past, he has had difficulty keeping the books in correct order. Because J. C. was never taught the proper way to catalog and store books, he has always put them into sections by subject: a COBOL section, a BASIC section, a systems analysis section, and so on. Within a subject area, books are stored alphabetically by title. Furthermore, because shelf space is at a premium, J. C. packs as many books on a shelf as will fit. Adding a new book is a major problem. Invariably, the new book belongs in the middle of the shelf, so every book to the

right has to be slid over to accommodate it. The last book on the right usually won't fit anymore, so it has to be moved to the first position on the next shelf. This process continues until J. C. finds room for an extra book on a shelf.

J. C. is about to try an experiment to help him store the first three new database books shown in Figure 3.1. He has some room at the ends of three shelves that are located on the first and third floors.

Figure 3.2 shows the actual locations where J. C. has finally stored the books. Although the books are no longer in title order, J. C. has devised a method whereby students can still retrieve them in title sequence. In fact, his new cataloging method allows students to also retrieve books alphabetically by author, something they couldn't do under the old method.

To accomplish this, J. C. has begun a new card catalog system, a portion of which is shown in Figure 3.3. Because the first card in-

FIGURE 3.1   Three Database Books to Be Cataloged in ICU's Library

FIGURE 3.2   Location of the New Database Books in ICU's Library

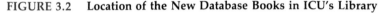

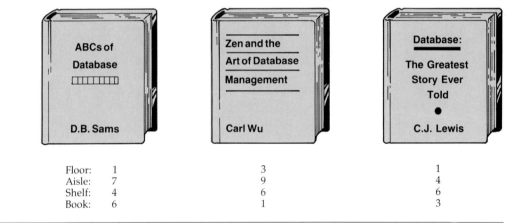

Floor:	1	3	1
Aisle:	7	9	4
Shelf:	4	6	6
Book:	6	1	3

dicates the location of the first new database book, sorted by title, he calls it the "First-Book-by-Title" card. By referring to the book locations (Figure 3.2), you can see that this card points to the book titled *ABCs of Database*. When a student goes to floor 1, aisle 7, shelf 4, book 6, he or she will find the desired book. The other card shown in Figure 3.3 J. C. calls his "First-Book-by-Author" card, because, like its "Title" counterpart that shows students the location of the first data-

base book by title, this card indicates the location of the first book by author.

Accompanying each book is another card, an example of which is shown in Figure 3.4. In fact, there are two cards accompanying *ABCs of Database*, one showing the location of the next book in title order and the other pointing to the next book by author. We will continue to follow the title sequence.

The "Next-by-Title" indicator that accompanies *ABCs of Database* tells the student to

FIGURE 3.3   **First-Book Cards for Title and Author**

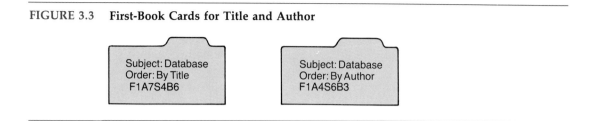

FIGURE 3.4   **Using Pointers to Relate Books in ICU's Library**

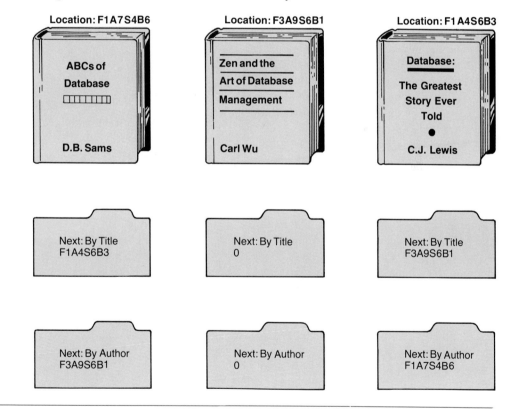

next go to floor 1, aisle 4, shelf 6 and look at book 3 on that shelf. Figure 3.4 shows that the book at that location is *Database: The Greatest Story Ever Told.* In fact, this title alphabetically follows the previous one; so far, so good. The "Next-by-Title" pointer with that book leads the student to the last database book, which is located on floor 3, aisle 9, shelf 6, book 1. When the now tiring student goes to this location, he or she discovers

Zen and the Art of Database Management, certainly the last book alphabetized by title. Notice that the "Next-by-Title" pointer associated with this book has a value of zero. J. C. has decided that this special value will designate that there are no more books according to the sequence being followed.

The student following the list of cards to access the books in alphabetical order by author would visit these locations: F1A4S6B3, where the book by C. J. Lewis is kept; then F1A7S4B6, where D. B. Sam's book is found; then to F3A9S6B1, where Carl Wu's book is located.

While the new system has been controversial, the ICU student body appreciates the fact that it enables them to easily (albeit not quickly) find books in two different sequences. J. C. is quick to point out that not only could his old system not do this, but the new system has also made it easy for him to add books. To prove this point, he shows anyone willing to listen what he has to do to add the title *Everything You Always Wanted to Know about Databases*, by I. M. Zanos. He has room for the book on floor 2, aisle 4, shelf 1, book 17. After placing the book there, he shows how only two cards have to be changed: the "Next-by-Title" card for *Database: The Greatest Story Ever Told* and the "Next-by-Author" card for *Zen and the Art of*

Database Management. Both cards must now "point" to the new book.

Unfortunately, just as acceptance of J. C.'s new idea is spreading, someone has taken both "first-book" pointer cards, leaving the interested students with no way to find the initial book in each list!

Discussion

1. Why couldn't J. C. physically put his database books in both title and author sequence?

2. What additional kind of pointer could J. C. use that, if added to each card, would enable him to determine the values on the cards that were stolen?

3. Why does J. C. even need the "first-book" cards?

4. Show the complete set of card values after adding the new book.

5. Suppose that J. C. also wants to be able to sequence the original three database books by publisher. How many total additional cards will be needed?

6. Assume that Sam's and Wu's books are published by Arnold Press while Lewis's book is published by MBI Publishing. Using your answer to Question 5, show the new cards for ordering the books by publisher.

This chapter is essential for understanding how a DBMS physically implements the conceptual designs in Chapter 2, especially those destined for implementation by either the hierarchical or network model. By using **pointers**—fields attached to records that relate records to one another—we can implement **data structures**—relationships among records. Both the hierarchical and network data models extensively use pointers to implement record relationships. The relational model also uses pointers, but it does so to help locate records, not to relate them.

Many of the examples in this chapter are based on the Suburban Hospital minicase in Chapter 2. Therefore, you may want to reread that minicase before reading this chapter.

At the conclusion of this chapter, you will be able to:

- List and discuss several ways to classify pointers.
- Describe three uses for data structures.
- Describe and implement the following data structures:

    Lists
    Rings
    Two-way lists
    Two-way rings
    Multilists
    Inversions
    Trees
    Networks

- Show how to add and delete records from lists.
- Determine the best way to search a multilist.
- Show how to use a list to sequentially organize a file on its key.
- Show how to use a multilist to process secondary keys.
- Use a binary tree to search for a primary or secondary key.
- Define the terminology used with hierarchical and network data structures.
- Implement hierarchical and network data structures.

3.1 POINTERS

The ICU library example uses pointers to allow students to access books in either of two orders. Remember that there are two special cards (pointers) that indicate the location of the first book for each ordering. J. C. calls these cards "first-book" cards. The two cards found alongside each book represent "next" pointers, because they indicate the next book for a particular sequence. One of these cards indicates the next book by title, and the other by author. To indicate that there are no more books in a given sequence, J. C. uses the value zero on the appropriate card.

Almost all relationships derived from the conceptual database design are of the 1:M type. To implement such relationships we, like J. C., need an initial pointer from the origin file (the "one" side) to the first related record in the destination file (the "many" side). We also need pointers to connect each of the subsequent related destination records to one another. We will now look at the different kinds of pointers and the role each plays in the physical design of the database.

We will use pointers to relate records of the same or different types. We will

---

FIGURE 3.5   **A Data Structure Diagram**

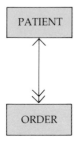

There is a 1:M relationship between a PATIENT and his or her ORDERs.

---

use the terms **pointer field** and **link field** interchangeably and refer to a group of related records as a **list,** which can relate a single record of one type to a collection of records of a different type or relate only records of the same type.

Figure 3.5 shows in condensed form the rather simple DSD we first saw in Figure 2.11. It depicts the conceptual 1:M relationship between a PATIENT and his or her pharmacy ORDERs. Using pointers, we can physically relate a PATIENT record to the group of related ORDER records. The complete set of related records will thus form the list. In constructing the different kinds of structures used to relate records, we use up to five different types of pointers:

- Next
- Prior
- Head
- Tail
- Origin

In addition, all of these pointer types can be embedded or carried in separate files called **directories,** or **indexes.**

Pointer Types

A **next** pointer connects records of the same type in a forward direction. A **prior** pointer does the same in the opposite direction. A **head** pointer provides the location of the initial record in the list; it is also called a **first** pointer. A **tail,** or **last,** pointer gives the location of the final record in the list. Finally, an **origin,** or **home,** pointer relates a destination record to its origin.

The ICU library cataloging system uses two head pointers, one for each of the two sequences. Also, each book is accompanied by two "next" cards, because there are two ways to access the next book—by title or by author. Based on this example, you may already have concluded that each ordering method requires a new pointer.

Similarly, to physically implement Figure 3.5, we need a head pointer to connect each PATIENT record occurrence to the initial ORDER occurrence for that PATIENT and a series of next pointers, one per ORDER, to relate the ORDERs for that PATIENT. One problem to be solved is: What do we mean by *first* and *next?* The answer depends on the desired sequence of ORDER (destination) records.

Choosing a Sequence. While this type of ordering is usually based on one of the fields contained in the record types being linked, it can be a time-based ordering, such as first-in, first-out. Figure 3.6 shows the description of both record types from Figure 3.5. The ORDER record type carries ORDER__NUMBER, STATUS, PATIENT__NO, MEDICATION__CODE, DATE__ENTERED, INITIALS, CHANGE__DATE, SCHEDULE, UNITS, and BILLING__UNITS. If it looks familiar it should, because it is the same record description used in Figure 2.5.

Some of the fields may require explanation. The DATE__ENTERED is the date the order initially was entered for the patient. The INITIALS are the initials of the pharmacist who entered the order. The CHANGE__DATE is the date the order was last modified. SCHEDULE tells how often to administer the medication. The UNITS field provides the amount of the medication to administer each time. The BILLING__UNITS field represents the number of medication units that have been administered to the patient but not yet billed.

Because we are attempting to relate a PATIENT with a collection of ORDER occurrences, we have to decide which of the ORDER fields to use as the basis for our ordering. Although we can sequence the ORDER occurrences on any of the fields (or on a combination of the fields), once we make our decision we cannot change our minds unless we want to add another pointer. Let's assume we decide to sequence the ORDER records for a given PATIENT by ORDER__NUMBER.

FIGURE 3.6   **Conceptual Record Descriptions for the Record Types of Figure 3.5**

PATIENT (<u>PATIENT__NO</u>, PATIENT__NAME, SEX, ADMIT__DATE)

The connection field (or foreign key)
↓

ORDER (<u>ORDER__NUMBER</u>, STATUS, PATIENT__NO, MEDICATION__CODE,
      DATE__ENTERED, INITIALS, CHANGE__DATE, SCHEDULE, UNITS,
      BILLING__UNITS)

FIGURE 3.7   **The Occurrence of Figure 3.5**

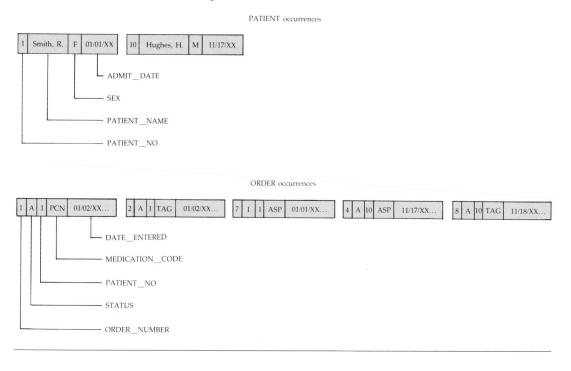

To continue with our example, we need some record occurrences. Figure 3.7 shows some of the data that we saw in Figure 2.5. Note that it contains some additional occurrences of ORDER and that some of the other data have been changed. The figure indicates that there are two occurrences of PATIENT and a total of five ORDER occurrences. Notice that PATIENT_NO 1 is related to three ORDER records—ORDER_NUMBERs 1, 2, and 7—and that PATIENT_NO 10 is related to two—4 and 8.

Head Pointers. Because we made the decision to relate a PATIENT to his or her ORDERs based on the ORDER_NUMBER field, the head pointer for each PATIENT must point to the ORDER record that contains the lowest ORDER_NUMBER value for that PATIENT, assuming that we want the ORDER occurrences to be in ascending order. Thus, the head pointer for PATIENT_NO 1 must point to the record containing ORDER_NUMBER 1. Similarly, PATIENT_NO 10's head pointer should point to the record containing ORDER_NUMBER 4.

FIGURE 3.8   **An Occurrence with Head (First) Pointers Stored in an Origin Record Occurrence**

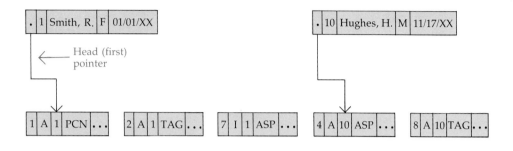

Problem 1. **Assume that ORDER occurrences are to be sequenced on DATE __ENTERED rather than on ORDER__NUMBER. What are the values for the head pointers for the two PATIENT occurrences? Also, what is the impact if we need both this and the original sequence?**

Solution. PATIENT__NO 1's orders were entered on January 1 (ORDER__NUM-BER 7) and January 2 (ORDER__NUMBERs 1 and 2), while those for PATIENT__NO 10 were entered on November 17 (ORDER__NUMBER 4) and November 18 (ORDER__NUMBER 8). Therefore, the head pointer for PATIENT__NO 1 would point to the record containing ORDER__NUMBER 7, and for PATIENT__NO 10 the value would be the record for ORDER__NUMBER 4.

The answer to the second question is that we will need two head pointers. Each additional sequencing requires a new head pointer.

Figure 3.8 shows the head pointer from each of the two PATIENT occurrences to the related ORDER record having the lowest ORDER__NUMBER value. Until we learn how to implement pointers, we will continue to use arrows to represent the pointers.

Next Pointers. Next pointers connect related records of the same type. Since we chose to relate the destination records (ORDERs) to one another based on ORDER__NUMBER, the next pointers must maintain an ascending sequence of ORDER__NUMBERs. Figure 3.9 shows the head and next pointer implementation for the simple database.

Prior Pointers. Because a prior pointer leads from one record to the related record having the next lower value for the sequencing field, in our example a prior pointer would lead from one ORDER record for a chosen PATIENT to the

FIGURE 3.9   Head (First) and Next Pointers

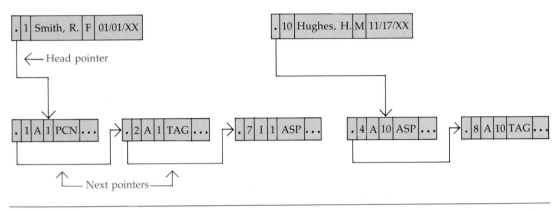

FIGURE 3.10   Head, Next, and Prior Pointers

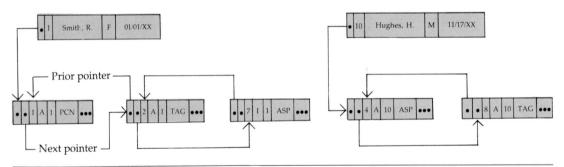

one that has the next lower ORDER_NUMBER value for that PATIENT. Figure 3.10 shows the prior pointers in place. Notice that ORDER_NUMBER 7 leads to ORDER_NUMBER 2, which in turn points to ORDER_NUMBER 1, and that all three are related to PATIENT_NO 1.

Tail Pointers. Can you see a problem associated with trying to use the structure depicted in Figure 3.10? The difficulty is related to the one we first saw in the minicase at the beginning of the chapter. Remember the problem J. C. had when someone took the "first-book" cards? Because no one knew where the first book was, none of the database books could be found. The problem here is that there is no way to determine where to begin the backward accessing of the ORDERs. We know that ORDER_NUMBER 7 points to ORDER_NUMBER 2, but how do we begin our chain of backward ORDERs? The answer lies in the use of a tail or last pointer, mentioned earlier. Figure 3.11 includes the tail pointers.

FIGURE 3.11   **Head, Tail, Next, and Prior Pointers**

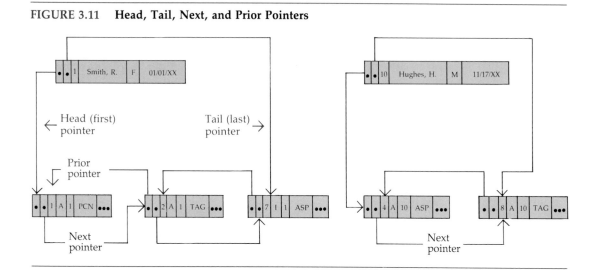

FIGURE 3.12   **Head, Tail, Next, Prior, and Origin Pointers**

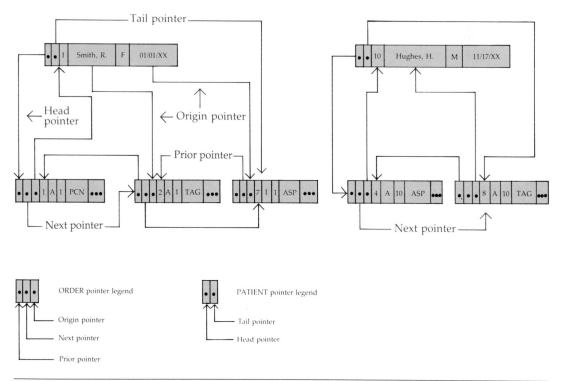

Notice that both the tail and head pointers are carried in the origin occurrence—PATIENT in this example.

Home Pointers. Earlier we saw that home, or origin, pointers point from a destination record to its related origin record. Thus, if we use origin pointers in our example, each of the ORDER records will point back to the PATIENT associated with the ORDER. We depict this situation in Figure 3.12, which also shows all the other pointers.

Implementation of Pointers

Although pointers can be implemented in several ways, we will usually assume they are relative record numbers. A **relative record number (RRN)** of a record is the record's displacement from the beginning of the file. The first record in a file has an RRN value of 0, the next record's RRN is 1, and so on. This is discussed in more detail in Appendix A.

Figure 3.13 shows an example of using RRNs. The figure assumes that records have been assigned consecutive record numbers beginning at 1. Technically, the first record in a file is assigned to RRN 0, but we use that value to designate that the last record has been reached. The figure uses two PATIENT pointers (head and tail) and three ORDER pointers (next, prior, and origin) per record. You can see from the example that we have treated PATIENT and ORDER records as if they were records within the same file. Record numbers 1 and 2 are used for PATIENT data, while record numbers 3 through 7 are used for ORDERs. In fact, most DBMSs treat the record types within a database in just this way: They do not differentiate record types from one another and store them in separate files; rather, in keeping with the conventions of the database approach, they view the different record types as simply records within a single file: the database.

Location

Two locations are used to store pointers: They can be embedded in record occurrences or in separate files called **indexes,** or **directories.** An index is a separate file that contains two elements: a field value and a collection of associated disk addresses, usually RRNs.

Figure 3.14 shows how to use an index together with the relative addressing scheme to create a file of directory pointers. First, we create a new file for the indexed field. Because in our example we are attempting to relate all of the ORDERs for a given PATIENT to one another, we need to index the ORDER file on PATIENT__NO. Next, we create a directory record for every possible value of the indexing field, with each record containing two components: a PATIENT__NO and the list of relative record numbers corresponding to the records that have that value. Notice that PATIENT__NO 1 has three associated

---

FIGURE 3.13   **Using Relative Record Numbers (RRNs) as Pointers to Relate a PATIENT Record to a Group of Related ORDER Records**

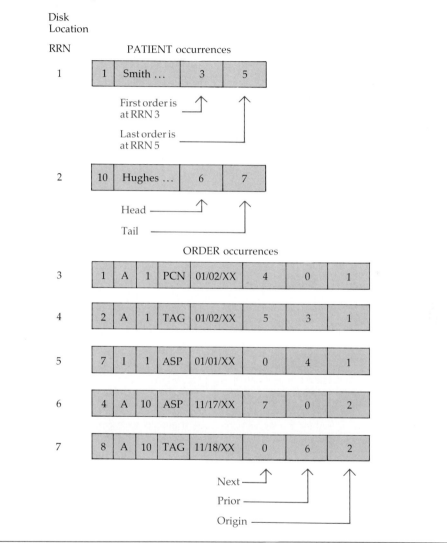

relative records: 3, 4, and 5, corresponding to ORDER_NUMBERs 1, 2, and 7, respectively. Because we still want to relate ORDERs to one another in ascending order of ORDER_NUMBER, the relative pointers are in the same sequence as the associated ORDERs.

The advantages that indexing offers are its potential ability to quickly answer queries without having to actually read the data records and its ability to let us

FIGURE 3.14   Using an Index File to Store Pointers

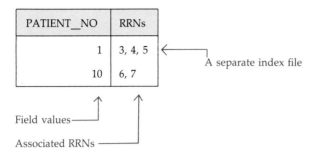

Field values

Associated RRNs

The RRN sequence maintains a logical order based on ORDER__NUMBER values.

FIGURE 3.15   Summary of Pointer Characteristics

Pointer Type	Database Management Uses
Head	Connects a record of one type to the initial record of a different type.
Tail	Connects a record of one type to the final record of another type.
Next	Connects two records of the same type in a designated order. Used to locate the "next" destination record.
Prior	Connects two records of the same type in the reverse direction; usually used to connect two destination records. Used to process destination records in a reverse direction and to facilitate repair of damaged pointers.
Origin	Connects a destination record to its origin. Provides fast access of an origin.

Location	Database Management Uses
Embedded	Used for sequential processing, especially for secondary keys.
Directory	Fast access to records having a particular secondary key value. Its primary disadvantage is difficulty of updating.

use a direct access of records on fields other than the primary key path. Its disadvantages are related to the difficulties in keeping the indexes current. Many DBMSs use both an indexing and an embedded-pointer scheme—the indexes for quick direct retrieval on nonprimary key fields and embedded pointers for normal sequential retrieval of records. In the upcoming section on data structures, we will again look at the advantages and disadvantages.

***Problem 2.* Index the ORDER records for PATIENT__NO 1 assuming the index is to be in order of DATE__ENTERED.**

Solution. Based on Figure 3.13, the associated relative record numbers would be 5, 4, and 3, in that order. Note that there are two records associated with January 2—RRNs 3 and 4—so an alternative answer would be 5, 3, 4.

This concludes our introduction to pointers. We have seen that there can be up to five kinds of pointers, each of which can be stored within the data records or in a separate directory or index file. Figure 3.15 summarizes the pointer types and associated uses for each. Now that we understand what pointers are, we will turn to the important concept of data structures.

3.2 DATA STRUCTURES: RELATIONSHIPS AMONG RECORDS

A **data structure** is a relationship among records. As you will eventually see, many of the ideas already discussed in this chapter are actually data structures. Data structures are used in a database context in the following ways:

- To process records on secondary keys.
- To relate records to one another in both inter- and intrafile relationships.
- To provide an efficient form of sequential processing based on primary keys where the logical and physical orderings are not the same.

First, data structures are a very efficient way to process secondary keys. Recall that a secondary key is a field that can have duplicate values and can be used as an alternate search path to the records. For example, the primary key for a purchase order (PO) master file would probably be the PO__NO field. However, it is quite likely that a purchasing department employee would also need to search the file on DATE__ISSUED. Because many POs could be issued on the same date, DATE__ISSUED qualifies as a secondary key.

Another example of a secondary key would be the PATIENT__NO field within the ORDER file that we discussed earlier in the chapter. By using a list data structure, it would be fairly simple to access all the purchase orders issued on a certain date or all the orders for a given patient.

Second, data structures are useful for creating inter- or intrafile relationships. Implementations of both the network and hierarchical database models must be able to relate records of different types (**interfile relationships**) and records of the same type (**intrafile relationships**). As you might expect, these relationships are accomplished through pointers.

Third, data structures provide end users with a primary key sequential processing capability without the inherent updating problems associated with physical sequential organization. Using the list data structure, for example, we could process the purchase orders in PO__NO sequence, even though the purchase order records were physically stored in a time-sequenced manner.

Regardless of which of the three uses for data structures we are discussing, the data structure will be used to relate records of the same type or of differing types. We begin our study of data structures with those that are particularly helpful in determining relationships among records of the same type:

- Simple lists
- Rings
- Two-way lists
- Two-way rings
- Multilists
- Inversions

3.3   SIMPLE LISTS

Simple lists, also called **simple chains** or **lists,** provide logical processing based on primary or secondary keys; they are collections of records of the same type that are logically related to one another based on a sequencing field. We will look first at what a list is and how to use one to sequentially process primary keys and then how to use one to process secondary keys.

Part (a) of Figure 3.16 shows a portion of a PURCHASE__ORDER file; part (b) shows the conceptual record description. Part (a) lists four purchase orders: PO__NOs 1, 4, 7, and 9. Each record occurrence has a primary key and two potential secondary keys. It should be apparent that the PO__NO is the primary key for the record type and the other two fields are secondary key candidates.

Figure 3.17 shows a sequential organization (see Appendix B for a thorough discussion of organization and access) of the PURCHASE__ORDER file, sorted on PO__NO. This organization cannot offer us the ability to process the records based on either of the two secondary keys and is difficult to update, especially when we are only adding or deleting a few records.

FIGURE 3.16   **Two Conceptual Views of a Purchase Order File**

(a) A tabular representation of a purchase order (PO) file

PO__NO	DATE__ISSUED	VENDOR__CODE
1	01/04/XX	103
4	01/04/XX	123
7	01/09/XX	103
9	01/10/XX	133

(b) The conceptual record types associated with Figure 3.16(a)

PURCHASE__ORDER (PO__NO, DATE__ISSUED, VENDOR__CODE)

FIGURE 3.17   A Sequential Organization of a PURCHASE__ORDER Master File, Reproduced from Figure 3.16

Using a Simple List to Sequentially Process Records Based on a Primary Key

Figure 3.18 shows both the conceptualization and the implementation of the link list that enables us to sequentially process the PURCHASE__ORDER records by their primary key, PO__NO. Part (a) shows what we must accomplish via the link field. The head pointer must point to RRN 9, which should point to 2, 2 to 8, and 8 to 6, which is the end of the list. Each record in part (b) of Figure 3.18 has three fields plus the link field that connects a given PURCHASE__ ORDER with the next one based on PO__NO.

The first physical record contains PO__NO 4 and has been assigned to RRN 2. The next record, which has an RRN value of 6, contains PO__NO 9. Next comes RRN 8, where PO__NO 7 is found. Finally comes RRN 9, which is the address for PO__NO 1. This means that the physical ordering of the PO__NOs is 4, 9, 7, and 1. Not exactly sequential is it? However, look at what happens when we follow the pointers.

The head of the list is RRN 9. You might feel a bit uncomfortable with the practicality of this approach at this time, because we still have no formal way to determine how we know this head value; but don't worry, we will see how to do this later. After accessing the head of the list, RRN 9, we use its link field value to determine the address of the next (logical) PURCHASE__ORDER record; it's at RRN 2. When we access the record at location 2, we find PO__NO 4. Continuing with the procedure, we next visit RRN 8, where we find PO__NO 7, and finally RRN 6, where PO__NO 9 is located. The pointer value associated with this last record is zero, indicating that there are no more PURCHASE__ORDER records.

We can generalize our example to develop a procedure for processing a list:

- Access the head pointer.
- Access the first record in the list based on the head pointer value.
- Use the link field to access the next record.
- Continue until the link field contains zero (or some other special designator, such as HIGH-VALUES).

FIGURE 3.18   Using a List to Order the Purchase__Order File

(a) A conceptualization of how to use a simple list to logically sequence the PURCHASE__ORDER occurrences on PO__NO

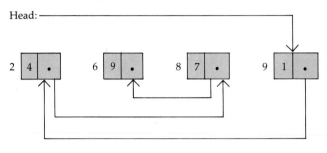

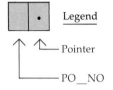

Legend

Pointer

PO__NO

(b) The implementation of the conceptual simple list shown in part (a)

Head: 9	PURCHASE__ORDER			
RRN	PO__NO	DATE__ISSUED	VENDOR__CODE	Link Field
2	4	01/04/XX	123	8
6	9	01/10/XX	133	0
8	7	01/09/XX	103	6
9	1	01/04/XX	103	2

Adding Records to a Simple List

Adding records to a list is conceptually very easy:

- Determine the RRN for the new record.
- Follow the list from the beginning to access the record that logically precedes the new one. (Note: Better approaches are possible.)
- Save its link field value.
- Set the link field value to the RRN of the new record.
- Rewrite the old record.

- Set the link field value of the new record to the saved value.
- Write the new record at its RRN.

Let's add a new PURCHASE_ORDER with a PO_NO value of 3. Assume the new PURCHASE_ORDER record has been hashed to location 11. Figure 3.19(a) shows the conceptual list before adding the new PURCHASE_ORDER. Figure 3.19(b) shows what we have to accomplish by using the record addition algorithm just described.

Logically, PO_NO 3 belongs after PO_NO 1 and before PO_NO 4. The figure also suggests that the pointer field for PO_NO 1 should contain the value 11, because that's the address of the new PURCHASE_ORDER record. Using our algorithm results in the new file shown in Figure 3.20. The figure shows the list both before the insertion (part a) and after (part b).

Notice that RRN 9's link value has been changed from 2 to 11, reflecting the new order. Also note that this is the only link field change necessary to add the new record.

FIGURE 3.19   Using a Link List to Order a File

(a) A conceptual list of PURCHASE_ORDER records. The number shown inside each record is the purchase order number. The number above each record is its RRN

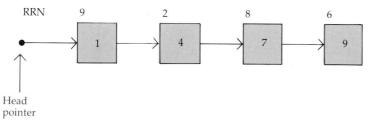

(b) The conceptual list from figure 3.19 (a) after adding PO_NO 3

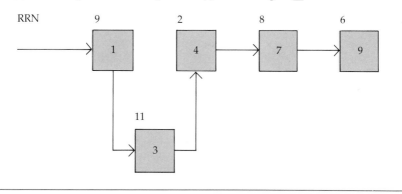

FIGURE 3.20   **Adding a New Record to a Link List**

(a) The list of PURCHASE__ORDER records before PO__NO 3 is added

Head: 9	PURCHASE__ORDER	
RRN	PO__NO	Link Field
2	4	8
6	9	0
8	7	6
9	1	2

(b) The list after adding the new purchase order—only one link change was necessary

Head: 9	PURCHASE__ORDER	
RRN	PO__NO	Link Field
2	4	8
6	9	0
8	7	6
9	1	11	◄————————— RRN of new record
11	3	2	◄————————— Old RRN value for PO__NO 1

Deleting Records from a Simple List

Deleting records from a list is even easier than adding them. The algorithm is:

- Access the record to be deleted.
- Save its link field value.
- Access the immediate logical predecessor.
- Set the link field of the predecessor to the saved value.
- Rewrite the record.

Because the record is still in the file or database, this kind of deletion is called a **logical delete.** If this is the only deletion procedure we use, the file will never decrease in size and, if it's a volatile one, could cause disk-space-related problems. Most organizations would use a **reorganization routine** that physically deletes records that have been logically deleted. This is accomplished by reading each record from the original file and writing it to a temporary file. Those records marked for deletion are omitted. When the entire file is transferred, the temporary file is copied back to the original file.

Let's delete PO__NO 7 from our original simple list. Figure 3.21 shows the conceptualization of what we want to accomplish. We need to change RRN 2's

FIGURE 3.21   The List from Figure 3.19(a) after Deleting PO__NO 7

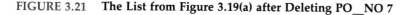
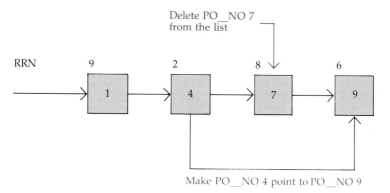

Notice that no record points to RRN 8; thus, there is no way to access PO__NO 7 even though the record is still in the physical file. The record has been logically deleted.

FIGURE 3.22   The Link List after Deleting PO__NO 7

Head: 9

RRN	PURCHASE__ORDER	
	PO__NO	Link Field
2	4	6	◄──── Was equal to 8
6	9	0	
8	7	6	◄──── Logically deleted
9	1	2	

Only one link field value has been changed. Notice that now there is no way to get to RRN 8, the deleted record, by using the link field values. However, the record is still physically stored.

link field value from 8 (the location of PO__NO 7) to 6, the new "next" PO__ NO value. Although PO__NO 7 still exists, there is no way to access it. Let's use the deletion algorithm to accomplish this. Figure 3.22 shows the list implementation of the procedure. The link field associated with PO__NO 4 has been changed from 8 to 6. While RRN 8 is still in the database, none of the link field values contain that value.

In summary, adding and deleting records for a simple list is much easier than doing so for a sequentially organized file. Adding a record requires changing the link field value of the record that immediately precedes the new one so that it points to the new record. Deleting a record is done in a logical sense and necessitates setting the link field value of the preceding record to that of the one being deleted.

Using a Simple List to Process Secondary Keys

The examples just discussed show how to use a simple list structure to chain records together based on values of primary keys. Earlier we suggested that a simple list can also be used to process secondary keys. Let's use a list to connect the PURCHASE__ORDER records on the secondary key, DATE__ISSUED.

There are two purchase orders issued on January 4 and one each on January 9 and 10 (see Figure 3.18). If we have to be able to quickly process just the purchase orders issued on a given date, we need three head pointers: one to point to the first order on January 4, one to point to the initial order on January 9, and one to point to the first order issued on January 10. Next, we need a way to connect the PURCHASE__ORDER records issued on the same date. In effect, we need three **sublists**—a subdivision of a list in which each record in the list has the same value for the relating field. In our case, the list is based on DATE__ISSUED and each sublist will contain records having the same value of DATE__ISSUED. However, only one pointer per record will be necessary to implement the three sublists.

Figure 3.23 suggests that if we want the PURCHASE__ORDER to be in ascending order by DATE__ISSUED, we need to access the following records. First, we retrieve the head of the 01/04/XX sublist. Next, we retrieve RRN 2, the record indicated by the head pointer. After accessing this record, we use its link field to access RRN 9, the last PURCHASE__ORDER issued on 01/04/XX. The figure suggests that the link value for this purchase order should be zero, because there are no more PURCHASE__ORDERs issued on 01/04/XX. If we wanted only the PURCHASE__ORDER records on this date, we would stop. However, because we want all the PURCHASE__ORDER records for every date, we must retrieve the other head sublist pointers and then follow their respective sublists.

Instead of sublists, we could have chosen to connect RRN 9 to RRN 8 and 8 to 6 rather than having the 01/04/XX sublist end at RRN 9 and the other sublists at 8 and 6. This would give one list instead of three sublists. However, this would make it more difficult to access the PURCHASE__ORDERs issued on a given date, because there would be no head pointer to the initial order on the desired date. However, it would make sequential processing by date quicker because there would be no need to read the head pointers for each date.

Figure 3.24 shows the implementation of Figure 3.23. Notice that we now have three head pointers, one for each sublist. Also, note that each sublist ends with a zero value for its next pointer.

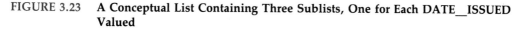

FIGURE 3.23   **A Conceptual List Containing Three Sublists, One for Each DATE__ISSUED Valued**

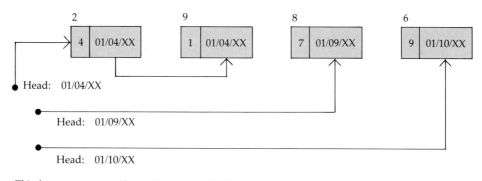

Head: 01/04/XX

Head: 01/09/XX

Head: 01/10/XX

This data structure provides rapid access to all POs issued on a given date.

FIGURE 3.24   **Using a Linked List to Relate Records Having the Same Secondary Key Values. The Key is DATE__ISSUED**

Head 01/04/XX: 2
Head 01/09/XX: 8
Head 01/10/XX: 6

RRN	PO__NO	DATE__ISSUED	VENDOR__CODE	Link Field
		PURCHASE__ORDER		
2	4	01/04/XX	123	9
6	9	01/10/XX	133	0
8	7	01/09/XX	103	0
9	1	01/04/XX	103	0

Although we have shown the example as a table, each row of the table actually would be a separate record.

How to Find the Head of a List

Now it's time to address the issue of determining the start of a list or sublist. There are three places to store the address of the head of a list or sublist:

- In a reserved record within the file
- In a separate file
- In an index

A common way to store the address of the first (or last) record in a list is to reserve record 0 for that purpose. To use this approach in Figure 3.18, we just add a new record with RRN 0. In that record, we store the value 9, the RRN of the head of the list. This method works best for lists without sublists.

A second, and better, approach is to designate a record in another file as the provider of this information. In a database setting, we use lists to connect destination records associated with the same origin record occurrence, so a logical place to store this information is in the origin record occurrences. In our earlier example, we tried to relate a PATIENT to all of his or her ORDERs. Recall that we related a patient's ORDERs to one another based on the primary key for the ORDER: ORDER__NUMBER. The logical place to store the head and tail ORDER pointers would be in each PATIENT occurrence.

Let's look at this in more detail by examining another 1:M relationship: DATE__ISSUED and PURCHASE__ORDER, which is shown conceptually in Figure 3.25. There would be three occurrences of DATE__ISSUED, one for each date in Figure 3.18, and four for PURCHASE__ORDER. The occurrence of DATE__ISSUED for 01/04/XX is associated with the two PURCHASE__ORDERs issued on that date. There is one PO associated with the other two dates. Figure 3.26 shows how we could use the DATE__ISSUED record occurrences to store head pointers to the first PURCHASE__ORDER issued on that date.

Notice that we have created three DATE__ISSUED records, one for each date value. One of the new records, 01/04/XX, has been assigned to RRN 10. It contains a head pointer value of 2, the location of the first PURCHASE__ORDER issued on that date. The other two records contain similar data: the RRN value of the first PURCHASE__ORDER record associated with that date.

Now let's see how we can use the third option, an index, to store sublist heads. As Figure 3.27 shows, we index on DATE__ISSUED as we did earlier, but instead of storing all the RRNs having that date value, we store only the sublist head pointer value. The first date in the index in Figure 3.27 is 01/04/XX, and the associated pointer value is 2. Because we can quickly search an index,

---

FIGURE 3.25   **Using a 1:M Relationship to Model a Secondary Key Relationship**

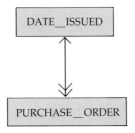

FIGURE 3.26   Storing Head Pointers in Origin Occurrences

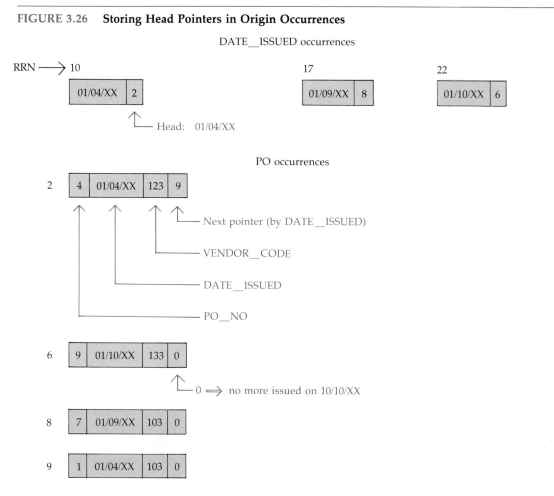

There are three DATE__ISSUED values, so three of its occurrences are shown. Each occurrence contains a head pointer to the first PO record issued on that date. As usual, RRN values are shown outside the record occurrences.

we can easily determine that PO__NO 2, which is stored at RRN 2, is the first PURCHASE__ORDER issued on that date.

To process the sublist containing a particular value of DATE__ISSUED, we use this algorithm:

Search the index for the desired DATE__ISSUED.

Use the associated RRN value as the address of the head of the sublist.

Access the RRN the index value points to.

FIGURE 3.27   **Using an Index to Store Head (and/or Tail) Pointers**

INDEX	
DATE__ISSUED	RRN
01/04/XX	2
01/09/XX	8
01/10/XX	6

The RRN corresponding to the first PO issued on the corresponding date

- Use the link field found with that record to retrieve the next PURCHASE__ ORDER.
- Stop when the link field has a value of zero.

This concludes our discussion of lists. All of the other data structures use lists for their implementations. Probably the next easiest structure to understand is the ring.

3.4 RINGS

Rings, also called **circular linked lists,** are lists in which the last record points back to the head of the list. As with simple lists, we can have rings that connect records based on primary or secondary key values. Let's first look at using a ring that connects records based on primary key values.

To convert Figure 3.18 into a ring, we just change the pointer value of RRN 6 from 0 to 9, the head of the list. Figure 3.28 shows the problem conceptually.

Converting sublists into subrings is equally easy: Instead of 0, the tail of the sublist should contain the RRN corresponding to the head of the sublist. Figure

FIGURE 3.28   **A Ring Data Structure of PURCHASE__ORDER Records**

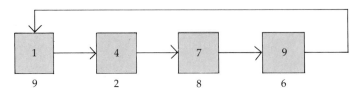

The last PO points back to the first one.

FIGURE 3.29   Converting Sublists to Subrings

Head 01/04/XX: 2
Head 01/09/XX: 8
Head 01/10/XX: 6

	PURCHASE_ORDER			
RRN	PO_NO	DATE_ISSUED	VENDOR_CODE	Link Field
2	4	01/04/XX	123	9
6	9	01/10/XX	133	6
8	7	01/09/XX	103	8
9	1	01/04/XX	103	2

The last PO issued on a given date now points to the first one.

FIGURE 3.30   A Variation of a Ring in Which Records of Two Types are Related

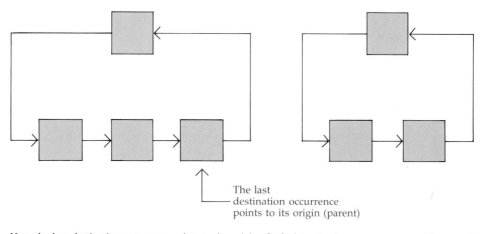

The last destination occurrence points to its origin (parent)

Here the last destination occurrence points to its origin. Such data structures are common with network DBMSs.

3.29 shows how we can convert Figure 3.24 into a series of three subrings, one for each value of DATE_ISSUED. Notice that RRN 6 points to itself, as does RRN 8. This is because there is only one record in each of the sublists for 01/09/XX and 01/10/XX. RRN 9 points to RRN 2, the head of the sublist for 01/04/XX.

Instead of lists, most network-based DBMSs usually use rings to implement 1:M relationships. By using a ring, we can have the first destination record point to the next related destination record, and so on. Instead of pointing back to the first one, the last destination record, as you would expect from the above discussion, actually points back to the origin of the 1:M relationship, as shown in Figure 3.30.

3.5   TWO-WAY LISTS AND RINGS

We will discuss the next two data structures together because, as we just saw, there is little difference between lists and rings. We will describe only two-way lists, but you should be able to extend the discussion to include two-way rings.

A **two-way list,** also called a **doubly linked list,** is a simple list with both next and prior pointers. The actual implementation of two-way lists will require us to use both head and tail pointers, because we must be able to process the list in either direction. Figure 3.31(a) shows the conceptualization of a two-way simple list as applied to our original PURCHASE__ORDER example. Figure 3.31(b) shows the actual implementation.

In practice, the tail pointers can be stored in the same locations that we suggested for the head pointers: in origin records, in a specially designated record in the list itself, or in an index. In most cases, we will assume the origin is used.

We use two-way lists for three purposes:

- To provide reverse-order sequential processing.
- To facilitate the deletion of records in a list.
- To fix damaged lists.

Reverse-order sequential processing means accessing records in the opposite order. It is seldom used to display or print complete files or record occurrences; rather, it serves to enable on-line applications to show a previous record. As an example, suppose a pharmacist is viewing an ORDER record for a given patient. Normally, each succeeding ORDER record would be accessed using the next link field. Suppose that while viewing an order the pharmacist forgets whether the prior order was active or discontinued. By using the prior pointer, the application can easily display the desired ORDER.

The second use for a two-way list is to make it easier to delete records in a list. When we described how to delete a member of a list, we saw that we have to start at the head of the list and sequentially read the records using the link field until we get to the record prior to the one being deleted. Using prior pointers, we can immediately go from the record being deleted to its predecessor, saving many steps and, consequently, much time.

The last use for backward pointers is a very important one: to fix lists damaged by invalid pointer values. The ability to fix damaged pointers must be designed into every DBMS. Using special utilities, the DBA can use the backward pointer

FIGURE 3.31 **Two-Way Link Lists**

(a) A conceptualization of a two-way linked list of POs. The list is sequenced by PO number, which is shown inside each record.

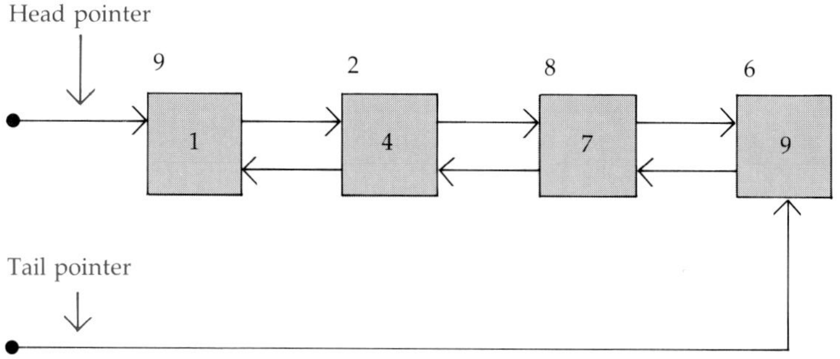

(b) The implementation of the two-way list shown in part (a)

Head: 9
Tail: 6

RRN	PO_NO	DATE_ISSUED	VENDOR_CODE	Next Link	Prior Link
	PURCHASE_ORDER				
2	4	01/04/XX	123	8	9
6	9	01/10/XX	133	0	9
8	7	01/09/XX	103	6	2
9	1	01/04/XX	103	2	0

values to repair lists that have been broken by the creation of "bad" forward pointers.

To illustrate, assume the next pointer for RRN 8 in Figure 3.31(a) is damaged in some way and we cannot read it. Unless we have the option to use a hashing algorithm to retrieve the PURCHASE_ORDER records in addition to following the pointers, there is no way to access the PURCHASE_ORDER that follows PO_NO 7: PO_NO 9. This situation is shown in Figure 3.32.

We can see from Figure 3.32 that the prior pointer from RRN 6 leads to the record containing the damaged link value. Thus, the bad forward link value must have been 6. This suggests the following algorithm:

- Access the tail pointer.
- Access the record the tail pointed to. Save its RRN.

FIGURE 3.32   A Broken Chain

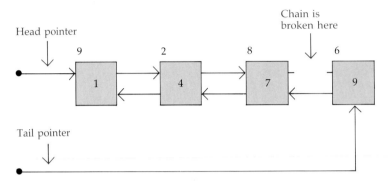

We assume that only one pointer is damaged. By reading the list backwards, we can determine the value of the damaged pointer.

- If that record is the one with the bad pointer, set the next pointer value to 0 because it is the last record in the chain, and stop. Otherwise, use the prior pointer to access the previous record. If it is the one with the bad pointer, set its pointer value to the saved value, rewrite the record, and stop.
- If there is still no match, save the current RRN and use the backward pointer to access the prior record.
- Continue until the record accessed by reading backward is the record with the bad forward pointer. At that time, set its next pointer value to the saved value and rewrite the record.

Problem 14 at the end of the chapter asks you to use this algorithm to correct the bad pointer in Figure 3.32.

3.6   MULTILISTS

Multilists are data structures in which two or more lists pass through the records. When the lists are used to connect secondary keys, each list will contain several sublists. Let's look at an example.

Figure 3.33 shows how we can construct a two-way multilist for the PURCHASE__ORDER example. One list connects the PURCHASE__ORDERs based on DATE__ISSUED, while the other is used for processing the records on VENDOR__CODE. Each record in the example has two next and two prior pointers. One pointer set is used for the DATE__ISSUED list; the other enables us to access the records via VENDOR__CODE. Notice that we use an index to store the head and tail pointers and also the number of records in each sublist. For example, there are two PO records for VENDOR__CODE 103, so the length

FIGURE 3.33   **Implementing a Multilist**

VENDOR__CODE Index

VENDOR__CODE	H	T	L
103	8	9	2
123	2	2	1
133	6	6	1

DATE__ISSUED Index

DATE__ISSUED	H	T	L
01/04/XX	2	9	2
01/09/XX	8	8	1
01/10/XX	6	6	1

PURCHASE__ORDER

RRN	PO__NO	DATE__ISSUED	VENDOR__CODE	NVC	PVC	NDI	PDI
2	4	01/04/XX	123	0	0	9	0
6	9	01/10/XX	133	0	0	0	0
8	7	01/09/XX	103	9	0	0	0
9	1	01/04/XX	103	0	8	0	2

NDI = next pointer, DATE__ISSUED
PDI = prior pointer, DATE__ISSUED
NVC = next pointer, VENDOR__CODE
PVC = prior pointer, VENDOR__CODE
  H = head pointer
  T = tail pointer
  L = length of sublist

The two lists are based on VENDOR__CODE and DATE__ISSUED. Notice that each list represents a secondary key and each multilist has three sublists. No ordering is assumed for the sublists.

of the sublist "owned" by 103 is 2—the value shown in the first record of the VENDOR index in Figure 3.33.

Processing a multilist is no different than processing a simple list, except that complicated queries can be processed in more than one way. By using the chain length field in the indexes, we can optimize our queries.

Problem 3. **Was the vendor with VENDOR__CODE 123 issued any purchase orders on 01/04/XX?**

Solution. To answer this query, follow either the sublist for 01/04/XX or the one corresponding to VENDOR__CODE 123. Which is better? The index entries indicate that VENDOR__CODE 123's sublist has one record in it, while that of 01/04/XX has two; follow the sublist for VENDOR__CODE 123. To finish the example, after reading the records in the sublist for VENDOR__CODE 123 (we have only one record to "follow"), test the DATE__ISSUED field for 01/04/XX. If the value matches, add 1 to an accumulator. When the pointer field value is zero, there are no more records to process.

Maintaining multilists can be quite complicated, as an example will show. Assume that when we entered PO_NO 4, we made a mistake: Instead of VENDOR_CODE 123, we should have used VENDOR_CODE 103. This means that we must remove this record from the sublist for 123 and add it to that of 103. As another example, assume we delete PO_NO 7. This will require us to patch several pointers so that all of our sublists will be properly maintained. We leave this for you as Problem 13 at the end of the chapter.

3.7   INVERTED DATA STRUCTURES

Long lists can create problems. It can take a very long time to read each record in a long list to find records having a desired primary or secondary key value. In on-line applications, this cannot be tolerated. Thus, we **invert,** or **index,** on secondary keys to permit quick access to records that satisfy complex queries (queries on more than one secondary key value). If we are not using an index to store head and tail pointers, an index will help us even for simple queries. We use the term *index* or *invert* in this context to mean the indexing method introduced at the beginning of the chapter, rather than the partial indexing method we have more recently been using to store and access head and tail pointers and list lengths.

When we invert on fewer than all the fields in a record, we perform a **partial inversion.** If we invert on every field in a record, we do what is called a **full inversion.**

Figure 3.34 shows the partial inversion of the PURCHASE_ORDER file on

---

FIGURE 3.34   **A Partial Inversion of the PURCHASE_ORDER File**

Invert on DATE_ISSUED		Invert on VENDOR_CODE	
DATE_ISSUED	RRNs	VENDOR_CODE	RRNs
01/04/XX	2, 9	103	8, 9
01/09/XX	8	123	2
01/10/XX	6	133	6

Notice that we end up with a variable-length record, which can be difficult to manage

We have inverted on two fields: DATE_ISSUED and VENDOR_CODE. Each index record carries an index value and the set of RRNs associated with records in the PURCHASE_ORDER file having that index value.

the two secondary keys, DATE__ISSUED and VENDOR__CODE. Each index contains records that carry a key value and a variable-length part that carries all the associated RRNs. To answer a complex query, we use the pointer values in the corresponding indexes rather than accessing the actual data records.

Problem 4. Which PURCHASE__ORDERs were issued on 01/04/XX to VENDOR__CODE 103?

Solution. Use a Boolean AND operation on the set of RRNs for DATE__IS-SUED:01/04/XX (RRNs 2 and 9) and for VENDOR__CODE 103 (RRNs 8 and 9). Mathematically, we can represent this as (2,9) AND (8,9) = (9). The only RRN that is a member of both sets is 9. After determining the RRNs that satisfy the request, use those values to directly access the records. In our case, this would result in reading RRN 9, where we find the only PURCHASE__ORDER that satisfies our query: PO__NO 1.

Answering "OR" queries can be done in a similar manner, as the following example shows.

Problem 5. Which PURCHASE__ORDERs were issued on either 01/04/XX or 01/09/XX?

Solution. Use a Boolean OR operator on the two sets, (2,9) and (8); that is, (2,9) OR (8) = (2,9,8). Reading the records at those locations results in the answer PO__NOs 4, 1, and 7.

In both examples, we can do the searches in memory rather than having to physically search the records on the disk, thus speeding up the search time.

3.8   HIERARCHICAL DATA STRUCTURES

Hierarchical data structures, also called **tree structures,** are the basis for IBM's popular DBMS:IMS and SAS's System 2000. The structure can also be used in data and file management systems for storing indexes of both primary and secondary keys.

A hierarchical data structure is characterized as one in which no record type is associated with more than one origin record type. We could alternatively say that a hierarchical data structure is one in which there is never more than one path (relationship) coming into an entity or record type. Figure 3.35 shows three examples of hierarchical data structures.

Hierarchical DSDs have been compared to upside-down trees, with the root of the tree at the top and branches leading to its leaves. In fact, much of the terminology associated with hierarchical data structures has been borrowed from "tree" terminology. Let's look at the hierarchical terminology more precisely.

FIGURE 3.35   **Three Hierarchical Data Structures**

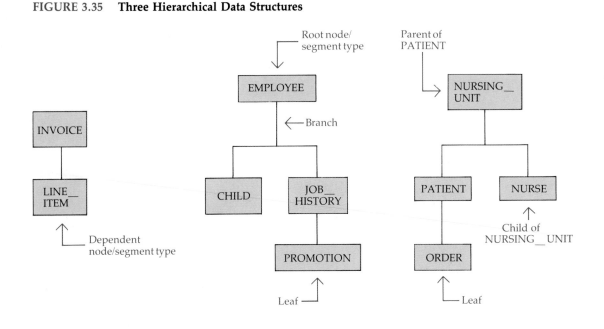

Each structure has a root and one or more dependent nodes or segment types. Each branch denotes a 1:M relationship between a parent and a child node. A leaf has no children.

Terminology

In hierarchical DSDs, record types are usually called **segment types,** or **nodes.** Vendor implementations of the hierarchical approach use the term *segment,* while *node* is used when talking conceptually. There are two categories of nodes: **root** and **dependent.** Each hierarchical data structure has but one root: the node at the top of the DSD. Every other node is a dependent.

In a 1:M relationship, the origin node is called the **parent** and the destination the **child.** This means that a 1:M relationship is always between a parent and a child segment type and that a hierarchical data structure can have no child with more than one parent. In fact, every segment type, except the root, must have one—and only one—parent segment type. As you might already have concluded, the root segment type can have no parent.

In Figure 3.35, the root nodes are INVOICE, EMPLOYEE, and NURSING _UNIT for parts (a), (b), and (c), respectively. All the other nodes in the figure

FIGURE 3.36   Two Tree Occurrences of Figure 3.35(c)

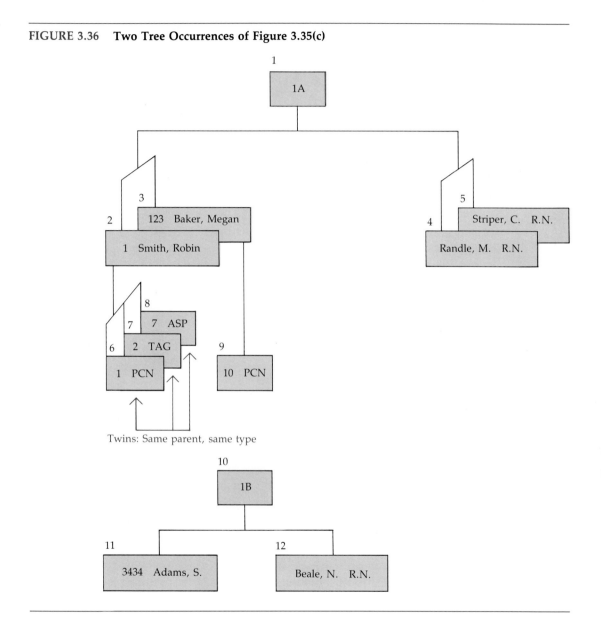

are dependents. Nodes that have no children are called **leaves** (of the "tree"). In part (c), ORDER and NURSE are leaves. The lines connecting the nodes are called **branches.** By following different sets of branches, beginning at the root, we can define several **hierarchical paths.** In Figure 3.35(c), there are four possible hierarchical paths:

- NURSING__UNIT
- NURSING__UNIT PATIENT
- NURSING__UNIT PATIENT ORDER
- NURSING__UNIT NURSE

The longest hierarchical path is the **height** of the tree—three in our example. The heights of the other two trees in Figure 3.35 are two and three.

A hierarchical data structure can have occurrences, consisting of a root occurrence and all its dependent node occurrences. Figure 3.36 shows two tree occurrences of Figure 3.35(c). Node occurrences of the same type are called **twins.** Like their human counterparts, twins must have the same parent. They must also be of the same type. In Figure 3.36, ORDER__NUMBERs 1, 2, and 7 are twins, as are PATIENTs 1 and 123.

Physical Representation of Trees

There are two ways to represent trees: using a first-child, next-child linked representation and using a preorder traversal.

The **first/next method** is the better of the two for speed of access and update. Each node occurrence has two link fields: a first child and a next child. The first-child link points to the head of a sublist, while the next pointer points to the next child of the parent. It is acceptable for the next-child pointers to point to nodes of a different type.

Figure 3.37 shows a first/next representation of the first tree occurrence in Figure 3.36. The address of the first child of the node at RRN 1 in Figure 3.36 is RRN 2. Similarly, the first child of RRN 2 is RRN 6. The next link for RRN 2 is RRN 3. Although RRNs 3 and 4 aren't twins, they are both children of RRN 1, so the next pointer associated with RRN 3 is 4. A pointer value of zero means that there is either no first child or no next node.

The **preorder traversal** method, also known as **left-list layout,** or **hierarchic order,** is a sequential representation of a tree occurrence and is used by IBM's IMS DBMS. To develop the preorder traversal of a tree occurrence:

- Start at the root and descend along the leftmost set of branches until you reach the bottom. Record the nodes that are visited.
- When you reach the bottom, back up one level and descend the next leftmost set of branches. Do not rerecord any nodes visited more than once.
- Stop when all nodes have been visited.

FIGURE 3.37   **A First/Next Representation of the First Tree Occurrence in Figure 3.36**

RRN	Contents	First Child	Next Child
1	1A	2	0
2	Smith, Robin	6	3
3	Baker, Megan	9	4
4	Randle, M.	0	5
5	Striper, C.	0	0
6	PCN	0	7
7	TAG	0	8
8	ASP	0	0
9	PCN	0	0

FIGURE 3.38   **A Preorder Traversal Implementation of Figure 3.36**

| 1A | Smith, Robin | PCN | TAG | ASP | Baker, Megan | PCN | Randle, M. | Striper, C. |

Applying the algorithm to the first occurrence in Figure 3.36, we begin with the nursing unit root node that contains the value "1A." Then we record the contents of that node. Next, we descend along the leftmost set of branches, resulting in the visitation of the nodes containing "Smith, Robin" and then "PCN." We record those nodes. Our representation now consists of three records: "1A," "Smith, Robin," and "PCN." We have reached the bottom, so we back up one level to "Smith, Robin" again. The next branch leads to "TAG." As we continue, the following branch will result in the recording of the node containing "ASP." There are no more unvisited branches that start at "Smith, Robin," so we back up one more level to the NURSING__UNIT root again. Next, we visit and record the nodes with the values "Baker, Megan" and "PCN." The final two nodes will be the two nurses. Figure 3.38 shows the complete preorder traversal.

This implementation method results in a sequential file containing all the inadequacies associated with sequential processing. As you might expect, the linked representation is easier to add to or delete from. It therefore might surprise you that IBM chose the latter implementation method for its IMS DBMS. The reason concerns the fact that it was developed in the 1960s before use of DASDs became widespread. Because most installations used tape, IBM needed a sequential way to represent tree occurrences and thus selected the preorder method.

Trees for Indexing: Binary and B-Trees

Binary trees and B-trees have some special properties that enable us to use them to store and retrieve record keys much more efficiently than we could using sequential indexes. Both binary trees and B-trees involve a single tree occurrence.

A **binary tree** is a tree occurrence in which each parent has only zero, one, or two children. One child is called the **left** child and the other the **right** child. Each child being pointed to is the parent of its own **subtree.**

Figure 3.39 shows both the conceptual binary tree and its implementation for a series of computer languages. As we discuss the example, remember that the binary tree is the structure used to facilitate the index; the actual language records would be stored in their own file and each assigned a location on the disk.

Each index node contains a primary key value: the language name. In reality, it would also contain the RRN of the record in the actual database where the language record is stored. In that record, we might find data such as the amount of memory required by the language, the language's vendor, and so on.

Characteristics that you should note about Figure 3.39(a) are:

- Each node has two ways out: left and right.
- Each node has one key value.
- Nodes (children) to the left of their parent have key values lower than those of their parent.
- Nodes to the right have key values higher than their parent's.

Searching a Binary Tree. To search a binary tree:

- Start at the root. If the search key matches the node's key value, stop; otherwise, compare the search key with the key at the node.
- If the search key is less than the node key, use the left-child pointer and search the left subtree; otherwise, use the right-child pointer to the right subtree, and search it.
- Continue until you get a match or encounter an unused pointer, indicating that there is no match.

Let's search the tree for "COBOL." We begin at the root; its key value is "FORTRAN." "COBOL" is less than "FORTRAN," so we use the left-child pointer to get to the next node. This leads to the language "C." Because "COBOL" is greater than "C," we use the right-child pointer, which leads to the node storing "COBOL," the desired key value. At this point, we can use the RRN stored as a field in the index to access the actual "COBOL" record in the database. In effect, we have used a binary search routine to eliminate half of the remaining subtree at each step. As you might expect, this method is more efficient than using a sequential search.

FIGURE 3.39   **A Binary Tree of Programming Languages**

(a) A conceptual binary tree of computer languages

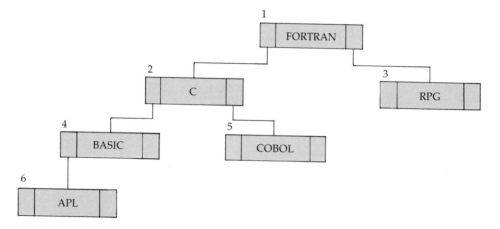

(b) The implementation of the binary tree. Notice the left and right child pointers

RRN	Language	Left Child	Right Child
1	FORTRAN	2	3
2	C	4	5
3	RPG	0	0
4	BASIC	6	0
5	COBOL	0	0
6	APL	0	0

Adding Records to a Binary Tree. To add records to a binary tree:

- Start at the root and proceed until you find an empty slot.
- For each node, compare the new key with the one found at the node. If the new key is less than the node key, go left; otherwise, go right.
- When you find an empty slot, store the new record.

Let's add the language "PILOT" to Figure 3.39. Because "PILOT" is greater than "FORTRAN" (the root), we go right. The right slot is occupied, so we go to RRN 3. "PILOT" is less than "RPG," so we go left. The left slot is empty, so we store "PILOT" there. Figure 3.40 shows the result. Part (a) shows the tree conceptually, part (b) shows its implementation as a data structure.

FIGURE 3.40   Adding a New Node to a Binary Tree

(a) The conceptual binary tree after adding "PILOT"

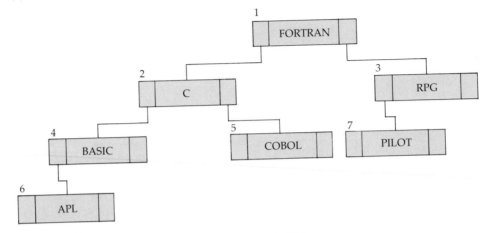

(b) The implementation of the binary tree from Figure 3.40(a)

RRN	Language	Left Child	Right Child
1	FORTRAN	2	3
2	C	4	5
3	RPG	7	0
4	BASIC	6	0
5	COBOL	0	0
6	APL	0	0
7	PILOT	0	0

B-Trees. A **B-tree** is an even more effective way to search for a given key value. It is similar to a binary tree, but instead of having only two ways to exit a node, it has *m*, where m is called the **degree** of the tree. Other characteristics of a B-tree of degree m are:

- Each node, except the root and leaves, has at least m/2 immediate children (subtrees); each node is at least one-half full.
- Each parent is connected to its m children via m or fewer pointers.
- All leaves of the tree are at the same level; the hierarchical path length is the same for all leaves.
- No node can have more than m children.

Figure 3.41 shows a B-tree of degree 3. Notice that some of the nodes have fewer than three ways to exit (pointers), because at the present time not all

FIGURE 3.41   A B-Tree of Degree 3

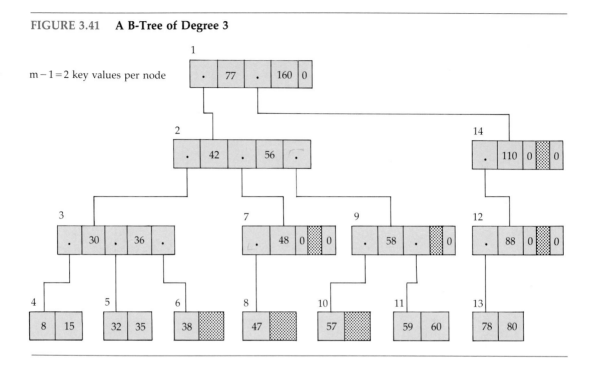

m − 1 = 2 key values per node

possible storage nodes are needed. Also, each node has a maximum of two key values (m − 1), which are used to decide which of the (up to) three subtrees starting at that node to examine next. Let's look for the key value 47.

- Because 47 is less than the first key value in the root node (RRN 1), we use the first pointer, which points to RRN 2.
- 47 is between 42 and 56, so we use the middle pointer in the node, which points to RRN 7.
- Because 47 is less than the first key at RRN 7, we use the first way out and go to RRN 8.
- We now have a match.

Before leaving the subject of trees, we should point out that there is a more sophisticated tree structure than the B-tree, called a *B+-tree*. In a B+-tree, the leaves are connected via a simple list (or two-way list) to provide sequential retrieval of the records in addition to the direct access made possible by searching the tree index. The leaves of the B+-tree carry RRNs to the actual record stored in the data file. The nonleaf nodes carry pointers to the leaves. This means that a key value appearing in a nonleaf node will be repeated in the leaf to which the node points.

3.9 NETWORK DATA STRUCTURES

A **network data structure** is one in which any record type can have an unlimited number of origin record types. Recall that with hierarchical structures, a record type cannot be the destination of more than one 1:M relationship. Figure 3.42 shows two network DSDs. In Figure 3.42(a), INVOICE is the destination of two 1:M relationships: DEPT:INVOICE and DUE__DATE:INVOICE. In Figure 3.42(b), PURCHASE__ORDER is the destination of two 1:M relationships: DEPT: PURCHASE__ORDER and DATE__ISSUED:PURCHASE__ORDER.

Notice that names have been assigned to the relationships. A relationship is called a **set type,** or simply a **set,** which is a named 1:M relationship between two or more record types. In Figure 3.42(a), there are three set types: ISSUED, IS__DUE, and CONTAINS. The record type that is the origin of a set is its **owner,** while the destination record type is its **member.** In Figure 3.42(b), DATE__ISSUED is the owner of the WERE__ISSUED set and PURCHASE __ORDER its member. Notice that in Figure 3.42(a), INVOICE is both an owner (of CONTAINS) and a member (of IS__DUE and ISSUED).

As we mentioned earlier, there are two kinds of networks: simple and com-

---

FIGURE 3.42   Two Network Data Structures

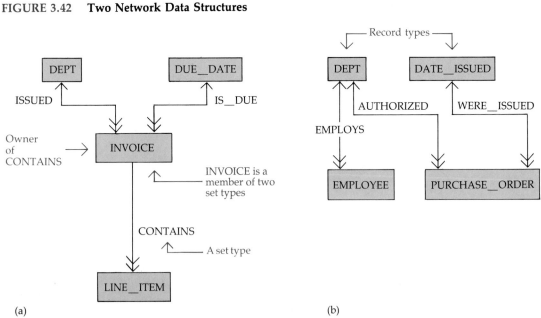

(a)

(b)

Notice that relationships now have names. In the first structure, INVOICE has two owners; thus, the structure is a network. INVOICE is both an owner (of CONTAINS) and a member (of IS__DUE and ISSUED). In the second structure, EMPLOYEE is only a member (of EMPLOYS).

FIGURE 3.43   **The INVOICE Database**

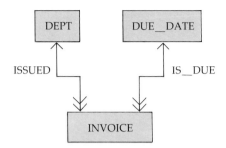

This is a simplified version of Figure 3.42(a), omitting the LINE__ITEM record type. Assume that ISSUED members are to be sorted by INO (a field in the INVOICE record), as are DUE__DATE members.

FIGURE 3.44   **The Data to Be Stored in the Conceptual INVOICE Database from Figure 3.43**

INVOICE	DEPT	AMOUNT	DUE__DATE
A10	ACTG	100.00	10/15/XX
B10	MIS	200.00	10/15/XX
C17	ACTG	150.00	10/31/XX
D19	ACTG	100.00	10/31/XX
A12	MIS	250.00	10/31/XX

plex. A **simple network** consists of only 1:M relationships. Both of the networks in Figure 3.42 are simple. A **complex network** contains one or more M:N relationships. Unfortunately, commercial implementations of the network data structure prohibit complex relationships.

Figure 3.43 shows an abbreviated DSD version of Figure 3.42(a). Figure 3.44 shows data to be stored according to the DSD.

There are five INVOICE occurrences, which have been issued by two different departments and are due on two different dates. We will have occasion to refer to **set occurrences**—owner occurrences of sets plus all their related members. Figure 3.45 shows the set occurrences that result from storing the data in Figure 3.44 according to the conceptual database in Figure 3.43. The number that appears near each record occurrence is its RRN. Notice that there are two occurrences of ISSUED, each owned by one of the two DEPT occurrences (parts [a] and [b] of Figure 3.45), and two occurrences of IS__DUE, one for each of the two DUE__DATE values (parts [c] and [d]). It is no coincidence that there are as many occurrences of ISSUED as there are of DEPT and as many of IS__DUE as there are of DUE__DATE. In fact, we can extrapolate this into a rule: *There are as many set occurrences of a given set as there are occurrences of the owner of the set type.*

FIGURE 3.45   Set Occurrences from Figure 3.43

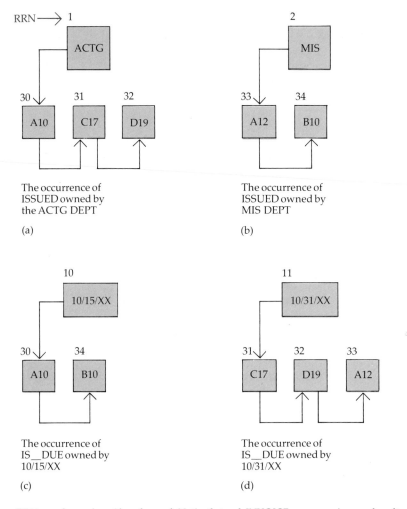

The occurrence of
ISSUED owned by
the ACTG DEPT

(a)

The occurrence of
ISSUED owned by
MIS DEPT

(b)

The occurrence of
IS__DUE owned by
10/15/XX

(c)

The occurrence of
IS__DUE owned by
10/31/XX

(d)

RRNs are shown alongside each record. Notice that each INVOICE occurrence is a member of two set occurrences.

Finally, notice that each INVOICE occurrence simultaneously participates in an occurrence of each set type of which it is a member. For example, INVOICE A10 is a member both of the ISSUED occurrence owned by ACTG and of the IS__DUE occurrence owned by 10/15/XX. The fact that each INVOICE is a member of two sets is more evident in Figure 3.46, which shows the complete database occurrence rather than just individual set occurrences.

FIGURE 3.46   The Complete Occurrence of the Database from Figure 3.45

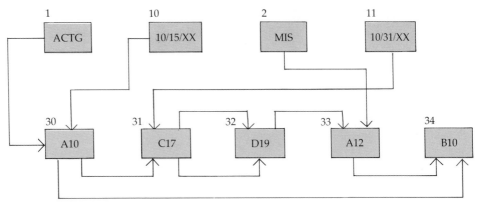

Member records participating in the IS__DUE set occurrences are shown in one color and ISSUED members by another color.

To implement a network data structure, we can use all five types of pointers. Figure 3.47 shows just the first and next pointers. The first pointer points to the first member of a given set occurrence, and next pointers relate member occurrences. Note that origin pointers are now called *owner pointers*, while tail and prior pointers retain their earlier names.

In creating Figure 3.47, we used the complete database occurrence from Figure 3.46 and assumed that each set was to be ordered on INO (invoice number). Problem 1 at the end of the chapter asks you to insert the other pointer types.

Simple Networks

In a simple network, all relationships are 1:M (or 1:1) and at least one member record type is a member of more than one set type. Figure 3.42 illustrated simple network DSDs.

Complex Networks

Complex networks are characterized as having two or more related record types, each participating in a one-to-many (1:M) relationship with the other. We can also state this as a single relationship—M:N, meaning the relationship may be 1:M in one direction but 1:N in the other. As an example, in Chapter 2 we looked at a database that Suburban Hospital was contemplating to help it provide better

FIGURE 3.47   Implementation of the Database Occurrence from Figure 3.46

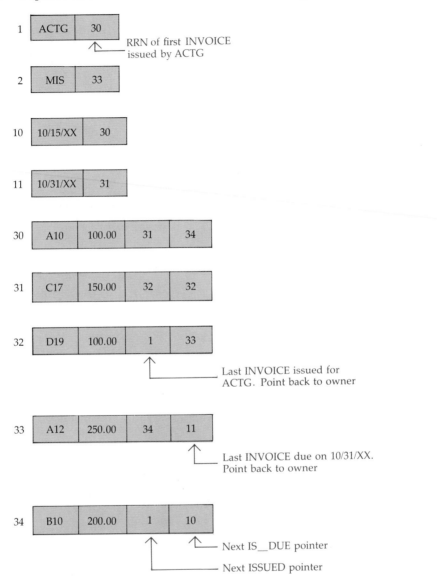

Only head and next pointers are used. The last member in a set occurrence points to its owner, which completes the ring structure.

patient care and recordkeeping. Figure 3.48 shows a complex relationship between two related entities: Order and Due__Time.

According to the DSD, a given Order is associated with zero, one, or several Due__Time occurrences, and a particular Due__Time occurrence is associated with zero, one, or several Orders. This means that a given Order may be due at several times (1:M) and that at a given Due__Time several pharmacy ORDERs may be due (1:N).

Figure 3.49 shows some occurrence data to be stored in the database resulting from the DSD. Each Order is associated with several Due__Times; for example, Order__No 10 is to be filled at 0200 and 1000—a 1:2 relationship. Also, many

---

FIGURE 3.48   A Complex Relationship

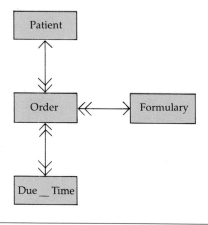

FIGURE 3.49   Sample Data to Be Stored in the Database Resulting from Figure 3.48

Order__ No	Patient__ Name	Patient__ Number (PID)	Medication__ Name	Med__ Code (MID)	Due__Time
10	Adams	174	Keflin	Kef	0200 1000
76	Adams	174	Penicillin	Pcn	0200
1	Cox	103	Penicillin	Pcn	1500
36	Cox	103	Valium	Val	0300
12	Cox	103	Vibrmycin	Vib	0300 1000
14	Davis	49	Penicillin	Pcn	0200 0600 1000
62	Davis	49	Tagamet	Tag	1500

of the Due__Times are associated with multiple Orders; for instance, at 0200, Order Nos. 10, 76, and 14 are to be filled—a 1:3 relationship, but in the reverse order from the previous one. This confirms that we have a M:N relationship.

Now let's see how we can reduce a complex relationship to a pair of 1:M simple relationships.

Reducing a Complex Network to a Simple One. The process of reducing a complex network to a simple one may seem almost trivial: Make each original record type (or entity) own a set that has a common member, called an **inter-**

FIGURE 3.50   **The Reduced Network and the Conceptual Record Types Resulting from Figure 3.49**

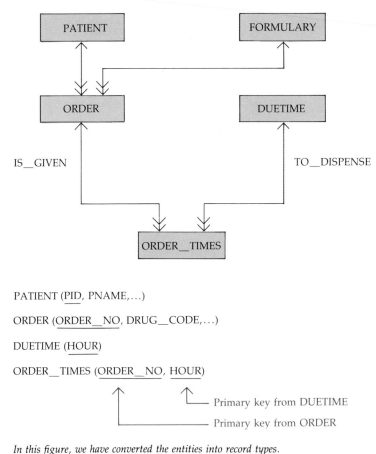

PATIENT (PID, PNAME,...)

ORDER (ORDER__NO, DRUG__CODE,...)

DUETIME (HOUR)

ORDER__TIMES (ORDER__NO, HOUR)

— Primary key from DUETIME

— Primary key from ORDER

In this figure, we have converted the entities into record types.

section record type. Figure 3.50 illustrates. The intersection record type, ORDER__TIMES, is a member of two new 1:M sets: IS__GIVEN and TO__ DISPENSE. At a superficial level, that's all there is to it. The complexity comes in when we try to analyze what this new record type means and what it should contain.

Its occurrences relate ORDER and DUETIME occurrences to each other, in effect cross-referencing a combination of ORDER and DUETIME. If this is so, there should be as many occurrences of ORDER__TIMES as there are combinations of ORDER and DUETIME. Based on Figure 3.49, there should be 11 such occurrences. For example, one occurrence would be for Order__No 10, Due__Time 0200, and another for Order__No 10 and Due__Time 1000. The other nine would be similarly derived. We will see all 11 occurrences a bit later.

The primary key for an intersection record will always be derived from the concatenation of the keys of its owners. Therefore, the primary key for ORDER__TIMES consists of ORDER__NO and HOUR, the keys for ORDER and DUETIME, respectively.

Note the following characteristics of the resulting data structure:

- A new record type has been added.
- Each original record type now owns a set, of which the intersection record type is the member.
- There are two one-to-many relationships in a single direction.
- Typically, the data items in the intersection record type include the keys of its owners and additional information that logically depends on knowledge of both owners.
- The intersection record type will also carry any additional sort keys needed to sequence its record occurrences.
- The record type may be called a **cross-reference** or **association** record type.

Let's examine the contents of an intersection record type in more detail. Because there often isn't an obvious correlation between an intersection record type and an entity in the real or logical world, it may be difficult to decide what kinds of data items should be stored in one. These record types typically contain:

- Pointers
- Connection data items (foreign keys)
- Sort keys
- Data logically dependent on both owners

The only data that must be in intersection record types is pointers, which are inserted by network- and hierarchy-based DBMSs as the records are stored. (Relational DBMSs don't use pointers to relate records.) These pointers are transparent to the programmer, the DBA, and the analyst, meaning that no overt action is necessary to create or use them. If pointers are the only data found in an intersection record type, that record type is called an **empty record.** Usually, additional items are required.

First, we will follow the rule that member record types in a 1:M relationship should include connection fields corresponding to the primary keys of their owners. These data items are concatenated and jointly constitute the composite primary key.

To formalize our discussion so far: Begin with two record types, R1(A1, A2, . . . AN) and R2(B1, B2, . . . BN), that share a M:N relationship. The reduction process results in a new record type that can be described this way: INTERSECTION(A1, B1). Finally, instead of the original M:N set, two 1:M sets result: R1_INTERSECTION and R2_INTERSECTION.

Next, we may need to add additional data items to support our sorting needs. Member occurrences can be sorted on any field contained in the member's definition. Here we are concerned with two sets and hence have two sort sequences to decide on. Remember that the intersection record type carries the two owner keys. A general rule is to sort each set on the portion of the concatenated member key that corresponds to the primary key of the owner of the other set. Using our notation, this means that the set R1_INTERSECTION would be sorted on B1 and the set R2_INTERSECTION, on A1. This is only a guideline, however; the real world situation may lead to a different sorting order.

Consider the IS_GIVEN set from Figure 3.50. Its owner is ORDER, which uses ORDER_NO as its primary key, and its member is ORDER_TIMES. Each occurrence of ORDER owns an IS_GIVEN set occurrence consisting of all the times that ORDER is due. The primary key of the owner of the other set, TO_DISPENSE, has HOUR as its primary key. Therefore, sort IS_GIVEN on HOUR. This means that for any given ORDER, all the ORDER_TIMES records will be in sequence by hour, and the set can be used for queries that start with "For a particular Order, list the times at which it is due, in sequence by hour." Similarly, the other set, TO_DISPENSE, will be sorted on ORDER_NO. Thus, for a given DUETIME, all the ORDER_TIMES records will be sequenced by ORDER_NO, and any request for all the orders due at a certain time, sorted by ORDER_NO, can be fulfilled.

Let's see what the ORDER_TIMES records will look like if we follow our general sorting rules. Figure 3.51 shows the data from Figure 3.49 as it would look if it were stored according to our conceptual database from Figure 3.50. As expected, there are 11 occurrences of ORDER_TIMES, one for each combination of ORDER and DUETIME. The arrows indicate the next pointers that would be associated with occurrences of ORDER_TIMES: one pointer for each set in which they participate. First, follow the occurrence of the IS_GIVEN set owned by ORDER_NO 10. According to our sorting rule, the ORDER_TIMES occurrences within this occurrence should be sorted by HOUR. The first record pointed

FIGURE 3.51   **All Occurrences of the Intersection Record Type, ORDER__TIMES, with One Occurrence Each of IS__GIVEN and TO__DISPENSE Also Indicated**

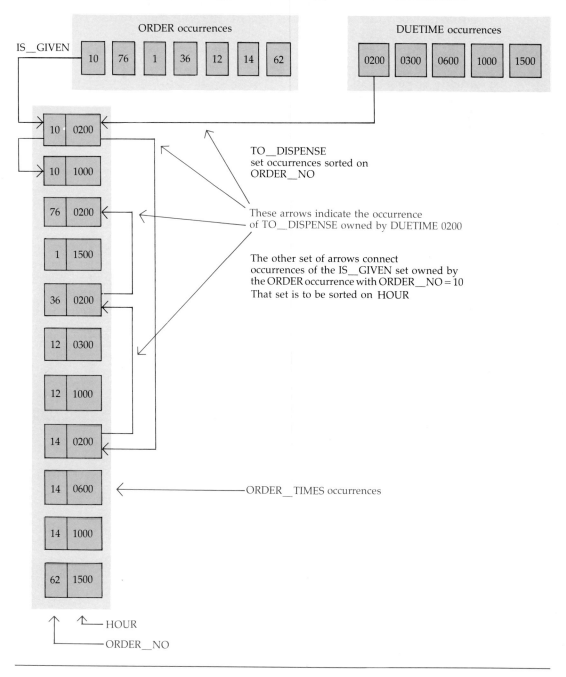

to from ORDER_NO 10 contains an HOUR value of 0200. The next record (and the last one) contains an HOUR value of 1000; the records are in ascending order by HOUR. We can verify that the sequencing for TO_DISPENSE is also correct, but remember that the member records for this set are in sequence by ORDER_NO rather than HOUR.

The final category of data found in these types of records is data that is logically dependent on both owners. As an example, assume the number of units of the drug to dispense varies by time. For instance, for ORDER_NO 13, three units of Keflin might be due at 0200 and five at 1000; the number of units to dispense depends on our knowledge of both the time and the drug. This means that the DBA will have to carry UNITS_TO_DISPENSE in the ORDER_TIMES record type.

3.10 MULTILISTS, SECONDARY KEYS, AND SET TYPES: A COMPARISON

Before concluding this chapter, we should note that multilists, secondary keys, and set types are really the same thing looked at in different ways. In our discussion of multilists, we looked at two lists that passed through a collection of PURCHASE_ORDER records: one for DATE_ISSUED and another for VENDOR_CODE. In that section, we also pointed out that these two fields were actually secondary keys. Finally, in the section on storing head pointers, we saw that we could turn DATE_ISSUED and, by similar reasoning, VENDOR_CODE, into owners of sets. Figure 3.52 illustrates.

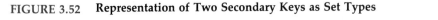

FIGURE 3.52   **Representation of Two Secondary Keys as Set Types**

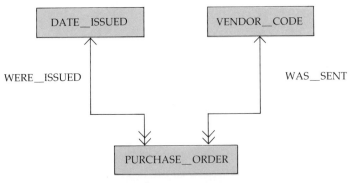

In the VENDOR file, both DATE_ISSUED and VENDOR_CODE are secondary keys.

3.11 SUMMARY

In this chapter, we examined two different ways to classify pointers: by type and by location. There are five types of pointers: first, next, tail, prior, and origin. Pointers can be embedded in records or stored in separate files called *indexes,* or *directories.*

Pointers are used to implement data structures, of which we looked at eight: lists, rings, two-way lists, two-way rings, multilists, inversions, trees, and networks. The first six data structures usually relate records at the same level on a DSD, while the last two relate records participating in two-level 1:M relationships.

Hierarchical structures, also called *trees,* are used by commercial implementations of the hierarchical data model. In addition, variations of trees are used to quickly locate records based on primary or secondary keys. These special trees are called *binary,* B-, and B$^+$-trees.

Hierarchy proponents call conceptual files *nodes* or *segment types.* In a hierarchical structure, no segment can be the destination of more than one 1:M relationship. There are two ways to represent tree occurrences: using first- and next-child pointers and using a sequential approach called *preorder traversal.* IBM's IMS package uses the latter method.

Network data structures are the most complicated. Entities are called *record types* and 1:M relationships *set types;* origins are known as *owners* and destinations as *members.* Each owner occurrence defines a set occurrence and one owner can own multiple set occurrences as long as the occurrences are of different types. To fully implement network occurrences, all five types of pointers can be used.

REVIEW QUESTIONS

1. What are first and last pointers used for? What other names are they called by?
2. What is the primary purpose of next pointers?
3. Of what practical use is an origin pointer?
4. What are some uses for prior pointers?
5. What is the advantage of indexed pointers? What kinds of applications should use them?
6. Which data structures relate records at a single level?
7. Which data structures relate records at two or more levels?
8. Describe three uses for data structures.
9. List three places to store head and tail pointers.
10. Of what use are sublist lengths?
11. Describe two uses for two-way lists.
12. What are the two kinds of network data structures?
13. What is the advantage of carrying connection data items?

PROBLEMS

1. Assume we are using forward and backward and origin pointers. Using the DSD that follows, fill in the following table by showing the total number of pointers of each type per record occurrence:

Record Type	First	Origin	Next	Prior
A				
B				
C				
D				
E				

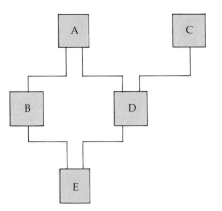

2. The following table shows several sports teams with their cities and sports:

Team	Sport	City
Indians	Baseball	Cleveland
Pirates	Baseball	Pittsburgh
Knicks	Basketball	New York
Cavaliers	Basketball	Cleveland
Giants	Baseball	San Francisco
Penguins	Hockey	Pittsburgh
49ers	Football	San Francisco
Steelers	Football	Pittsburgh
Mets	Baseball	New York

Assume the first team is assigned RRN 1, the next RRN 2, and so on, and that letters sort before numbers.

a. Create two lists for each team, one for Sport and the other for City. In each list (sublist), keep the teams in alphabetical order by name. Be sure to specify all the relevant head pointers.

b. Invert on Sport so that the teams are ordered alphabetically.

   c. Invert on City so that the teams are ordered alphabetically.

   d. Draw a suitable DSD.

Now assume we have implemented your DSD and assigned the following additional RRNs.

Cleveland	15
Pittsburgh	16
New York	17
San Francisco	18
Baseball	21
Basketball	22
Football	23
Hockey	25

   e. Draw the conceptual Sport occurrence for Baseball and the City occurrence for New York. Your solution should resemble Figure 3.30.

   f. Using head (first), tail, next, and prior pointers, construct the complete occurrence of your DSD. Again assume that every set is to be ordered on team name. Be sure to label each pointer and use the modified ring structure, in which the last destination occurrence points to its origin.

   g. Assume we have added the New York football team, the Giants, at RRN 10. Update your answer to part *f* by showing just the necessary changes.

3. Add a new PURCHASE__ORDER record to Figure 3.33. Its RRN is 10, its PO number is 2, it was issued on 01/09/XX, and it was sent to a vendor with code 123. Be sure to change all necessary pointers. How many pointers require changing? What conclusion do you draw?

4. Delete PO__NO 1 from your answer to Problem 3. Again be sure to change all necessary pointers.

5. Redraw Figure 3.26 relating the records based on VENDOR__CODE. Assume VENDORs are stored at consecutive RRNs beginning with 30.

6. Redraw Figure 3.31(b) using VENDOR__CODE as the basis.

7. Use Figure 3.33 to answer the following questions. Assume that any PO record can be randomly accessed using the PO__NO field. Explain how you could best resolve each question.

   a. How many PURCHASE__ORDERs were issued on 01/10/XX?

   b. Was PO__NO 1 issued on 01/09/XX?

   c. Assume the total amount of each PURCHASE__ORDER is carried in a field called TOT__AMT. What is the total amount of PURCHASE__ORDERs issued on 01/04/XX?

   d. What is the total amount of PURCHASE__ORDERs issued on 01/04/XX to VENDOR__CODE 133?

8. Redo all parts of Problem 7 based on the partial inversions shown in Figure 3.34.

9. Describe the possible hierarchical paths for Figure 3.35(b).

10. Indicate which records and which pointers must be used to access the record with key value 80 in Figure 3.41.

11. Add the language Assembler to both parts of Figure 3.40.

12. Use the algorithm discussed in Section 3.3 that adds new records to a simple list. Apply it to Figure 3.19(b), assuming we added PO__NO 3. Specifically, show the result from each of the seven steps of the algorithm. What mechanism could be used to accomplish step 3?

13. Figure 3.21 shows how to conceptually delete PO__NO 7 from the file. Figure 3.22 shows the file after the deletion. Use the deletion algorithm discussed in Section 3.3, and describe each step as you explain how to accomplish the deletion.

14. Apply the algorithm for repairing broken chains to the example in Figure 3.32.

15. Add prior, tail, and origin pointers to Figure 3.47. (You will find Figure 3.46 useful as you complete the solution.)

16. Redraw Figure 3.47 assuming that each set is to be sequenced by AMOUNT in descending order.

17. Assume there is a M:N relationship between ALBUM and ARTIST. ALBUM is defined as (ALBUM__ID, ALBUM__NAME, ALBUM__PUBL, COST, ON__HAND). ARTIST is defined as (ARTIST__NAME). Eliminate the M:N relationship, and show the resulting data structure.

PART II

Database Design

In Part II, we examine one of the many ways to design a database. We take a three-step approach: design the conceptual, then the logical, and finally the physical database.

In Chapter 4, we see how to design the conceptual database using either a data structure diagram or an entity-relationship diagram, both of which we discussed in Chapter 2. Chapter 4 emphasizes that the resulting database is a model of the organization and that one of the primary benefits of the approach is an understanding of the semantics of the organization's data.

In Episode 3, which follows Chapter 4, we see how Community Hospital modifies its preliminary design from Episode 2 based on a set of rules developed in the chapter. We will use this design in later episodes as we see how the hospital develops certain applications using a representative DBMS from each of the three models.

In Chapter 5, we examine the remaining two design steps. First, we map the conceptual design into a logical one, that is, adapt it to suit the particular model chosen. Then we illustrate how to perform this task with relational, hierarchical, and network databases. Finally, we design the physical database and adapt the technique to each model.

4

An Introduction to Database Design

The Conceptual Database and Normalization

MINICASE Fred's Pharmacy

Fred Angelino has been the only pharmacist in his store since he opened it in 1970. Like many of today's retail pharmacies, Fred's not only fills prescriptions; it also sells many non-drug items from the storefront, such as toiletries, sunglasses, and greeting cards. Keeping track of the inventory of almost 300 such items, together with over 1,000 drug items, is becoming increasingly difficult for Fred and his two clerks, Colleen and Nancy. On a typical day, he fills about 10 new prescriptions and 75 refills; approximately 10 people buy 25 nondrug items per hour.

Fred currently maintains profiles for 1,000

customers. Each patient's profile is kept on an 8 1/2"-×-11" card. The top shows static customer information such as name, address, phone number, and so on. The bottom carries prescription information for as many of the prescriptions for that customer as will fit: prescription number, name of drug, date the prescription was first filled, refill information, and associated charges. Fred doesn't accept commercial bankcards, but maintains a manual credit system for his regular customers. His accounts receivable system, like his profiling system, is a manual, card-oriented one, with each card showing only the total amount and date of each purchase. It also carries running subtotals, so customers can always find out their current balances by simply asking Fred.

Recently Fred contracted with Laurel Mountain Software (LMS) to develop a system to help him manage both his pharmacy and his storefront. LMS sent Bob Gall to interview Fred so they could set up a database for the proposed pharmacy management information system.

Bob began, "Fred, tell me about the prescription side of your business first. What are the usual kinds of things that go on?"

"Well, Bob, typically a customer comes in with several prescriptions to fill. Some of these are new, while others are refills. On the new prescriptions, we first check for the valid physician's signature, then find the customer's profile card. Of course, if it's a new customer, we have to type up a new profile card. We add the new prescription to the profile, determine the charge by looking the drug up in a master listing I get from my drug wholesaler, and then enter it into the profile. Computing the actual customer charge is a real pain because of insurance company policies—you know, medicare, insurance copays, and so on. Anyway, next I fill the bottle and put a label on it. Besides the directions and the drug information, the label shows the remaining refills. This number also goes on the profile card. I really hate typing the labels for those bottles. I never learned to type, and I always seem to mess up a label before I get it right.

"Before I finish, I have to ask the customer if it's a charge or not. If it isn't a charge, I just give the customer the prescription and the bill. If it is a charge, I give one of the clerks a sheet showing my computed charges. The clerk then takes the sheet to the cash register to add any storefront purchases.

"If the prescription is a refill, I first check

the expiration date of the prescription. Then I see how many refills were permitted and if the refill would cause the total number to exceed the allowable limit. If everything is OK, I adjust the refill number by adding 1 to it and decrease the number of remaining refills. The remaining steps are pretty much like I described for you for new prescriptions.

"Bob, before I forget, I'd like to be able to give each customer an end-of-the-year record of all drug purchases for tax purposes. I get a lot of those requests during January through April, and it's just too much work to do it manually. Any problems with that?"

Bob responded, "No, I don't think so. Let me ask you a few questions about what you've told me so far. Correct me if I'm wrong. A typical customer can have several prescriptions that are open, and each prescription is assigned to just one customer—right?"

"Right, Bob. I assign a unique prescription number to each prescription. When all the allowed refills have been used, we discontinue the prescription, forcing the customer to contact his or her doctor for a new one."

"Can a customer have more than one insurance company?"

"Unfortunately, yes. Each customer can have several, each with a different payment policy. We ask the customer to tell us which is the primary insurer, then work from there."

"OK. Now tell me about the storefront operation."

"Well, it's typical of any store. When a customer makes a purchase, we just ring it up on the cash register. The problem comes in when they want to charge. The clerk manually writes up a charge slip, which my accountant eventually transcribes onto a ledger card. If the customer also charged a prescription, all the transactions are combined onto a single charge slip that we give to the customer. I send statements at the end of the month.

"Manually keeping track of my storefront inventory units and their value is a nightmare. I'd really like to be able to have an inventory control module with the system we're talking about. It should subtract the units purchased from the on-hand amount, and so on."

"I have no trouble with that," Bill replied. "How about sales commissions?"

"I compute a sales commission for each clerk for the storefront merchandise she sells. I can give you the formula later. I pay the clerks their commissions at the end of each month, but it's based on the retail dollar amounts."

"Thanks, Fred, I think I have enough information for now. How about showing me all the manual documents you use, and I'll get back to you after I develop a tentative design for your system."

Fred and Bob spent the next several hours reviewing the documents. Then Bob left to return to the LMS office, where he began contemplating his database design.

Discussion

1. List as many of Fred's entities as you can.
2. Construct a DSD or E-R diagram using your entities from Question 1.
3. See if you can assign an identifier to each entity.

As we saw in Chapter 2, there are three levels of database abstraction: the conceptual, the external, and the physical database. The conceptual database is essentially a graphical representation of all the organization's entities and their relationships to one another. Included in this design is the assignment of attributes to the entities or conceptual files. Not too long ago, database theoreticians advocated a single conceptual database. Practitioners, on the other hand, claimed this was impossible because of a lack of adequate hardware and software, but most of all, it was just too complex. As a result, an organization in today's database environment might have several conceptual databases, one for each functional area or for each "subject" area.

The external databases are those seen by specific users and are sometimes called *user views* or *subschemas*. They can be unlimited in number and are subsets of the conceptual database(s).

The physical database refers to the methods used to implement the conceptual and external designs. It includes such things as which fields should be indexed or hashed, which access method should be used for which record types, and so on.

This chapter suggests one of the several ways organizations can design their conceptual and external databases. Unfortunately, there is no universally agreed-upon "best" step-by-step procedure for achieving the optimal design. The process of designing the conceptual and external databases is largely an art, with a few "good" rules sprinkled in.

The conceptual design focuses on entities, relationships, and attributes and attempts to meet certain guidelines. The primary input to this process is usually a series of interviews with end users. The output is a data structure diagram (DSD), an entity-relationship (E-R) diagram, or some other graphical representation of the entities and their relationships. The design process should also assign attributes to entities to ensure that the potential problems arising from the addition of new records and the deletion and updating of existing records do not occur. As you will learn, these potential problems are called **anomalies.** This technique of properly assigning attributes to entities to reduce anomalies is called **normalization.**

Although normalization is intended to help design relational databases, many companies use it to design all their files regardless of the underlying data model. We will follow this trend by developing a conceptual design based on the results of the normalization theory without worrying about which data model the organization actually uses. We will look at six normal forms—results of the normalization process—first from a practical approach and then from a technical view. The technical treatments, shown for all but the first rule, are optional, so you can skip them if your instructor permits.

The logical design attempts to map the conceptual design to the model appropriate to the chosen DBMS. Thus, for example, if the organization's DBMS is based on the network model, the design must be adapted to the needs and requirements of that model. The most restrictive of the three data models is the hierarchical one. Mapping the DSD or E-R results to a hierarchical diagram can be very time-consuming and result in much redundancy. The relational model is the most adaptable, requiring almost no additional steps, provided the normalization in the conceptual design has been done correctly.

The final step is to design the physical database. This necessitates deciding when and where to use pointers and indexes, which fields should be hashed, and so on. It also requires that the DBA describe record types, attributes, and entity relationships.

At the conclusion of this chapter, you will be able to:

- Distinguish among the conceptual, the logical, and the physical database designs.
- List the objectives of the conceptual design.
- List the 11 conceptual design steps.
- Discuss the need for subject databases.
- Apply the six rules for assigning attributes to entities.
- Determine whether a conceptual design is in domain/key normal form.

4.1   CONCEPTUAL DATABASE DESIGN: AN INTRODUCTION

The primary objectives of the conceptual design of a database are:

- To develop a graphical representation of the organization's entities and their relationships that is independent of the DBMS and hardware.
- To improve communications.
- To assign attributes to entities in an "optimal" way.
- To determine the characteristics of the attributes.

The primary purpose of the conceptual design is to formulate a model of the organization's data requirements. This model must be independent of the organization's hardware and DBMS, because both of these items can, and will, change over time. Because we want to preserve our investment in the database, we don't want to have to change it every time the organization acquires new hardware or switches DBMS vendors. By making the model reflect the organization's business, we build in flexibility. Historically, IS personnel designed files to optimize their own (that is, information systems) needs. This resulted in frequent file reorganization and high maintenance charges. By modeling the database on the organization's data needs, however, we minimize the need for such changes.

The next objective is to improve communications between IS personnel and end users and among end users themselves. Remember that one of the requirements of the database approach is cooperation. Because we are sharing data throughout the organization, we must foster an atmosphere of cooperation. During the development of the conceptual design, IS employees will meet with one another and with groups of end users. These meetings will force the organization to face the problems resulting from the sharing of data, to create solutions to the political and personal problems emanating from the database approach, and to make end-user groups more cognizant of the data and informational needs of other groups. All of this will make the organization deal with these problems during the design phase of the database—a situation much preferable to tackling them during the implementation phase, when users are actually beginning to use and rely on the data within the database.

The third objective is to assign attributes to entities so as to minimize the problems resulting from the database's dynamic nature. Only after collecting the data from users and designing the graphical model do we attach attributes to the entities. In performing this step, we must take care that our designs don't lead us to potential updating problems. By following some guidelines developed by the relational theoreticians we can, in fact, guarantee that problems arising from updating our database will be minimized.

Finally, we want to make sure that everyone in the organization understands the semantics of our design components. What do we mean by "An invoice can have several line items" or "What is a line item?" It is quite likely that this will be the first time the organization has looked at these kinds of questions, and the very process of asking and answering them will be beneficial.

To accomplish these objectives, we will follow these 11 steps:

- Determine the scope of the design.
- Determine the relevant transactions that the database must support.
- Determine the organization's business rules.
- From the previous two steps, determine the entities.
- Determine the identifier for each entity.
- Draw the DSD and/or E-R diagram.
- Make sure the diagram(s) supports both the business rules and the organization's transactions.
- Add attributes to the entities following the proper guidelines.
- Add anticipated attributes.
- Revise and refine the design.
- Determine user views.

4.2   STEP 1. DETERMINE THE SCOPE OF THE DESIGN: WHAT ARE THE BOUNDARIES?

During the formative years of the database approach, "experts" preached about the benefits of developing a single database that would serve the needs of the entire organization. They often suggested that the design team spend several years (often this took two to four years) to develop a conceptual model of all the organization's entities, their attributes, and the entities' relationships to one another. This should still be the ideal goal, because it is the one that guarantees the greatest flexibility and adaptability. Unfortunately, as DBAs who have followed this suggestion have found out, neither the hardware nor the software (DBMS) is likely to be fast enough to handle the updating problems, nor may the software be sufficiently sophisticated to adapt to changing needs, especially those discovered after the design is physically implemented. If a relationship is left out of the conceptual design, adding it to the organization's physical database will be quite difficult, especially with databases built on either the hierarchical or network data model. As more entities are incorporated into the global conceptual design, this inability to adapt will become even more significant.

These considerations aside, the most important problem associated with this approach is a people one. Few, if any, employees have a sufficiently broad knowledge of both the organization and the database technology to develop such a grandiose plan, and few programmers are able to cope with the complex programming environment that results from the global organizational conceptual design. Today, while we agree with the goal of developing an organizational design, we take a more practical approach. By developing several smaller databases, we can more easily adapt to changing requirements. Also, smaller-scale databases are easier for individuals to understand, control, and manage.

Determining the exact scope of each database is not a straightforward procedure. Some organizations limit their databases to the application level, but this is probably too narrow a view, leading to redundancy and limited adaptability to users' changing informational needs, especially across functional areas. A better approach is to develop "subject" databases. Choosing the subject areas should be done only after considering the overall organization's business plans and those of the information systems department.

We will develop a conceptual database to support Fred's Pharmacy, introduced in the minicase at the beginning of the chapter. It is usually helpful to state the scope of the design and the aspects of the organization it excludes. Therefore, we will limit the design to one that will support prescription processing and sales of storefront items and exclude Fred's payroll, accounts payable, and financial reporting needs.

4.3 STEP 2. DETERMINE THE RELEVANT TRANSACTION THE DATABASE MUST SUPPORT: WHAT DOES THE ORGANIZATION DO?

A **transaction** is a sequence of steps defining a business event. For practicality, we will classify reports and events as transactions. Only by documenting and understanding the organization's transactions can we ensure that our design will support the informational needs of the organization's end users.

Figure 4.1 shows the transactions on which Bob and Fred have agreed. After we look at Bob's initial conceptual design for Fred's Pharmacy, we will compare it to the list of transactions to ensure that we can indeed satisfy the data requirements of each of its transactions.

4.4 STEP 3. DETERMINE THE BUSINESS RULES: CONSTRAINTS AND DOMAINS

Business rules, sometimes simply called **constraints,** are statements about the cardinality of relationships among entities, referential integrity, and domain restrictions. Chapter 2 discussed all of these constraints.

Returning to our example, Bob has summarized the business rules for Fred's Pharmacy. Figure 4.2 shows some of those rules. The rules for the pharmacy have been divided into two groups: rules that pertain to prescription processing and those that relate to storefront sales. Notice that the emphasis is on the cardinality of the relationships among the pharmacy's entities. These rules will be instrumental in determining the entities and their relationships. For example,

---

FIGURE 4.1   **Transactions for Fred's Pharmacy**

Prescription-Filling Transactions

1. Enter, delete, or change customers.
2. Enter and fill new prescriptions for a customer.
3. Refill an existing prescription.
4. Bill for a new prescription or a refilled one.
5. Send forms to insurance companies to recover copays and insurance monies.
6. Update drug inventory when an item is sold.
7. Update inventory when items are purchased from drug wholesaler.
8. Update inventory when physical inventory is taken.
9. Print year-end summaries for each customer, showing drugs purchased for the year.

Nonprescription Inventory Processing

1. Record a sale. It can be for credit or cash.
2. Update inventory when an item is sold or purchased, or when a physical inventory is taken.
3. Print inventory profitability reports.
4. Record commission for each sale.
5. Calculate each salesperson's commission at the end of each month.
6. Print monthly customer statements.

FIGURE 4.2   **Rules for Fred's Pharmacy**

Prescription Rules

1. Each prescription can contain only one drug.
2. Many prescriptions can have the same prescribed drug.
3. A prescription can be refilled a limited number of times.
4. A customer can receive several prescriptions.
5. Each customer can have several insurance companies, each with a different copay amount.
6. Only a single licensed pharmacist is responsible for a prescription filling or refilling.

Nonprescription Sales Rules

1. Each sale can be associated with many inventory items.
2. One employee is designated as responsible for the sale.
3. An item is uniquely identified by its code.
4. A customer's code uniquely identifies a customer.

---

from rules 1, 2, and 4, Bob has deduced that he needs three entities: DRUG, CUSTOMER, and PRESCRIPTION. (Note that it has been our custom to capitalize only the first letter of an entity name. However, once the name is entered into the data dictionary, all letters are usually capitalized. This is the format we will adopt in this chapter.)

The first two rules suggest that the relationship between the entities DRUG and PRESCRIPTION is 1:M. We make this cardinality determination because rule 1 states that one PRESCRIPTION occurrence is associated with exactly one DRUG, while rule 2 states that each DRUG is associated with several PRE-SCRIPTION occurrences. Rule 4 tells Bob that he needs the third entity, CUS-TOMER, and that the CUSTOMER:PRESCRIPTION relationship is 1:M. Study-ing the rules derived from the detailed process of interviewing the end users of the system is probably the best way to discover the entities and their relation-ships.

4.5   STEP 4. DETERMINE THE ENTITIES: WHAT ARE THE ORGANIZATION'S OBJECTS?

One approach to determining the organization's entities is called the **top-down approach,** because it first focuses on the organization's entities, then attaches attributes to them only after ensuring that the entities and their relationships are correct and that they correctly model the organization's rules and support the informational needs of the transactions. This methodology, also called **entity analysis,** is a derivative of corporate planning, which also follows this approach.

A **bottom-up approach,** in contrast, first focuses on end user data require-ments, then aggregates them into entities. This approach is also called **attribute synthesis.**

Neither approach has been proven superior to the other, and, in fact, it usually is advocated that both be used, with one serving as a check on the other. Used in this manner, the top-down approach develops the forest, while the bottom-up method shows us the trees within it. Currently, we are discussing the top-down approach. In Section 4.13, we will demonstrate the differences resulting from the bottom-up approach.

To determine the entities and their relationships, the DBA should focus on the transactions and business rules pertinent to each prospective end user of

---

FIGURE 4.3   **Entities in Fred's Pharmacy Database**

Entity

ALLERGY
CUSTOMER
DRUG
NON_DRUG_INVENTORY
EMPLOYEE
PRESCRIPTION
REFILL
SALE
INSURANCE_CO

---

the database. Through a combination of experience, studying the transactions, and analyzing the business rules that he collected, Bob has summarized the entities as shown in Figure 4.3.

The list of entities discovered by examining the business rules and transactions may be incomplete, or it may include items that actually are not entities. When we get to step 7, we will see how we can determine whether the list is adequate. Now we will look at one way to determine whether all the items on the list are actually entities.

4.6 STEP 5. DETERMINE THE IDENTIFIER OF EACH ENTITY: FINDING A PRIMARY KEY

The next step is to determine the identifiers of the entities to ensure that the entities are really entities. Unless we can determine a unique data item, or combination of data items, that identifies a particular occurrence of the hypothesized entity, we probably do not have an entity. Figure 4.4 shows the identifier for each of the entities in Figure 4.3.

The choice of key attribute should not be made based on a few occurrences of the entity. Merely looking at a few records or rows and selecting the key based on that observation can lead to erroneous results. Instead, the DBA has to make this choice based on the application being studied.

While most of the entity identifiers in Figure 4.4 are atomic, REFILL's is a composite one. In our example, while interviewing Fred, Bob has determined that each REFILL occurrence has a sequential number assigned to it. Thus, the first filling is assigned refill number 1, the next filling (refill) is assigned number 2, and so on. Because every prescription can be refilled multiple times, the refill number by itself doesn't uniquely determine a specific refill. For example, pre-

---

FIGURE 4.4   **Identifiers for Each Entity Shown in Figure 4.3**

Entity	Identifier
ALLERGY	ALLERGY_CODE
CUSTOMER	CUSTOMER_NO
DRUG	DRUG_CODE
NON_DRUG_INVENTORY	ITEM_NO
EMPLOYEE	EMP_NO
PRESCRIPTION	PNO
REFILL	REFILL #, PNO
SALE	SALES_NO
INSURANCE_CO	COMPANY_ID

scriptions 10 and 100 may have been filled four times. Thus, there are at least two prescriptions having a REFILL value of 4. The other component of the identifier is the unique prescription number, PNO. Also, every refill of a given prescription will carry the same value of PNO, so that data item doesn't uniquely define a specific refill either. The combination of these two data items does, however. For example, a PNO of 4455 and a REFILL of 3 uniquely determine a specific refill. The identifier value is 445503, where the first four characters are the prescription number and the last two are the refill number.

4.7   STEP 6. DRAW THE DSD AND/OR E-R DIAGRAM: GRAPHICAL DATABASE MODELS

Next, we need to determine the relationships among the entities and document our findings. In doing so, we will rely heavily on the business rules and transactions developed earlier.

While relationships with cardinalities of 1:1 or 1:M can immediately be drawn on the E-R diagram or DSD, those with M:N relationships cannot. For those relationships, we must create an intersection entity, which represents the M:N relationship. We saw how to do this in Chapter 3.

Figure 4.5 shows Bob's initial DSD for Fred's Pharmacy. It tells us there is a 1:M relationship between EMPLOYEE and SALE. Bob reasons that each employee can be responsible for several sales, but a particular sale can be the responsibility of only one employee. This relationship is a direct result of studying the second nonprescription-sales rule in Figure 4.2. Because it was of the 1:M type, Bob can immediately represent it on the diagram.

After determining the relationship between the SALE and the NON__DRUG__INVENTORY entities, Bob correctly decides that it is M:N, because a sale can be for many items and a given item can appear as an item on several sales. As we just suggested, we must decompose all M:N complex relationships to two 1:M simple relationships, one each between the original entities and the intersection record type. Bob calls the new entity SALES__TR for "sales transaction." With his new entity, Bob will have to use a composite primary key consisting of the identifiers of both NON__DRUG__INVENTORY and SALE. In addition, he should carry any other attributes "belonging to," or determined by, the key—the units sold, for example. We will return to consider which attributes should be stored in an entity in a later step.

By studying prescription rule number 5 in Figure 4.2, Bob realizes there is another M:N relationship: between INSURANCE__CO and CUSTOMER. He concludes that each customer can have coverage from several insurance companies and, based on his experience, that each company can insure several of Fred's customers. To avoid M:N relationships in the design, Bob creates a new entity, CUST__INS, that will, after he assigns attributes in step 8, have a com-

FIGURE 4.5   Tentative DSD for Fred's Pharmacy Database

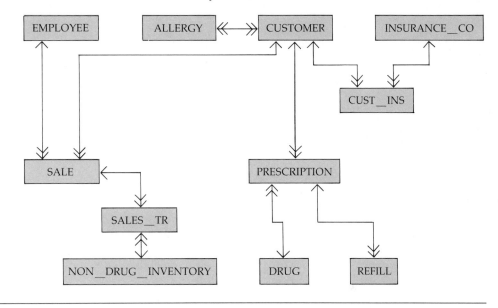

posite key consisting of the customer's code as well as that of the insurance company.

In addition to the key fields, we often carry other pertinent attributes in the new entity. For example, because the SALES__TR entity records data about the details of a sale, Bob should carry the SALES__AMOUNT and UNITS__SOLD attributes in there. The other relationships shown in Figure 4.5 are 1:M and can be derived from the rules presented in Figure 4.2.

The actual construction of the DSD isn't an easy task for the DBA. To facilitate the process, some of the end users of the new system should be involved with its design. Like a systems analysis project, early and continued involvement by end users helps foster cooperation and commitment. In fact, without their continued involvement, the approach will fail. Equally important is determining which users to involve in the project. Only motivated, committed employees from the user groups should be included. To do otherwise will lead to pessimism, lengthy arguments about the merits of the approach among the project's members, a general lack of morale, and other roadblocks.

As we mentioned earlier, many organizations today use E-R diagrams rather than DSDs to model entities and their relationships. Figure 4.6 shows the E-R diagram that Bob has developed for Fred's Pharmacy. It is similar to the DSD, but it makes it easier for us to determine the exact nature of the relationships among the entities.

FIGURE 4.6   The Entity-Relationship Diagram that Corresponds to the DSD in Figure 4.5

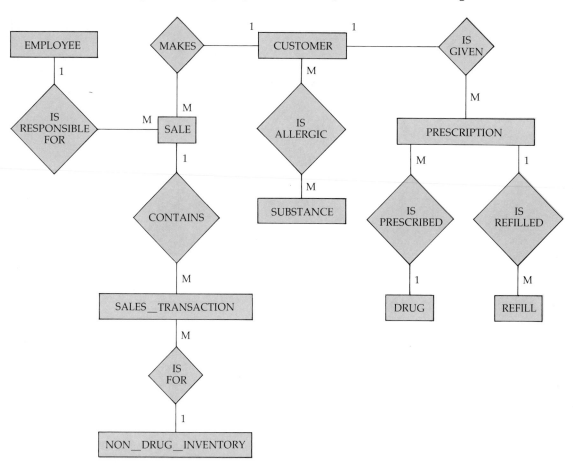

4.8   STEP 7. ENSURE THAT THE CONCEPTUAL DESIGN SATISFIES THE BUSINESS RULES AND TRANSACTIONS' NEEDS: HOW GOOD A MODEL DO WE HAVE?

The conceptual database must supply the organization's data needs as the organization carries out its day-to-day operations. As we saw earlier, we can understand these operations by defining the transactions that occur within each. The DBA should now compare the conceptual design against the list of transactions prepared earlier to ensure that the diagram models the transactions satisfactorily.

For example, one of the transactions in Figure 4.1 is to record a storefront sale. This transaction first involves determining whether or not the customer is a regular one. We can determine this by looking at the CUSTOMER entity, provided we carry a CREDIT__STATUS attribute. Next, the transaction suggests that the customer can be billed, provided he or she has an account. This means we will have to store some billing data—date of purchase, item purchased, payment date, amount of payment, and so forth. Where can we store this billing and payment information? It appears our design may be faulty, because we have no entity assigned that can represent the customer's payment transactions. The SALE entity should contain only attributes pertaining to the actual sale, not those pertaining to payments. In short, we need another entity. Let's call it PAYMENT. This entity is included in the revised diagram shown in Figure 4.7.

Let's look at one more transaction and see whether or not the diagram supports it. Prescription transactions 2 through 5 imply that we need to be able to relate customers with their prescriptions and prescriptions with their refills. Bob's design includes a 1:M relationship between CUSTOMER and PRESCRIPTION and a 1:M relationship between PRESCRIPTION and REFILL. From the diagram, we can conclude that each customer can have several prescriptions, but a particular prescription can be associated with only one customer. The

FIGURE 4.7   Revised DSD for Fred's Pharmacy Database

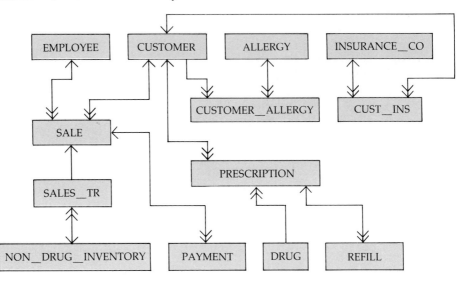

diagram also suggests that each prescription is associated with several refills, but a particular refill is associated with only one prescription. Bob's design successfully models these four transactions.

Let's assume that all the remaining transactions are modeled correctly. At this time, we must choose the attributes for each entity on our diagram.

4.9   STEP 8. ADD ATTRIBUTES TO ENTITIES: A DIFFICULT, ERROR-PRONE STEP

Only after we have determined the entities and their relationships and chosen the identifier for each entity do we add the remaining attributes. It is often suggested that a list of attributes be developed independently of the entities and that attributes be assigned to entities from this list. Figure 4.8 lists the attributes that pertain to Fred's Pharmacy.

FIGURE 4.8   A List of Attributes for Fred's Pharmacy

CUSTOMER__ADDRESS
CUSTOMER__ALLERGY__CODE
CUSTOMER__CODE
CUSTOMER__NAME
CUSTOMER__NUMBER
CUSTOMER__PHONE
CUSTOMER__TYPE
CUST__INS__CO__CODE
CUST__INS__CO__COVERAGE__TYPE
DRUG__CODE
DRUG__DESCRIPTION
DRUG__COST
DRUG__PRICE
DRUG__ON__HAND
DRUG__USAGE__YTD
PRESCRIPTION__REFILL__NO
PRESCRIPTION__DRUG
PRESCRIPTION__CHARGE
PRESCRIPTION__DATE
PRESCRIPTION__UNITS
REFILLS__ALLOWED
PAYMENT__DATE
PAYMENT__SALES__NO
PAYMENT__AMT
PAYMENT__CUST__NO

ITEM__CODE
ITEM__DESC
ITEM__COST
ITEM__PRICE
ITEM__USAGE__YTD
ITEM__QTY__ON__HAND

EMPLOYEE__CODE
EMPLOYEE__NAME
EMPLOYEE__COMMISSION

ALLERGY__CODE
ALLERGY__DESCRIPTION

INSURANCE__CO__CODE
INSURANCE__CO__NAME
INSURANCE__CO__ADDRESS
INSURANCE__CO__CO__PAY__AMT

SALES__NO
SALES__DATE
SALES__CUST__NO
SALES__EMP__CODE
SALES__TOT__AMT

SALES__ITEM__CODE
SALES__ITEM__UNITS
SALES__ITEM__CHARGE

REFILL__NO
REFILL__DATE
REFILL__PRESCRIPTION__NO
REFILL__AMT

Determining the attributes for an organization might seem to be an overwhelming task. However, it is similar to the process of developing a data dictionary, which a systems analyst must do in the course of developing an information system. The major difference is in the scope of the discovery process. Rather than focusing on one application, as the systems analyst does, the DBA considers the attributes for the entire organization or for several subject areas. The total number of attributes will vary from organization to organization but will be smaller than you might think—probably in the 1,000-to-2,000 range for a large organization and in the hundreds or even fewer for a smaller one.

As we have mentioned several times, we must not assign the attributes to the entities in an arbitrary way. Unless we are very careful about which attributes we associate with which entities, we can expect to experience problems related to modifying the files based on the entities. The next section looks at these problems.

Modification Anomalies

Assigning the attributes to the entities must be done in a way that will result in a minimal number of **modification anomalies**—problems related to the adding, deleting, or updating of record occurrences. The Standards Committee of CODASYL has identified 13 anomalies. We will discuss three: insertion, deletion, and update.

Insertion Anomalies. An **insertion anomaly** occurs when an attempt is made to add a record to a database or file and is rejected because of a missing value for one or more fields. Specifically, this will occur when a component of the primary key is null, which, according to the entity integrity rule we discussed in Section 3 of Chapter 2, isn't permitted. The cause of such problems is usually the mixing of attributes from two or more entities.

Deletion Anomalies. A **deletion anomaly** means that the deletion of a record occurrence causes an unintended deletion of information about another record of a different type. This too is due to an entity design in which attributes from two or more entities were mixed together.

Update Anomalies. An **update anomaly** occurs when updating a given file is made needlessly complicated due to redundancy. It manifests itself in the following manner: The process of updating an attribute of a single logical entity occurrence results in the updating of several.

Let's now look at an example of each type of anomaly.

Examples of Modification Anomalies. Part (a) of Figure 4.9 shows a poorly designed conceptual CUSTOMER file for Fred's Pharmacy. Part (b) shows a tabular occurrence of it. The composite key consists of the customer's number

FIGURE 4.9   **A File Design that Contains Modification Anomalies**

(a) A conceptual file containing potential modification anomalies

CUSTOMER (CUSTOMER__NO, DRUG__CODE, CNAME, PHONE, SIZE, UNITS, COST__PER__UNIT, CHARGE)

(b) A tabular occurrence of Figure 4.9(a)

CUSTOMER_NO	DRUG_CODE	CNAME	PHONE	SIZE	UNITS	COST_PER_UNIT	CHARGE
10	PCN	YANG	555-7676	250mg	20	.20	10.00
10	TAG	YANG	555-4545	500mg	50	.05	5.00
12	PCN	FROST	555-7879	100mg	10	.25	10.00

(CUSTOMER__NO) plus a drug code (DRUG__CODE). Let's call the components of a composite key **subkeys.** The key had to be composite because, as you can see from some of the occurrences in part (b), each customer can have several prescriptions, each for a different drug. For example, CUSTOMER__NO 10 occurs twice because that customer is associated with two prescriptions, and CUSTOMER__NO doesn't distinguish the first from the second occurrence. Similarly, two occurrences contain PCN as a DRUG__CODE value. Hence, that attribute isn't sufficient as an atomic key either; only a composite key will suffice.

Now for the addition anomaly. Assume that a customer has come into the pharmacy and informed Fred that he is a new member of the community and will be having all of his family's prescriptions filled there. As yet, however, none of the family members have prescriptions to be filled. Fred wants to enter the new customer into his CUSTOMER file. In Chapter 2, we discussed *entity integrity,* a term meaning that none of the key fields can be null (unknown). In this situation, if the customer has no prescriptions as yet, the associated customer record cannot be inserted into the file because there is no value for one of the subkey attributes, DRUG__CODE.

As an example of a deletion anomaly, assume Fred wants to delete the CUSTOMER records associated with CUSTOMER__NO 10. Furthermore, assume this is the only customer on penicillin and the CUSTOMER file is the only one that carries a drug's COST__PER__UNIT. Fred has two choices. First, in order to keep information about the drug, Fred can try to set the CUSTOMER__NO field value for every record pertaining to CUSTOMER__NO 10 to null. However, he cannot do so because of the entity integrity rule. Alternatively, Fred can delete all the records associated with the customer. However, if he does this, he will lose information not only about the customer but also about the cost of that particular drug. So, if he deletes customer 10, he will also delete the cost information about penicillin. The best solution is to remove the drug-related fields from the CUSTOMER file.

Finally, as an example of an update anomaly, consider the problems involved if customer number 10's phone number changes. Although only two records must be changed in our example, in a real-world situation it could be hundreds, because a pharmacy usually keeps records for several years.

The identification of anomalies, like that of primary keys, cannot be done by merely observing the data. More often it is only after listing the business's rules and constraints and making the necessary assumptions that the anomalies can be detected, and only then after studying the underlying relationships among the attributes. In all cases, the problems are due to undesirable functional dependencies among the attributes, a topic we discuss next.

Functional Dependencies

Several of the rules we will develop for assigning attributes pertain to functional dependencies. A **functional dependency** between two attributes, A and B, is a relationship such that knowing a value of A enables us to determine the corresponding value or values for B. We denote this as A → B, read as: A **determines** B, attribute A is the **determinant** of B, or B is **dependent** on A. For example, knowing a drug's code enables us to determine its cost; drug code is a determinant of drug cost. Figure 4.10 shows another way to depict functional dependencies. We call this kind of diagram a **functional dependency diagram (FDD).**

FIGURE 4.10   **A Functional Dependency Diagram (FDD) for Two Attributes**

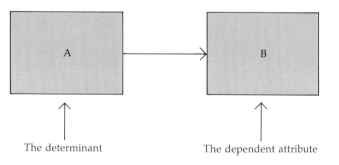

Sometimes we must use multiple attributes as a determinant. When an attribute is determined only by the complete combination of attributes and not by a subset of them, the attribute is said to be **fully functionally dependent** on that combination. Usually we use this term with respect to composite primary keys. For example, the CUSTOMER entity in Figure 4.9 contains a composite primary key or **prime**: CUSTOMER_NO + DRUG_CODE. However, COST_PER_UNIT is determined by the subkey attribute DRUG_CODE and hence is not fully functionally dependent on the composite prime. Figure 4.11 illustrates this using the FDD technique. By illustrating functional dependencies using diagrams like the one in the figure, the fact that a subkey is a determinant of a nonkey attribute is visually easy to see.

One of our design objectives is that all nonprime attributes be dependent on the entire composite key. If this isn't the case, the possibility for modification anomalies exists.

Next, let's consider an example that shows a fully functional dependency. Because only by knowing the customer's number (CUSTOMER_NO) and drug (DRUG_CODE) can we determine the CHARGE, CHARGE is dependent on the entire prime. Figure 4.12 shows the FDD.

Figure 4.13 shows the FDDs for the dependencies within the CUSTOMER definition in Figure 4.9. Notice that CUSTOMER_NO 10 is always associated with a single name, Yang. Also, CUSTOMER_NO 12 is always associated with the name Frost. This means that CUSTOMER_NO → CUSTOMER_NAME, a fact shown as the first functional dependency in Figure 4.13. Now think about the reverse. Is it possible for Fred to have several customers with the name "Smith," each having a different value of CUSTOMER_NO? The answer, of course, is yes. This means that over a period of time, a particular value of CUSTOMER_NAME can be associated with more than one value of

---

FIGURE 4.11   A Functional Dependency that Is Not Fully Dependent

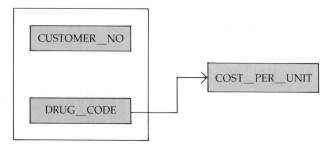

Even though we have a composite key, COST_PER_UNIT is functionally dependent only on a subkey.

FIGURE 4.12   A Fully Functional Dependency

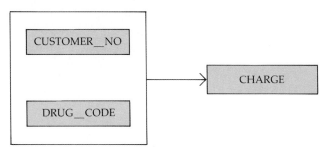

Only when we know the values for both the customer's number and the associated drug code can we ascertain the charge.

FIGURE 4.13   Examples of Functional Dependencies Found in Figure 4.9

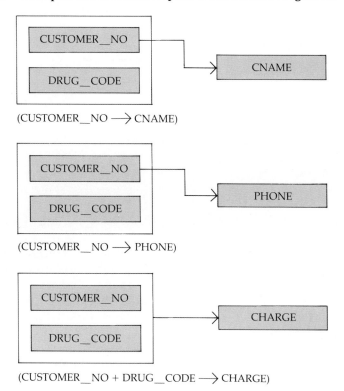

(CUSTOMER__NO $\longrightarrow$ CNAME)

(CUSTOMER__NO $\longrightarrow$ PHONE)

(CUSTOMER__NO + DRUG__CODE $\longrightarrow$ CHARGE)

FIGURE 4.13   (concluded)

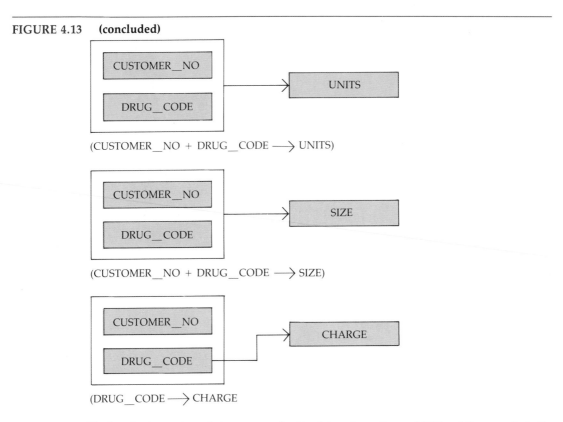

(CUSTOMER__NO + DRUG__CODE ⟶ UNITS)

(CUSTOMER__NO + DRUG__CODE ⟶ SIZE)

(DRUG__CODE ⟶ CHARGE

The dependencies are shown twice, once as a functional dependency diagram (FDD) and then parenthetically in a symbolic form.

CUSTOMER__NO and, therefore, that CUSTOMER__NAME does not determine CUSTOMER__NO.

A more complicated functional dependency can occur when an entity contains several **multivalued dependencies (MVDs).** In this situation, a value for attribute A is always associated with the same set of values of B. For example, assume Fred always buys penicillin from two vendors having codes 3 and 7. Thus, we can say that DRUG__CODE →→ VENDOR__NO, read as "DRUG__CODE multidetermines VENDOR__NO."

There is nothing wrong with an MVD unless there are three or more attributes and the following is true: Assume we have three attributes, A, B, and C, and each value of A is always associated with the same set of B and C values, but

B's values are independent of C's. This is called an **independent multivalued dependency** and leads to a proliferation of redundancy.

Let's look at an example. Figure 4.14 shows an entity DRUG__VEND__DIST, which contains data about drugs, vendors, and distributors. Assume the following rules:

- For each drug, there can be several vendors and several distributors.
- There is no relationship between vendors and distributors.

The first MVD is the relationship between DRUG and VENDOR. Each DRUG__CODE is associated with the same set of VENDOR__NO values. The second MVD in the figure is DRUG__CODE →→ DIST. For example, from part (b) of the figure, TAG is distributed by DRUGS R US and THE GENERIC CO. Part of the semantics behind the data (and not discoverable from the data) is that TAG is always acquired from these two distributors regardless of which vendor actually makes the drug.

A commonly asked question is: How does an MVD differ from the earlier example in which the name "Smith" seemed to be associated with many CUSTOMER_NO values? It might appear that because "Smith" is related to many different values of CUSTOMER_NO, CNAME multidetermines CUSTOMER_NO; that is, CNAME →→ CUSTOMER_NO. This illustrates the dangers in attempting to discern functional dependencies by merely looking at the data.

First, with an MVD, the same set of dependent values (in the hypothetical MVD, this would be CUSTOMER_NO) must always be associated with a single value of the determinant, in our case CNAME. Surely over time the set of CUSTOMER_NO values associated with "Smith" will not be the same. Sec-

---

FIGURE 4.14   **A File Design that Contains Two Independent Multivalued Dependencies**

(a) A conceptual file containing two multivalued dependencies

DRUG__VEND__DIST (<u>DRUG__CODE</u>, <u>VENDOR__NO</u>, <u>DIST</u>)

(b) A tabular occurrence of Figure 4.14(a)

DRUG__CODE	VENDOR__NO	DIST
TAG	3	DRUGS R US
TAG	7	THE GENERIC CO
PCN	5	THE GENERIC CO
ASP	3	PRICED RIGHT

TABLE 4.1   Rules to Follow When Assigning Attributes to Entities

1. There can be no repeating attributes in the entity.
2. Nonkey attributes must be dependent on the entire key.
3. Nonkey attributes must be determined only by the primary key.
4. All determinants must be candidate keys.
5. There can be no multivalued, independent attributes within the entities.
6. Constraints must be enforceable by either a key relationship or a domain constraint.

---

ond—and more important—functional dependencies must be based on the semantics of the data. It makes no sense to hypothesize that by knowing the value of a customer's name we will always be able to determine the same set of customer number values.

There is nothing wrong with multivalued dependencies, as long as there is a relationship between them. In our example, there is no such relationship between the attributes VENDOR__NO and DIST; they are independent of each other.

We are now ready to look at the entity design rules, which are summarized in Table 4.1.

Eliminating Modification Anomalies: Rules for Assigning Attributes to Entities

The entity design rules are based on the principles of normalization, which were developed during the 1970s and early 1980s as guidelines to follow while designing relational databases. However, the general goal of normalization is to design files (actually tables) that have a minimum number of potential modification anomalies—certainly a worthwhile goal regardless of the data model chosen.

This section summarizes the results of normalization theory and shows how we can use those results to properly assign attributes to entities. As you read over the rules and see examples of how they can be applied to incorrectly designed conceptual files, you will notice that the result is usually two or more conceptual files, each of which meets the rule being illustrated. Sometimes the treatment gets formal in tone. These sections have been boxed off and can be omitted without loss of continuity.

Rule 1: No Repeating Attributes (1NF). The *first normal form (1NF)* rule means that there can be no repeating attributes. The result is called a **relation,** or **flat file.**

When Bob first thought about the design of the CUSTOMER entity, he considered setting up a repeating aggregate called PRESCRIPTION. Each occurrence of the aggregate would contain data items such as PRESCRIPTION__DATE, DRUG__CODE, PHYSICIAN__NO, and so on. If a CUSTOMER had four prescriptions, there would be four occurrences of the PRESCRIPTION aggregate. However, Bob has realized that this design would violate the first rule, so he has set up a separate file for prescriptions.

When we detect a repeating aggregate or atomic attribute, we remove it and place it into a new entity. We also store the primary key from the original entity in the new entity so that the two can be related to each other. Of course, this

---

FIGURE 4.15   Using Decomposition to Eliminate Repeating Fields from a Conceptual File

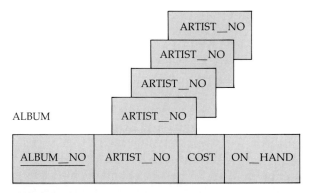

ALBUM design number 1. This design is unacceptable because it contains a repeating field.

ALBUM

ALBUM__NO	COST	ON__HAND

ALBUM__ARTIST

ALBUM__NO	ARTIST__NO

Design number 2 has decomposed the original conceptual file into two: one containing the original fields, but not the repeating one, and a second containing the original primary key plus the repeating field. This second file uses a concatenated primary key.

means that we will have created some redundancy, because the original entity will also retain the primary key attribute(s).

The first part (a) of Figure 4.15 illustrates an entity with repeating fields; the second part (b) shows how it can be decomposed into two separate ones without repeating attributes.

The entity is called ALBUM and might be useful in a record store sales application. The primary key is ALBUM__NO. Notice the repeating attribute, ARTIST__NO. This exists because an album can be created by more than one artist. The decomposed entities are called ALBUM and ALBUM__ARTIST, which represent a cross-reference of albums with artists. The primary key of the new entity is a composite one consisting of ALBUM__NO and ARTIST__NO. Neither of the new entities has repeating attributes, so the revised design complies with the first rule.

A conceptual file that isn't in 1NF is said to be **unnormalized.** Such a file has two problems. First, its semantics create difficulty. When shown in the usual manner, TABLE (A1, A2, . . . AN), there is no clue as to whether or not an attribute is a repeating one. If, on the other hand, we agree that every conceptual file that is in 1NF has only nonrepeating attributes, this problem disappears. Second, the relational operators used with the relational model work only for flat files. So, even if we agreed on a semantic indicator for a repeating attribute (a line above the attribute, for example), we would still face the more serious problem that the file can't be manipulated by the relational operators.

Rule 2: Nonkey Attributes Must Be Dependent on the Entire Prime (2NF). The only time we have to worry about violating the *second normal form (2NF)* rule is when the key is a composite one. Under these circumstances, we need to ensure that all nonkey attributes are fully functionally dependent on the prime and not on a sub-key. We saw an example of a composite key in Figure 4.9, where the two subkeys are CUSTOMER__NO and DRUG__CODE. However, as we saw in Figure 4.13, CUSTOMER__NO, a subkey, determines CNAME and another subkey, DRUG__CODE, determines COST__PER__UNIT, both clear violations of the rule.

Failure to follow rule 2NF will inevitably lead to anomalies. First, if Fred attempts to add a new CUSTOMER who has no prescription yet, there will be no value for DRUG__CODE, a subkey that cannot be null, and we will have an update anomaly. Next, as we discussed earlier, if Fred attempts to delete an existing customer, he will also delete information about a drug—a deletion anomaly. Last, suppose a customer's phone number changes. Because of Fred's poor design, PHONE is carried with every CUSTOMER:PRESCRIPTION combination. Thus, updating a CUSTOMER's phone number will result in a change to all the CUSTOMER occurrences for that CUSTOMER (there will be as many changes as that customer has prescriptions—an update anomaly).

A better plan would be to decompose the entity into the two shown in Figure 4.16. Now the design complies with the second rule, because all nonprime attributes are fully functionally dependent on primes.

FIGURE 4.16   A Revised Design of Figure 4.9(a) that Satisfies Rule 2: All Nonkey Attributes Must Be Dependent on the Entire Key

CUSTOMER (<u>CUSTOMER__NO</u>, CNAME, PHONE)
DRUG (<u>DRUG__CODE</u>, COST__PER__UNIT)
CUST__DRUG (<u>CUSTOMER__NO</u>, <u>DRUG__CODE</u>, SIZE, UNITS, CHARGE)

Let's check back on the anomalies. First, assume Fred wants to add a new customer who hasn't yet had a prescription filled. This presents no problem, because Fred can assign a CUSTOMER__NO and then add a new record to the CUSTOMER file. With this new design, he has a value for the complete CUS-TOMER prime and thus is in compliance with the entity integrity rule. Next, look at a deletion of a customer. Because CUSTOMER contains information only about customers, the deletion of a CUSTOMER record won't mean the loss of information about drugs, unlike the situation with the original design in Figure 4.9. Finally, a change in a customer's phone number will result in an update to a single CUSTOMER occurrence, not several.

As we proceed from one normal form to the next higher one, one of the common characteristics is that if a relation is in the nth normal form, it is also in (n–1) form. For example, a table in fourth normal form is also in third normal form.

Second Normal Form Rule (2NF)
Technical Treatment

For a conceptual file to be in second normal form, it must be in first normal form and nonkey attributes must be dependent on the entire key; that is, every nonkey attribute must be fully dependent on the primary key. Formally, we can state this as follows: For the conceptual file R (<u>A</u>,<u>B</u>,C,D . . . N),

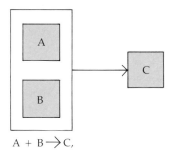

A + B $\rightarrow$ C,

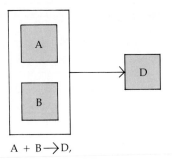

A + B $\rightarrow$ D,

$\vdots$

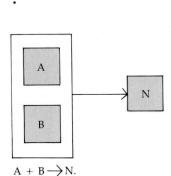

A + B $\rightarrow$ N.

assume that B $\rightarrow$ F. This means that a subkey attribute determines a nonprime, and the entity fails the test. Based only on an entity's definition, we cannot determine whether or not it is in 2NF. We also need to know the functional dependency rules. This is true for all the normal forms except 1NF.

If a conceptual file isn't in 2NF, we can convert it by decomposing the original relation into two separate relations, each of which meets the test for 2NF; that is, if in the relation R (A, B, C,D):

A + B $\rightarrow$ C,

but

A $\rightarrow$ D,

split R into two relations, R and S, where:

R (A, B, C)
S (A, D).

Rule 3: Nonkey Attributes Must Be Determined Only by the Primary Key (3NF). In essence, the *third normal form (3NF)* rule means that the nonkey attributes must be independent of one another; that is, a nonkey attribute cannot be functionally dependent on another nonkey attribute, even transitively (a term we define in the next paragraph).

Suppose we change the definition of CUSTOMER to:

CUSTOMER (<u>CUSTOMER_NO</u>,<u>DRUG_CODE</u>, CNAME, PHONE, SIZE,
    UNITS, COST_PER_UNIT, CHARGE, EMPLOYER,
    EMPLOYER_ADDRESS)

The new functional dependency is EMPLOYER → EMPLOYER_ADDRESS, and one nonprime attribute determines another. A fact that probably isn't obvious to you is that CUSTOMER_NO → EMPLOYER and, since EMPLOYER → EMPLOYER_ADDRESS, indirectly CUSTOMER_NO → EMPLOYER_ADDRESS. This means that a **transitive dependency,** also called an **intermediate dependency,** exists between CUSTOMER_NO and EMPLOYER_ADDRESS. This is illustrated in Figure 4.17 by the dotted line. Another way to state rule 3 is "Eliminate all transitive dependencies."

Again, failure to comply with the rule can lead to anomalies. Look at the last definition of CUSTOMER as we examine update anomalies. Every CUSTOMER record will contain a redundant copy of the employer's address. Think of how many occurrences might need updating if the customer changes jobs or the employer's address changes! Next, assume Fred deletes the only CUSTOMER occurrence that contains IBM's address. Then he loses information about an employer as well as a customer. This illustrates a deletion anomaly. Last, assume Fred wants to add a new company in town but can't because there are no customers working there yet. Remember that in order to add the employer, he must have values for the complete prime: CUSTOMER_NO and DRUG_CODE.

To eliminate the problems, we decompose the entity by creating a new one containing both the determinant (EMPLOYER) and the dependent attribute (EMPLOYEE_ADDRESS). This is illustrated in Figure 4.18. In the new CUSTOMER file, we dropped the EMPLOYER_ADDRESS attribute but retained EMPLOYER so that we can relate the two entities to each other—a necessary operation for determining the address of the customer's employer.

There will be times when it appears that a table isn't in 3NF when it really is. Consider this relation: DRUG (<u>DRUGCODE</u>, DRUGNAME, NDC#). There is a unique NDC (National Drug Code) number for every drug sold in America. Thus, we can say that NDC# → DRUGNAME and that the relation appears to have a nonprime attribute determining another nonprime attribute. However, our definition allows for this situation, provided the dependency is between a candidate key and a nonprime attribute. Certainly, we could have selected NDC# as the key. Hence, it is a candidate key, and the relation is in fact in 3NF.

FIGURE 4.17   An FDD Showing a Transitive Dependency

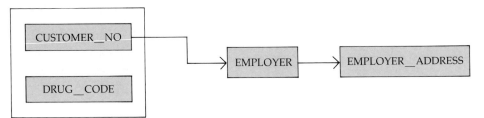

Therefore, indirectly:

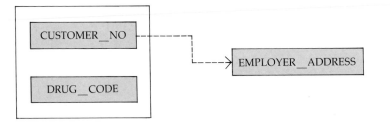

*CUSTOMER_NO → EMPLOYER, and EMPLOYER → EMPLOYER_ADDRESS; therefore,
CUSTOMER_NO → EMPLOYER_ADDRESS.*

FIGURE 4.18   A Decomposed Design for the Modified CUSTOMER Entity

(a) Original CUSTOMER design

CUSTOMER (<u>CUSTOMER_NO</u>, <u>DRUG_CODE</u>, CNAME, PHONE, SIZE, UNITS,
         COST_PER_UNIT, CHARGE, EMPLOYER, EMPLOYER_ADDRESS)

Nonprime attribute ——⌐   Nonprime ——————⌐
    (determinant)   dependent attribute
          of EMPLOYER

(b) New CUSTOMER design

CUSTOMER (<u>CUSTOMER_NO</u>, <u>DRUG_CODE</u>, CNAME, PHONE, SIZE, UNITS,
         COST_PER_UNIT, CHARGE, EMPLOYER)

EMPLOYER (<u>EMPLOYER</u>, EMPLOYER_ADDRESS)

This design satisfies rule 3: Nonkey attributes must be determined only by prime attributes.

Third Normal Form Rule (3NF)
Technical Treatment

A relation in 3NF has the following properties: (1) It is in 2NF and (2) all nonkey attributes are functionally dependent on the primary key only. Using the more formal approach, given a relation R ($\underline{A}$, B, C, . . . N), if for any two attributes, X and Y, where X is not equal to A, X → Y, the relation isn't in 3NF. This means that a relation is in 3NF if for all functional dependencies of the form A → B, either A is a key or all the attributes of B (it may be composite) are part of a (candidate) key.

A relation that isn't in 3NF is decomposed by splitting it into several, each of which is in 3NF. For the relation R ($\underline{A}$, B, C), A → B and B → C, we can split R into two tables, R and S: R ($\underline{A}$, B) and S ($\underline{B}$, C).

As a practical matter, many database designers make compliance with these first three rules their objective. Compliance can be checked only by studying the semantics behind the data, not by merely looking at the data.

Rule 4. All Determinants Must be Candidate Keys (BCNF). Even if rules 1, 2, and 3 have been satisfied, there can still be anomalies in the data. The next rule, developed by R. F. Boyce and E. F. Codd, can remove them. This rule is a stronger statement than rule 3 and is usually called *Boyce-Codd normal form (BCNF)*. The BCNF rule states that no key, subkey, or nonprime value can be determined by a nonprime attribute.

To illustrate, let's consider the simple VENDOR entity design in Figure 4.19. Assume that vendor names (VNAME) are unique, a fact we know only from the semantics concerning vendors. The FDD for the VENDOR design is shown in Figure 4.20 and illustrates the fact that either VNO or VNAME can be considered as primes; both determine the remaining attributes and hence are candidate keys. Let's select VNO as the key, leaving VNAME and VSTATUS as nonprimes. Based on the FDD, this means that a nonprime attribute (VNAME) determines another nonprime attribute (VSTATUS). However, the BCNF rule permits this because VNAME is a candidate key.

When candidate keys share one or more attributes, they are said to **overlap.** Only when overlapping candidate keys are present do we have the potential for anomalies. If a relation has nonoverlapping candidate keys, it will be in BCNF. A relation with only one candidate key, in which case it must also be the primary key, will also always be in BCNF.

FIGURE 4.19   **A Tentative VENDOR Design with Candidate Keys**

VENDOR (VNO, VNAME, VSTATUS)

None of the attributes are underlined because the prime has not yet been decided on.

FIGURE 4.20   **The FDD for the VENDOR Entity in Figure 4.19**

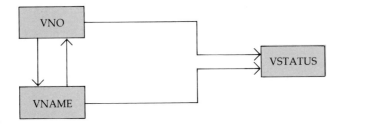

Boyce-Codd Normal Form Rule (BCNF)
Technical Treatment

Symbolically, a relation is in BCNF if for the relation R ($\underline{A}$, $\underline{B}$, C, D, . . . N) none of the nonprime attributes, C, D, . . . N, are determinants of either A or B. Conversely, given a relation R ($\underline{A}$, $\underline{B}$, C), if:

A + B and A + C are keys (A + C is a candidate key)

A + B → C

C → A,

the relation is in 3NF but <u>not</u> in BCNF.

To decompose a relation such as R above into BCNF, we split it into two, each satisfying the BCNF test. Thus, R becomes R and S: R ($\underline{A}$, $\underline{B}$) and S ($\underline{C}$, A).

Rule 5: Remove All Independent Multivalued Attributes (4NF). The fourth normal form (4NF) rule states that to check for compliance, we must be sure that if an MVD exists, only candidate keys are determinants. As discussed earlier, Figure 4.14 has two MVD attributes: DRUG__CODE →→ VENDOR__NO and VENDOR__NO →→ DIST. The problem is that VENDOR__NO and DIST are independent of each other and are not candidate keys.

To solve the problem, we decompose the original entity into two: one with DRUG__CODE and VENDOR__NO and one containing VENDOR__NO and DIST. Figure 4.21 illustrates.

When we have multivalued dependencies in an entity, we check to see if they are independent of each other. If they are, we decompose the entity.

It isn't the presence of the multivalued dependencies that causes the relation to fail the 4NF test. Only when the multivalued attributes have no relationship to each other does the test fail.

FIGURE 4.21   Decomposition of an Entity that Contains Two Independent MVDs in Two Entities

The conceptual design, shown below, contains two independent MVDs.

DRUG__VEND__DIST (DRUG__CODE, VENDOR__NO, DIST)

This can be substantiated by constructing the relevant FDDs:

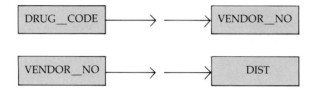

The problem is not that two MVDs exist, rather that there is no relationship between a vendor and a distributor. The solution is to decompose the original design into two relationships:

DRUG__VENDOR (DRUG__CODE, VENDOR__NO)

VENDOR__DIST (VENDOR__NO, DIST)

Fourth Normal Form Rule (4NF)
Technical Treatment

A relation is in 4NF if it is in BCNF and if there are no independent, multivalued dependencies. If a relation is in 4NF, all multivalued dependencies are related, and we again eliminate some potential anomalies. A relation that fails the test for 4NF can be decomposed into two or more relations that do satisfy it; that is, if in the relation R ($\underline{A}$, B, C),

$A \twoheadrightarrow B$

$A \twoheadrightarrow C$

B and C are independent,

we should decompose R into

$$R\ (\underline{A},\ \underline{B})$$
$$S\ (\underline{A},\ \underline{C}).$$

Rule 6: Constraints Must Be Enforced as a Consequence of Either a Key Relationship or a Domain Constraint (DK/NF). If every business rule and constraint is enforceable through primary dependencies and domain constraints, we can forget about the other five rules! This establishes what is known as a *domain/key normal form (DK/NF)*, and any entity or file exhibiting its characteristics will never have modification anomalies. Unfortunately, while this rule is easy to state, compliance with it is difficult to verify. Perhaps the best way to determine whether the design is in domain/key normal form is to use a model like

TABLE 4.2   A Model for Determining Whether a File Is in Domain/Key Normal Form

		Satisfied by	
Constraint	Key	Domain	Other
1.			
2.			
3.			
.			
.			
.			

FIGURE 4.22   A File that Fails the Test for Being in Domain/Key Normal Form

SALE (SALES__ID, ITEM__CODE, CUST__ID, DATE, CUST__NAME, CUST__TYPE, EMP__ID,
CHARGE__PER__ITEM, UNITS__PURCHASED)

		Satisfied by	
Constraint	Key	Domain	Other
SALES__ID → DATE			X
SALES__ID → EMP__ID			X
SALES__ID → CUST__ID			X
SALES__ID + ITEM__CODE → UNITS__PURCHASED	X		
CUST__ID → CUST__NAME			X
CUST__ID → CUST__TYPE			X
ITEM__CODE → CHARGE__PER__ITEM			X
A sale can be for cash or credit		X	

that shown in Table 4.2. In each row, we put one of two kinds of business rules: a cardinality rule or a domain constraint. Next, we put an X in one of the three enforcement columns: Key, Domain, or Other. An X indicates that the constraint can be enforced by the method corresponding to the title of the column. If any marks appear in the third column, the file is not in domain/key normal form, and one or more attributes must be removed and put into a new file (or files).

As an example of checking a design to see if it is in domain/key normal form, look at Figure 4.22. It lists some of the non-drug-related constraints from Figure 4.2 and assumes the existence of a file called SALE, which appears at the top. We assume the file is meant to satisfy the seven constraints.

The first constraint says we must be able to determine the date of a sale by its number. The mark in the third column indicates that we cannot satisfy this constraint either as a consequence of a functional dependency involving the key of the SALE entity or by imposing a domain restriction on its attributes. Actually, the date of the sale can be determined by means of a subkey field: SALES__ID. If we know the sales number, we can find out its date.

The next constraint says that the SALES__ID attribute should uniquely determine the employee responsible for the sale. Again, because SALES__ID is a subkey attribute, the constraint cannot be satisfied using either a key or domain enforcement policy.

The third constraint states that the combination of sales number and item code should determine the number of units purchased. This particular constraint does follow from a functional dependency involving the key, and it is the only one that satisfies the test for compliance.

FIGURE 4.23   A Conceptual File that Satisfies the Test for Being in Domain/Key Normal Form

SALE (SALES__ID, CUST__ID, DATE, EMP__ID)

SALES__TR (SALES__ID, ITEM__CODE, UNITS__PURCHASED)

ITEM (ITEM__CODE, ITEM__DESC, ITEM__CHARGE)

CUSTOMER (CUST__ID, CUST__NAME, CUST__TYPE)

Constraint	Satisfied by		
	Key	Domain	Other
SALES__ID → DATE	X		
SALES__ID → EMP__ID	X		
SALES__ID → CUST__ID	X		
SALES__ID, ITEM__CODE → UNITS__PURCHASED	X		
CUST__ID → CUST__NAME	X		
CUST__ID → CUST__TYPE	X		
ITEM__CODE → CHARGE__PER__ITEM	X		
A sale can be for cash or credit		X	

Enforcement of constraints four through six requires methods other than using the primary key or domain restrictions and, hence, they failed the test. The last constraint, which is an example of a domain constraint, can be enforced through a domain enforcement on the field CUST_TYPE.

As we have seen, several of the constraints in Figure 4.22 cannot be satisfied as a consequence of a functional dependency involving a primary key or a domain enforcement; it can be satisfied only through functional dependencies involving nonkey attributes. This means that our design is faulty and could possess modification anomalies. Figure 4.23 shows a better design. There, enforcement of every constraint is a consequence of a domain or key.

Suitability for Computer Applications. The normalization process is a mathematically sound method for eliminating anomalies. There may be times when the practical issue of adapting a design to the computer takes precedence. You may have noticed that normalization leads to many small (few-column) tables. Because these tables will be stored on a disk, the underlying files must be opened, indexes searched, pointers followed, and so on, before the requested records can be forwarded to the end user. Generally, the fewer the disk I/Os, the faster the application will run. Although normalization requires splitting a table into two or more, performance may dictate otherwise.

Consider this PATIENT relation:

PATIENT (PATNUM, PATNAME, PATSTREET, PATCITY, PATSTATE, PATZIP).

The problem is that PATZIP $\rightarrow$ PATSTATE and PATZIP $\rightarrow$ PATCITY; knowing a zip code value enables us to determine the corresponding state and city. According to 3NF rules, we should create a second relation such as this:

ZIPTABLE (ZIP, CITY, STATE).

The PATIENT relation would now look like this:

PATIENT (PATNUM, PATNAME, PATZIP).

While it is true that the design is "better" in that it is in 3NF, from a performance view, every time we need to know what city a PATIENT lives in, we will have to access the ZIPTABLE relation. It makes more sense to access the PATIENTs' addresses, along with their names and so on, thus reducing the number of I/Os.

If ignoring one of the normalization rules improves performance but leads to serious modification anomalies, we must consider performance issues as secondary and take care to eliminate the possible anomalies. Is it likely that we would want to add a ZIP code for which we have no PATIENTs? Probably not. Similarly, we should experience no deletion or update anomalies. In this example, we should violate our normalization guidelines and keep our original PATIENT design.

FIGURE 4.24   **An Illustration of Link, or Connection Fields**

(a) The DSD for the relationship between a customer and the associated prescriptions

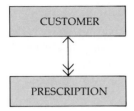

(b) The result of storing the origin key (changed from CUSTOMER__NO to PCUST) in the destination record type

CUSTOMER (<u>CUSTOMER__NO</u>, PHONE, ADDRESS)

CUSTOMER

CUSTOMER_NO	PHONE	ADDRESS
10	357-3434	8086 Main St.
12	454-7812	8088 Elm St.

└─ Connection attribute (foreign key)

PRESCRIPTION (<u>PNO</u>, <u>PCUST</u>, PDRUG, PUNITS, PDOCTOR, PDATE)

PRESCRIPTION

PNO	PCUST	PDRUG	PUNITS	PDOCTOR	PDATE
100	10	PCN	20	Adams	11/10/XX
110	10	TAG	50	Adams	11/30/XX
150	12	PCN	10	Quincy	12/02/XX

While the PCUST values are redundant, they permit us to relate a PRESCRIPTION to the associated PATIENT, regardless of which data model is used.

Adding Link Attributes

Link, or **connection, attributes,** are used to relate entities to one another. They result from the 1:M relationships depicted on either the DSD or E-R diagrams. In all cases, the link attribute will be the key (identifier) attribute of the origin entity; the attribute can be considered a foreign key.

For each 1:M relationship, we use the key from the origin entity and add it to the destination entity. Consider the DSD in part (a) of Figure 4.24. It represents a 1:M relationship between a CUSTOMER and his or her PRESCRIPTIONs. Part (a) shows that CUSTOMER is the origin of the relationship, while PRESCRIPTION is the destination. Assume the original design for CUSTOMER looked like this: (CUSTOMER__NO, PHONE, ADDRESS). Similarly, assume the initial PRESCRIPTION design looked this way: (PNO, PDRUG, PUNITS, PDOCTOR, PDATE). It should be obvious that there is no way to relate a PRESCRIPTION occurrence to the correct customer. Although this is an unrealistic situation, because a DBA would automatically assume that one of a prescription's attributes is the customer's number, it will serve to illustrate the need for the linking attribute.

Part (b) of Figure 4.24 shows that we have added PCUST (for prescription customer number) to the destination (PRESCRIPTION) table. Notice that the PCUST column values are clearly redundant. For example, the first two rows have the same PCUST value. However, it is this value that relates a row to its origin and should be carried.

Figure 4.25 shows how Bob attached the attributes from Figure 4.7 to the entities in compliance with the rules we have just developed. To complete the design, he must consider transactions and rules that are not currently important, but that could be so in the future.

FIGURE 4.25   The Attributes Associated with Each Entity for Fred's Pharmacy Design

SALES (SALES__ID, CUST__ID, DATE, TOT__AMT, EMP__ID)

SALES__TR (SALES__ID, ITEM__CODE, UNITS__PURCHASED, UNIT__PRICE)

NON__DRUG__INVENTORY (ITEM__CODE, ITEM__DESC, ITEM__COST,
       ITEM__PRICE, ON__HAND__USAGE__YTD)

CUSTOMER (CUST__ID, CUST__NAME, CUST__PHONE, CUST__ADDRESS,
    CUST__TYPE)

PAYMENT (SALES__ID, DATE, AMOUNT)

DRUG (DRUG__CODE, DRUG__DESC, DRUG__COST, DRUG__PRICE,
   ON__HAND, USAGE__TYD)

ALLERGY (ALLERGY__CODE, ALLERGY__DESCRIPTION)

CUSTOMER__ALLERGY (ALLERGY__CODE, CUST ID)

EMPLOYEE (EMP__ID, E__NAME, E__COMMISSION)

INSURANCE__CO (CO__CODE, CO__NAME, CO__ADDRESS, CO__PHONE,
     CO__PAY__AMT)

CUST__INS (CUST__ID, INS__CO, TYPE__OF__COVERAGE)

PRESCRIPTION (PNO, PDRUG, PCUST, PDATE, CHARGE, NO__OF__REFILLS)

REFILL (PNO, REFILL__NO, RDATE, CHARGE)

4.10   STEP 9. ADD ANTICIPATED ATTRIBUTES: BACK FROM THE FUTURE

As already indicated, Bob's conceptual design, shown in Figures 4.7 and 4.25, is adequate because it can meet the data needs of Fred's Pharmacy and is in domain/key normal form. Unfortunately, a database must serve not only the present business transactions and needs, but also those of the future. During this step, the DBA must "blue-sky" with the end users, asking them to cite operations and transactions that are not performed at present but would enhance their ability to do their jobs. For example, Fred wants to be able to produce year-end statements for all customers who purchased prescriptions from him during the year. This consideration must be included in Bob's design. Let's see if our design can produce this report.

We start by using the SALE entity and process all the occurrences for a given customer for the current year. From each occurrence, we extract the SALES__ID and use it to find the matching SALES__TR occurrences. After extracting the CUST__ID from the SALE file, we look up the corresponding customer in the CUSTOMER file to find his or her address. Our present design can handle this "blue-sky" request. Usually, however, this will not be the case, and the design will need to be modified.

4.11   STEP 10. REVISE AND REFINE THE DESIGN

Undoubtedly there will be transactions or rules that were omitted during steps 2 or 3 or uncovered during the "blue-sky" step we just discussed. As we uncover new ones, we must assimilate them into the conceptual design. Remember, the conceptual database must reflect the actual organization. If the model is incomplete, our ability to handle the chore of supplying the organization's data needs through the use of the database will be limited. One way to verify completeness is through a discovery process, in which we attempt to develop all user views as a consequence of the conceptual design.

4.12   STEP 11. IDENTIFY USER VIEWS: THE DATABASE THROUGH THE END USER'S EYES

At this point, we must identify external or user views of the database. Recall that we are advocating a top-down design approach. If you prefer a bottom-up approach, you must perform this step very early in the process and integrate the various views to form the organization's conceptual design. In the top-down approach, we use the user views as a check to ensure that our design is complete.

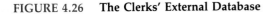

FIGURE 4.26   **The Clerks' External Database**

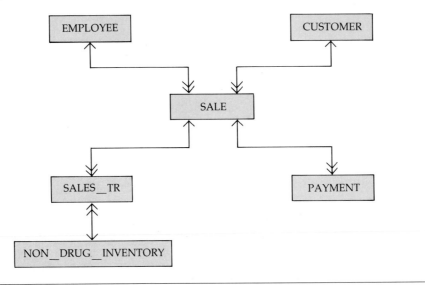

They subsequently become the basis for the external databases that we must define to the DBMS.

From Bob's discussion with Fred, it appears that Fred, Colleen, and Nancy will be the users. Bob's view is that of the entire database, but, as Figure 4.26 shows, the clerks' view is not. The clerks appear to have a much narrower view of the entities than Fred does, and some attributes are not to be made available to them. In addition to a DSD or E-R diagram, a view may include information about attributes—their names and formats. We have seen that different end user views can have attributes that differ from the entity or entities on which the views are based. The definition of the view might therefore consist of a DSD or E-R diagram, a view name, entity names, and attribute names and formats.

4.13   A BOTTOM-UP ALTERNATIVE

The bottom-up approach begins with user views and proceeds to the more general global model. The first three steps correspond to those of the top-down approach. The remaining steps are:

- Determine the complete set of user views.
- Include future considerations.

- Assign attributes for each entity such that each results in at least a 3NF relation.
- Consolidate the views.

Instead of focusing on an end user, we will look at specific transactions. One view would be that associated with filling new prescriptions. A customer walks into Fred's store and submits a request for a new prescription. Assuming the customer has had prescriptions filled before, the pharmacist retrieves the appropriate profile card and enters the new prescription data onto it. Next, the pharmacist fills the bottle, prints a label, and affixes it to the bottle. The label includes the customer's name, the drug name, the amount of the drug, the frequency of consumption, and the number of units to be taken. We extend the scenario by assuming that if the pharmacist notes that the inventory level is low, he or she adds the name of the drug to a list kept by the phone.

The required entities can be defined as:

CUSTOMER (CUST__ID, CNAME)
PRESCRIPTION (RXNO, CUST__ID, DRUG__NAME, SIZE, UNITS,
                FREQUENCY, REFILLS)
DRUG (DRUGID, DRUG__NAME, SIZE, UNITS__ON__HAND,
      REORDER__POINT)
REORDER__LIST (DRUGID, UNITS__TO__ORDER)

Because we are considering only one transaction, we have listed just the attributes necessary for its success. The graphical model is shown in Figure 4.27.

Another view is that necessary to support the production of a bill. As a prescription is filled, the pharmacist asks how the prescription is to be paid. If it is to be charged, a charge slip containing the customer's number and name, drug code, description, unit price, units filled, and total price is created. If the customer has no insurance, the total price will equal the product of PRESCRIP-

---

FIGURE 4.27   The Graphical Model of the User View to Support Prescription-Filling Transaction Number 2: Fill a New Prescription

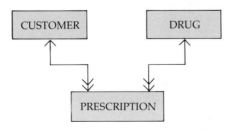

TION.UNITS and DRUG.CHARGE. (Note that the above DRUG definition had no CHARGE component.) Otherwise, the amount is determined by looking up the copay amount in an INSURANCE__CO file. On the last working day of the month, all charges for a given patient are grouped and an invoice prepared and mailed. The invoice contains the customer's name and address as well as the data associated with the charge slip.

If the item is to be paid for by cash, the same data is printed on a customer invoice, which is then given to the customer along with the prescription. Once paid, the amount is added to the profile for that customer.

Among the resulting entities are:

CUSTOMER(CUST__ID,CNAME,CSTREET,CCITY,CSTATE,CZIP,$\overline{\text{CINSC__CO}}$)
PRESCRIPTION (RXNO, CUST_ID, DRUG__NAME, SIZE, UNITS, FRE-
               QUENCY, PAY__METHOD, AMOUNT__PAID)
DRUG (DRUGID, DRUG__NAME, CHARGE)
INSURANCE__CO (INSCO, INS__NAME, INS__CO__PAYAMT)

We intentionally omitted the invoice entity from the above list. Notice that CUSTOMER isn't in 3NF because of the repeating attribute. Accordingly, we decompose CUSTOMER into two entities, resulting in:

CUSTOMER (CUST__ID, CNAME, CSTREET, CCITY, CSTATE, CZIP)
CUST__INS (CUST__ID, CINSC__CO)

The conceptual view is shown in Figure 4.28.

The next step in the bottom-up procedure is to consolidate attributes for identical entities. This results in the following entities:

CUSTOMER(CUST__ID,CNAME,CSTREET,CCITY,CSTATE,CZIP,$\overline{\text{CINSC__CO}}$)
PRESCRIPTION (RXNO, CUST__ID, DRUG__NAME, SIZE, UNITS, FRE-
               QUENCY, PAY__METHOD, AMOUNT__PAID, REFILLS)
DRUG (DRUGID, DRUG__NAME, CHARGE, SIZE, UNITS__ON__HAND,
      REORDER__POINT)
REORDER__LIST (DRUGID, UNITS__TO__ORDER)
INSURANCE__CO (INSCO, INS__NAME, INS__CO__PAYAMT)

Notice that for both views, CUSTOMER has the same primary key; hence, it must be the same entity. Also, we have consolidated CUSTOMER attributes, selecting CUST__ID and CNAME from the first view, and the other attributes from the second view. Finally, notice that even though CNAME was present in both views, we carry it only once. The presence of a repeating field, CINSC__CO, causes us trouble and must be removed during the normalization step.

This consolidation procedure is duplicated for each entity. The result is a complete list of entities and a graphical model that shows the relationships

---

FIGURE 4.28   The Entities and DSD Resulting from the Fourth Prescription Transaction: Bill for a New or Existing Prescription

CUSTOMER (CUST__ID, CNAME, CSTREET,CCITY,CSTATE,CZIP)

PRESCRIPTION (RXNO,CUST__ID, DRUG__NAME, SIZE, UNITS, FREQUENCY,

                PAY__METHOD, AMOUNT__PAID)

DRUG (DRUGID, DRUG__NAME, CHARGE)

INSURANCE__CO (INSCO, INS__NAME, INS__CO__PAYAMT)

CUST__INS (CUST__ID, CINSC__CO)

Notice that the repeating attribute CINSC__CO has been eliminated from CUSTOMER and inserted into a new entity: CUST__INS, which is an intersection entity.

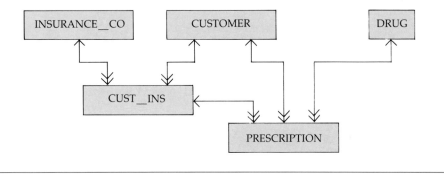

---

among them. Probably the primary advantage of this procedure is that it almost guarantees to be able to support the user views, since they are the source of the data.

There is no prescription for deciding which approach to choose. The top-down approach probably results in a more general model, because it is done somewhat independently of the individual views. This results in attributes and entities that may not be needed for any view. Consequently, the bottom-up approach would not have yielded these entities and attributes. All of this means that the approach probably results in a more flexible model, but initially may contain extraneous attributes and entities.

On the other hand, the bottom-up approach most likely results in a model that is better able to handle the day-to-day transactions. This is because the conceptual database is an amalgam of the individual views: it is unlikely that data needed by an existing view would be omitted.

4.14 SUMMARY

Designing a database is a three-step process:

- Design the conceptual database
- Design the logical database
- Design the physical database

This chapter was concerned primarily with the top-down approach, which results in a set of 11 rules that, if followed, leads to a suitable conceptual database design. First, we establish boundaries for the design. Then, by interviewing end users, we determine the transactions each one performs. During this discovery process, we also determine the business rules, or constraints. While these are usually cardinality statements, they can also be referential integrity or domain statements.

Based on an analysis of the transactions and business rules, we next determine the entities of the database. To help ensure that all the stated entities are in fact entities, we try to determine the identifier attribute for each one. If we are able to do so, we go on to the next step: representing the design as either a DSD or an E-R diagram. If we cannot find an identifier, we probably have failed to identify a proper entity.

This graphical representation of the database is independent of both the hardware and the DBMS software the organization uses. If the diagram is sufficient, it can be used to meet the data needs of each organizational transaction and will successfully model the business rules developed during the earlier design step. After verifying that this is so, we then complete the most difficult step: assigning the remaining attributes.

Using a general listing of all the organization's attributes, we assign them to entities such that the entities are in domain/key normal form, meaning that all constraints (business rules) are satisfied as a direct consequence of either a functional dependency involving the key attribute or of enforcing a domain attribute constraint. Any entity having this equality will be free from modification anomalies. An alternative objective is 3NF or BCNF.

After putting the entities into either form, we assign additional connection attributes to enable us to relate entities to one another. Based on the 1:M relationships among entities, we store a link attribute—the primary key of the origin of the relationship—in the destination entity.

Once we have assigned all attributes, we go back to the end users and determine if there are any transactions they do not currently perform, but which they may in the future. By including future considerations in our design, we (hopefully) reduce the chances of needing to change it once it is physically implemented. After completing the design, we develop the data dictionary that all programmers and analysts must use.

The final step is to prepare DSDs or E-R diagrams for the end users of the database. These external databases, like the conceptual database, are now ready to be transformed into new structures that conform to the requirements of the particular data model used by the DBMS the organization has chosen.

REVIEW QUESTIONS

1. What are the objectives of the *conceptual database design?*
2. What is meant by the *logical database design?*
3. Why have some organizations given up on the idea of a single, all-encompassing conceptual database design?
4. What is the purpose of determining the organization's transactions?
5. List the three kinds of business rules.
6. What is meant by *cardinality?*
7. Explain two independence qualities of the E-R diagram or DSD.
8. What is the rule for choosing a link attribute?
9. What is a functional dependency? A multivalued dependency?
10. Describe the three kinds of anomalies.
11. What is a subkey?
12. What is meant by the statement "Nonkey attributes must be dependent on the entire key"?
13. What is the benefit of including future types of transactions in the conceptual design?
14. What is meant by an *external database?*
15. Describe the components of a user view.
16. Describe some examples of when normalization might lead to performance degradation.
17. Discuss the advantages of the bottom-up (versus top-down) approach to database design.

PROBLEMS

1. List the transactions used for registration at your school.
2. Using your answer to Problem 1, list the entities and a suitable identifier for each.
3. Draw a DSD diagram for your answer to Problem 1. Then draw an E-R diagram.
4. List each transaction from Problem 1 and state how your design satisfies it.

5. Assume the following M:N relationship:

ALBUM

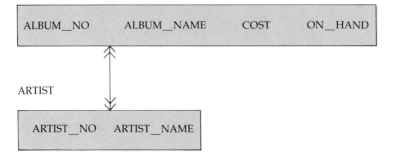

Convert the DSD into one that has no complex relationships.

6. Using your answer to Problem 5, list the identifier for each entity.

7. Again using your answer to Problem 5, indicate all attributes for each entity.

8. Which of the "attribute assignment" rules are violated by these designs?

    a. STUDENT (<u>STUDENT__NO</u>, NAME, MAJOR, DORM__ID, DORM__CHARGE)

    b. COURSES__TAKEN (<u>STUDENT__NO</u>, <u>COURSE__NO</u>, COURSE__DEPT, STUDENT__GRADE)

    c. STUDENT (<u>STUDENT__NO</u>, PARENT__NAME, MAJOR)

9. Convert each of the three faulty designs in Problem 8 into acceptable ones.

10. The following shows a typical invoice sent out by Computers R Us:

```
Invoice No.: 9999
Vendor: XXXXXXXXXXXXXXXXXXXXXXXXXXXXX
Address: XXXXXXXXXXXXXXXXXXXXXXXXXXX
         XXXXXXXXXXXXXXXXXXXXXXXXXXX
         XXXXXXXXX, XX 99999
Invoice Date: 99/99/99                          Terms:
Total Amount Due: 99,999.99                     Salesperson: XXX
```

Item Code	Description	Units	Price Per Unit	Total Charge
XXXXX	XXXXXXXXXX	999	9,999.99	99,999.99
XXXXX	XXXXXXXXXX	999	9,999.99	99,999.99

Subtotal:	99,999.99
Tax:	999.99
Shipping:	999.99
Insurance:	999.99
Total Amount:	99,999.99

    a. List the possible entities.

    b. Draw the E-R diagram.

    c. Assign attributes to the entities.

    d. Show how your design can support these two transactions:
       (1) List the invoices sent to the ACME Wrecking Company (code is ACME).
       (2) What are the names of the items on invoice number 100?

11. What is the normal form of each "relation" that follows?

    a. VHSTAPE (<u>TAPENO</u>, TDESC, TMEMNO, TMEMNAME, TDATE)
    if:

        TAPENO $\rightarrow$ TDESC
        TMEMNO $\rightarrow$ TMEMNAME
        TAPENO $\rightarrow\rightarrow$ TDATE
        TAPENO + TMEMNP $\rightarrow$ TDATE

    where TMEMNO is a tape club member number, TMEMNAME is the member's name, and TDATE is the date on which the tape was rented.

    b. INVOICE (<u>INVNO</u>, <u>ITEMCODE</u>, INVDATE, ITEMCOST, VENDNO)
    if:

        INVNO $\rightarrow$ INVDATE
        INVNO, ITEMCODE $\rightarrow$ ITEMCOST
        INVNO $\rightarrow$ VENDNO

    c. SHOE (<u>SHOENO</u>, STYLEID, COLORID, COST, ONHAND)
    STYLE (<u>STYLEID</u>, STYLE)
    COLOR (<u>COLORID</u>, COLOR)
    if:

        SHOENO $\rightarrow$ COLORID
        SHOENO $\rightarrow$ STYLEID
        SHOENO $\rightarrow$ COST
        SHOENO $\rightarrow$ ONHAND
        COLORID $\rightarrow$ COLOR
        STYLEID $\rightarrow$ STYLE

12. Split the relations given in Problem 11 into one or more 4NF relations.

13. Draw an E-R diagram or DSD showing your results for each part of Problem 12.

14. Consider this relation:

    STUDENT (STUNO, SNAME, SMAJORID, SADVISORID, SQPA, COURSE#,
            CNAME, SECTION#, STAUGHTBYID, SGRADE, SLOCATION)

    if:

    STUNO $\rightarrow$ SNAME
    STUNO $\rightarrow\rightarrow$ SMAJORID
    STUNO $\rightarrow\rightarrow$ SADVISORID
    STUNO $\rightarrow$ SQPA
    COURSE# $\rightarrow$ CNAME

COURSE# →→ SECTION#
STUNO, COURSE#, SECTION# → SGRADE
COURSE#, SECTION# → STAUGHTBYID
COURSE#, SECTION# → SLOCATION

Decompose the above relation into several, each of which is in 4NF.

15. For each of the following relations,

    a. State the normal form.

    b. Give an example of an insertion, update, and deletion anomaly.

    c. Split the relation into as many 4NF relations as are necessary.

(1) EMPLOYEE (<u>EMPNO</u>, EMPNAME, TITLE, COURSE_TAKEN_ID, CNAME)

EMPNO	EMPNAME	TITLE	COURSE_TAKEN_ID	COURSE
1	JOHN	PROGRAMMER	C1	COBOL I
1	JOHN	PROGRAMMER	AC	ADV COBOL
1	JOHN	PROGRAMMER	J1	JCL
2	MARY	PROGRAMMER	AC	ADV COBOL
2	MARY	PROGRAMMER	SP	STRUCTURED PROGRAMMING

EMPNO → EMPNAME
EMPNO → TITLE
COURSE_TAKEN_ID → CNAME

(2) FRANCHISE (<u>CITY</u>, <u>PRODUCT</u>, OWNER_NAME)

CITY	PRODUCT	OWNER_NAME
Chicago	Brooms	Gravely
Cleveland	Brooms	Robinson
Chicago	Brushes	Gravely
Cleveland	Brushes	Jackson

OWNER_NAME → CITY
PRODUCT, CITY → OWNER_NAME

In the above table, each franchise owner is in one city. For each product, each city that sells that product has only one franchise.

16. Consider this database:

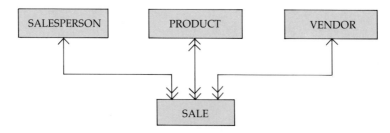

The current definitions of the conceptual files are as follows:

SALESPERSON (SID, SNAME, SADDRESS, SPHONE, SCHILDREN)
VENDOR (VNAME, VID, VADDRESS)
PRODUCT (PNAME, PAVGCOST, PID, PONHAND, PONORDER)
SALE (VID, SID, SNAME, PID, PRICE, UNITS, PNAME, DATE)

The rules are:

SID → SNAME, SADDRESS, SPHONE
SID →→ SCHILDNAME
SPHONE → SID, SNAME, SADDRESS
VID → VNAME, VADDRESS
PID → PNAME, PAVGCOST, PONHAND, PONORDER
VID, SID, PID, DATE → PRICE, UNITS

a. Redesign the conceptual files so that they are all in BCNF. Be sure to specify the primes.

b. Redraw the conceptual database, adding any new tables you developed from part *a*.

⠿ EPISODE 3

Barb Redesigns Her Database

In Episode 2, Barb had just been asked by her manager, Bill Moore, to redesign the database for Community Hospital. In this episode, she will use the 12 rules developed in this chapter to help her develop a better design.

Step 1: Determine the Scope of the Design

In general, Barb's project team decided to keep their database's boundaries exactly where they were before: They would include all entities and relationships necessary to determine patient charges.

Most of the patient charges are generated from two departments: pharmacy and materials management. The materials management department supplies non-drug items such as compresses, splints, crutches, and so on. Barb decided to strike a compromise between what was recommended in the text and what she had to do for expediency purposes. Rather than do a complete design, she settled on a two-phase approach. The first phase, which is the one we will follow for the remainder of the case, would encompass the two subject areas just mentioned, while the second would expand on these two areas to include the emergency room, the operating rooms, lab tests, and radiology.

While considering the consequences of her actions, Barb decided that these two areas account for over 80 percent of the patient charges for the hospital and almost 90 percent of the IS work. She also realized that this two-phase approach would require some extra work later on, but she estimated that implementing a complete design would require from 24 to 30 months, while phase 1 would require only 12 to 18—a more favorable time frame. Like Barb, you should not be afraid to deviate from our rules, provided there is a logical reason for the departure and your supervisor is informed prior to your action.

Step 2: Determine the Relevant Transactions

Because Bill Moore had criticized Barb for not considering the requirements of the end users of the database, Barb directed her team to interview John Baker and Judy Rankin, directors of the pharmacy and materials management departments, respectively. Exhibit 1 shows most of the pharmacy transactions derived from several meetings with John, his pharmacists,

and his pharmacy technicians. Exhibit 2 shows the transactions determined through interviews with Judy and her subordinates.

Many of the terms in Exhibit 1 are peculiar to the pharmacy profession, so some further explanation may be necessary. A unit dose order is one that is usually filled for 24 hours. Thus, if a patient receives two 250 mg aspirins three times a day, the unit dose amount is six. A patient profile shows all medications for a particular patient. An MAR is a report used by nurses. It shows each patient on the nursing unit and all the medications due for each patient for a 24-hour period. When a nurse administers a medication, he or she notes it on the patient's MAR. The final term that may be new to you is DRG. There are 467 DRGs, each specifying a possible patient diagnosis. DRGs are important to hospitals because medi-

---

EXHIBIT 1   Relevant Pharmacy Department Transactions

1. Admit a patient.
2. Discharge a patient.
3. Transfer a patient.
4. Enter an IV order.
5. Stop an IV order.
6. Change an IV order.
7. Produce IV labels.
8. Charge for filled IV orders.
9. Give extra IVs.
10. Credit IVs.
11. Enter a unit dose order.
12. Stop a unit dose order.
13. Change a unit dose order.
14. Produce unit dose fill list.
15. Give extra unit dose medications.
16. Credit a unit dose order.
17. Update formulary when medications are charged.
18. Update formulary when new inventory arrives.
19. Print Medication Administration Record (MAR).
20. Print patient profiles.
21. Print inventory usage report.
22. Print inventory valuation report.
23. Print costs by Diagnostic Related Group (DRG).
24. Print costs by physician.

EXHIBIT 2   Relevant Materials Management Department Transactions

1. Admit, discharge, transfer patients.
2. Update inventory when charging a patient for an item.
3. Update inventory when items received.
4. Charge patients for items used.
5. Credit patients.
6. Enter new purchase orders (POs).
7. Change POs.
8. Close POs when all items received.
9. Cancel portions of POs.
10. Print POs.
11. Print open POs by date.
12. Print open POs by vendor.
13. Print open POs by requesting department.
14. Check vendor's invoice against PO for accuracy.
15. Track dollar purchases by vendor.

care pays a flat amount per patient based on the patient's DRG rather than the actual costs incurred by the patient.

The materials management department uses a bar code system for inventory and patient charging. When an item arrives, it is labeled with a piggyback label having a six-character item code encoded using a bar code. A piggyback label is one that can be peeled away from its backing and restuck onto another substance.

Each patient has a charge card that is maintained by a nurse on the patient's nursing unit. When a patient uses an item from materials management, the piggyback label is removed from the item and stuck onto the patient's charge card. Once a day, all cards are collected and sent to the IS department for processing. By using a light pen, an IBM PC reads each patient card and the labels associated with the items used.

Step 3: Determine the Business Rules

Although Barb's complete list of rules was too long to reproduce, Exhibit 3 shows most of them. As we saw in

Chapter 4, these rules are statements about cardinality or domains.

Some of the rules may require some further explanation. For example, a patient who is suspended will not have any orders filled. This usually occurs when the patient is in surgery. When the surgery is finished, the patient is unsuspended (made active). Another possible unclear issue is that of standard medication times. An IV or unit dose order is assigned a unique SIG (a Latin abbreviation of SIGNATURE) and each SIG has a set of standard times associated with it. For example, one of the SIGs used by Community is TID, meaning "three times a day." The associated standard times are 0800, 1600, and 2400 hours. The hospital uses 55 such SIGs.

Step 4: Determine the Entities

Barb discovered that step 4 sounded more difficult than it actually was. She first listed the entities that were obvious from the transactions and rules she documented in the previous steps. This resulted in Exhibit 4. Later we will see that Barb needs some additional entities.

EXHIBIT 3   Business Rules for Community Hospital

General Rules

1. The patient number is a seven-digit code plus a check digit based on mod 11.
2. Nursing units are 1E, 1W, 1N, 1S, 2E, 2W, 2N, 2S, COU, ICU, LCU.
3. Room numbers are four digits long, with the first digit being 1, 2, C, I, or L.
4. Bed numbers are two digits long.
5. There are 15 hospital departments, each with a four-character code. See the hospital form number DZ56.R2 for current codes.
6. A patient's status is active or discharged.
7. There are 55 standard times for medications.
8. A patient has one DRG.
9. A patient has one primary physician and up to two secondary ones.

Pharmacy Rules

1. A patient can have several IV orders.
2. An IV order can be active, suspended, or stopped.
3. An IV order contains a solution and up to 12 additives (medications).
4. Every IV order has a unique five-digit order number, and each order is unique.
5. An IV can be given up to six times per day, based on its SIG.
6. Every patient can have several unit dose orders.
7. A unit dose order is active, suspended, or stopped.
8. Each unit dose order is for one medication only.
9. A unit dose order can be given up to 12 times per day, based on its SIG.
10. Medications have a six-character code.
11. A profile contains many orders for each patient.
12. An MAR contains several orders for each patient.

Materials Management Rules

1. Inventory items have a six-character code.
2. A PO contains up to 15 detail lines.
3. A PO can be sent to one, and only one, vendor.
4. Each PO has a unique eight-character code. The first two digits are the last two digits of the current year.
5. POs are classified as open, closed, partial, or canceled.
6. Each PO can have items requested from several departments.
7. A patient can be charged for several items per day and for several of the same item.

Step 5: Determine the Identifier for Each Entity

As we suggested in Chapter 4, Barb next tried to find a suitable identifier for each entity. The results of her efforts are shown in Exhibit 5. Notice that the Purchase Order Detail and Invoice Detail Item entities have composite identifiers. Also, in both cases the second subkey attribute is a sequential number. This is necessary because the first item on a purchase order or invoice is assigned sequential number 1, the second number 2, and so on. The Invoice Detail Item's other subkey attribute is a voucher number assigned by the accounts payable (AP) department. Because several vendors could send invoices with the same number, the AP department assigns its own sequential number, which it calls a *voucher number*.

EXHIBIT 4   Entities for Community Hospital

1. Patient
2. IV Order
3. IV Additive
4. Unit Dose Order
5. Physician
6. DRG
7. Nursing Unit
8. Room
9. Bed
10. Formulary
11. SIG
12. Purchase Order
13. Purchase Order Detail
14. Inventory Item
15. Vendor
16. Invoice
17. Invoice Detail Item
18. Department
19. Patient Usage

EXHIBIT 5   Identifiers for the Entities in Exhibit 4

Entity	Identifier
1. Patient	Patient No
2. IV Order	Order No
3. IV Additives	Order No, Additive No
4. Unit Dose Order	Order No
5. Physician	Doc No
6. DRG	DRG Code
7. Nursing Unit	Nu Code
8. Room	Room No
9. Bed	Bed No
10. Formulary	Med Code
11. SIG	SIG Code
12. Purchase Order	Po No
13. Purchase Order Detail	Po No, Seq No
14. Inventory Item	Item No
15. Vendor	Vendor No
16. Invoice	Voucher No
17. Invoice Detail Item	Voucher No, Seq No
18. Department	Dept Code
19. Patient Usage	Patient No, Item No

Step 6: Draw the DSD and/or E-R Diagram

Step 6 is an iterative one. Barb drew the DSD several times before she was satisfied with the design. Her final design is shown in Exhibit 6.

One of the problems Barb found with her initial design was a M:N relationship between Patient and Physician. She detected the relationship from general rule 9, which says that each Patient can have up to two secondary Physicians (of course, each Physician can treat more than one Patient). Using the technique shown in Chapter 4, Barb set up two 1:M relationships between those entities and a new intersection entity she called Patient Physician. Because the entity was derived from the M:N relationship and not directly from either the rules or the transactions, it does not appear in Exhibit 5.

Step 7: Compare the DSD and E-R Diagram to the Transactions

Step 7 is very important, because it tells us whether or not the design can support the data needs of the organization. To help her determine the suitability of the design, Barb called a meeting with Alan Jones and Karen Vance, her two database technicians. The purpose of the meeting was to have the team look at the transactions in Exhibits 1 and 2 and at the rules shown in Exhibit 3 and make certain the design could support them. Since her technicians did much of the design work, she asked them to go over each transaction and rule and show how the design could support it.

"Alan, show me how we represent general rule 8," she began.

Alan responded, "Look at Exhibit 6. We have a 1:M relationship between DRG and Patient. This is because each DRG can be assigned to several Patients, but each Patient has only one DRG."

"Very good, Alan. How about the third pharmacy rule?" Barb asked.

"Well, let me expand my answer to your question to include the first five rules. First, notice the 1:M relationship between Patient and IV Order. This allows each Patient to have many IV Orders but each IV Order to be associated with exactly one Patient. I think the first rule is covered. The second rule is a domain constraint, so I can't look at it until we add the attributes. Rule 3 means we should allow each IV Order to be associated with several additives. Even though the pharmacy uses a maximum of only 12 medications per order, our design is more general because we have a 1:M relationship between the IV Order entity and the IV Additive one. Because each IV must have a solution, we will carry that medication in the IV Order entity. Also, both the solution and the IV additives are drugs, so we have set up a 1:M relationship between the Formulary and those two entities. Finally, rule 5 means that each IV Order is associated with a SIG. This is shown in Exhibit 6 by the 1:M relationship between SIG and IV Order. Well, how'd I do, Barb?"

"Excellent! Karen, it's your turn. How about going over how to handle materials management transaction numbers 11 through 13?"

Karen replied, "OK. Oops—I think we left out an entity! We need a Date entity that is the origin for a 1:M relationship with Purchase Order, don't we?"

Barb realized there were at least two ways to handle transaction number 11. One would be to do as Karen suggested: Set up a new entity called Date. By establishing a 1:M relationship between Date and Purchase Order, the report could be provided. Another alternative would be to index the Purchase Order occurrences on the Date attribute, then read the Pur-

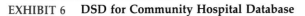
EXHIBIT 6   DSD for Community Hospital Database

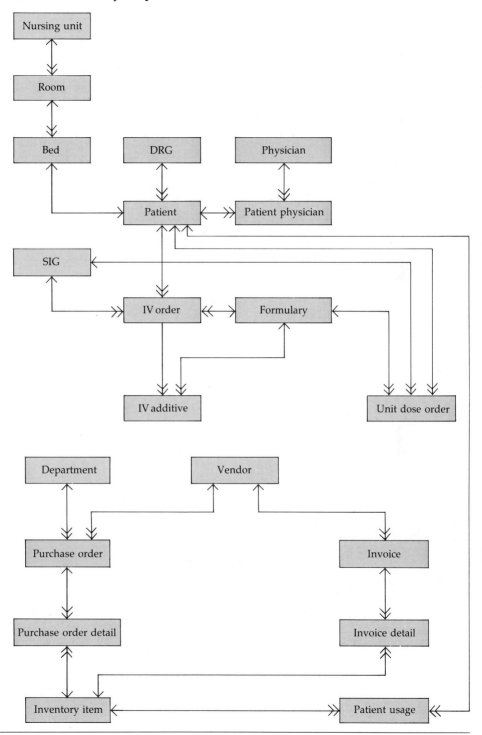

chase Orders using the index. Because Barb wanted the design to reflect the actual data requirements, she decided Karen's solution was the correct one.

"You're right, Karen. Let's modify our design to include a Date entity. Go ahead with the other transactions."

"Thanks. The next transaction, number 12, will be easy. We retrieve each Vendor occurrence, then access all the associated Purchase Orders using the relationship between the two entities. As we reach each Purchase Order, we just test a status attribute for "Open" POs.

"I just had a thought. Barb, why not set up an entity called Open PO and establish a 1:M relationship with it and Purchase Order?"

"That's not a bad idea, Karen, but I see a problem. What will be the identifier?"

"I see what you mean," said Karen. "I guess it's not an entity. OK, it was just a thought. I'll finish with transaction 13. Here we'll just read each Department occurrence, then retrieve the related POs and check the Status indicator. I think I'm finished!"

"You are. You did a really good job of showing how our design supports the materials management transactions. Alan, I guess it's your turn again."

The meeting continued until each rule and transaction had been studied and the DSD examined to verify that it could support each one. By the conclusion of the meeting, the team had established a new design, which is shown in Exhibit 7.

One of the new entities in Exhibit 7 is Med Charge. It seems the original design had no way to account for Pharmacy Patient charges. When the IV or Unit Dose Orders are filled, the occurrences of Med Charge will be created.

Eliminated from the original design is the Bed entity. Because there is a 1:1 relationship between a Patient and a Bed,

Barb decided there was no need to carry Bed as a separate entity; rather, the bed number should become an attribute for a patient.

Step 8: Add the Remaining Attributes

Barb's team decided to use the domain/key approach to add the remaining attributes to the entities. Exhibit 8 shows the design.

Let's look at some of the entities. The Med Charge entity will contain the data necessary to bill the Patients. Each occurrence will have the Patient's number, medication code, and total dollars billed. The Patient No will be determined from the relevant IV Order entity. For example, by using the SIG Code in an IV Order, we can find the times at which the IV Order is to be filled by matching the SIG Code to the primary key for the SIG entity (file). Next, we use the Med Code attribute to match the prescribed medication against the Formulary entity (file) to determine the charge per dose. By multiplying the frequency of administration by the charge per dose, the total amount to charge can be determined and put into the entity (file).

The SIG entity has a composite key, because a particular SIG might be associated with several times. For example, the SIG "TID" is associated with 0600, 1600, and 2400 hours, because those are the standard times that a medication with a SIG of TID is given.

Finally, let's look at Patient Physician. This entity resulted from the complex relationship between Patient and Physician. When such an entity is created, it will have a composite key consisting of the keys from the original entities—Patient No and Doc No in this example. Notice that we preceded the attribute names with an "X" (for cross-reference).

After much discussion among the pro-

EXHIBIT 7   Revised DSD for Community Hospital Database

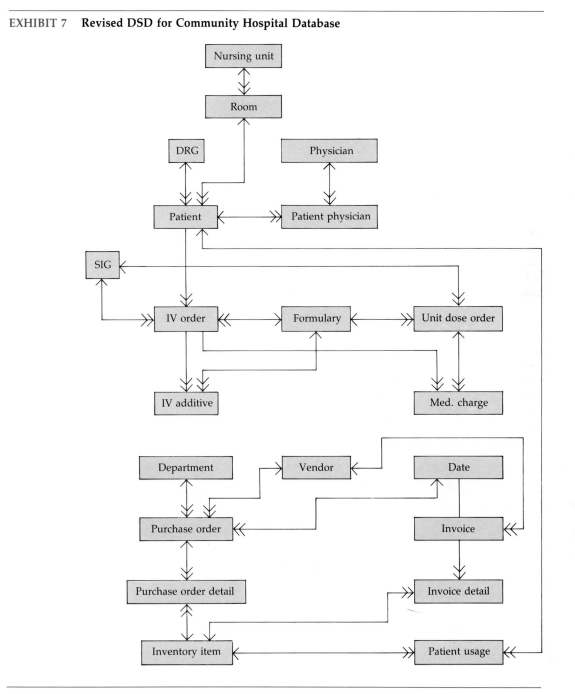

EXHIBIT 8   Complete Entity Design for Community Hospital

Patient (<u>Patient No</u>, Name, Sex, Age, Weight, Height, Religion, Address, Phone, DRG, Ins Co, Room No, Bed No, Status)

IV Order (<u>IV Order No</u>, Patient No, Pharmacist Initials, Date Entered, Date Changed, SIG Code, Solution Code[1], Flow Rate[2], Status)

IV Additive (<u>AIV Order No</u>, <u>Additive No</u>, Med Code, Amount)

Unit Dose Order (<u>UD Order No</u>, Patient No, Med Code, Amount, SIG Code, Pharmacist Initials, Date Entered, Date Changed, Status)

Med Charge (<u>MPatient No</u>, <u>MMed Code</u>, Dollars Charged)

Physician (<u>Doc No</u>, Doc Name, Phone, Room No, Home Address, Medicaid Number)

Patient Physician (<u>X Doc No</u>, <u>X Patient No</u>)

DRG (<u>DRG Code</u>, DRG Description)

Nursing Unit (<u>NU Code</u>, Phone)

Room (<u>Room No</u>, Number Of Beds)

Formulary (<u>Med Code</u>, Description, Cost, Charge, Package Size, Strength, GL Account, Standard SIG, Units Used YTD)

SIG (<u>SIG Code</u>, <u>Time</u>)

Purchase Order (<u>PO No</u>, Date, Dept Code, Vendor Code, Total Amount, Status)

Purchase Order Detail (<u>DPO No</u>, <u>Seq No</u>, DItem Code, Units Ordered, Cost Per Item, Units Received, Units Canceled, Date Last Arrived)

Inventory Item (<u>Item Code</u>, Item Description, Item Cost, Item Charge, Qty On Hand, Usage YTD, Primary Vendor Code, GL Account, Lead Time, EOQ, EOP, Critical Level)

Vendor (<u>Vendor No</u>, Name, Address, Contact, Dollars YTD)

Invoice (<u>Voucher No</u>, Due Date, Total Amt, Vendor Code, Vendor Invoice Number)

Invoice Detail (<u>DVoucher No</u>, <u>Seq No</u>, Item Code, Charge Per Unit)

Department (<u>Dept Code</u>, Department Name, Manager Name)

Patient Usage (<u>UPatient No</u>, <u>Uitem Code</u>, Units Used, Total Dollars)

Date (<u>Date</u>)

---

[1]A Solution Code represents the substance in which the additives are mixed. A common solution is dextrose (sugar).

[2]A Flow Rate represents the rate at which the medicine is administered. An example would be 100 milliliters/second.

ject team members concerning what constituted a suitable design objective, they decided that domain/key normal form, while difficult to implement and verify, represented the ideal design. The team members discussed this issue among themselves and even talked with other organizations in the area. At first, the members felt that since most of the other firms had stopped at 3NF, that 3NF should be their goal as well. However,

after weighing its pros and cons, they decided to aspire to DK/NF.

Exhibit 9 illustrates the resulting design for Community Hospital. It shows just a small portion of the model. Notice that Barb did not include the rules from Exhibit 3 that pertained to relationships. For example, pharmacy rule number 1 says that each Patient can have several IV Orders. This might seem to imply that Patient No $\rightarrow\!\!\!\rightarrow$ Order No. However, this

EXHIBIT 9   Checking Some of the Constraints to See If the Design in Exhibit 7 Is in Domain/Key Normal Form

Constraint	Consequence of	
	Key	Domain
Patient No → Patient Name	X	
Patient No → Bed	X	
Patient No → DRG	X	
SIG Code → → Due Time	X	
IV Order No → Solution Code	X	
IV Order No → Flow Rate	X	
IV Order No, Additive No → Med Code	X	
An IV Order status is:		
Active		
Suspended		
Stopped		X
IV Order No is 5 digits		X
Purchase Order No → Vendor Code	X	

really says that there is a 1:M relationship between the two entities: Patient and IV Order. When constructing a domain/key model, you must be sure to include only constraints on attributes.

The final phase in this step is to add connection attributes: identifier attributes from origin entities participating in 1:M relationships. The entities in Barb's design already contain these connection attributes. For example, the Purchase Order entity is associated with Date, Department, and Vendor. If you look at the entity for Purchase Order, you can see that Barb has included the keys from each of those parent or origin entities in the Purchase Order design.

Step 9: Consider the Future

Barb had already considered future needs, realizing that many additional entities would be required before the design was complete. To this end, she made a list of entities that are not included in Ex-

hibit 7, but that would be needed in the future. They included Lab Test, Diet, Radiology Test, Emergency Room Treatment, Operating Room Treatment, Operating Room, Nurse, and Employee.

In terms of the present design, Barb determined, through meetings with Judy and John, that both primary end users were satisfied. Furthermore, she verified that all the transactions within the scope of her project could be satisfied. Thus, Barb decided to go ahead with the design illustrated in Exhibit 7.

Step 10: Revise and Refine the Design

Because Barb's design was acceptable by all the end users—and, more important, because it supported all the required transactions—she did not have to modify it at this time. As she moves into phase 2, she may have to make substantial changes to include other applications.

EXHIBIT 10   A Material Management Clerk's Database View

Purchase Order (<u>PO No</u>, Date, Dept Code, Vendor Code, Total Amount, Status)
Purchase Order Detail (<u>DPO No</u>, <u>Seq No</u>, DItem Code, Units Ordered, Cost Per
                  Item, Units Received, Units Canceled, Date Last Arrived)
Inventory Item (<u>Item Code</u>, Item Cost, Item Charge, Qty On Hand, Usage YTD,
             Primary Vendor Code, GL Account, Lead Time, EOQ, EOP, Critical Level)
Vendor (<u>Vendor No</u>, Name, Address, Contact, Dollars YTD)
Invoice (<u>Voucher No</u>, Due Date, Total Amt, Vendor Code)
Invoice Detail (<u>Voucher No</u>, <u>Seq No</u>, Item Code, Charge Per Unit)
Department (<u>Dept Code</u>, Name, Manager Name)

Step 11: Determine User Views

Again, Barb deviated from the text: Rather than show DSDs for each user, she instructed her project team to use conceptual views. Exhibit 10 shows the view of one of the clerks in materials management. Because the clerks are not permitted to see patient charges, that entity has been eliminated from their access.

Before finishing the design, Barb defined views for every end user of the database. These included the two directors, the pharmacy technicians, secretaries for both departments, and a billing clerk in the pharmacy.

In later episodes, we will see how to implement Barb's design for each of the three major data models: network, hierarchical, and relational.

CHAPTER

5

Logical and
Physical
Database
Design

In Chapter 4, we developed three general steps for designing a database: (1) Design the conceptual database, (2) design the logical database, and (3) design the physical database. There we focused on designing the conceptual database. In this chapter, we examine steps 2 and 3.

The chapter is divided into three main sections: relational, network, and hierarchical database design. In each section, we discuss first how to map the conceptual model to the specific database model. Then we see how to physically implement it. At the conclusion of this chapter, you will be able to:

- Map a logical database design to the relational, network, or hierarchical model.
- Design a relational, network, or hierarchical physical database.

The conceptual database design is independent of hardware and DBMS software; it models the informational needs of the organization. Unfortunately, some customization may be necessary while adapting it to the specific DBMS the organization uses. Each of the three data models has a unique set of requirements. The process of accommodating those requirements is part of the logical design—the adaptation of the conceptual design to meet the needs of a specific data model.

Once the model has been adapted to the requirements of the underlying data model, the DBA is ready to implement it on a disk drive. Unlike the network and hierarchical models, the relational model has no standard physical storage techniques. We will discuss the standard approaches as well as some of the relational techniques used by the prominent vendors of relational products.

We will begin by examining how to transform the conceptual design into one suitable for implementation with the relational approach.

5.1 RELATIONAL DATABASE DESIGN

Of the three database models, the relational model requires the least amount of work in mapping to the logical model and implementing the results on a disk drive.

Mapping to the Logical Database

To map the conceptual database model to the relational model, we begin with the conceptual model and follow these steps:

1. Convert each entity into a table, including the intersection entities.
2. Map each attribute of the entity to a column of the table.
3. Identify the primary key and map each relationship to a foreign key.
4. Normalize the design (if not done already).
5. Decide which deletion integrity rule to use.
6. Determine the indexes.

Convert Each Entity into a Table. This step is straightforward: We transform each entity on the DSD or E-R diagram into a table and assign it a suitable name. (We eliminated the M:N relationships during the conceptual design process.) The result is a logical model that mirrors the conceptual model. When we examine the physical design, you will see examples of how further refinements can result in designs that differ from the conceptual one.

Map Attributes to Columns. Recall that we depict conceptual tables like this:

PATIENT (<u>PATNUM</u>, PATFIRST, PATLAST, PATLOC, PATINSCODE)
ORDER (<u>ORDERNO</u>, PATNUM, DRUGCODE, AMOUNT)
DOCTOR (<u>DOCCODE</u>, DNAME, DPHONE)

Since our procedure for conceptual database design was built on relational principles, this step is simple.

Identify the Primary Key and Map Each Relationship to a Foreign Key. Once we have identified the columns that pertain to the table, we specify the primary key and add all the connection columns (foreign keys) we need to relate the table to the others. Recall that the table containing the foreign key is called the *dependent table*, and the table to which it refers is the *parent table*. For every 1:M relation of which this table is a dependent, we add a foreign-key column consisting of the primary key of its parent. The relational model uses these foreign keys to establish relationships. If this sounds familiar, it's because this was part of step 8 in our design process. We repeat the step for emphasis because, while it is beneficial for the hierarchic and network models, it is essential for the relational.

Let's look at an example. Suppose there is a 1:M relationship between DOCTOR and PATIENT. This means we should carry the primary-key column for DOCTOR in the PATIENT table, because PATIENT plays the role of dependent in the relationship. The above PATIENT table now looks like this:

PATIENT (<u>PATNUM</u>, PATFIRST, PATLAST, PATLOC, PATINSCODE,
      DOCCODE)

Note these two points:

- DOCCODE is a foreign key, because we cannot have a DOCCODE value in a PATIENT row for which there is no matching code in the DOCTOR table.
- Relationships are implied by the foreign keys; that is, there is an implied relationship between DOCTOR and PATIENT, because DOCCODE appears in both tables. Similarly, there is a relationship between PATIENT and ORDER because of the foreign-key column, PATNUM, in the ORDER table. In the hierarchical and network models, the relationships are explicit because they are implemented via pointers or other physical mechanisms.

At the conclusion of this step, we must make sure that each table has a primary key and that we have identified all foreign keys.

Normalize the Design. Because we normalized the design during our conceptual design, this step shouldn't be necessary. We include it because some organizations do not normalize their conceptual designs and, hence, must do so at this point. Remember that failure to perform this step can result in insertion, deletion, and update anomalies. All three anomalies occur because of undesirable functional dependencies, a concept we introduced in Section 4.9 of Chapter 4.

Decide Which Deletion Integrity Rule to Use. In Section 2.3 of Chapter 2, we discussed three deletion integrity rules: restrict, set to NULL, and cascade. The DBA should decide which rule to apply for each parent/dependent table combination. Recall that *restrict* prevents the deletion of a parent row when that row is related to one or more dependent rows through a foreign key. If *cascade* is used, deleting a parent row results in the deletion of all the related dependent rows. Finally, if the DBA chooses *set to NULL*, all the related foreign-key values are set to NULL when a parent row is deleted.

The trend today is to use relational implementations that support both insertion and deletion integrity, and to select the rules in advance. Failure to do so can result in inconsistent data among the tables.

Determine the Indexes. First, we should point out that if indexes are available to a relational DBMS (RDBMS), the RDBMS will determine on its own which, if any, to use. Neither the end user nor the programmer need be concerned with their existence. In fact, some DBMS packages even create indexes "on the fly" on an as-needed basis.

An index should be created on the primary key for each table and should specify that no duplicate values are permitted. Indexes for the more frequent search path columns (secondary keys) should also be established, and duplicate values for these columns should be allowed for. Finally, an index should be defined for each foreign-key column that is used as the basis for combining two or more tables. This operation is called a *join*, and we will discuss it in the next chapter.

Physical Design of Relational Databases

Each vendor has its own unique set of physical options plus a standard set used by most. Among the standard tools are *partitioning* and *clustering*.

Partitioning. **Partitioning** means subdividing a table occurrence, either horizontally or vertically, and creating additional tables to accommodate the results. A **vertical partitioning** splits a single table vertically into two or more tables, leaving some columns in the original table and placing others in the new one. In this case, the physical design differs from the logical one. This technique is useful when some columns have a higher frequency of activity than others. The high-activity columns are placed in one table and the others in a second one. In this way, the DBMS won't have to retrieve infrequently needed columns. If the tables must be viewed as one, the relational join operator can be used to combine them. Notice that this type of partitioning can result in unnormalized results, and thus unexpected complications can occur. However, a rule can be violated if all trade-offs are considered and the rule's violation is considered justified.

A second situation that often results in a vertical partitioning occurs when different groups of users access different sets of columns in the same table. After a vertical partitioning, each user group has a table with columns that only it uses. When these groups are geographically diverse, the result may be tables that actually reside on different computers under the control of different but related DBMSs—an environment called *distributed database management*, which we will discuss later in the text.

Horizontal partitioning refers to splitting tables along their row dimension.

This may be necessary if the DBA feels that some rows are more frequently accessed than others. Placing the infrequently accessed rows into another table will enhance the performance of the frequently accessed table. Horizontal partitioning can also be useful in distributed environments in which one set of users accesses one set of rows and another group a different set.

Clustering. In its simplest form, **clustering** means storing frequently accessed tables near one another on the same disk drive. For example, a purchase order (PO) and its associated items (PO_DETAIL) presumably would be accessed together; thus, the DBA might cluster the two tables.

A variation of clustering is used by ORACLE, a vendor of one of the primary relational DBMSs. Here, a linked list is used to relate associated records. Continuing the purchase order example, each PO_DETAIL row should contain a purchase order number (PO_NO) column—a foreign key. If one purchase order contains 50 items, 50 rows in PO_DETAIL will contain the same PO_NO value. With ORACLE, the clustering of PO and PO_DETAIL will result in the following benefits:

- The PO number will be stored only once.
- A simple list relating each PO value with its associated PO_DETAIL rows will be maintained.
- Search time will decrease, because the PO and PO_DETAIL tables will be stored as close together as possible.

Organization Optimization. While most RDBMSs use a B-tree to organize indexes, that is not always the optimal retrieval organization. INGRES, another RDBMS vendor, offers the DBA several index options. For example, if rows are almost always accessed by search criteria based on =, a **hashed** organization and retrieval will be preferable. Hashing means there is a predictable relationship between a record's primary key and the disk address of the record. It is discussed in detail in Appendix A. For very small tables, a **heap** organization—an unordered organization in which duplicate rows are permitted and all insertions are at the end of the table—may be more beneficial. Finally, the DBA can use a compression algorithm.

Compressed Indexes. A **compressed index** maintains only enough information to guarantee uniqueness and truncates everything else. Consider the data in Table 5.1. The second row contains the name SMITH. This varies from the previous name by the single character *H*, so in the compressed form, the index will carry only that letter. This is evident in Table 5.2. Because SMITHTON differs from SMITH only by its last three letters, only the letters *TON* are carried in the associated row. While this technique saves a considerable amount of storage and can be used with any indexing scheme, it forces the RDBMS to go to the actual table to verify that a search key actually *exists* in the database.

TABLE 5.1 **Names to Be Stored in a Compressed Index**

SMIT
SMITH
SMITHTON
SMITS
SMYTHE

TABLE 5.2 **The Compressed Index**

	Number of Characters that Are the Same as in the Previous Entry	Result of Compression
SMIT	0	SMIT
SMITH	4	H
SMITHTON	5	TON
SMITS	4	S
SMYTHE	2	YTHE

5.2 NETWORK DATABASE DESIGN

Before we begin discussing network database design, let us quickly review some terminology. An origin of a 1:M relationship is called an *owner* and a destination a *member*. A 1:M relationship is a *set type* and is given a name; entities or conceptual files are called *record types*. The CODASYL model allows for *primary* and *secondary keys* for each record type. A *set occurrence* consists of an *owner* occurrence and all associated *member* occurrences. Finally, *member records* can be sequenced.

Mapping to the Logical Database

The steps the DBA follows to prepare the conceptual model for network implementation are as follows:

1. Map each entity to a record type.
2. Map each 1:M relationship to a set type.
3. Map each attribute to a field or data item.
4. Determine the primary and secondary keys.
5. Add additional sets to accommodate reporting needs.
6. Choose a sequence for each set type.
7. Add a "dummy" owner, if necessary.
8. Assign record types to areas, if necessary.

Map Entities to Record Types and 1:M Relationships to Set Types. Each entity on the DSD or E-R diagram becomes a record type, and each 1:M relationship becomes a set type. If any 1:1 relationships are detected, we collapse the member data items into those of the owner. As an example, suppose we have determined that there is a 1:1 relationship between EMPLOYEE and SPOUSE. Instead of creating a SPOUSE and an EMPLOYEE record type and a set called HAS-A, we expand the definition of EMPLOYEE to include the SPOUSE data items.

Figure 5.1 reproduces a portion of the resulting DSD from Fred's Pharmacy shown in Figure 4.7. We have shortened it to simplify our discussion. The figure shows four entities, each of which has been mapped to a record type, and three 1:M relations, each converted into a set type.

Map Each Attribute to a Field or Data Item. In this step, we convert all the attributes to fields. In addition to the attributes determined during the conceptual design phase, we add the connection data items (foreign keys) to each member

---

FIGURE 5.1   **A Portion of the DSD for Fred's Pharmacy**

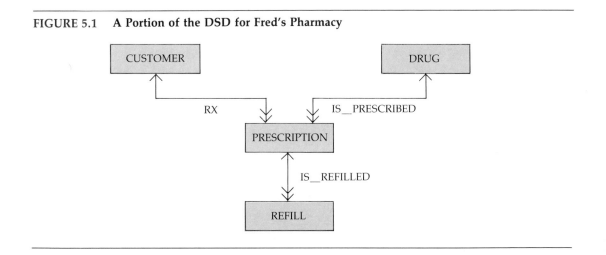

FIGURE 5.2   **The Conceptual Record Type Definitions Associated with Figure 5.1**

CUSTOMER (<u>CUST__ID</u>, CUST__NAME, CUST__PHONE, CUST__ADDRESS, CUST__TYPE)

DRUG (<u>DRUG__CODE</u>, DRUG__DESC, DRUG__COST, DRUG__PRICE, ON__HAND, USAGE__YTD)

PRESCRIPTION (<u>PNO</u>, PDRUG, PCUST, PDATE, CHARGE, NO__OF__REFILLS)

Connection fields ⎯⎯⎯⎯⎯⎯

REFILL (<u>PNO</u>, <u>REFILL__NO</u>, RDATE, CHARGE)

record. Figure 5.2 shows our familiar representation of conceptual files as applied to the Fred's Pharmacy example. This time we refer to the items as *conceptual record types* in keeping with the CODASYL terminology.

Determine Primary and Secondary Keys. The CODASYL model, the most popular implementation of the network approach, permits each record type to have a primary key and several secondary keys. When using the relational model, primary keys are required for each table. With the CODASYL model, they are optional; however, in most cases, they should be used.

If secondary keys are to be used, they must be identified in advance so that the DBA can specify them as such when defining the conceptual database to the DBMS. Notice that this isn't so with the relational model. In that case, we can use any column as a secondary key and need not specify this in advance.

Add Additional Sets to Accommodate Reporting Needs. New sets may be needed to accommodate reporting needs, especially for different sort sequences of the same 1:M relationship. Member records in a set can be sequenced in only one way. Thus, if two different sorts of the same set are desired, a new set must be added. For example, assume that PRESCRIPTIONs in the RX set are sorted by PDATE within CUSTOMER. If another sort is required by, say, PNO, another set will have to be established between CUSTOMER and PRESCRIPTION.

Choose a Sequence for Each Set Type. Each set type can be sorted in one of several ways. The most popular method is to sort on a field within the member record. Other sequencing options include last-in-first-out, first-in-first-out, and no sequencing at all. Because the DBA must specify the desired sequence when defining and coding the logical design for implementation by the DDL portion of the DBMS, it is important that he or she decide this before doing the actual coding.

Establish a Dummy Owner, If Necessary. DBMSs based on CODASYL specifications prior to 1981 can sequence only member occurrences, not records that are only owners. This means that only member records can be sequentially accessed. For example, we could not sort CUSTOMER occurrences in Figure 5.1, because CUSTOMER is not a member of any set. However, we can make CUSTOMER into a member of a set by establishing a "dummy" owner called SYSTEM, meaning that the DBMS system is its owner.

To illustrate, let's assume we need sequential access to both DRUG and CUSTOMER occurrences. This will result in the modified DSD shown in Figure 5.3.

FIGURE 5.3   A Revised DSD that Permits Sequential Retrieval of CUSTOMER and DRUG Occurrences

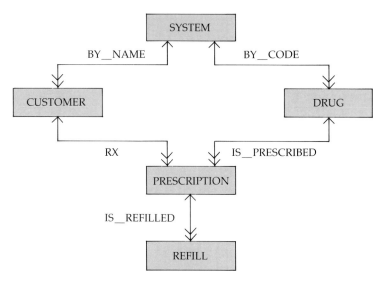

The new record type, SYSTEM, was necessary because (1) we assumed an early version of the CODASYL model was used, and (2) we needed sequential (or sorted) access to CUSTOMER and DRUG occurrences.

Assign Record Types to Areas, If Necessary. When most of the commercial DBMSs were developed, CODASYL advocated the controversial use of **areas,** or **realms**—physical subdivisions of a database to which record types are assigned. For example, we could assign PRESCRIPTION and REFILL occurrences to one area, CUSTOMERs to a second, and DRUGs to a third.

   Areas were used for the following purposes:

- To improve DBMS performance by effectively storing frequently accessed records near one another.
- To enhance DBMS performance by placing specific areas at locations of the disk that have faster average seek times—beneath fixed heads, for example. Appendix A discusses these disk concepts in detail.
- To permit records in the various areas to have differing security levels. In our example, we could assign PRESCRIPTIONs and REFILLs one password and the other record types different ones.

   The area concept was dropped from the more recent CODASYL-based standards.

Mapping to the network model isn't difficult when one begins with a sound conceptual design. If we hadn't taken care with our conceptual design, the mapping process would have been more complex. Specifically, there can be no complex network structures in the logical design; we eliminated them during the previous design step.

Physical Design of Network Databases

The CODASYL network model uses next, prior, and owner pointers, all stored within member records, to implement set occurrences. In addition, it uses a first (head) pointer, carried in owner records, to indicate the first member occurrence. Its counterpart is a last (tail) pointer, which indicates the last member record and is also stored in the owner occurrence.

Set Representations: How Set Occurrences Are Maintained. Figure 5.4 shows a network DSD that we will use to examine how to implement a set and to see how physical design changes can affect application performance.

First and Next Member Pointers. Two pointer types are always used: first and next. The CODASYL-based DBMSs implement sets as linked lists with embedded next pointers or with the pointers carried in the owner of the set as an index. Although the exact number of bytes per pointer varies from one commercial system to another, most require from two to four bytes. Each owner record occurrence contains a first pointer to the first member record for each set it owns. For example, because INVOICE owns just one set type, CONTAINS, each INVOICE occurrence will have one first pointer, indicating the initial DETAIL item the INVOICE CONTAINS.

Figure 5.5 shows some sample data that are to be stored according to the DSD in Figure 5.4. Figure 5.6 shows the data stored in the database. Note that the occurrence of CONTAINS owned by INVOICE number A12 has three members, one for each of its DETAIL records. One of those items is number 77, which is also a member of IS__ORDERED. The fact that a DETAIL occurrence has two owners verifies that we have a network data structure. We assumed that CONTAINS member records were sorted by invoice number (INO) values and IS__ORDERED member occurrences in descending order by units ordered. For example, in the IS__ORDERED occurrence owned by item 111, the initial member is the DETAIL item that carries 3 units, while the next one carries 2 units.

The number associated with each record is its RRN. To follow the CONTAINS set owned by INVOICE number A12, the program would retrieve RRNs 100, 200, 204, and 206. Implementation of such a structure can be accomplished via next pointers. With next pointers, the member records in a set occurrence are linked together, with the last one pointing back to its owner. We saw several examples of this kind of data structure in Chapter 3 and identified it as a modified

FIGURE 5.4   A Network DSD

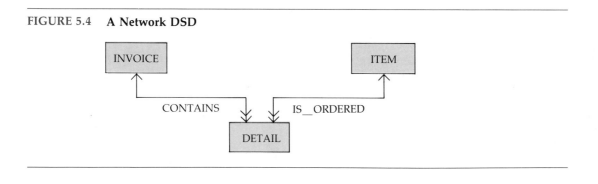

FIGURE 5.5   Sample Invoice Data to Be Stored in the Conceptual Database in Figure 5.4

Invoice Summary

Invoice Number	Vendor Code	Amount Due	Due Date	Terms
A12	ACME	$128.00	04/15/XX	2/10 net 30
A19	ACME	80.00	04/15/XX	2/10 net 30
A22	ACME	145.00	04/15/XX	2/10 net 30
A23	ACME	50.00	04/30/XX	2/10 net 30
BX1	BYARS	100.00	04/30/XX	2/10 net 30
BY7	BYARS	120.00	04/15/XX	2/10 net 30

Invoice (line item) Contents

Invoice Number	Item Code	Item Description	Quantity	Cost per Item
A12	14	DSDD Diskettes	20	3.00
	77	SSSD Diskettes	10	2.00
	10	Ribbon	12	4.00
A19	111	11 × 15 Paper	2	40.00
A22	77	SSDD Diskettes	20	2.00
	111	11 × 15 Paper	3	35.00
A23	90	RS-232 Cable	1	50.00
BX1	17	8088-2	20	5.00
BY7	100	8086	20	2.00
	103	80386	20	4.00

ring. Each DETAIL occurrence therefore would contain two next pointers: one to refer to the next DETAIL for a given INVOICE (CONTAINS) and one to indicate the next occurrence of the same item (IS_ORDERED).

Prior and Last Pointers. Prior pointers point backwards. To fully implement them, a last pointer must be stored with the owner record so that the chain (ring) can be followed backwards.

FIGURE 5.6   Relationship of Several Set Occurrences to One Another

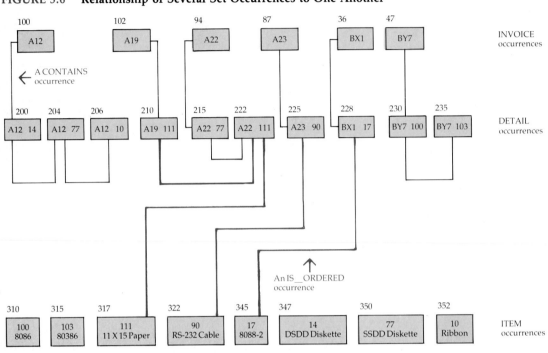

The figure is based on the data from Figure 5.5 and the conceptual model shown in Figure 5.4. The numbers above each occurrence are RRNs. One color is used to designate IS_ORDERED set occurrences and the other color CONTAINS.

Owner Pointers. An owner (home) pointer directly connects a member to its owner. As expected, this results in yet another pointer for each member record. However, it can greatly speed up the accessing of an owner, because otherwise the ring must be followed to its logical end, which would then point to its owner. Figure 5.7 shows our database from Figure 5.6 with all the embedded pointers.

To determine how many pointers are necessary per record occurrence, let's look at Table 5.3, which summarizes the number of pointers required for owner and member record types. To use the table, we look at the DSD and determine in how many sets a given record type participates as an owner and a member. Then we add the resulting values. For instance, DETAIL is a member of two sets and an owner of none. Table 5.3 indicates that for each set it owns, a maximum of two pointers are needed—a first and a last pointer. Similarly, for each set of which it is a member, three are possible—next, prior, and owner. Thus, there can be up to six pointers per occurrence of DETAIL.

FIGURE 5.7   **Physical Implementation of Figure 5.6**

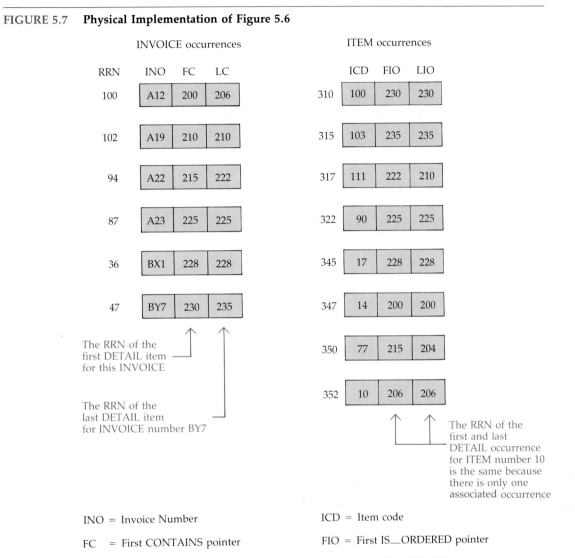

INO = Invoice Number

FC   = First CONTAINS pointer

LC   = Last CONTAINS pointer

ICD = Item code

FIO = First IS__ORDERED pointer

LIO = Last IS__ORDERED pointer

FIGURE 5.7   *(concluded)*

DETAIL occurrences

		NC	PC	OC	NIO	PIO	OIO
200	A12 14	204	100	100	347	347	347
204	A12 77	206	200	100	350	215	350
206	A12 10	100	204	100	352	352	352
210	A19 111	102	102	102	317	222	317
215	A22 77	222	94	94	204	350	350
222	A22 111	94	215	94	210	317	317
225	A23 90	87	87	87	322	322	322
228	BX1 17	36	36	36	345	345	345
230	BY7 100	235	47	47	310	310	310
235	BY7 103	47	230	47	315	315	315

NC = Next CONTAINS pointer

PC = Prior CONTAINS pointer

OC = Owner CONTAINS pointer

NIO = Next IS__ORDERED pointer

PIO = Prior IS__ORDERED pointer

OIO = Owner IS__ORDERED pointer

TABLE 5.3   **Determining the Maximum Number of Pointers per Record Occurrence**

Pointer Type	Number per Set of Which Record Is a(n)	
	Member	Owner
First	0	1
Last	0	1
Next	1	0
Prior	1	0
Owner	1	0

The DBA can choose whether or not to employ prior and owner pointers. This decision can have a large impact on the physical performance of the database. Prior pointers make it easy to read a set backwards, but, more important, they facilitate the deletion of records from a set occurrence. The disadvantages are increased storage and increased updating complexity.

Today, the trade-off of storage space for processing efficiency is a less difficult choice than it was in the past. Disk storage cost per megabyte is declining almost monthly. Each additional prior and owner pointer requires from two to four bytes per member record occurrence for each set type, a relatively small storage penalty for features so potentially valuable.

Let's look at the total overhead associated with the two optional pointers for a realistic example. Assume 10,000 records of a particular type are stored in a database and each is a member of six set types. This would result in extra pointer-related storage of 2 pointers/occurrence/set type × 6 set types × 10,000 occurrences × 4 bytes/pointer = 480,000 bytes. With DASD costs per KB at around 1 to 2 cents, the additional storage costs are almost negligible. The nonmonetary costs associated with the additional pointers may not be.

If a record is a member of 10 sets, each with prior and owner pointers, adding a new record will require the determination of values for 10 next, 10 prior, and 10 owner pointers for the record being stored. Additionally, as we saw in Chapter 3, the record logically preceding the new one for each of the 10 sets will need to have its next-member pointer changed to the RRN of the new record. Also, the record logically following the new one in each set will need to have its prior pointer adjusted so that it points to the new one. This could require that 20 additional records be read and then rewritten. In a multiuser environment, all the reads and writes must be physical ones so that the updates are immediately available to all users.

This means that the insertion of a new record occurrence might consume a considerable amount of time. However, the extra pointers will facilitate the retrieval of owner occurrences and provide the ability to repair broken chains— features that probably offset the reduced insertion performance and additional storage requirements.

Pointer Arrays. Another option for the DBA is to use pointer arrays instead of lists. In this case, member records contain no next or prior pointers but may contain owner pointers. The next and prior pointers are now stored as an index in the owner record or in a separate index.

Figure 5.8 shows the pointer array implementation of the CONTAINS set. The first row of pointers represents the collection of next CONTAINS pointers. By following the pointers associated with the first INVOICE occurrence, the DBMS will retrieve DETAIL records stored at RRNs 200, 204, and 206. Backwards retrieval will be done using the lower set of pointers.

Embedded Pointers versus Pointer Arrays. Let's compare the two options. To process all the DETAIL items for INVOICE number A12 using the pointer array, we would execute the following steps:

1. Access the INVOICE owner (RRN 100) using a hashing routine.
2. Use the first CONTAINS pointer value (200) to access the initial DETAIL record, which is for the item with code 14.

FIGURE 5.8   Implement a Set Occurrence through a Pointer Array

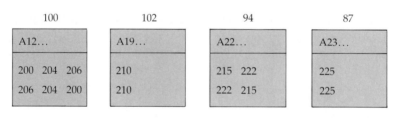

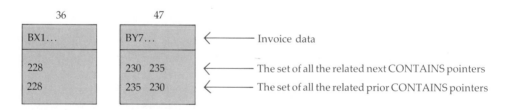

Each INVOICE carries a pointer array of next and prior CONTAINS pointers. The first row of pointers contains next pointers and the second row prior pointers. For example, INVOICE BY7 should have two forward (next) pointers, one for each DETAIL item. The values are 230 and 235.

3. Access the owner again to determine the next CONTAINS pointer value (204). (This could be a logical disk I/O, meaning that the INVOICE record was already in a buffer. See Appendix A for a more thorough treatment.)
4. Access RRN 204.
5. Repeat steps 3 and 4 until there are no more index values to follow.

Using a pointer array to retrieve the data results in six I/Os (input/output operations): The INVOICE record is retrieved three times and each of the associated DETAIL occurrences one time.

Contrast this with the steps necessary to follow the embedded-pointer option:

1. Perform a hashed access of INVOICE number A12.
2. Determine the first CONTAINS pointer value (RRN 200), then access the indicated record.
3. Use the embedded next CONTAINS pointer in the record (204) to access the next DETAIL item.
4. Repeat step 3 until a status indicator returns an end-of-set condition.

This alternative results in four I/Os. It appears that chaining is preferable to pointer arrays, especially if the list must always be followed from start to finish. However, if access to the nth record in a set occurrence is required, the pointer array method is faster.

If the set occurrence is implemented as a chain, we must process every record in the list prior to the desired one, always starting at the beginning of the list. With the pointer array method, however, we can determine the exact index value and go directly to that disk address. As an example, using a chain to access the third DETAIL item in the occurrence of CONTAINS owned by INVOICE number A12 would require four I/Os:

1. Access the INVOICE record for number A12 using a hashing routine.
2. Retrieve the initial DETAIL item as indicated by the first CONTAINS pointer. The first CONTAINS pointer value is 200.
3. Retrieve the next CONTAINS record pointed to by RRN 200, 204. This is the second DETAIL item.
4. Use the next pointer to retrieve the detail record at RRN 206.

If we used a pointer array instead, we would first access the INVOICE owner, then use the third pointer (value 206) to directly access the proper record. In this case, a pointer array would be preferable to a chain.

The decision about which method to use depends on the circumstances. If frequent sequential retrieval of member records is indicated, a chain is preferable. If random access to specific members is needed often, the pointer array method should be selected. As is the case with most design options, there is no one best choice for all conditions.

5.3   THE HIERARCHICAL MODEL

Recall that owners are known as *parent segments* and members as *child segments*. Entities are mapped to segment types rather than to record types (network) or tables (relational). Each segment contains one or more fields known as a **key sequence field (KSF),** which is essentially a sorting mechanism used to order child occurrences. The conceptual database determines its hierarchical order.

Mapping to the Logical Database

The steps for mapping to the logical database are as follows:

1. Map each entity to a segment type.
2. Reduce any network structures to a collection of trees or to a logical relationship.
3. Choose the hierarchical order.
4. Map each attribute to a field and choose a category for each field.

Map Each Entity to a Segment Type. This part of the mapping process is easy. Each relationship results in a parent-child relationship. Less easy is what to do with nonhierarchical structures.

Reduce Each Network Substructure to a Collection of Trees or to a Logical Relationship. A network substructure (a portion of a data structure that contains a network) can be reduced to a collection of tree structures, but this results in redundancy. To see this, let's look again at Figure 5.1. Because PRESCRIPTION is the child of two 1:M relationships, the structure qualifies as a network and cannot be directly implemented using a hierarchical model. One way to deal with this situation is to construct two tree structures from the original one, as shown in Figure 5.9. Now there are two hierarchical data structures: one containing CUSTOMER, PRESCRIPTION, and REFILL and the other DRUG, PRESCRIPTION and REFILL. Notice that there is quite a bit of redundancy: PRESCRIPTION and REFILL occurrences appear in both tree structures.

With IBM's hierarchical DBMS, IMS, both structures would result in separate databases, so the organization would find that two sets of PRESCRIPTION and REFILL occurrences would have to be maintained—not a very good solution. An alternative is to use logical pointers. As long as there are no more than two parents of a segment, a **logical pointer** can be used to associate:

- A child in one segment of a database to a parent in another database
- A parent in one database to a child in another database
- Two children in the same or different databases

FIGURE 5.9   **The Equivalent Set of Two Trees Resulting from Figure 5.1**

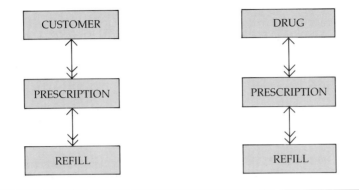

Figure 5.10 shows two ways to use logical pointers to transform a network into a tree structure. Even though PRESCRIPTION is shown twice, it would be stored only once. PRESCRIPTION has two parents—one is called the physical parent (it actually exists) and the other the logical parent. Part (a) uses a **logical parent pointer** to connect a PRESCRIPTION occurrence to its logical parent. In this case, the actual PRESCRIPTION occurrences would be stored in the DRUG database, and a pointer in each CUSTOMER occurrence would relate it to its first PRESCRIPTION.

Part (b) of the figure uses a **logical child pointer** within the DRUG segment, which points from a DRUG occurrence to the initial PRESCRIPTION for that medication. Now the PRESCRIPTION data is stored in the CUSTOMER database, and a pointer in DRUG relates a specific DRUG occurrence to the initial PRESCRIPTION for that drug.

In both cases, a dotted line indicates the logical relationship. The choice of whether to use a logical child or a logical parent should be based on performance. It is faster to access physical children than logical ones. Thus, if PRESCRIPTION data is more often accessed through CUSTOMER, Figure 5.10(a) is the preferred design; otherwise, Figure 5.10(b) is preferable.

Choose the Hierarchical Order. After transforming the data structures into one or more hierarchical structures, we decide on the hierarchical ordering of the segments. In Chapter 3, we called this ordering a *preorder traversal sequence*. Because of the storage implications of the hierarchical ordering, some conceptual designs are better than others.

Occurrences of segments appearing on the left side of the data structure can be accessed more quickly than those on the right. Consider the two hierarchical designs in Figure 5.11.

FIGURE 5.10   Using Logical Pointers to Implement a Limited Network Structure

(a) Using a logical parent pointer to map the network structure in Figure 5.1 to the hierarchical model. In this case, the actual PRESCRIPTION occurrences would be stored only in the DRUG hierarchy.

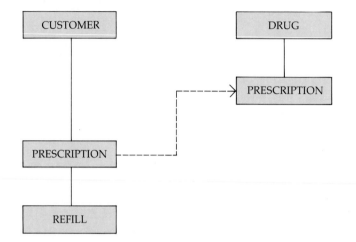

(b) Using a logical child pointer to map network structure to the hierarchical model. In this case, the PRESCRIPTION occurrences would be stored in the CUSTOMER hierarchy.

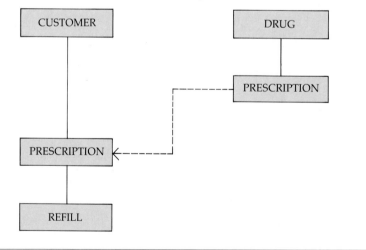

FIGURE 5.11   **Two Similar Conceptual Designs that Result in Two Different Physical Databases**

(a) A hierarchic design with ORDER segments on a hierarchic path along a left-branch of the root.

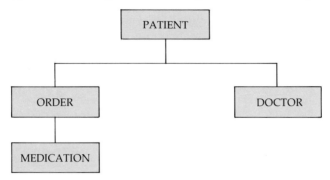

(b) An alternative design where ORDER segments are found on a hierarchic path that lies on a right-branch of the root. If ORDERs of a PATIENT are more frequently accessed than DOCTORs, this design will be seen to be less efficient than that shown in part (a).

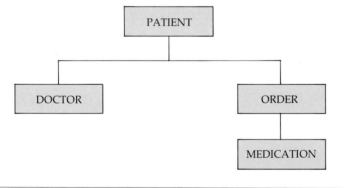

The hierarchical order associated with part (a) is PATIENT, ORDER, MEDI-CATION, DOCTOR. For part (b), the order is PATIENT, DOCTOR, ORDER, MEDICATION. This order also dictates the sequence of segment occurrences. For example, in part (b), the database occurrences would begin with the initial PATIENT occurrence, then all of that PATIENT's DOCTORs, followed by the first ORDER, then all the MEDICATIONs prescribed for that ORDER. The subsequent occurrence would be the next ORDER for that PATIENT, followed by MEDICATIONs, and so on. Once all the ORDERs were stored, the next PATIENT occurrence would be stored. Child segments of the same type would be sequenced according to their KSF. For example, if the ORDER KSF were ORDER_NO, all ORDERs for a given PATIENT would be in that sequence. We assume the KSF for PATIENT, DOCTOR, ORDER, and MEDICATION are

PATIENT__NO, DOCTOR__ID, ORDER__NO, and MEDICATION__ID, respectively. The **hierarchical sequence** refers to the ordering of segments based on the hierarchical order plus each segment's KSF.

Figure 5.12 shows the hierarchical sequence resulting from part (a) of Figure 5.11. Figure 5.13 shows the hierarchical sequence resulting from part (b). In both figures, the number next to each segment occurrence is a value designating its position in the hierarchical sequence. For example MEDICATION M11 is the third segment in Figure 5.12 but the fifth in Figure 5.13.

Although it is far more likely that end users would access a PATIENT's ORDERs than his or her DOCTORs, if the DBA elected to use the design in Figure 5.11(b), an end user would first retrieve all the DOCTOR occurrences prior to any ORDERs (see Figure 5.13). Hopefully, you can see that this hierarchical ordering of segment types can dramatically affect the performance of the database.

Contrast this with the results of using the design in Figure 5.11(a). Now, according to Figure 5.12, immediately following each PATIENT would be the first associated ORDER. After each ORDER occurrence, all the MEDICATION occurrences would be stored. Only after all ORDER and MEDICATION occurrences were stored would DOCTOR occurrences be stored. Assuming that an end user would access a PATIENT's ORDERs more frequently than that

FIGURE 5.12   **The Hierarchical Sequence of Occurrences Based on Figure 5.11(a)**

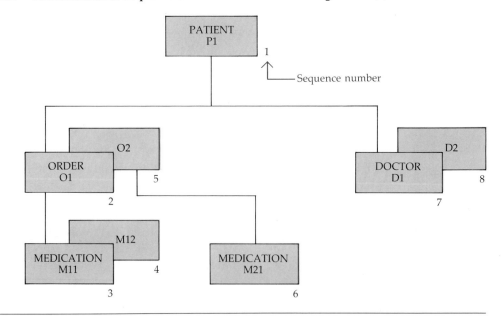

FIGURE 5.13   **The Hierarchical Sequence of Occurrences Based on Figure 5.11(b)**

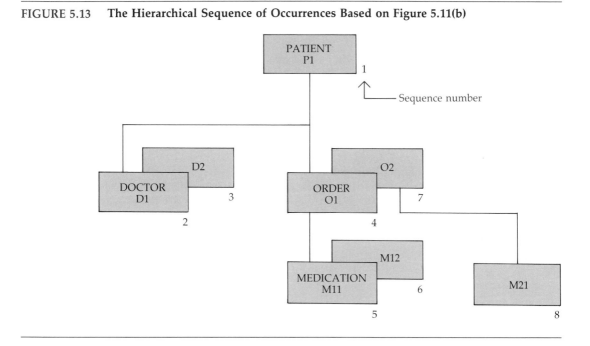

PATIENT's DOCTORs, the design in part (a) is more efficient. To summarize: We place more frequently accessed segments to the left of those needed less often.

Map Each Attribute to a Field and Select a Category for Each Field. Next, we map each attribute to a field. There are three kinds of IMS fields: key-sequence, search, and nonsearch. A **key-sequence field** is usually used to order child occurrences, but it can also be used to provide hashed or indexed access to root occurrences. A **search field** is a field that can be used as an access path by an application, while a **nonsearch field** cannot. In essence, a nonsearch field is like a COBOL "FILLER"; it occupies space but cannot be referenced in the PRO-CEDURE DIVISION.

This completes our discussion of how to map the conceptual design to a logical one. The relational model requires the fewest adjustments and work, while the hierarchical model usually necessitates a substantial change in the conceptual design. The network model is easily accommodated, but it requires that the DBA specify many more items than is necessary with the other two models.

Hierarchical (IMS) Physical Database Design

The method used by IMS to store the segments and any associated overhead depends on the *physical storage structure,* referred to by IBM as *access methods.* These access methods will be discussed in the IMS portion of the text in Section 11.5. In this section, we will discuss only their general features.

In Chapter 3, we saw that one way to implement a tree is to use the preorder traversal, or hierarchical order, technique. This is the approach IBM uses.

We can use one of three implementation methods: a physical approach, a linked list of the segments in their hierarchical order, or a child/twin linked list.

Physical Implementation of the Hierarchical Order. Figure 5.14 shows the physical representation of the hierarchical sequence that results from the logical database design in Figure 5.13. The first component is PATIENT P1, followed by its two DOCTOR child occurrences, then ORDER O1 followed by its two MEDICATION child occurrences, and so on. As we pointed out in Chapter 3, this is a sequential file that will be very slow to update when new segments are added or existing ones deleted. An alternative is to use pointers to implement the structure, discussed next.

Forward Hierarchical Pointer Implementation of the Hierarchical Order. Figure 5.15 shows the linked-list implementation using **forward hierarchical pointers.** Notice that the hierarchical order is preserved by using forward (next) pointers to associate related segment occurrences. Each record now contains a pointer that relates it to the next one in the hierarchical sequence: The first PATIENT record contains a pointer that relates it to the initial DOCTOR; that DOCTOR occurrence contains a pointer to its twin DOCTOR. The last MEDICATION occurrence for the PATIENT points to the next PATIENT. This results in a physical structure that is much more responsive to updating and has the additional benefit of allowing random (hashed or indexed) access to root occurrences, a topic we cover later in the text.

Yet another option is to use a two-way list in which both forward and backward hierarchical pointers are used to implement the tree. As usual, use of such pointers facilitates the deletion of segment occurrences. We leave its implementation to you as one of the problems at the end of the chapter.

FIGURE 5.14   **Sequential Representation of the Hierarchical Sequence from Figure 5.13**

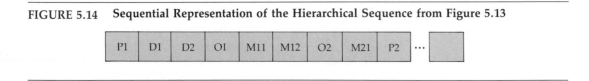

FIGURE 5.15   Forward Hierarchical Pointers Used with the Database in Figure 5.13

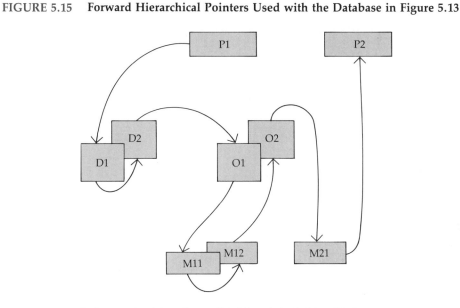

Each segment points to the one that follows it in the hierarchical sequence.

Physical Child/Twin Implementation of the Hierarchical Order. The final option is to use **physical child** and **twin pointers.** Here a pointer connects a parent occurrence to the first child occurrence of its different child segment types. This means that if a segment is the parent of four segment types, four first child pointers will be necessary. A second pointer type relates each segment to its next twin.

Figure 5.16 shows how this works. Now a patient occurrence points to its first DOCTOR child and to its first ORDER child. Similarly, each ORDER occurrence points to its initial MEDICATION child. None of the MEDICATION occurrences contain child pointers, because MEDICATION is not a parent. Each ORDER occurrence also has a pointer to the next ORDER (its **physical twin**). The last ORDER for a given PATIENT contains a null twin pointer.

Variations of this approach include the use of a physical last child pointer and backward physical twin pointers, both of which can facilitate retrieval performance. However, this will slow down insertion or deletion of segments because of the additional overhead necessary to maintain all the pointers. Again, we leave its implementation to you.

FIGURE 5.16   Physical First Child and Twin Pointers Used with the Database in Figure 5.13

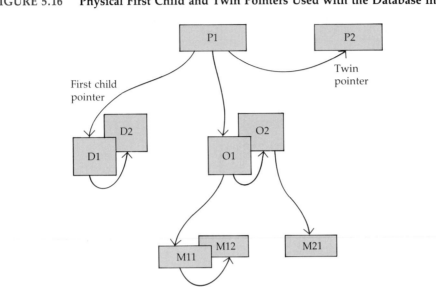

Each parent contains one or more child pointers, which connect it to the first child of each of its direct descendent segment types. Each child occurrence also contains a pointer to its next twin.

5.4 SUMMARY

This chapter completes our brief look at database design. In Chapter 4, we saw that database design begins with a sound conceptual design. Here we looked at how the DBA maps that design to the specific DBMS, a process dictated by the model used by the vendor of the package.

Mapping to the relational model is fairly easy. It consists of these steps:

1. Convert each entity into a table.
2. Map each attribute of the entity to a column for the table.
3. Identify the primary and foreign keys for each table.
4. Normalize the design.
5. Decide which deletion integrity rule should apply.
6. Determine on which columns to index.

The process of mapping to the network model is also relatively easy:

1. Map each entity to a record type.
2. Map each 1:M relationship to a set type.

3. Map each attribute to a field or data item.
4. Determine the primary and secondary keys.
5. Add additional sets to accommodate reporting needs.
6. Choose a sequence for each set type.
7. Add a "dummy" owner, if necessary.
8. Assign record types to areas, if necessary.

When mapping to the hierarchical model, substantial changes may be necessary due to nonhierarchical structures. By transforming such structures into two or more trees, the problem can be eliminated—but at the expense of redundancy. An alternative is to use logical pointers, an approach that eliminates the redundancy. Unfortunately, this approach is limited because it cannot accommodate more than two parent segment types for a given child. The steps we developed were:

1. Map each entity to a segment type.
2. Reduce any network structures to a collection of trees or to a logical relationship.
3. Choose the hierarchical order.
4. Map each attribute to a field and choose a category for each field.

The other topics we discussed were physical designs for each of the three models. The relational approach is the most nebulous, because ANSI has left its physical implementation to the individual vendors. Some of the techniques we looked at include clustering, partitioning, index optimization, and compressed indexing.

The CODASYL network model allows for embedded pointers or for arrays of pointers, both of which are used to implement 1:M relationships between an owner and the set of related member occurrences. We saw how both methods are implemented and examined the benefits of each.

The final section was devoted to the physical design choices available under IMS, IBM's hierarchical database manager. We saw that although the underlying structure is always a hierarchical ordering, there are three ways to implement it: physically; using hierarchical pointers; or using first child/twin pointers.

REVIEW QUESTIONS

1. Why does mapping to a relational model require that a primary key be identified?
2. When should indexes be considered for relational databases?
3. How difficult is it for end users to use relational indexes?
4. What do we call 1:M relationships with the network model?
5. Differentiate between a set type and a set occurrence.

6. When might it be necessary to add sets when the need to do so wasn't discovered during the conceptual design? Why isn't this a concern with the relational approach?

7. Describe the hierarchical equivalent of an owner and a member.

8. Explain the two methods for mapping a network structure to something that can be implemented using the hierarchical approach.

9. List and define the three kinds of hierarchical fields.

10. Explain why segments on the left side of a hierarchy are faster to access than those on the right side.

11. Explain when clustering and partitioning are useful.

12. Of what benefit is an owner pointer? What are its disadvantages?

13. Discuss the advantages and disadvantages of pointer arrays.

14. Define *hierarchical order* and *hierarchical sequence*. What is the difference between them?

15. Describe the three ways to implement the hierarchical sequence for a hierarchical database.

PROBLEMS

Use the following DSD for Problems 1 through 3:

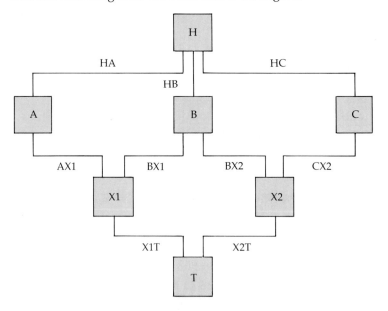

1. Assuming that all possible network pointers are used, how many pointers would each occurrence of B have? List them.

2. Assume there is one occurrence of H, 10 of A, 20 of B, and 25 of C. How many occurrences would there be of the set HA?

3. How many occurrences would there be of BX1?

4. Modify Figure 5.4 to allow for the relationship between a VENDOR and an INVOICE.

5. Assuming the set you added in Problem 5 was called HAS-SENT and the set is to be sorted by invoice number, show all of its occurrences as we did in Figure 5.6. Use the data from Figure 5.5.

6. Modify Figure 5.7 to include the new set. Assign ACME to RRN 3 and BYARS to RRN 6.

7. Assume we need to be able to produce a sequential report of all VENDORs by name. Modify your solution to Problem 4 to permit this.

8. Repeat your answer to Problem 6, but use a pointer array instead. (An array would be carried within each VENDOR occurrence.)

9. Assume that we need the second ACME INVOICE. Use your answer to Problem 6 to show each necessary I/O.

10. Do the same as in Problem 9, but use the pointer array solution you developed for Problem 8.

Use the following DSD for Problems 11 through 17:

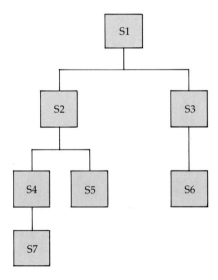

11. Give the hierarchical order.

12. Reverse the subtrees for which S2 and S3 are the parent—that is, S2 will be to the right of S3. Move all children as needed.

13. Give the hierarchical order resulting from Problem 12.

14. Explain when the design of Problem 13 is preferred to that of Problem 11.

15. Assume that segment types S5 and S7 are no longer needed for the original database. The following occurrence diagram shows the hierarchical sequence for one root:

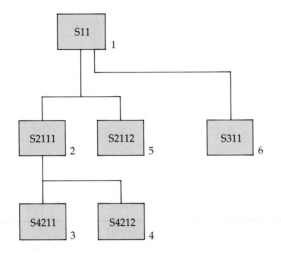

Show the sequential form of the physical implementation of the hierarchical sequence.

16. Show the forward hierarchical pointer implementation of Problem 15.

17. Repeat your answer to Problem 16 using physical child and twin pointers.

18. Modify Figure 5.15 to include backward hierarchical pointers.

19. Modify Figure 5.16 to show (just) backward twin and last child pointers.

P A R T

III

The Relational Model

Part III focuses on the most recent and popular of the three data models: the relational model. Following publication of a paper by an IBM employee, Dr. E. F. Codd, many researchers began to look for ways to implement his promising approach. Initial implementation efforts focused on the mathematical techniques of relational algebra and calculus. Later, IBM developed a graphical approach called *Query-By-Example* (QBE). Chapter 6 introduces the general characteristics of the relational model. Then it explores the three approaches to data manipulation.

During the 1970s, IBM began a project to bring Codd's ideas to the marketplace through a language first called Structured English Query Language (SEQUEL), then simply Structured Query Language (SQL). IBM currently markets four DBMSs that use this language: SQL/DS for its mid-size mainframe customers, DB2 for its large mainframe customers, SQL/400 for its AS/400 minicomputer line, and Data Manager, which runs under OS/2 Extended Edition, for its microcomputer customers. SQL has also been adopted by ANSI as the standard relational DBMS language. Many other companies now market DBMS packages that also contain SQL, including ORACLE, Informix, and Relational Technology, Inc.

IBM's DB2 is the most dominant of the SQL implementations. Chapter 7 describes how to define relations (tables) and manipulate them using an interactive form of DB2. Even though DB2 is a proprietary IBM product, because it uses SQL, almost all of the chapter's contents apply to the other SQL-based products.

Chapter 8 examines how to embed SQL calls into a COBOL host program running under DB2. It also looks at how Informix-4GL integrates SQL into its language.

The fourth episode in our continuing case, which follows Chapter 8, gives a complete example of a COBOL program that contains embedded SQL calls.

6

An Introduction to the Relational Model

Concepts and Manipulation via Relational Algebra and Calculus and Query-By-Example

This chapter reconsiders the Suburban Hospital case introduced in Chapter 2. It begins our in-depth study of the relational approach to data modeling and expands the discussion in Chapters 2 and 3.

At the conclusion of this chapter, you will be able to:

- State the benefits of the relational approach.
- Describe the four types of relational languages.
- Differentiate between a base table and a virtual table.
- Discuss the two relational assertions.
- List the steps for mapping the conceptual database design to the logical relational model.
- Manipulate a relational database by means of relational algebra.
- Use Query-By-Example (QBE) to access, add to, and modify tables.

6.1   FEATURES OF THE RELATIONAL MODEL

The network and hierarchical models rely heavily on physical characteristics of the stored data. Network implementations require users to know about indexes, set names, owners, members, and so on. Hierarchical users must contend with access methods, child/parent relationships, secondary indexes, and so forth. In contrast to both, the relational approach is almost devoid of physical data considerations. Furthermore, the nonrelational approaches require that end users be aware of the underlying data structures and be capable of record-oriented file searching.

To end users of the relational approach, it appears that all data is stored in two-dimensional *tables,* called *relations* or *flat files.* The rows, also called *tuples,* represent records, while the columns, also called *attributes,* represent the fields. Common columns relate tables to one another. In other words, relationships are represented by foreign keys in the dependent (child) tables.

In reality, the data may not be stored as two-dimensional tables. But, in order for the DBMS to be considered relational, it must appear to the users that all data is represented as tables. Characteristics of this relational approach include:

- Data independence.
- Flexibility.
- Ease of use by end users and IS personnel.
- File rather than record operators.
- Security.
- **Symmetry of access,** meaning that the ease with which queries are constructed is not a function of the underlying data structure or of the record connection facilities.

The data independence comes from the fact that users need not have information about items such as which are the primary and/or secondary keys, what are the allowable search paths, which tables are origins and which are destinations of 1:M relationships, where the tables are stored, and so on. Furthermore, columns can be added or deleted, their sequences changed, or column specifications altered, all with minimal effect on existing users.

Both the network and hierarchical models are based on a rigid data structure that relates record occurrences in a tightly coupled manner, in which relationships are usually implemented using pointers—a methodology called **pointer based.** With this approach, new relationships can't be accommodated without redefining the schema and then reloading the database.

Whereas the network and hierarchical models store both pointers and values, the relational approach uses only values; thus, it is **value based.** Also, the network and hierarchical models are **static** in that relationships must be predefined. However, the relationships in the relational approach aren't defined until a query is made; it is a **dynamic** approach offering maximum query flexibility. Because with the relational approach relationships are determined when a query is made, almost any relationship can be accommodated as long as there are common connection columns in the various tables.

All of the above means that the relational model is more forgiving of some kinds of conceptual database design errors when those errors are related to missing relationships. With the network or hierarchical model, in contrast, such design errors would necessitate defining a new schema, unloading the database to a tape, and reloading the data according to the new schema. Such tasks are often error prone and time-consuming and can lead to downtime for applications that depend on the database. This means that the DBA spends a considerable amount of time ensuring that all relationships are correctly identified during the conceptual design phase, which could reduce the amount of time spent properly defining the entities and the domains of their attributes.

As we saw in Chapter 3, if the entities are defined to meet the business rules, and if the attributes are assigned to the entities in accordance with normalization rules, the resulting database will be able to support the organization. With the relational approach, the DBA can allocate more time to entities and domains and less time to determining all the relationships among the entities.

By introducing a high degree of data independence, coupled with flexibility and tabular representation of data, users of the relational approach have a much easier time expressing their data needs than do those using either the network or hierarchical approach.

Instead of forcing users to understand a *record-oriented procedural approach,* in which steps such as entering the search criteria, reading a record, testing for end of file, testing for the record that satisfies the search criteria, testing for error codes, printing if the record matches the search criteria, reading the next record, and so on, are used, the user in the relational approach employs a *set-oriented, nonprocedural* syntax to state *what* is needed, not *how* to retrieve it. It is unfortunate that the word *set* is also used in the network model, but with a different meaning. That model calls a 1:M relationship between two entities a *set type.* Here, the word *set* refers to a collection of rows (records) from a table (file).

When implemented by means of a commercial package, the relational approach also has many security features. Typical of these are user views (external databases, or subschemas), passwords, tuple (row or record) locking, table (file) locking, and backup/recovery facilities. Finally, the relational approach is mostly impervious to the relationship of the request for data, the structure of the tables from which the data is extracted, and the connection columns that relate the tables to one another. In CODASYL and hierarchical database implementations, searches are easiest to complete if the requests begin at a specific origin occurrence and then move down to the associated destination occurrences. Queries that begin at a destination and then flow upward or across from one record type to another are more difficult to state and implement. Because all data is represented as values with the relational approach, there is no "best" query construct, at least from the user's perspective. "Behind the scenes," the DBA might decide to implement an index or the DBMS may optimize a particular path, depending on the query.

Most of the relational terminology can be traced to a series of papers written by Dr. E. F. Codd during the early 1970s, when he first applied the concepts of set theory and logic to databases. The following section looks at his contributions to this model and also at some early attempts to develop relational database management systems (RDBMSs).

6.2   AN HISTORICAL PERSPECTIVE

In 1970, Dr. Edgar F. Codd, an IBM employee, published a paper titled "A Relational Model of Data for Large Shared Data Banks." In that paper, he discussed several ideas. First, he described the advantages of data independence and symmetry of access and how the relational approach supplies both of these qualities. Next, he described two relational approaches: the relational calculus and the relational algebra. Finally, he discussed the problems associated with redundancy, which laid the groundwork for his work on normalization.

Let's look first at the two data manipulation languages proposed by Codd, relational calculus and algebra, then at two other relational approaches: transform oriented and graphics oriented.

Relational Calculus Implementations

Relational calculus is a nonprocedural collection of operators that can be used by any user to simply state what data is desired without having to worry about how to implement the access strategy; this is done by the RDBMS. Based on the mathematical theory of predicate calculus and first applied to relational databases by Codd in 1971, two specific implementation strategies have evolved: tuple and domain calculus.

Tuple calculus was first proposed by Codd and formed the theoretical basis for his proposed language, ALPHA. Other early 1970s packages included QUEL (QUEry Language, University of California, 1975) and RIL (Representation Independent Language, IBM, 1973). RIL never achieved popularity, but QUEL became the basis for INGRES (INteractive Graphics and REtrieval System), a DBMS that is still popular today and marketed by Relational Technology, Inc. (RTI).

Domain calculus utilizes a concept whereby a variable is allowed to take on values over the range of its domain. IBM's Query-By-Example, discussed later in the chapter, illustrates a graphical implementation of domain calculus.

Relational Algebra Implementations

The **relational algebra approach** is more procedural than the calculus approach. It requires users to provide a series of relational algebra operators, each of which results in a new relation, or table. Some of the operators combine tables, while others result in subsets of the original tables, both horizontally and vertically.

Languages based on this approach have been developed at IBM (IS/1, 1972), MIT (MACAIMS, 1970), and General Motors (Relational Data Management System, 1972). Currently, there are no RDBMSs completely based on the relational algebra approach. However, IBM's Structured Query Language (SQL) uses a method of data manipulation that is similar, called a mapping or transform-oriented approach.

Transform-Oriented Implementations

Transform-oriented, or **mapping-oriented, languages** are less procedural than those based on relational algebra and thus are easier to use by programmers and especially by end users. They are just as powerful as the relational calculus and algebra-based languages, but they don't require mathematical notation or understanding and they are set oriented, providing for insertion, deletion, updating, and reporting of data.

With a transform-oriented language, a user inputs a request for some desired output by means of a well-defined structure. Then the RDBMS transforms those input statements into the desired output.

Two early transform-oriented languages were SQUARE (Specifying Queries As Relational Expressions, R. F. Boyce, 1975) and SEQUEL (Structured English Query Language, IBM, 1974). SEQUEL later became the foundation of IBM's System R, a complex language that provided for multiuser support, support for environments having large volumes of transactions, logging, authorizations, views, and data integrity enforcement. This package also provided for both host-language and end user usage. Eventually, it was produced as a viable product but renamed Structured Query Language/Data System, or SQL/DS (still pronounced *Sequel*) in 1980. SQL was first released for DOS/VSE and VM/CMS in April 1982, and a similar package, DB2 (Database 2), was released in 1983 for large IS departments using MVS. In 1988, IBM also released a microcomputer version called the Database Manager, which runs under its OS/2 Extended Edition operating system. Finally, in 1988, IBM announced SQL/400, which runs on its AS/400 minicomputer.

Graphics-Oriented Implementations

The final category of data manipulation languages is the **graphics-oriented languages,** with which end users use visual display terminals (VDTs) or hard-copy terminals to interactively enter commands into tabular representations of the relations. The best example of such a language is IBM's QBE (Query-By-Example,

1980), which is an implementation of domain calculus. To use QBE to retrieve data from a relation, the user is presented with a table with the column names as headings and a table body consisting of a series of blank rows. By entering appropriate QBE commands below the desired columns, the user is presented with the records that match the request.

6.3   TERMINOLOGY AND CONCEPTS

Figure 6.1 shows two relations, PATIENT and ORDER, each expressed first structurally and then as an occurrence. We will use the two relations as a basis for a relational review.

FIGURE 6.1   Two Ways to Depict Relations: Conceptually and as an Occurrence

(a) A relation named PATIENT

PATIENT (<u>PATNUM</u>, PATFIRST, PATLAST, PATLOC, PATINSCODE)
↑
└──── A relation (table) named PATIENT

Attributes (columns)

PATNUM	PATFIRST	PATLAST	PATLOC	PATINSCODE
100	JOHN	JONES	1A-101	10
110	MARY	ROBERTS	1B-123	10
103	EDGAR	THOMAS	2A-231	10
102	GORDON	GORDON	2A-231	12

Tuples (rows)

↑
└────An occurrence of the PATIENT relation

(b) A relation named ORDER

ORDER (<u>ORDERNO</u>, PATNUM, DRUGCODE, AMOUNT)
↑
Conceptual relation ─┘
named ORDER

ORDERNO	PATNUM	DRUGCODE	AMOUNT
1	100	TAG	50mg
2	100	ASP	500mg
10	103	TAG	100mg

Occurrence of the ORDER relation

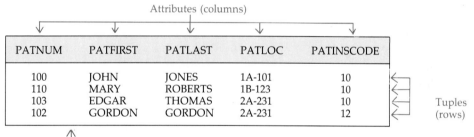

The figure shows two relations, each presented two ways: once as a conceptual table, then as a table occurrence.

Relations

A **relation** can be formally defined as a series of rows, each taking its first element from column 1's domain, its second from column 2's domain, and so on. For our purposes, a more appropriate definition is a file that consists of a series of unique records, each having the same number and type of fields.

Relations can be described using the familiar notation:

NAME(<u>PRIMARYKEYCOLUMN,</u> COL2, COL3, . . . ,COLn)

Each relation has one or more columns, called the **primary key,** that uniquely identifies row occurrences of that relation; that is, no two rows can ever have the same value for the primary key. When there is more than one such key, each is identified as a **candidate key.** The primary key is underlined and can consist of either a single column, in which case it is called an **atomic key,** or two or more columns, where it is known as a **composite key.** Both of the relations in Figure 6.1 have atomic keys. The key for PATIENT is PATNUM, because it is impossible for two PATIENTs to have the same code. If the LOCATION column included the bed number it would be a candidate key, because no two PATIENTs can have the same LOCATION (NURSING__UNIT + ROOM + BED).

Occurrences of Relations

An occurrence of a relation is represented in a tabular form with columns representing fields and rows depicting the records. If a column's value is unknown, recall that we assign the value NULL to it.

The number of rows in the table's occurrence defines its *cardinality,* while the number of columns associated with each row defines its **degree,** or **arity.** Notice that the cardinality of a relation changes over time, while its degree does not, and that this definition of cardinality differs from the one we discussed in Chapter 2. When a relation has a single column, it is said to be of degree one, or a **unary** relation. If a table is of degree two, we sometimes say it is a **binary** relation, while the general relation is often referred to as an **n-ary** relation.

Base and View Tables

Tables like those in Figure 6.1 may also be called **base tables, real tables,** or **stored tables,** meaning that:

- They have names.
- They actually exist.
- They are almost always stored on a disk drive.

When any of the four kinds of relational languages are used, tables called **derived tables, views,** or **virtual tables** may also result. These are tables that appear to exist but aren't stored as such. While to the end user they appear to be base tables, they are not actually stored on a disk as two-dimensional tables. Instead, the rows that are presented to the user when a query of a view is requested are derived from other (base) tables.

Relational Rules

There are several general features of relations:

- Each table must have one or more candidate keys.
- The table's row ordering is immaterial.
- The column ordering is immaterial.
- There can be no repeating columns, either atomic or composite.

In keeping with the premise that the relational approach is easier to understand, let's substitute the more "friendly" term, *table*, for *relation*.

First, each table must have a primary key that uniquely identifies the table's rows. If there are several candidate keys, one must be selected as the primary key. As a result, no two rows can be identical.

Next, it makes no difference in what order the rows are stored or in which sequence the columns are defined. Furthermore, the ordering of the rows and columns can be changed at any time. Finally, every row must have the same number of columns; thus, the term *flat file* is often used to describe relations.

6.4 RELATIONAL ASSERTIONS

To help ensure the integrity of data stored in relations, two **assertions**—constraints or rules that are applicable to a data model—have been developed. They are the referential integrity and primary key assertions.

Referential Integrity Assertions

In Chapter 2, we discussed the three kinds of **referential integrity assertions:** insertion, modification, and deletion. Consider the two tables in Figure 6.1. ORDER.PATNUM is a foreign key. Application of the foreign-key assertion would mean that the ORDER.PATNUM values can either be NULL or, if present, must match some PATIENT.PATNUM value. In addition, we should state which of the three deletion rules—cascade, set to NULL, or restriction—to apply when a PATIENT is deleted. Finally, there should be a statement about what action to take for ORDER.PATNUM values if a PATIENT.PATNUM value changes and that a patient has some associated orders.

Primary Key Assertions

The **primary key assertion,** sometimes called the **entity integrity assertion,** states that no component of the primary key can be null. Had we chosen LOCATION as the PATIENT key, and if LOCATION consisted of NURSING__UNIT + ROOM + BED, none of the three components would ever be permitted to be null.

6.5   RELATIONAL ALGEBRA

Relational algebra is a *procedural* methodology, meaning that users must know not only *which* data is desired but *how* to retrieve it. Most of the high-level languages used in IS departments are of the same family; for example, COBOL, FORTRAN, BASIC, and PL/1 are all procedural languages. In contrast, relational calculus is descriptive, or *nonprocedural,* meaning that the user need only describe what he or she desires and the language will determine how to retrieve the information.

Relational algebra works with entire tables at a time (called *high-level processing*) rather than with the more familiar "record-at-a-time" (low-level) processing that COBOL and most other high-level languages perform.

Figure 6.2 shows two groups of algebraic operators. Group I consists of special relational operators, while Group II consists of the familiar set operators.

In the rest of this section, we will discuss and apply these operators in the context of the Suburban Hospital example introduced in Chapter 2. Let's look at some table occurrences from that example.

The tables in Figure 6.3 provide some additional information about the hospital. The PATIENT table is of degree four. The semantics concerning the columns should be obvious except for DCODE and DID. DCODE represents the code associated with that patient's diagnosis, while DID is the patient's doctor identification.

Recall that we must be able to relate tables to one another. To relate patients to their physicians, we must carry a doctor identifier (DID) in the PATIENT table. This column is the connection column for the 1:M relationship between DOCTOR and PATIENT. Alternatively, it can be thought of as a foreign key.

The next table, DIAGNOSIS, carries the information about the various diagnoses that can be assigned to a patient. The first column is the code and the second a description.

The MEDICATION table carries columns for medication code, name, and cost. The meanings of the columns in DOCTOR, a binary table, are obvious.

The DOSAGE table contains a row for every patient-drug-time combination. Notice that patient 174 receives Keflin at 0200 and again at 1000. You might wonder why we didn't construct this table with the columns PID, MID, DOSAGE, TIME__1, TIME__2, . . ., TIME__24. However, the repeating field is prohibited by the atomic field rule we discussed earlier.

FIGURE 6.2   **Summary of the Relational Algebra Operators**

Group I

SELECT SELECT extracts rows from a table that match specified search criteria. Sometimes called **RESTRICT.**

PROJECT PROJECT reduces the number of columns in a table. It is particularly useful when displaying output and for making tables union-compatible.

JOIN JOIN creates a new table that has all the columns of both the first and second tables. Usually we use a natural join, which eliminates one of the joining columns from the result. The tables are joined (matched) over a common column called the *joining column*. Typically, the join is based on an equality operator. We use this operator when we need to combine tables.

Group II

UNION UNION combines two tables into a third one. The resulting table has all the rows that were in either the first or the second table.
   The two tables must be *union-compatible,* which means:
1. Both tables must be of the same degree.
2. The corresponding columns from both tables come from the same respective domains.

INTERSECTION INTERSECTION combines two union-compatible tables into a new one consisting of those rows that were in both the first and second tables.

DIFFERENCE DIFFERENCE is defined on two union-compatible tables and produces a third table that contains all the rows that were in the first table but **not** in the second.

PRODUCT With PRODUCT, every row of the first table is concatenated with each row in the second table.

The ROOM table has only two columns: room number and patient number. Notice that there is no one in room 110, so the special value NULL is used. This means that the exact value of the column is unknown. It should not be confused with blanks or zeros, as it designates that the value is truly not known.

The next two tables, CRITICAL__CONDITION and SERIOUS__CONDI-TION, contain patient numbers for those patients having certain conditions. The last table shows the patients who are diagnosed as having heart ailments.

The SELECT Operator

The SELECT, or RESTRICTION, operator is used to extract a horizontal subset of rows from a table. It retrieves those rows whose column values match criteria specified as part of the operator syntax. This—and all—operators can create a temporary query table or send the output directly to the default display device (a VDT or printer).

The relational model is based on set theory and possesses a quality known as *closure.* One of the borrowed-set theory rules is that there can be no duplicate rows. **Closure** means that the application of a relational operator on a relation

---

FIGURE 6.3   Definition and Occurrence of the Tables from the Suburban Hospital Minicase in Chapter 2

PATIENT (<u>PID</u>, PNAME, DCODE, DID)

PATIENT

PID	PNAME	DCODE	DID
174	ADAMS	ANG	10
103	COX	ANG	10
49	DAVIS	CF	12

DIAGNOSIS (<u>DCODE</u>, DIAGNOSIS)

DIAGNOSIS

DCODE	DIAGNOSIS
ANG	Angina
CF	Compound Fracture
PNM	Pneumonia

MEDICATION (<u>MID</u>, MNAME, MCOST)

MEDICATION

MID	MNAME	MCOST
KEF	KEFLIN	2.00
TAG	TAGAMET	3.00
PCN	PENICILLIN	.50
VAL	VALIUM	.50
VIB	VIBRAMYCIN	1.50

DOCTOR (<u>DID</u>, DNAME)

DOCTOR

DID	DNAME
10	STARZEL
12	LONG
13	ROBERTS

FIGURE 6.3   **(concluded)**

DOSAGE (<u>PID</u>, <u>MID</u>, <u>TIME</u>, DOSAGE)

DOSAGE

PID	MID	TIME	DOSAGE
174	KEF	0200	100mg
174	KEF	1000	100mg
103	PCN	0200	50mg
103	VAL	0300	20mg
103	VIB	0300	50mg
103	VIB	1000	50mg
49	PCN	0200	50mg
49	PCN	0600	50mg
49	PCN	1000	50mg
49	TAG	1500	100mg

ROOM (<u>RNO</u>, <u>PID</u>)

ROOM

RNO	PID
102	174
102	103
104	49
110	NULL

CRITICAL_CONDITION (<u>PID</u>)   SERIOUS_CONDITION (<u>PID</u>)

CRITICAL_CONDITION   SERIOUS_CONDITION

PID
174

PID
103

HEART_ILLNESS (<u>PID</u>)

HEART_ILLNESS

PID
174
103

yields another relation; that is, there can never be duplicate rows in a table. Therefore, the result of a SELECT will always be a relation without duplicate rows. The SELECT syntax we will use is as follows:

> *Format 1.* Table__name__2 = Table__name__1 WHERE condition
>
> *Format 2.* Table__name__1 WHERE condition

Format 1 is used to create a query table, while Format 2 is used to send the results directly to a display device. With both formats, only those rows that meet the stated condition are retrieved.

The condition is of the form:

$$\text{Column\_\_name} \left\{ \begin{array}{c} < \\ > \\ = \\ <= \\ >= \\ \langle\rangle \end{array} \right\} \text{Value}$$

Value is usually a constant, but it can include the Boolean operators AND, OR, and NOT, as well as calculations.

Problem 1. What is the result of ROOM WHERE RNO = 102?

In this problem, the search criterion is RNO = 102, and the table is ROOM. Figure 6.4 shows the result.

FIGURE 6.4   Satisfying the Algebraic Statement ROOM WHERE RNO = 102

ROOM

RNO	PID
102	174
102	103
104	49
110	NULL

←—— Two rows match the search criterion RNO = 102

Therefore, the result will be:

RNO	PID
102	174
102	103

FIGURE 6.5   **Satisfying the Statement T1 = DOSAGE WHERE TIME = 0200 OR TIME = 0300**

DOSAGE

PID	MID	TIME	DOSAGE
174	KEF	0200	100mg
174	KEF	1000	100mg
103	PCN	0200	50mg
103	VAL	0300	20mg
103	VIB	0300	50mg
103	VIB	1000	50mg
49	PCN	0200	50mg
49	PCN	0600	50mg
49	PCN	1000	50mg
49	TAG	1500	100mg

Rows that match
TIME = 0200 or 0300

T1

PID	MID	TIME	DOSAGE
174	KEF	0200	100mg
103	PCN	0200	50mg
103	VAL	0300	20mg
103	VIB	0300	50mg
49	PCN	0200	50mg

Solution. We have just answered the query "What are the patient numbers for the patients in room number 102?" The operator matched the search criterion (RNO = 102) against the RNO values in the table. Only two matching rows were found.

The next problem shows how we can use Boolean operators.

Problem 2. **What is the result of T1 = DOSAGE WHERE TIME = 0200 OR TIME = 0300?**

Solution. This will result in the query table T1 shown in Figure 6.5, which has all the columns of the DOSAGE table but contains only those rows that match the time criteria of 0200 or 0300.

Problem 3. **Which patients receive Keflin (code KEF) at 0200 hours?**

Solution. DOSAGE WHERE MID = "KEF" AND TIME = 0200
    This time we are given a query and must develop the algebra to respond to it. The solution says to use the DOSAGE table and display only those rows

---

FIGURE 6.6   **The Result of DOSAGE WHERE MID = "KEF" AND TIME = 0200**

DOSAGE

PID	MID	TIME	DOSAGE
174	KEF	0200	100mg
174	KEF	1000	100mg
103	PCN	0200	50mg
103	VAL	0300	20mg
103	VIB	0300	50mg
103	VIB	1000	50mg
49	PCN	0200	50mg
49	PCN	0600	50mg
49	PCN	1000	50mg
49	TAG	1500	100mg

⟵——— The only row having TIME = 0200 and MID = "KEF"

Therefore, the result is:

PID	MID	TIME	DOSAGE
174	KEF	0200	100mg

---

whose MID values match KEF and whose TIME column equals 0200. The result of the query is shown in Figure 6.6.

The PROJECT Operator

The PROJECT operator creates vertical subsets (columns) of tables. We will use the following syntax:

> *Format 1.* Table__name__2 = Table__name__1 [column__1,
> column__2, . . . , column__n]
> *Format 2.* Table__name__1 [column__1, column__2, . . . ,column__n]

The names inside the square brackets are the columns to be carried in the query table (Format 1) or to be shown to the user (Format 2).

Problem 4. **What is the result of ROOM [RNO]?**

Solution. Here we are requesting that the room numbers be shown on the default display device. Figure 6.7 shows the result.

Due to the closure characteristic, the PROJECT operator cannot return duplicate rows. Thus, each room number is shown once, even though room number

FIGURE 6.7   Illustration of the PROJECT Operator for the Statement ROOM [RNO]

Extract RNO column only

ROOM

RNO	PID
102	174
102	103
104	49
110	NULL

The results are as follows:

RNO
102
104
110

102 was in the original table twice. We should point out that IBM's SQL products sometimes violate this rule, resulting in duplicate rows being returned, much to the consternation of relational purists such as Dr. Codd.

Recall that another relational rule is that column ordering is immaterial. Another use for PROJECT is to alter the sequence of the columns in the table to suit a given user's needs.

Problem 5. **Show the result of T2 = DOSAGE [MID,PID].**

Solution. This creates a new table, T2, with all the original rows but only two columns. Notice that the column order differs from that of the base table:

T2

MID	PID
KEF	174
PCN	103
VAL	103
VIB	103
PCN	49
TAG	49

The query we answered was "What are the patient numbers and medication codes for those patients receiving a medication?"

Problem 6. **What are the patient numbers of those patients assigned to a room?**

Solution. T3 = ROOM [PID]

This results in a new table, T3, with the following rows:

T3

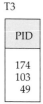

The JOIN Operator

Consider the two tables ROOM and PATIENT. If you were asked "What are the names of the patients in each room?" how would you manipulate the two tables to answer the request? Hopefully, you would answer that you would find the first patient number in ROOM, then match it against the PATIENT table to determine that patient's name. Then each subsequent ROOM.PID would be matched against PATIENT.PID until all ROOM.PID values had been matched. This matching is the chief characteristic of the JOIN operator.

JOIN combines two tables into a third one by matching values for a common column, called the **joining column.** While the joining columns need not have the same name in both tables, they must come from the same domain. The rows in the new table will consist of the rows extracted from the first table concatenated with every row of the second table, where there was a match on the joining column.

Types of Joins. We will discuss four kinds of joins:

- Natural
- Equi
- Theta
- Outer

When the new table contains all the columns from the first table plus all the columns from the second but does not redundantly carry the joining column, the result is called a **natural join.** The resulting table will therefore be of degree m + n − 1. While this will be our usual assumption, at times we will carry the joining column twice.

Usually, the joining condition will be an equality, which results in an **equijoin.** Sometimes the condition will be an inequality, resulting in a **theta join.** Finally, we can also have an **outer join,** in which every row from the first table is part of the result. When there is no match for the joining condition in the second table, the column values in the result that come from the second table are set to NULL.

The general JOIN syntax we will use is:

Format 1. Table__name__3 = Table__name__1 JOIN (joining condition) Table__name__2
Format 2. Table__name__1 JOIN (joining condition) Table__name__2

The JOIN operator is **commutative,** meaning that A JOIN B is the same as B JOIN A. This is important, because it means that we need not worry about the sequence of table names in the joining operation.

Natural Joins and Equijoins.

Problem 7. What results from ROOM JOIN (ROOM.PID = PATIENT.PID) PATIENT?

Joining columns

Assume a natural join.

Solution. The problem results in a natural equijoin (because of the =). Figure 6.8 shows how the operator would proceed and the result.

The number of columns in the resulting table is 5, the sum of the degrees of PATIENT and ROOM, minus 1. The join has matched each patient number from the ROOM table with the PATIENT.PID values.

Problem 8. Show the results of T4 = MEDICATION JOIN (MID = MID) DOSAGE.

Solution. We did not qualify the joining column names in this example. The assumption is that the first column comes from table 1, while the second column belongs to table 2.

The operation will match the medication code for every row of MEDICATION with every DOSAGE row having the same medication code. Figure 6.9 shows how the operator would proceed. Since KEF in MEDICATION matched two DOSAGE rows, T4 contains two rows with an MID value of KEF. Similarly, there were four matches for PCN.

You should consider the JOIN operator whenever you need to add information to a table. For example, if we were asked for a report showing the patient numbers and names as well as their physicians' numbers and names, we might

FIGURE 6.8   **Example of a Natural Equijoin**

The two tables to be JOINed are:

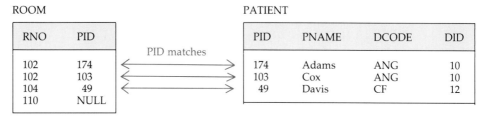

ROOM

RNO	PID
102	174
102	103
104	49
110	NULL

PID matches

PATIENT

PID	PNAME	DCODE	DID
174	Adams	ANG	10
103	Cox	ANG	10
49	Davis	CF	12

The result will contain all the ROOM columns plus all the PATIENT columns. The rows will be just the matches from above:

RNO	PID	PNAME	DCODE	DID
102	174	Adams	ANG	10
102	103	Cox	ANG	10
104	49	Davis	CF	12

The duplicate (PID) column is carried only once. The query was ROOM JOIN (ROOM.PID = PATIENT. PID) PATIENT.

conclude that such a report is impossible to produce because the physician name is not in the PATIENT table and there is no patient information in the DOCTOR table. However, by joining the two tables over DID, we can add the missing data by creating the new table that will contain all the columns from PATIENT plus all the columns from DOCTOR.

Problem 9. **Give the number, name, diagnosis code, and doctor identification code for those patients in critical condition.**

Solution. To answer this query, we join CRITICAL__CONDITION and PA-TIENT. This is necessary because no single table has all the required data. The joining column has to be PID, since it is the common column. Our solution is CRITICAL__CONDITION JOIN (PID = PID) PATIENT. The operator would proceed as shown in Figure 6.10.

The result would be the same if we reversed the names of the tables to be joined; that is, PATIENT JOIN (PID = PID) CRITICAL__CONDITION would give the same result.

FIGURE 6.9   **Results of the Relational Algebra Statement T4 = MEDICATION JOIN (MID = MID) DOSAGE**

MEDICATION

MID	MNAME	MCOST
KEF	Keflin	2.00
TAG	Tagamet	3.00
PCN	Penicillin	.50
VAL	Valium	.50
VIB	Vibramycin	1.50

There are two KEF matches

DOSAGE

PID	MID	TIME	DOSAGE
174	KEF	0200	100mg
174	KEF	1000	100mg
103	PCN	0200	50mg
103	VAL	0300	20mg
103	VIB	0300	50mg
103	VIB	1000	50mg
49	PCN	0200	50mg
49	PCN	0600	50mg
49	PCN	1000	50mg
49	TAG	1500	100mg

There are four PCN matches

The above tables show how two of the five MEDICATION.MID values are matched against the DOSAGE.MID values. The complete result follows.

T4

MID	MNAME	MCOST	PID	TIME	DOSAGE
KEF	Keflin	2.00	174	0200	100mg
KEF	Keflin	2.00	174	1000	100mg
TAG	Tagamet	3.00	49	1500	100mg
PCN	Penicillin	.50	103	0200	50mg
PCN	Penicillin	.50	49	0200	50mg
PCN	Penicillin	.50	49	0600	50mg
PCN	Penicillin	.50	49	1000	50mg
VAL	Valium	.50	103	0300	20mg
VIB	Vibramycin	1.50	103	0300	50mg
VIB	Vibramycin	1.50	103	1000	50mg

FIGURE 6.10   **Results from Coding CRITICAL_CONDITION JOIN (PID = PID) PATIENT**

CRITICAL_CONDITION

PID
174

PATIENT

PID	PNAME	DCODE	DID
174	Adams	ANG	10
103	Cox	ANG	10
49	Davis	CF	12

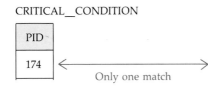

Only one match

Therefore, the resulting table will be:

PID	PNAME	DCODE	DID
174	Adams	ANG	10

Theta Joins. While any nonequality join condition would qualify as a theta join, consider this format:

X JOIN (X.ATTRIB > Y.ATTRIB) Y

This will display a table constructed of all the rows from X concatenated with all the rows from Y, but only if the value of ATTRIB in X is greater than the corresponding value of ATTRIB in Y.

To show an example, we need to modify two tables: MEDICATION and DOSAGE. Assume that MEDICATION and DOSAGE are now defined this way:

MEDICATION (<u>MID</u>, MNAME, MCOST, ONHAND)

DOSAGE (<u>PID</u>, <u>MID</u>, <u>TIME</u>, DOSAGE, UNITS)

The ONHAND column stores the on-hand amount of medications, while UNITS represents the quantity of the medication to dispense to a patient.

Now assume we need to join DOSAGE and MEDICATION, but in the result we want only those rows in which patients receive a number of units greater than 2 percent of the total units on hand for that medication. The command is:

DOSAGE JOIN (DOSAGE.UNITS > .02 * MEDICATION.ONHAND) MEDICATION

Outer Joins. The final join type is the outer join. The only difference between a natural join and an outer join is in how nonmatching rows are handled. Instead of leaving them out, they are included in the result, but all column values for the nonmatching table are set to NULL. For example, if we used an outer join for PATIENT JOIN (DID = DID) DOCTOR, the result would be:

PID	PNAME	DCODE	DID	DNAME
174	Adams	ANG	10	Starzel
103	Cox	ANG	10	Starzel
49	Davis	CF	12	Long
NULL	NULL	NULL	13	Roberts

←— 13 didn't match, so set column values from PATIENT table to NULL

The UNION Operator

The UNION operator combines two union-compatible tables and creates a new one consisting of rows that were in *either* the first table *or* the second table. *Union-compatible* means that:

- Each table is of the same degree.
- Each corresponding column comes from the same domain.

We will use the following syntax:

> *Format 1.* Table__name__3 = Table__name__1 UNION
> Table__name__2
> *Format 2.* Table__name__1 UNION Table__name__2

The operator is commutative.

Problem 10. Show the result of CRITICAL__CONDITION UNION SERIOUS__CONDITION.

Solution. The result, shown in Figure 6.11, is the list of patient numbers of those patients who are in critical or serious condition. Let's check for union compatibility.

CRITICAL__CONDITION has one column, as does SERIOUS__CONDITION. The single column in both tables comes from the same domain. Therefore, the tables are union-compatible and the operation is legitimate.

Problem 11. Which patients are either in critical condition or are in the hospital for a heart ailment?

Solution. There are two keys that lead us to use the UNION operator: use of the word *or* and the necessity to search two tables. Take the UNION of CRITICAL__CARE and HEART__ILLNESS, like this:

CRITICAL__CARE UNION HEART__ILLNESS.

FIGURE 6.11   Result of CRITICAL__CONDITION UNION SERIOUS__CONDITION

CRITICAL__CONDITION   SERIOUS__CONDITION

The result will contain all the rows from *either* CRITICAL__CONDITION *or* SERIOUS__CONDITION:

PID
174
103

FIGURE 6.12   Execution of CRITICAL__CONDITION UNION HEART__ILLNESS

CRITICAL__CONDITION   HEART__ILLNESS

The result will again be all the rows from both tables:

PID
174
103

The two input tables and the result are shown in Figure 6.12. Despite the fact that 174 appears in both tables, the closure rule precludes there being duplicate rows, so 174 appears in the resulting table just once.

The UNION operator can also be used to add new rows to an existing table. To add a new row, 15 Kim, to the DOCTOR table, the following two steps are necessary.

First, we must create a table, TEMPDOC, containing only the single row to be added, as follows:

TEMPDOC

DID	DOCTOR
15	KIM

Sometimes a table occurrence with cardinality one will be shown this way:

⟨15, Kim⟩

Second, we must use the UNION operator: DOCTOR = DOCTOR UNION TEMPDOC. Figure 6.13 shows how this would work. Notice that TEMPDOC's second column, DOCTOR, has a different name than that of the corresponding column in DOCTOR, DNAME. However, the columns have the same domain.

There will be times when we need to take the UNION of tables that aren't union-compatible. Under these circumstances, we must first use the PROJECT operator on one or both tables to reduce them to the same set of columns. Because this requires a nested set of operators, we will defer presenting examples until we discuss nesting operators.

FIGURE 6.13   Using UNION to Add a Row to the DOCTOR Table

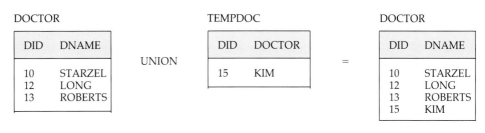

The INTERSECTION Operator

The INTERSECTION operator combines two union-compatible tables into a third one containing rows that were in the first *and* second tables. The syntax is as follows:

> *Format 1.* Table__name__3 = Table__name__1 INTERSECTION
> Table__name__2
> *Format 2.* Table__name__1 INTERSECTION Table__name__2

***Problem 12.* Who are the patients who are in critical condition and have a heart ailment?**

Solution. Because we are interested in an "anding" operation involving two tables, the INTERSECTION operator is the correct one to use. The solution is:

T9 = HEART__ILLNESS INTERSECTION CRITICAL__CONDITION

Figure 6.14 shows how this would be executed.

The DIFFERENCE Operator

The difference of two union-compatible tables is a third table that contains the rows that were in the minuend but *not* in the subtrahend. Here is the syntax:

> *Format 1.* Table__name__3 = Table__name__1 −
> Table__name__2
> *Format 2.* Table__name__1 − Table__name__2

As is true with the arithmetic difference operator, $A - B \langle\rangle B - A$, and the operator isn't commutative.

FIGURE 6.14   Execution of T9 = HEART__ILLNESS INTERSECTION CRITICAL__CONDITION

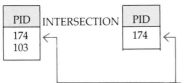

HEART__ILLNESS   CRITICAL__CONDITION

There is only one row that completely matches

Therefore, the result is:

PID
174

FIGURE 6.15   Results of HEART__ILLNESS − CRITICAL__CONDITION

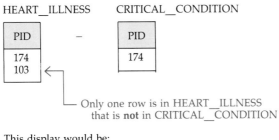

HEART__ILLNESS   CRITICAL__CONDITION

Only one row is in HEART__ILLNESS that is **not** in CRITICAL__CONDITION

This display would be:

PID

PID
103

Problem 13. **Show the results of HEART__ILLNESS − CRITICAL__CONDI-TION.**

Solution. The result would proceed as indicated in Figure 6.15. Since the two tables are union-compatible, this query will correctly show the numbers of the patients who are in Suburban Hospital for a heart ailment but are not in critical condition.

FIGURE 6.16   **Result of DOCTOR = DOCTOR − TEMPDOC**

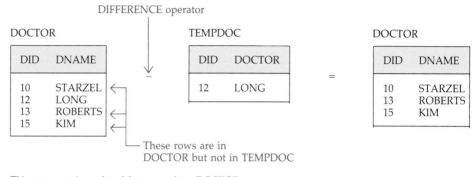

This statement is used to delete a row from DOCTOR.

Problem 14. **Who are the patients in critical condition who are not in for a heart ailment?**

Solution. T10 = CRITICAL__CONDITION − HEART__ILLNESS. The occurrence of T10 is as follows:

T10

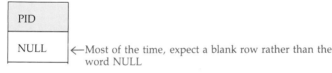

There are no patients who satisfy our request. Problems 13 and 14 also show that DIFFERENCE is not commutative.

The DIFFERENCE operator can be used to delete rows from tables. Let's delete the row ⟨12, Long⟩ from the DOCTOR table. Two steps are necessary:

- Create a new temporary table, TEMPDOC, containing the row to be deleted: TEMPDOC = ⟨12, Long⟩.
- Use the DIFFERENCE operator: DOCTOR = DOCTOR − TEMPDOC. Figure 6.16 shows how this would work.

The PRODUCT Operator

The last set operator—PRODUCT or, more properly, **Cartesian product**—concatenates *every* row of one table with *every* row of a second table. The columns in the new table will consist of *all* the columns from both tables. If the degrees of the tables whose product is being taken are m and n, respectively, the resulting table is of degree m + n.

FIGURE 6.17   How the PRODUCT Operator Determines Which Rows to Include in the Resulting Table

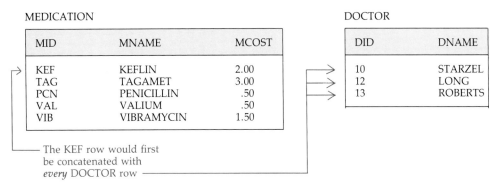

MEDICATION

MID	MNAME	MCOST
KEF	KEFLIN	2.00
TAG	TAGAMET	3.00
PCN	PENICILLIN	.50
VAL	VALIUM	.50
VIB	VIBRAMYCIN	1.50

DOCTOR

DID	DNAME
10	STARZEL
12	LONG
13	ROBERTS

The KEF row would first be concatenated with *every* DOCTOR row

This first row in table 1 is concatenated with every row in table 2. This would result in the new table having three rows with <KEF, Keflin, 2.00> as the first three column values. This can be seen in the resulting table (below).

Next, row 2 of MEDICATION would be concatenated with every row from DOCTOR. This would continue until there were no more rows in MEDICATION to concatenate.

T10

MID	MNAME	MCOST	DID	DNAME
KEF	KEFLIN	2.00	10	STARZEL
KEF	KEFLIN	2.00	12	LONG
KEF	KEFLIN	2.00	13	ROBERTS
TAG	TAGAMET	3.00	10	STARZEL
TAG	TAGAMET	3.00	12	LONG
TAG	TAGAMET	3.00	13	ROBERTS
PCN	PENICILLIN	.50	10	STARZEL
PCN	PENICILLIN	.50	12	LONG
PCN	PENICILLIN	.50	13	ROBERTS
VAL	VALIUM	.50	10	STARZEL
VAL	VALIUM	.50	12	LONG
VAL	VALIUM	.50	13	ROBERTS
VIB	VIBRAMYCIN	1.50	10	STARZEL
VIB	VIBRAMYCIN	1.50	12	LONG
VIB	VIBRAMYCIN	1.50	13	ROBERTS

The three KEF rows

The example is T11 = MEDICATION × DOCTOR.

Assume the cardinality of tables 1 and 2 are a and b, respectively. This means the result has a × b rows. The format we will use is:

Format 1. Table__name__3 = Table__name__1 × Table__name__2
Format 2. Table__name__1 × Table__name__2

Problem 15. What is the result of T11 = MEDICATION × DOCTOR?

Solution. The result would be developed as shown in Figure 6.17.

You should take care when using this operator, because it can result in misleading information. Table T11 seems to imply that every physician prescribes every medication, which is an incorrect conclusion.

Nesting Operators

Like operators in any algebra, the relational operators can be combined to form more complex expressions. The result of nesting the operators is always another table (relation). Parentheses may be used to reduce ambiguity concerning the ordering of operators. Let's consider some examples.

Problem 16. What are the physician names and numbers of the patients they treat? Use the original DOCTOR table from Figure 6.3.

Solution. Because we want information from two tables, it should be apparent that the JOIN operation is required. Also, the user wants only two columns to appear in the result, so we must also do a PROJECT operation.
Figure 6.18 indicates that the query requires two steps:

- Join two tables on DID.
- PROJECT the result on the desired columns (PID and DNAME).

Because there was no single table with physician names and patient numbers, we had to create one via the JOIN operation. The joining column must be DID, since it is the only common one for the two tables. The resulting table will have five columns: PID, PNAME, DIAGNOSIS, DID, and DNAME. Before displaying the result, the PROJECT operation will eliminate the unwanted columns, leaving only PID and DNAME. The parentheses ensure that the join is done first.

FIGURE 6.18   **A Nesting Operation that Satisfies the Request: For Each Patient in the Hospital, Show the Patient Number and Doctor Name**

(PATIENT JOIN (DID = DID) DOCTOR) [PID,DNAME]

First, JOIN PATIENT
and DOCTOR to add
the doctor's name

Next, PROJECT on
the desired columns

Let's examine the two steps in sequence of operation.

Step 1: PATIENT JOIN (DID = DID) DOCTOR (intermediate result).

PID	PNAME	DCODE	DID	DNAME
174	ADAMS	ANG	10	STARZEL
103	COX	ANG	10	STARZEL
49	DAVIS	CF	12	LONG

Step 2: Project the results from step 1 over PID and DNAME.

PID	PNAME
174	STARZEL
103	STARZEL
49	LONG

Problem 17. What are the patient numbers and physician names for those patients being treated for heart ailments?

Solution. This query requires two JOINs. First, we join PATIENT and HEART_ILLNESS over PID. Next, we JOIN the result with DOCTOR over DID. Finally, we PROJECT on the desired columns, PID and DNAME. Let's show the answer first as a series of operations, then as a single line command.

T12 = PATIENT JOIN (PID = PID) HEART_ILLNESS
T13 = T12 JOIN (DID = DID) DOCTOR
T14 = T13 [PID, DNAME]

The single-line equivalent is shown in Figure 6.19.

FIGURE 6.19   The Relational Algebra for the Query: What Are the Patient Numbers and Physician Names for Those Patients Being Treated for Heart Ailments?

Match PATIENT and HEART_ILLNESS rows ⟶   Match the result with DOCTOR rows ⟶   PROJECT

((PATIENT JOIN (PID = PID) HEART_ILLNESS) JOIN (DID = DID) DOCTOR) [PID, DNAME]

Problem 18. **What are the names of the patients who are in critical or serious condition?**

Solution. Again note the use of OR plus the fact that two tables are involved. This means that a UNION operation is necessary. Unfortunately, after taking the union of CRITICAL__CONDITION and SERIOUS__CONDITION, we will not yet have the patient names, so we must perform subsequent JOIN and PROJECT operations.

Figure 6.20 shows the solution. The outer set of parentheses is necessary to ensure that the PROJECT is done last. Without them, Figure 6.20 might be misinterpreted to mean "Take the projection of PATIENT over PNAME" first, giving us a unary table, which consists of only the patient name column. This would prevent us from taking the JOIN with the query table resulting from the UNION.

FIGURE 6.20   The Relational Algebra that Satisfies the Request: What Are the Names of Patients in Critical or Serious Condition?

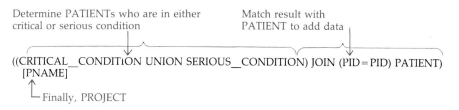

Determine PATIENTs who are in either critical or serious condition

Match result with PATIENT to add data

((CRITICAL__CONDITION UNION SERIOUS__CONDITION) JOIN (PID = PID) PATIENT) [PNAME]

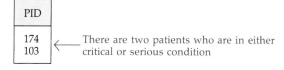

Finally, PROJECT

The result of executing the UNION statements inside the first set of parentheses would be:

PID
174
103

← There are two patients who are in either critical or serious condition

The JOIN produces this table:

PID	PNAME	DCODE	DID
174	ADAMS	ANG	10
103	COX	ANG	10

Finally, the PROJECT results in:

PNAME
ADAMS
COX

Problem 19. **Give the patient numbers of those patients on penicillin (coded PCN).**

Solution. The solution is shown in Figure 6.21.

Suppose we do not know the code for penicillin. This means we must determine it before we can use Figure 6.21. This has been done in Figure 6.22.

To better understand Figure 6.22, let's break it up into smaller components and examine each one. First, we do the SELECT and PROJECT operations inside the innermost set of parentheses. This gives us the following table:

Next, we select those rows from DOSAGE whose value for MID matches PCN (the result of the previous step). Finally, we PROJECT on the patient name.

FIGURE 6.21   **The Relational Algebra for: What Are the Patient Numbers of Those Patients on Penicillin?**

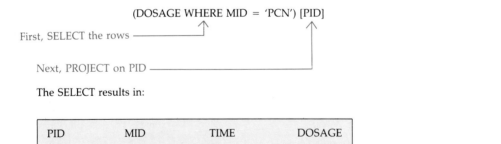

The SELECT results in:

PID	MID	TIME	DOSAGE
103	PCN	0200	50mg
49	PCN	0200	50mg
49	PCN	0600	50mg
49	PCN	1000	50mg

←—All MID values are PCN

The PROJECT result is:

FIGURE 6.22   The Relational Algebra Statements to Resolve Problem 19 (Figure 6.9) Assuming Penicillin's Code Is Unknown

(DOSAGE WHERE MID = (MEDICATION WHERE MNAME = 'Penicillin' [MID])) [PID]

First, extract the row from
MEDICATION that has MNAME = 'Penicillin'

Next, PROJECT on MID ('PCN')

Extract the matching DOSAGE rows

PROJECT on PID

The inner (first) SELECT — "MEDICATION WHERE MNAME = . . ." — results in:

MID	MNAME	MCOST
PCN	PENICILLIN	.50

The PROJECT that immediately follows results in:

MID
PCN

The inner SELECT is now, in effect, DOSAGE WHERE MID = 'PCN', which results in:

PID	MID	TIME	DOSAGE	
103	PCN	0200	50mg	← All MID values are 'PCN'
49	PCN	0200	50mg	←
49	PCN	0600	50mg	←
49	PCN	1000	50mg	←

Therefore, the final result, after projecting on PID, is the same as in the previous problem:

PID
103
49

This concludes the section on relational algebra. The concept has never been completely implemented as a commercial product, but its basic ideas appear in actual relational languages, such as SQL, that have the SELECT, PROJECT, JOIN, and UNION operators but are used in a more user-friendly manner. Finally, relational algebra is procedural in that users must state their data needs and how to extract the data as a series of consecutive steps. In contrast, the relational calculus, briefly discussed next, is nonprocedural.

6.6   RELATIONAL CALCULUS

The relational calculus method for manipulating tables is much closer to English and at the same time is more intuitive for users than relational algebra. Rather than specifying the precise ordering of several operators, we use a precise notation to define the query.

Relational calculus is **descriptive, or nonprocedural,** in that we simply describe what we want, rather than **prescriptive, or procedural,** like relational algebra, which makes us define in minute detail exactly how to answer a particular query.

The syntax of Codd's calculus is ambiguous. Therefore, we will use the INGRES adaptation, shown in Figure 6.23. The calculus methodology combines JOIN, PROJECT, and SELECT into a single command: RETRIEVE. Following the RETRIEVE clause, we list the columns to be displayed. The INTO clause permits us to create query tables that store the result. We use the WHERE clause to restrict the search to just those rows matching the "relationship" following the WHERE verb. To specify the tables to be used in the search, we precede the column names with the table name. For example, to display the names of patients with angina, we might code:

RETRIEVE PATIENT.PNAME WHERE DIAGNOSIS = 'ANG'

Joins are implicitly performed by using more than one table name in the WHERE clause, which is also used to specify the joining condition.

Problem 20. Retrieve the patient numbers for Dr. Starzel.

Solution.

Joining condition
↓
RETRIEVE PATIENT.PID WHERE PATIENT.DID = DOCTOR.DID AND
DOCTOR.DNAME = 'STARZEL'

Two table names indicates a join

FIGURE 6.23   **The Relational Calculus Syntax as Represented by the Programming Language QUEL**

RETRIEVE column__1, column__2, . . . INTO [Table__name] WHERE Relationship

---

Problem 21. **Retrieve the patient numbers of those patients who receive penicillin.**

Solution. Because presumably we don't know penicillin's code, we must tell the calculus how to determine it, much like we did with the algebra:

RETRIEVE DOSAGE.PID WHERE DOSAGE.MID = MEDICATION.MID AND MEDICATION.MNAME = 'Penicillin'.

Problem 22. **List the patient name and dosage amount for those patients retrieved in Problem 21.**

Solution.

RETRIEVE PATIENT.NAME, DOSAGE.DOSAGE WHERE PATIENT.PID = DOSAGE.PID AND
DOSAGE.MID = MEDICATION.MID AND MEDICATION.MNAME = 'Penicillin'

Thus far, we have seen how to manipulate relations by using relational algebra and calculus. The next section looks at a graphical approach marketed by IBM called *Query-By-Example (QBE)*.

6.7   END USER INTERACTION WITH DB2: QBE

Query Management Facility (QMF) is an IBM product that is intended for use by end users for either of IBM's mainframe relational DBMSs: DB2 or SQL/DS. It includes the ability to either enter SQL statements or use **Query-By-Example (QBE),** a graphical technique first suggested by M. M. Zloof, an IBM employee.

Besides the IBM offering, other vendors market QBE-like systems. For example, Borland offers PARADOX for microcomputer users and INFORMIX markets QBE as part of its SQL-based package that runs on all classes of computers from micros to mainframes. Even Lotus 1-2-3's data management query facility uses a QBE-like approach for defining search criteria. This section examines only IBM's offering.

FIGURE 6.24   **The Empty QBE Table that Results from the Command DRAW MEDICATION**

MEDICATION	MID	MNAME	MCOST	ONHAND	MED_CATEGORY	UNITS_ USED

Identifying the Desired Tables

After invoking QMF with a procedure we won't show here, we request the framework of the desired table by entering the command DRAW table-name on a command line. For example, to specify the MEDICATION table, we would enter DRAW MEDICATION. A blank MEDICATION **example table** containing all of its columns, as in Figure 6.24, will then appear.

In the blank MEDICATION table, some of the column names have been adjusted so that the complete table will fit onto one page. The actual QBE column widths are a function of the data type and width associated with each column. However, the displayed column sizes can be modified by using the REDUCE or ENLARGE commands. REDUCE can also be used to remove a column and ENLARGE to create a new one.

Retrieval

After specifying the table's columns, we use the **P.** operator to present the columns for display on the terminal. There is a program function key (PFK) that we can use to produce hard copy. If we enter a **P.** in the box directly below the table's name, all the columns associated with that table will be displayed.

Following the **P.** operator, we can specify one of two sort sequence indicators: **AO** (for ascending order) or **DO** (for descending order). We use **UNQ** to show only the unique values or **ALL,** which is the default value, to show all values.

***Problem 23.* Display the MEDICATION codes, names, and on-hand amounts in ascending name order.**

Solution. The solution is shown in Figure 6.25.

Multilevel sorting can be done by enclosing integers in parentheses, where (1) indicates the primary sort column, (2) means the secondary sort column, and so on. Figure 6.26 shows Problem 23 sorted by MED_CATEGORY (ascending) and MNAME (also ascending) and also displays the MED_CATEGORY values.

FIGURE 6.25   **Using QBE to Display the MID, MNAME, and ONHAND Columns from the MEDICATION Table, Sorted in Ascending Order by MNAME**

MEDICATION	MID	MNAME	MCOST	ONHAND	MED_CATEGORY	UNITS_USED
	P.	P. AO		P.		

Ascending order

FIGURE 6.26   **Specifying a MEDICATION Report Sorted by MED_CATEGORY, by MNAME**

MEDICATION	MID	MNAME	MCOST	ONHAND	MED_CATEGORY	UNITS_USED
	P.	P. AO (2)		P.	P. AO (1)	

Retrieval of Selected Rows: Implementing Algebra's SELECT Operator

To restrict the rows to be presented, we enter the desired value into the table below the column that is to be searched.

Problem 24. **Display the names of the IV medications.**

Solution. Figure 6.27 shows one solution. The IV in the MED_CATEGORY column means that we want to search for that particular value. Because there is no P. preceding the IV, QBE will not display the category values; it will only search on them.

QBE also supports **variables** (not to be confused with *example elements,* a topic covered later), elements whose values are supplied at run time. For example, suppose we want to be able to enter the desired medication category when the query is run. To do so, we place the & symbol before the variable's name, which

FIGURE 6.27   **A QBE Request that Uses an "Example" to Specify that Only the IV Medications Are Desired**

MEDICATION	MID	MNAME	MCOST	ONHAND	MED_CATEGORY	UNITS_USED
		P.			IV	

Use this method to implement the SELECT (RESTRICT) algebraic operator.

FIGURE 6.28   **Using a Variable to Display the IV Medications**

MEDICATION	MID	MNAME	MCOST	ONHAND	MED_CATEGORY	UNITS_USED
		P.			&MEDCAT	

Indicates a variable ⟶

When the query is executed, QBE will request a value for the variable. By entering IV, the results will be the same as those from Figure 6.27.

is entered below the desired column name. To illustrate, Figure 6.28 changes the previous problem's solution to use a variable. Now when the query is run (by entering RUN on the command line), QBE will prompt for a value of MEDCAT, then use the entered value as the basis for its search.

Alternatives for Complicated Queries: Condition Boxes. Instead of specifying the search conditions in the table space, we can draw a **condition box** and use example elements in the table's framework. The search condition is entered into the condition box and must use **example elements,** or values, which are indicated much like desired values. They can be up to 18 characters in length, but they must be preceded with the underline character. You can think of example values as a kind of variable. For example, if we enter __MC under the MED_CATE-GORY column, we define it as any value that might appear in the MED__

FIGURE 6.29   A Blank Condition Box Resulting from Entering the Command DRAW COND

CONDITIONS

FIGURE 6.30   Specifying a Sample Value

MEDICATION	MID	MNAME	MCOST	ONHAND	MED_CATEGORY	UNITS_USED
		P.			__MC	

Sample value ──────────────────────────

We assign a value to it in the condition box, which is shown in Figure 6.31.

CATEGORY column. IBM suggests that you think of example elements as substitutes for the column name under which they appear. Example elements are used twice: once in the example table and again in the conditions box.

To draw the conditions box, we enter the command DRAW COND, which will result in the display shown in Figure 6.29. Next, we create example values in the desired table. In Figure 6.30, we show how to use a sample value to search the MED_CATEGORY column for IVs. Notice the __MC below the MED_CATEGORY column name. Used in this manner, __MC means "a sample value called MC."

After entering the example elements, we enter the search condition in the condition box, as illustrated in Figure 6.31.

Allowable condition operators are AND, OR, NOT, IN, LIKE, and NULL. We can also use the arithmetic operators +, >, <, and so on. Quotation marks can be omitted when specifying alphanumeric values. That is why there are no quotation marks around the IV in the previous two examples.

We use condition boxes when:

- The condition includes two or more columns.

- Parentheses are necessary to alter the normal precedence of operators.

FIGURE 6.31   Condition Box that Specifies the Value of MC to Search for

CONDITIONS
__MC=IV

FIGURE 6.32   Example of a Compound Search Condition

MEDICATION	MID	MNAME	MCOST	ONHAND	MED_CATEGORY	UNITS_USED
		P. AO	P. > 2.00	P.	IV	

When search criteria appear on the same line, it means AND. Thus, the QBE statement says to find all the MEDICATIONs that have MED__CATEGORY = 'IV' AND cost over $2.00.

- It is undesirable to widen a column to accommodate a complex condition.
- A built-in function is necessary.
- It is necessary to use example elements along with AND or OR.

Retrieval with Compound Search Conditions. The previous example required a single search argument. To implement a query that involves **conjunction (AND),** we place all the desired values on the same line.

Problem 25. **Get the MEDICATION name, cost, and on-hand amounts for the IVs costing over $2.00.**

Solution. Figure 6.32 demonstrates one possible solution. Because both >2.00 and IV appear on the same line, QBE interprets this as meaning AND.

You might be wondering why we didn't include the = operator in the MED__CATEGORY column. The reason is that = is the default operator.

The next example shows how to implement a compound search condition with **disjunction (OR).** As you will see, each search criterion is now placed on a separate line.

Problem 26. **Show all the MEDICATION information for those items that cost under \$2.00 or are of the PO or IV categories.**

Solution. Figure 6.33 presents two solutions. The first one uses OR, and the second illustrates the IN operator. This example not only demonstrates how to implement disjunctions but shows how to request that all columns be displayed.

While the next example may not be very practical, it does show how to use expressions in conditions. Suppose we want to show only those medications

---

FIGURE 6.33   **Two QBE Solutions for Responding to the Query: Show the MEDICATIONs that Cost Less than \$2.00 or Have MED__CATEGORY = PO OR IV**

Solution 1: Use separate lines to designate OR

MEDICATION	MID	MNAME	MCOST	ONHAND	MED__CATEGORY	UNITS__USED
P. P. P.			<2.00		PO IV	

Solution 2: Use a condition box

MEDICATION	MID	MNAME	MCOST	ONHAND	MED__CATEGORY	UNITS__USED
P.			__COST		__MC	

Substitute name for MCOST, ⟶
or an **example element**

CONDITIONS
__COST >2.0 __MC IN ('PO', 'IV')

Because the two criteria are on separate lines, QBE interprets them as meaning OR.

for which the amount ONHAND plus the UNITS__USED exceeds 1,000 units. The query could be stated as shown in Figure 6.34.

As another example illustrating expressions and conditions, assume it is March. To display the average monthly usage of all MEDICATIONS having an average usage of at least 100, we enter the commands shown in Figure 6.35.

The solution to the next example will require both AND and OR.

FIGURE 6.34   Using QBE to Display Those MEDICATIONs for Which the Sum of ONHAND and UNITS__USED Exceeds 1,000

MEDICATION	MID	MNAME	MCOST	ONHAND	MED__CATEGORY	UNITS__USED
		P. AO		P. __OH		P. __UU

CONDITIONS
__OH + __UU > 1000

The solution requires that a calculation be performed within the condition box. The sum could have been displayed by adding a blank column after UNITS__USED, then entering this command below the new column: P. __OH + __UU.

FIGURE 6.35   Displaying Those MEDICATIONs Having an Average Monthly Usage of at Least 100

MEDICATION	MID	MNAME	MCOST	ONHAND	MED__CATEGORY	UNITS__USED
		P. AO				__UU

CONDITIONS
__UU/3 >100

We make the assumption that it was March—hence the division by 3 in the condition box. The solution illustrates a compound condition and a calculation.

FIGURE 6.36   A Query that Requires an AND and an OR

MEDICATION	MID	MNAME	MCOST	ONHAND	MED_CATEGORY	UNITS_USED
		P. AO	_M	_OH	_MC	

CONDITIONS
(_M>2.00 AND _MC=IV) OR (_MC=PO AND _OH<25)

The problem could be solved without use of a condition box, but this would result in much more complexity.

FIGURE 6.37   The QBE Commands to Retrieve Those MEDICATIONs Costing over $2.00 but under $4.01 Regardless of the Value of MED_CATEGORY

MEDICATION	MID	MNAME	MCOST	ONHAND	MED_CATEGORY	UNITS_USED
		P. AO	_M	P.		

CONDITIONS
_M>2 AND _M<4.01

The query requires that we perform an AND operation on a single column. As an alternative, we could have constructed a duplicate MCOST column and entered >2 in one and <4.01 in the other.

Problem 27. **Display the names of MEDICATIONs that are of type IV and cost over $2.00 or that are PO and of which there are fewer than 25 on hand.**

Solution. The solution is shown in Figure 6.36.

Problem 28. **Resolve Problem 27, but retrieve only those medications costing over $2.00 but under $4.01 regardless of the value of MED_CATEGORY.**

Solution. This is an example of an AND on a single column. The search condition we require is:

(MCOST >2.00 AND MCOST<4.01).

To implement this in QBE, we enter the commands shown in Figure 6.37.

Adding New Rows: The I. Operator

To add a new row:

- Key the values into the spaces provided below the column names.
- Enter the **I** operator below the table's name.

Problem 29. **Add a new MEDICATION whose code is TAP, is named TAPAZOLE, costs $3.50, is of category PO, and of which there are 100 on hand.**

Solution. Figure 6.38 shows the solution.

Any columns that don't have values are assigned the value NULL. Also, multiple rows can be added at one time by entering them as separate lines in the example table.

Changing Existing Rows: The U. Operator

To change the value of an existing element, we precede its new value with the operator **U.** and enter the value of the primary key in the appropriate column.

Problem 30. **Change the cost of TAGAMET to $3.50.**

Solution. First, we enter the value TAG in the MID box. This specifies the row to be retrieved. Next, in the box below MCOST, we enter U. 3.50. The complete solution appears in Figure 6.39.

FIGURE 6.38   **Using the I. Operator to Insert a New Row**

MEDICATION	MID	MNAME	MCOST	ONHAND	MED_CATEGORY	UNITS_ USED
I.	TAP	TAPAZOLE	3.50	100	PO	

FIGURE 6.39   Using the U. Operator to Change the Value of One or More Columns in a Given Row

MEDICATION	MID	MNAME	MCOST	ONHAND	MED_CATEGORY	UNITS_USED
	TAG		U. 3.50			

             └ U. → update this column
                     ──── Find rows with MID = 'TAG'

The example changes the cost of TAGAMET to $3.50.

FIGURE 6.40   Updating Multiple Rows

MEDICATION	MID	MNAME	MCOST	MCOST	MED_CATEGORY
			_CST	U. _CST∗1.1	IV

Sample value: ────────────────
We could have used a value like: _123.45

Notice that the column names have been altered. First, the MCOST column is shown twice. This is done by adding a blank column, then keying MCOST as its name. Next, some of the columns have been omitted. This can be done using QMF and often makes the query more readable.

As intended, the query retrieves the sample value, _CST, then multiplies it by 1.1 before updating it.

The above example shows how to update a single row. However, QBE can also update many rows, although the procedure is a bit more complex.

Problem 31.   Increase the cost of all IV medications by 10 percent.

Solution. Figure 6.40 shows the solution.

Problem 32.   Change the cost of all IVs by adding a flat fee of $3.00, and add $2.50 to the PO MEDICATIONs.

Solution. Figure 6.41 presents the solution.

FIGURE 6.41   **Multiple Simultaneous Updates**

MEDICATION	MID	MNAME	MCOST	MCOST	MED_CATEGORY
			_CST _CST2	U. _CST+3 U. _CST2+2.5	IV PO

We are to add $3.00 to all IV MEDICATIONs and $2.50 to all POs. Line 1 says to retrieve the sample value, _CST, then add $3.00 to it, but only for those rows that contain MED_CATEGORY = 'IV'. Line 2 is similar in meaning.

FIGURE 6.42   **Using the D. Operator to Delete One or More Rows**

DOSAGE	PID	MID	TIME	DOSAGE
D.	174	TAG	200	

In this case only one row is actually deleted, because there is only one match for the three conditions specified.

Deleting Rows: The D. Operator

First, we will look at an example of deleting a single row. We will qualify the query by keying in a value for the primary key, then enter the **D.** operator below the table name.

Problem 33. **Delete the DOSAGE row for patient 174's dose of TAGAMET at 0200.**

Solution. The solution is presented in Figure 6.42.

Deletion of several rows is equally easy, as the next problem demonstrates.

Problem 34. **Delete all of patient 174's rows from the DOSAGE table.**

Solution. Rather than qualifying the query to the drug and time level, which uniquely identifies a single row, we simply enter the patient's number, as in Figure 6.43.

FIGURE 6.43   **Deleting More Than One Row Using the D. Operator**

DOSAGE	PID	MID	TIME	DOSAGE
D.	174			

The difference between this and the previous solution is that this one finds multiple rows because there are several rows in DOSAGE that have PID = 174.

This section looked briefly at the end user product QBE. Among the topics we omitted were joins and the built-in functions. If you are interested in more details, consult the appropriate IBM manuals.

6.8 SUMMARY

The relational model is appealing in its simplicity. Every file is thought of as a two-dimensional table, or flat file. These tables have several properties:

- Each table has a set of candidate keys.
- There can be no repeating columns.
- Their row ordering is immaterial.
- Their column ordering is immaterial.

Instead of requiring users to know about the underlying data structures, this approach allows users to simply state their data needs. Rather than dealing with variable-length records, pointer names, indexes, and the like, the applications need know only the table names and the names of their columns. With any of the four relational approaches, search criteria are simply stated, the relations searched, and the results presented to the user.

Every table's occurrence consists of a collection of records, also called *tuples* or *rows*, each having the same number of columns. The number of columns defines the table's degree or arity, and the number of rows defines its cardinality. One or more columns must be designated as the primary key. This is a column, or collection of columns, that uniquely identifies a row. Another kind of key is a foreign key. This is a column whose values either must be NULL or must match the value of a primary key for some other table.

Once we have constructed relations, we need ways to manipulate them. Two of Codd's methods are relational algebra and relational calculus. Relational algebra offers eight operators to precisely define the steps necessary to retrieve the desired information. It is called a *procedural*, or *prescriptive*, methodology. Relational calculus, on the other hand, is more intuitive, because we need not be concerned with how to retrieve our results, only with how to define what we want.

The next section looked at IBM's Query Management Facility. Users can use either SQL or QBE to enter queries from a terminal. QBE is a graphical technique first suggested by an IBM employee in 1975. For simple queries, the product is an excellent choice; it combines ease of use with significant power. We discussed only IBM's implementation, but other vendors offer similar products.

REVIEW QUESTIONS

1. Define *relation*.
2. What is symmetry of access?
3. Differentiate between cardinality and degree.
4. List two relational assertions, and give an example of each.
5. Differentiate among *primary key, foreign key,* and *candidate key.*
6. Explain how to implement a 1:M relationship.
7. Why do we say that relationships are implicit in the relational model? Use your answer to Question 6 as a guide.
8. Differentiate between a base and a view table.
9. What possible computer implementation problems do you foresee with the relational model?
10. What is a procedural methodology?
11. List the traditional set operators.
12. List the special set operators.
13. What is meant by *commutative?* Which algebraic operators have this characteristic?
14. Give two kinds of joins. What is their difference?
15. Explain the difference between JOIN and INTERSECTION.
16. Define *union-compatible.*
17. What are the QBE commands that are used to display a table and a condition box?
18. What do the QBE commands ALL and UNQ do?
19. How are the AND and OR operators indicated without using condition boxes?
20. What is the QBE operator for:
    a. Display?
    b. Update?
    c. Delete?
21. Define a sample value. How is one indicated? When should we use one?

PROBLEMS

Use relational algebra to solve Problems 1 through 14. For problems 1–4, assume you don't know the physician's code. For problems 1–7, use Figure 6.3 for the table definition.

1. What are the names of Dr. Starzel's patients?
2. What are the names of Dr. Starzel's patients in room 102?
3. What are the names of Dr. Starzel's patients in room 102 with angina?
4. What are the names of Dr. Starzel's patients in room 102 in critical condition with angina?
5. What are the names of the patients receiving medication at 0200?
6. What are the patient and doctor names of those patients getting penicillin?
7. What are the patient numbers of those patients getting a drug costing under $2.00?

Use the following relations to answer Problems 8 through 14.

PO (<u>PONUM</u>, PODATE, POVENDNO, POSTATUS, EMPCODE, TOTITEMS, TOTVALUE)

PODETAIL (<u>PONUM</u>, <u>ITEMCODE</u>, UNITS_ORDERED, PRICE_PER_UNIT)

INVENTORY (<u>ITEMCODE</u>, ITEM_DESC, CHARGE_AMT, LAST_COST, ONHAND, ONORDER, CATEGORY)

DEPT (<u>DEPT_CODE</u>, DNAME)

TRANSFER (<u>DEPT_CODE</u>, <u>ITEM_CODE</u>, DATE_TRANSFERRED, UNITS_TRANSFERRED, ONHAND)

VENDOR (<u>VENDNO</u>, VNAME, VSTREET, VCITY, VSTATE, VZIP, VPHONE)

EMPLOYEE (<u>EMPCODE</u>, EMPNAME)

The POSTATUS column in PO contains one of three values: O for open, C for closed, or P for partial. A PO is assigned a P status if only a portion of the PO items have been received.

When employees set up a PO, they are asked for their initials. These initials are called EMPCODE in the PO and EMPLOYEE tables. As the items are added to a PO, the number of items (TOTITEMS) and the total value (TOTVALUE) are accumulated. We should point out that this generally is not a good idea, because it is easy to forget to perform these calculations and thus produce incorrect data.

The INVENTORY column, CHARGE_AMT, is the price charged to customers. The LAST_COST column stores the latest cost for that item, determined from a purchase order. Because the same item can be ordered many times on different POs, this column is used to track the latest cost.

Once received, items are transferred to departments within the organization. The TRANSFER table keeps track of these transfers by recording the department code, item code, units transferred, and date of transfer each time a transfer is performed. At that time, the inventory ONHAND is reduced and the TRANSFER ONHAND column value increased.

8. List all the PO numbers and associated item codes and descriptions for those purchase orders that are not closed.

9. Display the PO number for all POs sent to the same vendor as PO number 7812.

10. List the codes of all vendors who have been sent an order (regardless of its status) for those orders not entered by employee JCS.

11. Show the item description for all items on PO number 17.

12. Show the PO number, date entered, employee name, and vendor name for those POs that do not contain item FRISB10.

13. Assume that we set up two new relations called CLOSED and PARTIAL. The CLOSED columns are PNO, DATE_CLOSED, and EMPCODE. The columns for PARTIAL are PNO and EMPCODE. Use the CLOSED and PO relations to list those PO numbers that are not closed.

14. Show the purchase order numbers of those POs that are either CLOSED or PARTIAL-ly complete.

Use relational calculus (INGRES) to solve Problems 15 through 20.

15. Repeat Problem 1 using relational calculus.

16. Repeat Problem 5 using relational calculus.

17. Repeat Problem 7 using relational calculus.

18. Repeat Problem 8 using relational calculus.

19. Repeat Problem 11 using relational calculus.

20. Repeat Problem 12 using relational calculus.

Use QBE to solve the remaining problems.

21. Use a single table to add two new PATIENTs with these values: ⟨177,Abarnathy,ANG,12⟩ and ⟨202,Thomas,CF,12⟩.

22. List the patient numbers for those patients who receive a medication at either 1200 or 1000.

23. Add one hour to the due time for all penicillin orders.

24. List the patients who are under the care of physician number 12 or who are being treated for angina. Do not use a condition box.

25. Resolve Problem 24 using a condition box.

26. Delete all medications costing over $15.00.

7

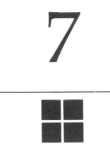

An Introduction to SQL Using Database 2 (DB2)

Database 2 (DB2) is IBM's relational database management system (RDBMS) for its MVS environment. The defining of attributes, the accessing and updating of rows, and the granting of rights are all done through SQL (Structured Query Language), a subset of DB2.

DB2 is the most popular mainframe implementation of SQL, with almost 2,000 installations by the end of 1988. This chapter focuses on Version 2, announced in April 1988 and released in October 1988. However, almost all of what you will learn in this chapter can easily be applied to other SQL-based products. We say "almost all" because, as with any standard language, IBM has added new, nonstandard features.

To use DB2 in an interactive mode, users must employ a product called DB2I (DB2 Interactive). IBM's other mainframe SQL product, SQL/DS, uses ISQL (Interactive SQL), which is more user friendly in that the user can enter the SQL statements directly at the keyboard. DB2I, in contrast, is menu driven and is intended more for application programmers than for end users. IBM suggests that end users of DB2 databases use QMF to query and report data. Although DB2I and ISQL use different user interfaces for their interactive facilities, we will show the SQL statements as though we were running ISQL because of its less cluttered Application Programming Interface (API).

The SQL statements for any of IBM's RDBMSs can also be embedded in host programs written in COBOL, PL/1, FORTRAN, or Assembler. In this case, the mode is called Embedded SQL (ESQL). One of the ease-of-use features of DB2 is that, with very minor differences, the syntax for DB2I and ESQL are identical.

TABLE 7.1   SQL-Based Packages

Vendor	Product	Computer Types
Ashton/Tate	dBASE IV	Micro
CINCOM	SUPRA	Mainframe and mini
Data General	DG-SQL	Mini
Hewlett-Packard	HP-SQL	Mini
IBM	SQL/DS	Mainframe
IBM	DB2	Mainframe
IBM	Data Manager	Micro (OS/2 Extended Edition)
Informix Software, Inc.	INFORMIX-SQL	Mainframe, mini, micro
Relational Technology, Inc.	INGRES	Mainframe, mini, micro
Oracle, Inc.	ORACLE	Mainframe, mini, micro

This permits programmers to develop the SQL portions of their programs interactively: entering SQL statements and viewing the results immediately. Any problems detected can be solved by an interactive procedure. After all such problems are removed from the SQL portion of the host program, the same SQL statements can be embedded into the final program.

Other SQL-based products are shown in Table 7.1. One of the packages in the table is ORACLE's product, ORACLE, which runs on microcomputers with 80286 or 80386 microprocessors and at least 1.8MB of RAM, on minicomputers, and on mainframes. INFORMIX and INGRES also run on all three computer types, but each of these packages can be run on microcomputers with the "standard" 640K of memory.

At the conclusion of this chapter, you will be able to:

- Define DB2 *objects*.
- Create, update, and delete definitions of tables, indexes, and views.
- Retrieve, update, and delete data from tables using the SELECT-FROM-WHERE (SFW) block.
- Use *predicates* in SFW blocks, including the "special" predicates LIKE, BETWEEN, IN, and NULL.
- Show how DB2 implements the relational SELECT, PROJECT, UNION, JOIN, INTERSECTION, and DIFFERENCE operators.
- Use the built-in column functions COUNT, AVG, MAX, MIN, and SUM.
- Use the built-in string functions LENGTH, SUBSTR, and VALUE.
- Sort queries.
- Group and subsequently report on similar rows within a table.
- Use subqueries and correlated queries.
- Implement the DB2 security facility.
- Discuss the DB2 concurrency facilities.
- Query the DB2 system tables.

7.1 DB2 CONCEPTS

DB2 was introduced for the MVS environment in June 1983. The most significant item concerning this announcement was the fact that it used the SQL language. This is also the language adopted by ANSI as the standard RDBMS, although there are some small differences between the standard and DB2. We will discuss these differences at the end of the chapter.

Before we examine how to use DB2, we must define some new concepts, notably *table types* and *objects*.

Table Types

There are three kinds of DB2 tables:

- Base
- View
- System

Base Tables. Both the values and definitions of *base tables* are physically stored on a disk drive. We will be concerned primarily with base tables in this chapter.

View Tables. The values associated with *view tables*, also called *logical tables,* are not actually stored; only their definitions are. The view values an end user sees are derived from base tables, other view tables, or a combination of base and view tables. Although the data associated with view tables aren't stored as values, it appears to end users that they are. This means that end users cannot tell whether they are querying a base table or a view table.

Views are used for two purposes:

- To simplify data retrieval
- To limit user access to data

As you will see later, retrieval from base tables can be quite involved. Instead of making end users learn a complicated query syntax, we can create a simpler one—that is, a view—that is based on the complicated query. Then, instead of using the complex query syntax, the end user will use the view.

Views are also a useful security mechanism for limiting user access to certain columns. Assume we have a table containing EMPCODE, EMPNAME, EMP-SALARY, EMPSTREET, and EMPCITY. Furthermore, suppose we don't want particular users to be able to see the EMPSALARY column. By defining a view that masks the undesirable EMPSALARY column, users of that view will be unable to see the salary values. This view would contain only the columns EMPCODE, EMPNAME, EMPSTREET, and EMPCITY.

TABLE 7.2   Some DB2 System Tables Found in the DB2 Catalog

SYSTABLES: Stores one row per table or view. The *columns* are:

NAME	The name of the table or view
CREATOR	The user ID of the creator of the table given in NAME
DBNAME	The database name (defined later when we discuss objects) associated with this table
TSNAME	The table space name (also defined later) to which the table is assigned
COLCOUNT	The number of columns associated with the table

Additional fields in SYSTABLES specify the number of rows in the table, the space available for growth, and so on.

SYSCOLUMNS: Stores one row for every table. Among its fields are:

NAME	The column's name
TBNAME	The name of the table that contains the column
COLTYPE	The field type—character, numeric, etc.
LENGTH	The number of bytes associated with the field

SYSTABAUTH: Contains the rights associated with both tables and views. Among its fields are:

GRANTOR	The "owner" of the table
GRANTEE	The user to whom rights are being granted

There are also fields for a time stamp, which shows the time and date when the right was granted, and the rights (called *functions*) being granted to the grantee.

View columns can be real (derived from the underlying base table), be based on column calculations within a particular row, or be based on a calculation derived from several rows.

System Tables. *System tables* are used by DB2 to record DDL-like data, such as table names, column names and specifications, user rights (also called *privileges*), and so on. The collection of all the system tables make up the **DB2 catalog,** which is IBM's data dictionary facility for DB2. Table 7.2 shows three of the catalog tables, together with most of their columns. Toward the end of the chapter, we will see how to query these tables.

Objects

Objects are anything that can be defined using the SQL DDL. They include tables, views, table spaces, indexes, databases, and storage groups. Typically end users, including programmers, are concerned only with the first two kinds of objects.

Tables. A (base) table is a collection of rows, each containing a set of specified fields, or columns. At the intersection of a row and column is a **field value—** the smallest unit of data that DB2 can manipulate.

Views. A view is an alternative way of representing table data. Only the definitions of views are stored, not their values.

Table Spaces. Table values are stored in **table spaces,** which contain from 1 to 64 VSAM entry-sequenced data sets. VSAM is discussed in detail in Appendix B. Each table space consists of one or more pages, each page 4K or 32K bytes in length.

When the table space is defined, the DBA must assign one of four possible bufferpools: BP0, BP1, BP2, or BP32K. A **bufferpool** is like a conventional buffer. When a row is requested, it is brought into the bufferpool. When a row is changed, it is placed in the bufferpool before being physically written to the table space. If the data already exists in the bufferpool, no physical I/O may be necessary.

Indexes. There are two reasons for indexes:

- To enforce the primary key assertion
- To improve search and join performances

Several times we have stated that a primary key must be unique. The only way to guarantee that there are no duplicate primary key values when using most SQL products is to establish a unique index on the primary key.

Indexes also decrease the time required to perform a search or to execute a join. You should establish an index for any column that will be frequently searched or often used as part of a joining condition.

An important SQL concept is that end users need not know that indexes exist and which columns comprise them. This contributes to SQL's high data independence.

If several indexes exist, there will be several alternative paths for resolving a query. DB2 uses an optimizer to choose the optimal path, but the end user does not see this or even have to specify which indexes to consider.

Database. A database is a collection of tables, indexes, views, and the spaces required to hold them.

Storage Group. A **storage group** is a collection of disk drives to which a name is given. By using storage groups, DB2 is forced to perform many of the physical storage operations, such as the defining and deleting of data sets.

Figure 7.1 shows the relationships among the various objects based on the Suburban Hospital example in previous chapters.

FIGURE 7.1   **Relationships among the DB2 Objects**

Storage group DSNSG001

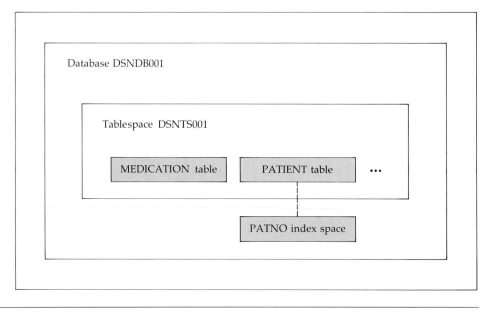

7.2   THE DATA DESCRIPTION LANGUAGE

DB2's data description language (DDL) is used to define (CREATE) all of the objects discussed in the previous section. It is also used to delete (DROP) objects and to modify (ALTER) them. When the DDL is used, DB2 automatically updates all relevant catalog entries.

Once invoked, DB2 can be used by anyone with proper authorization to perform either DDL or DML functions. Through its security system, DB2 restricts the rights of most users to actually carry out many DDL functions, but this fact remains: DB2, and thus SQL, contains both a DDL and a DML, and both are accessible within an application.

Defining Objects: The CREATE Statement

The general syntax for initially defining an object is shown in Figure 7.2.

You may have noticed that the CREATE statement ends with a semicolon. This is true for all SQL statements.

FIGURE 7.2   **Standard Syntax Used to Define All DB2 Objects**

```
CREATE  object-name
        parameters;
```

TABLE 7.3   **DB2 Naming Conventions**

Item	Naming Convention
Bufferpool	BP0, BP1, BP2, BP32K
Column	Long-id; unique to table
Database	Short-id
Index	Long-id
Storage group	Short-id
Table	Long-id
Table space	Short-id
View	Long-id

Naming Conventions. Object names fall into one of two categories: short-ids and long-ids. *Short-ids* are from one to eight characters long; the first must be alphabetic (A–Z, @, #, or $) and the rest alphabetic or numeric. Long-ids are from 1 to 18 characters long, with the first being alphabetic and the rest being alphabetic or numeric or containing the underline character, __. DB2 objects must be named according to Table 7.3.

Defining Storage Groups, Bufferpools, and Databases.[1] To create a storage group, we use the syntax shown in Figure 7.3.

Problem 1. **Define a storage group named DSNSG001.**

Solution.

CREATE STOGROUP DSNSG001
VOLUMES (DSNV01)⟵ Device serial number
VCAT DSNCAT ⟵ VSAM catalog alias name
PASSWORD DSNSESAME; ⟵ VSAM password

The volume serial number is assumed to be DSNV01, the catalog name DSNCAT, and the password DSNSESAME. If the password is omitted, the VSAM catalog

_____

[1]This describes technical features useful primarily to a DBA. It can be skipped without loss of continuity.

FIGURE 7.3   **Defining a Storage Group**

```
CREATE STOGROUP storage-group-name
      VOLUMES (serial-number1, sn2, . . .)
      VCAT vsam-catalog-name
      PASSWORD vsam-password;
```

FIGURE 7.4   **The DB2 Statement for Defining a Database**

```
CREATE DATABASE database-name
      STOGROUP storage-group-name
      BUFFERPOOL BPx;
```

where BPx is BP0, BP1, BP2, or BP32K

---

will be accessed without one. We will no longer be concerned with storage group definitions, because defining storage groups, like defining bufferpools and databases, is usually left to the DBA.

To create a database, we use the syntax shown in Figure 7.4.

Problem 2. **Define a database called DSNDB001 that is to be stored within the storage group from Problem 1. None of the rows in the tables to be assigned to this database will be over 4K in size.**

Solution.

CREATE DATABASE DSNDB001
STOGROUP DSNSG001 ⟵—— Default storage group
BUFFERPOOL BP1; ⟵——— Default bufferpool

If a subsequent table space or index definition doesn't contain a bufferpool specification, DB2 will use the default bufferpool, BP1. Similarly, if subsequent table definitions don't specify a storage group, DB2 will use DSNSG001 as the default value. Notice that this is where we assign the bufferpool; there is no CREATE BUFFERPOOL entry.

To create a table space, we use the syntax shown in Figure 7.5. The CREATE TABLESPACE entry predefines space on the DASD for table rows to be stored. Its size is "limited" to 64 gigabytes. The IN clause specifies the database, the USING clause determines which storage group to use, and the storage group's "other parameters" specify the sizes of the primary and secondary spaces to be allocated for the named storage group. The LOCKSIZE parameter has three

FIGURE 7.5   **Defining a DB2 Table Space**

```
CREATE TABLESPACE table-space-name
  IN database-name
  USING STOGROUP storage-group-name
  (other parameters)
  LOCKSIZE ANY | PAGE | TABLESPACE
  (other parameters);
```

options and is used to specify the lock granularity, a term we discussed in Chapter 1.

Use of LOCKSIZE ANY leaves to DB2 the choice of whether to lock at the PAGE or TABLESPACE level. Using either of the other two options forces the application to always lock at that level. As a general rule, select LOCKSIZE ANY.

Problem 3. **Define a table space called DSNTS001 for the database in Problem 2. Perform locking at the page level.**

Solution.

CREATE TABLESPACE DSNTS001
  IN DSNDB001
  USING STOGROUP DSNSG001 . . .
  LOCKSIZE PAGE;

The next section shows how to define DB2 tables. Much of the syntax follows the standard SQL specification.

Defining Tables. Every table must be defined using the CREATE TABLE statement. The complete syntax is shown in Figure 7.6.

Column Names. Following the table name, we list all the column names and data types for each column, each separated by a comma and enclosed within a single set of parentheses. Use of the optional NOT NULL prevents the storing of column occurrences that don't have values.

Data Types. Allowable DB2 data types are shown in Table 7.4.

The PRIMARY KEY Clause. New with Version 2 (and not available with the other SQL products at the time of this writing), the optional PRIMARY KEY clause explicitly specifies which column or columns constitute the primary key. Implicitly it also says that this column or columns must have unique values. The clause is required if you want automatic enforcement of referential integrity.

FIGURE 7.6   **Defining a DB2 Table**

```
CREATE TABLE table-name-1
   (column-name1 data-type [NOT NULL] [WITH DEFAULT],
   column-name2 data-type [NOT NULL] [WITH DEFAULT],
   . . .)
   [PRIMARY KEY (column-name)]
   [FOREIGN KEY [relationship-name]
      (column-name1, . . .,column-namen)
   REFERENCES table-name-2 (primary-key-2)
   ON DELETE RESTRICT | CASCADE | SET NULL]
   IN database-name, table-space-name
   EDITPROC edit-routine
   VALIDPROC validation-routine;
```

The standard SQL implementation provides only for the column names. The PRIMARY KEY clause defines a primary key and is optional. If it is used and a unique index over the key is also defined using the CREATE INDEX statement, DB2 will enforce entity integrity. The FOREIGN KEY clause is used to define foreign keys, while EDITPROC and VALIDPROC are routines that are to be automatically executed prior to or after certain DML calls.

TABLE 7.4   **Allowable DB2 Data Types**

Data Type	Internal Representation
CHAR (n)	Fixed-length character, n bytes long
DATE	Format will be YYYYMMDD
DECIMAL (m,n)	Packed decimal with m (limited to 1–15) total digits, n of which follow the decimal point
FLOAT	64-bit floating point
INTEGER	31-bit signed binary
LONG VARCHAR	DB2 will use the system maximum
SMALLINT	Halfword (15-bit) signed binary
TIME	Format is HHMMSS (hour, minute, second)
TIMESTAMP	Same as DATE plus TIME; also includes microseconds
VARCHAR (n)	Variable-length character, n (maximum 4K) bytes long

The next three clauses are used only when foreign keys are being defined and, like the PRIMARY KEY clause, are available only with DB2 at the time of this writing.

The FOREIGN KEY Clause. The FOREIGN KEY clause specifies a foreign-key relationship and contains the optional ability to name it. All relations are stored in the system catalog. If no name is assigned, a default value will be used. Inside the parentheses, we list the columns that make up the foreign key. The data type and length of the foreign key must be the same as the primary key it references.

The REFERENCES Clause. Remember that a foreign key establishes a relationship between a dependent table and a parent table. The REFERENCES clause
specifies both the parent table and the primary key to which the foreign key
relates. This clause also is necessary only when defining foreign keys.

The ON DELETE Clause. The ON DELETE clause defines the integrity rule to
be used when the parent row of a foreign key is deleted. Use of RESTRICT will
make users unable to delete a parent row if there are matching dependent rows.
If CASCADE is used and a parent row is deleted, all dependent rows that contain
a matching foreign key value will also be deleted. Finally, SET NULL will force
DB2 to set the foreign-key values in the dependent table to NULL if the parent
row is deleted. The result of this choice is sometimes called a **dangling reference,**
because it leaves a foreign key that doesn't refer to anything. In a later section,
we will discuss referential integrity and DB2 in more detail.
    The next three clauses are also peculiar to DB2.

The IN Clause. The IN clause specifies the database and table space names to
which to assign the table. If no table space name is given (the second parameter),
DB2 will assign and define a default table space.

The EDITPROC Clause. The EDITPROC clause is a routine that cannot contain
any DB2 statements and is automatically invoked immediately following the
retrieval of a row or just prior to the storing of one. It is used for data compression, decompression, and encryption purposes.

The VALIDPROC Clause. The VALIDPROC clause is the name of an executable
module that will be invoked just before a row is stored. Like EDITPROC, it can
contain no DB2 statements and typically is used for data validation.

    Like the PRIMARY KEY, FOREIGN KEY, REFERENCES, and ON DELETE
clauses, the last three clauses just discussed aren't used with SQL-based products
other than DB2. If we used ORACLE, for example, we would omit the IN,
EDITPROC, and VALIDPROC lines from the table definition syntax.

Problem 4. **Define the following tables (from Chapter 6): PATIENT, MED-
ICATION, ROOM, DOCTOR, DOSAGE, CRITICAL__CONDITION, SERI-
OUS__CONDITION, and HEART__ILLNESS.** Ignore referential integrity at
this time.

Solution. Figure 7.7 shows the definition of each table. One of the tables, MED-
ICATION, has been expanded to include three new columns: ONHAND,
MED__CATEGORY, and UNITS__USED. The ONHAND column represents the
units of that medication that are presently in the pharmacy. MED__CATEGORY
represents a medication category. There are two categories: IV ("intravenous")
and PO (a Latin abbreviation meaning "by mouth"). UNITS__USED accumulates

FIGURE 7.7   Some Table Definitions for the Suburban Hospital Example in Chapter 6

```
CREATE TABLE PATIENT
  (PID         CHAR(10) NOT NULL,
   PNAME       CHAR(25) NOT NULL,
   DCODE       CHAR(3),
   DID         INTEGER,
   PRIMARY KEY (PID))
 IN DSNDB001.DSNTS001;  ←───────────── Database and table space names

CREATE TABLE MEDICATION
  (MID         CHAR(3) NOT NULL,
   MNAME       CHAR(20) NOT NULL,
   MCOST       DECIMAL(7,2),
   ONHAND      INTEGER,      ←───────── A new attribute
   MED_CATEGORY CHAR(4),     ←───────── These are also new attributes,
   UNITS_USED  INTEGER,      ←─────┘       not found in Chapter 6
   PRIMARY KEY (MID))
 IN DSNDB001.DSNTS001;

CREATE TABLE ROOM
  (RNO         CHAR(4)  NOT NULL,
   PID         CHAR(10) NOT NULL,
   PRIMARY KEY (RNO,PID)),
 IN DSNDB001.DSNTS001;

CREATE TABLE DOCTOR
  (DID         INTEGER    NOT NULL,
   DNAME       CHAR(25)   NOT NULL,
   PRIMARY KEY (PID))
 IN DSNDB001.DSNTS001;

CREATE TABLE DOSAGE
  (PID         CHAR(10)  NOT NULL,
   MID         CHAR(3)   NOT NULL,
   TIME        SMALLINT  NOT NULL,
   DOSAGE      CHAR(7)   NOT NULL,
   PRIMARY KEY (PID, MID, TIME))
 IN DSNDB001.DSNTS001;

CREATE TABLE CRITICAL_CONDITION
  (PID         CHAR(10) NOT NULL)
 IN DSNDB001.DSNTS001;

CREATE TABLE SERIOUS_CONDITION
  (PID         CHAR(10) NOT NULL)
 IN DSNDB001.DSNTS001;

CREATE TABLE HEART_ILLNESS
  (PID         CHAR(10) NOT NULL)
 IN DSNDB001.DSNTS001;
```

TABLE 7.5   The New MEDICATION Table Occurrence

MEDICATION

MID	MNAME	MCOST	ONHAND	MED_CATEGORY	UNITS_USED
KEF	KEFLIN	2.00	10	PO	1000
TAG	TAGAMET	3.00	5	PO	10
PCN	PENICILLIN	.50	100	IV	14000
VAL	VALIUM	.50	300	IV	24980
VIB	VIBRAMYCIN	1.50	100	PO	456
D5W	DEXTROSE 5%	2.00	150	IV	2450

FIGURE 7.8   DB2 Syntax for Defining Indexes

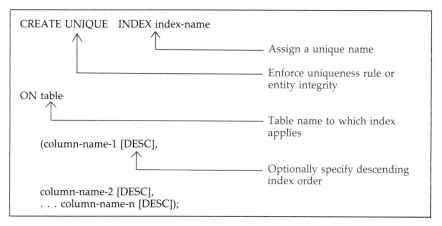

CREATE UNIQUE   INDEX index-name
— Assign a unique name
— Enforce uniqueness rule or entity integrity

ON table
— Table name to which index applies

(column-name-1 [DESC],
— Optionally specify descending index order

column-name-2 [DESC],
. . . column-name-n [DESC]);

Use of UNIQUE is required for all PRIMARY KEY columns if it is desired that DB2 enforce entity integrity.

the total amount of the medication used to date. Table 7.5 shows the new occurrence of the MEDICATION table.

Defining Indexes. As we saw earlier, there are two reasons for defining indexes: to improve efficiency and to enforce a uniqueness constraint. The syntax is shown in Figure 7.8.

Use of the optional UNIQUE clause forces DB2 to reject new rows containing an index value that matches one already stored. The table on which the index is defined follows the word ON. The column names specify the components of the index. Each component can be in ascending (the default) or descending (DESC) order. There are five other parameters that we won't discuss.

When the index is created, the space is automatically allocated and the index built from the base table's contents. Typically, such indexes are defined before a table is loaded with data.

Let's define an index on the PATIENT table, using PID. It is coded as follows:

CREATE UNIQUE INDEX PIDIDX
    ON PATIENT
        (PID);

Because we used the optimal parameter UNIQUE, any attempt to add a new patient having the same number as an existing one will result in an error.

Defining Views. Because of the dependence of one of the clauses on a statement not yet introduced (SELECT), we will defer discussing view definition until later in the chapter.

Deleting Objects: The DROP Statement

Any of the objects defined via the CREATE statement can be deleted by using the syntax in Figure 7.9. For example, to DROP the PATIENT table, we would code DROP TABLE PATIENT;.

When a table is dropped, all related indexes and views associated with it are also dropped.

Problem 5. **Delete database DSNDB001.**

Solution.

DROP DATABASE DSNDB001;

In this case, all associated tables, views, and indexes are also deleted.

When you use DROP INDEX index-name, you delete both the definition of the index and its contents.

FIGURE 7.9   **General Syntax Used to Delete Any DB2 Object**

```
DROP object-type object-name;
```

Changing a Table's Structure: The ALTER TABLE Statement

We can change any of the objects using the syntax shown in Figure 7.10.

We will limit the scope of the ALTER command to tables only. Its functionality is restricted to adding new columns, a new primary key, or new foreign keys and to changing a validation routine's name. The syntax is illustrated in Figure 7.11.

We will limit our discussion to those cases where we need to add new columns. When a new column is added, all of its values are set to NULL and will be found at the logical end of the table. Some SQL implementations permit us to specify where to place the new column; IBM's does not. Because all of the new column's values are initially set to NULL, its data type specification cannot use the NOT NULL option. Column values are later changed from NULL by using the UPDATE command, which we will examine later.

This is the second aspect of DB2's (and thus SQL's) data independence. As we saw in Chapter 1, adding a new field to a conventional VSAM or sequential file can be a chaotic process. With DB2, however, the DBA can add a new column to an existing table while users are using the database without having to perform a complicated unload-reload procedure.

Thus far, we have seen how to define a table, how to drop one, and how to add a column to an existing one. The procedure for deleting a column is a multistep one and is discussed later in this chapter.

FIGURE 7.10   **Syntax Used to Signify that a Change to an Object Follows**

```
ALTER object-type object-name;
```

FIGURE 7.11   **DB2 Command for Adding a New Column, a Primary Key, or a Foreign Key, or Changing the Name of a Validation Routine to an Existing Table**

```
ALTER TABLE table-name
  ADD column-name data-type
  [PRIMARY KEY . . .]
  [FOREIGN KEY . . .]
  VALIDPROC   validation-routine-name;
```

7.3 DATA RETRIEVAL FROM A SINGLE TABLE: THE SELECT-FROM-WHERE STATEMENT

A simplified form of the statement that is used to extract data from a table appears in Figure 7.12. A **search-condition** is made up of one or more *predicates* connected by OR, AND, and NOT. The complete SELECT-FROM-WHERE syntax is shown in Figure 7.13.

Because we did not see the ALL | DISTINCT option with the simpler SELECT-FROM-WHERE (SFW) format, you should conclude that one of the two choices is the default—and it is. DB2 assumes that unless DISTINCT is used, the query is to return every row that satisfies the query. If DISTINCT is specified as part of the query, DB2 displays only unique rows.

At this point, you may wonder about the need to specify DISTINCT, because every row in a relation must be unique and, therefore, there should never be duplicate rows. However, two factors refute this expectation. First, DISTINCT pertains to the query result, not to the original table. Second, DB2 does permit duplicate rows unless we use the UNIQUE index capability. In this case, while we can prohibit the base table from having duplicate rows, queries can still have them, as some later examples will illustrate.

A **select-list** consists of combinations of:

- Column names separated by commas
- SQL built-in functions
- Literals
- Arithmetic expressions

The **ordering-specification** is one or more column names: sequence-specification pairs, each pair separated by a comma. The sequence-specification can be either ASC (ascending—the default) or DESC (descending).

We will discuss the GROUP BY and HAVING options later.

FIGURE 7.12   **A Simplified Form of the SELECT-FROM-WHERE (SFW) Statement**

```
SELECT column-name1, column-name2, . . ., column-namen
                                                            Column(s) to be
                                                            displayed
FROM table-name
                                                            Table name
WHERE search-condition;
```

FIGURE 7.13   The Complete DB2 SELECT-FROM-WHERE Syntax

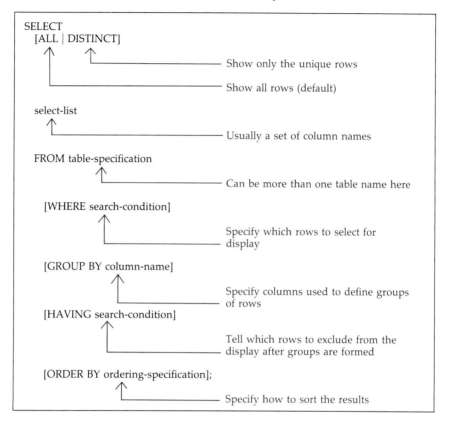

Predicates

A **predicate** is any logical expression that can be tested via the rows of the table. The general syntax of a predicate is:

expression comparison-operator expression

An **expression** is a field name, a constant, or a combination of both, connected by +, −, *, or /. A **comparison-operator** is one of the following: >, > =, <, < =, =, ¬=, ¬>, ¬<. The symbol ¬ means "not." Let's look at some examples of predicates.

Problem 6. **Define the predicate for finding all patients who are prescribed Keflin (code KEF) or who receive aspirin (code ASP) at 0900. The column name to use for medication code is MID and for the hour TIME.**

Solution. This requires three predicates, connected as follows:

MID = 'KEF' OR (MID = 'ASP' AND TIME = 0900).

The three predicates are MID = 'KEF', MID = 'ASP', and TIME = 0900. The predicates inside the parentheses are evaluated first.

Special Predicates. In addition to the normal predicates, there are four special ones:

- LIKE
- NULL
- BETWEEN
- IN

LIKE. LIKE causes DB2 to match for patterns in a character string. The syntax is shown in Figure 7.14.

The **pattern** can obtain any character string we want to find. It can also contain the special characters %, and __. The % character means to match any string regardless of length, while __ means to match any single character at that position.

Problem 7. **Give the predicate for finding patient names (column name PNAME) containing MITH in bytes 2–5.**

Solution. The predicate is

PNAME LIKE '__MITH'

FIGURE 7.14   Syntax Used to Search for Patterns

column-name [NOT] LIKE 'pattern'

Column name to search

Optional NOT

Keyword

What to search for

Had we coded PNAME LIKE '%MIT%', DB2 would find names containing the three letters MIT anywhere, regardless of their byte positions. Names such as SCHMIT, SMITH, and GROSCHMIT would be accessed.

NULL. The NULL predicate is used to access rows that either do or do not contain NULL values for the designated column depending on the syntax chosen. The syntax is shown in Figure 7.15.

Problem 8. **What predicate will find all medications containing NULL cost (MCOST) values?**

Solution. The predicate is

MCOST IS NULL.

BETWEEN. We use BETWEEN when searching for a range of field values. The syntax is presented in Figure 7.16.

Problem 9. **Give the predicate that will search for all medications costing between $1.00 and $5.00.**

Solution. The predicate is

MCOST BETWEEN 1.00 AND 5.00.

Note that we could have used the $>=$ and $<=$ operators to accomplish the same thing:

MCOST $>=$ 1.00 AND MCOST $<=$ 5.00

FIGURE 7.15   Predicate for Extracting Rows that Do or Do Not Contain NULL Column Values

column-name IS [NOT] NULL

FIGURE 7.16   Predicate Used to Search for Column Values within a Range

FIGURE 7.17 **Predicate for Searching Rows Based on a Specified Set of Column Values**

```
                column-name [NOT] IN (value-1, value-2, . . ., value-n)
                                          ↑        ↑             ↑
First value to search for ────────────────┘        │             │
Next value to search for ──────────────────────────┘             │
Last value to search for ────────────────────────────────────────┘
```

IN. The IN predicate enables us to easily phrase queries where we want DB2 to search a column for a list of values. The syntax is shown in Figure 7.17.

Problem 10. **What predicate will search for all medications having codes ASP, FEL, or KEF?**

Solution. Based on Figure 7.17, the predicate is

MID IN ('ASP', 'FEL', 'KEF')

If you are getting impatient to see how these predicates are used, your wait is over. The next section shows several examples. We begin by showing how the SQL SFW block can be used to access data in a single table and how to effect the relational algebraic operators PROJECT and SELECT.

SQL and the Relational PROJECT

To project a table on specified columns, we follow the DB2 SELECT clause (that's right, to execute a project, SQL uses SELECT!) with the desired column names. There are three SELECT options, with only the first two corresponding to the algebraic project. They are presented in Figure 7.18.

The optional parameter DISTINCT results in query results that contain unique rows. As we discussed earlier, unlike theoretical relations, SQL query results can contain duplicate rows. To prevent this, use DISTINCT when specifying the query format.

Problem 11. **Display the numbers and names of all patients.**

Solution.

```
SELECT PID, PNAME
       FROM PATIENT;
```

Figure 7.19 shows the result.

When DB2 displays the results, it shows the column's name above its values—in this example, PID and PNAME.

FIGURE 7.18   The Three SELECT Options

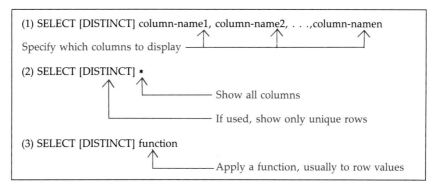

(1) SELECT [DISTINCT] column-name1, column-name2, . . .,column-namen

Specify which columns to display

(2) SELECT [DISTINCT] *

Show all columns

If used, show only unique rows

(3) SELECT [DISTINCT] function

Apply a function, usually to row values

The first format is the one most often used and which most closely corresponds to the relational algebra PROJECT operator; it displays the columns specified. The second format shows all of the columns in a table. The third format applies the built-in functions to column values.

FIGURE 7.19   Execution of the SQL Statement SELECT PID, PNAME FROM PATIENT;

Column names to be displayed

The SQL statement is: SELECT PID, PNAME
                         FROM PATIENT;

Table name

which says to extract only the specified columns and display them.
The PATIENT table appears below.

Extract these columns only

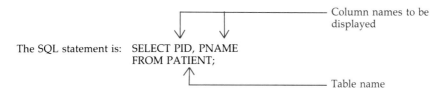

PID	PNAME	DCODE	DID
174	ADAMS	ANG	10
103	COX	ANG	10
49	DAVIS	CF	12

The results that will appear on the default display device are:

PID	PNAME
174	ADAMS
103	COX
49	DAVIS

The statement is the solution to the query: Display the numbers and names of all patients. We have taken some liberties with the actual output display, as DB2 does not draw lines on the display device and the actual size conforms to that of a standard display device: 24 rows by 80 columns.

FIGURE 7.20   Execution of the Statement SELECT * FROM DOCTOR;

The DOCTOR table is shown first:

DOCTOR

DID	DNAME
10	STARZEL
12	LONG
13	ROBERTS

The SELECT statement SELECT * FROM DOCTOR; says to extract all columns. Therefore, the display will match the one above.

The statement solves the query: Show all the data in the DOCTOR table.

Problem 12. **Show all the data in the DOCTOR table.**

Solution.

SELECT *
    FROM DOCTOR;

The result is shown in Figure 7.20.

Problem 13. **List the patient numbers of those patients receiving a drug.**

Solution.

SELECT PID
    FROM DOSAGE;

Figure 7.21 shows the results.

Notice that the query shows the rows in the same order as that in which they are stored. Later we will see how to specify a more desirable order. Also, notice that DB2 presented us with a result that contains duplicate rows. This is because the default value for the scope of the result is ALL. To override this, we use DISTINCT in the SELECT clause. Doing so will change our previous solution to:

SELECT DISTINCT PID
    FROM DOSAGE;

This will result in the following display:

PID
174
103
49

FIGURE 7.21   Execution of the Statement SELECT PID FROM DOSAGE;

The SQL statement is:

SELECT PID
FROM DOSAGE; ⟵ ――――――――――

Because the optional clause, DISTINCT, is
omitted, DB2 may return duplicate rows

Because we omitted the word DISTINCT from the SELECT clause, DB2 will return a table that
can contain duplicate rows. Theoretically this is incorrect, because the result isn't a relation.
However, for information processing purposes, this is often necessary. The effect of SELECT PID
is:

―――――――――――――― Extract the PID values

DOSAGE

PID	MID	TIME	DOSAGE
174	KEF	0200	100mg
174	KEF	1000	100mg
103	PCN	0200	50mg
103	VAL	0300	20mg
103	VIB	0300	50mg
103	VIB	1000	50mg
49	PCN	0200	50mg
49	PCN	0600	50mg
49	PCN	1000	50mg
49	TAG	1500	100mg

This will result in the following display:

PID
174
174
103
103
103
103
49
49
49
49

The example illustrates the problem that can arise if DISTINCT isn't used.

Built-in SQL Functions

As part of the third SELECT format, we saw "function." There are eight built-in functions we can use in the SELECT clause:

COUNT	Determines the number of values in a column
SUM	Determines the sum of values in a column
AVG	Determines the average of values in a column
MAX	Determines the largest value in a column
MIN	Determines the smallest value in a column
LENGTH	Determines the length of the argument
SUBSTR	Returns a substring
VALUE	Returns either argument 1 or argument 2, depending on whether or not argument 1 has a NULL value

The first five functions are called **column functions,** while the last three are known as **string functions.** Note that when retrieving individual rows from a table, you cannot use a column function and a column name at the same time. This forbids queries like:

SELECT MID,AVG(MCOST)
    FROM MEDICATION;

However, string functions can be used along with column names in a SELECT clause.

COUNT. One purpose of COUNT is to determine how many rows exist in a table; the result is always an integer. The format is shown in Figure 7.22.
    To illustrate the format, query:

SELECT COUNT (*)
    FROM PATIENT;

would display the following result:

where 3 is the number of rows in the PATIENT table.
    The second use for COUNT is to determine the number of unique values within a given column. In this case, we use the syntax illustrated in Figure 7.23.

FIGURE 7.22   **Using COUNT (∗) to Determine the Number of Rows in a Table**

> SELECT COUNT (∗)

FIGURE 7.23   **Using COUNT to Determine the Number of Unique Values in a Column**

> COUNT (DISTINCT column-name)

Problem 14. **How many different patients receive a drug?**

Solution. Using the format in Figure 7.23 results in this formulation:

SELECT COUNT (DISTINCT PID)
    FROM DOSAGE;

This will result in displaying the value 3, the number of different PID values in the DOSAGE table.

AVG. The AVG function calculates the arithmetic average of the column specified. It will present the result with a precision of 15 digits, and no name will appear above the result.

Problem 15. **What is the average cost of all drugs in the inventory?**

Solution.

SELECT AVG(MCOST)
    FROM MEDICATION;

The result is shown in Figure 7.24.

MAX, MIN, and SUM. The MAX, MIN, and SUM column functions result in an answer that has as many digits of precision as the underlying data. We won't show examples here, because their usage is identical to that of AVG, discussed above. However, some of the later problems include them.

LENGTH. The LENGTH function displays the length of the string (alphanumeric) argument. For example:

SELECT LENGTH(PNAME)
    FROM PATIENT
    WHERE PID = '103';

FIGURE 7.24   **Execution of the Statement SELECT AVG(MCOST) FROM MEDICATION**

The MEDICATION table is shown first:

MEDICATION

MID	MNAME	MCOST	ONHAND	MED_CATEGORY	UNITS_USED
KEF	KEFLIN	2.00	10	PO	1000
TAG	TAGAMET	3.00	5	PO	10
PCN	PENICILLIN	.50	100	IV	14000
VAL	VALIUM	.50	300	IV	24980
VIB	VIBRAMYCIN	1.50	100	PO	456
D5W	DEXTROSE 5%	2.00	150	IV	2450

The average cost (unweighted by the number of units of each) is: (2.00 + 3.00 + .50 + .50 + 1.50 + 2.00)/6 = 9.5/6 = 1.583. The actual display is:

AVG (MCOST)
1.58333333333333

This statement solves the query: What is the (unweighted) average cost of the inventory?

---

would show the value 3, which is the number of letters in COX, the name associated with PATIENT 103 (we discuss the WHERE clause in a later section).

SUBSTR. SUBSTR performs the same function as its counterpart in COBOL: It extracts substrings from string arguments. There are three arguments: S, N, and L. The first argument, S, is the column name, N the starting byte, and L the length of the desired substring. As an example, this query would display the first letter of all PATIENT names:

SELECT SUBSTR(PNAME,1,1)
    FROM PATIENT;

VALUE. We use VALUE when we want to substitute our own description for NULL values. For example, to attach the description "Unknown" to null MEDICATION MCOST values, we would use this syntax:

SELECT MID, VALUE(MCOST, 'Unknown')
    FROM MEDICATION;

Concatenation

Recent releases of DB2 permit the use of the concatenation operator (‖) as part of the SELECT clause. Suppose that instead of a single PATIENT name column, PNAME, we use two: PLAST for the last name and PFIRST for the first. To display all names as LAST, FIRST, we code:

```
SELECT PLAST ‖ ',' ‖ PFIRST
    FROM PATIENT;
```

DATE and TIME Functions

DAYS can be used to determine the number of days between two dates or the number of days since December 31, 0000. MICROSECOND, SECOND, MINUTE, HOUR, DAY, MONTH, and YEAR extract those items from DATE, TIME, or TIMESTAMP columns. For example, assume there is a column called WHEN associated with each DOSAGE row. It is a TIMESTAMP data type used to record when a particular order was initially saved. To show the DATE portion of the WHEN values, we use this syntax:

```
SELECT DATE(WHEN)
    FROM DOSAGE;
```

A DATE is shown in this format: YYYY-MM-DD. The DAY function extracts only the day (DD) portion of a column value, while MONTH and YEAR extract the MM and YYYY portions, respectively.

Assume there are two new PATIENT columns: DATE_ADMIT and DATE_DISCHARGED. We can perform subtraction or addition on DATE or TIME columns. For example, to determine how long a particular patient was in the hospital, we would code the following:

```
SELECT DATE_ADMIT - DATE_DISCHARGED
    FROM PATIENT . . .
```

We can also use constants with those functions. For example, suppose a patient is expected to be released one month after being admitted. To determine when this will be, we use:

```
SELECT DATE_ADMIT + 1 MONTHS
    FROM PATIENT . . .
```

In addition to MONTHS, we can use the keywords DAYS, YEARS, HOURS, MINUTES, and SECONDS as part of the SELECT statement. When used, such expressions are called **labeled durations.**

SQL and the Relational SELECT: SQL with Predicates

To effect the relational operator, SELECT, we use the WHERE clause, which, as we saw earlier, contains one or more predicates.

Problem 16. **How many patients receive the drug Keflin (code KEF)?**

Solution.

SELECT COUNT (DISTINCT PID)
    FROM DOSAGE
    WHERE MID = 'KEF';

Figure 7.25 shows both the query and its result. This query results in the value 1 being shown, because only patient 174 receives the drug. Note that if we used COUNT (*), we would see the value 2 rather than 1, because patient 174 receives the drug at two different times.

Problem 17. **Which medications cost over $1.50?**

Solution.

SELECT MID,MNAME,MCOST
    FROM MEDICATION
    WHERE MCOST > 1.5;

The result is:

MID	MNAME	MCOST
KEF	KEFLIN	2.00
TAG	TAGAMET	3.00
D5W	DEXTROSE 5%	2.00

Problem 18. **List all the medication data for those drugs beginning with the letter *V*.**

Solution. Figure 7.26 shows the solution.

This example showed the use of the LIKE operator with the % option. The next one demonstrates an example of the other LIKE option: '__'.

Problem 19. **List the three-byte codes for those Medications whose MID value begins with *V* and ends with *L*.**

FIGURE 7.25   Answering the Query: How Many Patients Receive the Drug Keflin, Code = 'KEF'?

The query statement is: SELECT COUNT (DISTINCT PID)
                                            FROM DOSAGE
                                            WHERE MID = 'KEF';

Extract just those rows that
have MID = 'KEF'

The DOSAGE table is shown next:

DOSAGE

PID	MID	TIME	DOSAGE
174	KEF	0200	100mg
174	KEF	1000	100mg
103	PCN	0200	50mg
103	VAL	0300	20mg
103	VIB	0300	50mg
103	VIB	1000	50mg
49	PCN	0200	50mg
49	PCN	0600	50mg
49	PCN	1000	50mg
49	TAG	1500	100mg

There are
two matches for MID
= 'KEF'

The effect of the WHERE clause is to generate a table with two rows:

PID	MID	TIME	DOSAGE
174	KEF	0200	100mg
174	KEF	1000	100mg

Now simply count how many different values of PID exist—obviously 1.
The display will be:

COUNT (DISTINCT PID)
1

Solution.

SELECT MID
    FROM MEDICATION
    WHERE MID LIKE 'V__L';

The second letter can be anything

FIGURE 7.26   **Answering the Query: Show the Medications Whose Code Begins with the Letter *V*.**

The SQL statement is:

SELECT *
    FROM MEDICATION
    WHERE MID LINE 'V%';

            Extract any rows that contain an MID value that begins with the letter *V* and is of any length

This produces the following display:

MID	MNAME	MCOST	ONHAND	MED_CATEGORY
VAL	VALIUM	.50	300	IV
VIB	VIBRAMYIN	1.50	100	PO

The only medication that satisfies this request is Valium, so the resulting display will be:

MID
VAL

Problem 20. **List those drugs costing between \$1.00 and \$3.00.**

Solution. Refer to the MEDICATION table in Problem 15.

SELECT MNAME,MCOST
    FROM MEDICATION
    WHERE MCOST BETWEEN 1.00 AND 3.00;

The display will be:

MNAME	MCOST
KEFLIN	2.00
TAGAMET	3.00
VIBRAMYCIN	1.50
DEXTROSE 5%	2.00

Problem 21. **List the numbers of those patients who receive medications having an MID value of either KEF or TAG.**

Solution.

SELECT PID
    FROM DOSAGE
    WHERE MID = 'KEF' OR MID = 'TAG';

The result is shown in Figure 7.27. Again, notice the duplicate rows. In this example, we have two predicates linked together using the keyword OR. As we discussed in the section on predicates, we can also use NOT and AND to link multiple predicates.

FIGURE 7.27   **Executing the query: SELECT PID FROM DOSAGE WHERE MID = 'KEF' OR MID = 'TAG';**

The WHERE clause says to extract those rows that satisfy the predicate: WHERE MID = 'KEF' OR MID = 'TAG';

DOSAGE

PID	MID	TIME	DOSAGE
174	KEF	0200	100mg
174	KEF	1000	100mg
103	PCN	0200	50mg
103	VAL	0300	20mg
103	VIB	0300	50mg
103	VIB	1000	50mg
49	PCN	0200	50mg
49	PCN	0600	50mg
49	PCN	1000	50mg
49	TAG	1500	100mg

There are two matches for MID = 'KEF'

There is one match for MID = 'TAG'

The resulting display will be:

PID
174
174
49

FIGURE 7.28   Sorting a Query

ORDER BY $\left\{ \begin{array}{l} \text{column-name1} \\ \text{rel-position-1} \end{array} \right.$ [DESC | ASC], $\left\{ \begin{array}{l} \text{column-name2} \\ \text{rel-position-2} \end{array} \right.$ [DESC | ASC] . . .

where DESC designates descending and ASC ascending.

Sorting Queries: The ORDER BY Clause

Unless specified otherwise, all SQL results are unsorted; that is, the rows will be in the same order as they were originally inserted. To change this, we use the ORDER BY clause. Its syntax is shown in Figure 7.28. Notice that we can substitute the column's relative position for the column name in the select-list.

Problem 22. **List all the medication names and costs, first in sequence by cost (ascending), then by name (descending).**

Solution.

SELECT MNAME,MCOST
    FROM MEDICATION
       ORDER BY MCOST ASC, MNAME DESC;

Because ASC is the default, had we coded the last line as ORDER BY MCOST, MNAME DESC, we would have seen the same result:

MNAME	MCOST
VALIUM	.50
PENICILLIN	.50
VIBRAMYCIN	1.50
KEFLIN	2.00
DEXTROSE 5%	2.00
TAGAMET	3.00

Before leaving this topic, we need to discuss the alternative way to specify the columns to be used for sequencing. As just mentioned, instead of the column's name, we can use the column's relative position, with *relative* referring to the position of the desired column in the select-list. The first column named in the SELECT clause has position 1, the next 2, and so on. Thus, in our last query, the last line might be stated as:

ORDER BY 2 ASC, 1 DESC

MCOST is the second column
named in the select list

Even though MCOST's position in the *original* table was 3, in the resulting query it is second; hence, the use of the digit 2 rather than 3.

Simple Queries with Calculations and Literals

In addition to using column names and functions in the select-list, we can use literals, calculations, or both. Literals are enclosed in single quotation marks. Calculations follow the conventional rules for programming languages.

Problem 23. **List the medication code and name, units on hand, and total dollar value for all drugs beginning with the letter *V*.**

                                                        ┌──── Perform and display a
                                                        │   calculation
                                                        ↓
SELECT MID,MNAME,ONHAND,MCOST*ONHAND
    FROM MEDICATION
    WHERE MID LIKE 'V%';

Solution.

The result is:

MID	MNAME	ONHAND	MCOST*ONHAND
VAL	VALIUM	300	150.00
VIB	VIBRAMYCIN	100	150.00

Here SQL will retrieve just the rows that contain the letter *V* as the first character of the MID value. Only two rows qualify. For each row, the three columns MID, MNAME, and ONHAND are then extracted. Finally, for each row, the product of ONHAND and MCOST is determined (to 15 places) and the result displayed.

Use of literals in the SELECT clause is similar to that in using calculations: We simply place the literal on the SELECT line enclosed in single quotation marks. Problem 24 will demonstrate this.

Table Aliases

There are times when we want to, or must, use a table name other than the one originally assigned. We can do this merely by adding a new name after the FROM table name(s). For example, if in the last query we wanted to use a shorter table name than MEDICATION, such as MED, we could have coded:

```
SELECT MID,MNAME,ONHAND,MCOST*ONHAND
    FROM MEDICATION MED
                                                                    Alias
    WHERE MED.MID LIKE 'V%';
                                                                    Use alias in WHERE clause
```

Retrieval of NULL Values

If we want rows that contain NULL values, we use IS NULL in the WHERE clause. For example, to display all the ROOM rows that don't have a patient assigned, we would use:

```
SELECT RNO
    FROM ROOM
    WHERE PID IS NULL;
```

A frequently made mistake in the above example is to code: WHERE PID = NULL instead of IS NULL. Remember that NULL values are never retrieved when using a predicate that doesn't contain IS NULL. Such a value is never less than, greater than, or equal to any other value, even another NULL value. The only way a row containing such a value can satisfy a search condition is to use the "column-name IS NULL" predicate.

SQL and UNION: The SQL UNION Statement

SQL has a UNION statement that does exactly what its relational algebra counterpart does. For two SQL tables to be union-compatible, both must have the same number of columns, and the corresponding columns from each table must be of the same data type. You should note that the union compatibility refers to the "table" resulting from the SQL SELECT and not the original tables.

Problem 24. **List the patient numbers who are on Keflin (code = 'KEF') or are in room 102.**

Solution.

```
SELECT PID, 'On Keflin'    A literal
    FROM DOSAGE
    WHERE MID = 'KEF'
```

UNION ⟵——— UNION operator
SELECT PID, 'In room 102'
    FROM ROOM
    WHERE RNO = '102';

Figure 7.29 shows how the above statement would be executed.

The UNION operator always eliminates duplicate rows, so we don't need DISTINCT. This example also shows the use of literals in the SELECT clause. Without this, the user would not know which patients were prescribed Keflin and which were in room 102. Patient 174 satisfies both search criteria. However, the message that is shown corresponds to the first match (on medication code).

If the query solution required the ORDER BY option, we would have been forced to use the relative column-number method, because this is the only option UNION supports.

You may be wondering if SQL also has the DIFFERENCE and INTERSECTION operators. The answer is a qualified yes. IBM's DB2 and SQL/DS do not, but ORACLE uses the operators INTERSECT and MINUS as substitutes, respectively. Like UNION, these ORACLE operators only present unique rows; all duplicates are removed. To implement DIFFERENCE and INTERSECTION using the IBM products, we can use combinations of other operators, as we will see later.

FIGURE 7.29   **Using DB2 to Take the UNION of Two Tables**

Step 1. Execute SELECT PID 'On Keflin'
                      FROM DOSAGE
                      WHERE MID = 'KEF'

———————————————————————— Extract just this
                                                                column

↓ DOSAGE

PID	MID	TIME	DOSAGE
174	KEF	0200	100mg
174	KEF	1000	100mg
103	PCN	0200	50mg
103	VAL	0300	20mg
103	VIB	0300	50mg
103	VIB	1000	50mg
49	PCN	0200	50mg
49	PCN	0600	50mg
49	PCN	1000	50mg
49	TAG	1500	100mg

There are
two matches for MID
= 'KEF'

FIGURE 7.29   (concluded)

After extracting the two rows that match and then the single column, PID, the resulting temporary table is:

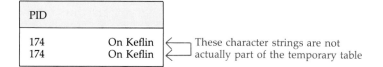

PID	
174	On Keflin
174	On Keflin

These character strings are not actually part of the temporary table

Step 2. Generate another temporary table according to:

```
SELECT PID, 'In room 102'
   FROM ROOM
   WHERE RNO = '102';
```

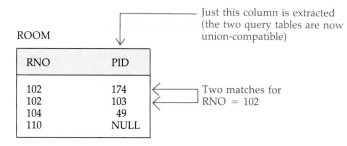

Just this column is extracted
(the two query tables are now
union-compatible)

ROOM

RNO	PID
102	174
102	103
104	49
110	NULL

Two matches for
RNO = 102

The result of this will be a second temporary table:

PID	
174	In room 102
103	In room 102

Notice that except for the character strings, the tables are now union-compatible. Therefore, when DB2 takes the UNION, the result will be:

PID	
174	On Keflin
103	In room 102

The original tables were not union-compatible, so a SELECT was used to make the query results compatible.

7.4   QUERYING MULTIPLE TABLES: SQL AND JOIN

To accomplish a join, we specify the following:

- The table names in the FROM clause, separated by commas.
- The joining condition in the WHERE clause. Because more than one table is involved, we qualify the column names by preceding them with the appropriate table name, followed by a period.

When we discussed the JOIN operator with respect to relational algebra, we saw that the domains of the joining attributes must be the same. With SQL, the joining columns must be only of the same data type.

Problem 25. **List the names of the patients receiving penicillin (code = 'PCN').
List the results in ascending patient name order.**

Solution. To solve the problem, we conceptually extract those DOSAGE rows that indicate that the patient receives penicillin (code PCN). Then, to determine the patient's name, we join those rows with PATIENT, using PID as the joining condition. Finally, we PROJECT over the desired columns, sorting by PNAME. Figure 7.30 shows the solution.

You can think of the extraction process this way. First, SQL extracts the DOSAGE rows that contain a medication code of PCN; there are four such rows. Next, those four rows are joined with PATIENT using PID as the joining condition. This will also result in a four-row table, with DAVIS being the patient name for three of the rows and COX for one. Finally, the unique names are presented in name order.

FIGURE 7.30   **Example of a SQL Join that Solves Problem 25**

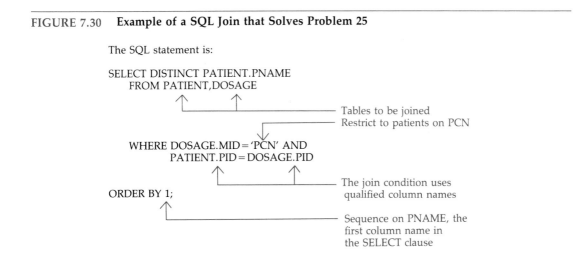

FIGURE 7.30   (concluded)

First, assume the restriction on MID is done first. This yields a temporary table based on DOSAGE (see Figure 7.29 for the DOSAGE occurrence) that looks like this:

PID	MID	TIME	DOSAGE
103	PCN	0200	50mg
49	PCN	0200	50mg
49	PCN	0600	50mg
49	PCN	1000	50mg

There are four DOSAGE rows that contain MID = 'PCN'

Now join PATIENT and the temporary table over PID:

PATIENT

PID	PNAME	DCODE	DID
174	ADAMS	ANG	10
103	COX	ANG	10
49	DAVIS	CF	12

join
(PID)

TEMP

PID	MID	TIME	DOSAGE
103	PCN	0200	50mg
49	PCN	0200	50mg
49	PCN	0600	50mg
49	PCN	1000	50mg

Using PID as the joining column, there will be no matches for PID 174, one for 103, and three for 49. The new (temporary) table that results from the join is:

PID	PNAME	DCODE	DID	MID	TIME	DOSAGE
103	COX	ANG	10	PCN	0200	50mg
49	DAVIS	ANG	12	PCN	0200	50mg
49	DAVIS	CF	12	PCN	0600	50mg
49	DAVIS	CF	12	PCN	1000	50mg

Finally, perform the SELECT, which results in this display:

PNAME
COX
DAVIS

Because SQL has a built-in optimizer, it makes no difference whether we specify the join condition (PATIENT.PID = DOSAGE.PID) first or second. In this case, we chose to specify first the algebraic SELECT operation (DOSAGE.MID = 'PCN'), then the join.

Problem 26. **What are the names of the patients who receive penicillin at 0600 or 1000? Assume we know the medication code is PCN.**

Solution.

SELECT DISTINCT NAME
    FROM PATIENT,DOSAGE
    WHERE (DOSAGE.MID = 'PCN'⟵— Restrict the search
    AND DOSAGE.TIME IN (0600,1000))
    AND PATIENT.PID = DOSAGE.PID; ————————————— Join condition

The result is:

PNAME
DAVIS

The only patient who receives penicillin at the specified times is patient number 49 (DAVIS). The other patient who receives penicillin gets it at 0200, a time that falls outside the desired set of values.

Sometimes tables must be joined to themselves. When this occurs, we must use aliases.

Problem 27. **List the patient numbers and room numbers for those rooms that contain more than one patient.**

Solution. One way to solve this is to imagine two tables, each having the same columns as ROOM. Then, by joining over RNO (room number), we would display only those patients who share a room with one or more other patients. Of course, we in fact have only a single table, ROOM, but we can "fool" SQL into thinking there are two tables by using aliases.

Figure 7.31 shows the answer. Notice there are two patients in room 102 and one in room 104; there are no patients in room 110. When we omit the second condition (ONE.PID < TWO.PID), SQL simply joins the two tables on RNO (room number). Thus, there are two matches for room 102 and one each for rooms 104 and 110.

Another occasion that requires a table being joined to itself arises when a query necessitates a search on one column for multiple values. For example,

---

FIGURE 7.31   Joining a Table to Itself

The SQL statement is:

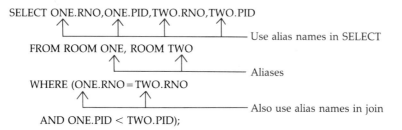

First, assume DB2 creates two temporary tables—ONE and TWO, both based on ROOM:

ONE

RNO	PID
102	174
102	103
104	49
110	NULL

TWO

RNO	PID
102	174
102	103
104	49
110	NULL

Now do the join:

RNO	PID	RNO	PID
102	174	102	174
102	174	102	103
102	103	102	174
102	103	102	103
104	49	104	49
110		110	

Notice that in row 1, both PIDs are the same. What we want are just those rows that have different PID values. Use ONE.PID < TWO.PID to do this. We could have used ONE.PID > TWO.PID or ONE.PID ¬ = TWO.PID, where "¬" is used to designate "NOT". In either case, the display would be:

RNO	PID	RNO	PID
102	103	102	174

This example solves Problem 27.

suppose we are asked to find the patients who are on both VAL and VIB. We might be tempted to code something like:

SELECT PID FROM DOSAGE WHERE MID = 'VAL' and MID = 'VIB';

This won't work, however, because there are no rows in which the value of MID is simultaneously VIB and VAL. The proper solution is:

SELECT A.PID
    FROM DOSAGE A, DOSAGE B
        WHERE A.MID = 'VAL'
        AND B.MID = 'VIB'
        AND A.PID = B.PID;

7.5   NESTED SELECT-FROM-WHERE BLOCKS: SUBSELECTS

A **subselect,** or **subquery,** is a SFW within a SFW; that is, a subquery contains two or more SFW blocks, one nested inside the other. Subselects:

- May return only one column.
- Are able to return data from one row or several.

FIGURE 7.32   **Example of a Subquery**

The SQL statement is:

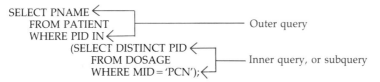

First, the inner SWF is executed: SELECT DISTINCT PID FROM DOSAGE WHERE MID = 'PCN':

DOSAGE

PID	MID	TIME	DOSAGE
174	KEF	0200	100mg
174	KEF	1000	100mg
103	PCN	0200	50mg
103	VAL	0300	20mg
103	VIB	0300	50mg
103	VIB	1000	50mg
49	PCN	0200	50mg
49	PCN	0600	50mg
49	PCN	1000	50mg
49	TAG	1500	100mg

There are four matches for MID = 'PCN'

FIGURE 7.32   **(concluded)**

After performing the SELECT DISTINCT PID on the restricted results above, the resulting table is:

PID
103
49

← Use of DISTINCT eliminated the other 49s

Notice that this results in the set of PID values 103,49. Now SQL substitutes these values inside the parentheses, yielding this equivalent query:

SELECT PNAME
    FROM PATIENT
    WHERE PID IN
        (103,49);

Let's see how this shortened form of the query proceeds:

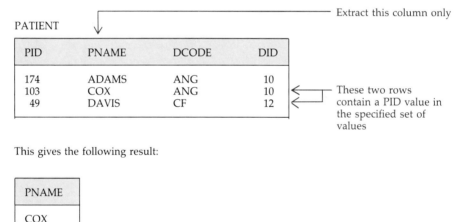

Extract this column only

PATIENT

PID	PNAME	DCODE	DID
174	ADAMS	ANG	10
103	COX	ANG	10
49	DAVIS	CF	12

← These two rows contain a PID value in the specified set of values

This gives the following result:

PNAME
COX
DAVIS

The query statement was: List the names of the patients receiving a drug with code = PCN.

- Are typically coded as part of a predicate containing =, which is used when they return a single value, or IN when they return several values.
- Often can be used as a substitute for a join when we want to display columns from a single table.

As a first example, we will use a subquery to answer the query: List the names of the patients who receive medication PCN. The solution is shown in Figure 7.32.

FIGURE 7.33   **A Three-Level SFW that Solves the Query: List the Names of the Patients Who Receive a Medication Costing over $1.00**

One answer to Problem 28, assuming we know which medications cost over $1.00, is:

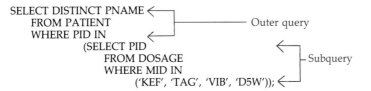

```
SELECT DISTINCT PNAME
    FROM PATIENT
    WHERE PID IN
            (SELECT PID
                FROM DOSAGE
                WHERE MID IN
                    ('KEF', 'TAG', 'VIB', 'D5W'));
```

Of course, we don't know those medication codes in advance. However, we do have a way to determine them—use a SFW like this:

```
SELECT MID
    FROM MEDICATION
        WHERE MCOST > 1.00;
```

Now we substitute this last SFW for the set of three values in our tentative solution. This gives the final solution:

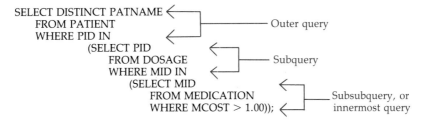

```
SELECT DISTINCT PATNAME
    FROM PATIENT
    WHERE PID IN
            (SELECT PID
                FROM DOSAGE
                WHERE MID IN
                    (SELECT MID
                        FROM MEDICATION
                        WHERE MCOST > 1.00));
```

Let's play back the query in reverse order. First, the innermost query is executed, resulting in:

MID
KEF
TAG
VIB
D5W

←All of these MID values are associated with medications costing over $1.00

The subquery is now:

```
SELECT PID
    FROM DOSAGE
    WHERE MID IN
        ('KEF', 'TAG', 'VIB', 'D5W')
```

FIGURE 7.33   (concluded)

The table that results from the above subquery is derived from DOSAGE and contains the PID values for those rows containing a MID value in the set of values above. The table is derived like this:

DOSAGE

PID	MID	TIME	DOSAGE		
174	KEF	0200	100mg	←	These are
174	KEF	1000	100mg		the matches
103	PCN	0200	50mg		
103	VAL	0300	20mg		
103	VIB	0300	50mg		
103	VIB	1000	50mg	←	
49	PCN	0200	50mg	←	
49	PCN	0600	50mg		
49	PCN	1000	50mg		
49	TAG	1500	100mg	←	

This results in:

PID
174
103
103
49

The final query (the outer one) is now equivalent to:

SELECT DISTINCT PNAME
    FROM PATIENT
    WHERE PID IN
        (174, 103, 103, 49);

This results in the end user display:

PNAME
ADAMS
COX
DAVIS

Except for the sorting, this example is the same as Problem 24. The solution to that problem used a join. In fact, the problem can be solved using either a subquery or a join, whichever is easier.

Problem 28. Show the names of patients who receive a drug costing over $1.00.

Solution. Before showing the solution, lets solve a simpler problem. Assume we already know that the medications costing over $1.00 have the codes KEF, TAG, VIB, and D5W. The problem now reduces to one of finding those patients receiving those medications. The solution is developed in Figure 7.33.

7.6 QUERIES USING ALL OR ANY

Although all subqueries using either ANY or ALL can be reformulated to avoid them, we will nevertheless present two examples that use them. Before we begin, note that some implementations of SQL substitute the ANSI SQL keyword SOME for ANY. Both operators usually follow an expression and a comparison operator. For example:

expression < ANY subquery

or

expression > ALL subquery

When < is used with ALL, it means the subquery will return several values, and the expression's value should be smaller than all of those values. If the statement is of the form expression < ANY subquery, the value of the expression should be less than at least one of the returned values. The other operators (>, =, etc.) work in a similar manner.

Problem 29. Show the name and cost of the medications that cost more than all the drugs in the IV category.

Solution 1. First we present the solution without using ALL:

```
SELECT MNAME,MCOST
    FROM MEDICATION
    WHERE MCOST >
        (SELECT MAX(MCOST)
            FROM MEDICATION
            WHERE MED_CATEGORY = 'IV');
```

Figure 7.34 shows the execution of this solution.

FIGURE 7.34   **Using a Subquery without Using the Qualifier ALL to Resolve the Query: Show the Name and Cost of the Medications Costing More than All the Drugs in the IV Category**

The MEDICATION table looks like this:

MEDICATION

MID	MNAME	MCOST	ONHAND	MED_CATEGORY	UNITS_USED
KEF	KEFLIN	2.00	10	PO	1000
TAG	TAGAMET	3.00	5	PO	10
PCN	PENICILLIN	.50	100	IV	14000
VAL	VALIUM	.50	300	IV	24980
VIB	VIBRAMYCIN	1.50	100	PO	456
D5W	DEXTROSE 5%	2.00	150	IV	2450

The SQL Statement is:

```
SELECT MNAME,MCOST
    FROM MEDICATION
    WHERE MCOST >
        (SELECT MAX(MCOST)
            FROM MEDICATION
            WHERE MED_CATEGORY = 'IV');
```

First, the innermost query is executed. The IV MEDICATION costing the most is D5W, which costs $2.00. Thus, our query effectively reduces to:

```
SELECT MNAME,MCOST
    FROM MEDICATION
    WHERE MCOST > 2.00;
```

Now DB2 will scan the MEDICATION rows looking for those rows containing an MCOST value > 2.00. You can see that only one medication costs more than $2.00—the one shown in the result below:

MNAME	MCOST
TAGAMET	3.00

Solution 2. This time, we use ALL:

```
SELECT MNAME,MCOST
    FROM MEDICATION
    WHERE MCOST > ALL
        (SELECT MCOST
            FROM MEDICATION
            WHERE MED_CATEGORY = 'IV');
```

First, all MCOST values corresponding to the IV medications are returned by the inner query. Next, DB2 scans the rows of MEDICATION looking for MCOST values that exceed all of the returned values.

Both of the above solutions will give the same result. Again, choose whichever one is easier for you to conceptualize.

Problem 30. **Show the names of the medications that cost more than any IV.**

Solution. This problem asks DB2 to list those medications that cost more than the minimum costing IV. Like Problem 29, we can solve this one using a nested

---

FIGURE 7.35   **Solution to the Query: List Those Medications Costing More than Any IV**

The MED__CATEGORY = 'IV' rows are:

MID	MNAME	MCOST	ONHAND	MED__CATEGORY	UNITS__USED
PCN	PENICILLIN	.50	100	IV	14000
VAL	VALIUM	.50	300	IV	24980
D5W	DEXTROSE 5%	2.00	150	IV	2450

The MCOST values resulting from SELECT MCOST
                                     FROM MEDICATION
                                     WHERE MED__CATEGORY = 'IV';

would therefore be:

MCOST
.50
.50
2.00

The outer query says that DB2 is to return those rows where the MCOST value is greater than any of the values in the set just shown: (.50, .50, 2.00). The result is:

MNAME	MCOST	
KEFLIN	2.00	⟵ > .50
TAGAMET	3.00	⟵ > All values
VIBRAMYCIN	1.50	⟵ > .50
DEXTROSE 5%	2.00	⟵ > .50

SFW but with the inner one containing MIN (MCOST) rather than MAX (MCOST). However, our solution contains the ANY operator:

SELECT MNAME,COST
    FROM MEDICATION
    WHERE MCOST > ANY
      (SELECT MCOST
        FROM MEDICATION
        WHERE MED__CATEGORY = 'IV');

Figure 7.35 shows how the solution unfolds.

7.7   QUERIES USING GROUP BY

Conceptually, "GROUP BY column-name" rearranges a table into groups of rows, with each row having the same value for the specified column name. (In practice, this physical restructuring isn't done.) DB2 then displays one row from each group. To restrict the rows that make up a group, we use the WHERE clause as a filter.

Earlier, we said that SQL functions cannot be mixed with column names in the same SELECT line. When using the GROUP BY option, this rule is relaxed.

Problem 31. What is the total dollar value of each medication category?

Solution. We want to use the SUM function to determine the total value of (ONHAND * MCOST) for each of the two categories. First, we group the medications by MED__CATEGORY. Next, we SELECT the MED__CATEGORY value associated with each group and calculate the total value by multiplying the ONHAND value by MCOST. The complete solution is:

SELECT MED__CATEGORY,SUM(ONHAND*MCOST)
    FROM MEDICATION
    GROUP BY MED__CATEGORY;

The result is:

MED__CATEGORY	SUM(ONHAND*MCOST)
PO	185.00
IV	500.00

First, imagine that DB2 rearranges the MEDICATION table by MED__CATEGORY, as in Figure 7.36. Next, for each row within the two groups (IV and PO), DB2 multiplies the cost by the units on hand and then totals this amount for each group. Finally, DB2 displays the MED__CATEGORY and totals.

FIGURE 7.36   **The Imaginary Restructuring of the MEDICATION Table Due to the SQL Clause GROUP BY MED__CATEGORY**

MID	MNAME	MCOST	ONHAND	MED__CATEGORY	UNITS__USED
KEF	KEFLIN	2.00	10	PO	1000
TAG	TAGAMET	3.00	5	PO	10
VIB	VIBRAMYCIN	1.50	100	PO	14000
PCN	PENICILLIN	.50	100	IV	24980
VAL	VALIUM	.50	300	IV	456
D5W	DEXTROSE 5%	2.00	150	IV	2450

When a column name is SELECTed and GROUP BY is used, the value of the SELECTed column must be the same for all rows in the group. This usually means that only the GROUP BY column can be SELECTed. In the above problem, all medications in the IV group also have the same MED__CATEGORY value: IV. Obviously, all medications in the PO group have the same MED__CATE-GORY value. As a result, we were permitted to display the MED__CATEGORY value for each group. Would DB2 permit us to display the ON__HAND amount for each group? The answer is no, because the ON__HAND value differs for each row within the two groups.

Problem 32. **Exclude from Problem 31 any medications for which there are fewer than 10 units on hand.**

Solution.

SELECT MED__CATEGORY,SUM(ONHAND*MCOST)
    FROM MEDICATION
       WHERE ONHAND>=10
   GROUP BY MED__CATEGORY;

When the groups are formed, they will exclude the second row because there are only five units of Tagamet on hand. The new result will be:

MED__CATEGORY	SUM(ONHAND*MCOST)
PO	35.00
IV	120.00

There is one more SFW clause that pertains to the GROUP BY option: "HAV-ING search-condition." This permits us to apply a condition to the groups, causing DB2 to display only those groups that satisfy the search-condition.

Problem 33. **Modify Problem 32 to report only those groups that contain more than three medications.**

Solution.

SELECT MED__CATEGORY,SUM(ONHAND*MCOST)
    FROM MEDICATION
     WHERE ONHAND>=10
   GROUP BY MED__CATEGORY
   HAVING COUNT(*)>3;

Because there are no such groups, SQL will report no values.

7.8   ADDING ROWS TO A TABLE: THE INSERT STATEMENT

There are two methods for adding rows to a table: Add the rows as values, one row at a time, or populate the table from another table. Let's look at the first method. Its syntax is shown in Figure 7.37.

The column list is optional. If provided, it defines a subset of columns to be given values. Those columns not specified will be assigned NULL values.

Problem 34. **Add a new DOCTOR with code 17 and name "Lundberg."**

Solution.

INSERT INTO DOCTOR
    VALUES (17, 'LUNDBERG');

No column names are provided, so SQL will assume we are giving each DOCTOR column a value. Had there been more than two DOCTOR columns, DB2 would have flagged the statement, saying that too few values were provided. To insert only the DID value at this time, we would code:

INSERT INTO DOCTOR
   (DID)
    VALUES (17);

In this case, the value for DNAME would be NULL.

FIGURE 7.37   **Format of the INSERT Statement**

```
INSERT INTO table-name  ←──────────── Table being added to
   [column-name list]   ←──────────── Optional column-list
   VALUES  (list of values); ←─────── A single row of values
```

FIGURE 7.38   **The INSERT Format Used to Populate One Table by Extracting Rows from Another Table**

```
INSERT INTO table-name-1
   [column-list]
      SELECT column-list
         FROM table-name-2
            WHERE search-condition;
```

The other INSERT method extracts values from one table and INSERTS them into another. Figure 7.38 shows the format.

Problem 35. **Create and then load a table that contains the MID and MNAME values for the IV medications.**

Solution. First, we create a new table with the desired columns:

```
CREATE TABLE IV_MEDS
    (MID CHAR(3) NOT NULL,
    MNAME CHAR(20) NOT NULL)
IN DSNDB001.DSNTS001;
```

Next, we populate the table by extracting the desired rows from the MEDICATION table:

```
INSERT INTO IV_MEDS
    SELECT MID,MNAME
        FROM MEDICATION
        WHERE MED_CATEGORY = 'IV';
```

7.9 DELETING ROWS FROM A TABLE: THE DELETE STATEMENT

To remove one or more rows from a table, we use the statement in Figure 7.39.

Problem 36. **Delete the doctor with the last name "COX" from the DOCTOR table.**

Solution.

```
DELETE
    FROM DOCTOR
    WHERE DNAME = 'COX';
```

FIGURE 7.39   **Format of the DELETE Statement**

```
DELETE
     FROM table-name
     WHERE search-condition;
```

Problem 37. Delete all medications for which fewer than 25 units have been used.

Solution.

```
DELETE
     FROM MEDICATION
     WHERE UNITS_USED<25;
```

The above statement would delete MEDICATION row 2, because only 10 units of Tagamet have been used. If the WHERE clause were omitted, *all* of the table's rows would be deleted—so don't forget to specify it!

7.10   CHANGING A TABLE'S ROW VALUES: THE UPDATE STATEMENT

We can change values in a table by using the UPDATE statement. Its syntax is shown in Figure 7.40. The SET clause specifies both the column's name and its new value. As in other cases, use of the WHERE clause restricts the action of the UPDATE statement.

FIGURE 7.40   **Format of the UPDATE Statement**

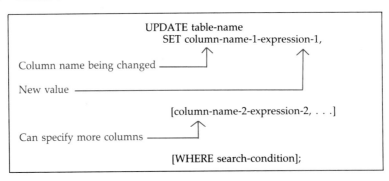

Problem 38. **Assume it is January 1. Change the UNITS__USED for all medications to zero.**

Solution.

UPDATE MEDICATION
    SET UNITS__USED = 0;

Problem 39. **The hospital has requested the pharmacy to increase all IV costs by 10 percent. Use DB2 to implement the change.**

Solution.

UPDATE MEDICATION
    SET MCOST = MCOST*1.10
    WHERE MED__CATEGORY = 'IV';

After selecting the rows that contain IV as the medication category, SQL will replace the existing MCOST values with the expression MCOST*1.10.

7.11 DELETING COLUMNS FROM TABLES

Earlier we saw that the ALTER TABLE statement can be used to add columns but not delete them. To remove a column from a table, we follow these steps:

1. Define a new table containing the same columns as the original one but without the column to be deleted.
2. Use the UPDATE . . . SELECT statement to populate the new table from the original one.
3. DROP the original table.

Problem 40. **The hospital has decided to eliminate the MED__CATEGORY column from the MEDICATION table. Show the steps necessary to accomplish this.**

Solution. First, we define the new table with MED__CATEGORY omitted:

CREATE TABLE NEW__MEDICATION
    (MID   CHAR   (3) NOT NULL,
    MNAME   CHAR(20) NOT NULL,
    MCOST   DECIMAL(7,2),
    ONHAND   INTEGER,
    UNITS__USED   INTEGER)
IN DSNDB001. DSNTS001;

Next, we load the new table from MEDICATION:

INSERT INTO NEW_MEDICATION
    SELECT MID,MNAME,MCOST,ONHAND, UNITS_USED
        FROM MEDICATION;

Finally, we DROP the original MEDICATION table:

DROP TABLE MEDICATION;

7.12   USE OF EXISTS AND NOT EXISTS

DB2 can test for the existence of rows in a table that match some specified condition. Such a test is usually performed within a subquery and is connected to the outer query by using the syntax shown in Figure 7.41.

If DB2 can find a row that satisfies the EXISTS clause (subquery), the expression is said to be "true"; otherwise, the expression is "false." Let's look at some examples.

Problem 41. **List the names of the medications that are prescribed for 1000 hours.**

Solution.

SELECT MNAME
    FROM MEDICATION
    WHERE EXISTS
        (SELECT * FROM DOSAGE
            WHERE MEDICATION.MID = DOSAGE.MID
            AND DOSAGE.TIME = 1000);

All subqueries that follow the EXISTS (or NOT EXISTS) use the same form, namely "SELECT * FROM table-name." The subquery is "true" if any rows that satisfy the search condition are found in the FROM table.

In our example, DB2 will examine each row in the MEDICATION table, one at a time. If the MEDICATION is given at 1000, the EXISTS clause is "true" and

---

FIGURE 7.41   **The EXISTS Format**

WHERE [NOT] EXISTS

the corresponding MEDICATION name is displayed. This procedure is repeated until every MEDICATION has been examined.

The first MEDICATION code is KEF. Are there any rows in the DOSAGE table that have MID = 'KEF' and TIME = 1000? The answer is yes. Therefore, the subquery evaluates to "true," and KEFLIN will be the first MEDICATION to be displayed. Similarly, VIBRAMYCIN and PENICILLIN satisfy the subquery and thus are also displayed. The complete result is:

MNAME
KEFLIN
VIBRAMYCIN
PENICILLIN

For those SQL implementations that do not directly support them, we can use NOT EXISTS to implement the DIFFERENCE operator and EXISTS to implement the INTERSECTION operator.

Problem 42. **Which patients are in critical condition and also have a heart ailment?**

Solution 1. The first solution pertains to ORACLE, which supports the INTERSECT operator.

```
SELECT PID
    FROM HEART__ILLNESS
INTERSECT
    SELECT PID
        FROM CRITICAL__CONDITION;
```

The INTERSECT operator returns the rows that are returned by both the first and the second queries. Like UNION, ORACLE's INTERSECT (and MINUS) operator requires union compatibility for the select-list. This solution, while acceptable for ORACLE, won't work for DB2 or SQL/DS.

Solution 2. Here is the DB2 solution:

```
SELECT PID
    FROM HEART__ILLNESS
    WHERE EXISTS
        (SELECT *
        FROM CRITICAL__CONDITION
        WHERE HEART__ILLNESS.PID = CRITICAL__CONDITION.PID);
```

Both queries give the same result:

PID
174

   As an example of the DIFFERENCE (MINUS in ORACLE) operator, consider the next problem.

Problem 43. **List the PIDs for patients who are in the hospital with a heart ailment but are not in critical condition.** We solved this problem (Problem 13) in Chapter 6.

Solution 1. The first solution applies to ORACLE:

SELECT PID
    FROM HEART__ILLNESS
MINUS
    SELECT PID
        FROM CRITICAL__CONDITION;

The result is:

PID
103

   The MINUS operator returns the rows that are in the first query but not in the second.

Solution 2. Here is the DB2 solution:

SELECT PID
    FROM HEART__ILLNESS
    WHERE NOT EXISTS
      (SELECT *
          FROM CRITICAL__CONDITION
          WHERE HEART__ILLNESS.PID =
          CRITICAL__CONDITION.PID);

7.13   CORRELATED SUBQUERIES

For all the subqueries we have examined thus far, DB2 first evaluated the innermost (last) query first. The evaluation of the subquery, or subselect, returned a single value (or set of values). It then substituted this value into the outer level's predicate. Only then did DB2 use those results to evaluate the next query. There are times, however, when this isn't desirable—situations where the inner query depends on a value or values determined by an outer query. In this case, the outer query is repeatedly evaluated and a value determined. Then the inner query is evaluated based on the previously determined value. This type of query is called a **correlated subquery.**

Problem 44. **Retrieve the code and name for any medication whose average cost exceeds the average cost of its category.**

Solution.

```
SELECT MID,MNAME
    FROM MEDICATION MED
    WHERE MCOST<
        (SELECT AVG(MCOST)
            FROM MEDICATION
            WHERE MED.MED__CATEGORY=
            MEDICATION.MED__CATEGORY);
```

The result is as follows:

MID	MNAME
TAG	TAGAMET
D5W	DEXTROSE 5%

The alias in this situation is sometimes called the **correlation name** and is required when such queries are constructed. Figure 7.42 shows how the solution works.

7.14   CREATING VIEWS: LOGICAL TABLES AND DOMAIN CONSTRAINTS

As we have discussed, a view is a logical table whose rows are derived from base tables, views, or combinations of both. They can also include derived values based on several rows of a base table (an average, for example). They are usually used to simplify a query or for security reasons. To define a view, we use the syntax shown in Figure 7.43.

FIGURE 7.42   **How a Correlated Subquery Works**

First, the correlation table is:

MED

MID	MNAME	MCOST	ONHAND	MED_CATEGORY	UNITS_USED
KEF	KEFLIN	2.00	10	PO	1000
TAG	TAGAMET	3.00	5	PO	10
PCN	PENICILLIN	.50	100	IV	14000
VAL	VALIUM	.50	300	IV	24980
VIB	VIBRAMYCIN	1.50	100	PO	456
D5W	DEXTROSE 5%	2.00	150	IV	2450

The correlated subquery now proceeds like this. The MED_CATEGORY value associated with the first row in MEDICATION is used to determine the average cost for that category. DB2 finds that the medication is Keflin, that it costs $2.00, and that it is in category PO.

Next, DB2 substitutes that value for MED.MED_CATEGORY in the last line of the query. Therefore, the innermost query is now equivalent to:

SELECT AVG(MCOST)
    FROM MEDICATION
    WHERE 'PO' = MEDICATION.MED_CATEGORY;

The above WHERE clause effectively reduces MEDICATION to:

MEDICATION

MID	MNAME	MCOST	ONHAND	MED_CATEGORY	UNITS_USED
KEF	KEFLIN	2.00	10	PO	1000
TAG	TAGAMET	3.00	5	PO	10
VIB	VIBRAMYCIN	1.50	100	PO	456

The SELECT clause gives a result of 2.167, the average cost of the PO medications.

Next, DB2 returns to the first row in the MEDICATION table. If the cost of that medication ($2.00) exceeds the computed average, the corresponding code and name are displayed. Because Keflin's cost is only 2.00, its row isn't shown.

The next row in MEDICATION is now checked the same way. Tagamet is also a PO medication, so we already know that the average cost of such drugs is 2.167 (although SQL doesn't and hence must recalculate it). Since its cost does exceed the average for its category, its code and name are displayed. SQL continues in this manner until all MEDICATION rows are examined.

The query is:

SELECT MID,MNAME
    FROM MEDICATION MED
    WHERE MCOST>   ↑————— Correlation name
        (SELECT AVG(MCOST)
        FROM MEDICATION
        WHERE MED.MED_CATEGORY = MEDICATION.MED_CATEGORY);

FIGURE 7.43   **The CREATE VIEW Statement**

```
CREATE VIEW view-name
   [(column-name-1, column-name-2, . . . )]
   AS SELECT [DISTINCT] select-list
       FROM table-name
       [WHERE search-condition]
       [GROUP BY column-name]
       [HAVING search condition]
       [WITH CHECK OPTION];
```

A view appears to an end user just like a base table. However, some operations may not be applicable, depending on the exact makeup of the view.

The AS SELECT clause actually defines the view. It can contain several table or view names (in the FROM clause), assign new column names (column-name-1, column-name-2, etc.), and contain a GROUP BY and a HAVING clause. If the view is based on a join, new column names **must** be given; otherwise, SQL will use the same names as the underlying tables.

As long as the view is a simple one, meaning that it is based on a single base table, views can be used to UPDATE, INSERT, and DELETE the underlying base tables. On the other hand, views based on joins, or functions, or that contain the GROUP BY or DISTINCT options cannot be updated.

DB2 does not directly support the idea of a domain constraint. However, by using a view that contains the WITH CHECK OPTION, we can force DB2 to support them.

Suppose a view is defined such that users of the view are able to process only those patients under the care of a particular physician. Unless the WITH CHECK OPTION is specified, it will be possible to add a new patient with a doctor code (DID) other than the one specified in the view or to change the patient's DID value to one different from the code associated with that view. Conversely, by using the optional clause, DB2 will permit to be added only those rows that contain values that satisfy the view definition, thus effectively implementing domain constraints.

Problem 45. **Create a view table that contains the patients under Dr. Long's care.**

Solution.

```
CREATE VIEW DRLONG
AS SELECT *
       FROM PATIENT
       WHERE DID = 12;
```

In this example, the view will contain the same column names as the underlying base table (PATIENT). However, only those patients treated by Dr. Long will be displayed when the view is queried. Thus, if this query is used:

SELECT *
   FROM DRLONG;

the result will be:

PATIENT

PID	PNAME	DCODE	DID
49	DAVIS	CF	12

Referring to our previous discussion, unless we use the WITH CHECK OPTION, it will be possible to add a new patient—"SHILDT," for example—who is not treated by Dr. Long, DID=12. For example, DB2 will permit this:

INSERT INTO DRLONG
   VALUES (100,'SHILDT','ANG',10)

even though DID 10 corresponds to Dr. Starzel. To prevent this from happening, we use the WITH CHECK OPTION when defining the view.

Problem 46. Create a view containing the MED__CATEGORY and average cost for each category.

Solution.

CREATE VIEW AVGM
   (CAT,AVGC)
   AS SELECT MED__CATEGORY,AVG(MCOST)
      FROM MEDICATION
      GROUP BY MED__CATEGORY;

This time, new column names are assigned. Instead of MED__CATEGORY, CAT is used. Also, rather than using the cumbersome name AVG(MCOST), the shorter name AVGC is substituted. The view's contents could be shown by:

SELECT *
   FROM AVGM;

This would result in:

CAT	AVGC
IV	1.0000000
PO	2.1666667

Because the view contains a built-in function, AVG, the MEDICATION table cannot be updated by using the view.

7.15 SECURITY: USER-IDs, GRANT, AND REVOKE

While views can facilitate the enforcement of security by limiting the users' ability to access particular columns, DB2 uses the GRANT and REVOKE statements to implement a secure environment more fully. Most users of DB2 access it from IBM's TSO (Time Sharing Option), a subsystem of IBM's MVS OPERATING SYSTEM. To log on to TSO, a user enters the following command at a VDT:

LOGON user-ID/password

The user-ID is assigned by someone in operations or by the system administrator.

Next, the user must access DB2 by entering the proper command. For example, to access DB2I, the interactive version of DB2 that we have been using, the syntax is: ISPF. This presents a menu from which the user selects choice 8 (DB2). At this time, DB2 knows the user-ID that the user entered. This user-ID is the basis of most of DB2's security.

The command GRANT gives privileges (rights) to users. The user-ID that GRANTs the privileges is known as the **grantor,** while the recipient is known as the **grantee.** The REVOKE command can subsequently delete those privileges, but only the grantor can issue it. Privileges can be assigned to a single user, to a group of users, or to all users (the user-ID is PUBLIC). Also, they can be applied to indexes, databases, views, columns, table spaces, and bufferpools. Finally, under certain circumstances, if a user is given particular rights, he or she can in turn GRANT those rights to others.

The GRANT syntax is shown in Figure 7.44.

The privilege-list is usually a DML command such as SELECT, UPDATE, ALTER, and so on. However, it can consist of several privileges, each separated by commas, or the phrase ALL PRIVILEGES.

Typical of the resource-list are TABLE (the default if none is specified), INDEX, DATABASE, and TABLESPACE. Authorization-ID-list is a list of user-IDs sep-

---

FIGURE 7.44   The GRANT Statement

```
GRANT privilege-list ON resource-list
   TO authorization-ID-list
      [WITH GRANT OPTION];
```

If the WITH GRANT option is used, the specified rights are transferable.

---

arated by commas. If the WITH GRANT OPTION is specified, the grantor can pass along his or her privileges to others.

Problem 47. Give Mary and Bill all privileges for the PATIENT and ROOM tables, and allow them to pass along their privileges to others.

Solution.

GRANT ALL PRIVILEGES ON TABLE ROOM,PATIENT
   TO MARY,BILL
   WITH GRANT OPTION;

Note that you cannot use WITH GRANT OPTION if the user-ID is the keyword PUBLIC, meaning "everyone."

Problem 48. Ann, a pharmacy clerk, is to be given the right to update the medication code, description and cost only.

Solution.

GRANT UPDATE ON MEDICATION(MID,MNAME,MCOST)
   TO ANN;

Ann is prohibited from deleting or inserting MEDICATION rows. Further, she can see only the three columns that are indicated in the GRANT statement and cannot pass along her privileges.

Problem 49. Allow Mary to create new indexes for the DOSAGE table.

Solution.

GRANT INDEX ON DOSAGE
   TO MARY;

Problem 50. Gordon is a new technician who has been hired to work in the IV room. Give GORDON the right to perform all operations to the MEDICATION table, but only for those medications designated as MED_CATEGORY IV.

Solution. This will require a two-step solution. First, we create a view for GORDON, then GRANT ALL PRIVILEGES to him:

CREATE VIEW GORDON_VIEW
   AS SELECT * FROM MEDICATION
      WHERE MED_CATEGORY = 'IV';

Next, we use the GRANT command:

GRANT ALL PRIVILEGES ON GORDON_VIEW
   TO GORDON;

Had we wanted to limit Gordon to being able to see only the MID, MNAME, MCOST, and ONHAND columns, we could have done so by coding:

GRANT SELECT ON GORDON_VIEW(MID,MNAME,MCOST,ONHAND)
    TO GORDON;

The following privileges can be GRANTed to base and view tables: SELECT, UPDATE, DELETE, and INSERT. In addition, privileges pertaining only to base tables are ALTER and INDEX. To allow a user to create a table, that user must have a database privilege called CREATETAB.

***Problem 51.* Give Bill the right to create new tables.**

Solution.

GRANT CREATETAB ON DATABASE DSNDB001 TO BILL;

7.16 DATA INTEGRITY: ENTITY INTEGRITY, REFERENTIAL INTEGRITY, AND CURRENCY CONTROL

Version 2 of DB2 has facilities for enforcing entity integrity, referential integrity, and concurrency control, three essential components of data integrity.

Entity Integrity

Recall that entity integrity is the enforcement of the rule that no part of the primary key can be NULL. With DB2, this is done by a two-step process:

- Specify a PRIMARY KEY clause in the table's definition.
- Define a unique index over that key.

Specifying Referential Integrity Rules

DB2 has implemented most of the insertion, update, and deletion integrity rules that we discussed in Chapter 2.

Figure 7.45 shows a foreign-key relationship between a VENDOR and an INVOICE table. The foreign key is in the INVOICE table. If we attempt to store an INVOICE, the value of VID must be NULL (if permitted) or must match some VENDOR.VENVID primary key value. We also want the following rules to apply:

- If an INVOICE is added, ensure that there is a row in VENDOR with the same vendor code as the foreign-key value in INVOICE (*insert integrity rule*).
- If someone attempts to delete a VENDOR, deny the request if there are any related INVOICEs (*delete integrity rule*).

FIGURE 7.45   Example of a Foreign Key Relationship

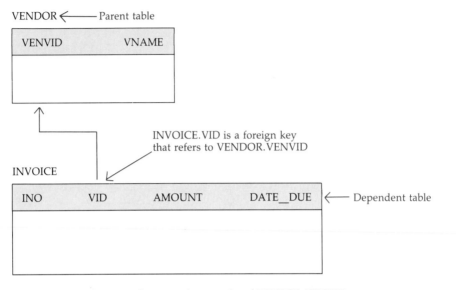

INVOICE.VID *values must always match some value of VENDOR.VENVID o*

- Do not permit a vendor code in the VENDOR table to be changed if there are matching INVOICE.VID values (*update integrity rule*).

  The establishment of referential integrity is done in two steps:

1. Specifying of a primary key and unique index over that key.
2. Defining of the foreign key and its deletion rule.

   Figure 7.46 shows how we have defined the VENDOR primary key. DB2 will then verify that the NOT NULL option has been specified, because this is a requirement. Prior to using the table for the first time, there must be a unique index defined over the primary key. How this is done was discussed in the section on index generation.

   Next, we define the foreign-key columns using the FOREIGN KEY clause. In Figure 7.46, the VID column of INVOICE has been specified as a foreign key. The REFERENCES clause is used to define the parent table and its primary key. In the example, the parent table is VENDOR and the VENDOR key to be matched is VENVID.

   Finally, we specify the deletion rule. The example uses RESTRICT. Recall that this prevents a user from deleting a parent if there are one or more dependent

---

FIGURE 7.46   Specifying the Relational Integrity Assertions

```
CREATE TABLE VENDOR
   (VENVID      CHAR(6)       NOT NULL,
    VNAME       CHAR(25)      NOT NULL,
    PRIMARY KEY (VENVID) );

CREATE TABLE INVOICE
   (INO         CHAR(7)       NOT NULL,
    VID         CHAR(6)       NOT NULL,
    AMOUNT      DECIMAL(8,2),
    DATE_DUE DATE,
    PRIMARY KEY (INO),
    FOREIGN KEY (VID) HASSENT
    REFERENCES VENDOR (VENVID)
              ON DELETE RESTRICT);
```

---

rows. In the example, any attempt to delete a VENDOR with a VENVID value that matches some VID value in INVOICE will be rejected.

Insertion Integrity. DB2 automatically enforces the following insertion rule: No row can be added into a row of a dependent table unless the foreign-key value is NULL, which implies an optional relationship, or unless it matches a primary key value for some row in the parent table. In our example, no INVOICE can be added unless the VID value matches some VENDOR.VENVID value.

Deletion Integrity. If a parent row is deleted and CASCADE is specified, all dependent rows containing matching foreign-key values will also be deleted. In the example, enforcement of this option would mean that when a VENDOR was deleted, so would all related INVOICEs.

Finally, SET NULL results in the foreign-key values being set to NULL if the parent row is deleted and if NOT NULL has not been specified for the foreign key.

Update Integrity. Update integrity is enforced this way. DB2 prevents the altering of any primary key value if there are dependent rows with matching values. Other primary key values can be changed. The VENDOR and INVOICE specifications found in Figure 7.46 satisfy the rules we want DB2 to enforce.

Concurrency Control

When we discussed the CREATE TABLESPACE statement, we said that there are three LOCKSIZE choices: PAGE, TABLESPACE, and ANY. We also said that if ANY is chosen, DB2 will select the better of the two lock units (page or table space) whenever locks are necessary. This choice is based on the number of pages affected by the intended DB2 operation. If only a few pages are affected, page locking is performed, but if many are affected, DB2 will lock at the tablespace level. All such locking is done automatically; the user/host program need not explicitly request/release locks.

There are four kinds of DB2 locks, each of which can be applied to a page or a tablespace, but we will discuss only types S (shared) and X (exclusive). If an application executes a SQL command that is "read only"—that is, it doesn't attempt to update the table—the lock is of type S and the table can be shared simultaneously with other "read-only" applications in memory. Should a second application attempt to place an exclusive (X) lock on the table, that application will be placed into a wait state. However, if the second application issues a type-S lock, it will be granted, and the application can continue.

An exclusive lock prevents any other applications from simultaneously accessing the tablespace or page until the lock is released. This is done when an application executes any statement that updates a table. If an application has caused DB2 to place a type-X lock on a table, all other applications that attempt to simultaneously lock that table, regardless of lock type, will be placed into a wait state until the first application releases the lock.

If the application wishes to explicitly perform the locking, the DB2 LOCK command can be used. Figure 7.47 shows the syntax. Although a table name is specified, it is the tablespace that stores the table that is actually locked.

Changes made to DB2 tables can be either physically applied to the database or discarded. As long as DB2 is being run under TSO, the COMMIT and ROLLBACK commands that we briefly discussed in Chapter 2 are available.

Use of COMMIT WORK physically updates all tables that have been changed since the last COMMIT. It also releases any locks applied by the application and makes all updated data available to other applications. Until the COMMIT is executed, updated data is available only to the application that changed it. This command is automatically executed at the normal conclusion of an application. At any other time, the application can issue the COMMIT command. We normally do so when a transaction has been processed successfully. If the processing of a transaction is unsuccessful, we need to discard all updates affected by the transaction. We do this by issuing the ROLLBACK command. The ROLLBACK command discards all changes made since the last COMMIT and makes the original table values available to all users. We will illustrate these concepts in the next chapter.

FIGURE 7.47   **The LOCK Statement**

```
LOCK TABLE table-name IN SHARE | EXCLUSIVE MODE;
```

7.17   QUERYING THE SYSTEM TABLES

Table 7.2 showed most of the important catalog tables. Like any base table, they can be queried, provided the user has that privilege. Although we never used it, DB2 requires that unless the creator of a table is issuing the query, the table name must be preceded by the creator's user-ID. For example, if MARY created the table PATIENT, all references to PATIENT by any user except MARY must look like this:

SELECT . . .
    FROM MARY.PATIENT
    WHERE . . .

   DB2 catalog tables are "created" by the user-ID: SYSIBM. Thus, all references to those tables must include that user-ID.

Problem 52. **Display the table names and creator of all the tables.**

Solution.

SELECT NAME,CREATOR
    FROM SYSIBM.SYSTABLES;

The result is:

NAME	CREATOR
PATIENT	JCSHEPHERD
MEDICATION	JCSHEPHERD
ROOM	JCSHEPHERD
DOCTOR	JCSHEPHERD
DOSAGE	JCSHEPHERD
CRITICAL_CONDITION	JCSHEPHERD
SERIOUS_CONDITION	JCSHEPHERD

Problem 53. **Display the column names associated with the CRITICAL_CONDITION table.**

Solution.

SELECT NAME
    FROM SYSIBM.SYSCOLUMNS
WHERE TBNAME = 'CRITICAL_CONDITION';

The result is:

NAME
PID

7.18   ANSI/IBM SQL DIFFERENCES

It remains to be seen whether or not vendors fully conform to the ANSI X.3H2 SQL standard. Thus far, the differences between DB2 and SQL/DS and the X.3H2 standard are small. In fact, there are only four.

First, IBM requires that the words INTEGER and DECIMAL be spelled out completely, while ANSI permits them to be abbreviated as INT and DEC. Second, IBM's columns must be explicitly assigned a length, while the ANSI standard assigns a standard length with the ability to optionally define one if the standard is unacceptable. Third, with DB2 the only way to enforce a uniqueness constraint for a column is to use a CREATIVE UNIQUE INDEX statement. ANSI, however, permits a uniqueness constraint to be defined when the table is described. Fourth, the number of reserved words varies between the IBM and ANSI SQLs.

7.19   SUMMARY

SQL is the ANSI relational database language. Many vendors offer commercial implementations of SQL, but we focused on the IBM package, DB2. Occasionally, we discussed another popular SQL product: ORACLE. While almost identical to DB2, ORACLE has extended the relational operators and uses a simpler format for defining tables.

There are six DB2 objects: tables, views, table spaces, indexes, databases, and storage groups. All six can be defined or deleted using the CREATE and DROP commands, respectively.

As each table, view, and index is defined, it is assigned to a database. When tables are defined, they are also assigned to a table space—the unit of storage that actually stores the tables' values. Finally, databases are assigned to storage groups.

Tables consist of columns and rows. Each column must be assigned one of seven data types and also must have its length defined. If the NOT NULL option is used when defining the column, any row added must contain a value for that column. Two optional clauses, EDITPROC and VALIDPROC, can be used to automatically invoke data compression/decompression or encryption and data validation (including referential integrity enforcement) automatically.

If we want to improve the efficiency of DB2 or to enforce a unique-key by constraint, we can define indexes. The availability of the indexes is shielded from the user, helping to provide data independence; if the indexes are found, DB2 will automatically use them.

The "workhorse" of DB2's DML, called SQL, is the WHERE clause, IBM's implementation of the relational SELECT operator. Using this, we can restrict the SELECT, INSERT, UPDATE, or DELETE commands to only those rows that satisfy the predicate conditions within the clause. In addition to the usual expressions, DB2 predicates can contain the four keywords NULL, IN, BETWEEN, and LIKE. These permit easy search methods for what otherwise would be cumbersome queries.

When retrieving table rows, we use the SELECT command. In effect, this is the DB2 version of the PROJECT operator from relational algebra. In addition to column names, the SELECT clause can contain built-in functions for performing simple mathematical calculations on the column values that are retrieved. DB2 also supports join operators by specifying two or more tables on the FROM clause and the JOIN condition on the WHERE clause. Also directly supported is the relational UNION operator. While ORACLE's SQL implementation directly supports the DIFFERENCE and INTERSECTION operators, DB2 requires that the EXISTS and NOT EXISTS options be used to implement them indirectly.

Any query can be sorted and/or grouped. A grouped query will usually show a single row from each group. If particular groups are desired, a filter can be applied by using the HAVING option with the SELECT command.

Adding new rows is done using the INSERT command. However, if INSERT is used with a table rather than a view, domain constraints cannot be enforced.

Deleting table rows is done by issuing the DELETE command. Like SELECT and INSERT, DELETE can contain a WHERE clause to restrict its action.

To add a new column to an existing table, we can use the ALTER command. To delete a column, we must follow a rather complicated, multistep procedure.

DB2 table security is ensured by using the GRANT and REVOKE commands. GRANT gives a user the right (privilege) to perform a given action, while REVOKE removes that right. If the WITH GRANT option is specified, rights can be transferred from one grantee to another.

DB2 contains a rather sophisticated concurrency facility. It automatically locks at one of two levels, but the user can override the automatic feature by using the LOCK command.

If DB2 detects a deadlock, or if a transaction fails to end normally, all of the changes affected can be undone by issuing a ROLLBACK command. On the other hand, successful transactions can be permanently posted to the database with the COMMIT command, which is automatically issued when an application session ends.

In the next chapter, we will see how to use DB2 within a host COBOL program.

REVIEW QUESTIONS

1. Define a view. When can the underlying base table be updated via the view?

2. What can we do through a view that we cannot do through a base table?

3. Under what circumstances do we use views?

4. What is a DB2 catalog? List the name and purpose of two of its tables.

5. What is the relationship among a storage group, a database, and a table?

6. Describe the data types supported by DB2.

7. Why are end users unaware that indexes exist? What is the reason for this?

8. Give two reasons for establishing indexes.

9. What is a predicate? Give examples of the four special predicates supported by DB2.

10. List the built-in functions that can be used in a SELECT clause.

11. Describe the DB2 equivalent of the relational operators SELECT, PROJECT, JOIN, UNION, INTERSECTION, and DIFFERENCE.

12. What do ALL and ANY mean when used in a subselect?

13. Describe the steps and commands necessary to delete a column. How do we delete a row(s)?

14. Discuss the concept of a correlated subquery.

15. Under what circumstances can a grantor grant his or her rights to others? When can a grantee transfer rights?

16. Discuss the differences between an exclusive lock and a shared lock.

17. If an application has a shared lock on a table, what kinds of processing can another application perform?

18. How does DB2 implement domain constraints? Referential integrity? Entity integrity?

19. What does ROLLBACK do? Describe two situations in which we should consider using it.

20. Explain the differences between DB2 and the ANSI standard for SQL.

PROBLEMS

Use DB2 to answer all of the following questions

1. What are the names of Dr. Starzel's patients? Assume you know that Dr. Starzel's identification number is 10. Finally, produce the report in name order.

2. What are the names of Dr. Starzel's patients in room 102 assuming you don't know Dr. Starzel's code?

3. What are the names of Dr. Starzel's patients in room 102 who are in critical condition and are being treated for angina? Answer the question assuming you know Dr. Starzel's code and angina's as well.

4. Show the names of patients receiving medication at 0200 hours. Answer the problem using first a join and then a subquery. Show the results alphabetically.

5. Display the names and room numbers of patients receiving a medication costing over $2.00.

6. Establish a view consisting of patient number and name, room number, medication code, medication description, due time, and amount to dispense. The view should contain only medications in the PO category.

7. Assume patient number 103 has been discharged. Delete the corresponding patient rows from the PATIENT, ROOM, and DOSAGE tables.

8. What is the average cost of medications being dispensed to patient number 103? What is the name of the most expensive medication being given to that patient?

9. Assume patient 103 has been discharged after being in the hospital for three days. Calculate the patient's bill. (This will require you to determine the cost for each medication for the patient and then multiply these values by the length of the stay.)

10. There has been a recall of the current lot of the 50mg size of penicillin. List the patient name, room number, and physician name of the affected patients.

The following tables are reproduced from the Problems section in Chapter 6:

PO (PONUM, PODATE, POVENDNO, POSTATUS, EMPCODE, TOTITEMS, TOTVALUE)
PODETAIL (PONUM, ITEMCODE, UNITS_ORDERED, PRICE_PER_UNIT)
INVENTORY (ITEMCODE, ITEM_DESC, CHARGE_AMT, LAST_COST, ONHAND, ONORDER, CATEGORY)
DEPT (DEPT_CODE, DNAME)
TRANSFER (DEPT_CODE, ITEM_CODE, DATE_TRANSFERRED, UNITS_TRANSFERRED, ONHAND)
VENDOR (VENDNO, VNAME, VSTREET, VCITY, VSTATE, VZIP, VPHONE)
EMPLOYEE (EMPCODE, EMPNAME)

11. Make whatever assumptions are necessary about the column data types, and show how to define the first three tables. Use neither the PRIMARY KEY nor the IN clause.

12. Define appropriate primary key indexes, one per table.

13. List all the PO numbers and associated item codes and descriptions for those purchase orders that are not closed.

14. Display the PO number for all POs sent to the same vendor as PO number 7812.

15. List the codes for all vendors who have been sent an order (regardless of its status) for those orders not entered by employee JCS.

16. Show the item description for all items on PO number 17. First use a join; then reanswer using a subquery.

17. What is the average amount of the closed purchase orders that contained item code FRISB10?

18. Use NOT EXISTS to determine the PO number for those POs that do not contain item FRISB10.

19. Display the PO numbers for all POs whose total amounts exceed those of all the POs entered by the employee with code JCS.

20. What is the total on hand at department IS of the item that has the description "3.5 in. Diskette"?

21. Assume purchase order 100 is now complete. Show how to update the INVENTORY and PO tables. (This will require you to update the ONHAND, LASTCOST, POSTATUS, AND ONORDER columns.)

22. Assuming we don't store the two total columns in PO, display the number of items and total value for PO number 1234.

23. Suppose we are finished with the current transactions. Save all updates to the database permanently.

24. Establish a view of the closed purchase orders that were entered by employee JCS.

8

Embedded SQL
COBOL and 4GLs

In the last chapter, we looked at the interactive form of the SQL component of DB2. As you may have noticed, SQL is not a complete programming language; it is a query language plus a DBMS that cannot be used for sophisticated application development without embedding it in a host program.

With few exceptions, what we learned in Chapter 7 about interactive SQL is applicable to the IBM SQL/DS or DB2 products and to most of the other SQL products on the market today.

Most of this chapter will discuss how to embed SQL calls into a COBOL program. Most of the chapter's contents can be directly transferred to any vendor having a COBOL/SQL interface—even to some on the microcomputer market. For example, ORACLE has a product that can be used with REALIA's COBOL compiler to develop COBOL/SQL applications on a microcomputer. The last section of the chapter briefly looks at the 4GL/SQL marriage.

At the conclusion of this chapter, you will be able to:

- List the steps necessary for embedding SQL in COBOL programs.
- Discuss the COBOL changes necessary for embedded SQL, including changes to the SQL statements themselves.
- Show how to determine whether or not a SQL call was successful.
- Discuss the roles that table declarations, host structures, precompilation, and binding play with embedded SQL.
- Use cursors to retrieve multiple rows from a table.
- Distinguish between static and dynamic SQL.
- Discuss the advantages of using a 4GL over COBOL for SQL processing.

8.1   THE EMBEDDED SQL ENVIRONMENT

To use the embedded form of SQL in a COBOL program, we follow these steps:

1. Create and test the SQL commands interactively.
2. Define, or INCLUDE from a library, table definitions and COBOL structures, called *host structures*, to be used to receive rows retrieved from DB2 and to transfer them to DB2 for storage.
3. Define, or INCLUDE, the SQL Communications Area, SQLCA.
4. Embed the debugged SQL statements from step 1 into the PROCEDURE DIVISION of the COBOL host program.
5. Precompile the program.
6. Compile and link-edit the application.
7. Bind the program.
8. Execute the program.

ιgure 8.1 shows the general structure of such a program. You will find it a useful reference as we look at the details.

The following SQL statements can be included in a host program: SELECT, UPDATE, DELETE, INSERT, FETCH, OPEN CURSOR, CLOSE CURSOR, and DECLARE CURSOR. We suggest that all of the SQL operations first be tested interactively and then added to the COBOL program at the appropriate locations. This is an important concept. Programmers can test row insertion, updating, deletion, and retrieval without the overhead burden imposed by a procedural language such as COBOL. Once the SQL calls are thoroughly tested, they are ready to be included in the COBOL program. All such SQL statements must be surrounded by the SQL delimiters EXEC SQL and END-EXEC. You can see this by looking at block 7 in Figure 8.1.

Although the tables in Figure 8.1 are already defined using DB2, they must be declared in the DATA DIVISION of the COBOL program. You can see how this is done by examining block 2 in the figure.

Host structures and **host variables** are program variables that typically hold a row or row portion returned by a SELECT statement. They can be individual data elements (host variables) or multilevel structures (host structures). For example, block 3 in Figure 8.1 contains two COBOL host structures: HOST-NAME-TABLE-1 and HOST-NAME-TABLE-2. Each of these could be used to receive a row from a DB2 table, because there is a data item defined for each column in the corresponding table.

Later we will examine another clause in the SELECT statement: "INTO :host-structure," which informs DB2 where to place the result of the query. For example, we might code:

```
EXECT SQL
     SELECT *
         FROM PATIENT
```

```
          INTO :COBOL-PATIENT
               WHERE PID = '100'
END-EXEC.
```

Here, COBOL-PATIENT would have to be a host structure (an 01-level, plus all the necessary 03-levels) so that DB2 could place a complete row into it. The statement would find the row with the designated PID value and place it into the COBOL-PATIENT record. Note that semicolons aren't used with embedded SQL.

Host variables (see block 4 in Figure 8.1) can be used with WHERE and SET clauses and also with INSERT statements. For example, block 5 in Figure 8.1 contains a **cursor** definition, which is a mechanism used whenever DB2 returns multiple rows. This subject is covered later. For now, look at the WHERE clause. Notice the :HOST-VARIABLE1 clause. The colon (:) designates that the variable following it is a COBOL one and not a DB2 column name.

The SQL Communications Area (see block 1), called *SQLCA*, is the area DB2 uses to communicate the results of the embedded SQL calls back to the host program. The most important data element in SQLCA is SQLCODE, whose value indicates the success or failure of the call to DB2. In Figure 8.1, we used 'INCLUDE SQLCA,' a SQL statement that specifies that SQLCA has previously been defined and its definition should be included at this time. It functions like the COBOL COPY statement.

With minor modifications, the SQL statements that are run interactively can be directly embedded into the COBOL program. Two changes are necessary. First, we must use the SQL delimiters, EXEC SQL and END-EXEC, mentioned earlier. Second, we must specify the host structures or variables. We will see examples of both later in this chapter.

Because COBOL compilers don't recognize SQL commands, imagine the number of syntax errors the COBOL compiler would return if it encountered statements like SELECT * FROM PATIENT. The solution is to have a **precompiler** scan the source code and substitute DB2 CALL statements for all SQL statements encountered. A precompiler is a program that substitutes valid COBOL commands for invalid ones, which in our case are SQL statements. To facilitate the finding of the SQL statements, we must surround them with EXEC SQL and END-EXEC delimiters, as we saw above. Everything between them is replaced with CALL statements to a DB2-COBOL interface module. The extracted statements are placed into a **Data Base Request Module (DBRM)** for inspection by the **bind** module.

The compile and link-edit steps are done in the normal manner, except that the libraries in which the DB2 modules can be found by the link-editor must be specified. Now we are ready to bind. The bind operation accomplishes these tasks:

- Validation of the SQL statements in the DBRM to ensure they can be executed.
- Determination of the resource authorizations.

FIGURE 8.1   General Format of a COBOL Program that Calls DB2

```
DATA DIVISION.
FILE SECTION.
********************************************************
* non-DB2 FDs go here
********************************************************
  .
  .
  .
WORKING-STORAGE SECTION.
********************************************************
* normal COBOL variables and structures go here
********************************************************
  .
  .
  .
```

```
********************************************************
* SQL include for SQLCA
********************************************************
          EXEC SQL INCLUDE SQLCA END-EXEC.
```
1

— Follows every SQL statement
— A communications area
— Precedes every SQL statement

```
********************************************************
* SQL declarations for DB2 tables next
********************************************************
          EXEC SQL
              DECLARE table-name-1 TABLE

                 (column-name-1    DB2-definition1,
                     column-name-2    DB2-definition2,
                     column-name-n    DB2-definitionn)
          END-EXEC.
```
2

```
********************************************************
* declare next table
********************************************************
          EXEC SQL
              DECLARE table-name-2 TABLE
                  (column-name-1    DB2-definition1,
                   column-name-2    DB2-definition2,

                     .

                     .
                   column-name-n    DB2-definitionn)
          END-EXEC.
********************************************************
* repeat for all tables to be used by application
```

FIGURE 8.1   (continued)

```
*********************************************************
        .
        .
        .

*********************************************************
* declare SQL host structures and variables
*********************************************************
           EXEC SQL BEGIN DECLARE SECTION END-EXEC.
*********************************************************
* define first table for COBOL usage
*********************************************************
 01 HOST-NAME-TABLE-1.
       03 COLUMN-NAME-1          PIC...
       03 COLUMN-NAME-2          PIC...
          .
          .
          .
       03 COLUMN-NAME-N          PIC...
*********************************************************
* define next table for COBOL usage
*********************************************************
 01 HOST-NAME-TABLE-2.
       03 COLUMN-NAME-1          PIC...
       03 COLUMN-NAME-2          PIC...
          .
          .
       03 COLUMN-NAME-N          PIC...
          .
          .
          .
```

```
*********************************************************
* declare host variables next
*********************************************************
 01 HOST-VARIABLE1          PIC...
 01 HOST-VARIABLE2          PIC...
    .
    .
    .
           EXEC SQL END DECLARE SECTION END-EXEC.
```

3

4

FIGURE 8.1   (concluded)

```
************************************************************
* declare cursors last
************************************************************
                 EXEC SQL DECLARE CURSOR-1 CURSOR FOR
                           SELECT *
5                              FROM...
                                  WHERE column-name1 LIKE :HOST-VARIABLE1
                                  AND...
                 END-EXEC.
.
.
.
```

Indicates a
host variable

```
PROCEDURE DIVISION.
```

```
************************************************************
* SQL return code handling
6  ************************************************************
        EXEC SQL WHENEVER SQLERROR    GOTO DBERROR END-EXEC
        EXEC SQL WHENEVER SQLWARNING GOTO DBERROR END-EXEC
        EXEC SQL WHENEVER NOT FOUND   CONTINUE     END-EXEC
```

```
                 EXEC SQL
7                      SQL statements here
                 END-EXEC.
```

```
   DBERROR.
   ************************************************************
8  *   error routine coded here
   ************************************************************
```

- Determination of the optimal search paths.
- Creation of an application plan, which is stored in the DB2 system catalog.

The last step—creation of the **application plan,** a compiled and link-edited version of the SQL statements that were extracted by the precompiler and stored in the DBRM—is the primary purpose of the bind operation. Later, when the run-unit version of the host program is loaded into main memory, the application plan is loaded as well. As the application runs, every time a DB2 CALL is detected, control passes to the application plan, which executes the SQL state-

---

FIGURE 8.2   **The Host Program Development Process with Embedded SQL Calls**

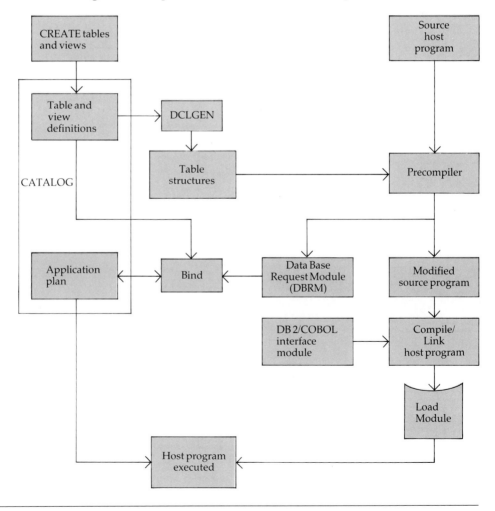

ments and then returns control to the host program, along with an error indicator, SQLCODE, and, if the statement was a SELECT, the requested rows, which are stored in the host structure. Figure 8.2 shows the relationships among these steps. The figure will be useful in the next section, where we look at the steps in more detail.

Create and Test the SQL Portion of the Host Program

Because we already have seen how to use interactive SQL, we will no.
this step here except to say that some modification of the debugged SQL .
mands will be necessary before we actually embed them. This is especially tr.
with SELECT statements, because we must provide a COBOL host structure to accept the row (record, in COBOL) passed to the program by DB2. The same host structure concept is used to pass a record from COBOL to DB2 for subsequent storage and, consequently, will also be encountered with the SET clause in the UPDATE statement.

Declare the DB2 Tables and the Associated Host Structures and Set Up the Communications Area: DATA DIVISION Requirements

Both the host structures and the table declarations are coded in the WORKING-STORAGE SECTION. We have two implementation choices: We can either code the required tables and host structures directly into the COBOL program using an editor or INCLUDE their definitions from a DB2 library. Additions to the library are made by running a program called DCLGEN.

Declaring Tables. All the DB2 tables and views to be processed by the host program should be declared. Because the DB2 tables presumably have been defined using interactive SQL (by means of the CREATE TABLE command), we need only **declare** them. The format for declaring a table is almost the same as that used to CREATE one. The only differences are:

- The requirement to enclose the definition within the delimiters
- A "DECLARE table-name TABLE" clause

The complete DECLARE TABLE syntax is shown in Figure 8.3. You can see its location in a program by looking at block 2 in Figure 8.1.

While technically optional, use of such declarations allows the precompiler to check the declared table against the SQL statements it later finds in the PROCEDURE DIVISION. This helps verify that the usage of the tables is correct. Errors can thus be detected prior to the bind operation. A second advantage is documentation, because the names and types of each column will then be recorded in the source program.

FIGURE 8.3   **The Syntax Used to Declare a Table in an Embedded SQL/COBOL Program**

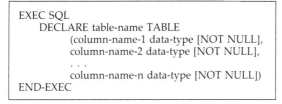

```
EXEC SQL
    DECLARE table-name TABLE
            (column-name-1 data-type [NOT NULL],
            column-name-2 data-type [NOT NULL],
            . . .
            column-name-n data-type [NOT NULL])
END-EXEC
```

Tables should be declared before referring to them in the PROCEDURE DIVISION.

Problem 1. **Declare the PATIENT, DOSAGE, and MEDICATION tables from Chapter 7.**

Solution. The solution is shown in Figure 8.4. Note that we have taken some liberties with the table names. In reality, the user-ID of the creator of the table precedes the table name. Thus, if JOHN CREATEd the MEDICATION table, the table's full name should be JOHN.MEDICATION.

Problem 2. **Declare a new table called DUETIMES, which is to contain two columns: SIG (a unique, four-character code) and DUETIME (a four-digit value).**

Solution. New tables should be defined using the interactive form of SQL, not the embedded one. Recall that a table is defined using the CREATE TABLE statement:

```
CREATE TABLE DUETIMES
    (SIG        CHAR(4)     NOT NULL,
    DUETIME   SMALLINT   NOT NULL,
PRIMARY KEY (SIG))
IN DSNDB001.DSNTS001;
```

Defining the Host Tables and Variables. Host structures are COBOL tables and variables used:

- In the INTO clause of a SELECT statement to receive the data retrieved
- As column name variables used in a SELECT column-name clause
- As variables used in search conditions for WHERE clauses
- As variables used to represent an attribute's new value within a SET clause
- As variables used to represent VALUES in an INSERT statement

FIGURE 8.4   **DB2 DECLARE Statements for the PATIENT, MEDICATION, and DOSAGE Tables**

```
EXEC SQL
  DECLARE PATIENT TABLE
    (PID        CHAR(10) NOT NULL,
     PNAME      CHAR(25) NOT NULL,
     DIAG_CODE  CHAR(3),
     DID        INTEGER)
END-EXEC.

EXEC SQL
  DECLARE MEDICATION TABLE
    (MID          CHAR(3) NOT NULL,
     MNAME        CHAR(20) NOT NULL,
     MCOST        DECIMAL(7,2),
     ONHAND       INTEGER,
     MED_CATEGORY CHAR(4),
     UNITS_USED   INTEGER)
END-EXEC.

EXEC SQL
  DECLARE DOSAGE TABLE
    (PID     CHAR(10)  NOT NULL,
     MID     CHAR(3)   NOT NULL,
     TIME    SMALLINT  NOT NULL,
     DOSAGE  CHAR(7)   NOT NULL)
END-EXEC.
```

- As a component of a WHERE clause to specify a predicate search-condition
- Following LIKE, NOT LIKE, or IN

Host structures are defined within the two SQL statements, BEGIN DECLARE SECTION and END DECLARE SECTION, and when subsequently used must be preceded by a colon. (Note: Theoretically, they need not be preceded by a colon except under certain circumstances. For simplicity, however, we will always use the colon.) However, they should not be preceded by a colon if they are used outside a SQL statement. Figure 8.5 shows the statements' general definitional structure.

The only requirements for host variables is that their names be unique (that is, there cannot be native COBOL variables with the same names) and their types be compatible with those defined within the CREATE TABLE statement.

The composition of the host structure depends on the level of aggregation of the data being processed by the application. If a single column, or even several columns, is desired, separate host variables are best, each defined as a separate 01-level (or 77-level) COBOL variable. However, when an entire row is to be SELECTed, it is more convenient to read that row into a single 01-level structure consisting of subordinate 03-level data elements, each data element corresponding to a column in the DB2 table.

When defining the host structures or variables, we must follow certain rules

---

FIGURE 8.5   Using the BEGIN/END DECLARE SECTION Statements to Define Host Structures

WORKING-STORAGE SECTION.

.
.
.

(normal COBOL variables defined here)

.

   EXEC SQL BEGIN DECLARE SECTION END-EXEC.

     (host structures declared here)
     .
     .
     .

   EXEC SQL END DECLARE SECTION END-EXEC.

---

so that the COBOL data element specifications will be compatible with the data stored by DB2. For example, using DB2 we might CREATE a table containing a column defined as DECIMAL (7,2) or SMALLINT. A question we must address is: What COBOL data specification should be used for each of them? Figure 8.6 shows how to map each DB2 data type to the equivalent COBOL data type.

Problem 3. **Define a host structure for the PATIENT table. (See Figure 7.7 for its SQL definition.)**

Solution.

```
01 PATIENT-DATA.
    03 PAT-ID              PIC X(10).
    03 PAT-NAME            PIC X(25).
    03 DIAGNOSIS-CODE      PIC X(3).
    03 DOC-ID              PIC S9(9) COMP.
```

Notice that the structure follows conventional COBOL rules. Most notably, the underline character isn't used, and the columns have been given more meaningful names. Although less efficient, we could have coded the four data elements as separate, unrelated host variables, each prefaced with an 01-level number.

As an example of how to use a host variable, look at the SET clause in Figure 8.7. It says to add the value of the host variable, COST-THIS-MONTH, to the column COST-YTD. The colon tells DB2 that the variable is a COBOL variable and not a DB2 column.

Generating Declarations: The DCLGEN Utility. Earlier, we said that we could alternatively use the INCLUDE statement to copy in the COBOL source statements required to declare the tables and define their host structures. The simplest

FIGURE 8.6 **DB2/COBOL Data Type Mapping**

DB2 Data Type	COBOL Data Type
SMALLINT	PIC S9(4) COMP.
INTEGER	PIC S9(9) COMP.
DECIMAL(p,q)	PIC S9(r)V(q) COMP-3., where r = p − q
FLOAT	COMP-2.
CHAR(n)	PIC X(n).
VARCHAR(m)	03 name-1.
	05 name-2 PIC S9(4) COMP. (length)
	05 name-3 PIC X(m). (data value)
LONG VARCHAR	Same as VARCHAR
DATE	01 name PIC X(10).
TIME	01 name PIC X(6). (X(8) if seconds are desired)
TIMESTAMP	01 name PIC X(19). (X(26) if microseconds are desired)

FIGURE 8.7 **Example of an UPDATE Statement that Contains a SET Clause with a Colon, Designating a Host Variable**

```
EXEC SQL
    UPDATE . . .
    SET COST-YTD = COST-YTD + :COST-THIS-MONTH
                                ↑
                                └── The colon specifies that
                                    COST-THIS-MONTH is a host (COBOL)
                                    variable
    END-EXEC.
```

way is to invoke DCLGEN (DeCLarations GENerator) from IBM's Time Sharing Option (TSO). To do so, we use the format shown in Figure 8.8.

We won't show an example of how to use DCLGEN. Please refer to the relevant IBM manuals for details on its use. Once defined, to subsequently INCLUDE either the table declarations or SQLCA, we use the syntax shown in Figure 8.9. For example, if the PATIENT table is stored in a library as PATDEF, we use this coding to INCLUDE it:

```
EXEC SQL
    INCLUDE PATDEF
END-EXEC.
```

Defining the SQL Communications Area: SQLCA. Another requirement is to define the SQLCA structure. We do this by directly coding it within the host program or including it from a library, as we just discussed.

FIGURE 8.8   DB2 Statements for Generating COBOL Table Declarations

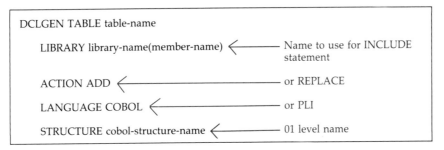

Instead of hard-coding the table declarations in the host programs, we can include them in the COBOL program by using the command "INCLUDE library-name."

FIGURE 8.9   The Syntax Used within a COBOL Host Program to Include either Table Declarations or SQLCA Source Statements

```
EXEC SQL
   INCLUDE member-name
END-EXEC.
```

As Figure 8.10 shows, the SQLCA structure contains 21 data elements, 6 of which are part of a table called SQLERRD. SQLCAID will always have the value SQLCA, which identifies the structure as the SQLCA. Next comes SQLCABC, an element that contains the length of the SQLCA, which is always 136 bytes. SQLCODE is the element we test after each call to DB2 to determine if it was successful. If SQLCODE contains a value of less than zero, it means the SQL call failed and we should invoke an appropriate error routine. A value of zero means that no unusual errors were detected, while positive values indicate that a nonfatal error occurred. Sometimes the "error" isn't an actual error. For example, the value 100 indicates that no row could be found that satisfies the SELECT statement. In this case, we might simply display a message to that effect, but no error-handling routine is necessary.

The SQLERRM element will contain descriptive information about the nature of the DB2 error. Of the six elements in SQLERRD, only the third one is relevant to us here. It will contain the number of rows affected by a DB2 INSERT, UPDATE, or DELETE statement. For example, after an INSERT of three rows, SQLERRD(3) would equal 3.

The final set of eight elements, SQLWARN0 through SQLWARN7, is used by DB2 to denote warnings. If the first one, SQLWARN0, is blank, there are no

---

FIGURE 8.10   COBOL Version of SQLCA, the Communications Area for DB2

```
01 SQLCA.
     05 SQLCAID          PIC X(8).
     05 SQLCABC          PIC S9(9) COMP.
     05 SQLCODE          PIC S9(9) COMP.
       05 SQLERRM.
           49 SQLERRML   PIC S9(4) COMP.
           49 SQLERRMC   PIC X(70).
       05 SQLERP         PIC X(8).
       05 SQLERRD        OCCURS 6 TIMES
                         PIC S9(9) COMP.

     05 SQLWARN.
         10 SQLWARN0     PIC X(1).
         10 SQLWARN1     PIC X(1).
         10 SQLWARN2     PIC X(1).
         10 SQLWARN3     PIC X(1).
         10 SQLWARN4     PIC X(1).
         10 SQLWARN5     PIC X(1).
         10 SQLWARN6     PIC X(1).
         10 SQLWARN7     PIC X(1).
     05 SQLTEXT          PIC X(8).
```

---

warnings and the remaining seven can be safely omitted from further processing. However, if the element contains a *W*, one of the other warning flags has been set to W and further processing is warranted. We won't look at the seven warnings except to mention that SQLWARN1 denotes that at least one column's value was truncated when it was transferred to the COBOL host variable.

Providing for NULL Values. For those columns that might contain such values, we define a special null-value indicator. When a NULL value is returned by DB2, this indicator will be set to a value of less than zero; otherwise, its value will be set to zero. To define such a variable, called an **indicator variable,** we use the syntax shown in Figure 8.11. For example, to be able to test for a NULL cost value in MEDICATION, we define NULL-COST as:

01 NULL-COST   PIC 9(4) COMP.

We then code:

SELECT MCOST
    INTO :WS-COST,: NULL-COST
    FROM MEDICATION . . .
IF NULL-COST < 0
    PERFORM NO-COST-ROUTINE. . .

Notice that the indicator variable immediately follows the host variable.
If NULL-COST is less than zero, DB2 will not update the host variable; that

---

FIGURE 8.11   **Defining a Variable Used to Receive Notification that a SQL Call Has Resulted in a NULL Value Being Returned**

```
01 null-indicator-name       PIC S9(4) COMP.
```

FIGURE 8.12   **An Example that Does Not Require a Cursor**

```
EXEC SQL                          ←SQL delimiter
   SELECT * FROM PATIENT          ←Retrieve all columns
     INTO :PATIENT-DATA           ←See Problem 3 for PATIENT-DATA composition
     FROM PATIENT                 ←DB2 table name
     WHERE PID = '103'            ←Just one row
END-EXEC.                         ←SQL delimiter
```

When a single row is returned, cursors are not necessary.

---

is, WS-COST has the same value it had before the SQL statement was executed. If a column contains a NULL value and no indicator variable is used, an error will result. Later in this chapter, we will see how to deal with a structure containing some data elements that can be NULL and others that cannot.

Defining Structures for Handling SELECTs that Return Multiple Rows: Defining Cursors.   The easiest kind of SQL SELECT to implement is one that results in a single row (record) being returned by DB2. That row is placed into the host structure specified as part of the new SELECT format. For example, to retrieve the single PATIENT row with the PID value 103, we use the PROCEDURE DIVISION statements in Figure 8.12.

The single row containing the PID value 103 is placed into the structure named PATIENT-DATA, which we defined earlier. Notice the use of the colon (:) signifying that PATIENT-DATA is a host table or variable. Much of the power of a relational DBMS comes from the fact that it can process a collection of rows—a "set-at-a-time" approach—instead of using the COBOL "record-at-a-time" method. This can create problems when we embed such statements into a COBOL program, because a COBOL structure can hold only one record, or row, at a time. For example, if we coded the program segment in Figure 8.13, we would end up with a problem. In that example, *every* PATIENT row would be returned by DB2. (Note that the syntax is for sample purposes only and contains errors.) Because this SELECT would return many rows, the PATIENT-DATA structure would be unable to receive them and the host program would terminate. We need a mechanism for accepting the rows one at a time. This is the purpose of

---

FIGURE 8.13   **A Program Segment that Returns Multiple Rows**

```
EXEC SQL
   SELECT *
   INTO :PATIENT-DATA
```

This structure can hold a single
row (record) only

```
FROM PATIENT
```

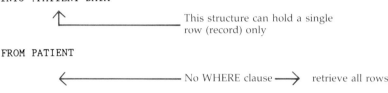

No WHERE clause ⟶   retrieve all rows

```
END-EXEC
```

However, PATIENT-DATA is a COBOL data structure that can hold only a single record. A cursor should have been used.

---

a **cursor structure,** or simply **cursor,** which as we saw earlier is coded in the DATA DIVISION.

In effect, a SELECT statement that uses a cursor results in a set of rows being retrieved—a "results table"—that is then processed like a sequential file. The cursor is the mechanism that makes the rows of the "results table" accessible to the host program. Through the FETCH command, each row is made sequentially available to the host program until the last one (SQLCODE = 100) is encountered.

Even though a cursor contains DML commands, it is coded in the DATA DIVISION. To define a cursor, we use the format shown in Figure 8.14. The statements are placed in the WORKING-STORAGE SECTION.

While the cursor format in Figure 8.14 shows only a simple SELECT, it can contain joins, subselects, or even correlated queries. The only time it is necessary to use the FOR UPDATE option is when you will be following the FETCH with an UPDATE. Each column to be updated must be specified. Don't be misled into thinking that all UPDATE operations must be done through cursors; later you will see this isn't so.

Problem 4. **Define a suitable cursor for the PATIENT example in Problem 3.**

Solution.

```
EXEC SQL
     DECLARE PAT-CURSOR CURSOR FOR
          SELECT *
               FROM PATIENT
END-EXEC.
```

FIGURE 8.14   The Syntax for Defining a Cursor

```
EXEC SQL
   DECLARE cursor-name CURSOR FOR
   SELECT column-list
    FROM table-name
        WHERE column-names = search predicates
          [FOR UPDATE OF column-list]
END-EXEC.
```

Even though it contains a procedural statement (SELECT), it is coded in the DATA DIVISION.

Remember: We code the cursor in the DATA DIVISION even though it contains DML statements. For now, the rule we will adopt is: Define a cursor for every SELECT that will return two or more rows. We won't yet concern ourselves with having to anticipate when to use cursors with UPDATE and INSERT operations.

Embed the Debugged SQL Statements into the Host Program

The SQL commands SELECT, UPDATE, DELETE, and INSERT are fully implemented in the embedded version of DB2. Like the SQL statements in the DATA DIVISION, all SQL statements must be enclosed between the EXEC SQL and END-EXEC delimiters. In addition, there are some new commands: OPEN CURSOR, CLOSE CURSOR, and FETCH, which are necessary when processing sets of rows.

Let's look briefly at the basic SQL commands as used within a COBOL program. Later we will examine them in more detail.

Retrieval of a Single Row. The steps for retrieving a single row are:

1. Define a suitable host structure.
2. Code the SELECT in the PROCEDURE DIVISION.
3. Enclose the SELECT between the delimiters.
4. Allow for the row not being found.

As a simple example, let's look again at a portion of the program to retrieve patient number 103:

```
EXEC SQL
    SELECT *
         INTO :PATIENT-DATA
         FROM PATIENT
            WHERE PID = '103'
```

END-EXEC.
    IF SQLCODE = 100
        PERFORM 2000-COULDNT-FIND-PATIENT.

Notice that the SELECT statement contains the clause INTO :PATIENT-DATA. After DB2 retrieves the desired PATIENT row, it places it into the PATIENT-DATA host structure, and the host program can then process it like any COBOL structure. The IF statement at the end checks for the possibility that the desired PATIENT row will not be found.

Retrieval of Multiple Rows. The steps for retrieving multiple rows are:

1. Define the cursor in the DATA DIVISION.
2. OPEN the cursor. This sets a pointer to the value zero, indicating that DB2 is ready to retrieve the first row. Think of this as executing the SELECT statement, with the results being placed into a temporary sequential file.
3. FETCH the next results row. Each successive FETCH statement retrieves the next "results table" row, one after another, placing it into the host structure specified in the FETCH statement, and updates the pointer value.
4. Test for the last row (SQLCODE = 100).
5. If it is the last row, CLOSE the cursor and stop.
6. If there are more rows to process, do so and go back to step 3.

Later we will show examples of how to implement these steps.

Updating and Deleting of Rows. There are two situations to consider when updating rows: UPDATEs to the "current" row and UPDATEs to sets of rows. To UPDATE the current row, the one most recently returned by a cursor, we use the syntax shown in Figure 8.15. For those situations where the UPDATE

FIGURE 8.15   **The Syntax Used to Update a Single Row**

```
EXEC SQL
  UPDATE table-name
    SET column-name1 = value1
    [column-name2 = value2. . .]
  WHERE CURRENT OF cursor-name
          ↑
          └──── Used only if a single row
                was returned via a cursor
END-EXEC.
```

The WHERE CURRENT clause says to update the row returned by a cursor.

FIGURE 8.16   **Updating Multiple Rows When a Cursor Wasn't Used to Retrieve the Rows Being Changed**

```
EXEC SQL
   UPDATE table-name
      SET column-name1 = value1
         [column-name2 = value2. . .]
      WHERE search-condition
END-EXEC.
```

FIGURE 8.17   **The Syntax Used to Delete Multiple DB2 Rows from within a Host Language**

```
EXEC SQL
   DELETE FROM table-name
   WHERE search-condition
END-EXEC.
```

applies to a set of rows rather than just the current row, we use the UPDATE statement discussed in the previous chapter. The syntax is shown in Figure 8.16.

There are also two DELETE situations: those that delete the current row and those that delete sets of rows. To DELETE the current row, use the format: DELETE FROM table-name WHERE CURRENT OF cursor-name. The syntax for deleting multiple rows is presented in Figure 8.17.

Adding New Rows. To add new rows to an existing table, we use the format shown in Figure 8.18.

This concludes our brief look at how to embed the SQL source statements within our COBOL program. Let's continue with the steps required to compile and execute it.

Precompile the Host Program

Now we are ready to **precompile** the application. As we saw earlier, the DB2 precompiler removes the SQL statements from the source program and substitutes appropriate CALL statements to the DB2-COBOL interface. The removed statements are placed into the DBRM and then compiled, or bound, into an object module called the *application plan*. The application plan later performs the actual SELECTs when the host program invokes a SQL statement.

FIGURE 8.18   **The Format for Adding a New Row into an Existing Table**

```
EXEC SQL
  INSERT INTO table-name
    (column-name1 [,column-name2] . . .)
    VALUES (value1 [,value2] . . .)
END-EXEC.
```

Specifically, the precompiler performs these tasks:

- Comparing the host structures with the SQL statements for validity
- Checking the syntax of every SQL statement
- Replacing the SQL statements with the appropriate COBOL-DB2 CALL statements
- Storing the extracted SQL statements in the DBRM, where they are kept for the BIND process

If the output is sent to a terminal, the results of the precompilation will immediately appear on the screen.

Assuming that no diagnostic errors are detected, we are now ready for the next step: compiling and link-editing.

Compile and Link-Edit the Host Program

Once the program is precompiled, it can be compiled and then link-edited in the normal manner. We must be sure to specify the DB2 library when linking the program.

Bind the Host Program: Creating the Application Plan

The next step is to bind the application. Earlier we saw that the primary purpose of this step is to create the application plan. **Binding** is the process that establishes the relationship between the DB2 tables and the application. There are four BIND functions:

- SQL/DBRM statement validation.
- Checking of authorizations—ensuring that the person invoking the BIND process is authorized to process the tables within the host program.
- Selection of the best access paths.
- Creation of the application plan.

The precompilation step can be done without DB2 being active, because it doesn't need DB2. One of the tasks performed by the bind operation is to compare the table, view, and column names found in the DBRM against the DB2 catalog for validity. Next, the processor compares the authorization of the person performing the bind against the DB2 catalog. Only those personnel authorized to access the data can bind the programs.

One of the most important bind tasks is optimizing the access to the desired data. Among the considerations that DB2 uses to select the best path to the data are the available indexes and the sizes of the tables.

The final function is the establishment of the application plan. This is the control structure that will be used to actually access the tables. It contains information about both the host program and the data it intends to access. Both the DBRM and the information about the application plan are kept in the DB2 catalog.

Execute the Host Program

The application is executed like any COBOL program. To execute it from TSO, we enter:

RUN PROGRAM (program-name)
    PLAN (plan-name)

We're now ready to look at some detailed examples of embedded SQL.

8.2 SINGLE-ROW PROCESSING: EMBEDDED SQL WITHOUT CURSORS

Single-row processing is the type of file processing we perform with a conventional COBOL program: One record (row) is read or updated at a time. This is the simplest kind of processing, because it doesn't require the use of a cursor. We saw an example of it at the beginning of the section on cursors.

Retrieval of One Row: Host Structures with the INTO Clause

Problem 5. **Display the name of the patient who has PID = 103.**

Solution. First, we must be sure that the table is declared and that we have a suitable host structure to receive the row. In this case, we do. The host structure was defined in Problem 3; its name is PATIENT-DATA. Also, the table was declared in Problem 1. We are therefore ready to embed the SELECT statement. The COBOL statements are shown in Figure 8.19.

When DB2 retrieves the desired PATIENT row, it places it into the host structure whose name(s) appears in the INTO clause—PATIENT-DATA in this

---

FIGURE 8.19   Procedural Statements for Displaying the Name of Patient 103

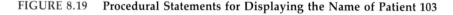

```
        EXEC SQL                        ←———— Delimeter
          SELECT *                      ←———— Retrieve ALL columns
            INTO :PATIENT-DATA          ←———— Host structure
            FROM PATIENT                ←———— DB2 table name
            WHERE PID='103'             ←———— Restriction
          END-EXEC.                     ←———— Delimiter
   *
   * the desired row is searched for, and if found, placed into
   *   the PATIENT-DATA host structure
   *
   * check for row-not-found condition
   *
        IF SQLCODE =100
          THEN
              DISPLAY 'PATIENT NOT FOUND'
   *
   * row found, display the PAT-NAME element
   *
          ELSE
            IF SQLCODE = 0
              THEN
                  DISPLAY 'THE PATIENT NAME IS: ',PAT-NAME
              ELSE
                  DISPLAY ' AN ERROR HAS OCCURRED'
            END-IF
        END-IF.
```

---

case. Because the problem asked for a single data element rather than the entire record (row), we could change the SELECT and INTO lines to reflect this:

```
SELECT PNAME
    INTO :PAT-NAME
    FROM PATIENT
        WHERE PID = '103'
```

In this case, only the patient's name would be passed to the host variable PAT-NAME. Because it is less efficient to retrieve all the columns, we should avoid using the "SELECT * . . ." format whenever possible.

Handling NULL Values: The NULL Indicator

To improve the validity of our program segment, we should also check for NULL values. Recall that NULL values are not returned to the host variables; rather, we must use an indicator variable. As part of the INTO clause, each column that can contain a NULL value must have associated with it a binary half-word data element. After the DB2 call, we test this indicator for a negative value. A negative value designates that a NULL value was returned.

Assume that a PATIENT's DIAGNOSIS value can be NULL and we are going to retrieve the DIAGNOSIS for patient 103. First, we set up the suitable NULL indicator:

01 NULL-DIAGNOSIS PIC 9(4) COMP.

Then we define a host variable to receive the DIAGNOSIS value:

01 WS-DIAGNOSIS PIC X(20).

Next, we modify the embedded SELECT statement to include the NULL indicator in the INTO clause:

```
        EXEC SQL
            SELECT DIAGNOSIS
            INTO :WS-DIAGNOSIS,:NULL-DIAGNOSIS
*
*   Note the two host variables.
*
        FROM PATIENT
            WHERE PID = '103'
        END-EXEC
*
*   Finally, we check for a NULL value:
*
        IF NULL-DIAGNOSIS < 0
            THEN
                DISPLAY 'NO DIAGNOSIS FOR THIS PATIENT'
            ELSE
                IF SQLCODE = 0
                    THEN
                        DISPLAY WS-DIAGNOSIS
                END-IF
        END-IF
```

When a host structure is used to receive a complete or partial row, and when at least one of the column values can be NULL, that structure must have associated with it a separate one-dimensional table with as many elements as the number of data elements in its structure. For example, because PATIENT has four elements, the corresponding NULL indicator structure will also have four. Even if not all of the elements can have NULL values, a spot must be reserved for them in the NULL table. If the program does not provide for handling NULL values and DB2 returns one, the application will ABEND.

FIGURE 8.20   Modifying the Solution to Problem 5 to Enable Us to Check for NULL Column Values

```
EXEC SQL
  SELECT *
    INTO :PATIENT-DATA,:NULLS
    FROM PATIENT
    WHERE PID='103'
END-EXEC.
```

Let's modify our answer to Problem 5 to test for NULL values. We will create a table with four elements, one for each of the four data elements in PATIENT:

01 NULLS OCCURS 4 TIMES PIC 9(4) COMP.

The SQL SELECT must now be modified, as in Figure 8.20.
Then we check to see if the DIAGNOSIS is NULL:

IF NULLS(4) < 0
    THEN
        DISPLAY 'NO DIAGNOSIS CODE'
END-IF.

We check NULLS(4) because DIAGNOSIS is the fourth element in PATIENT. Because of the complexity introduced by checking for NULLS, we will omit such steps in the remainder of the chapter. In an actual application, however, we cannot do this; we must always allow for NULL values whenever applicable.

Updating a Row

Conceptually, updating is done just as in the previous problem:

1. Set up the proper DATA DIVISION structures.
2. Embed the necessary SQL statements inside the delimiters.

The only difference is the use of UPDATE instead of SELECT.

***Problem 6.* Change the ONHAND amount of Keflin (code KEF) to 512.**

Solution. The solution to this problem illustrates the use of host variables in the SET clause. Therefore, we need to define one.
Assume we have a host variable called WS-NEW-ONHAND and it has been assigned the value 512. Also, assume the host structure for MEDICATION has been defined and the table declared. The PROCEDURE DIVISION portion of the solution is presented in Figure 8.21.

FIGURE 8.21   **Example of an Embedded UPDATE**

```
    EXEC SQL
        UPDATE MEDICATION
        SET ONHAND = :WS-NEW-ONHAND
*
* note the host variable
*
        WHERE MID='KEF'
    END-EXEC.
```

The new value for ONHAND is stored in a host variable; hence the colon that precedes the WORKING-STORAGE variable name.

The SET clause can also use constants instead of host structures. As an example, in the solution to Problem 6, we could change the line containing SET to:

SET ONHAND = 512

How would we change the solution to Problem 6 if the value of MID were determined by means of a variable? First, instead of the constant KEF, we would change the WHERE clause to use a host variable. Assume that a variable WS-MID has been defined. Next, we must alter the program to somehow input a value for MID. We will use the interactive ACCEPT verb:

ACCEPT WS-MID

The UPDATE portion of Figure 8.21 would now look like this:

UPDATE MEDICATION
SET ONHAND = :WS-NEW-ONHAND
    WHERE MID = :WS-MID

Later, we will see how to UPDATE a row that has been accessed by a cursor and how to UPDATE a set of rows.

Adding a Row

Let's add a new row to the table defined in Problem 2. It contains two columns: SIG and DUE-TIME. Recall that SIG is a Latin term pharmacists use to mean "schedule-code." It specifies the exact times that medications associated with an order having that SIG are to be dispensed to the patient. The other column is for the associated due time. A complication is that a given SIG can have several associated times. For example, BID means "twice a day"; thus, there would be two times to be entered.

The COBOL program must contain two host variables, one for SIG and the other for DUE-TIME. Because each value of SIG is associated with several values of DUE-TIME, we use a single-part, single-dimensional table as the host structure for DUE-TIME:

```
01   WS-SIG                              PIC X(4).
01   WS-DUE-TIMES   OCCURS 10 TIMES      PIC 9(4) COMP.
```

Assume that WS-SIG has now been assigned the value TID (meaning "to dispense a medication three times a day") and that WS-DUE-TIMES (1), (2), and (3) have been initialized to the three values 0800, 1200, and 2000—the three due times for this SIG.

Problem 7. **Add the new rows to the DUETIMES table.**

Solution. Three rows must be added, one for each element of WS-DUE-TIMES. The values will be ⟨TID, 0800⟩, ⟨TID, 1200⟩, and ⟨TID, 2000⟩. As you look at the solution in Figure 8.22, notice that it illustrates how to use host variables as VALUES in an INSERT statement.

FIGURE 8.22   Illustration of an Embedded INSERT Statement

```
* EXECUTE A LOOP THREE TIMES
      PERFORM 100-ADD-DUE VARYING I FROM 1 BY 1
          UNTIL I > 3.
*
*   we assume that we know in advance that three due times are
*    to be added. In practice this loop would be more complex.
*
  .
  .
  .

 100-ADD-DUE.
      MOVE WS-DUE-TIMES(I) TO WS-DUE
      EXEC SQL
        INSERT INTO DUETIMES
          VALUES (:WS-SIG,:WS-DUE)
* Note the colons, and the subscripts
      END-EXEC.
      IF SQLCODE = -803
          THEN
              DISPLAY 'DUPLICATE SIG/TIME COMBINATION...ROW NOT ADDED'
      END-IF.
```

The program segment adds three new rows to the DUETIMES table. The values to be added are stored in a COBOL table called WS-DUE-TIMES. We assume the values already have been read into that table.

FIGURE 8.23   **Deleting Patient 103 from the PATIENT Table**

```
EXEC SQL
   DELETE
    FROM PATIENT
    WHERE PID='103'
END-EXEC.
```

The first time through the loop, I has the value 1, so it stores the values TID (the value of WS-SIG) and 0800 (the value of WS-DUE-TIMES(1)). You may wonder why we MOVE the value of WS-DUE-TIMES(I) to another data element within the loop rather than using the subscripted variable directly in the VALUES clause. The reason is that a host structure cannot contain an OCCURS clause.

The next time through the loop, I has the value 2. The final time it has the value 3. All of the due times are thus stored.

The test for SQLCODE value -803 is to determine if an attempt to add a duplicate row has been made. Recall that through the CREATE INDEX statement, we can specify that a primary key have unique values. When a SQLCODE value of -803 is returned by DB2, it means that an attempt to add a duplicate index key value has been made. If any error other than -803 is detected, the insertion will also fail and SQLCODE will return a value that corresponds to the error.

Deleting a Row

Deleting a row is procedurally the same as SELECTing one, only we use DELETE instead of SELECT. For example, Figure 8.23 shows how to DELETE the PATIENT row for patient 103.

In the next section, we will see an example in which several rows are deleted.

8.3   MULTIPLE ROW PROCESSING: EMBEDDED SQL WITH AND WITHOUT CURSORS

When SELECTing more than one row, we *must* use a cursor structure. If we UPDATE or DELETE more than one row, a cursor may or may not be necessary. We begin by showing how to retrieve more than one row.

Retrieval of Multiple Rows

When a SELECT involves more than one row, we use the cursor concept introduced earlier. In Problem 4, we set up a cursor that we can now use to retrieve all the PATIENT rows.

FIGURE 8.24   Using a Cursor to Retrieve All the PATIENT Rows

```
DATA DIVISION.
     .
     .
     .
 WORKING-STORAGE SECTION.
*
* host structure definition
*
     EXEC SQL BEGIN DECLARE SECTION END-EXEC.
 01 PATIENT-DATA.
     03 PAT-ID      PIC X(10).
     03 PAT-NAME    PIC X(25).
     03 DIAG-CODE   PIC X(3).
     03 DOC-ID      PIC S9(9) COMP.
     EXEC SQL END DECLARE SECTION END-EXEC.
*
* declare PATIENT table next
*
     EXEC SQL
      DECLARE PATIENT TABLE
     (PID         CHAR(10) NOT NULL,
      PNAME       CHAR(25) NOT NULL,
      DIAG_CODE   CHAR(3),
      DID         INTEGER)
    END-EXEC.
*
* add SQLCA
*
     EXEC SQL
          INCLUDE SQLCA
     END-EXEC.
*
* define cursor last
*
     EXEC SQL
        DECLARE PAT-CURSOR CURSOR FOR
           SELECT *
              FROM PATIENT
        END-EXEC.
 PROCEDURE DIVISION.
*
* open the cursor
*
     EXEC SQL
        OPEN PAT-CURSOR
*
* see problem 4...pointer value now = 0
*
     END-EXEC.
```

FIGURE 8.24   (concluded)

```
*
* Issue a priming FETCH
*
      EXEC SQL
        FETCH PAT-CURSOR
*
* pointer = 1
*
        INTO :PAT-DATA
      END-EXEC.
      IF SQLCODE = 100
        THEN
            DISPLAY 'NO PATIENTS FOUND'
*
* specifies what to do if no rows in results table
*
        ELSE
*
* OK. execute  the DISPLAY/FETCH-NEXT loop until SQLCODE=100
*
            PERFORM 300-SHOW-AND-READ
            UNTIL SQLCODE=100
        END-IF.
*
* all done...close cursor and stop
*
      EXEC SQL
        CLOSE PAT-CURSOR
      END-EXEC.
      STOP RUN.
*
* DISPLAY/FETCH NEXT loop defined next
*
 300-SHOW-AND-READ.
*
* only DISPLAY if SQLCODE = 0
*
      IF SQLCODE=0
        THEN
            DISPLAY PAT-ID,PAT-NAME, DOC-ID,DIAGNOSIS
        END-IF
*
* FETCH the next row regardless of previous SQLCODE value
*
            EXEC SQL
              FETCH PAT-CURSOR
*
* increments pointer value
*
              INTO :PAT-DATA
            END-EXEC
```

Problem 8. **Retrieve all the rows in the PATIENT table.**

Solution. The solution is shown in Figure 8.24. Notice that inside the loop we display the rows only if the value of SQLCODE is zero. However, regardless of the value of SQLCODE, we FETCH the next row. When the cursor is empty, SQLCODE will have a value of 100, and the loop will terminate.

The cursor can be as complex as needed. Suppose Problem 8 called for the physician's name instead of his or her code. To solve this problem would require us to perform a join of PATIENT and DOCTOR. The new cursor is shown in Figure 8.25. Remember that this cursor is coded in the DATA DIVISION, not the PROCEDURE DIVISION. Because we are now going to extract the physician name, we must set up another host variable. The coding to do so might be:

01 DOCTOR-NAME PIC X(25).

Two PROCEDURE DIVISION changes to Figure 8.24 are necessary. First, we must specify the new cursor name. Second, we must change the lines containing the INTO clause to reflect the fact that we are to place the data into three host variables (the patient's number and name and the doctor's name). Both of these changes must be made in two locations: in the line containing the priming FETCH and in paragraph 300, where the "FETCH next" line is located. The changes are:

FETCH PAT-CURSOR2 ———————————————————————— New cursor name

INTO :PAT-NUMBER, :PAT-NAME, :DOCTOR-NAME ———————— Doctor's name will be placed into this host variable

Suppose we want to make the cursor in Figure 8.25 more flexible by permitting the user to specify the patient's name at run-time through a variable. The cursor would therefore need to include a host variable for the name and would look like this:

DECLARE PAT-CURSOR2 CURSOR FOR
SELECT PATIENT.DID, DOCTOR.DNAME
  FROM PATIENT, DOCTOR
  WHERE PATIENT.DID = DOCTOR.DID AND
      PATIENT.PNAME = :WS-PAT-NAME

Then, in the PROCEDURE DIVISION, prior to the open PAT-CURSOR2 statement, the program would MOVE the desired value to WS-PAT-NAME. The final change would be to the FETCH statements because we would be retrieving one less column.

FIGURE 8.25   **A More Complicated Cursor Containing a Join**

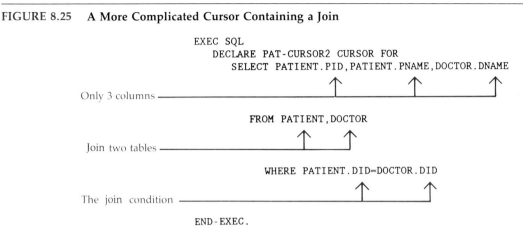

The structure could be used in the PROCEDURE DIVISION to DISPLAY a physician's code and name and the names of patients treated by the physician.

Updating Multiple Rows

There are two situations in which we update multiple rows:

- Those where we UPDATE without a previous cursor operation
- Those based on a previous cursor operation

First, let's look at an example in which no cursors are used to retrieve a row and we want to change the value of more than one row based on a search-condition.

Problem 9. **Increase the cost of all IV MEDICATIONS by 10 percent.**

Solution. This will not require the use of a cursor. Figure 8.26 shows the coding.

As we have seen, we can also use host variables in the SET line. Suppose we also want to add a flat fee of $2.00 to every IV. First, we assign a value to a previously defined data element:

MOVE 2.00 TO FLAT-FEE

Now we change the SET line to:

SET MCOST = MCOST * 1.1 + :FLAT-FEE

If DB2 encounters an error while updating multiple rows, SQLCODE will return a suitable value and all updating will stop. All rows that have been changed will be restored to their previous values.

FIGURE 8.26   Updating Several Rows

```
        EXEC SQL
          UPDATE MEDICATION
*
* no need for host variables...use table column name (MCOST)
*   only
*
          SET MCOST = MCOST * 1.1
          WHERE MED_CATEGORY='IV'
        END-EXEC.
```

The next example shows how to update the most recently accessed row. This concept requires the use of a DB2 clause called "CURRENT OF cursor-name," which is used in the WHERE clause. The value of "CURRENT OF cursor-name" indicates the last row retrieved by means of a FETCH statement.

***Problem 10.* Resolve Problem 9 using the CURRENT OF clause.**

Solution. We use a cursor to FETCH the MEDICATION rows one at a time into three host variables: MED-CODE, MED-COST, and MED-CAT. Then we test the host variable MED-CAT to see if it equals IV. If so, we UPDATE the current row. Figure 8.27 demonstrates one possible solution.

When defining cursors to be used for updating, we must use the FOR UP-DATE OF clause. If several column values are to be changed, we must specify all of them similarly. For example, assume the value of ONHAND as well as that of MCOST is to be modified. The last line of the cursor would therefore be changed to:

FOR UPDATE OF MCOST, ONHAND.

Before leaving our current coverage of cursors, we should point out that they are particularly useful in on-line programming situations. For example, assume a pharmacist has called up a particular patient and wants to page through all of that patient's orders, one at a time. Our program would use a cursor to sequentially FETCH the orders, then display them and allow the pharmacist to move around the screen making changes to the displayed fields (columns). After indicating that all changes are complete, the pharmacist could hit a designated function key and the program would update the currently displayed record using the UPDATE WHERE CURRENT syntax.

FIGURE 8.27   Using the CURRENT OF Option to Update a Row Previously FETCHed Via a Cursor

```
      DATA DIVISION.
      WORKING-STORAGE SECTION.
*
* Code the host variables
*
          EXEC SQL BEGIN DECLARE SECTION END-EXEC.
      01 MED-CODE      PIC X(7).
      01 MED-COST      PIC S9(5)V99.
      01 MED-CAT       PIC X(4).
          EXEC SQL END DECLARE SECTION END-EXEC.
*
* DECLARE the MEDICATION TABLE next
*

      EXEC SQL
        DECLARE MEDICATION TABLE
        (MID            CHAR(3)      NOT NULL,
         MNAME          CHAR(20)     NOT NULL,
         MCOST          DECIMAL(7,2),
         ONHAND         INTEGER,
         MED_CATEGORY   CHAR(4),
         UNITS_USED     INTEGER)
      END-EXEC.
*
* now include SQLCA
*

      EXEC SQL
          INCLUDE SQLCA
      END-EXEC.


*
* define the cursor last
*
      EXEC SQL
        DECLARE MED-CURSOR CURSOR FOR
           SELECT MID,MCOST,MED_CATEGORY
           FROM MEDICATION
           FOR UPDATE OF MCOST
      END-EXEC.
*
* notice that we haven't restricted the search to
*    MED_CATEGORY value 'IV'. This will be done in
*    the PROCEDURE DIVISION
* Also note the "FOR UPDATE" option
*
      PROCEDURE DIVISION
           .
           .
           .
```

FIGURE 8.27   (continued)

```
*
* open the cursor
*
              EXEC SQL
              OPEN MED-CURSOR


          END-EXEC.
*
* priming FETCH next
*
          EXEC SQL
                FETCH MED-CURSOR
              INTO :MED-CODE,:MED-COST,:MED-CAT
              END-EXEC.
*
* note that the "INTO" variables correspond to
*   the columns that are SELECTed via the cursor
*
*
* check for IV
*
              IF SQLCODE = 100
              THEN
                 DISPLAY 'NO MEDICATION ROWS FOUND'
                 PERFORM 200-CLOSE-CURSOR
              ELSE
                 IF MED-CAT ='IV'
                   THEN
                       PERFORM 400-UPDATE
                     END-IF
          END-IF
*
* loop through remainder of rows
*
          PERFORM 500-READ-AND-PROCESS
            UNTIL SQLCODE=100.
*
* all finished, CLOSE cursor
*
  200-CLOSE-CURSOR.
          EXEC SQL
              CLOSE MED-CURSOR
          END-EXEC.
        STOP RUN
*
* Routine that actually issues UPDATE
*
  400-UPDATE.
          EXEC SQL
              UPDATE MEDICATION
            SET MCOST=MCOST* 1.1
```

FIGURE 8.27   (concluded)

```
*
* UPDATE current row
*
                WHERE CURRENT OF MED-CURSOR
        END-EXEC.
*
* Routine to FETCH next row and process it
*
  500-READ-AND-PROCESS.


*
* FETCH next row and test for MED-CAT = 'IV'
*
        EXEC SQL
            FETCH MED-CURSOR
            INTO :MED-CODE,:MED-COST,:MED-CAT
        END-EXEC.
        IF SQLCODE NOT = 100
          THEN
            IF MED-CAT = 'IV'
                THEN
                    PERFORM 400-UPDATE
            END-IF
        END-IF.
```

Deleting Multiple Rows

Rows can be deleted by using a cursor or by simply issuing the DELETE FROM statement without using cursors. Because we just discussed cursors, we will begin by showing how to use a cursor to delete all IV MEDICATIONs.

We can use our previous program provided we make these changes:

- Inside paragraph 400, change the word UPDATE to DELETE.
- Delete the SET clause.
- Remove the FOR UPDATE line in the cursor definition.

There is an even easier method that doesn't involve cursors. It is shown in the solution to the next problem.

Problem 11. **Delete all the IV MEDICATIONs without using cursors.**

Solution. We code the PROCEDURE DIVISION statements shown in Figure 8.28. As with UPDATE, if an error is returned, all rows are restored to their original state.

Thus far, all of our examples have assumed that the exact SQL statements were known ahead of time and could thus be "hard-coded" into the host pro-

---

FIGURE 8.28   Example of Embedded SQL Statements for Deleting Multiple Rows

```
EXEC SQL
  DELETE FROM MEDICATION
    WHERE MED_CATEGORY ='IV'
END-EXEC.
```

The example deletes all the IV MEDICATIONs.

---

gram. However, in an interactive, on-line environment in which end users interact with a host program, this assumption may not always be true. End users can enter their own SQL statements, to which our program must then respond. This will create a major problem for DB2. Because the precompiler can't possibly extract the SQL statements (they will be entered at run-time by an end user), there will be no DBRM, which means there will be no application plan. Situations like this require a dynamic environment, a subject we briefly discuss next.

8.4   DYNAMIC SQL

When the SQL statements are embedded in the host program, they are called **static** SQL statements. However, if the SQL statements are input from a terminal, they are called **dynamic** SQL statements. We will discuss the latter case next.

The following SQL statements cannot be executed dynamically: CLOSE, DECLARE, DESCRIBE, EXECUTE, EXECUTE IMMEDIATE, FETCH, INCLUDE, OPEN, PREPARE, ROLLBACK, and WHENEVER. However, all the other SQL statements can be executed using one of two modes: EXECUTE IMMEDIATE or PREPARE and EXECUTE. EXECUTE IMMEDIATE means that the SQL statement is to be dynamically prepared for execution and then executed, all at run-time. The other option essentially does the same thing, but in two steps.

The application has several responsibilities:

- To include SQLCA.
- To generate the desired SQL statement. This can be done via a literal (01 WS-SQL-STATEMENT PIC X(20) VALUE 'SELECT * FROM PATIENT WHERE PID = 103'), by input from a user (ACCEPT WS-SQL-STATEMENT), or by any other acceptable means.
- To execute the statement using either of the two methods above.
- To handle any errors reported.

In some situations, we want the end user to be able to enter the complete SQL statement and have our host program execute it. Under these circumstances, we can use the EXECUTE IMMEDIATE option. Provided we define a variable-length host variable (let's call it WS-SQL-STATEMENT) and assign a value to the variable, we can use the syntax in Figure 8.29 to execute it. The statement will then be dynamically prepared and executed at run-time.

As an example, suppose the end user encounters a prompt message from these COBOL statements:

DISPLAY 'ENTER A SQL STATEMENT'
ACCEPT WS-SQL-STATEMENT

and enters this character string value:

DELETE FROM MEDICATION WHERE MED-CATEGORY = 'IV'

The EXECUTE IMMEDIATE statement shown above will then delete all the IV medications after DB2 has prepared and bound the statement.

At times we would like to repeatedly execute a statement based on a value entered by the end user. For example, we may want a program to repeatedly request a patient number value, then delete that patient from the PATIENT table. Of course, we could use static SQL to perform this request, but let's see how dynamic SQL would solve the problem.

Our solution will demonstrate the PREPARE and EXECUTE statements, both of which can be used only within applications. The format for PREPARE is quite simple:

PREPARE statement-name
FROM host-variable.

The host variable value (a character string containing a portion of a SQL statement) cannot contain references to other host variables; we need another mechanism whenever we require that a parametric value be included in the SQL

FIGURE 8.29   Example of a Dynamic SQL Statement

```
EXEC SQL

    EXECUTE IMMEDIATE :WS-SQL-STATEMENT

END-EXEC.
```

where WS-SQL-STATEMENT is assumed to be the variable-length variable discussed previously.

The end user can input the SQL statement to be executed.

---

statement. For example, assume we want the end user to input values for PID, PNAME, DIAG-CODE, and DID for a new PATIENT row. We also want the entire INSERT statement to be executed dynamically. Executed statically, we would code:

INSERT INTO PATIENT
    VALUES (' . . . ', ' . . . ', . . .);

where we would insert the actual values into the VALUES clause.

With dynamic SQL, not only can the INSERT statement come from the end user, but so can the values. Because a dynamic SQL statement cannot include a host variable, we need a new mechanism for denoting parametric values. Dynamic SQL uses the question mark (?) for this purpose, and this is called a **parameter marker.** Assume the variable WS-SQL-STATEMENT now has the value:

'INSERT INTO PATIENT VALUES (?,?,?,?)'

FIGURE 8.30   The Structure that Enables an Application to Dynamically Prepare a SQL Statement for Execution

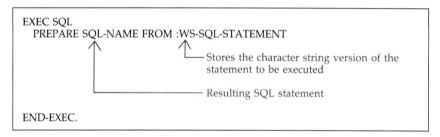

The PREPARE statement results in an executable SQL statement that is derived from a host variable containing a character string. The character string cannot contain CLOSE, COMMIT, DECLARE CURSOR, DESCRIBE, EXECUTE, EXECUTE IMMEDIATE, FETCH, INCLUDE, OPEN, PREPARE, ROLLBACK, or WHENEVER.

FIGURE 8.31   Declaring the Variable that Will Be Converted into the Actual SQL Statement to Be Executed

```
EXEC SQL
   DECLARE SQL-NAME STATEMENT
END-EXEC.
```

The PREPARE statement will prepare the character string for execution, while the EXECUTE statement will run it. Think of this pair of statements as an EXECUTE IMMEDIATE done as two steps.

To prepare the string for execution, we use the format presented in Figure 8.30. The variable SQL-NAME will become the actual SQL statement that is executed and must be DECLAREd in the DATA DIVISION as shown in Figure 8.31.

To run the PREPAREd statement, we use the format shown in Figure 8.32. For example, to execute the above insertion statement, we could code the statements shown in Figure 8.33.

If the SQL statement is always the same and no parametric values are needed, we can use EXECUTE IMMEDIATE; otherwise, we use the PREPARE/EXECUTE steps. Situations involving a SELECT are even more complex.

Here the DESCRIBE statement must be used, along with a new communication area called the *SQL Descriptor Area* (*SQLDA*), which is coded in the WORKING-STORAGE SECTION. It is an 11-element structure that will contain information about which columns the end user requested. The DESCRIBE statement can be used to query the SQLDA to determine how large the host variables must be to accept the columns requested.

Dynamic SQL is a facility that allows end users to input their own SQL statements and have them executed by a COBOL program that calls DB2. IBM's VS COBOL II is capable of executing all dynamic statements, but OS/VS COBOL cannot run queries that involve SELECTs containing undeterminable numbers and names of columns—a situation known as a **variable SELECT list.** The interaction of these components is quite complex, and we intentionally omit the details from this text. If you need to use dynamic SQL, we suggest that you read the appropriate IBM DB2 manuals.

8.5   AUTOMATIC ERROR HANDLING: THE WHENEVER STATEMENT

DB2 has a facility for having the application automatically call an error routine when SQLCODE contains a nonzero value. It is invoked by using the WHENEVER statement. (See block 6 in Figure 8.1 for an example.)

FIGURE 8.32   The EXECUTE Statement Used to Execute a Prepared SQL Statement

```
EXEC SQL
   EXECUTE statement-name
     [USING host-variable argument-list]
END-EXEC.
```

Where the optional argument list supplies values for any parameter markers.

FIGURE 8.33   A Program Segment that Illustrates Dynamic Insertion of a PATIENT Row

```
MOVE 'INSERT INTO PATIENT VALUES (?,?,?,?)' TO WS-SQL-STATEMENT.
```

Parameter markers ⟶ ⋀⋀⋀

```
*
* PREPARE the statement
*
EXEC SQL
   PREPARE SQL-NAME FROM :WS-SQL-STATEMENT
END-EXEC.
*
* next EXECUTE it, but be sure to supply the desired PID value
*
DISPLAY 'ENTER PATIENT NUMBER, NAME, DIAGNOSIS CODE AND PHYSICIAN ID'
ACCEPT PAT-ID, PAT-NAME, DIAGNOSIS-CODE, DOC-ID
EXEC SQL
   EXECUTE SQL-NAME
     USING :PAT-ID, :PAT-NAME, :DIAGNOSIS-CODE, :DOC-ID
```

↑⟶ Host variable that contains the PID
value of the PATIENT row to be inserted

```
END-EXEC.
```

The PAT-ID variable contains the PID value of the patient to be added.

The WHENEVER statement allows the application to take one of two courses of action—to pass control to the next statement or to transfer control to a specified paragraph—depending on the value of SQLCODE. There are three formats, all of which are shown in Figure 8.34.

If there are two WHENEVER NOT FOUND statements in a single program, the first remains active until another one of the same type is encountered, at which time it assumes control of all subsequent SQL statements. This means that the WHENEVER statements must precede the SQL statements they are to control.

The first format in Figure 8.34 says to either transfer control to the next statement or transfer control to the indicated paragraph (see block 8 in Figure 8.1) when SQLCODE has a value of 100. Recall that this is the value DB2 returns when it cannot satisfy a SELECT or FETCH.

The next WHENEVER choice says to either CONTINUE processing or transfer control to the indicated paragraph whenever SQLCODE contains a positive value. This clause will also be executed if SQLWARN0 has a value of W. The last statement specifies what to do if the value of SQLCODE is negative.

FIGURE 8.34   The Three WHENEVER Formats Used to Trap SQL Errors Automatically

```
(1) EXEC SQL
        WHENEVER NOT FOUND
        CONTINUE | GOTO paragraph-name
    END-EXEC.

(2) EXEC SQL
        WHENEVER SQLWARNING
        CONTINUE | GOTO paragraph-name
    END-EXEC.

(3) EXEC SQL
        WHENEVER SQLERROR
        CONTINUE | GOTO paragraph-name
    END-EXEC.
```

Once a WHENEVER statement is activated, it remains so until another one of the same type is encountered.

Because WHENEVER is, in effect, a GO TO, many organizations do not use it, since it violates structured-programming guidelines. In this case, the application programmer is responsible for all error detection and correction.

8.6   TRANSACTION PROCESSING STATEMENTS: LOCK, COMMIT, AND ROLLBACK

Using embedded SQL, we can also issue the SQL commands shown in Figure 8.35. The three statements shown in the figure typically are used in a transaction processing environment in which several users simultaneously input short transactions that update multiple tables.

The LOCK TABLE statement names the table to be locked. If the SHARE MODE is selected, all other concurrent users can issue only SELECTs; they cannot update until the lock is removed by means of the COMMIT statement. If the EXCLUSIVE MODE is chosen, concurrent users can execute no SQL statements against the named table.

Recall from Chapter 7 that the COMMIT WORK statement posts all database changes made by the application. The complete sequence of SQL statements effected by the statement at that time is called a **unit of recovery.** The unit of recovery begins when the application begins or upon the termination of a previous unit of recovery. The end of the unit of recovery occurs when a COMMIT or ROLLBACK is issued or the application ends. The COMMIT statement affects only the unit of recovery, in effect the statements issued since the last COMMIT

FIGURE 8.35   Other SQL Statements that Can Be Embedded in a Host Language

LOCK TABLE table-name IN SHAPE | EXCLUSIVE MODE

COMMIT WORK

ROLLBACK WORK

---

or ROLLBACK. All changes made due to ALTER, CREATE, DELETE, DROP, GRANT, REVOKE, INSERT, ROLLBACK, and UPDATE are posted.

Changes made by a program aren't made available to other programs until a COMMIT is issued. Thus, if many rows are being updated, added, or deleted, be sure to issue the COMMIT command frequently.

The ROLLBACK statement backs out all changes made by a unit of recovery. All uncommitted changes are invisible to concurrent users, but they can be backed out. Committed changes cannot be backed out. Figure 8.36 illustrates the COMMIT/ROLLBACK concepts by applying them to Problem 9, where we updated the costs for the IV MEDICATIONs.

8.7 SQL AND 4GLS

In many ways, embedding SQL calls in a procedural language is self-defeating. While SQL was designed to respond to a single command by operating on sets of records, COBOL was designed to operate with a single record at a time. As a result, the cursor concept was necessary, which in many ways reduces the power of SQL to that of the COBOL-based access methods. Many of the SQL vendors, other than IBM, include a 4GL with their products. These 4GLs have been designed to work in harmony with their SQL products, are more capable of processing the multiple records the products return, and make programming much simpler.

4GLs are much more than just SQL processors; they are better able to process multiple rows at a time than COBOL. Typically, they also include modules for screen definition and maintenance, including window management, report writers, a form of Query-By-Example (QBE), and a combination of procedural and nonprocedural statements.

As a simple example, Figure 8.37 shows an Informix-4GL program that establishes a cursor, then processes the results. The program first identifies the desired database (PHARMACY), then specifies that three program records (host tables, in effect)—pr__medication, px__order, and pr__patient—are based on the MEDICATION, ORDER, and PATIENT tables, respectively. Program records

FIGURE 8.36   Example of a Transaction Processing Program that Illustrates the LOCK, COMMIT, and ROLLBACK Commands

```
        PERFORM 1000-UPDATE.
        STOP RUN.
1000-UPDATE.
        EXEC SQL
            LOCK TABLE MEDICATION IN EXCLUSIVE MODE
        END-EXEC.
*
* locks the table so no one else can use the table while
*   it is being updated
*
        EXEC SQL
            UPDATE MEDICATION
            SET MCOST = MCOST * 1.1
            WHERE MED_CATEGORY='IV'
        END-EXEC.
*
* the statements above perform the UPDATE (see problem 9)
*
*
* see if OK
*
        IF SQLCODE NOT=0
            THEN
*
* problem.. back out changes
*
                ROLLBACK WORK
            ELSE
*
* OK. COMMIT changes
*
                COMMIT WORK

*
* COMMIT also unlocks the table
*
        END-IF.
```

are storage locations used to hold new rows to be inserted, rows to be changed, or rows returned by a SELECT. The * following the table name indicates that the program records are to have the same data items as the tables on which they are based. Furthermore, the word LIKE means that the data item is to be of the same type as the corresponding column of the underlying table. Such a statement helps enforce data independence, because if a table's column speci-

---

FIGURE 8.37   **A Simple Informix-4GL Program that Joins Three Tables and Displays Resulting Medication Code and Name and the Patient Number and Name for Each Order in a DOSAGE Table**

```
DATABASE PHARMACY
MAIN
DEFINE pr_dosage RECORD LIKE dosage.*
DEFINE pr_medication LIKE RECORD medication.*
DEFINE pr_patient RECORD LIKE patient.*
DECLARE c_cursor CURSOR FOR
    SELECT mid, mname, pid, pname
        INTO pr_medication.mid, pr_medication.mname,
            pr_patient.pid, pr_patient.pname
        FROM medication, dosage, patient
        WHERE dosage.mid = medication.pid AND
            patient.pid = dosage.pid
FOREACH c_cursor
    DISPLAY pr_medication.mid, pr_medication.mname,
            pr_patient.pid, pr_patient.pname
END FOREACH
END MAIN
```

---

fication changes, the programs do not even have to be recompiled. This isn't true for COBOL and SQL.

The cursor that follows serves the same purpose as the one we saw earlier in the chapter. In the example, it joins PATIENT, DOSAGE, and MEDICATION, producing a results table called c__cursor.

The main part of the program follows next. The FOREACH loop is used to process each row in the results table. Informix is to display the medication code and description, as well as the number and name of the patient receiving the medication.

The next three figures show the power of the Informix-4GL more clearly. Figure 8.38 shows a portion of a program that processes PATIENT data. It displays a ring menu (like that in Lotus 1-2-3), then takes the appropriate action depending on what the user chooses from the menu. It also displays a form called PATIENT, which is defined in Figure 8.40, and shows the coding for the routine to add a new patient. One of the menu choices presented in Figure 8.38 refers to the ability to perform a QBE search. Figure 8.39 shows the coding to implement this using the Informix-4GL.

Figure 8.38 includes a lot of comments, but let's take just a general look at the program. It first displays the PATIENT form using yellow for all of its captions. There are many other color choices to choose among, and they can be mixed for emphasis.

Next, the MENU structure is used to define a ring menu at the top of the

FIGURE 8.38   An Informix-4GL Program Segment that Contains a Menu and Coding for Inputting PATIENT Data from the Screen

```
database PHARMACY
MAIN
DEFINE  pr_patient RECORD LIKE patient.*
```
⟶ Define a program record based on the PATIENT table to hold PATIENT rows

```
OPEN FORM patient FROM "patient"
DISPLAY FORM patient
```
⟶ Display blank patient form (screen)

```
ATTRIBUTE (yellow)
```
⟶ Use yellow captions

```
MENU "Patient Processing"
```
⟶ Set up a ring menu

```
COMMAND "Add-patient" "Enter a new patient"
```
⟶ First choice is to Add a new patient

```
  CALL add_pat()
```
⟶ Call this procedure if "Add" is selected

```
COMMAND "Find a patient using QBE"
  CALL q_pat()
```
⟶ Allow user to use QBE to locate a patient based on any criteria

```
  . . .other menu choices would go here

  COMMAND "Exit" "Exit to DOS"
    CLEAR SCREEN
    exit menu
END MENU

FUNCTION add_pat()
```
⟶ Define the "Add-Patient" routine

FIGURE 8.38   (continued)

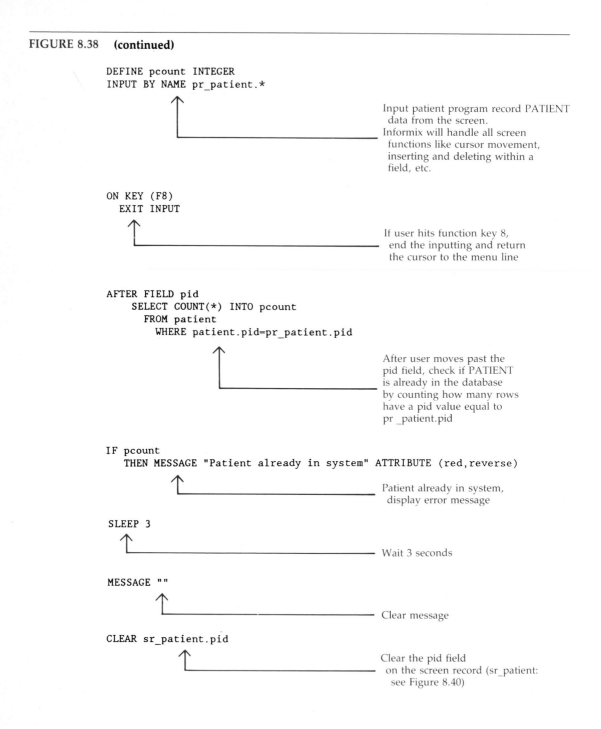

```
DEFINE pcount INTEGER
INPUT BY NAME pr_patient.*
```

Input patient program record PATIENT
data from the screen.
Informix will handle all screen
functions like cursor movement,
inserting and deleting within a
field, etc.

```
ON KEY (F8)
  EXIT INPUT
```

If user hits function key 8,
end the inputting and return
the cursor to the menu line

```
AFTER FIELD pid
    SELECT COUNT(*) INTO pcount
      FROM patient
        WHERE patient.pid=pr_patient.pid
```

After user moves past the
pid field, check if PATIENT
is already in the database
by counting how many rows
have a pid value equal to
pr _patient.pid

```
IF pcount
    THEN MESSAGE "Patient already in system" ATTRIBUTE (red,reverse)
```

Patient already in system,
display error message

```
SLEEP 3
```

Wait 3 seconds

```
MESSAGE ""
```

Clear message

```
CLEAR sr_patient.pid
```

Clear the pid field
on the screen record (sr_patient:
see Figure 8.40)

FIGURE 8.38   (concluded)

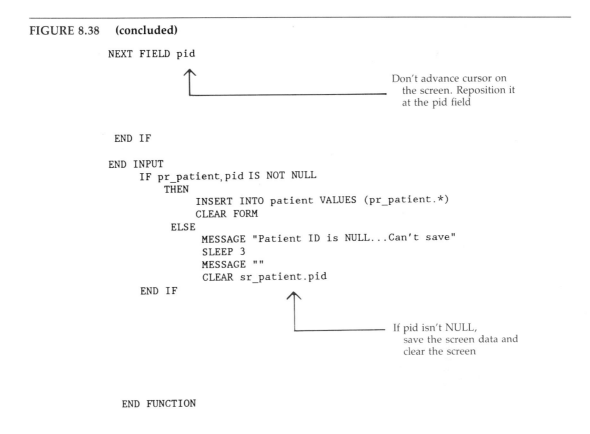

```
NEXT FIELD pid
```
Don't advance cursor on
the screen. Reposition it
at the pid field

```
        END IF

END INPUT
    IF pr_patient,pid IS NOT NULL
        THEN
                INSERT INTO patient VALUES (pr_patient.*)
                CLEAR FORM
          ELSE
                MESSAGE "Patient ID is NULL...Can't save"
                SLEEP 3
                MESSAGE ""
                CLEAR sr_patient.pid
        END IF
```
If pid isn't NULL,
save the screen data and
clear the screen

```
        END FUNCTION
```

screen. The menu's name is "Patient Processing," and three of its choices are shown, each following a COMMAND operator: "Add-patient," "Find a patient using QBE," and "Exit to DOS."

The remainder of the figure shows how we might code the "Add" routine. The "input by name" line says to take all the field values from the screen and put them into the program record, pr-patient. When the user strikes the F8 key (ON KEY (F8)), the input routine ends, the screen data is saved (discussed later), and control returns to the menu line at the top of the screen.

As the cursor leaves the pid field on the screen, we check to see if there already is a patient in the table having the same pid value as that entered on the screen. If so, it is an error, because the user has chosen Add, and, therefore, an appropriate error message is shown for three seconds before it is erased. The cursor is then repositioned at the pid field rather than at the next field.

After all the data is entered, we check to see if the pid value is NULL. If it

---

FIGURE 8.39   The Informix Routine to Construct and Execute a QBE

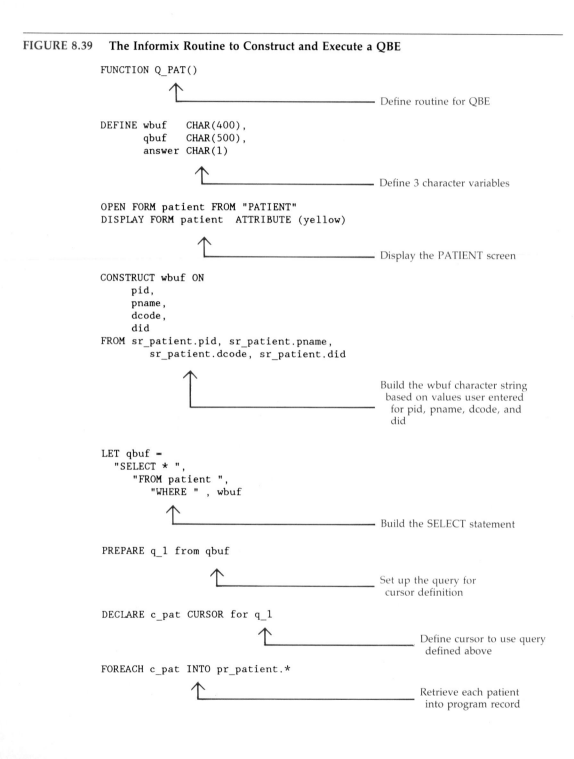

```
FUNCTION Q_PAT()
                                                    ———— Define routine for QBE

DEFINE wbuf    CHAR(400),
       qbuf    CHAR(500),
       answer CHAR(1)
                                                    ———— Define 3 character variables

OPEN FORM patient FROM "PATIENT"
DISPLAY FORM patient  ATTRIBUTE (yellow)
                                                    ———— Display the PATIENT screen

CONSTRUCT wbuf ON
     pid,
     pname,
     dcode,
     did
FROM sr_patient.pid, sr_patient.pname,
        sr_patient.dcode, sr_patient.did

                                                    Build the wbuf character string
                                                    based on values user entered
                                                    for pid, pname, dcode, and
                                                    did

LET qbuf =
   "SELECT * ",
      "FROM patient ",
         "WHERE " , wbuf
                                                    ———— Build the SELECT statement

PREPARE q_1 from qbuf
                                                    ———— Set up the query for
                                                         cursor definition

DECLARE c_pat CURSOR for q_1
                                                    ———— Define cursor to use query
                                                         defined above

FOREACH c_pat INTO pr_patient.*
                                                    ———— Retrieve each patient
                                                         into program record
```

FIGURE 8.39   (concluded)

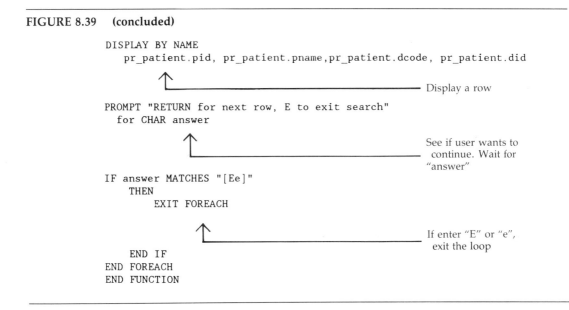

```
DISPLAY BY NAME
     pr_patient.pid, pr_patient.pname,pr_patient.dcode, pr_patient.did
```
———————————————————————————————— Display a row

```
PROMPT "RETURN for next row, E to exit search"
  for CHAR answer
```
———————————————————————————————— See if user wants to continue. Wait for "answer"

```
IF answer MATCHES "[Ee]"
     THEN
          EXIT FOREACH
```
———————————————————————————————— If enter "E" or "e", exit the loop

```
     END IF
END FOREACH
END FUNCTION
```

isn't, we execute the SQL INSERT command and clear the screen. Otherwise, an error message is displayed in red with reverse-video attributes.

Figure 8.39 shows the coding for executing a QBE based on what the user has entered on the PATIENT form. The character string "wbuf" will contain all the field names and their search values once the user finishes filling in the form. For example, if the user enters ">100" in the pid field and "ang" for dcode, wbuf's value will be "pid > 100 AND dcode = 'ang'". The building of the character string is done via the CONSTRUCT statement shown in the figure.

After the string is built, we use it to construct the complete SELECT statement, which is stored as "qbuf." Using the above example, qbuf will look like this: SELECT * FROM PATIENT WHERE pid > 100 AND dcode = 'ang';. The PRE-PARE statement converts the character string into a legitimate Informix SQL statement, suitable for execution. Rather than directly executing it, however, we use the statement to define a cursor. The remainder of the routine fetches each cursor row and prompts the user as to whether or not to continue.

We have only scratched the surface of the 4GL/SQL marriage in this section. However, the future appears to be headed this way, with more and more organizations using the power of a 4GL coupled with the power of SQL. Instead of retrofitting a record-oriented language like COBOL with the capabilities for dealing with the set-oriented approach of SQL, why not use a language built specifically to interface with SQL? With 4GL compilers, hardware independence, prototyping, faster development cycles, and so on, the future of such marriages appears bright indeed.

FIGURE 8.40   **The PATIENT Screen Definition**

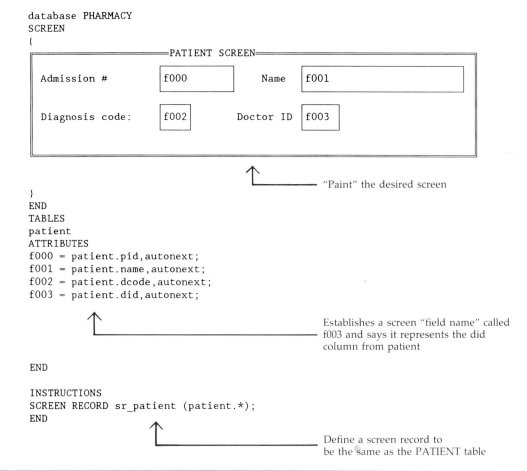

```
database PHARMACY
SCREEN
(
                            =PATIENT SCREEN=

    Admission #        f000          Name     f001


    Diagnosis code:    f002       Doctor ID   f003


```
——————— "Paint" the desired screen

```
)
END
TABLES
patient
ATTRIBUTES
f000 = patient.pid,autonext;
f001 = patient.name,autonext;
f002 = patient.dcode,autonext;
f003 = patient.did,autonext;
```
Establishes a screen "field name" called f003 and says it represents the did column from patient

```
END

INSTRUCTIONS
SCREEN RECORD sr_patient (patient.*);
END
```
Define a screen record to be the same as the PATIENT table

8.8   SUMMARY

In this chapter, we examined the embedded form of SQL, especially in COBOL applications. Most of the interactive SQL statements can be used in such programs as long as they are surrounded by the delimiters EXEC SQL and END-EXEC. We also saw that a host structure must be provided for rows returned by SELECT statements.

Using embedded SQL is simple when cursors aren't necessary:

1. In the DATA DIVISION, define the host structures, declare the tables, and INCLUDE SQLCA.

2. Embed the desired SQL statements between the delimiters.
3. Precompile, compile, link-edit, bind, and then run the host program.

The following kinds of statements do not require the use of cursors:

- Retrieval of a single row
- INSERT
- UPDATE, unless "CURRENT OF cursor-name" is used
- DELETE, again unless "CURRENT OF cursor-name" is used

When SELECT returns more than one row, a cursor must be used. After defining it in the DATA DIVISION, it must be opened before it can be used. A FETCH statement is employed to retrieve the rows one at a time through the cursor. Each FETCH statement contains a host structure name into which the actual row is placed. When there are no more rows, a SQLCODE value of 100 is returned, and at that time the cursor should be closed.

A cursor is required for:

- Retrieval of multiple rows
- DELETE, when "CURRENT OF cursor-name" is used
- UPDATE, when "CURRENT OF cursor-name" is used

We also looked at how to UPDATE and DELETE rows from within a COBOL program. If such modifications are applied to rows retrieved using a cursor, the line "CURRENT OF . . . " must be used. Otherwise, modifying rows using embedded SQL is done in the same way as with the interactive form.

Finally, we briefly looked at an example of a 4GL with embedded SQL statements. That environment offers more data independence and a simpler interface to SQL, because the languages were initially designed with the objective of integrating SQL statements in them. The future appears headed this way, with more and more organizations doing new development work using such 4GLs.

REVIEW QUESTIONS

1. Give two differences between embedded and interactive SQL.
2. What are the functions of:
   a. The precompiler?
   b. The bind operation?
3. What is the DBRM? What is its purpose?
4. Explain why a precompiler is needed for embedded SQL. Which SQL command causes the most COBOL-related problems?
5. What is a host structure? Where can it be used? How do we designate a host structure in PROCEDURE DIVISION statements?

6. Consider SQLCODE. Fill in the following table:

SQLCODE Value	Meaning	Programming Action to Take
<0		
=0		
>0		

7. What does a negative value for a NULL indicator mean?

8. Under what circumstances is a cursor necessary?

9. What does the FETCH statement do?

10. Which rows do you think would be UPDATEd in Problem 10 in the chapter if we omitted the "WHERE CURRENT OF MED-CURSOR" line in paragraph 400-UPDATE?

11. What are some problems associated with the WHENEVER statement?

12. Would you expect a program with embedded SQL statements to perform slower or faster than one containing DBMS statements related to a hierarchical or network database? Explain your answer.

13. Describe the purpose of the COMMIT statement. When should it be used?

14. If a COMMIT has just been executed, what would a ROLLBACK do if issued?

15. What portions of a COBOL program must be changed if a table's definition is altered? How does Informix overcome this problem?

PROBLEMS

For Problems 1 through 10, give the relevant COBOL and embedded SQL statements to answer the stated queries.

1. Change patient 103's room number to 345. Use the ROOM table from Chapter 7.

2. Change the 1000 time that patient 174 receives Keflin to 1100, and change the quantity to 150mg.

3. Input an adjustment for the quantity on hand for any medication. Show how to account for this adjustment while updating the MEDICATION table. (*Hint:* Ignore the sign of the adjustment.)

4. Display the diagnosis for patient 174.

5. Show the medication codes for those drugs prescribed to patient 103.

6. Resolve Problem 4 showing the medication names.

7. Display the names and room numbers of patients receiving a medication costing over $2.00. (*Hint:* This question was answered in Chapter 7 using ISQL.)

8. Write a program that inputs a patient number and displays the names of all medications prescribed to that patient. Do not show a medication more than once.

9. Delete the DOSAGE rows for patient 174 without using a cursor.

10. Use a cursor to resolve Problem 10 from the chapter.

▮▮ EPISODE 4

A Purchase Order Program Is Written Using DB2

Community Hospital recently acquired DB2 in order to evaluate it. As part of a pilot study, Barb asked Alan to use DB2 to write a purchase order program.

Alan first used interactive DB2 to define the conceptual files in Exhibit 1 as DB2 tables. Exhibit 2 shows the coding he used to generate them. (Note: The IN clause that specifies the database and table space has been omitted.)

Let's listen as Alan describes the program (Exhibit 3) to his co-workers.

"The program first requests a PO number from the end user. It then attempts to retrieve that PO from the PO table and, in turn, displays all the related detail records. Within the loop that shows the detail items, I ask for the units of each item that have been received. I then add that figure to the PO detail units previously received and also to the inventory units on hand.

"Now let me describe the program in detail.

"Since DB2 is a new package for us, I guess I'd better say something about the DATA DIVISION changes first. Each table that is to be processed must be declared using a syntax much like that used to create the table. Although I haven't as yet used all five tables in the program, I probably will do so eventually, so you can see that I coded five DECLARE TABLE structures, each enclosed within the two delimiters EXEC SQL and END-EXEC.

"Following each table declaration, I also coded a COBOL host structure that will hold rows going to or from DB2. I was careful to use the data conversion rules for DB2-COBOL. For example, even though the INVENTORY cost column is DECIMAL (7,2) in DB2, I used PIC 9(5)V99, because the first integer within

---

EXHIBIT 1 **Current Conceptual File Design for the Purchase Order Portion of Community Hospital's Schema**

PURCHASE__ORDER (PO__NO, DATE, DEPT__CODE, VENDOR__CODE, TOTAL__AMT, STATUS)

PURCHASE__ORDER__DETAIL (PO__NO, SEQ__NO, DITEM__CODE, UNITS__ORDERED, COST__PER__ITEM, UNITS__RECEIVED, UNITS__CANCELED, DATE__LAST__ARRIVED)

INVENTORY__ITEM (ITEM__CODE, ITEM__DESCRIPTION, ITEM__COST, ITEM__CHARGE, QTY__ON__HAND, USAGE__YTD, PRIMARY__VENDOR__CODE, GL__ACCOUNT, LEAD__TIME, EOQ, EOP, CRITICAL__LEVEL)

VENDOR (VENDOR__NO, NAME, ADDRESS, CONTACT, DOLLARS__YTD)

DEPARTMENT (DEPT__CODE, DEPARTMENT__NAME, MANAGER__NAME)

EXHIBIT 2   The DB2 Tables for the Purchase Order Portion of the Community Hospital Database

```
CREATE TABLE PO

    (PONUM          CHAR(10)       NOT NULL,

     CREATEDATE     DATE,

     DEPTCODE       CHAR(7),

     VENDNO         CHAR(7)        NOT NULL,

     TOTAL          DECIMAL(9,2),

     STATUS         CHAR(1),


CREATE TABLE PODETAIL

    (PONUM          CHAR(10)       NOT NULL,

     SEQNO          SMALLINT,

     ITEMCODE       CHAR(7)        NOT NULL,

     UNITSORDERED   SMALLINT,

     UNITCOST       DECIMAL(7,2)   NOT NULL,

     UNITSRCVD      SMALLINT,

     UNITSCANCLD    SMALLINT,

     DATEARVD       DATE


CREATE TABLE INVENTORY

    (ITEMCODE       CHAR(7)        NOT NULL,

     DESC           CHAR(25),

     COST           DECIMAL(7,2)   NOT NULL,

     CHARGE         DECIMAL(7,2)   NOT NULL,

     QOH            SMALLINT,

     YTDUSAGE       SMALLINT,

     VENDCODE       CHAR(7),

     GLNO           CHAR(10),

     LEADTIME       SMALLINT,

     EOQ            SMALLINT,

     EOP            SMALLINT,

     CRITLEVEL      SMALLINT,
```

EXHIBIT 2   (concluded)

```
CREATE TABLE VENDOR

      (VENDNO        CHAR(7)

       VNAME         CHAR(25),

       VSTREET       CHAR(25),

       VCITY         CHAR(25),

       VSTATE        CHAR(2),

       VZIP          SMALLINT,

       CONTACT       CHAR(25),

       DOLLARSYTD    DECIMAL(9,2))


CREATE TABLE DEPT

      (DEPTCODE      CHAR(7),

       DNAME         CHAR(25),

       DMANGR        CHAR(25))
```

---

the DECIMAL clause refers to the total length of the column, not just the digits before the decimal point as with COBOL. Also, the DATE data types must be set up as PIC X(10), because they are represented in COBOL as '1995-12-25'.

"The final DATA DIVISION item I want to point out is the cursor definition for retrieval of the PODETAIL rows associated with a particular PO number. When a set of rows is retrieved by DB2, those rows are kept in a 'results table,' a sequential-like file. To process such rows, we 'define' the results table in the DATA DIVISION by setting up a cursor containing a suitable SELECT clause. We then process these rows in the PROCEDURE DIVISION by using a command called FETCH. In my case, I also wanted to update the PODETAIL table attribute UNITSRCVD (units received), so I

needed the clause FOR UPDATE as part of the cursor.

"Any questions so far?"

"Yes," said Barb. "I noticed that you changed some of the SMALLINT attributes to COBOL PIC 9(3) and others to 9(5). Why the discrepancies?"

Alan replied, "Well, as long as the host variable is large enough to hold the actual column's value, there's no harm in making it as small as needed. For example, even though the WS-LEADTIME element is only PIC 9(3), this is large enough to hold up to 999 days. Certainly that's large enough, or we shouldn't be doing business with that vendor! Besides, I can always check the value of SQLWARN1 to determine if a value has been truncated."

Alan continued, "Now for the PROCEDURE DIVISION. Paragraph 200-ASK-

EXHIBIT 3   The DB2 Program for Displaying and Updating a Purchase Order

```
      IDENTIFICATION DIVISION.
         .
         .
         .
      ENVIRONMENT DIVISION.
    * set up CRT as a special name
      SPECIAL-NAMES.
      system-name IS CRT.
      DATA DIVISION.
         .
         .
         .
      WORKING-STORAGE SECTION.

    *
    * SQLCA first. Hard code it instead of using INCLUDE SQLCA
    *
      01 SQLCA.
            05 SQLCAID            PIC X(8).
            05 SQLCABC            PIC S9(9) COMP.
            05 SQLCODE            PIC S9(9) COMP.
            05 SQLERRM.
                49 SQLERRML       PIC S9(4) COMP.
                49 SQLERRMC       PIC X(70).
            05 SQLERP             PIC X(8).
            05 SQLERRD            OCCURS 6 TIMES
                                  PIC S9(9) COMP.

            05 SQLWARN.
                10 SQLWARN0       PIC X(1).
                10 SQLWARN1       PIC X(1).
                10 SQLWARN2       PIC X(1).
                10 SQLWARN3       PIC X(1).
                10 SQLWARN4       PIC X(1).
                10 SQLWARN5       PIC X(1).
                10 SQLWARN6       PIC X(1).
                10 SQLWARN7       PIC X(1).
            05 SQLTEXT            PIC X(8).
    *
    * DECLARE THE PO TABLE NEXT
    *
          EXEC SQL
            DECLARE PO TABLE
              (PONUM             CHAR(10)   NOT NULL,
               CREATEDATE        DATE,
               DEPTCODE          CHAR(7),
               VENDNO            CHAR(7)    NOT NULL,
               TOTAL             DECIMAL(9,2),
               STATUS            CHAR(1))
          END-EXEC.
    *
    * CODE THE HOST STRUCTURE
    *
```

EXHIBIT 3   (continued)

```
        EXEC SQL BEGIN DECLARE SECTION END-EXEC.
   01   WS-PO.
        03 WS-PONUM                 PIC X(10).
        03 WS-CREATEDATE            PIC X(10).
        03 WS-DEPTCODE              PIC X(7).
        03 WS-VENDNO                PIC X(7).
        03 WS-TOTAL                 PIC 9(7)V99 COMP-3.
        03 WS-STATUS                PIC X(1).
        EXEC SQL END DECLARE SECTION END-EXEC.
 *
 * PODETAIL ITEMS NEXT
 *
        DECLARE PODETAIL TABLE
            (PONUM                  CHAR(10)  NOT NULL,
             SEQNO                  SMALLINT,
             ITEMCODE               CHAR(7)   NOT NULL,
             UNITSORDERED           SMALLINT,
             UNITCOST               DECIMAL(7,2) NOT NULL,
             UNITSRCVD              SMALLINT,
             UNITSCANCLD            SMALLINT,
             DATEARVD               DATE)
        EXEC SQL BEGIN DECLARE SECTION END-EXEC.
   01 WS-PO-DETAIL.
        03 WS-PONUM                 PIC X(10).
        03 WS-SEQNO                 PIC 9(3).
        03 WS-ITEMCODE              PIC X(7).
        03 WS-UNITSORDERED          PIC 9(5).
        03 WS-UNITCOST              PIC 9(5)V99 COMP-3.
        03 WS-UNITSRCVD             PIC 9(5) COMP-3.
        03 WS-UNITSCANCLD           PIC 9(5) COMP-3.
        03 WS-DATEARVD              PIC X(10).
        EXEC SQL END DECLARE SECTION END-EXEC.
 *
 * INVENTORY INFORMATION CODED NEXT
 *
        EXEC SQL
           DECLARE INVENTORY TABLE
            (ITEMCODE               CHAR(7)        NOT NULL,
             DESC                   CHAR(25),
             COST                   DECIMAL(7,2)  NOT NULL,
             CHARGE                 DECIMAL(7,2)  NOT NULL,
             QOH                    SMALLINT,
             YTDUSAGE               SMALLINT,
             VENDCODE               CHAR(7),
             GLNO                   CHAR(10),
             LEADTIME               SMALLINT,
             EOQ                    SMALLINT,
             EOP                    SMALLINT,
             CRITLEVEL              SMALLINT)
        END-EXEC.
        EXEC SQL BEGIN DECLARE SECTION END-EXEC.
   01 WS-INVENTORY.
```

EXHIBIT 3   (continued)

```
            03 WS-ITEMCODE              PIC X(7).
            03 WS-DESC                  PIC X(25).
            03 WS-COST                  PIC 9(5)V99 COMP-3.
            03 WS-CHARGE                PIC 9(5)V99 COMP-3.
            03 WS-QOH                   PIC 9(5) COMP-3.
            03 WS-YTDUSAGE              PIC 9(5) COMP-3.
            03 WS-VENDCODE              PIC X(7).
            03 WS-GLNO                  PIC X(10).
            03 WS-LEADTIME              PIC 9(3) COMP-3.
            03 WS-EOQ                   PIC 9(5) COMP-3.
            03 WS-EOP                   PIC 9(5) COMP-3.
            03 WS-CRITLEVEL             PIC 9(5) COMP-3.
            EXEC SQL END DECLARE SECTION END-EXEC.
    *
    *   NEXT, CODE VENDOR INFORMATION
    *
            EXEC SQL
                DECLARE VENDOR TABLE
                    (VENDNO                CHAR(7),
                     VNAME                 CHAR(25),
                     VSTREET               CHAR(25),
                     VCITY                 CHAR(25),
                     VSTATE                CHAR(2),
                     VZIP                  SMALLINT,
                     CONTACT               CHAR(25),
                     DOLLARSYTD            DECIMAL(9,2))
            END-EXEC.
            EXEC SQL BEGIN DECLARE SECTION END-EXEC.
        01 WS-VENDOR.
            03 WS-VENDNO                PIC X(7).
            03 WS-VNAME                 PIC X(25).
            03 WS-VSTREET               PIC X(25).
            03 WS-VCITY                 PIC X(25).
            03 WS-VSTATE                PIC X(2).
            03 WS-VZIP                  PIC 9(5) COMP-3.
            03 WS-CONTACT               PIC X(25).
            03 WS-DOLLARSYTD            PIC 9(7)V99 COMP-3.
            EXEC SQL END DECLARE SECTION END-EXEC.
            EXEC SQL
    *
    *   DEPARTMENTS NEXT
    *
            DECLARE TABLE DEPT
                    (DEPTCODE              CHAR(7),
                     DNAME                 CHAR(25),
                     DMANGR                CHAR(25))
            END-EXEC.
            EXEC SQL BEGIN DECLARE SECTION END-EXEC.
        01 WS-DEPT.
            03 WS-DEPTCODE              PIC X(7).
            03 WS-DNAME                 PIC X(25).
            03 WS-DMANGR                PIC X(25).
```

EXHIBIT 3   **(continued)**

```
        EXEC SQL END DECLARE SECTION END-EXEC.
*
* NORMAL WORKING-STORAGE VARIABLES NEXT
*
 01 WS-PO-NO                  PIC X(10).
 01 UNITS                     PIC 9(5).
 01   SWITCHES.
      03 DETAIL-SW            PIC X.
         88 NO-MORE-DETAIL    VALUE 'N'.
      03 ACTION              PIC X    VALUE 'N'.
         88 USER-WANTS-TO-QUIT      VALUE 'Y'.


*
* CURSOR TO FIND ALL DETAIL ROWS
*   FOR A GIVEN PO
*
      EXEC SQL
        DECLARE PODETAIL CURSOR FOR
          SELECT *
            FROM PODETAIL
            WHERE PODETAIL.PONUM = :WS-PO-NO
            FOR UPDATE OF UNITSRCVD
      END-EXEC.
 PROCEDURE DIVISION.
      PERFORM 200-ASK-FOR-PO
        UNTIL USER-WANTS-TO-QUIT.
      PERFORM 1000-WRAP-UP.
 200-ASK-FOR-PO.
      DISPLAY 'ENTER PO. #     (0 TO QUIT)'
          UPON CRT.
      ACCEPT WS-PO-NO FROM CRT.
      IF WS-PO-NO = 0
          THEN
              MOVE 'Y' TO ACTION
          ELSE
* FIND THE PO
              PERFORM 600-FIND-THE-PO
              IF SQLCODE=100
                  THEN
                      DISPLAY 'NO SUCH PO...TRY AGAIN' UPON CRT
                  ELSE
                      IF SQLCODE NOT = 0
                          THEN
                              DISPLAY ' ERROR FINDING PO    UPON CRT
                              DISPLAY 'ERROR WAS: ', SQLCODE UPON CRT
                          ELSE
* MOVE AND PRINT THE PO HEADING WOULD GO HERE
* NEXT FIND ALL THE DETAIL ITEMS
                              MOVE 'Y' TO DETAIL-SW
                              PERFORM 300-F-DETAIL
*
* CLOSE THE CURSOR, UNTIL THE NEXT PO IS REQUESTED
```

EXHIBIT 3 **(continued)**

```
                                          EXEC SQL
                                              CLOSE PODETAIL-CUR
                                          END-EXEC
                                      END-IF
                              END-IF
              END-IF
          END-IF.
      300-F-DETAIL.
      *
      * OPEN THE CURSOR
      *
          PERFORM 400-OPEN-CURSOR
      *
      * FETCH UNTIL SQLCODE = 100
      *
          PERFORM 350-FETCH
              UNTIL NO-MORE-DETAIL.
      350-FETCH.
          EXEC SQL
              FETCH PODETAIL-CUR
              INTO :WS-PO-DETAIL
          END-EXEC.
          IF SQLCODE = 100
      *
      * SQLCODE = 100
      * SET SWITCH AND TERMINATE LOOP
      *
              THEN
                  MOVE 'N' TO DETAIL-SW
                  PERFORM 550-COMMIT
              ELSE
                  IF SQLCODE NOT = 0
                      THEN
      *
      * NON-100 VALUE DETECTED:
      *    1. DISPLAY MESSAGE
      *    2. DISPLAY ERROR CODE VALUE
      *    3. ROLLBACK
      *    4. SET SWITCH TO ABORT PROCESSING THIS PO
      *
                          DISPLAY 'ERROR FINDING DETAIL' UPON CRT
                          DISPLAY 'ERROR CODE WAS: ', SQLCODE UPON
                              CRT
                          PERFORM 500-ROLLBACK
                          MOVE 'N' TO DETAIL-SW
                      ELSE
      *
      * EVERYTHING OK...CONTINUE
      * INSERT CODE TO MOVE WS-PO-DETAIL DATA AND PRINT IT...HERE
      *  ASSUME THE PO IS A PARTIAL SHIPMENT, ASK HOW MANY UNITS ARRIVED
      *
                          DISPLAY 'HOW MANY UNITS ?'UPON CRT
```

EXHIBIT 3   (continued)

```
                            ACCEPT UNITS FROM CRT
    * NOW FIND INVENTORY ROW AND UPDATE QTY ON HAND
                        EXEC SQL
                            UPDATE INVENTORY
                                SET QOH = QOH + :UNITS
                                WHERE ITEMCODE = :WS-ITEMCODE
                        END-EXEC.
                        IF SQLCODE NOT = 0
    *
    * UPDATE FAILED:
    *   1. ROLLBACK CHANGES THUS FAR
    *   2. SET SWITCH
    *
                            THEN
                                DISPLAY 'MODIFY OF INVENTORY FAILED'
                                    UPON CRT
                                DISPLAY ' THE ITEM WAS:
                                    WS-ITEMCODE UPON CRT
                                DISPLAY 'THE ERROR WAS: ',SQLCODE
                                    UPON CRT
    *
    * ROLLBACK THE CHANGES THUS FAR
    *
                                PERFORM 500-ROLLBACK
                                MOVE 'N' TO DETAIL-SW
                            ELSE

    *
    * NOW UPDATE UNITS RECEIVED COLUMN IN PODETAIL
    *
                                EXEC SQL
                                   UDATE PODETAIL
                                     SET UNITSRCVD = UNISTRCVD +
                                         :UNITS
                                       WHERE CURRENT OF PODETAIL-CUR
                                END-EXEC.
                                IF SQLCODE NOT = 0
    *
    * UPDATE FAILED:
    *   1. ROLLBACK CHANGES THUS FAR
    *   2. SET SWITCH
    *
                                THEN
                                    DISPLAY 'MODIFY OF PODETAIL FAILED
                                        UPON CRT
                                    DISPLAY 'THE ITEM WAS:
                                        WS-ITEMCODE   UPON CRT
                                    DISPLAY 'THE ERROR WAS: ',SQLCODE
                                        UPON CRT
    *
    * ROLLBACK THE CHANGES THUS FAR
    *.
```

EXHIBIT 3   (concluded)

```
                                                 PERFORM 500-ROLLBACK
                                                 MOVE 'N' TO DETAIL-SW
                                      END-IF
                        END-IF
                    END-IF
                END-IF.
        400-OPEN-CURSOR.
            EXEC SQL
                OPEN PODETAIL-CUR
            END-EXEC.
        500-ROLLBACK.
            EXEC SQL
                ROLLBACK
            END-EXEC.
        550-COMMIT.
        *
        * COMMIT THE WORK THUS FAR...SHOULD CHECK SQLCODE AGAIN...
        *
            EXEC SQL
                COMMIT WORK
            END-EXEC.
        600-FIND-THE-PO.
            EXEC SQL
                SELECT *
                    FROM PO
                    INTO :WS-PO
                    WHERE PONUM = :WS-PO-NO
            END-EXEC.
        1000-WRAP-UP.
            CLOSE.
            STOP RUN.
```

FOR-PO asks the user for a purchase order number, which is accepted into the variable, WS-PO-NO. If its value is zero, a termination switch is set and the program ends.

"Once I have input the desired purchase order number, I look it up in the PO table within paragraph 600-FIND-THE-PO. That paragraph extracts all the columns for the desired order and stores them in the WORKING-STORAGE host structure, WS-PO. Notice that the WHERE clause contains a host variable, WS-PO-NO. This is indicated by the colon. In effect, this paragraph says to find the purchase order that has a number equal to the value of WS-PO-NO and, if it is found, to place the row into WS-PO.

"Upon returning from the paragraph, I test SQLCODE for a value of 100, which would indicate that the order couldn't be found. In that case, I display an error message. Then the paragraph falls through to the end of paragraph 200-ASK-FOR-PO.

"Assuming the order was found, paragraph 200-ASK-FOR-PO next checks for any other nonzero SQLCODE values. If it finds any, it displays an appropriate error message. I thought about using the WHENEVER statement that automatically responds to errors, but I decided I'd rather do my own error checking.

"Finally, if everything is OK, I perform paragraph 300-F-DETAIL, which opens the cursor, then sequentially processes the PODETAIL rows. The first thing it does is PERFORM paragraph 400-OPEN-

CURSOR, where the OPEN is executed. Next, the paragraph repeatedly executes paragraph 350-FETCH until SQLCODE = 100 (which is indicated by a loop control switch, DETAIL-SW). Let's look at that paragraph next.

"The first thing it does is FETCH the next row from the 'results table.' Notice that the row is returned to WS-PO-DETAIL and that one of its elements is WS-ITEMCODE, the part number that was ordered. This element will be used later to look up the INVENTORY row.

"If SQLCODE = 100, this means there are no more PODETAILs, so I COMMIT the work done since the last COMMIT by calling paragraph 550-COMMIT, then set the loop control switch, and return.

"Next, if SQLCODE has any other non-zero value, I ROLLBACK the changes since the last COMMIT by calling paragraph 500-ROLLBACK.

"If SQLCODE's value is zero, I'm ready to ask how many units of the detail item arrived. The ACCEPT statement stores the value in the UNITS variable. We now know how many units have arrived, and there are two tables to update: INVENTORY and PODETAIL. The INVENTORY update is done first and looks like a conventional SQL UPDATE command. First, I look up the INVENTORY item by matching INVENTORY.ITEMCODE against WS-ITEMCODE. Recall that WS-ITEMCODE is a COBOL variable that is part of the host structure, WS-PO-DETAIL. As each detail item is fetched in paragraph 350-FETCH, it is

inserted into this structure. Thus, WS-ITEMCODE is the primary key associated with each fetched detail item.

"Assuming that the item was found, I next add the ACCEPTed value of UNITS to the INVENTORY table's value of QOH (quantity on hand), then store the updated row. If the UPDATE fails, I ROLLBACK the changes made thus far and reset the DETAIL-SW switch so that another PO can be requested.

"The last thing the paragraph does is update the PODETAIL row from the cursor. After adding the value of UNITS to UNITSRCVD, I request to update the current PODETAIL row. As usual, I check SQLCODE for nonzero values which, if found, cause the program to ROLLBACK all the transactions, then set the exit switch.

"Notice that the update of PODETAIL used the "WHERE CURRENT . . . " clause, while the update of INVENTORY used the more familiar "WHERE ITEM-CODE = . . . ". The reason is that I used a cursor to retrieve the PODETAIL row but used the SQL WHERE clause to find the INVENTORY ROW. You should also note that I used the clause FOR UPDATE OF UNITSRCVD when the cursor was defined. This is the only column value that I changed in 350-FETCH.

"Unless there are any questions, I suggest that you all take a copy of the program with you so that you can use it as a guide as you learn more about embedded SQL calls using DB2."

IV

The CODASYL Network Model

Part IV focuses on the most popular network model implementation: that of CODASYL. Chapter 9 describes the CODASYL terminology and shows how to define a database using the schema data description language (DDL). Then it describes how to code subschemas. The basis for all the examples is the Microtech Luggage Company, the subject of the minicase at the beginning of the chapter.

Episode 5 of the Community Hospital case follows Chapter 9. There we see a complete example of how to code a schema and several subschemas. However, rather than using the conceptual CODASYL model, the episode uses Cullinet's DBMS, known as IDMS/R. This product is probably the most widely used of all the commercial CODASYL implementations.

Chapter 10 discusses the CODASYL data manipulation language (DML). We will see how to invoke the proper subschema, add new records, and find, modify, and delete existing records. The retrieval mechanisms are quite extensive, providing the ability to retrieve records using a hashing routine or sequentially. As we examine each command, we will consider the impact of some of the schema DDL decisions on the DML. The last section of the chapter examines transaction processing and concurrency control using examples based on the Microtech minicase.

Episode 6 follows Chapter 10. It uses IDMS/R to develop a COBOL application. You'll see that there are few differences from the CODASYL standard. The program is the same one that we saw in Episode 4, so a comparison of the two may be useful.

The CODASYL Network Model

Theory and Implementation

MINICASE Microtech Luggage Company

Microtech Luggage Company wishes to develop a database to help it manage its accounts payable. At present, it does business with about 100 vendors. Historical data has revealed that Microtech owes an average of five invoices per vendor, with each invoice containing charges for several items. Microtech accounts payable manager, Kevin Thomas, pays invoices on the 15th and last day of each month and has asked for two reports, one showing all the invoices owed all vendors and the other the invoices due on a given date. A third report has been requested by Sandy Hill, Microtech's purchasing director. Figures 9.1 through 9.3 show the three reports the data structure must support.

Gordon Reid, one of Sandy's clerks, has also made a request to the IS department. He will need a listing of all the vendors with

which Microtech does business for a Christmas mailing he has been asked to do.

Mary Robbins, an analyst with Microtech, has been given the task of designing the database to support the payables needs. She designed the reports shown in Figures 9.1 through 9.3. Let's listen in as she discusses the reports with Kevin.

Mary Thank you for agreeing to meet with me this morning. I know you're quite busy, because tomorrow's the 15th.

Kevin That's OK. I know how important it is for us end users to take part in the design of information systems.

Mary Let's start with the Vendor Owed Report. Let me see if I have it correct. You need to have this report printed on demand, right?

Kevin That's right. However, I'll use it most

FIGURE 9.1   **The Vendor Owed Report Layout**

```
                    Microtech Luggage Co.
                    Vendor Owed Report          Page: XXX
                      As of: XX/XX/XX


        Vendor:  XXXXX     Name: XXXXX---X

        Invoice         Amount          Due
        No.             Due             Date

        XXXX            99999.99        XX/XX/XX
        XXXX            99999.99        XX/XX/XX
        .
        .
        .


        Total this vendor ** $999,999.99 **
```

FIGURE 9.2   **The Due Date Report Layout**

```
                        Microtech Luggage Co.                    Page: XXX
                        Due Date Report
                          As of: XX/XX/XX

        Due Date: XX/XX/XX

        Invoice         Vendor          Vendor                          Amount
        No.             No.             Name                            Due

        XXXX            XXXXX           XXXXXXXXXXXXXXXXX                99999.99
        XXXX            XXXXX           XXXXXXXXXXXXXXXXX                99999.99
        .
        .
        .
        Total this date: ** $999,999.99 **
```

often about 10 days prior to the pay dates so that I can see how much we owe each vendor. I know I originally wanted to select only a single vendor, but I now think I also want to be able to print the report for all the vendors.

Mary That's no problem. Your statement also answers what was going to be my next question about sorting. I've designed the report so that when a detailed report of all vendors is printed, the primary sort is on vendor code and the secondary sort is on invoice number. That way all invoices to a particular vendor will be grouped together, in ascending order by invoice number.

Kevin I have a problem with the sorting. I

FIGURE 9.3   **The Invoice Analysis Report Layout**

```
                    Microtech Luggage Co.                    Page: XXX
                    Invoice Analysis Report
                       As of: XX/XX/XX

      Invoice No: XXXXXXXXX                      Date received: XX/XX/XX

      Vendor: XXXXX                              Total: 99999.99
              XXXXXXXXXXXXXXXXXXXXXXXXXXXXX
      Vendor address: XXXXXXXXXXXXXXXXXXXXX
                      XXXXXXXXXXXXXXXXXXX
                      XXXXXXXXXXXXX XX 9999

      Item        Description        Price      Units      Extension
      XXXXX       XXXXXXXXXXXXXX      9999.99    9999       99999.99




                                               Total       _____
                                                           99999.99
```

---

might want the secondary sort on due date instead of invoice number. Since I was never able to sort at all before this, I'm not sure which is more useful to me.

Mary That's OK. With the new database package we purchased, I don't think the sorting order will have much impact on my design.

Before we look at report two, I want to be sure you don't need the details about the invoices on this report. Notice that I'm only going to print totals.

Kevin That's no problem.

Mary The second report is designed to enable you to select any date and receive a report showing all the invoices due on that date, sorted by invoice number. Again, there is to be no detail. The individual items can be seen by requesting the third report. Any problems?

Kevin None. Let's get to the third report. I'm late for a meeting already.

Mary I've designed the third report to assist you and Sandy when you need detailed information about a particular invoice or a complete listing of all the invoices. This is the only place where the detail items appear. I'd better caution you about the need to keep your inventory data accurate. Instead of carrying the item description in the detail record, I'm going to look it up in the INVENTORY master. This also means that you can't enter detail invoice data into the database if the item isn't in the INVENTORY file.

Kevin OK. I don't think that will be a problem. If you don't have any more questions, let's end the meeting.

Mary reluctantly agreed to end the meeting and set off to consult with the DBA about how to design the accounts payable database.

Discussion

1. What are the entities necessary to support each report?

2. List the transactions the database must support.

3. Draw a suitable DSD or E-R diagram.

4. Add as many attributes to each entity as you can.

5. Why do you think Mary was reluctant to end the meeting?

6. Based on Mary's last statement, how can we label the relationship between an inventory item and an invoice detail item?

In Chapter 2, we introduced the idea of the three database views: the conceptual, the external, and the physical. In Chapter 5, we saw that the conceptual database may need to be modified to suit the particular model used by the DBMS. We called the result the *logical database*. In this chapter, we present most of the CODASYL terms and examine how the conceptual (logical) and external databases are implemented.

At the conclusion of this chapter, you will be able to:

- Discuss CODASYL terminology
- Define a conceptual database using the schema DDL
- Discuss and implement CODASYL integrity enforcement methods
- Define an external database using the subschema DDL

9.1 HISTORICAL PERSPECTIVE

During the 1960s, efforts to develop a standard database theory were evolving along many paths. In 1965, the Conference on Data Systems Languages (CODASYL) formed a committee known as the Database Task Group (DBTG) in an attempt to develop a standardized approach. The committee contained three representatives from IBM, three from Honeywell Information Systems, two from Computer Sciences Corporation, and one each from 14 other enterprises, including General Electric, the U.S. Navy, and Bell Labs.

At about the same time, General Electric was marketing a product called Integrated Data Store (IDS), developed by a project team headed by Charles Bachman, who had also invented the DSD method for describing conceptual databases. The product was later bought by Honeywell Information Systems and is still marketed as IDS II. Notice that the committee's membership was well represented by these two companies, which might help explain the similarities between the IDS product line and the results of the committee.

The DBTG released its most important document, *The DBTG April 1971 Report*, in April 1971. This report called for a data description language (DDL), known as the *schema DDL*, which was to be used for describing databases; a similar DDL for describing external databases, called the *subschema DDL*; and a data manipulation language (DML) to be used by the host program to store, access, and maintain the records in the database. The DBTG also suggested that vendors develop a device media control language (DMCL) for defining the physical database.

By 1978, CODASYL had disbanded the DBTG in favor of an organization constructed along schema and DML lines. The Data Description Language Committee (DDLC) now had responsibility for schemas and storage requirements, while the Programming Language Committee was responsible for the DML and subschema definitions. The continuing efforts of CODASYL were announced about every two years in its *Journal of Development (JOD)*. *JOD* released updates to the 1971 CODASYL model in 1973, 1978, and 1981. The last release is the basis for most of the discussion in this portion of the text. By 1984, the DDLC was disbanded because its data definition language had been chosen as a network standard by the X3H2 committee of ANSI (see Chapter 2 for a discussion of the ANSI organization).

9.2   THE CODASYL ARCHITECTURE

The current CODASYL architecture calls for conceptual databases to be defined through the schema data description language, or schema DDL; for external databases, or subschemas, to be defined through the subschema DDL; and for the internal, or physical, database to be defined through the data storage description language (DSDL).

We can compare these three tool sets to those of the relational model. For example, the schema DDL would roughly correspond to the CREATE command. Recall that this command can be used to define (and physically create) databases, tables, and indexes.

It is more difficult to find a parallel for the subschema DDL. The primary purpose of the subschema is the specification of those record types, data items, and relationships that can be accessed by host programs. Two relational comparisons come to mind. First, the DBA, through the creation of views, can restrict relational end users to selected table columns or to combinations of tables. Second, by using the relational GRANT command, only specified users are permitted access to the designated tables. With the network model, only record types and data items listed in the subschema DDL are accessible.

It is even more difficult to compare the relational model's hardware-specific, physical database tools to the network's DSDL, because there is no one relational standard in this area. Instead, as we saw in Chapter 5, each vendor is free to implement its own tools and methods. Techniques that we addressed, such as clustering and partitioning, serve the same purpose as the DSDL. The DSDL also permits the DBA to choose between embedded lists and pointer arrays, to decide if a journal is to be used, and so on. Because it is quite vendor specific, we won't discuss it in detail.

FIGURE 9.4   The CODASYL Conceptual Database Management System

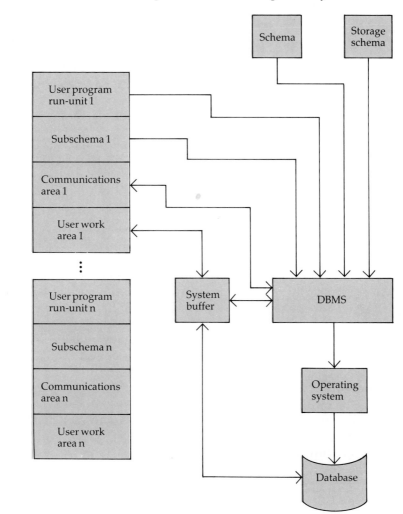

Figure 9.4 shows conceptually how the CODASYL components interact with a host program to access and store data in a database.

A **schema** defines the database and consists of specifications of three kinds of objects: record types, data items, and relationships among the records, called *set types*. Until 1981, the schema also included information about *areas*, or *realms*. Because of the physical connotations of realms, their definitions were moved to the DSDL.

Schemas are defined using the schema DDL. The **database** is the collection of records and sets controlled by a single schema. This implies that CODASYL recognizes the fact that several organizational databases can exist, each with its own schema.

Records, or **record types,** are named collections of data items and are defined via the schema DDL using a RECORD entry. They correspond to the relational tables. In keeping with the terminology of Chapter 2, we will use the term *record types*.

As each record occurrence is stored, it is assigned a **database key,** or **DBKEY,** which is the disk address associated with the record. In Section 5.2 of Chapter 5, we assumed that these were RRNs. In reality, they can be more complicated than this, with each CODASYL-compliant vendor devising its own scheme for physically defining them.

Data items are the smallest units of named data and are the CODASYL realization of attributes, or the relational columns. Using the TYPE clause of the RECORD entry, they are defined as belonging to one of three categories.

A **set type** is a named relationship between an origin record type and one or more destination record types. It is defined in the schema DDL using a SET entry. The CODASYL terms for origin and destination are **owner** and **member,** respectively. Unlike the relational approach, where relationships are dynamically defined as records are retrieved, CODASYL DBMS relationships must be predefined.

A **set occurrence** consists of one owner occurrence and all the related member occurrences. Within a set occurrence, members can be sorted on a member data item or arranged according to a time sequence.

A **subschema** is what we have been calling an external, or user, view and is defined as the host program's description of the record and set types and the data items it requires. The subschema is defined by the subschema DDL.

The **run-unit** is the executing host program, which contains a mixture of DML calls and procedural statements (we assume COBOL in this chapter). Run-units can have their own subschema or can share them. Record occurrences are transferred to the run-unit through the **user work area (UWA).** Communication to and from the DBMS is accomplished by the establishment of several system communication locations. One of these is DB-STATUS, which, after a call to the DBMS, may or may not contain an error code. The embedded SQL structure, SQLCA, which we saw in Chapter 8, plays this communication role with the relational model. The relational host structures are the functional equivalent of the UWA.

Finally, the **storage DSDL** describes the physical database. Its tasks include determining whether pointers are embedded or stored in an index, whether or not hashing is necessary, what devices to use to store the records, and so on. We discussed most of these matters in Section 5.2 of Chapter 5.

A typical sequence of events, triggered by a DML call, proceeds like this.

First, the DBMS analyzes the DML statement to determine its type. Then the DBMS adds further information to the call through its referencing of the schema and subschema descriptions. Next, the DBMS makes a call to the operating system for the physical I/O, which fetches or stores the record in the database. Upon completion of the operating system call, the DBMS updates the value of DB-STATUS and the other communications variables, then places the record into a *system buffer*. The **system buffer** is shared by all run-units but is controlled exclusively by the DBMS. Finally, the record is transferred between the system buffer and the UWA as required.

Let's look at these concepts more closely.

Record Types: The Conceptual Files, or Entities

Figure 9.5 shows one possible conceptual database based on the Microtech minicase. It is a more complex form of Figure 5.4, with which we introduced the physical design of network databases in Chapter 5.

FIGURE 9.5   Conceptual Database for the Microtech Accounts Payable Application

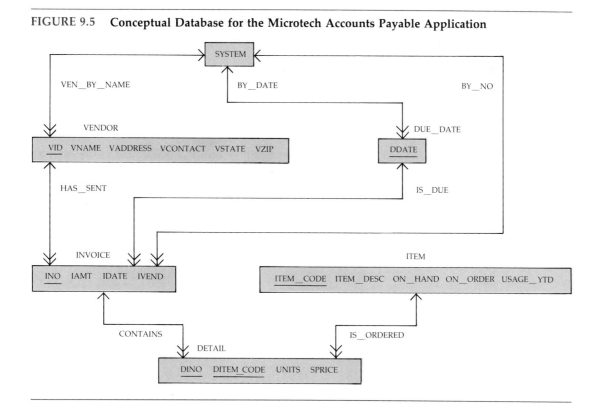

Record Keys: Primary, Secondary, and Ordering. The schema DDL provides the ability to define two kinds of keys: RECORD and RECORD ORDER.

A **record key** is used for direct access of the records and defines either a primary or secondary key. There can be multiple record keys per record. **Record order keys** are used to logically order the records and can consist of the same data item(s) as the record key. When the records are accessed sequentially, we can use the record order key to ensure the record ordering. An unusual feature of both key types is that each must be given a unique **key name.**

Database Keys: Disk Addresses. A **database key** is the disk address of a record. As each record is initially stored in the database, it is assigned a database key value that allows the DBMS to subsequently access that record; it is also used as the pointer data item to other related records. The implementation of database keys varies from vendor to vendor. As a result, there is no one accepted representation. In this text, we will usually use an RRN as a surrogate for a record's database key value.

Record Occurrences. Specific VENDORs, INVOICEs, and so on are called **record occurrences,** or **record instances.** Each record contains several data items.

Data Items: The Fields, or Attributes

Data items are the smallest accessible unit of named data. They represent the implementation of the attributes attached to the entities during the conceptual design of the database and are usually called *fields* when using COBOL terminology and *columns* in the relational model. Data items are aggregated to form a record type and, like the record types, are defined through the schema DDL. We can group data items into **data aggregates** in much the same way we can aggregate 05 levels in COBOL into a single 03 level.

FIGURE 9.6   **Numeric Data Item Characteristics**

Base
  Decimal
  Binary
Scale
  Fixed
  Floating point
Mode
  Real
  Complex
Precision
  A length and the number of decimal places

There are three permissible data types: numeric, Boolean, or string. Figure 9.6 shows the additional characteristics that can be associated with numeric data items. Boolean data types always have one of two values, TRUE or FALSE, and are sometimes called **logical data items.** As an example, the ITEM record type could contain a data item called BACK_ORDERED. When an item is ordered but the shipment hasn't yet arrived, the BACK_ORDERED value of the record associated with that item would be TRUE; otherwise, it would be FALSE. The final data type is string. Such data items can be character or bit strings. In this text, we will always select the character string option.

As part of the definition of any data item, we can specify that the values of that item can never be NULL, a feature that derives from the relational concept with the same name. In addition, data items can be assigned default values.

Set Types: Named 1:M Relationships

Set types are one-to-many named relationships among record types. Each set type has one owner record type and one or more record types designated as its members.

For example, the arrow in Figure 9.5 from VENDOR to INVOICE indicates that VENDOR is the owner of the HAS_SENT set and INVOICE the member. There are no restrictions on limiting record type participation as owners or members. For example, INVOICE is a member of three sets and an owner of one, while DETAIL is only a member.

Although we will always show a set as a relationship between two record types, it can have more than one member record type, like the one shown in Figure 9.7. The set HAS_DEPENDENTS is owned by EMPLOYEE and has two members: SPOUSE and CHILDREN.

FIGURE 9.7   **A Set with Two Member Record Types**

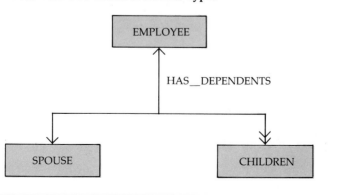

Set Categories. Set types are sometimes classified as being either value based or information bearing. In an occurrence of a **value-based set,** the value of one or more data items in the member record occurrence must match the value of one or more data items in its owner. It is what the relational model calls a *foreign key* or a *referential integrity constraint*. For example, in the Microtech minicase, Mary has established the policy that each IDATE value in INVOICE (see Figure 9.5) must match a value of DDATE for some occurrence of DUE__DATE. This means we cannot store an INVOICE occurrence that has an IDATE value that doesn't match some DDATE value. Therefore, IS__DUE is a value-based set type.

In an **information-bearing set,** there is no such connection between owner and member. In Figure 9.5, if we removed the IDATE data item from INVOICE, the IS__DUE set would become information bearing, because we would have removed the connection data item and thus have no way to match values from the two record types.

The CODASYL model also permits **recursive sets,** in which the owner and the member record types are the same. In Chapter 2, we called these sets *loops* or *recursive relationships.*

Set Occurrences. A **set occurrence** consists of an occurrence of the owner of the set and all of its associated member records. Each such occurrence is usually implemented as a modified ring structure, with the head pointer carried in the owner occurrence and next pointers carried in each member. Next, prior, and owner pointers can be embedded in the member records. As discussed in Section 5.2 of Chapter 5, the last member customarily points back to its owner. If a record occurrence is a member of two or more sets, the resulting data structure can be considered a multilist (or multiring) and will contain a set of pointers for each set of which it is a member.

Let's look at some examples. To do so, we need to store some data in the database. Consider the data we looked at in Figure 5.5, reproduced here as Figure 9.8.

Figure 9.9 shows several of the set occurrences resulting from the data presented in Figure 9.8 and stored according to the conceptual database depicted in Figure 9.5. It is an extension of Figure 5.6, with additional sets included.

Look first at the portion of the figure that shows the ACME occurrence of the VENDOR record type and the four associated INVOICE occurrences. This graphically illustrates the "HAS__SENT set occurrence owned by ACME." Like all set occurrences, it consists of an owner occurrence (the VENDOR with VID = ACME) and all the associated member records (INVOICEs that ACME HAS__SENT).

Characteristics of set occurrences are as follows:

■ A set occurrence consisting of only an owner record occurrence is called an **empty set.** As an example, Microtech might have no invoices from the

FIGURE 9.8 **Sample Invoice Data**

Invoice Number	Vendor Code	Amount Due	Due Date	Terms
A12	ACME	$128.00	04/15/XX	2/10 net 30
A19	ACME	80.00	04/15/XX	2/10 net 30
A22	ACME	145.00	04/15/XX	2/10 net 30
A23	ACME	50.00	04/30/XX	2/10 net 30
BX1	BYARS	100.00	04/30/XX	2/10 net 30
BY7	BYARS	120.00	04/15/XX	2/10 net 30

Invoice Number	Item Code	Item Description	Quantity	Cost/Item
A12	14	DSDD diskettes	20	3.00
	77	SSSD diskettes	20	2.00
	10	Ribbon	12	4.00
A19	111	11 × 15 paper	2	40.00
A22	77	SSDD diskettes	20	2.00
	111	11 × 15 paper	3	35.00
A23	90	RS-232 cable	1	50.00
BX1	17	8088-2	20	5.00
BY7	100	8086	20	2.00
	103	80386	20	4.00

The figure was previously shown as Figure 5.5.

VENDOR named BROWN. Thus, the set occurrence of HAS__SENT owned by BROWN would be empty.

- In addition to the occurrence of its owner, a set occurrence may have an arbitrary number of member occurrences. For example, there are four member occurrences in the HAS__SENT occurrence owned by ACME, but none in BROWN's.

- A set that occurs only one time is called a **singular set.** In our example, BY__NO, VEN__BY__NAME, and BY__DATE are all singular sets. Every set that has SYSTEM as its owner is singular. This rule can be applied to the three sets just mentioned. The first portion of Figure 9.9 shows there is only one occurrence each of VEN__BY__NAME, BY__DATE, and BY__NO, confirming the fact that all are singular sets.

- Member occurrences in a set must be ordered. Choices include sorting on a member data item or placing new records first, last, or after some other member record. If a record type is a member of two different sets, its occurrences can be sorted differently in each set, but each set can be sorted in only one way.

FIGURE 9.9   The Set Occurrences for Microtech

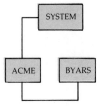

The occurrence of
VEN__BY__NAME. The fact that there is
only one occurrence means that VEN__BY__NAME
is singular

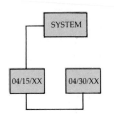

The occurrence of
BY__DATE. Sorting
is by date value

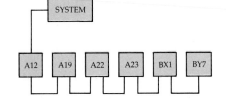

The occurrence of BY__NO. Sorting
is by invoice number value

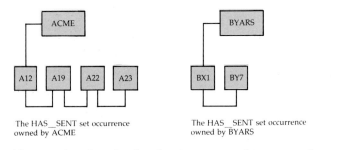

The HAS__SENT set occurrence
owned by ACME

The HAS__SENT set occurrence
owned by BYARS

No attempt is made to show how the set occurrences relate to one another.

- A particular record occurrence may not appear in more than one occurrence of that set. For example, ACME can own only one occurrence of HAS__SENT, and a particular INVOICE can be sent by only one VENDOR.
- There are as many occurrences of a set as that set has owner record occurrences. This means there are as many occurrences of HAS__SENT as there are VENDORs and as many occurrences of CONTAINS as there are INVOICEs.

FIGURE 9.9   (concluded)

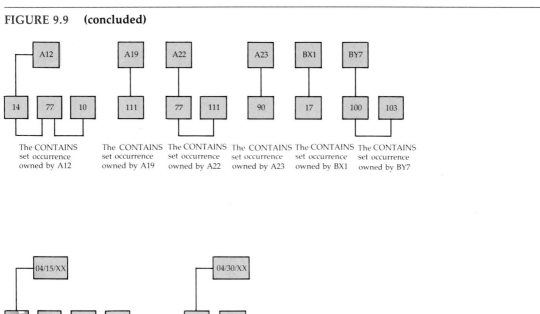

The CONTAINS set occurrence owned by A12

The CONTAINS set occurrence owned by A19

The CONTAINS set occurrence owned by A22

The CONTAINS set occurrence owned by A23

The CONTAINS set occurrence owned by BX1

The CONTAINS set occurrence owned by BY7

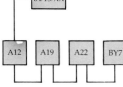

The IS__DUE occurrence owned by 04/15/XX

The IS__DUE occurrence owned by 04/30/XX

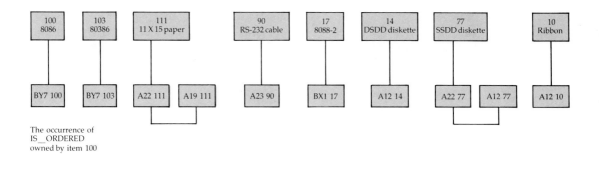

The occurrence of IS__ORDERED owned by item 100

Many commercial DBMSs (those based on pre-1981 standards) permit only member records to be sequentially accessed. If a record is not a member of a set and sequential access of its occurrences is necessary, we must construct an artificial set with SYSTEM as the owner. The 1981 guidelines provided for record order keys, which can serve the same purpose. However, because most DBMSs are based on the earlier guidelines, we will follow the practice of establishing singular sets with SYSTEM as the owner whenever we require a sequential retrieval of occurrences of a given record type.

Now look at the set occurrence of HAS__SENT owned by BYARS. Notice there are only two member records in it. That there would be a similar set occurrence (with a different number of member occurrences) for every VENDOR in the database hopefully is clear. This suggests there eventually will be a total of 100 occurrences of the set HAS__SENT, one for each VENDOR. Each of these set occurrences will consist of a single VENDOR record and all the INVOICEs the vendor HAS__SENT.

Next, look at the set type IS__DUE. Consider the occurrence of IS__DUE owned by the DUE__DATE record with DDATE = 04/15/XX. Figure 9.8 shows that four invoices are due on that date. Thus, in Figure 9.9, there are four member occurrences in the occurrences of IS__DUE owned by 04/15/XX. The second occurrence of IS__DUE is owned by the DUE__DATE record with DDATE = 04/30/XX. The figure indicates there are two member records in this set occurrence.

The data presented in the Microtech minicase indicates that the company pays on the 15th and last working day of each month. Thus, there should be 24 occurrences of DUE__DATE, each owning a set occurrence of IS__DUE, and 24 occurrences of the IS__DUE set.

Figure 9.10 shows how the set occurrences from Figure 9.9 relate to one another, and it provides the assumed database key (RRN) values. First, look at the ACME record. It owns all four of the INVOICEs sent by that VEN-DOR. Notice that the first INVOICE in the set is number A12, followed by A19, A22, and A23 (remember that the minicase specified that INVOICES are to be sorted by invoice number, INO, within a particular VENDOR__CODE). Now look at the INVOICE record with INO equal to A12. It is owned by both ACME and 04/15/XX. (The IS__DUE arrow is omitted to avoid clutter-ing the diagram.) All of the INVOICE records are members of two different sets and hence have two owners. It is this fact that necessitated using the network model.

Currency Indicators: Keeping Track of the Most Recently Accessed Logical Unit

CODASYL DBMSs maintain several **currency indicators**, pointers to positions within its three main logical units: the run-unit, record types, and set types. There are three corresponding groups of currency indicators:

- Current of run-unit
- Current of record
- Current of set

FIGURE 9.10   Relationship of Several Set Occurrences to One Another

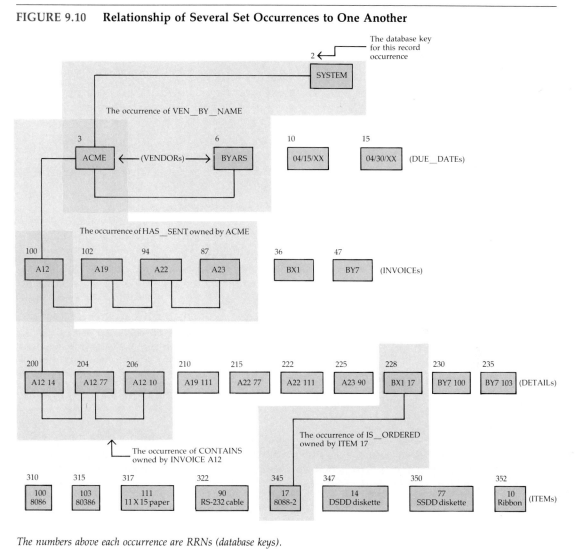

The numbers above each occurrence are RRNs (database keys).

Each currency indicator's value corresponds to the DBKEY of some record. This means that the current of INVOICE, for example, would be the DBKEY associated with the most recently accessed INVOICE record.

Current of Run-Unit. Current of run-unit is the database key associated with the most recently accessed record regardless of type. By *access* we mean any of the following: retrieval, storage, or deletion. Assume the DBMS just accessed the INVOICE record for number A12. According to Figure 9.10, the RRN of the record is 100. Thus, the current of run-unit will equal 100.

Current of Record. The DBTG used the term *current of record* to mean the database key associated with the most recently accessed record occurrence of a given record type. There is a current of record for each record type in the database, but any record type not as yet accessed will have a NULL value.

As an example, if the first record accessed by a host program is the DUE__ DATE record having DDATE = 04/15/XX, the current of DUE__DATE and run-unit both become 10, since 10 is the database key associated with the DUE__ DATE occurrence. Because we wouldn't have yet accessed VENDOR or DETAIL records, their currency indicators would be NULL.

Current of Set. The value of current of set, of which there is one per set type, will equal the database key associated with the record last accessed in the set. There are two ways to do this: access an owner or access a member. This means there are two ways to establish the current of the CONTAINS set: access an INVOICE record or access a DETAIL record. Notice that when we access the INVOICE record for invoice number A12, it simultaneously becomes the current of set for CONTAINS and for HAS__SENT, because it participates in both sets. In fact, that record also becomes the current of run-unit and INVOICE.

9.3   WRITING THE SCHEMA: USING THE DDL TO DESCRIBE THE CONCEPTUAL DATABASE

A schema consists of the complete series of DDL statements that fully define the conceptual database. It includes three entry types: one schema entry and as many record and set entries as are required. Once the schema is coded using the DDL, it, like any other "program," must be compiled into machine language. We won't show this step, since CODASYL left this to the commercial implementors.

Throughout the remainder of this chapter, you will see references to seven DML commands. They will be capitalized and used in a processing context. These commands are:

- STORE—inserts new records
- FIND—locates records but doesn't transfer them to the UWA
- GET—physically transfers records to the UWA after they have been located using the FIND command
- MODIFY—changes field values in records previously STOREd
- REMOVE or DELETE—deletes records previously STOREd

FIGURE 9.11   **A Schema DDL Using 1981 CODASYL JOD Guidelines**

```
SCHEMA NAME IS A_P
RECORD NAME IS VENDOR
```

1
```
        KEY VENDOR_KEY IS ASCENDING VID
            DUPLICATES ARE NOT ALLOWED
```
— Record ordering key
— Primary key

2
```
        KEY VNAME IS ASCENDING VNAME
            DUPLICATES ARE FIRST
```
— Secondary key

3
```
    ACCESS CONTROL LOCK FOR STORE FIND IS 'IKNOWIT'
```
— Password needed

4
```
    03 VID          TYPE IS CHARACTER 5

                    CHECK IS NOT NULL
```
— Don't permit NULLs

```
    03 VNAME        TYPE IS CHARACTER 30
    03 VADDRESS     TYPE IS CHARACTER 40
    03 VCONTACT     TYPE IS CHARACTER 20
    03 VSTATE       TYPE IS CHARACTER 2
    03 VZIP         TYPE IS CHARACTER 5

RECORD NAME IS DUE_DATE
        KEY DUEDATE_KEY IS ASCENDING DDATE
        DUPLICATES NOT ALLOWED
    03 DDATE        TYPE CHARACTER 8

RECORD NAME IS INVOICE
        KEY INO IS ASCENDING INO
        DUPLICATES NOT ALLOWED
    ACCESS CONTROL LOCK FOR STORE IS 'UKNOWIT'


    03 INO          TYPE IS CHARACTER 5
                    ACCESS CONTROL LOCK FOR MODIFY IS 'APACHE'
```

FIGURE 9.11   **(continued)**

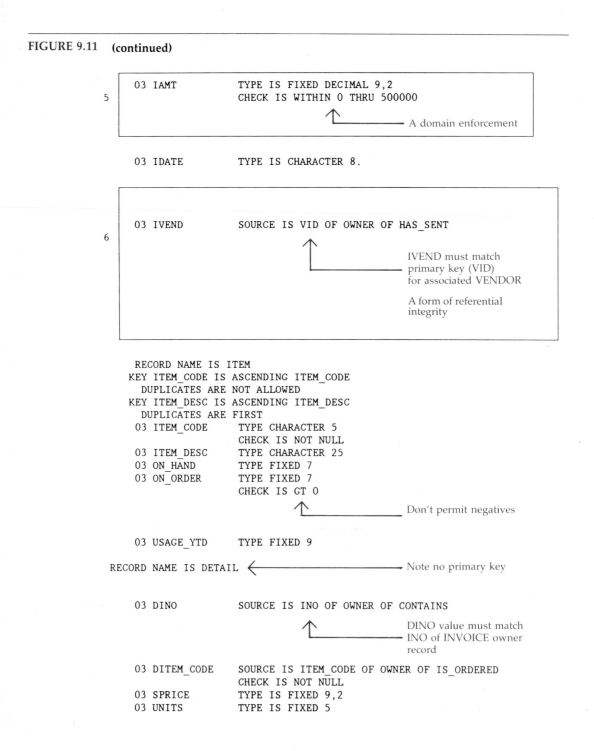

```
5     03 IAMT          TYPE IS FIXED DECIMAL 9,2
                       CHECK IS WITHIN 0 THRU 500000
                                        ↑
                                        |_____ A domain enforcement


      03 IDATE         TYPE IS CHARACTER 8.


6     03 IVEND         SOURCE IS VID OF OWNER OF HAS_SENT
                                 ↑
                                 |        IVEND must match
                                 |_____ primary key (VID)
                                          for associated VENDOR

                                          A form of referential
                                          integrity
```

```
      RECORD NAME IS ITEM
      KEY ITEM_CODE IS ASCENDING ITEM_CODE
        DUPLICATES ARE NOT ALLOWED
      KEY ITEM_DESC IS ASCENDING ITEM_DESC
        DUPLICATES ARE FIRST
        03 ITEM_CODE     TYPE CHARACTER 5
                         CHECK IS NOT NULL
        03 ITEM_DESC     TYPE CHARACTER 25
        03 ON_HAND       TYPE FIXED 7
        03 ON_ORDER      TYPE FIXED 7
                         CHECK IS GT 0
                                  ↑
                                  |_____ Don't permit negatives

        03 USAGE_YTD     TYPE FIXED 9
      RECORD NAME IS DETAIL ←_____ Note no primary key

        03 DINO          SOURCE IS INO OF OWNER OF CONTAINS
                                  ↑
                                  |        DINO value must match
                                  |_____ INO of INVOICE owner
                                           record
        03 DITEM_CODE    SOURCE IS ITEM_CODE OF OWNER OF IS_ORDERED
                         CHECK IS NOT NULL
        03 SPRICE        TYPE IS FIXED 9,2
        03 UNITS         TYPE IS FIXED 5
```

FIGURE 9.11   **(continued)**

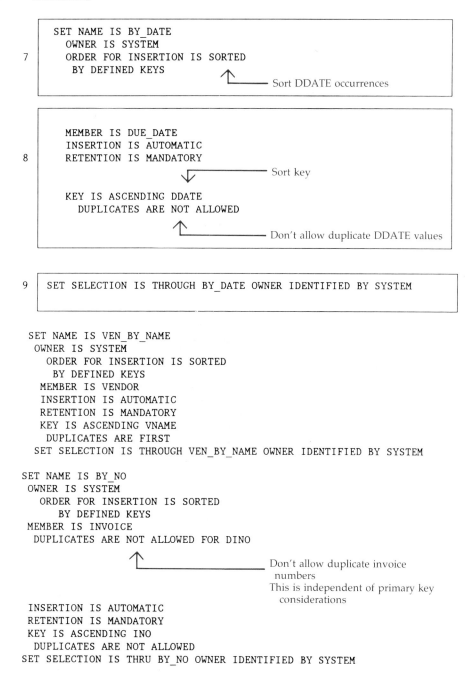

```
    SET NAME IS BY_DATE
       OWNER IS SYSTEM
7      ORDER FOR INSERTION IS SORTED
       BY DEFINED KEYS
```
↑ —— Sort DDATE occurrences

```
       MEMBER IS DUE_DATE
       INSERTION IS AUTOMATIC
8      RETENTION IS MANDATORY
```
↓ —— Sort key

```
       KEY IS ASCENDING DDATE
          DUPLICATES ARE NOT ALLOWED
```
↑ —— Don't allow duplicate DDATE values

```
9   SET SELECTION IS THROUGH BY_DATE OWNER IDENTIFIED BY SYSTEM
```

```
    SET NAME IS VEN_BY_NAME
     OWNER IS SYSTEM
       ORDER FOR INSERTION IS SORTED
       BY DEFINED KEYS
      MEMBER IS VENDOR
      INSERTION IS AUTOMATIC
      RETENTION IS MANDATORY
      KEY IS ASCENDING VNAME
        DUPLICATES ARE FIRST
     SET SELECTION IS THROUGH VEN_BY_NAME OWNER IDENTIFIED BY SYSTEM

    SET NAME IS BY_NO
     OWNER IS SYSTEM
       ORDER FOR INSERTION IS SORTED
          BY DEFINED KEYS
      MEMBER IS INVOICE
       DUPLICATES ARE NOT ALLOWED FOR DINO
```
↑ —— Don't allow duplicate invoice
     numbers
     This is independent of primary key
          considerations

```
      INSERTION IS AUTOMATIC
      RETENTION IS MANDATORY
      KEY IS ASCENDING INO
        DUPLICATES ARE NOT ALLOWED
     SET SELECTION IS THRU BY_NO OWNER IDENTIFIED BY SYSTEM
```

FIGURE 9.11   **(continued)**

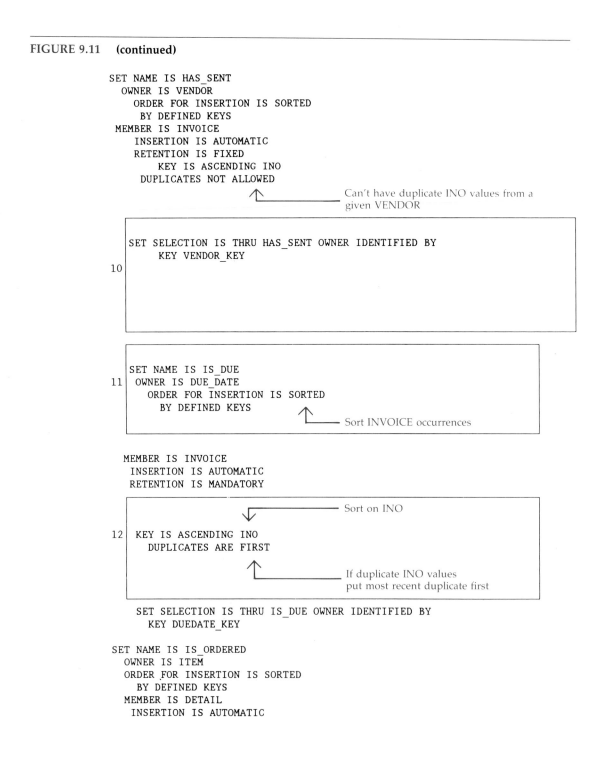

```
SET NAME IS HAS_SENT
  OWNER IS VENDOR
    ORDER FOR INSERTION IS SORTED
      BY DEFINED KEYS
  MEMBER IS INVOICE
    INSERTION IS AUTOMATIC
    RETENTION IS FIXED
        KEY IS ASCENDING INO
      DUPLICATES NOT ALLOWED
```
                                    Can't have duplicate INO values from a
                                    given VENDOR

```
    SET SELECTION IS THRU HAS_SENT OWNER IDENTIFIED BY
        KEY VENDOR_KEY
10
```

```
    SET NAME IS IS_DUE
11    OWNER IS DUE_DATE
        ORDER FOR INSERTION IS SORTED
          BY DEFINED KEYS
```
                                    Sort INVOICE occurrences

```
  MEMBER IS INVOICE
    INSERTION IS AUTOMATIC
    RETENTION IS MANDATORY
```
                                    Sort on INO

```
12    KEY IS ASCENDING INO
        DUPLICATES ARE FIRST
```
                                    If duplicate INO values
                                    put most recent duplicate first

```
    SET SELECTION IS THRU IS_DUE OWNER IDENTIFIED BY
        KEY DUEDATE_KEY

SET NAME IS IS_ORDERED
  OWNER IS ITEM
  ORDER FOR INSERTION IS SORTED
    BY DEFINED KEYS
  MEMBER IS DETAIL
    INSERTION IS AUTOMATIC
```

FIGURE 9.11 (concluded)

```
RETENTION IS MANDATORY
 KEY IS DESCENDING IUNITS
    DUPLICATES ARE FIRST
 SET SELECTION IS THRU IS_ORDERED OWNER IDENTIFIED
    BY APPLICATION
```

Run-unit will tell DBMS which set occurrences to add new member occurrences to

```
Note: the definition of CONTAINS is left as an exercise
```

- CONNECT—adds records into a set occurrence
- DISCONNECT—removes member records from a set occurrence

The next chapter will look at the DML in detail.

Our discussion of the schema DDL will be both top-down and bottom-up. Figure 9.11 shows the (almost) complete schema DDL corresponding to Figure 9.5. Subsequent figures will illustrate each of the entries in more detail, but it will be helpful to see the big picture before looking at the details.

The SCHEMA Entry

The first line in every schema is the schema entry. It is coded according to Figure 9.12.

There is one such schema entry per schema. As an example of this entry, look at Figure 9.11. The schema's name is A__P. Note the use of the underscore in the schema name. Prior to 1981, the DDL did not support the hyphen for any of the programmer-supplied names, and we will follow that rule here.

The CALL feature forces the DBMS to call a **database procedure** whenever the specified operation is executed. A **database procedure** is a routine, link-edited with the run-unit, that the DBMS can call.

An ACCESS CONTROL LOCK is a security feature and is usually a password (literal) that a user must supply when attempting a particular operation on a given database resource. More specifically, a user (run-unit) must supply an **access control key,** which the DBMS then compares to the specified access lock. If they match, permission to proceed is granted, and the operation begins. In addition to applying to the schema as a whole, access control locks can be applied to records and data items, although the operations to which they apply will differ.

A lock FOR ALTER means that anyone attempting to change the schema would have to supply the proper control key. Use of FOR DISPLAY prevents anyone from displaying the schema without a valid password. COPY forces anyone trying to copy the schema to know the corresponding control key.

FIGURE 9.12   The Schema Entry

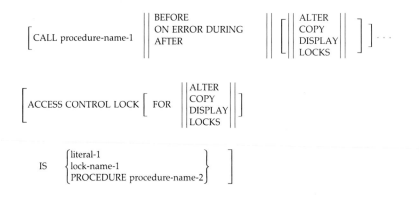

SCHEMA NAME IS schema-name

The Record Entries

Each record type in the conceptual database, which we have been representing as a DSD or E-R diagram, must be defined by coding a RECORD entry, using the syntax shown in Figure 9.13.

RECORD NAME Subentry. In COBOL, we define a record by assigning a 01-level name to it. CODASYL uses the RECORD NAME clause instead. In Figure 9.11, the first record's name is VENDOR, the second DUE__DATE, and so on. It isn't necessary to define the SYSTEM record type, nor does the sequence of record definitions matter. We suggest a top-to-bottom, left-to-right sequence based on the conceptual database.

The KEY Subentry. The KEY clause specifies primary, secondary, and order keys. As Figure 9.13 indicates, a record key is defined by following the word KEY with a unique key name, then the data item(s) that comprise the key. If a logical ordering is necessary, we code the optional ASCENDING/DESCENDING clause. As noted earlier, this feature provides sequential accessing of records independently of their participation as members. Next, if the key is a primary one, we enter the line DUPLICATES ARE NOT ALLOWED. For secondary keys, we use either DUPLICATES ARE FIRST or LAST. If we choose FIRST, the most recent duplicate key value will be placed first in the list of duplicates. Use of LAST is similar, except that the most recent duplicate secondary key will be stored after all the others. We cannot use DUPLICATES ARE FIRST or LAST unless we select either ASCENDING or DESCENDING. For example, to set up VID as a primary key, we could code:

FIGURE 9.13   The RECORD Entry Syntax

RECORD NAME IS record-name

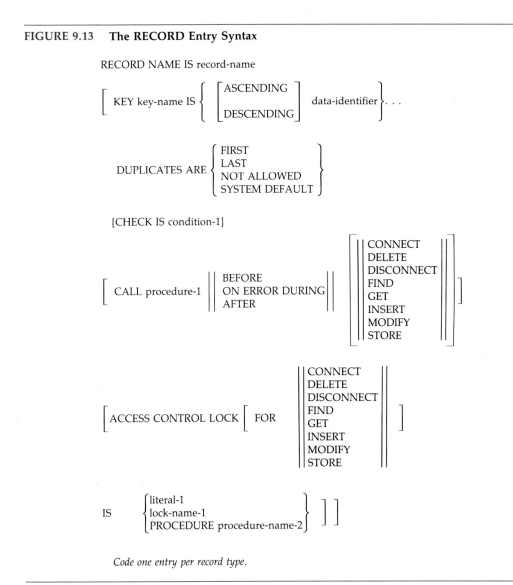

Code one entry per record type.

KEY VENDOR__PRIMARY__KEY IS VID
DUPLICATES NOT ALLOWED

Although we omitted the word ARE in the DUPLICATES clause, this is acceptable because it's optional. To also sequence the VENDOR records by VID, we would code these lines instead:

KEY VENDOR__KEY IS ASCENDING VID
DUPLICATES ARE NOT ALLOWED

"ASCENDING" ⇒ record order key

"not" ⇒ primary key

This specification would permit sequential access to the VENDORs, sorted by vendor code, plus direct access, also based on a vendor's code. Remember that we can also establish a singular set to permit sequential retrieval, and, in fact, this is the method usually adopted.

As an example of a secondary key, assume Microtech needs to be able to access VENDOR occurrences by name. This would be specified as:

KEY VENDOR__SECONDARY__KEY IS ASCENDING VNAME
DUPLICATES ARE FIRST

Record order key

"FIRST" ⇒ secondary key

Next, let's examine the actual schema in Figure 9.11 and look at the VENDOR keys. In block 1, the atomic key, VENDOR__KEY, is both a primary key and a record order key and is defined on VID. The other VENDOR key (block 2) is a secondary one and is used to sequence the VENDOR records by name.

The CHECK IS Subentry: Enforcing an Integrity Constraint. The CHECK IS feature is used to specify a validation rule (domain) that must hold in order for the DBMS to store the record. This clause can also be applied at the data item level. If a violation occurs, instead of returning a zero value for DB-STATUS, the DBMS will return a value indicating that the value for the data item wasn't within the specified domain. We will discuss this clause further in another section as it pertains to data items.

The ACCESS CONTROL LOCK Subentry: Specifying Passwords. Like its counterpart in the schema definition, the ACCESS LOCK subentry assigns locks (passwords) to record operations. The DBA can assign a different lock for each of the DML operators listed in Figure 9.13. For example, block 3 states that anyone attempting to STORE or FIND a VENDOR record must supply the access control key value IKNOWIT.

The CALL Feature: Invoking Integrity Routines Automatically. The CALL feature causes the DBMS to call a programmer-supplied routine before or after the execution of any of the operators listed. For example, assume that prior to storing an INVOICE, we want the DBMS to invoke a validation routine that checks for missing data item values. As part of the RECORD entry for INVOICE, we would code:

CALL MY__ROUTINE BEFORE STORE.

This would result in the routine MY__ROUTINE being invoked prior to storing a new INVOICE record.

The TYPE Clause: Defining Data Items. Figure 9.14 shows most of the TYPE choices. Let's look at the data items for the INVOICE record type. The first item, INO, is a string type, with a length of five bytes. Users attempting to MODIFY

FIGURE 9.14   **The Data TYPE Subentry**

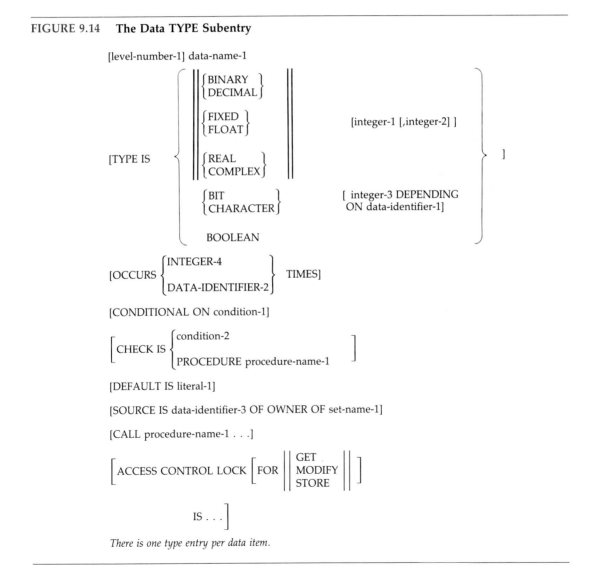

There is one type entry per data item.

an INO value must supply the control key APACHE. The next item, IAMT, has a decimal base (TYPE IS DECIMAL), is of fixed scale (FIXED), and has a precision of nine total digits, with two places after the decimal point (9,2).

The CHECK IS Subentry: Enforcing Domain and Integrity Constraints. The CHECK IS feature is used to specify a domain or an entity integrity rule. As we saw with the RECORD clause having the same name, if that rule is violated, the record won't be stored. As an example of using the clause in the RECORD entry, assume that as part of the RECORD entry for the ITEM record type, we code:

CHECK IS ON_HAND GT 0

Now if a user attempts to store an ITEM with a negative ON_HAND value, the DBMS will reject it and place a suitable value into DB-STATUS.

Block 5 in Figure 9.11 shows how to establish a domain check for a data item. It says that the INVOICE value of IAMT must be within 0 and 500,000. Any attempt to STORE a new INVOICE, or to MODIFY an existing one, that causes the value for IAMT to fall outside the given range will be rejected, and DB-STATUS will be given a suitable value.

Recall that entity integrity refers to the fact that no part of a primary key can be NULL. In block 4, you can see how we applied the NOT NULL clause to the VENDOR.VID data item. We can extend this to a rule: To specify entity integrity, code CHECK IS NOT NULL when defining the data items that make up the primary key.

The SOURCE IS Subentry: Enforcing Referential Integrity Constraints. To enforce referential integrity, we use SOURCE IS to specify that the value of the data item being defined has to match that of the specified data item, which must be stored in a record type that owns the one being defined. No TYPE clause can be specified if SOURCE IS is used.

As an example, look at block 6 in Figure 9.11. It says that when an INVOICE record is stored or modified, the IVEND value is to be set equal to the VID value of its HAS_SENT owner, which is VENDOR. This is another way of saying that INVOICE.IVEND is a foreign key that refers to VENDOR.VID.

The SET Entry: Defining Set Types

Figure 9.15 shows the syntax for describing set types. Each 1:M relationship must be described next. Remember that relationships are called *set types* in the CODASYL network model.

The following items must be defined for each set:

- Name of the set.
- Name of its owner record type.

FIGURE 9.15   **The SET Entry**

SET NAME IS set-name-1

OWNER IS $\begin{cases} \text{record-name-1} \\ \\ \text{SYSTEM} \end{cases}$

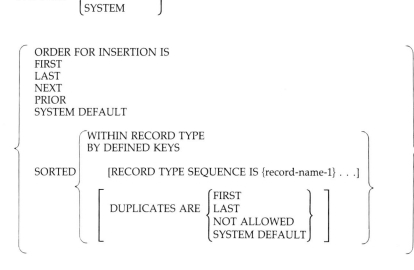

[CALL procedure-name-1 . . .]

[ACCESS CONTROL LOCK . . .]

Notice that the MEMBER clause isn't shown; it is described later. Code one SET entry per set type.

- Desired sequence of member records in the set's occurrences.
- Name of set's member record type.
- Membership rule for new records.
- Membership rule for existing records.
- Responsibility and method for identifying and accessing a set occurrence.

The SET NAME Subentry: Assigning a Name to the 1:M Relationship. Set names can be directly taken from the E-R diagram. However, they will probably have to be established at this time if a DSD was used, because that method doesn't normally associate a name with a relationship.

The name should be meaningful and follow a standard convention. Some organizations use the first few letters of the set owner's name plus the first few letters of the member's name. For example, a set between an EMPLOYEE and his or her PROJECTs might be given the name EMP__PROJ. Other organizations use a verb plus a preposition. The set's name based on this policy might be WORKS__ON.

The OWNER IS Clause: Specifying the Owner Record Type. The purpose of the OWNER IS clause is to identify the set's owner. All singular sets should specify SYSTEM. This is done within block 7 of Figure 9.11, which indicates that the owner of BY__DATE is SYSTEM.

The ORDER IS Subentry: Sequencing Member Records in a Set Occurrence. A rule that defines the sequence of member records in a given set occurrence must be stated. Implications of this are:

- Each set can be sequenced in one—and only one—way.
- Every set definition results in several linked lists, one per set occurrence. A first (head) pointer will be stored in each owner of an occurrence and a next (forward) pointer stored in each related member record occurrence, where first and next are determined by this option.

A set occurrence is usually a linked list, with its first pointer (database key) stored in the owner of the occurrence. Thus, for instance, each VENDOR record would contain a pointer to its initial INVOICE and each INVOICE a pointer to the first associated DETAIL item, where "first" is determined by the sequencing option we select.

Each member then contains a next pointer to the member record having the next higher sequence value. The sequencing implication is that the ordering option we select here determines how the records in the list are sequentially retrieved. For example, if HAS__SENT is sequenced by INVOICE.INO, any report that sequentially navigates that set will find INVOICEs in this order.

Thus, the CODASYL databases physically maintain the desired ordering at all times, resulting in fast sequential retrieval in the correct order. The trade-off is that only one such sequence can be maintained at a time per set, implying that additional sort sequences require additional sets. With the relational model, sorting of results is specified at run-time, providing much more flexibility. This flexibility can come at the expense of speed, however, if there is no index that matches the desired order.

If a record type is a member of several sets, the occurrences of that record type can be sequenced differently in each set. For instance, we could sequence INVOICEs by invoice number (INO) within the IS__DUE set and by amount (IAMT) for the HAS__SENT set. This means that sequential retrieval of IN-VOICEs could lead to two different orderings, depending on which set was used. Traversing the HAS__SENT set to the associated INVOICEs would yield records ordered by amount, while traversing the IS__DUE set would produce INVOICEs within a given due date ordered by invoice number.

We have just seen that the sequence method that we choose for a set completely determines the sequential retrieval order of that set's member records. What we haven't yet seen is how to specify that order.

There are three general ways to sequence member record occurrences:

- Sort on data items within the member record type.
- Sequence the member records according to their chronological relationships to one another.
- Sequence records with respect to their current positions in the set.

Sorting. Sorting is the most common choice. Here we sequence member records based on a data item carried in the member record type. Three items must be defined:

- The fact that members are to be sequenced this way.
- The sort key(s) and their sequence (ascending or descending).
- Whether or not to permit duplicate sort keys.

The sort option is specified by using the clause ORDER FOR INSERTION IS SORTED BY DEFINED KEYS. The specification of sort keys, their sequence, and acceptance or rejection of duplicates are all coded in the MEMBER clause, which

Let's look at the BY__DATE set defined in Figure 9.11. Block 7 simply indicates that occurrences of DUE__DATE (the member) in the BY__DATE set are to be sorted. Block 8 states that the sort key is DDATE, that the DUE__DATE records are to be in ascending order, and that there cannot be two or more DUE__DATE occurrences with duplicate DDATE values.

Next, look at block 12, which is a portion of the definition for the IS__DUE set. The owner of the set is DUE__DATE, and its member is INVOICE. The block specifies that the sort key for the set is INO and, if there are two or more INVOICEs with the same INO value due on the same date, to place the latest duplicate at the beginning of the list of duplicates (DUPLICATES ARE FIRST). The DUPLICATES clause refers to whether or not duplicate sort keys are permitted in a given set occurrence.

Composite sort keys are easy to specify. For example, to sort INVOICEs within a given DUE__DATE in ascending order by amount and then in descending order by invoice number, we would code the member KEY IS clause as:

KEY IS ASCENDING IAMT, DESCENDING INO

If we specify DUPLICATES ARE NOT PERMITTED and a run-unit attempts to STORE a member record within a set occurrence that has the same sort key value as another member already stored, the DBMS will return an error code in DB__STATUS and will not store the record. Unfortunately, this code is usually the same value as the one we get when we STORE a record with a duplicate primary key value. This can create debugging problems, because it is difficult to determine which situation prevails—a duplicate sort key or a duplicate primary key.

Chronological Ordering. There are two time-based options:

- LAST, which means that the most recently stored record is logically the last one in the set.
- FIRST, which has the opposite effect.

   Use of FIRST results in a chronological last-in, first-out sequence of member records, while LAST results in a first-in, first-out sequence.

Current of Set Sequencing. There are also two choices here:

- PRIOR, which means that the record being stored is to be logically placed just before the most recently accessed member record in the set.
- NEXT, which means that the record being stored is to be logically placed after the most recently accessed member record.

   Both PRIOR and NEXT depend on the current position within the set. To discuss examples using the PRIOR and NEXT options with the IS__DUE set, we need to assume which INVOICE represents the current of the IS__DUE set. Imagine that the INVOICE with INO = BY7 has just been stored and the host program is about to store the INVOICE record with INO = A22. Using PRIOR would logically place A22 before BY7, while the NEXT option would logically STORE it after BY7.

   The last sequencing option, SYSTEM DEFAULT, says that the DBMS can sequence the member records in any sequence. In effect, it means that no specific sequencing is required.

The MEMBER IS Clause: Assigning a Name to the Destination Record Type. Figure 9.16 shows the complete MEMBER subentry. We will discuss these four clauses:

- INSERTION/RETENTION
- DUPLICATES ARE [NOT] ALLOWED
- KEY IS
- SET SELECTION

   Recall that an entity's participation in a relationship can be optional or required. On a DSD, we use a small circle to denote optional membership in the relationship and a line to designate required membership. Next, we look at how the CODASYL model implements these two kinds of membership rules through the INSERTION and RETENTION clauses.

FIGURE 9.16   **Most of the CODASYL MEMBER Clauses and Subentries**

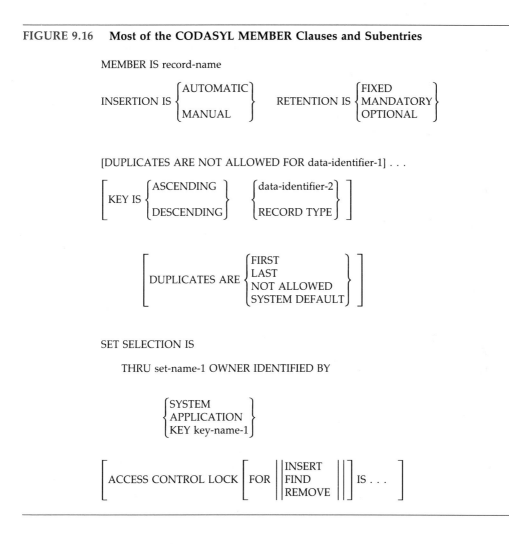

MEMBER IS record-name

INSERTION IS { AUTOMATIC / MANUAL }   RETENTION IS { FIXED / MANDATORY / OPTIONAL }

[DUPLICATES ARE NOT ALLOWED FOR data-identifier-1] . . .

[KEY IS { ASCENDING / DESCENDING }   { data-identifier-2 / RECORD TYPE }]

[DUPLICATES ARE { FIRST / LAST / NOT ALLOWED / SYSTEM DEFAULT }]

SET SELECTION IS

THRU set-name-1 OWNER IDENTIFIED BY

{ SYSTEM / APPLICATION / KEY key-name-1 }

[ACCESS CONTROL LOCK [FOR || INSERT / FIND / REMOVE ||] IS . . .]

The INSERTION Subentry: Specifying the Membership Rule for New Records. The
INSERTION subentry determines the DBMS actions when new member records are
added. There are two possibilities: The DBMS is either to provide values for all the
pointers associated with this set or to simply add the record and provide pointer
values later, when the host program uses the CONNECT command.

There are two corresponding INSERTION options: AUTOMATIC and MAN-
UAL. If a set type has AUTOMATIC membership, any member record that is
stored will be related to its owner and to the next logical member record in that
set occurrence. As an example, consider the HAS_SENT set, which uses the
INSERTION IS AUTOMATIC clause and whose member records in each set
occurrence are to be sorted on INO.

When an INVOICE is stored, it will be related, through a pointer, to the next INVOICE in INO order from the same VENDOR. The DBMS will determine this pointer value before storing the record. If owner and prior pointers are also used, their values also will be determined prior to storing the INVOICE.

Sometimes this option cannot be used. Assume a set named ADVISES between two record types, FACULTY and STUDENT, where FACULTY is the owner and STUDENT the member. Now suppose a particular student has been admitted into the university and has no advisor, but we wish to store the student anyway. If we select AUTOMATIC for the set, the DBMS must be able to determine all pointer values before inserting a record into the set. In this case it can't be done, because there is no FACULTY owner and thus no ADVISES set occurrence in which to store this STUDENT. Any attempt to store such a STUDENT will be rejected. In this situation, we will have to specify MANUAL, because membership in the relationship is optional.

Using MANUAL enables member records to be added to the database without being connected to any owner. We would use MANUAL for optional membership or when the exact owner is as yet unknown. When sets are specified this way, member records are not inserted into a set occurrence until the DML CONNECT command is issued by the run-unit.

Another use for the MANUAL option is in situations like that shown in Figure 9.17, where a cycle is present. There, record type B is a member of a set owned by A. In turn, C is a member of a set owned by B, and A a member of a set owned by C; we have a cycle. If all three sets have automatic INSERTION, we have an impossible situation.

We cannot store a B record unless its A owner is already stored, so let's try to store all the A records first. However, this creates a problem: We cannot store the A records unless the C records are stored, because C owns the set of which A is a member. So let's revise our plan and store all the C records first. But this is also impossible, because B owns the set of which C is a member, and so on. To break this loop, we must define one of the sets as MANUAL and, after storing its members, issue the CONNECT command, which will link the new record into its proper set occurrences.

The RETENTION Subentry: Specifying the Membership Rule for Existing Records. The RETENTION option specifies the rule that applies to existing member records. There are three choices:

- Don't permit a member to switch owners.
- Do permit a member to switch owners.
- Permit a member to be associated with no owner at all.

The three options FIXED, MANDATORY, and OPTIONAL correspond to each of the three choices.

FIGURE 9.17   **Example of a Cycle, Where We Cannot Use INSERTION IS AUTOMATIC for All Sets**

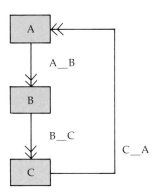

If a member's retention is FIXED, once a member record is stored in a set occurrence, that record must always be in that set occurrence; in other words, the record cannot switch owners. For example, if we choose RETENTION IS FIXED for the IS__DUE set, once an INVOICE is associated with a given DUE__DATE, it must always be associated with the same owner; it cannot be associated with a different DUE__DATE later. This means we cannot disconnect the INVOICE from a set occurrence owned by one DUE__DATE and connect it to one owned by another date. The only way to effect this change would be to physically delete the INVOICE occurrence and store it again, this time in the correct IS__DUE set occurrence.

Using MANDATORY means the record occurrence must always be associated with some owner, but not necessarily with the original one. If we used it for the IS__DUE set, we could change the DUE__DATE owner of an INVOICE record once it had been inserted into the database. To do so, we would DISCONNECT it from the incorrect set occurrence and CONNECT it to the correct one.

The MANDATORY option can also assist with deletion integrity. A consequence of using MANDATORY is that any attempt to DELETE an owner of a nonempty set results in an error being returned to DB-STATUS. This is the restrict option for deletion referential integrity that we discussed in Section 2.3 of Chapter 2. Let's look at an example.

Assume we want to delete the DUE__DATE record with a DDATE value of 04/15/XX. Remember, there are four INVOICEs in the IS__DUE set occurrence owned by this DUE__DATE record. If the set IS__DUE has MANDATORY retention, the delete attempt will be rejected, because there are member records in the IS__DUE set owned by 04/15/XX; it isn't empty. The database will be in the same state it was prior to the attempt.

When class membership is optional, we use RETENTION IS OPTIONAL. This permits members to be totally disassociated from owners at any time. For example, suppose that after adding INVOICE A12, we discover that its DUE_ DATE of 04/15/XX is incorrect, but we do not know the proper value. If we had used RETENTION IS MANDATORY, we would be forced to leave the INVOICE connected to some owner. Choosing FIXED would be even worse, because the INVOICE would have to stay connected to 04/15/XX, its present owner. Either choice could result in the INVOICE being paid incorrectly. However, if we use OPTIONAL membership, we can DISCONNECT the INVOICE from 04/15/XX without CONNECTing it to another DUE_DATE owner.

In summary, we use INSERTION IS AUTOMATIC and RETENTION IS MANDATORY for required membership. For sets whose member record types' membership is optional, we use INSERTION IS MANUAL and RETENTION IS OPTIONAL.

The SET SELECTION Subentry: Identifying a Set Occurrence. The SET SELECTION clause defines the process for identifying and accessing a given set occurrence. For example, when a new INVOICE is to be STOREd, the DBMS must be told to which DUE_DATE and VENDOR to connect it, that is, to which set occurrence of IS_DUE and HAS_SENT it should be linked. Although the general syntax for set types shown in Figure 9.16 shows four options, we will cover only the first three.

The first option is SYSTEM. This is used when SYSTEM is the set's owner and was used for the example in block 9 in Figure 9.11. If APPLICATION is used, the DBMS will add the new member record to the set occurrence last selected by the run-unit. Suppose we have just stored an INVOICE into the occurrence of IS_DUE owned by the date 05/15/XX. Also, assume we have just read a new INVOICE record from an input file that is due on 06/15/XX, and we want to store it. If we don't access the proper DUE_DATE owner (06/15/XX) prior to issuing a STORE command, the DBMS will add the INVOICE into the current IS_DUE set—the one for 05/15/XX! This shows the importance of always properly identifying all owners before storing the new member record. When APPLICATION is chosen, this responsibility lies completely with the run-unit. This is usually done by moving the primary key value of the owner of the record being stored to the owner's key field and performing a hashed access using one of the FIND command formats. Failure to issue the FIND command will result in the member being inserted into the current set occurrence. If BY KEY is chosen, the MOVE will still be necessary, but the FIND won't.

The BY KEY option transfers some of this responsibility to the DBMS, because after the run-unit moves values to the specified key-name components of the owner record, the DBMS will make that owner the current of set. Let's look at some examples.

First, look at block 10 in Figure 9.11. The SET SELECTION clause says to use

KEY VENDOR__KEY. Now look at block 1. There is only one component of VENDOR__KEY: VID. Thus, in an application in which we wanted to store a new INVOICE record, we would code something like:

```
    MOVE WS-VENDOR-CODE TO VID
* Assume WS-VENDOR-CODE is the code for the VENDOR
* who sent the INVOICE
* Not necessary to "FIND" the corresponding VENDOR, the DBMS will
* do so for us
*
* Next, MOVE values to the data items in INVOICE here
*

    STORE INVOICE
```

There is no need to actually locate the VENDOR owner by means of a FIND command as with the previous example; the DBMS does it for us.

9.4 DDL INTEGRITY ENFORCEMENT

In Chapter 2, we saw that there are several ways to protect the integrity of data. Among these are:

- Domain constraints
- Entity integrity
- Referential integrity
- Passwords
- User views

Let's review the DDL clauses that address these issues.

Domain Constraints

First, let's look at domain constraints. The CHECK IS feature can be used for this purpose. Recall that there are two ways to specify domains: implicitly and explicitly. Implicit domains are specified by giving a type and a range, while explicit domains are indicated by enumerating all possible choices.

To illustrate implicit domains, review the discussion on p. 436, in which we constrained the values of the IAMT data item to be within the range of $0 to $500,000 (see block 5 in Figure 9.11).

To set up an explicit domain check, we list the possible values in the CHECK IS clause. Assume we want to define an EMPLOYEE data item for SEX. To have the DBMS automatically enforce the explicit domain ("M","F"), we code the data item definition this way:

```
03 SEX     TYPE IS CHARACTER 1
           CHECK IS "M","F"
```

Entity Integrity

Entity integrity is the rule that no element of the primary key can be NULL. Like domain enforcement, this quality can be implemented by the CHECK IS clause. We add the line CHECK IS NOT NULL to the TYPE IS clause when defining the primary key data item (see block 4 in Figure 9.11, where we describe VID).

Referential Integrity Constraint Enforcement: Foreign Keys

Insertion and update integrity is provided by using the SOURCE IS option while defining data items. In this way, to use the terminology of Chapter 2, the dependent data item's value will always equal that of the parent. CODASYL calls the parent the **source** data item and the dependent the **object.**

Block 6 in Figure 9.11 specifies that the value of INVOICE.IVEND, the object data item, or foreign key, must always equal that of its source, VENDOR.VID. Any time the value of VID changes, the DBMS will adjust the IVEND value of all the related INVOICES. Also, when storing an INVOICE, the DBMS will guarantee that the two vendor code values match.

We can specify the restrict deletion integrity rule by selecting the member clause RETENTION IS MANDATORY. If we do so, any attempt to delete an owner of a nonempty set will result in a nonzero DB-STATUS value. Unfortunately, CODASYL does not provide for the cascade and set-to-NULL deletion integrity options. Their implementation is left to the applications programmer.

Data Security: Passwords

As we have seen, guarding against unauthorized access of data is accomplished through the use of ACCESS CONTROL LOCKs. Examples of CONTROL LOCKs appear in block 3 in Figure 9.11 and in the general syntax for setting such locks for records, data items, and sets.

Data (User) Views

Data views are useful for restricting the ability of users to see specific data items or combinations of data items and for limiting their ability to see specific record types. The CODASYL model provides this with its subschema concept. Because an unlimited number of subschemas are permitted, each end user theoretically can have a different view. Section 9.6 discusses subschemas.

9.5   PRE-1981 DDL DIFFERENCES

The most significant feature of the pre-1981 DDLs was the inclusion of some physical considerations. Among these are:

- Areas, or realms
- Specification of pointer implementation
- Specification of pointer types
- Specification of hash (CALC) fields

One of the often debated aspects of the pre-1981 CODASYL specifications was that of **areas,** or **realms.** These are physical constructs and represent the actual files in which the database is stored. These realms were defined in the schema DDL, and each record type was assigned to one of them as it was defined. The JOD felt that physical considerations should not be part of the DDL, so realms were dropped from the 1981 specifications.

The earlier DDLs also called for the schema to specify whether to use a linked list or an index to maintain the set occurrences. We discussed the implications of these specifications in Chapter 5. Let's briefly see how this was done in the earlier DBMSs.

The MEMBER clause contained two options: CHAIN [LINKED TO PRIOR] and POINTER ARRAY. With the CHAIN option, the owner record of each occurrence of the set being defined had an embedded first and last pointer, and each member record had an embedded next pointer. (You might want to review Section 5.2 at this time.) Using the optional clause, LINKED TO PRIOR, forced the DBMS to establish an embedded prior pointer in each member record, which connected a member to the previous one according to the specified sequence.

The other MODE IS option, MODE IS POINTER ARRAY, resulted in the DBMS using an index (which was called a pointer array) rather than an embedded pointer to relate owners to members and members to other members. This choice also resulted in both forward and backward member pointers.

The other major difference in the earlier guidelines was that the RECORD clause specified the storage method to be used to physically store the records. There were two main choices:

- Use a CALC data item for hashed storage and access
- Use a VIA set-name SET option to physically store member records near their owners

The choice of "LOCATION MODE IS CALC USING data-item name" established a primary key and instructed the DBMS to hash on the specified data item and STORE the record at the resulting database key location. This option also specified whether or not to allow for duplicate primary key values by using a DUPLICATES ARE [NOT] ALLOWED clause. The typical specification was that duplicates were not permitted.

The other LOCATION MODE option, "LOCATION MODE IS VIA set-name," instructed the DBMS to store the member record occurrences as close to the set owner as possible—a form of clustering. If there was no need for random access of a record, this choice could lead to very efficient processing, provided the correct set name was chosen. Let's see how this efficiency resulted.

An area is divided into physical units called **pages,** which can be made large enough to hold many logical records. When a physical read of the database is executed, an entire page is transmitted. If VIA is used, several member records might be on the same page (often on the same page as their owners), and a single physical read will therefore transfer many logical records. A major problem with VIA was that the only way to access such record occurrences was through their participation in sets; that is, we could not access such record occurrences randomly.

This completes our discussion of how to code a schema. We have seen that there is a SCHEMA entry and as many RECORD and SET entries as the conceptual database design dictates. A point you should remember is that each set represents a 1:M relationship and must be defined in the schema DDL. As we saw in Chapter 5, each set is implemented as a linked list (or pointer array), so we can say that all relationships are physically maintained by the network DBMSs. This isn't so with the relational model, in which relationships are seen as implicit and not even specified until a query is made. With the network model, adding a new relationship would mean a complete restructuring of the database to provide new storage locations for the additional pointers—a formidable task.

9.6   EXTERNAL DATABASES: SUBSCHEMAS

External database descriptions are defined using the subschema DDL. There is no limit to the number of subschemas that can be defined over any schema.

Designing the External Databases: Determining User Requirements

The external databases must be based on the original schema, but records, sets, and data items can be omitted and/or renamed. In some CODASYL implementations, access paths can even be changed or added.

The procedure begins by first reviewing the user DSDs. During the conceptual design phase, we base the conceptual database on transactions from end users. However, if we don't do this or if new transactions have occurred, we can still use the technique developed earlier: check the DSD against the end users' transactions and ensure that the DSD supports them. Figure 9.18 shows a DSD suitable for Sandy Hill's needs in the Microtech minicase. Figure 9.19 shows the brief DSD developed for Gordon Reid's requirements.

Next, we identify the access path through the DSD that is necessary to provide

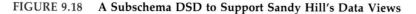

FIGURE 9.18   **A Subschema DSD to Support Sandy Hill's Data Views**

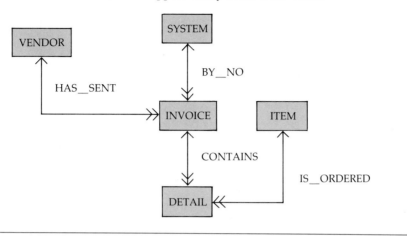

FIGURE 9.19   **A Subschema DSD to Support Gordon Reid's Application**

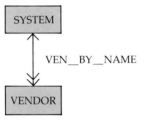

the desired information. This technique is sometimes called a **logical access map (LAM).** To determine this, it might be helpful to first think through the logic to support a given application. Let's do this for Sandy's application.

Sandy needs a report that shows all INVOICEs, associated VENDOR information, and all the DETAIL data, including item descriptions (see Figure 9.3). The general plan is:

1. Access SYSTEM. This is where the head pointer for the first INVOICE in the BY__NO set will be located.
2. Sequentially access all the INVOICE records in the BY__NO set. This will be done using the BY__NO next pointers.
3. For each INVOICE, locate the VENDOR owner of HAS__SENT (we can use an owner pointer).

4. For each INVOICE, sequentially access each DETAIL record in the CON-TAINS set.

5. For each DETAIL record, access its ITEM owner by using the IS__ORDERED set.

This suggests the LAM shown in Figure 9.20.

Let's look at the above logic in more detail. First, we access SYSTEM. Finding the SYSTEM record establishes the current of set for BY__NO as 2, the database key value for SYSTEM (see Figure 9.10). Next, we loop through the BY__NO set, checking for an end-of-set value for DB-STATUS. Each pass through the loop will establish a new current of set for BY__NO and CONTAINS.

The first thing this loop will do is FIND the VENDOR owner of the HAS__SENT set. This is necessary for retrieving VENDOR information. The next thing we will find in this loop is a second loop that processes all the DETAIL records for the current CONTAINS. Within this inner loop we must access ITEM, the owner of IS__ORDERED, to retrieve the description information.

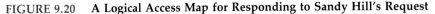

FIGURE 9.20   A Logical Access Map for Responding to Sandy Hill's Request

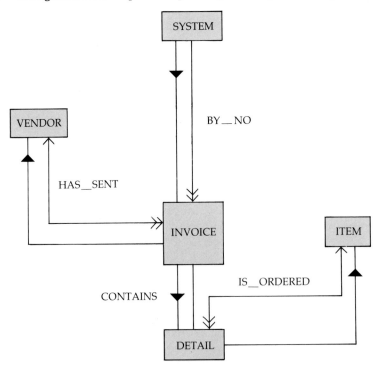

FIGURE 9.21   Pseudocode to Support Sandy Hill's Transaction

```
 1.  MORE-INVOICES = "Y"
 2.  FIND SYSTEM RECORD
 3.  DO WHILE MORE-INVOICES-BY-NO
 4.      FIND NEXT INVOICE IN BY-NO SET
 5.      IF END-OF-SET FOR BY-NO
 6.          MORE-INVOICES = "N"
 7.      ELSE
 8.          GET INVOICE
 9.          FIND OWNER VENDOR OF HAS-SENT SET
10.          MORE-DETAIL = "Y"
11.            DO WHILE MORE-DETAIL-THIS-INVOICE
12.                FIND NEXT DETAIL IN CONTAINS SET
13.                IF END-OF-SET FOR CONTAINS
14.                    MORE-DETAIL = "N"
15.                ELSE
16.                    GET DETAIL
17.                    FIND OWNER ITEM OF IS-ORDERED SET
18.                    GET ITEM
19.                    MOVE DATA TO PRINT LINE AND PRINT
20.                END-IF
21.            END DO
22.      END-IF
23.  END DO
24.  STOP
```

Figure 9.21 shows our general logic converted to pseudocode. The outer loop is controlled by the switch MORE-INVOICES. We are assuming a condition name called MORE-INVOICES-BY-NO when the switch is set to Y (see line 3). As long as the switch is Y, the outer DO loop (lines 3 through 23) will be executed.

Line 4 accesses the "next" INVOICE record in the BY-NO set. To transfer a record from the database to the UWA, we must first FIND it, then GET it. Line 4 merely establishes the current of INVOICE. The next line checks for the end of the BY-NO set, and, if encountered, sets the MORE-INVOICES switches to N. If there are more INVOICEs, we retrieve one (line 8). Line 9 locates the VENDOR occurrence that owns this INVOICE. Notice that to do this, we issued a FIND of the owner of the HAS-SENT set. Next, MORE-DETAIL, the switch that controls the inner loop, is set. It must be reset before executing the inner loop each time.

The inner loop begins at line 11 and concludes with line 21. It processes all the DETAIL items for the current INVOICE. Alternatively, we might say that it processes the member records in the current of the CONTAINS set until it encounters an end-of-set. As long as there are more DETAIL records for this INVOICE, the DETAIL record is found (line 16), the ITEM owner found (line 17), and the ITEM retrieved (line 18), and then everything is printed. If there are no more DETAIL items for this INVOICE (the end-of-set for CONTAINS has been reached), the inner loop switch is set accordingly (line 14), and we are ready for the next INVOICE in BY-NO.

In keeping with the COBOL spirit of this text, all underscores were replaced with hyphens for the pseudocode example. You will see this again in the next chapter.

Defining the External Databases: The Subschema DDL

Like the schema DDL, the subschema language has undergone several revisions with each new CODASYL JOD release. In the 1981 release, there are three DIVISIONs: TITLE, MAPPING, and STRUCTURE. Figure 9.22 shows Sandy Hill's subschema using those guidelines.

The SS Entry. The SS entry is a subschema entry and is used primarily to name the subschema. All run-units accessing this subschema must use this name. The name following the WITHIN clause is the underlying schema name, A__P in Figure 9.22.

The MAPPING DIVISION. The next entry is the MAPPING DIVISION, where aliases are defined. In Figure 9.22, the data item IAMT is renamed INVOICE-AMOUNT. The AD entry is short for "alias description," and the delimiters (= =) specify which schema-defined names are to be redefined. Besides data items, records and sets can be given new names.

The STRUCTURE DIVISION. The first entry in the STRUCTURE DIVISION is the RECORD SECTION. Here we list just the records and data items applicable to this subschema. In addition, we can define a new record key or record order key. For instance, to use the vendor's address as a record key that was not specified as such in the schema but is needed in the subschema, we just code:

```
01 VENDOR
KEY VADDRESS IS VADDRESS
DUPLICATES FIRST
```

After identifying the record, we continue with the data item definitions.

The final section is the SET SECTION, where the desired sets and their SET SELECTIONs are defined. Each set definition begins with SD, which stands for "set description." Notice that we are specifying four sets: BY-NO, CONTAINS, HAS-SENT, and IS-ORDERED. Also note that, except for the schema's name, all underscores have been converted to hyphens.

This completes our discussion of defining subschemas. In the next chapter, we look at what the internal (physical) database is and how to define it.

FIGURE 9.22   **Sandy Hill's Subschema DDL**

```
TITLE DIVISION.
  SS SANDY WITHIN A_P.
MAPPING DIVISION.
  ALIAS SECTION.
    AD = = IAMT = =       BECOMES  INVOICE-AMOUNT
STRUCTURE DIVISION.
  RECORD SECTION.
    01 INVOICE.
           03 INO              PIC S9(5) COMP-3.
           03 IAMT             PIC S9(7)V99 COMP-3.
           03 IDATE            PIC X(8).
           03 IVEND            PIC X(5).
    01 VENDOR.
           03 VEN-CODE         PIC X(5).
           03 VEN-NAME         PIC X(20).
           03 VEN-ADDRESS      PIC X(40).
           03 VEN-CONTACT      PIC X(20).
           03 VEN-STATE        PIC X(2).
           03 VEN-ZIP          PIC X(5).
    01 ITEM.
           03 ITEM-CODE        PIC X(5).
           03 ITEM-DESC        PIC X(25).
           03 ON-HAND          PIC S9(7) COMP-3.
           03 ON-ORDER         PIC S9(7) COMP-3.
           03 USAGE-YTD        PIC S9(9) COMP-3.
    01 DETAIL.
           03 DINO             PIC S9(5) COMP-3.
           03 DITEM-CODE       PIC X(5).
           03 UNITS            PIC S9(7) COMP-3.
           03 SPRICE           PIC S9(5)V99 COMP-3.
  SET SECTION.
  SD BY-NO.
  SD CONTAINS.
  SD HAS-SENT.
  SD IS-ORDERED.
```

9.7 SUMMARY

The conceptual or logical schema is defined by specifying three types of entries within the schema DDL:

- One schema entry
- Several record type entries
- Several set entries

    Record types are defined first. Each entry has several clauses, including ones that specify primary, secondary, and order keys and the data items themselves.

Use of the CHECK feature while defining data items can enforce domain and entity integrity constraints. The SOURCE clause enables us to implement update referential integrity.

Sets are defined last. Besides identifying the owner and member of each set, we must specify how a set occurrence is to be identified (SET SELECTION), along with the rules that govern how new member records are to be inserted and existing ones moved about from one set occurrence to another. One of the MEMBER clauses, RETENTION IS, can help us implement restriction deletion integrity.

All entries provide the ability to establish passwords to restrict access to the database. This is done by specifying an ACCESS CONTROL LOCK that must match a control key value to be supplied by the run-unit.

Any operation that violates a referential integrity constraint or an ACCESS CONTROL LOCK will cause a value to be returned by the DBMS in a special variable called DB-STATUS. This variable will also be used to detect other kinds of abnormalities, such as failure to find a record when a hashed access is executed or when the end of a set is reached.

Each network structure contains record types and set types. Each set has an owner and one or more member record types. By following occurrences of those sets, we can respond to sequential queries. Using a hashing routine permits random access to any of the records in the database, provided we have designated the records as having primary and/or secondary keys.

Next, we looked at the external databases. During the conceptual design phase, or on an as-needed basis, user DSDs are constructed. Then logical access maps are defined depicting the path needed to carry out the transactions defined by the end user, which the DSD hopefully supports.

To implement user views, subschemas must be coded using the subschema DDL. We looked at the 1981 version of this language. To provide security, integrity, and privacy for end user data, subschemas can omit records, sets, or data items not needed by a given user. Furthermore, any of these items can be renamed, or new ACCESS CONTROL LOCKs can be applied.

REVIEW QUESTIONS

1. Distinguish between record types and record occurrences.

2. Differentiate between set types and set occurrences.

Refer to Figure 9.5 for Questions 3 through 5.

3. How many times can the record INVOICE occur?

4. In words, how many set occurrences of CONTAINS exist?

5. Why did we carry IVEND in the INVOICE record when the vendor's code is also carried in the VENDOR record?

6. In Figure 9.9, in the set occurrence of IS__ORDERED owned by the part having code 77, why is the detail line item designated as A22 77 the first one?

7. What is a value-based set? An information-bearing set?

8. What is a singular set?

9. When is a singular set necessary?

10. If a set is singular, is sorted on the member's primary key (ORDER FOR INSERTION IS SORTED . . .), and the DUPLICATES ARE NOT PERMITTED clause for the sorting sequence is specified, why would this prohibit duplicate primary keys?

11. Explain how the CODASYL model provides for integrity protection through value-based sets.

12. Explain the benefits and problems associated with the RECORD subentry LOCATION MODE IS VIA in the pre-1981 DBMSs.

13. What is a LAM? Why is it useful?

14. What is an external database? Which CODASYL language defines it?

15. Describe the subschema DIVISIONs and their purposes.

PROBLEMS

1. Assume an end user at Microtech wants a report by due date by vendor (in vendor name), showing all invoices in decreasing order by amount. Modify the DSD in Figure 9.5 to accommodate this new database transaction. Specify how each new set is to be sorted.

2. For the Microtech schema, code the CONTAINS set entry.

3. Draw a LAM for Gordon Reid's application.

4. Give the pseudocode necessary to implement the LAM from Problem 3.

5. Code the resulting subschema.

Assume the DSD on p. 456 is to be used as a starting point for the development of a database for albums and compact discs (CDs) for a record store. We have made the simplifying assumption that each CD and album is produced by a single artist.

The number of albums for any one title (AUNITS) should never exceed 100 or be less than 10. The upper and lower limits for CDs are 25 and 5, respectively. All codes are 7-byte alphanumeric data items, and all names are 25 bytes long. The units-on-hand data item for both CDs and albums is to be two-digit numeric. Assume whatever is appropriate for the other data items.

The store requires a report listing all ALBUMs in album order (ANO) and others that do the same for CDs (CNO) and ARTISTs (by artist name).

6. Add the additional sets, indicate their sorting sequence, and, assuming that record order keys are not used, add the new record type that will permit these sequential reports.

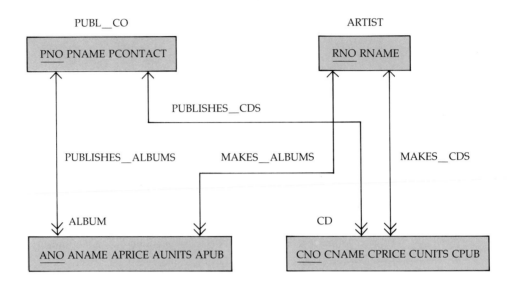

7. Code the record description for ALBUM assuming that a primary key is needed, access by name is required, and the APUB item is virtual.

8. Assume that the PUBLISHES__CD set is to be sorted by CD code. Show the schema DDL entries necessary to completely specify the set.

9. A new store manager has requested a report by ARTIST code by ALBUM description. Can our present DSD support this transaction? If not, modify the DSD to do so.

10. Assuming that all possible pointers (first, next, prior, last, and owner) are used, how many pointers will each occurrence of ALBUM contain? Use the original DSD above.

11. How many pointers will each ARTIST record occurrence contain? Use the same assumptions that we made for Problem 10.

12. How many occurrences of PUBLISHES__CDS will there be? Assume there are 1,500 CD titles and 150 PUBL__COs.

13. Assume we have directly retrieved an ALBUM with code S&G101. How can we determine the contact from the corresponding publishing company?

14. Show a graphical LAM for the following report: Display all the ALBUMS produced by the artist having code BEAT101. For each ALBUM, list the publishing company name and address.

15. Show the pseudocode for your answer to Problem 14.

▪▪ EPISODE 5

Defining the Schema Using IDMS

This episode should be considered independently of Episode 4, where we saw how to use DB2 in an embedded mode. In this episode, Barb Scholl discusses the implementation of the hospital's database using Release 10.0 of IDMS/R, which is a Cullinet product. This episode illustrates some of the differences between IDMS and the CODASYL schema DDL from Chapter 9.

IDMS was originally developed at B. F. Goodrich but acquired by Cullinet (known as Cullinane at the time). It is an almost complete implementation of the CODASYL model, which includes an Integrated Data Dictionary system and an optional set of Cullinet's 4GL products. In 1983, Cullinet added many relational features to IDMS and renamed the product IDMS/R.

Let's return now to Community Hospital.

Barb has a logical design to explain and a new DBMS to implement it. Her design is shown in Exhibit 1.

The diagram is essentially the same as Exhibit 7 in Episode 3, but set names have been assigned to the 1:M relationships. One change was made: the addition of a set, PAT__CHARGE, between PATIENT and MED__CHARGE. Although the set could have been left off, Barb wanted to be able to quickly move from the MED__CHARGE occurrence back to the associated PATIENT without having to traverse the intervening record types, UNIT__DOSE__ORDER and IV__ORDER.

Although not shown in Episode 1, Barb also decided to have several of the record types owned by the SYSTEM. Because IDMS does not support RECORD ORDER keys, she had to explicitly define the singular sets. Exhibit 2 shows them, together with their associated sort keys.

At a meeting with Alan Jones and Kevin Vance, Barb was asked to describe some of the IDMS/CODASYL schema DDL differences. She began, "For the most part, they are similar. However, there are three major differences: (1) the existence of a new entry, AREA; (2) several changes in the RECORD entry; and (3) several in the SET entry. In the schema DDL, we have to define one or more physical units, called *areas*, which are subdivisions of the database that map to the external files managed by the operating system. Each area is in turn divided into a series of contiguous pages.

"A page corresponds to a physical block on a DASD [direct access storage device, or disk] and contains logical records and some overhead. Page sizes are defined via the Device Media Control Language (DMCL). Once the areas are defined, each record type must be assigned to one of them using the WITHIN AREA clause.

"Any questions so far?"

There weren't any, so Barb then told her team about the RECORD changes:

"Here there are three major differences: (1) We need to assign records to areas; (2) each record type must have a LOCATION MODE; and (3) each record type must be assigned a unique RECORD ID.

"First, the requirement to assign the record to an area. This isn't a difficult concept, and I won't go into the rationale for it. Suffice it to say that we'll set up a single area for our database and assign all records to it.

"Next, each record must have a LOCATION MODE, which specifies how

EXHIBIT 1   The CODASYL DSD for the Community Hospital Conceptual Database

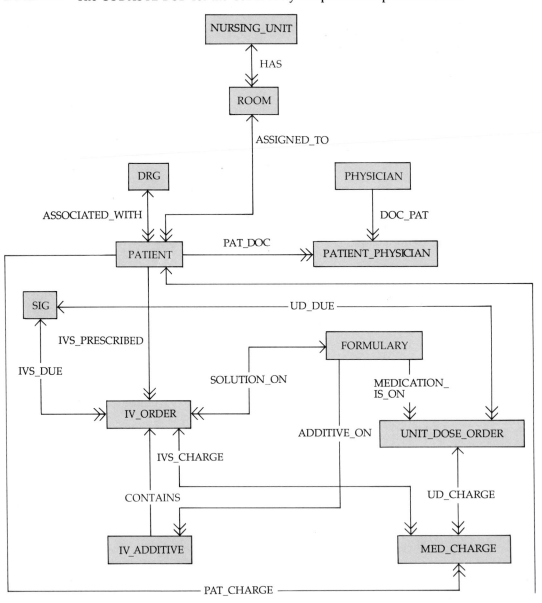

EXHIBIT 1   (concluded)

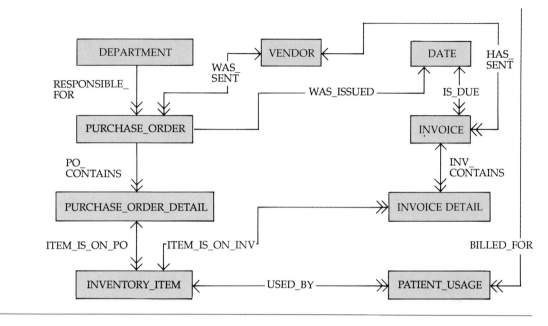

EXHIBIT 2   Sets Not Shown in Exhibit 1

Set Name	Member	Sequence Method	Sort Key
BY_NU	NURSING_UNIT	S	NU_CODE
BY_DRG	DRG	S	DRG_CODE
BY_DOC_NAME	PHYSICIAN	S	DOC_NAME
BY_DOC_NO	PHYSICIAN	S	DOC_NO
ALL_PATS	PATIENT	S	PATIENT_NO
IVS_BY_NO	IV_ORDER	S	IVORDER_NO
FORMULARY_BY_ID	FORMULARY	S	MED_CODE
FORMULARY_BY_DESC	FORMULARY	S	MED_DESC
UD_BY_NO	UNIT_DOSE_ORDER	S	UDORDER_NO
DEPTS_BY_ID	DEPARTMENT	S	DEPT_CODE
DEPTS_BY_NAME	DEPARTMENT	S	DEPT_NAME
INV_BY_NO	INVOICE	S	VOUCHER_NO
ALL_DATES	DATE	S	DATE
ALL_ITEMS_BY_ID	INVENTORY_ITEM	S	ITEM_CODE
ALL_ITEMS_BY_NAME	INVENTORY_ITEM	S	ITEM_DESC

All sets are owned by the SYSTEM.

records are to be stored. This is quite a bit different than the 1981 JOD guidelines, because it limits us to a single primary key per record type. The clause also influences our ability to retrieve records. We will choose between two options: 'CALC' for hashed storage and access and 'VIA set-name,' which causes IDMS to store member records near the current of set when the record is stored.

"Choice of 'LOCATION MODE IS CALC USING data-item-name' means IDMS will hash on the specified data item(s) and STORE the record at the resulting database key location. This choice offers random access of records based on the CALC data item and is probably the more frequently chosen option. When we look at my schema, you will notice that I also had to specify whether or not to allow for duplicate hash item values.

"The second LOCATION MODE option, 'LOCATION MODE IS VIA set-name,' means to store the record occurrences as physically close as possible to the current of set at the time the record is stored. Usually, the current of set will be the owner, and the member will therefore be stored on the same page as its owner. This offers quick access of member records, because they are often on the same pages as their owners. When this happens, if we access an owner, the members will also be in the buffer; it's a form of blocking. Unfortunately, using the VIA LOCATION MODE means that the only way to access the records is through their participation in sets. We can't randomly access them."

Barb continued, "Let me explain this in more detail. Because a page is the unit of data transmitted to and from the disk, it may be beneficial to have an owner and as many member records on a page as possible. For example, it makes sense that when we access an IV__ORDER, we will also want to see all the associated

drugs in that IV, which are carried in the related IV__ADDITIVE occurrences. I want the order and its associated additives to be retrieved as quickly as possible by placing them on the same page. Furthermore, there is no reason to ever access an IV__ADDITIVE occurrence without first retrieving the related IV__ORDER occurrence, which means we can live without hashed access to the additives. All of these characteristics result from using the VIA LOCATION MODE."

Much of the group's remaining discussion centered on the technical details of how IDMS physically stores the pages, but this isn't relevant to our episode. We will pick up the narrative as Barb Scholl returns to her discussion about the RECORD entry differences between IDMS and CODASYL.

"The last IDMS/CODASYL record difference is the requirement to assign each record a unique record ID, an internal number necessary for the DBMS. Version 10.0 of IDMS has an option for automatically assigning them, but earlier versions forced us to assign the ID as the record was defined. This was a pain, because we had to keep track of which numbers had been used.

"A similar IDMS peculiarity is the need to assign a number to each pointer that results from a set's definition. I guess I'll talk about sets next, unless there are any questions."

There weren't any, so Barb continued (much to the disappointment of her team members, who felt the meeting was going a bit long):

"First, there are three new clauses that you didn't see in the CODASYL training you had: MODE IS, DBKEY POSITION, and LINKED TO OWNER. Also, there are two omissions from the '81 standards. We can't use FIXED RETENTION, and there isn't a SET SELECTION clause.

"First, in the MEMBER entry of each

set definition, one of two MODEs must be selected [Note: These were discussed in Chapter 5]. They are MODE IS CHAIN [LINKED TO PRIOR], or MODE IS INDEXED."

Kevin interrupted, "Is the INDEXED option like the pointer array the earlier CODASYL models talked about?"

"You're right, Kevin," Barb replied. "If we choose this option, IDMS will construct an array within the owner occurrence, where the next and previous pointers will be stored. Sounds like you have a good grasp of the CODASYL model. Let's see how you react to this next feature.

"The relative position of each pointer must be specified through a clause that begins 'NEXT DBKEY POSITION IS . . .' Its purpose is to associate a relative number with each pointer in the owner and member records. Remember that within a particular set, each member can have a next, prior, and owner pointer and each owner can have a head and tail pointer. Not only must these pointers be accounted for and assigned a relative number, the numbering must be consistent from set to set. Before release 10.0 of IDMS, the assignment of these pointers was difficult and error prone. The current release permits us to use an automatic (AUTO) method for assigning them. Just be sure that you provide the schema with the correct number of pointers, and IDMS will assign the relative values. I'll have more to say when we look at the schema I've brought with me.

"The last set difference is the need to specify whether a member record is to use owner pointers. If this is desirable, code LINKED TO OWNER within the MEMBER clause.

"I think we need a break. Let me give both of you a copy of the schema [Exhibit 3]. Take it to your offices, and let's meet again next Tuesday at 9:00. I appreciate

your coming today and hope we can finish this schema discussion at our next meeting."

The topic of the next meeting focused on the schema and on some of Barb's design decisions. Again, Barb led the discussion.

"Let me begin by saying that I want all of you to use IDMS's Integrated Data Dictionary whenever possible. I admit that my schema didn't, but after making numerous coding errors, I can see the wisdom in using it.

"Now let's go down the copy of the schema I gave each of you last week. I've added a number to several areas on your listing that you'll find helpful as we discuss it.

"First, I named the schema and specified that the record IDs are to be automatically assigned by IDMS, beginning with number 500 [item 1 in Exhibit 3]. The INCLUDE TECH clause says that the user with name TECH must be defined in the data dictionary (REGISTERED) and has all rights to the schema. Use of 'PUBLIC ACCESS . . . ' [item 2] says that all other end users may only DISPLAY the schema.

"The next entry, FILE NAME [item 3], defines the external files that the operating system will manage. My schema uses only one such file, HOSPFILE. The ASSIGN TO clause [item 4] is necessary for IBM's file-related JCL and won't be discussed.

"Next comes the AREA entries. Code one for each area, and also specify a name, how many pages to reserve, and where to place the pages in the external file.

"My schema includes a single area, AREA__1, which is to be stored in the HOSPFILE file and is to contain 2,000 pages. The records are to occupy pages 1 through 2,000 within the file [see item 5].

"The next collection of entries are for

EXHIBIT 3   **A Portion of the Schema DDL for Community Hospital**

```
SCHEMA NAME IS PAT_CARE VERSION IS NEXT HIGHEST

  ASSIGN RECORD IDS FROM 500
```

Each record must have a unique ID. This provides a starting value of 500

```
  INCLUDE TECH...

    REGISTERED FOR ALL
```

A form of security. User must be registered in the IDMS Data Dictionary and has all rights to the schema

```
    PUBLIC ACCESS IS ALLOWED FOR DISPLAY
```

Anyone may display the schema

```
FILE NAME IS HOSPFILE
```

Physical name of database file

```
  ASSIGN TO DDNAME
```

Necessary for IBM JCL

```
AREA NAME IS AREA_1

  TYPE IS STANDARD

  PAGE RANGE IS 0001 THRU 2000
```

2000 pages reserved for AREA_1

```
    WITHIN HOSPFILE
```

AREA_1 can be found in HOSPFILE

```
  FROM 1 FOR ALL
```

Records stored beginning at first page

```
RECORD NAME IS PATIENT.
  RECORD ID IS AUTO
```

Prior to release 10.0 the DBA had to assign a unique ID

```
    LOCATION MODE IS CALC USING PATIENT_NO
```

Hashed access is specified

EXHIBIT 3   **(continued)**

```
          DUPLICATES ARE NOT ALLOWED

WITHIN AREA AREA_1.
```
———————————————————————————— Must assign every record to an area

```
     03  PATIENT_NO        PIC X(10).
```
———————————————————————————— Uses COBOL-like PICTURE clauses

```
     03  PAT_NAME          PIC X(25).
     03  SEX               PIC X.
     03  AGE               PIC 9(3).
     03  WEIGHT            PIC X(3).
          .
          .
          .
     03  PAT_STATUS        PIC X(1).
RECORD NAME IS IV_ORDER
     RECORD ID IS AUTO
     LOCATION MODE IS CALC USING IVORDER_NO
          DUPLICATES ARE NOT ALLOWED
     WITHIN AREA AREA_1.
     CALL IDMSCOMP        BEFORE STORE
```
———————————————————————————— A database procedure to be
called prior to a STORE of
IV_ORDER. It compresses the data,
saving storage space

```
     CALL IDMSDCOM AFTER OBTAIN, GET
```
———————————————————————————— Decompress the data when
a record is retrieved

```
     03  IVORDER_NO        PIC 9(5).
     03  IV_PAT_NO         PIC X(10).
     03  PHARM_INIT        PIC X(3).
     03  IV_ENT_DATE       PIC X(8).
     03  IV_CHG_DATE       PIC X(8).
     03  IV_SIG_CODE       PIC X(4).
     03  SOLN_CODE         PIC X(7).
     03  FLOW_RATE         PIC 9(3).
     03  IV_STATUS         PIC X.
RECORD NAME IS IV_ADDITIVE
     RECORD ID IS AUTO
     LOCATION MODE IS VIA CONTAINS
```
←——————————————————————————— No "DUPLICATES" clause with VIA

EXHIBIT 3   **(continued)**

```
            WITHIN AREA AREA_1.
            03 ADD_IVORDER_NO   PIC 9(5).
            03 ADDITIVE_NO      PIC 99.
            03 ADD_MED_CODE     PIC X(7).
            03 AMOUNT           PIC X(7).
        RECORD NAME IS UNIT_DOSE_ORDER
            RECORD ID IS AUTO
            LOCATION MODE IS CALC USING UD_ORDER_NO
                DUPLICATES ARE NOT ALLOWED
            WITHIN AREA_1.
            03 UD_ORDER_NO      PIC 9(5).
            03 UD_PAT_NO        PIC X(10).
            03 UD_MED_CODE      PIC X(7).
            03 UD_AMOUNT        PIC X(7).
            03 UD_SIG_CODE      PIC X(4).
            03 UD_PHARM_INIT    PIC X(3).
            03 UD_DATE_ENT      PIC X(8).
            03 UD_DATE_CHG      PIC X(8).
                .
                .
                .

        RECORD NAME IS PO
            RECORD ID IS AUTO
            LOCATION MODE IS CALC USING PO_NO
                DUPLICATES ARE NOT ALLOWED
            WITHIN AREA AREA_1.
            COPY PO RECORD VERSION 1
```

Would result in these items being copied in from the Data Dictionary

```
            03 PO_NO        PIC X(10).

            03 PO_DATE      PIC X(8).

            03 PO_DEPT_RESP PIC X(5).
                                .
                                .
                                .
```

```
        RECORD NAME IS MED_CHARGE
            RECORD ID IS AUTO
            LOCATION MODE IS VIA PAT_CHARGE
```

No need for hashed access, choose VIA the set most often used: PAT_CHARGE

EXHIBIT 3   (continued)

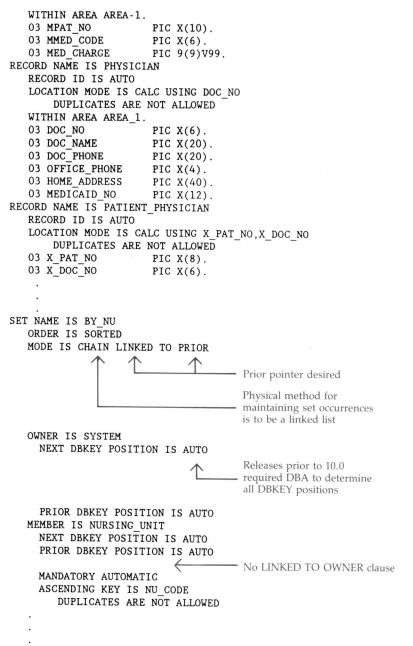

```
                WITHIN AREA AREA-1.
                03 MPAT_NO         PIC X(10).
                03 MMED_CODE       PIC X(6).
                03 MED_CHARGE      PIC 9(9)V99.
            RECORD NAME IS PHYSICIAN
                RECORD ID IS AUTO
                LOCATION MODE IS CALC USING DOC_NO
                    DUPLICATES ARE NOT ALLOWED
                WITHIN AREA AREA_1.
                03 DOC_NO          PIC X(6).
                03 DOC_NAME        PIC X(20).
                03 DOC_PHONE       PIC X(20).
                03 OFFICE_PHONE    PIC X(4).
                03 HOME_ADDRESS    PIC X(40).
                03 MEDICAID_NO     PIC X(12).
            RECORD NAME IS PATIENT_PHYSICIAN
                RECORD ID IS AUTO
                LOCATION MODE IS CALC USING X_PAT_NO,X_DOC_NO
                    DUPLICATES ARE NOT ALLOWED
                03 X_PAT_NO        PIC X(8).
                03 X_DOC_NO        PIC X(6).
                 .
                 .
                 .

            SET NAME IS BY_NU
                ORDER IS SORTED
                MODE IS CHAIN LINKED TO PRIOR
```

— Prior pointer desired

— Physical method for maintaining set occurrences is to be a linked list

```
                OWNER IS SYSTEM
                NEXT DBKEY POSITION IS AUTO
```

— Releases prior to 10.0 required DBA to determine all DBKEY positions

```
                PRIOR DBKEY POSITION IS AUTO
                MEMBER IS NURSING_UNIT
                    NEXT DBKEY POSITION IS AUTO
                    PRIOR DBKEY POSITION IS AUTO
```

← — No LINKED TO OWNER clause

```
                MANDATORY AUTOMATIC
                ASCENDING KEY IS NU_CODE
                    DUPLICATES ARE NOT ALLOWED
                 .
                 .
                 .
```

EXHIBIT 3   **(continued)**

```
SET NAME IS IVS_PRESCRIBED
   ORDER IS SORTED
   MODE IS CHAIN LINKED TO PRIOR
   OWNER IS PATIENT
      NEXT DBKEY POSITION IS AUTO
      NEXT DBKEY POSITION IS AUTO
   MEMBER IS IV_ORDER
      NEXT DBKEY POSITION IS AUTO
      PRIOR DBKEY POSITION IS AUTO
      LINKED TO OWNER
         OWNER DBKEY POSITION IS AUTO
      MANDATORY AUTOMATIC
      ASCENDING KEY IS IVORDER_NO
         DUPLICATES ARE NOT ALLOWED
SET NAME IS CONTAINS
   ORDER IS SORTED
   MODE IS INDEX BLOCK CONTAINS 12 KEYS
```
                                                    ⟶ Use a pointer array
```
   LINKED TO PRIOR
   OWNER IS IV_ORDER
      NEXT DBKEY POSITION IS AUTO
      PRIOR DBKEY POSITION IS AUTO
   MEMBER IS IV_ADDITIVE
      INDEX DBKEY POSITION IS AUTO
      NEXT DBKEY POSITION IS AUTO
      PRIOR DBKEY POSITION IS AUTO
      LINKED TO OWNER  ⟵                 ── Use an owner pointer
         OWNER DBKEY POSITION IS AUTO
      MANDATORY AUTOMATIC
      ASCENDING KEY IS ADDITIVE_NO
         DUPLICATES NOT ALLOWED
SET NAME IS SOLUTION_ON
   ORDER IS SORTED
   MODE IS CHAIN
   OWNER IS FORMULARY
      NEXT DBKEY POSITION IS AUTO
      PRIOR DBKEY POSITION IS AUTO
   MEMBER IS IV_ORDER
      NEXT DBKEY POSITION IS AUTO
      PRIOR DBKEY POSITION IS AUTO
      LINKED TO OWNER
         OWNER DBKEY POSITION IS AUTO
      OPTIONAL MANUAL
      ASCENDING KEY IS IVORDER_NO
         DUPLICATES NOT ALLOWED.
```

EXHIBIT 3   **(concluded)**

```
SET NAME IS ASSOCIATED_WITH
   ORDER IS SORTED
   MODE IS CHAIN LINKED TO PRIOR
   OWNER IS DRG
      NEXT DBKEY POSITION IS AUTO
      PRIOR DBKEY POSITION IS AUTO
   MEMBER IS PATIENT
      NEXT DBKEY POSITION IS AUTO
      PRIOR DBKEY POSITION IS AUTO
      LINKED TO OWNER
         OWNER DBKEY POSITION IS AUTO
      OPTIONAL MANUAL
      ASCENDING KEY IS PATIENT_NO
         DUPLICATES NOT ALLOWED
      .
      .
      .

VALIDATE
```

defining records. Following the record's name must be the unique record ID, a numeric value above 100 that associates the record type with that number. The schema I gave you uses the AUTO feature I mentioned last week, so I didn't have to worry about accidentally assigning two records the same value. Since PATIENT is coded first, its RECORD ID will be 500.

"Now look at item 8. It says that PATIENT occurrences are to be stored using a hashing algorithm based on PATIENT_NO and that there cannot be two PATIENTs with the same PATIENT_NO value. When a PATIENT is stored, IDMS will generate a page number from 1 to 2,000, the allowable page values, and store the record on that page. Synonyms are automatically handled by IDMS by chaining them together in a linked list that Cullinet calls a 'CALC set.' Contrast this with item 11, which shows use of VIA for the IV_ADDITIVE record type.

"There is no need for hashed retrieval of IV_ADDITIVEs. Also, by using VIA, the IV_ADDITIVE occurrences will be near one another on the DASD and also near the IV_ORDER that owns them, yielding fast retrieval of an order's additives.

"So far, I've discussed how to name the record, assign it a record ID, specify the LOCATION MODE, and assign it to an area. Next, define the data elements. As item 9 shows, data items are defined using the familiar COBOL PICTURE clauses rather than TYPE IS, as with the CODASYL standard.

"Again I apologize for not doing what I expect both of you to do: use the Integrated Data Dictionary. However, I did use it for the PO record definition. The line that says: COPY PO RECORD VERSION 1 [item 12] means to do just that: When the schema is translated [converted into object code], the first version of the record definition for PO within the Data Dictionary should be retrieved and inserted at this point.

"The IV_ORDER record definition [item 10] illustrates the ability to CALL database procedures before or after DML commands. IDMSCOMP is a routine that compresses data in order to save room on the DASD. The other procedure, IDMSDCOM, reverses the compression and is to be invoked after a record is retrieved by an OBTAIN [FETCH in 1981 CODASYL] or GET command.

"Most of the SET entries are similar to or, in some cases, the same as the '81 standard. I'll emphasize the differences, unless anyone objects."

Although Alan and Kevin were getting overwhelmed by the technical nature of Barb's discussion, they had no objections, so she continued.

"I'll begin with the first set, BY__NU. First, note the slight difference in the way the sorting sequence is indicated. Simply code: ORDER IS SORTED. The sort key is specified in the MEMBER clause, as was the case with the CODASYL examples you've both seen.

"Next, look at item 13. It says that the set is to be physically implemented as a linked list [MODE IS CHAIN] and that backwards, or prior, pointers are to be used [LINKED TO PRIOR]. As an example that uses a pointer array, look at the CONTAINS set [item 16].

"Let me talk a bit about owner pointers and the LINKED TO OWNER clause. I didn't use it with the BY__NU set [item 15], because we don't need to access the SYSTEM from the NURSING__UNIT occurrence very often. However, I did specify it with the SOLUTION__ON set [item 18], which relates a given drug—actually a FORMULARY occurrence—with the related IV orders. I carry only the drug's code in IV__ORDER; if we need the drug's description, we'll have to FIND the FORMULARY owner of the IV__ORDER by means of this set. I realized the LINKED TO OWNER would result in an owner pointer being stored in the IV__

ORDER occurrences—it's the member of the set—but it will provide the fastest possible retrieval of the drug's description.

"A problem that results from the optional pointer options like LINKED TO PRIOR and LINKED TO OWNER is that the relative position of each pointer in the owner and member records must be defined by the DBKEY POSITION clause I mentioned last week.

"Look at SOLUTION__ON again. Within the OWNER IS clause, notice the two DBKEY clauses, one beginning with NEXT and one with PRIOR [item 17]. Both use the AUTO option and state that IDMS is to determine a sequential, relative value for these pointers and that they are associated with the FORMULARY record type, the owner of the set. Let me describe what these owner [FORMULARY] pointers are. Each FORMULARY occurrence will have a head and a tail SOLUTION__ON pointer, indicating the first and last IV__ORDER associated with the medication. It is these two pointers that NEXT and PRIOR refer to. I think Cullinet should have called them by their more descriptive terms.

"The NEXT and PRIOR pointers mentioned in the MEMBER clause of the set refer to forward and backward SOLUTION__ON pointers that will be stored in occurrences of IV__ORDER, the member of the set. Use of AUTO here means that IDMS is to determine which of the pointers within the IV__ORDER occurrences refer to the SOLUTION__ON next and prior pointers. As I discussed earlier, each occurrence of IV__ORDER will also have an owner pointer. The OWNER DBKEY POSITION clause tells IDMS to determine for us which of the IV__ORDER pointers to associate with the owner pointer. You ought to be glad we didn't have to use an earlier release of

IDMS, because we would have had to come up with actual values for these pointer positions. Believe me when I say this was a difficult task!

"I want you to look quickly at the last line. It contains the single statement VALIDATE, which begins the schema compilation. Once compiled, the object module is stored in the IDMS Data Dictionary.

"I think that's enough. Any problems?"

Kevin had a question about her logical design: "Barb, we learned in the training course that probably the most important objective of a DMBS is to control redundancy. Yet, when I look at the design we came up with, I see redundancy all over the place. Can you tell me why?"

"Good question, Kevin. The redundancy is because of my desire to carry connection fields. Look at the IV__ORDER record type. There is a 1:M relationship between a PATIENT and his or her IV__ORDERs. In a CODASYL database, the set represents this relationship, and we gave it the name IVS__PRESCRIBED. Now, as you know, if we are processing a particular IV__ORDER, and we need to know the PATIENT to whom the order pertains, we could use the FIND OWNER WITHIN IVS__PRESCRIBED command to access the proper PATIENT. So you're right, the patient number data item in the IV__ORDER record is clearly redundant. However, it is likely that we will be converting to a relational database at some time, and I don't want to have to restructure the database. Also, we have a couple of 4GLs that we are trying out, and they also need connection items to work properly. Finally, by using value-based sets, we guarantee that the foreign-key constraints are enforced."

Alan had a question: "Barb, could you go over a couple of the set definitions? I noticed that while most of them are similar, several of them, including ASSOCIATED__WITH, appear different."

Barb replied, "OK, start with BY__NU. This set is used to process all the nursing units in nursing unit code order. Remember that it was one of the SYSTEM-owned sets we talked about earlier. I made the set's insertion AUTOMATIC and its RETENTION MANDATORY because I wanted the DBMS to always tie the NURSING__UNIT records to the SYSTEM for me, and there's no need to ever delete one or change owners.

"A similar set is CONTAINS. It relates IV__ORDERs to their IV__ADDITIVEs. Because each IV prepared by the pharmacy can have many medications added to it, we needed the set. The INSERTION/RETENTION clauses are the same as for BY__NU. Because it's impossible for there to be an IV__ADDITIVE without a corresponding IV__ORDER, I wanted the DBMS to automatically connect an additive record with its corresponding order, and once an additive is associated with an order, I don't want anyone to be able to remove it. I thought about using OPTIONAL retention, but that would have created the possibility of an IV__ADDITIVE being in the database without being connected to *any* order—a situation I wanted to prevent. By the way, the IDMS retention options, MANDATORY and OPTIONAL, mean the same things they do in the CODASYL model.

"Look at ASSOCIATED__WITH. It's got a couple of differences from the other sets. First, it is possible for us to not know which DRG [diagnosis-related group] has been assigned to a PATIENT at the time of admission. Furthermore, after assigning a DRG to a PATIENT, Admissions often calls and says the DRG was incorrect, but they don't know which one to use. Thus, I couldn't use AUTO-

MATIC. Since it's possible for a PATIENT to be without an associated DRG, I had to use OPTIONAL retention.

"I think that's all I have. Any other questions before we tackle the subschemas?"

Because there were no questions, the meeting concluded, but not before Barb asked her two employees to begin coding the subschemas.

The Subschemas Are Defined

After several meetings with Joe South, the billing manager, and Judy Rankin, manager of materials management, Barb's team developed 10 conceptual subschemas for just those two departments. Exhibits 4 and 5 show two of them.

Exhibit 4 represents the conceptual subschema that will be used by the receiving function. When a truck arrives with supplies, the receiving clerk will use a VDT to call up the applicable purchase orders and their associated detail items. If the order is complete, the clerk will designate this on the screen. Any shortages will be noted immediately, as will any items that weren't ordered.

Exhibit 5 shows the conceptual subschema for the billing function. This subschema is used to produce that portion of a patient's charges applicable to the use of items other than medications. A comparable subschema, not shown, is used to generate the pharmacy's patient charges.

When a patient uses an inventory item, a PATIENT-USAGE record is created that contains the patient's number, the item code that was used, the number of items, and the unit price. The occurrences of PATIENT-USAGE eventually are combined with those of MED-CHARGE for the billing system, which produces the patient's bill. The subschema for producing the final bill is not shown.

Exhibits 6 and 7 show the subschema DDLs corresponding to Exhibits 4 and 5. Although the subschemas don't have the

---

EXHIBIT 4   A Conceptual External Database for the Receiving Function

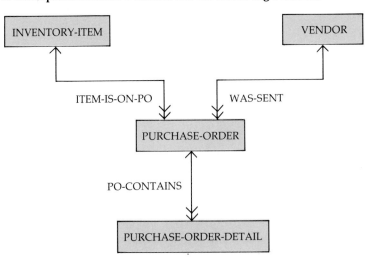

EXHIBIT 5   A Conceptual External Database for Materials Management's Billing Function

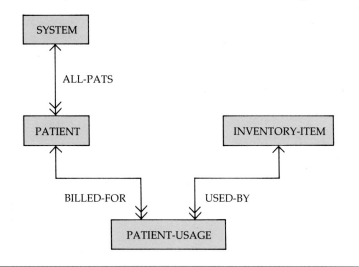

EXHIBIT 6   The IDMS Subschema DDL for the Conceptual External Database in Exhibit 4

```
ADD
SUBSCHEMA NAME IS RECEIVING
 OF SCHEMA PAT-CARE
 DMCL NAME IS HOSP-DMCL
 PUBLIC ACCESS IS ALLOWED FOR ALL.
ADD
AREA NAME IS AREA-1
  DEFAULT USAGE IS SHARED UPDATE.
ADD
RECORD NAME IS PURCHASE-ORDER
   ELEMENTS ARE ALL.
ADD
RECORD NAME IS PURCHASE-ORDER-DETAIL
    ELEMENTS ARE ALL.
ADD
RECORD NAME IS INVENTORY-ITEM
   ELEMENTS ARE ALL.
ADD
RECORD NAME IS VENDOR
   ELEMENTS ARE ALL.
ADD
    SET NAME WAS-SENT.
ADD
    SET NAME PO-CONTAINS.
ADD
    SET NAME ITEM-IS-ON-PO.
GENERATE
```

EXHIBIT 7   The IDMS Subschema DDL for the Conceptual External Database in Exhibit 5

```
ADD
SUBSCHEMA NAME IS MM-BILLS
   OF SCHEMA PAT_CARE.
   DMCL NAME IS HOSP-DMCL
   PUBLIC ACCESS IS ALLOWED FOR ALL.
ADD
AREA NAME IS AREA-1
   DEFAULT USAGE IS SHARED UPDATE.
ADD
RECORD NAME IS  PATIENT
   ELEMENTS ARE ALL.
ADD
RECORD NAME IS INVENTORY-ITEM
   ELEMENTS ARE ALL.
ADD
RECORD NAME IS PATIENT-USAGE
   ELEMENTS ARE ALL.
ADD
SET NAME ALL-PATS.
ADD
SET NAME BILLED-FOR.
ADD
SET NAME USED-BY.
GENERATE
```

CODASYL subschema DIVISIONs, the general structure is the same as that which we saw in Chapter 9.

Because Barb decided not to restrict the ability of anyone in the billing or receiving functions to see data items within the records, she was able to simply copy in all the elements for each record from the IDMS Data Dictionary. Also copied in were the record and set definitions.

To omit some data elements, Barb would have listed just those that were desired. For example, to include just a VENDOR's name and address into a VENDOR definition, she might have coded:

```
ADD RECORD NAME IS VENDOR
    ELEMENTS ARE
        VNAME
        VADDRESS
        VSTATE
        VZIP.
```

One difference from the 1981 standard is the need to specify the DMCL name. Although we chose not to show the coding for you, we assumed its name to be HOSP-DMCL.

The last statement, GENERATE, causes the subschema to be compiled.

CHAPTER

10

The CODASYL Data Manipulation Language

MINICASE Microtech Luggage Company—Continued

Mary Robbins just received an information systems request from her director. It seems that Jenny Harris, the production manager, asked for a system that will tie in with the schema Mary has already designed. (See the minicase in Chapter 9.)

Jenny wanted to track the costs associated with luggage as it is being produced. Much of Microtech's business was project oriented, and production runs often were specific to the requirements of individual customers. As a result, Jenny needed to be able to tie the costs from the payables database to a particular project or product line.

After discussions with Jenny and her staff, Mary decided to modify her schema by defining three new entities, Customer, Project, and Line, and two new sets, Customer__Project and Project__Line. It was easy for her to change the conceptual schema. All she did was draw the three conceptual records and two relationships on her old DSD, then connect the existing DETAIL record type to PRO-

JECT. Thus, each PROJECT could be associated with costs from several DETAIL items. When asked how she was going to implement the changes on the existing database, she replied, "Don't worry. The database approach makes it easy to add relationships or entities. I'll worry about implementation when I begin coding."

However, Mary was beginning to worry about referential integrity, especially deletion integrity. As the conceptual database grew, she correctly reasoned that it was becoming too easy for someone to, for example, delete a VENDOR record without realizing that several INVOICE records were associated with the vendor or to delete an INVOICE but forget to delete the related DETAIL items.

To compound the problem, Microtech had just acquired a query program that worked with its CODASYL-compliant DBMS. Although its ability to navigate the sets was limited, it could easily be used to query a single record type. Unfortunately, it transparently interfaced with the DBMS to update and insert into individual record types, that is, users weren't aware that the package called the DBMS. Mary wanted to prevent end users from adding items to member record types without the DBMS checking all foreign keys, and she wanted to ensure that all domains were correct before record occurrences were added. Because the query package bypassed the normal editing routines, Mary felt that the DBMS should be responsible for domain and referential integrity.

Discussion

1. Under what circumstances is Mary right about the ease with which the database approach can assimilate new transactions?

2. Based on your knowledge from the previous chapter, what changes to the physical database will be necessary? Will such changes be easy to implement assuming that all changes must be made by writing COBOL programs? How might these be accomplished?

3. Is it easier to accommodate changes with the relational model or the network model? Why?

4. What kind of deletion integrity is justified for the VENDOR/INVOICE relationship? For the INVOICE/DETAIL? (You might need to review Chapter 2.)

5. What DDL features can Mary use to assist with insertion integrity? With domain enforcement?

This chapter looks at the programmer's interface to a CODASYL-based DBMS. It uses COBOL as the host language, but the concepts described apply regardless of the language used to develop the run-unit.

Most implementations of CODASYL DBMSs require the use of a precompiler like the one we saw with DB2. The input to the precompiler is the source program containing the DML statements. These DML statements aren't recognizable by the compiler, so the precompiler substitutes CALL statements to the DBMS, changing the original source statements into comments so that the programmer can see what was originally coded. The altered source program is then compiled and linked normally, resulting in a run-unit.

The run-unit first invokes the appropriate subschema through a new SECTION in the DATA DIVISION. Once it does so, the run-unit has access not only to all the defined sets, records, and data items but also to some new variables, which CODASYL calls *registers*.

The DBMS maintains the data in the database through DML calls it receives from the run-unit. The calls can be grouped into five categories:

- Housekeeping
- Retrieval
- Storage

- Maintenance
- Transaction processing

  At the conclusion of this chapter, you will be able to:

- Invoke a subschema
- Use the error codes returned to a run-unit
- Add, delete, or modify records using the DML with a COBOL host language
- Write transaction processing programs
- Use DECLARATIVES to automatically trap errors
- Discuss how the CODASYL network model implements data integrity
- Show how concurrency can be controlled

10.1 INVOKING THE SUBSCHEMA: HOW TO ACCESS THE DESIRED USER VIEW

Before we can begin the DML to maintain our database, we must inform the DBMS about which subschema to use. We do this by adding a new database SECTION at the beginning of the DATA DIVISION, which is coded as shown in Figure 10.1.

Notice the substitution of the hyphen for the underscore, because the underscore is not an acceptable COBOL character. Had an ACCESS CONTROL

FIGURE 10.1   **Defining the Subschema to Use**

```
DATA DIVISION.
SUBSCHEMA SECTION.
DB subschema-name WITHIN schema-name.
FILE SECTION.
 .
 .
 .
```

For instance, to invoke Sandy's subschema, code:

```
SUBSCHEMA SECTION. ⟵
DB SANDY WITHIN A-P.
```

⟵ Source subschema statements are copied into here in the COBOL source listing

A new SECTION is coded in the DATA DIVISION.

LOCK been specified for the subschema in the DDL, the corresponding control key value would be coded immediately following the DB statement.

When the program is compiled, many of the commercial DBMSs copy the subschema source statements into the source program directly after the DB statement. This makes debugging easier, because the source program listing will contain the definition of all the records, sets, and data items from the subschema.

10.2   THE SPECIAL REGISTERS: COMMUNICATING WITH THE DBMS

The DBMS creates several special storage areas, called **registers,** which collectively represent a facility with which the run-unit can communicate with the DBMS and, more important, with which the DBMS can communicate with the run-unit. In Chapter 9, we called these registers the *communications area* (see Figure 9.4).

DB-STATUS: Determining the Success or Failure of a DML Call

DB-STATUS, the most important register, is a seven-byte item whose value indicates the status of the result of a call to the DBMS. A value of zero indicates that the call was successful; any other value is called a **database exception.**

The first two bytes, which are called the **statement code,** designate the type of call that was in progress when the error was trapped. Table 10.1 shows the possible statement code values.

The remaining five bytes, called the **database status code,** specify the kind of error. Some of the important database status codes are listed in Table 10.2.

Problem 1. **How can we detect the end of a set occurrence while executing a FIND operation?**

Solution. FIND is used to locate a record in the database. The value of DB-STATUS will be 0502100.

Problem 2. **How can we determine if a hashed access was unsuccessful?**

Solution. Again, we will encounter this condition only when issuing a FIND. Thus, the value of DB-STATUS will be 0502400.

Problem 3. **How can we determine if a record being added to the database contains a duplicate primary key value?**

Solution. We use the STORE command to insert a new record. The value of DB-STATUS will be 1505100. The statement code is 15, because the statement

TABLE 10.1   **The First Two Bytes in DB-STATUS**

DML Command	Two-Byte Statement Code
COMMIT	01
CONNECT	02
DISCONNECT	03
ERASE (DELETE)	04
FIND	05
FINISH	06
GET	08
KEEP	10
MODIFY	11
ORDER	12
READY	13
ROLLBACK	14
STORE	15

TABLE 10.2   **Summary of the Major Database Status Codes**

Status Code	Meaning
01100	A deadlock prevents completion of the operation
01300	A database key contains a NULL value
02100	An end of set or end of area has been detected
02200	A request for an unavailable area has been detected
02400	No record that satisfies the record selection criterion can be found
03200	The current of run-unit is NULL
05100	The record contains a duplicate data item
05300	A data item violates a CHECK clause
07100	Access of a deleted record has been attempted
07200	Deletion of a nonempty MANDATORY set occurrence has been attempted
09400	A concurrent run-unit has caused a READY conflict
90100	The resource is locked due to a PRIVACY LOCK

involved STORE. The database status code was 05100, indicating a duplicate. Had we been attempting to change an existing record (MODIFY), the database exception would have been 1105100.

Problem 4. **What value of DB-STATUS indicates a duplicate sort key value (ORDER IS SORTED. DUPLICATES NOT ALLOWED) when adding a new record?**

Solution. The solution is the same as that in Problem 3. There is only one error code that designates a duplicate data item condition.

The Other Registers

The other registers, while less important than DB-STATUS, are useful when DB-STATUS indicates an error.

DB-SET-NAME. If DB-STATUS is not equal to zero and the operation causing the error involved a set, the DB-SET-NAME register will contain the set's name.

DB-RECORD-NAME. The name of the current of record is moved to the DB-RECORD-NAME register following a FIND command. The value of this register is independent of the value of DB-STATUS.

DB-DATA-NAME. Following any operation that accesses data items, the DB-DATA-NAME register will contain the name of a data item. The value of this register is also independent of the value of DB-STATUS.

When a nonzero value of DB-STATUS is found, you can display or print these registers to help determine which data might have caused the error. An example might be:

```
IF DB-STATUS NOT = 0
    THEN
            DISPLAY 'ERROR DETECTED, STATUS WAS: ', DB-STATUS
            DISPLAY 'ERROR OCCURRED WHILE PROCESSING SET ',
            DB-SET-NAME
            DISPLAY 'RECORD WAS: ',DB-RECORD-NAME
            DISPLAY 'THE DATA ITEM WAS: ',DB-DATA-NAME
            DB-SET-NAME
END-IF
```

We are now ready to study the DML. It is procedural and requires that the programmer have intimate knowledge not only of record and data names but of set (access path) names. Table 10.3 summarizes the commands we will be discussing.

10.3 HOUSEKEEPING COMMANDS: READY AND FINISH

The housekeeping commands function like the COBOL OPEN and CLOSE commands. We READY a database at the beginning of a program and (usually) FINISH it at the end. Recall from our earlier discussions that a database is divided into physical units called *areas*, or *realms*, and that these realms represent the physical files to the operating systems. Each record type is assigned to an area through either the DDL (pre-1981) or the DSDL (1981 and later).

TABLE 10.3   **Summary of the CODASYL DML**

DML Command	Meaning
COMMIT	Physically post all database activity since last quiet point (last COMMIT)
CONNECT	Add record into specified set occurrences that use MANUAL or OPTIONAL set clauses in DDL
DISCONNECT	Remove member record from specified set occurrence provided the set uses OPTIONAL membership
ERASE	Delete record from database
FIND	Locate a record and make it current of run-unit, record, and all sets in which it is a member or owner
FINISH	Close a realm
GET	Place a record into the UWA
MODIFY	Change contents of a record by transferring UWA to the database
READY	Open a realm
RECONNECT	DISCONNECT a record from one set occurrence and CONNECT it to another
ROLLBACK	Remove all changes to a database that haven't been committed
STORE	Insert a new record into the database by transferring contents of UWA

To make a realm available to the run-unit, we use the READY command. The format is:

$$\text{READY [realm-name] USAGE-MODE IS} \begin{bmatrix} \text{EXCLUSIVE} \\ \text{PROTECTED} \end{bmatrix} \begin{Bmatrix} \text{RETRIEVAL} \\ \text{UPDATE} \end{Bmatrix}$$

To close a realm, we use the FINISH command. Its format is:

$$\text{FINISH [realm-name]}$$

Use of RETRIEVAL results in the records within the realm (area) being read only; they cannot be updated. On the other hand, UPDATE permits new records to be stored and existing ones to be modified or retrieved.

The other choices, EXCLUSIVE and PROTECTED, are more difficult to understand. They are concerned with concurrent processing controls. EXCLUSIVE means that only one run-unit at a time can use records in the specified realm. If a second concurrent run-unit attempts to READY the area, a DB-STATUS of 1309400 will result. While the PROTECTED option prohibits concurrent updating, it does permit concurrent retrieval of records within the realm.

If the database has been divided into multiple realms, each realm must be opened by a separate READY statement, assuming that the run-unit requires access to it. When the realm is closed by issuing the FINISH call, it and all of its associated records become available for other run-units to use regardless of whether EXCLUSIVE or PROTECTED is selected.

10.4   RETRIEVAL COMMANDS: FIND AND GET

To make a record available to a run-unit, we use the pair of commands FIND and GET. The 1981 JOD added FETCH, a command that combines the functions of FIND and GET.

FIND establishes the current of run-unit, the current of all sets in which the record participates, and the current of record. GET retrieves the current of run-unit and then transfers it to the UWA, the structures found in the DB SECTION discussed above.

Included in the record selection options for FIND are the abilities to access records:

- Randomly
- Sequentially, based on the record's participation as a member
- Sequentially, based on RECORD ORDER key values
- That are owners
- That were previously accessed

When a FIND is issued, it makes that record the:

- Current of record
- Current of set (for all sets in which it participates)
- Current of realm
- Current of run-unit

To transfer the record to the UWA after issuing a FIND, we code:

GET identifier

In all cases, the GET command transfers the current of run-unit into that record's UWA. The "identifier" can be a record's name, in which case the entire record is transferred; a series of data item names, which causes just those items to be transferred; or omitted entirely, in which case the entire record is transferred again.

The FETCH command combines a FIND and a GET. When it isn't necessary to actually transfer a record to the host program, we use FIND. Most of the time we need to perform both a FIND and a GET, so we can usually use FETCH when available. Most DBMSs do not have the FETCH command, however, so we have chosen to use the more cumbersome FIND/GET method. Some commercial DBMSs substitute OBTAIN for FETCH

Random Access

To find a record based on its primary key, we use this syntax:

FIND ANY record-name USING key-name

Before issuing the call, we MOVE the desired key value into the RECORD KEY component(s). If the call is unsuccessful because there is no record that matches the item's value, DB-STATUS will have a value of 0502400.

Problem 5. **Retrieve the INVOICE record with INO = 'A12'.**

Solution. Figure 10.2 shows the COBOL syntax necessary for solving this problem. For this example— and most of the remaining ones— we assume the records to be retrieved are in a realm that is opened as UPDATE.

Notice in Figure 10.2 that immediately after the FIND ANY command, we first check for a DB-STATUS value of 0502400, then for any other nonzero value. The figure also shows how the source statements from the subschema have been copied into the application.

Sequential Retrieval

We will discuss two types of sequential retrieval: member records in a set occurrence and retrieval based on a record order key. In addition, there is a way to retrieve records sequentially based on *any* data item. Let's look at the sequential retrieval of member records first.

Set Sequential Retrieval of Member Records. To retrieve member occurrences in a given set occurrence, we use one of the following formats:

$$\text{FIND} \begin{Bmatrix} \text{FIRST} \\ \text{LAST} \\ \text{nth} \\ \text{NEXT} \\ \text{PRIOR} \end{Bmatrix} \text{record-name WITHIN set-name}$$

FIGURE 10.2   Random Retrieval of the INVOICE Record with INO = 'A12'

```
DB SANDY WITHIN A-P

    01 INVOICE.

        03 INO              PIC S9(5) COMP-3.

        03 IAMT             PIC S9(7)V99 COMP-3.

        03 IDATE            PIC X(8).

        03 IVEND            PIC X(5).

    01 ITEM.

        03 ITEM-CODE        PIC X(5).

        03 ITEM-DESC        PIC X(25).

        03 ON-HAND          PIC S9(7) COMP-3.

        03 ON-ORDER         PIC S9(7) COMP-3.

        03 USAGE-YTD        PIC S9(9) COMP-3.

    01 DETAIL.

        03 DINO             PIC S9(5) COMP-3.

        03 DITEM-CODE       PIC X(5).

        03 UNITS            PIC S9(7) COMP-3.

        03 SPRICE           PIC S9(5)V99 COMP-3.

    *

    * sets would be copied in also

    *

        .

        .

        .

    PROCEDURE DIVISION.

        MOVE 'A12' TO INO
```

FIGURE 10.2   (concluded)

```
* move desired key value to primary key data item

     FIND ANY INVOICE USING INO
```

↑ This is the name
of the RECORD KEY
in the schema DDL

```
* try to find the invoice

     IF DB-STATUS = 0502400

* not found...print message

          THEN

               DISPLAY 'NO SUCH INVOICE'

          ELSE

               IF DB-STATUS NOT = 0

* check other non-zero values

                    THEN

* an error was detected

                         DISPLAY 'ERROR FINDING INVOICE ',INO

                         DISPLAY 'ERROR WAS: ',DB-STATUS

                    ELSE

* OK...retrieve it

                         GET INVOICE

*

*   record now in INVOICE record in UWA above

*

                    move and print


               END-IF

     END-IF
```

FIND FIRST causes the initial occurrence in the specified set to become current of that set. Similarly, LAST will cause the last record in the set occurrence to become the current of that set.

Let's look at the role of the currency indicators on a FIND NEXT command. Complicating our discussion is the fact that we want to read a record, but the record is part of a set. It is the current of set rather than record that determines which record will be retrieved. We will examine two scenarios: the current of set points to an owner, and the current of set points to a member.

FIGURE 10.3   A Reproduction of Figure 9.10, the Physical Database for Microtech

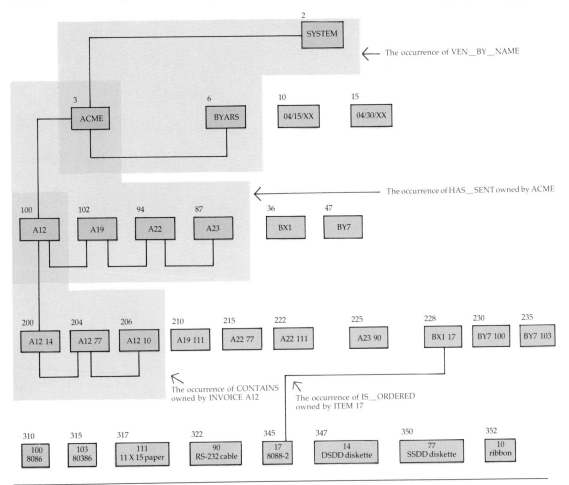

Effect of Using FIND NEXT When the Current of Set Is an Owner. When the set's currency indicator points to the owner of the set occurrence, the initial FIND NEXT will retrieve the first member record according to the specified sequence for that set. Subsequent repeated execution of the command will sequentially access the remaining member records.

Problem 6. **Print the DETAIL items associated with INVOICE number A12.**

Solution. At this time, we will show only the pieces that solve this problem; we will put the pieces together in our solution to the next problem. The purpose of our discussion is to reintroduce you to the currency indicators that we discussed in the last chapter.

Figure 10.3 reproduces the Microtech physical database from the previous chapter. We will use the RRN values as surrogates for the DBKEY values.

The algorithm we will use is as follows:

1. Randomly access the INVOICE with INO = 'A12'.
2. Use FIND NEXT to sequentially access the DETAIL records in the CONTAINS set owned by the INVOICE.
3. Stop when a DB-STATUS code of 0502100 is returned by the DBMS.

The first thing the run-unit should do is randomly find the INVOICE record with INO = 'A12', which we saw how to do in Problem 5. As Figure 10.4 shows, this makes the current of HAS-SENT, CONTAINS, run-unit, and INVOICE, all equal to 100, the DBKEY of the accessed INVOICE record.

FIGURE 10.4   **Currency Indicator Values after Issuing the Statements MOVE 'A12' TO INO and FIND ANY INVOICE USING INO**

Current of:	
Run-unit	100
INVOICE	100
DETAIL	NULL
VENDOR	NULL
CONTAINS	100
VEN-BY-NAME	NULL
HAS-SENT	100

To sequentially retrieve the DETAIL items associated with this INVOICE, the run-unit should repeatedly execute this command: FIND NEXT DETAIL WITHIN CONTAINS. The first time the command is executed, the DBMS will locate the initial DETAIL item associated with the INVOICE, making the current of run-unit, DETAIL, CONTAINS, and IS-ORDERED all equal to 200. This is illustrated in Figures 10.5 and 10.6.

Figure 10.5 shows that the current of CONTAINS (200) is associated with the first DETAIL item in the set owned by INVOICE number A12. Figure 10.6 shows the values for all of the currency indicators.

Effect of Using FIND NEXT When the Current of Set is a Member. When a currency indicator points to a member record, as it does in Figure 10.5, execution of "FIND NEXT WITHIN set-name" will retrieve the next member record in the set's occurrence according to the sequence specified in the DDL. This means that if we issue a second FIND NEXT DETAIL WITHIN CONTAINS, the DBMS would retrieve the record at DBKEY 204, the address of the DETAIL record with DITEM-CODE = 77.

FIGURE 10.5   A Pictorial Representation of the Currency Indicator for CONTAINS after Accessing the First Member of the Occurrence of CONTAINS Owned by INVOICE A12

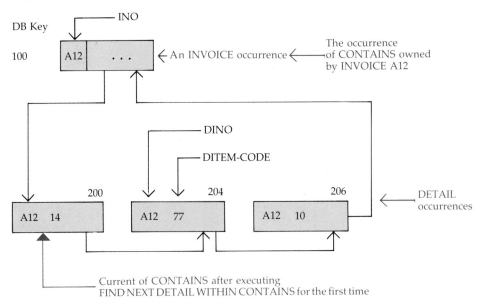

The command was: FIND NEXT DETAIL WITHIN CONTAINS. We could have used FIND FIRST DETAIL WITHIN CONTAINS.

FIGURE 10.6   **Currency Indicator Values Corresponding to the State of the Run-Unit as Depicted in Figure 10.5 after Executing the Statement FIND NEXT DETAIL WITHIN CONTAINS for the First Time**

Current of:	
Run-unit	200
INVOICE	100
DETAIL	200
VENDOR	NULL
CONTAINS	200
IS-ORDERED	200
HAS-SENT	100

The Other FIND Options. FIND PRIOR does the opposite of FIND NEXT, so it won't be discussed. It should be obvious what FIND LAST does, but perhaps not so obvious what FIND nth means. After substituting an integer value for n, it might be more meaningful to you. Can you determine what FIND 5 DETAIL WITHIN CONTAINS might do? It would retrieve the fifth occurrence of DETAIL in the current occurrence of CONTAINS, provided there are at least five occurrences to access.

When using any of the formats, the value of DB-STATUS will be 0502100 if there are no more member records to find.

Let's see some complete examples of how to sequentially process records in a set occurrence. Our general algorithm will be:

1. Establish the current of set at the desired location. If you want to begin at the first member, make the owner current.
2. Use "FIND NEXT record-name WITHIN set-name" inside a PERFORM UNTIL loop that terminates when a DB-STATUS value of 0502100 is returned.

Problem 7. **Retrieve all the VENDOR records by name.**

Solution. This is the report Gordon Reid needs for his Christmas mailing. It requires that we sequentially process the complete VEN-BY-NAME set, beginning with the first VENDOR in the set. Figure 10.7 shows the code to produce it. Figure 10.8 will be useful to you as you walk through the program. It looks

---

FIGURE 10.7   A Sequential Retrieval of VENDOR Records that Solves Problem 7

```
01    PROBLEM-SWITCH             PIC X VALUE 'N'.

      88 NO-PROBLEMS                   VALUE 'N'.

      88 HAD-A-PROBLEM                 VALUE 'Y'.

01    END-OF-VENDOR-SET-SWITCH   PIC X VALUE 'N'.

      88 NO-MORE-VENDORS VALUE 'Y'.

          .

          .

          .

      PROCEDURE DIVISION.

1         PERFORM 100-HOUSE-KEEPING

2         IF NO-PROBLEMS

3             THEN

    * initialize switch

4                 MOVE 'Y' TO MORE-VENDORS

    * priming access

5                 FIND FIRST VENDOR WITHIN VEN-BY-NAME

6                 IF DB-STATUS NOT = 0

    * any non-zero status...terminate

7                     THEN

8                         PERFORM 1000-WRAP-UP

9                         STOP RUN

10                    ELSE

    * OK... transfer to UWA and print

11                        PERFORM 300-GET-AND-PRINT

12                        PERFORM 200-FIND-VENDORS UNTIL NO-MORE-VENDORS

13                ELSE
```

FIGURE 10.7   **(continued)**

```
       * couldn't READY the realm

14             PERFORM 1100-ERROR

15             PERFORM 1000-WRAP-UP

16             STOP RUN

17        END-IF

18  100-HOUSE-KEEPING.

19        READY AREA-1 USAGE-MODE IS PROTECTED RETRIEVAL

20        IF DB-STATUS NOT = 0

     * problem...abort

21            THEN

22                MOVE 'Y' TO PROBLEM-SWITCH

23        END-IF.

24  200-FIND-VENDORS.

     * access next VENDOR

25        FIND NEXT VENDOR WITHIN VEN-BY-NAME

26        IF DB-STATUS = 0502100

     * end of set

27            THEN

28                MOVE 'Y' TO END-OF-VENDOR-SET-SWITCH

29            ELSE

30                PERFORM 300-GET-AND-PRINT

31          END-IF.

32  300-GET-AND-PRINT.

33        GET VENDOR

34  *    place statements to MOVE data to print line and print it here.

35  1000-WRAP-UP.
```

FIGURE 10.7   (concluded)

```
36        FINISH.

37   1100-ERROR.

38        DISPLAY 'COULDNT OPEN DATABASE...PLEASE TRY LATER'

39        DISPLAY 'ERROR WAS: ',DB-STATUS
```

FIGURE 10.8   The Evolving Concurrency Tables as the Program in Figure 10.7 is Executed

	Line Numbers		
Current of:	5	25	25
Run-unit	3	6	6
INVOICE	NULL	NULL	NULL
DETAIL	NULL	NULL	NULL
VENDOR	3	6	6
CONTAINS	NULL	NULL	NULL
VEN-BY-NAME	3	6	6
HAS-SENT	3	6	6
DB-STATUS	0	0	0502100

The second time line 25 is executed

The first time line 25 is executed

like the other currency tables, but the top line now contains line numbers from Figure 10.7 and the bottom row the DB-STATUS values.

In Figure 10.7, the housekeeping paragraph, lines 18 through 23, uses the RETRIEVAL option for the READY command in line 19 because records are only to be read, not updated. If, after attempting to READY the realm, DB-STATUS isn't zero, in line 22 we immediately set PROBLEM-SWITCH to Y.

We need to access the VENDOR records alphabetically by name. The set to follow is VEN-BY-NAME, and we will use the FIND NEXT syntax within a loop for our sequential retrieval. It is up to the run-unit to ensure that the current of VEN-BY-NAME points to the owner of the set before the initial execution of the loop. Because it is owned by SYSTEM, there is no need to formally FIND the owner.

After control returns to line 1 in Figure 10.7, we test to see if any errors were detected. If errors were found, we perform a routine that closes the open realm and stops the execution of the run-unit (see lines 14 through 16).

If no errors were detected with the READY command, we can loop through the VENDOR records. We begin with a priming read in line 5. We could have substituted FIND NEXT VENDOR WITHIN VEN-BY-NAME, because the current of CONTAINS points to SYSTEM, following a READY command.

After the priming FIND, the current of VEN-BY-NAME will be 3 (ACME). Because the end of set isn't detected in line 6, we transfer the record to the record name (UWA) using GET and then print it (lines 32 through 34).

The loop at line 12 controls the accessing of the remainder of the VENDOR records. It will be executed twice: once successfully for BYARS and then unsuccessfully, which will result in a DB-STATUS of 0502100. Let's look at the specifics.

The initial FIND NEXT VENDOR WITHIN VEN-BY-NAME in line 25 accesses the next VENDOR in the set, which would make 6 (BYARS) the current of VEN-BY-NAME. On the next attempt to locate the next VENDOR, the THEN clause of paragraph 200-FIND-VENDORS will be executed, because both VENDORs will have been accessed.

Problem 8. Print a report by vendor (in name sequence) by invoice (in invoice number order).

Solution. Our approach will be as follows:

1. Sequentially loop through each VENDOR using the VEN-BY-NAME set.
2. For each VENDOR, loop through all the INVOICEs from that VENDOR by traversing the HAS-SENT set occurrence owned by the VENDOR.

Figure 10.9 shows an appropriate subschema for this problem. Figure 10.10 shows the portion of the physical database the solution will navigate. You will find it useful for the discussion that follows.

This is basically the same problem that we saw in Problem 7 except that after finding each VENDOR, we must include another FIND NEXT loop that processes all the INVOICEs in the HAS-SENT set for that VENDOR. The DBMS should first access DBKEY 3 (ACME), then the INVOICEs at DBKEYs 100, 102, 94, and 87, at which point a DB-STATUS of 0502100 will be returned.

Next, the second VENDOR should be accessed. This has a DBKEY value of 6, corresponding to BYARS. The INVOICEs related to this VENDOR are at DBKEYs 36 and 47. Let's see how to do this in a COBOL program. For the complete solution, refer to Figure 10.7 and insert the lines from Figure 10.11.

Lines 32 through 34 of Figure 10.7 are reproduced in Figure 10.11. Assume the program is executing from the beginning. According to line 25 of Figure 10.7, VENDORs are retrieved by navigating the VEN-BY-NAME set. Thus, the first VENDOR retrieved will be ACME. After printing ACME in line 34 of Figure 10.11, the next line initializes MORE-INVOICES-THIS-VENDOR, a switch used

FIGURE 10.9   A Subschema for Problem 8

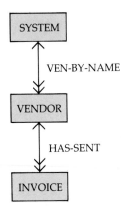

FIGURE 10.10   The Portion of the Microtech Database Needed for Problem 8

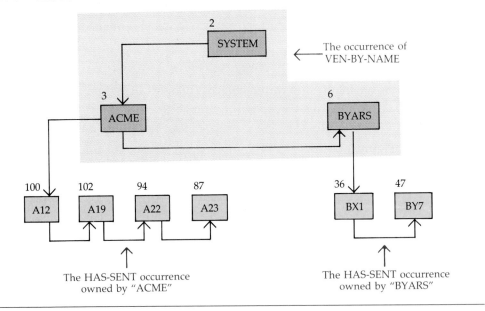

to test whether there are more INVOICE occurrences in the HAS-SENT occurrence owned by the current of VENDOR. As with any program containing multiple nested loops, we must reset the loop control switch prior to the PERFORM statement.

Next, a priming read is executed in line 36. The line could have been coded

FIGURE 10.11   Modifications to Figure 10.7 that Enable Us to Solve Problem 8

```
32   300-GET-AND-PRINT.

33       GET VENDOR

34 *     place statements to MOVE data to print line and print it here.

     * initialize switch for inner loop

35       MOVE 'Y' TO MORE-INVOICES-THIS-VENDOR

     *

     * see if there is at least one INVOICE for this VENDOR

     *

36       FIND NEXT INVOICE WITHIN HAS-SENT

37       IF DB-STATUS = 0502100

     *

     * no

     *

38           THEN

39               DISPLAY 'NO INVOICES FOR THIS VENDOR: ',VENDOR-ID

40               MOVE 'N' TO MORE-INVOICES-THIS-VENDOR

41           ELSE

     * found one... transfer and print

42                   PERFORM 600-GET-AND-PRINT-INVOICE

     *

     * process remainder of INVOICES, this VENDOR

     *

43                   PERFORM 700-PROCESS-REST

44                       UNTIL NO-MORE-INVOICES-THIS-VENDOR

45           END-IF

46   600-GET-AND-PRINT-INVOICE.
```

FIGURE 10.11   (concluded)

```
47      GET INVOICE
 *      Statements to move data to the print line and print it go here
48   700-PROCESS-REST.
49      FIND NEXT INVOICE WITHIN HAS-SENT
50      IF DB-STATUS = 0502100
  * end of set...set switch
51      THEN
52          MOVE 'N' TO MORE-INVOICES-THIS-VENDOR
53      ELSE
54          IF DB-STATUS NOT = 0
  * found another kind of error
55              THEN
56                  DISPLAY 'ERROR FINDING INVOICE RECORD'
57                                  DISPLAY 'ERROR WAS: ',DB-STATUS
58                  MOVE 'N' TO MORE-INVOICES-THIS-VENDOR
59              ELSE
  * transfer and print
60                  PERFORM 600-GET-AND-PRINT-INVOICE
61          END-IF
62      END-IF
63   1000-WRAP-UP.
64      FINISH.
65   1100-ERROR.
66      DISPLAY 'COULDNT OPEN DATABASE...PLEASE TRY LATER'
67      DISPLAY 'ERROR WAS: ',DB-STATUS
```

---

as FIND FIRST INVOICE WITHIN HAS-SENT, since we want to access the initial INVOICE sent by the VENDOR (ACME). Figure 10.10 indicates that the current of run-unit, INVOICE, and HAS-SENT would all be 100, corresponding to the address of the first INVOICE from ACME.

Had there been no INVOICEs for ACME, DB-STATUS would have been equal to 0502100 and the message in line 39 would be printed and the switch set accordingly. However, there was an INVOICE, so the program PERFORMs paragraph 600-GET-AND-PRINT-INVOICE (lines 46 and 47), where the first INVOICE record is transferred to the UWA and printed. Finally, the program repeatedly executes paragraph 700-PROCESS-REST until there are no more IN-VOICEs for ACME, at which time a value of N is moved to the switch, MORE-INVOICES-THIS-VENDOR. The first time through 700-PROCESS-REST, the DBMS would access DBKEY value 102, then DBKEYs 94 and 87 (see Figure 10.10). The next time through, the DB-STATUS register will contain 0502100, since there are no more INVOICEs for ACME. Now MORE-INVOICES-THIS-VENDOR will be set to N.

Control will now return to line 44, then back to paragraph 200-FIND-VEN-DORS, which will retrieve the next VENDOR, BYARS. The inner loop again will be processed, this time retrieving the INVOICEs sent by BYARS. This will complete the program, because when the DBMS attempts to access the next VENDOR in VEN-BY-NAME in line 25, it will discover a DB-STATUS of 0502100, so the END-OF-VENDOR-SET-SWITCH will be set.

Sequential Retrieval of Records Based on a Record Order Key. Using this feature allows us to perform sequential processing of records without requiring that they be members of a set. The expression is:

> FIND NEXT record-name [USING record-key-name]

Because there is no set name following the FIND NEXT, the DBMS will use the record-key-name search path. For example, in Figure 9.11 we coded part of the VENDOR record within the schema DDL this way:

KEY VNAME IS ASCENDING VNAME
    DUPLICATES ARE FIRST

These statements establish VNAME as an order key, enabling us to use the above FIND syntax to retrieve the VENDORs by name, without regard for set membership. To do so, we enclose the following line in a loop: FIND NEXT VENDOR USING VNAME or, more simply, FIND NEXT VENDOR. If the US-ING option isn't used, the retrieval will be based on the RECORD KEY data item.

Sequential Retrieval of Records Based on a Nonkey Data Item. There is a brute-force, nonpointer, nonindexed retrieval method we can use to sequentially access records based on any data item. The format is:

$$\text{FIND} \begin{Bmatrix} \text{FIRST} \\ \text{NEXT} \end{Bmatrix} \text{record-name USING identifier-name}$$

For instance, to search the DETAIL records for the first one that has a DITEM-CODE value 10, we would code:

MOVE 10 TO DITEM-CODE
FIND FIRST DETAIL USING DITEM-CODE.

To access the next DETAIL record containing this item, we would code:

FIND NEXT DETAIL USING DITEM-CODE

Finding the Owner of a Set Occurrence: FIND OWNER

There are many occasions when we need to determine the owner occurrence of a given member. This operation makes sense only when the currency indicator of the set is pointing to a member. Trying to find the owner of a set occurrence when the current of the set is NULL will result in a DB-STATUS value of 0503100. Attempting to find the owner of a set occurrence when the current of that set is already an owner will result only in finding the owner again.

The syntax is:

$$\boxed{\text{FIND OWNER WITHIN set-name}}$$

Because a record can have multiple owners, it is necessary to specify the set name to use.

Let's look at an example. Recall that Sandy Hill wants a detailed listing of INVOICEs that contain both item codes and descriptions. The algorithm to solve her problem would be:

1. Sequentially process all INVOICEs by navigating the BY-NO set.
2. For each INVOICE in the set, sequentially process the DETAIL items owned by that INVOICE by using the CONTAINS set.
3. For each DETAIL occurrence, FIND the owner of IS-ORDERED, which will access the associated ITEM, so that the description can be retrieved.
4. Display the information.

Figure 10.12 reproduces this subschema.

As an example showing this syntax, let's modify the example slightly to make it shorter to code. Assume that Sandy wants all the DETAIL items, complete

---

FIGURE 10.12   **The Subschema for Sandy Hill's Report**

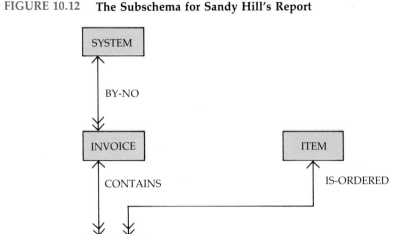

---

with item description and quantity on hand, for the items on a single INVOICE, A12. The statements for accomplishing this are illustrated in Figure 10.13.

The program begins by finding the INVOICE, establishing CONTAINS currency at the INVOICE record. Next, a loop control switch is set and paragraph 200-FIND-DETAIL is repeatedly executed until there are no more DETAIL items, indicated by a DB-STATUS value of 0502100. Inside paragraph 200, we access the NEXT DETAIL record contained on INVOICE A12. If it isn't the end of the set, we GET the record. Note that we used a short form of the GET command, which GETs the current of run-unit. In the ELSE clause, you can also see how we access the ITEM owner of the DETAIL record. DETAIL is a member of two sets: CONTAINS and IS-ORDERED. The respective owner records are INVOICE and ITEM. Because we need the ITEM owner, we used " . . . OWNER WITHIN IS-ORDERED." The second GET transfers the ITEM record into the UWA.

You might have noticed that the record's name isn't specified in the format when an owner is accessed. This is because by definition every set occurrence has one owner.

10.5   ADDING NEW RECORDS: THE STORE COMMAND

Adding new records can be quite complex, depending on the following options:

- The SET SELECTION for the set
- The INSERTION IS option

FIGURE 10.13   **A Program Segment that Includes a FIND OWNER Statement**

```
* first initialize the loop switch

    MOVE 'A12' TO INO

    FIND ANY INVOICE USING INO

    IF DB-STATUS = 0

* found it; retrieve all DETAIL items

        MOVE 'Y' TO MORE-DETAIL-THIS-INVOICE

        PERFORM 200-FIND-DETAIL

            UNTIL NO-MORE-ITEMS.

    PERFORM 1000-WRAP-UP

    STOP RUN

 200-FIND-DETAIL.

    FIND NEXT DETAIL WITHIN CONTAINS

    IF DB-STATUS = 0502100

* no more DETAIL items

    THEN

        MOVE 'N' TO MORE-DETAIL-THIS-INVOICE

    ELSE

        GET

* access ITEM owner of IS-ORDERED set

        FIND OWNER WITHIN IS-ORDERED
```

Access ITEM that owns the current of run-unit: a DETAIL occurrence

```
        GET

*

*   Place all pertinent statements to MOVE data and print it here

*

    END-IF
```

The command that adds new records is:

> ### STORE record-name

The basic algorithm for storing records is:

1. Read the record to be added from an input file or from a terminal.
2. Identify the proper owners.
3. Move the fields from the FILE SECTION record description area or from WORKING-STORAGE to the data item names in the subschema (UWA).
4. Issue the STORE command and test for duplicates and other relevant errors.

Storing Records that Are Owners Exclusively or Are Members of Singular Sets Only

If the record to be added is an owner only, or if it is a member of singular sets only, and the INSERTION clause is AUTOMATIC, the algorithm is quite simple:

1. READ the record to be added from a terminal or input file
2. MOVE the fields to the corresponding subschema names in the UWA
3. STORE

Let's write a COBOL program that will STORE the VENDOR records. The only owner of VENDOR is SYSTEM. Therefore, it is a member of a singular set, and our three-step algorithm will work. Assume the records to be stored are in a batch file called VENDOR-IN. Figure 10.14 shows the program.

The program uses the READ INTO format so that the record is not only placed into the input buffer area and transferred to the 01-level name, VENDOR-RECORD, but is also placed into a WORKING-STORAGE record called VENDOR-REC.

In line 13, if the test for the end of the input file is true, the program sets VENDOR-EOF-SWITCH to indicate this. The program assumes there is an 88-level item associated with VENDOR-EOF-SWITCH, called NO-MORE-TO-READ, because line 14 tests for it. When the end-of-file is detected, an undefined paragraph, called 1000-WRAP-UP, is performed, which will FINISH the database and CLOSE any open COBOL files.

If an input record is available, paragraph 300-READ-AND-STORE-VENDORS calls paragraph 100-ADD-IT, which STORES it. The coding is straightforward: MOVE each field from WORKING-STORAGE to the corresponding subschema data item name, then STORE VENDOR. The DB-STATUS check in line 33 is

---

FIGURE 10.14   **Example of a Program Segment that Stores VENDORS, Illustrating How to Insert New Records that Are Owned Only by SYSTEM or Have No Owners**

```
1  FILE SECTION.

2  FD    SELECT VENDOR-IN

3        ASSIGN TO...

4  01    VENDOR-RECORD PIC X(95).

5  WORKING-STORAGE SECTION.

6  01    VENDOR-REC.

7        03 VENDOR-NUMBER-IN   PIC X(5).

8        03 VENDOR-NAME-IN     PIC X(30).

9        03 VENDOR-ADDRESS-IN  PIC X(40).

10       03 VENDOR-CONTACT-IN  PIC X(20).

11 PROCEDURE DIVISION.

   * read input record into WORKING STORAGE

12     READ VENDOR-IN INTO VENDOR-REC

13            AT END  MOVE 'Y' TO VENDOR-EOF-SWITCH.

14     IF VENDOR-EOF

15        THEN

16            DISPLAY 'NO VENDORS IN INPUT FILE'

17            PERFORM 1000-WRAP-UP

18            STOP RUN

19        ELSE

20            PERFORM 300-READ-AND-STORE-VENDORS

21               UNTIL NO-MORE-TO-READ

22                  PERFORM-1000-WRAP-UP

23                  STOP RUN

24
```

FIGURE 10.14   (concluded)

```
25           .

26           .

27        100-ADD-IT.

   * move fields from WORKING-STORAGE to data item names in database

28           MOVE VENDOR-NO-IN TO VID

29           MOVE VENDOR-ADDRESS-IN TO VADDRESS

30           MOVE VENDOR-NAME-IN TO VNAME

31           MOVE VENDOR-CONTACT-IN TO VCONTACT

32           STORE VENDOR

33           IF DB-STATUS = 1505100

   * duplicate detected

34               THEN

35                   DISPLAY 'DUPLICATE VENDOR CODE', VID

36                   DISPLAY 'SKIPPING TO NEXT ONE'

37        300-READ-AND-STORE-VENDORS.

38           PERFORM 100-ADD-IT

39           READ VENDOR-IN INTO VENDOR-REC

40               AT END MOVE 'Y' TO VENDOR-EOF-SWITCH.


   * 1000-WRAP-UP not shown
```

where the test for duplicates is done. If we had imposed any domain constraints (CHECK IS), we could test for violations of them with a statement like:

```
IF DB-STATUS = 1505300
    THEN
            . . . DISPLAY 'INVALID VALUE FOR ',DB-DATA-NAME
END-IF.
```

Storing Records that Have Owners

Let's store the INVOICE records next. INVOICE is a member of two AUTO-MATIC sets that have non-system-related owners: HAS-SENT and IS-DUE. It is also a member of BY-NO, but that set is singular and the DBMS will ensure that all pointers are inserted for it automatically. The respective owners of the other two sets are VENDOR and DUE-DATE, which means that before issuing the STORE INVOICE command, we must be sure that the currents of both owners are correct so that the INVOICE will be inserted into the proper set occurrences.

The insertion algorithm is now:

1. READ an input record from the batch file or terminal.
2. Ensure that the proper occurrence of the owner record type for each set is current of its record type.
3. MOVE data from the input fields to the subschema data items.
4. STORE the record.
5. Test for duplicates and other errors.

There are two possibilities to consider: The set uses (1) SELECTION is THRU KEY or (2) BY APPLICATION.

Storing Records When Set Selection Is Thru Key. Let's set the stage. Figure 9.11 established the INSERTION of IS-DUE as AUTOMATIC and its SET SELECTION as THRU KEY DUEDATE-KEY. The use of "THRU KEY . . . " means that the DBMS will automatically find the proper owner provided the host program MOVEs the correct values to the data items making up the KEY. It isn't necessary to code a statement to FIND the owner, because the DBMS will do so. The other set that owns INVOICE, HAS-SENT, is similarly defined, but the owner's key is VENDOR-KEY, which consists of VID.

In order for an INVOICE to be stored, its input record must contain enough data for us to locate both of its owners: DUE-DATE and VENDOR. The primary keys for the owners are DDATE and VID, respectively. Thus, the input record for an INVOICE must contain a due date and a vendor code value. We MOVE values from the input record area to the two schema key fields, then issue the STORE. Because SELECTION was BY KEY, we don't have to issue a FIND ANY to establish currency of DUE-DATE and VENDOR.

To add a new INVOICE, we use the program segment shown in Figure 10.15. The first DB-STATUS check, after the STORE INVOICE line, looks for a duplicate. Remember, a code of 1505100 means duplicate, but doesn't differentiate between a duplicate sort key value and a duplicate primary key. The next DB-STATUS check is for any other nonzero value. Among the reasons such a value would be returned are a CHECK IS violation on IAMT and failure to FIND one or both owners. If this occurs, DB-STATUS will be 0502400 but our program will not determine which situation caused the error.

FIGURE 10.15   Adding a Member Record to a Set in Which All Owners Use SET SELECTION IS BY KEY

```
WORKING-STORAGE SECTION.

      .

      .

      .

01   WS-INVOICE.

      03 INVOICE-NO        PIC 9(5).

      03 INVOICE-AMOUNT     PIC 9(7)V99.

      03 INVOICE-DATE      PIC X(8).

      03 INVOICE-VEND      PIC X(5).

   .

   .

   .


   PROCEDURE DIVISION.

   .

   .

   .


      READ INVOICE-IN INTO WS-INVOICE
* move a value to the key item for VENDOR-KEY (VID)
      MOVE INVOICE-VEND TO VID
* move a value to the key item for DUEDATE-KEY
      MOVE INVOICE-DATE TO DDATE
*
*   Next, MOVE values to the INVOICE database record data
*     items.
*
*   but don't MOVE values to IVEND.
```

FIGURE 10.15   (concluded)

```
*  It will take its value from VID in VENDOR

*  because in figure 9.11 we coded IVEND as:

*  SOURCE IS VID OF OWNER OF HAS_SENT

*

       MOVE INVOICE-DATE TO IDATE

       MOVE INVOICE-AMOUNT TO IAMT

       MOVE INVOICE-NO-IN TO INO

*  Finally, just issue the STORE INVOICE command, without

*     FINDing the two owners

       STORE INVOICE

     IF DB-STATUS = 1505100

     THEN

         PERFORM 20000-DUPLICATE

     ELSE

         IF DB-STATUS NOT=0

            THEN

                 PERFORM 20000-GENERAL-ERROR-ROUTINE

         END-IF

             END-IF
```

Storing Records When Set Selection Is Thru Application. If the SET SELEC-TION clause uses THRU . . . APPLICATION, as did IS__ORDERED in Figure 9.11, we must explicitly FIND the owner; otherwise the DBMS will connect the new record to whichever owner is current. This means that our last algorithm is still valid, but we are responsible for issuing the FINDs necessary to make the proper owner current of record type and set.

Assume that IS-DUE and HAS-SENT are both THRU APPLICATION. We add the statements in Figure 10.16 immediately before the STORE INVOICE in Figure 10.15.

FIGURE 10.16   **Modifications to Figure 10.15 Necessary If the Sets to Which INVOICE Belongs Use the SET SELECTION Clause THRU . . . APPLICATION**

```
FIND ANY DUE-DATE USING DUEDATE-KEY

    IF DB-STATUS NOT = 0

        THEN

            MOVE 'Y' TO PROBLEM-SWITCH

            IF DB-STATUS = 0502400

                THEN

                    DISPLAY 'DUE DATE NOT FOUND ',DDATE

    END-IF

        END-IF

FIND ANY VENDOR USING VID

    IF DB-STATUS NOT = 0

        THEN

            MOVE 'Y' TO PROBLEM-SWITCH

            IF DB-STATUS = 0502400

                THEN

                    DISPLAY 'VENDOR NOT FOUND: ',

                        INVOICE-VEND-NO-IN

        END-IF

* test to be sure both owners were found

    IF FOUND-NO-PROBLEM

        THEN

* continue with STORE INVOICE line, figure 10.15
```

The major change is the requirement to explicitly FIND the owners using FIND ANY.

The Impact of Automatic versus Manual Set Insertion. If the record being stored is a member of a set with AUTOMATIC INSERTION, the DBMS will determine values for all the necessary pointers when storing the record. However, if the set uses MANUAL, although the record will still be added to the database and stored, no pointers will be given values until we issue a CONNECT command. We will discuss the CONNECT command later.

10.6   MAINTENANCE OF EXISTING RECORDS: THE MODIFY, DISCONNECT, CONNECT, AND ERASE COMMANDS

We use the MODIFY command to change data item values for existing records. Like the GET command, MODIFY will work only on the current of run-unit. DISCONNECT is used to remove a record from a set occurrence but works only when the set has RETENTION IS OPTIONAL. The third DML command we will see in this section is CONNECT, which inserts an existing record into a MANUAL set occurrence. Finally, we will see how to delete a record using the ERASE command.

Changing Data Item Values: The MODIFY Command

To change data items of existing records, we follow this algorithm:

1. FIND and GET the desired record.
2. Use conventional COBOL MOVE, COMPUTE, and other statements to make the desired changes to the subschema data items.
3. Issue the MODIFY command.

The format of the MODIFY command is:

MODIFY [record-name]

Use of the record name is only for information purposes, because the command will change only the current of run-unit.

Problem 9. **A correction to INVOICE number A12 is necessary. The number of units ordered of item 10 has been changed from 12 to 11. Each of these items costs $4.00, so the amount due must also be changed from $128.00 to $124.00.**

Solution. This will require two MODIFY commands: one to MODIFY INVOICE and one to MODIFY DETAIL. As with any program, there are several ways to approach the problem. We will use a FIND ANY hashed access of the INVOICE, then use a FIND NEXT loop to locate the proper DETAIL (there is no DETAIL primary key). The program segment for doing this is shown in Figure 10.17.

FIGURE 10.17 **A Program Segment for Changing the Amount Value for INVOICE A12 and the Units Field for One of Its Associated DETAIL Line Items**

```
        MOVE 'A12' TO INO

        FIND ANY INVOICE USING INO

        IF DB-STATUS = 0

            PERFORM 100-CHANGE

        ELSE

            DISPLAY 'ERROR FINDING INVOICE. CODE WAS: ',DB-STATUS.

        PERFORM 1000-WRAP-UP

        STOP RUN.

    100-CHANGE.

        GET INVOICE

        MOVE 124.00 TO IAMT

        MODIFY INVOICE

        MOVE 'N' TO FOUND-SWITCH

        MOVE 'N' TO END-OF-CONTAINS-SET-SWITCH

        PERFORM 200-FIND-THE-DETAIL

            UNTIL FOUND-IT OR NO-MORE-DETAIL.

        IF NO-MORE-DETAIL

            DISPLAY 'COULDNT FIND DETAIL RECORD...UPDATE NOT

        COMPLETED'

    200-FIND-THE-DETAIL.

        FIND NEXT DETAIL WITHIN CONTAINS

        IF DB-STATUS = 0502100

            THEN

                MOVE 'Y' TO END-OF-CONTAINS-SET-SWITCH

            ELSE

    * must GET before using any data items

                GET
```

FIGURE 10.17   (concluded)

```
    IF DINO = 10

        THEN

        MOVE 10 TO IUNITS

        MODIFY DETAIL

        MOVE 'Y' TO FOUND-SW

    END-IF

END-IF
```

The solution would be much simpler if DETAIL records contained a primary key. However, none was specified in Figure 9.11, so we must sequentially scan the DETAIL records associated with INVOICE A12 until we find the desired item. We begin by randomly accessing the proper INVOICE record. If DB-STATUS has a nonzero value, we stop processing. In paragraph 100-CHANGE we first GET the current of run-unit, INVOICE, alter its amount field, and rewrite it using MODIFY. Next, we initialize some switches, then begin our loop of paragraph 200-FIND-THE-DETAIL to locate the desired DETAIL record.

That paragraph uses the FIND NEXT format to sequentially access and test all the DETAIL items associated with INVOICE A12. After first testing for the end of the CONTAINS set and determining that it is not, we GET the DETAIL record so that we can test for the desired item code. If the code is 10, we change the value of its units item and issue the MODIFY command.

However, there is a problem with our approach and also some missing statements. First, what should we do if the INVOICE is found and modified but the DETAIL item cannot be located? The total due for the INVOICE will not balance to the sum of the DETAIL line items. One approach would be to not MODIFY the INVOICE until we are sure that the DETAIL item can be found. Another approach would be to change the INVOICE back to the original amount if the DETAIL cannot be located.

As for the missing code, after we issue the MODIFY command, we should check DB-STATUS to ensure that the MODIFY was successful.

Removing a Member Record from a Set Occurrence: The DISCONNECT Command

At times we will need to remove an existing member record from a set occurrence. Either the record currently has no owner or we need to remove it from one occurrence so that we can connect it to another owner. The DISCONNECT command is applicable only if the set has been specified with RETENTION IS OPTIONAL. The format is:

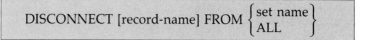

$$\text{DISCONNECT [record-name] FROM} \left\{ \begin{array}{l} \text{set name} \\ \text{ALL} \end{array} \right\}$$

The first format option disconnects the current of run-unit record from the current of the specified set, while the second removes it from all sets in which it participates as a member. In both cases, the record is still in the database but is no longer connected to the owner(s) or to the other members.

The algorithm to remove a member from a set is:

1. FIND the record.
2. DISCONNECT it from the set.

To use an example with the Microtech database, we need to assume two changes to the schema of Figure 9.11:

- The HAS-SENT set has RETENTION IS OPTIONAL.
- The IVEND data item is no longer based on the SOURCE item, VID, in VEN-DOR.

Having made those assumptions, suppose the vendor code associated with INVOICE A12 was incorrectly entered but the proper vendor isn't known. We need to remove the INVOICE from the HAS-SENT set occurrence owned by ACME but leave the INVOICE in the database.

First, we access the INVOICE record. Then we change the value of IVEND to blanks (however, NULL would be better). Next, we issue a MODIFY IN-VOICE, then DISCONNECT it from HAS-SENT. The code is shown in Figure 10.18. (We have omitted the MODIFY step).

If a set uses the FIXED option, its member records can never be disassociated with their original owners. In this case, we must delete the record and then STORE it again, this time into its proper set occurrence. If MANDATORY is specified, the member records must always be associated with some owner; hence DISCONNECT won't work either.

Inserting a Record into a Set Occurrence: The CONNECT Command

When a set has been defined with INSERTION/RETENTION options—AUTO-MATIC OPTIONAL, MANUAL OPTIONAL, OR MANUAL MANDATORY—the CONNECT command will add the current record into the current of set. The format is:

$$\text{CONNECT [record-name] TO set-name}$$

FIGURE 10.18   **Coding to Remove INVOICE A12 from the HAS-SENT Occurrence Owned by ACME, but Leave the INVOICE in the Database Not Connected to Any VENDOR**

```
        MOVE 'A12' TO INO

*  try to find the invoice

        FIND ANY INVOICE USING INO

        IF DB-STATUS = 0

*  status = 0 means found it

          THEN

*  the statements to modify the INVOICE would go here

            DISCONNECT INVOICE FROM HAS-SENT

*  see if disconnect was OK

            IF DB-STATUS NOT = 0

** oops...it wasn't

            THEN

                DISPLAY 'UNSUCCESSFUL DISCONNECT. ERROR WAS:',

        DB-STATUS

            END-IF

        END-IF
```

Assume the IS-DUE set uses MANUAL OPTIONAL. Now let's DISCONNECT INVOICE number A12 from membership in the set occurrence of IS-DUE owned by the DUE-DATE record with DDATE = 04/15/XX and CONNECT it to one owned by 04/30/XX. The necessary coding is shown in Figure 10.19.

The first line is pseudocode telling us to find the INVOICE as we have done several times. Next, we alter the value of the due date data item (IDATE) in the INVOICE record because it is a member of a value-based set, and we want the data to be consistent. If we disconnect the INVOICE from the old DUE-DATE owner and connect it to the new one, we want the IDATE value to match the DDATE value of its new owner. Using SOURCE IS in the DDL would accomplish the same thing, and more easily.

After the MODIFY is issued, the program tests DB-STATUS to make sure the

---

FIGURE 10.19   **A Program Segment to Change a Member Record from One Set Occurrence to Another**

```
* first find the INVOICE so the due date item can

*  be changed and the record disconnected from the

*  original due date owner

*    find invoice A12 as shown before, and check DB-STATUS

* assuming the find was OK, issue the DISCONNECT

      DISCONNECT INVOICE FROM IS-DUE

* now change the INVOICE due date data item value to maintain

*  the integrity of the value-based set

      MOVE '04/30/XX' TO IDATE

      MODIFY INVOICE

      IF DB-STATUS = 0

* modify was ok...connect to new due date

         THEN

            MOVE '04/30/XX' TO DDATE

* make proper DUE-DATE record the current of set

*  by finding it

         FIND ANY DUE-DATE USING DDATE-KEY
```

Not necessary if IS_DUE uses "…BY KEY" SET SELECTION

```
         IF DB-STATUS = 0

            THEN

* make the record being CONNECTed the current of

*  run-unit

*    find the INVOICE again

               FIND ANY INVOICE USING INO
```

FIGURE 10.19   (concluded)

```
* everything OK...CONNECT

              CONNECT INVOICE TO IS-DUE

          IF DB-STATUS NOT = 0

            THEN

                DISPLAY 'UNSUCCESSFUL CONNECT..CODE WAS: ',

                    DB-STATUS

            END-IF

          ELSE

              DISPLAY 'COULD NOT RETRIEVE THE INVOICE'

              DISPLAY 'CODE WAS: ',DB-STATUS

        END-IF

      ELSE

          DISPLAY 'MODIFICATION OF INVOICE WAS UNSUCCESSFUL'

          DISPLAY 'CODE WAS: ',DB-STATUS

    END-IF
```

Here we move INVOICE number A12 from the IS-DUE occurrence owned by 04/15/XX to 04/30/XX.

modification was successful. If it was, it locates the new DUE-DATE occurrence and makes it the current of DUE-DATE, IS-DUE, and run-unit. However, this creates a problem, because the record that is CONNECTed, INVOICE, must be the current of run-unit. After a FIND of DUE-DATE, that record is current of run-unit. Thus, we will have to refind the INVOICE record. Only then do we issue the CONNECT.

Deleting Records: The ERASE Command

We use ERASE to delete a record occurrence. The format is:

ERASE [ALL] record-name

Deleting a Member Record. To remove a member record from the database, we simply make it the current of run-unit, then code "ERASE record-name." Because under our assumption the record is only a member of a set, it will be deleted, and the pointers for all the sets in which it participates will be updated to bypass the deleted record. For example, let's delete a DETAIL item from INVOICE number A12: item 77. According to Figure 10.3, the record has a DBKEY value of 204 and logically follows the DETAIL occurrence with item code value 14 (DBKEY 200) and precedes item 10 (DBKEY 206).

First, we find the INVOICE using FIND ANY. This makes the INVOICE the current of CONTAINS. Next, we make the record we wish to delete the current of run-unit by sequentially issuing FIND NEXT DETAIL WITHIN CONTAINS statements until the desired record is accessed. As discussed above, the DETAIL item will be accessed on the second pass through the loop. Now we issue the command ERASE DETAIL. This not only deletes the record; it also causes the DBMS to update all set occurrences in which it participates. If we ERASE the DETAIL record with item 77 on it, the next CONTAINS pointer associated with DBKEY 200 should point to DBKEY 206. Similarly, the prior CONTAINS pointer for DBKEY 206 must be changed to 200.

A complication is that the DETAIL occurrences also participate in IS-OR-DERED occurrences. Specifically, the record we are deleting is owned by item 10. In Figure 10.3, you can see that there are two DETAIL occurrences in the IS-ORDERED set for item 77. The second occurrence is at DBKEY 215. This means that there will be only one occurrence after the deletion, and the following changes must be made:

1. The first and last IS-ORDERED pointers for DBKEY 350 must be changed by the DBMS to 215.
2. The next and prior pointers for DBKEY 215 must be set to 350 (the owner).

When an ERASEd record owns a set, the situation is more complicated and deletion integrity is called for.

Deleting an Owner and Deletion Integrity Enforcement. If the record being deleted owns a nonempty set and ALL is not used, the impact on the members, and on DB-STATUS, depends on the RETENTION clause used in the schema's DDL. Remember that there are three RETENTION choices: FIXED, OPTIONAL, and MANDATORY.

If we use FIXED, the members will also be deleted, because a FIXED relationship means that a member must always be connected to the original owner; thus, deleting the owner implies deleting the members. This is the cascade deletion integrity rule we originally saw in Chapter 2.

If the record being deleted owns a set that uses OPTIONAL RETENTION, the members will be disconnected only; they will still be in the database but will be left "dangling," that is, connected to no owner. This is similar to the "set-to-NULL" deletion integrity option. Such records can later be connected to another owner by the CONNECT command.

Finally, if the set uses MANDATORY membership and the set is nonempty, the request for deletion of the owner will result in a database exception value of 0407200. This is the restrict deletion integrity option.

If we use the optional word ALL, a cascade deletion will be implemented and all affected members deleted regardless of class membership.

Problem 10. Delete INVOICE A12.

Solution. First, we need to be aware of the sets that INVOICE owns. There is only one: CONTAINS. Figure 9.11 indicates that the CONTAINS set uses FIXED membership, meaning that DETAIL line items must always be associated with their original INVOICES. Thus, when we delete the INVOICE, all the associated DETAIL records will also be deleted. This deletion, in turn, affects the IS-ORDERED set, because the deleted ITEM records also participate in occurrences of that set. Since the DETAIL items are members of IS-ORDERED according to our discussion about deleting members, they will be removed from any IS-ORDERED set occurrences in which they participate.

The coding for deleting the DETAIL item is shown in Figure 10.20. The ERASE command will remove the INVOICE from the database as well as all of its associated DETAIL items.

FIGURE 10.20   **Deleting INVOICE Number A12 from the Database**

```
* first find the invoice as before

    MOVE 'A12' TO INO

    FIND ANY INVOICE USING INO

* should check DB-STATUS...assume OK

*

* delete the record

    ERASE ALL
```
↑
⌐ The record name is omitted...Current
  of run-unit assumed

Because the optional clause ALL is used, a cascade deletion results in the removal of all associated DETAIL occurrences.

Problem 11. Which records will be affected if we delete one of the DETAIL line items from INVOICE A19 and do not specify ALL?

Solution. DETAIL records are only members of sets, so only they are affected by an ERASE command. Specifying ALL will have no bearing on our answer.

10.7 TRANSACTION PROCESSING COMMANDS: COMMIT AND ROLLBACK

The CODASYL model uses the same two transaction processing commands that we saw with DB2: COMMIT and ROLLBACK.

Establishing a Quiet Point: The COMMIT Command

Recall the problem we had in the example in which we changed the amount on an INVOICE, then tried to change the quantity on a DETAIL item, but failed. When we attempted to find the proper DETAIL item, we discovered that it didn't exist and the integrity of the data in the database was violated because the INVOICE amount didn't balance to the DETAIL items. Use of COMMIT and ROLLBACK could have solved this problem.

The COMMIT command creates a **quiet point,** a time when all changes made since the last COMMIT are actually posted to the database. ROLLBACK will remove all changes made since the last COMMIT.

Removing Updates Since the Last Quiet Point: The ROLLBACK Command

If the run-unit issues a ROLLBACK, changes made since the previous COMMIT will be removed. In the INVOICE/DETAIL update examples, we would COMMIT only after both parts of our transaction were completed. If after issuing the MODIFY INVOICE we discovered that the desired DETAIL record wasn't in the database, we would issue a ROLLBACK, removing the change to the amount data item in the INVOICE. If, on the other hand, the DETAIL item was found and the change to the quantity was successful, issuing COMMIT would post both changes to the database.

We use COMMIT to end the processing of a transaction. Typically, we read a transaction from a terminal or batch file, update the database, and then COMMIT, which posts the transaction not only to the database but to the journal, or log, file provided one has been specified in the DSDL. Changes made but not yet committed are kept in internal buffers or temporary files. Only when we issue COMMIT or FINISH are the buffers flushed and the transactions posted.

The effect of ROLLBACK is to remove all of the postings to the database since the last quiet point. The ability to recover the data in the database comes from the log file. Remember that we can store before- and after-images together with transactions in this file, which can be on tape or disk. When we issue a ROLL-BACK, the before images will be read from the log and reposted to the database.

Use of COMMIT and ROLLBACK with Transaction Processing

A transaction is an event that enters the system, is posted to the database, and is then terminated. It can come from a batch input file or from an on-line terminal. A typical application reads a transaction, posts it, then requests another. Several things can go wrong: incorrect data is posted, a concurrent user interferes, or an error is detected in DB-STATUS. COMMIT and ROLLBACK, however, provide a mechanism for protecting the integrity of the data from the kinds of problems just mentioned.

An application should use the COMMIT command at the conclusion of every update transaction posting, which usually ends with a STORE or MODIFY. The approach is:

1. Read a transaction
2. Update the database
3. COMMIT

If the application detects a problem at any point in the process, we issue a ROLLBACK, which will restore the database to the previous quiet point.

10.8   RETAINING CURRENCY: ENSURING THAT THE DBMS DOES NOT UPDATE ONE OR MORE CURRENCY INDICATORS[1]

When we discussed the FIND command, we did not mention the optional clause RETAINING CURRENCY. There are times when we do not want the DBMS to update its currency indicators, because doing so will result in the processing of an incorrect set occurrence. The format of this clause, which can be attached to both FIND and STORE, is:

$$
\text{RETAINING CURRENCY FOR } \begin{Bmatrix} \text{REALM} \\ \text{set-name(s)} \\ \text{SETS} \\ \text{RECORD} \end{Bmatrix}
$$

---

[1]This section contains advanced material and can be omitted without loss of continuity.

FIGURE 10.21   An Incorrect Program Segment that Displays All the Other INVOICEs Containing the Items Associated with INVOICE A12.

```
 1  *    code to find the Invoice as before goes here

 2  *

 3  * now loop through the DETAIL items for that INVOICE

 4  *

 5      MOVE 'Y' TO MORE-DETAIL-SWITCH

 6      PERFORM 100-FIND-DETAIL

 7          UNTIL NO-MORE-DETAIL-ITEMS.

 8      STOP RUN

 9   100-FIND-DETAIL.

10      FIND NEXT DETAIL WITHIN CONTAINS

11      IF DB-STATUS = 0

12          THEN

13  * find the ITEM owner

14          FIND OWNER WITHIN IS-ORDERED

15  * now find the other INVOICE records having this item

16          MOVE 'Y' TO MORE-INVOICE-SWITCH

17          PERFORM 200-FIND-OTHERS UNTIL NO-MORE

18      ELSE

19          MOVE 'N' TO MORE-DETAIL-SWITCH

20      END-IF

21   200-FIND-OTHERS.

22      FIND NEXT DETAIL WITHIN IS-ORDERED

23  * the above statement updates current of:

24  *  run-unit, IS-ORDERED, DETAIL, and CONTAINS

25      IF DB-STATUS = 0

26          THEN
```

FIGURE 10.21   (concluded)

```
27              GET DETAIL

28              DISPLAY DINO

29          ELSE

30              MOVE 'N' TO MORE-INVOICE-SWITCH

31          END-IF
```

FIGURE 10.22   **A Currency Table for Figure 10.21**

	Line number in Figure 10.21								
Current of	1	10	14	22	22	10	14	22	22
Run-unit	100	200	347	200	200	204	355	204	215
INVOICE	100	100	100	100	100	100	100	100	100
DETAIL	NULL	200	200	200	200	204	204	204	215
ITEM	NULL	NULL	347	347	347	347	355	355	355
CONTAINS	100	200	200	200	200	204	204	204	215
IS-ORDERED	NULL	200	347	200	200	204	355	204	215
HAS-SENT	100	100	100	100	100	100	100	100	100
DB-STATUS	0	0	0	0	502100	0	0	0	0

In the situations we will examine, only the set-name option will be used. If the clause is used with a FIND command, the currency indicator value applicable to the named set will be left unchanged after the FIND is executed.

Let's look at an example. An end user at Microtech wants to look at all the line item DETAIL information for INVOICE number A12. For each line item on that INVOICE, the end user wants to know the invoice number of all the other invoices that contain the same item. For example, one of the items is number 77. This item also appears on INVOICE number A22. The (incorrect) code for implementing this is shown in Figure 10.21. As we walk through the program, follow along with Figure 10.22, which shows the relevant currency indicator values, and Figure 10.23, which shows the relevant portion of the physical database.

First, we find the INVOICE using the pseudocode in line 1 of Figure 10.21. Since INVOICE is a member of HAS-SENT and CONTAINS, the currency indicator for both sets is set to 100, the DBKEY for the INVOICE. As the first column in Figure 10.22 shows, the DBKEY for run-unit and INVOICE are also 100.

FIGURE 10.23   **Some of the Records Involved in the Program in Figure 10.21**

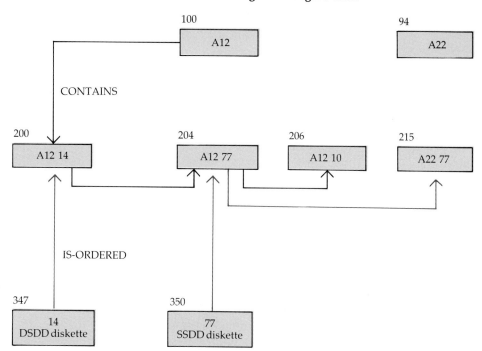

One of the colored lines indicates records in the CONTAINS set. The other color indicates IS-ORDERED occurrences.

In paragraph 100-FIND-DETAIL, the program begins to loop through the DETAIL items in the CONTAINS set occurrence owned by the INVOICE. In line 10, the first DETAIL item encountered is item 14, with a DBKEY value of 200. Because DETAIL is a member of CONTAINS and IS-ORDERED, the currency indicators in Figure 10.22 associated with both sets have been set to 200. Line 14 finds the IS-ORDERED owner. Its DBKEY is 347, which as Figure 10.23 shows, is the address of a DSDD diskette.

Next, paragraph 200-FIND-OTHERS is executed to find the other invoices. This loop sequentially accesses all the DETAIL records in the current of the IS-ORDERED set. Because we carry the INVOICE/DETAIL connection data item, DINO (the invoice number) in each DETAIL record, line 28 can display its value.

The first time through the loop, the DBMS again encounters the record at DBKEY 200, since this is the first detail record owned by item 14. The DINO value A12 is thus displayed. The next time line 22 is executed, a DB-STATUS of 0502100 will be returned.

Control then returns to line 10, where the next DETAIL item on INVOICE A12 is found to be item 77. Now the currency values for DETAIL, run-unit, CONTAINS, and IS-ORDERED are all 204. The ITEM owner of the IS-ORDERED set is found in line 14, making the current of run-unit, ITEM, and IS-ORDERED all equal to 350 (SSDD diskette).

The first time through paragraph 200-FIND-OTHERS, the DBMS will locate the original DETAIL line item containing item 77, as shown by the next to last column in Figure 10.23.

Look carefully at what happens next. The next time through the loop, the DBMS accesses DBKEY 215, the location of the next DETAIL record containing a SSDD diskette. As the last column in Figure 10.22 shows, the current of CONTAINS is now 215. Notice which INVOICE is the owner of CONTAINS—INVOICE number A22. This means that when control returns to paragraph 100-FIND-DETAIL and line 10 is executed again, it will FIND the next DETAIL record for INVOICE A22, not A12.

The problem is that the currents of both IS-ORDERED and CONTAINS are now 215. This occurred when we executed the FIND NEXT DETAIL statement in line 22. We need a way to prevent the current of CONTAINS from being updated when the statement is executed. That's the purpose of "RETAINING CURRENCY FOR set-name." The solution to the problem is to change line 22 to:

FIND NEXT DETAIL WITHIN IS-ORDERED
    RETAINING CURRENCY FOR CONTAINS.

10.9 DECLARATIVES AND THE USE COMMAND

When we attempt to FIND, STORE, or MODIFY a record, we should follow the DML command with a series of statements beginning with "IF DB-STATUS = . . . ". Because coding such statements can be tedious and the statements can be difficult to understand unless we know what each value of DB-STATUS means, we can take advantage of COBOL's facility for DECLARATIVES to reduce the coding effort and improve program readability.

A DECLARATIVE is a set of PROCEDURE DIVISION statements that is invoked only under certain circumstances, which are specified via the USE FOR clause. To tell the run-unit to use special code whenever a nonzero value for

---

FIGURE 10.24   **Informing the DBMS that Automatic Error Handling Is to Be Used**

DECLARATIVES.
DATABASE-ERRORS SECTION. USE FOR DB-EXCEPTION.

The SECTION must be the first one encountered in the PROCEDURE DIVISION.

FIGURE 10.25 **Defining When Automatic Error Processing Is to Be Executed and What Actions to Take**

```
WORKING-STORAGE SECTION.

        03  WHAT-HAPPENED           PIC X(3).

            88  END-OF-SET          VALUE 'EOS'.

            88  RECORD-NOT-FOUND    VALUE 'RNF'.

            88  CHECK-VIOLATION     VALUE 'CHK'.

            88  DUPLICATE           VALUE 'DUP'

            88  OTHER-ERROR         VALUE 'OTH'.

    .

    .

    .


    PROCEDURE DIVISION.

    .

    .

    .


    9999-ERROR-PROCESSING.

        IF DB-STATUS = 0502100

        THEN

            MOVE 'EOS' TO WHAT-HAPPENED
*
* end of set
*
        ELSE

            IF DB-STATUS = 0502400

                THEN

                    MOVE 'RNF' TO WHAT-HAPPENED
*
* record not found
```

FIGURE 10.25   (concluded)

```
            *

                        ELSE

                            IF DB-STATUS = 1505300

                                THEN

                                    MOVE 'CHK' TO WHAT HAPPENED

            *

            * CHECK violation

            *

                            ELSE

                                IF DB-STATUS = 1505100

                                    THEN

                                        MOVE 'DUP' TO WHAT-HAPPENED

            *

            * duplicate

            *

                                    ELSE

                                        MOVE 'OTH' TO WHAT-HAPPENED

            *

            * some other error

            *

                                    DISPLAY 'DB-STATUS was: ',DB-STATUS

                                    END-IF

                            END-IF

                    END-IF

                END-IF

            END DECLARATIVES.
```

FIGURE 10.26   Taking Advantage of the Error-Handling Facility Defined in Figures 10.24 and 10.25

```
MOVE 'A11' TO INO

FIND ANY INVOICE USING INO

IF RECORD-NOT-FOUND

  THEN

    DISPLAY 'No such Invoice', INO.

  END-IF
```

DB-STATUS is detected, we use the syntax in Figure 10.24 as the first SECTION in the PROCEDURE DIVISION. The lines indicate that the run-unit is to use whatever statements follow whenever a nonzero DB-STATUS is detected. Like any DECLARATIVE COBOL condition, the DB-EXCEPTION is the condition under which the DECLARATIVE is to be invoked. Following this line, we might code as in Figure 10.25.

As an example of how to use this, let's FIND the INVOICE record with INO = A12. Figure 10.26 illustrates this. When a DECLARATIVE of this type is used, we don't need to be concerned with how to set the switch, because it is done for us automatically.

10.10   CONCURRENCY CONTROL

There are several ways to control concurrency. The first method is to properly READY the realms. An abbreviated COBOL program segment that opens an area using EXCLUSIVE UPDATE while checking for other concurrent users is shown in Figure 10.27.

The main paragraph is 200-OPEN-AREA. It is executed until the realm is successfully opened (OPEN-SWITCH has the value Y), the database cannot be opened (PROBLEM will have the value Y), or the area is currently locked by a second user and the first user wants to quit waiting (the USER-RESPONSE value will be Y, and ANSWER will have the value Q). All of this controlling is defined in the PERFORM . . . UNTIL statement.

Within paragraph 200-OPEN-AREA, we first attempt to READY the area. If a DB-status of 1309400 is detected, we ask the user whether he or she wishes to continue waiting, in which case the loop is executed again, or to quit. If the user wants to wait, control returns to the 100-MAIN paragraph. Because no

---

FIGURE 10.27   A COBOL Open Routine for Detecting Concurrent Run-Units and Avoiding a Deadlock

```
01 ANSWER                    PIC X.

01 SWITCHES.

    03 USER-RESPONSE         PIC X VALUE 'N'.

        88 USER-WANTS-TO-WAIT        VALUE 'N'.

        88 USER-WANTS-TO-QUIT        VALUE 'Y'.

    03 OPEN-SWITCH           PIC X VALUE 'N'.

        88 DATABASE-IS-OPEN          VALUE 'Y'.

    03 PROBLEM               PIC X VALUE 'N'.

        88 CANT-OPEN                 VALUE 'Y'.


    .

    .

    .




PROCEDURE DIVISION.

100-MAIN.

    PERFORM 200-OPEN-AREA

        UNTIL USER-WANTS-TO-QUIT OR DATABASE-IS-OPEN

            OR CANT-OPEN

    IF USER-WANTS-TO-QUIT OR CANT-OPEN

        PERFORM 900-WRAP-UP

        STOP RUN

    END-IF

            remainder of program...
```

FIGURE 10.27   (concluded)

```
200-OPEN-AREA.

    READY AREA-1 USAGE-MODE EXCLUSIVE UPDATE

    IF DB-STATUS = 1309400

        THEN

            DISPLAY 'AREA IS LOCKED...C>ONTINUE OR Q>UIT ?'

            ACCEPT ANSWER FROM TERMINAL

            IF ANSWER = 'Q'

              THEN

                  MOVE 'Y' TO USER-RESPONSE

            END-IF

        ELSE

            IF DB-STATUS NOT = 0

                THEN

                    PERFORM 400-CANT-OPEN

                ELSE

                    MOVE 'Y' TO OPEN-SWITCH

            END-IF

    END-IF

400-CANT-OPEN.

    DISPLAY 'ABORTING...CANT OPEN THE DATABASE'

    DISPLAY 'STATUS WAS: ',DB-STATUS

    MOVE 'Y' TO PROBLEM

900-WRAP-UP.

    FINISH

    (  close any conventional COBOL files here )
```

switches have been set, the program will then repeat the procedure of attempting to READY the database. However, if the user wants to quit, the program first sets the USER-RESPONSE switch to Y before passing control back to 100-MAIN.

If DB-STATUS is any value other than 1309400, the switch that indicates a problem is set. Finally, if the DB-STATUS register contains a zero, OPEN-SWITCH, the switch indicating a successful open, is set accordingly.

The use of EXCLUSIVE or PROTECTED to control locking is of a coarse granularity, because it locks all records in the realm. However, if each record type is assigned to its own realm, locking will now be at the file level. While not as good as record locking, locking at the file level is much better than locking at the realm level.

Using READY and FINISH in this way can implement a suitable multiuser environment. As an example, assume two run-units are concurrently attempting to READY a realm called INVOICE-AREA, which is used exclusively for IN-VOICE records. Here is a scenario illustrating how file locking (realm locking) might work:

1. User 1 opens INVOICE-AREA as EXCLUSIVE UPDATE.
2. User 1 retrieves the INVOICE record with INO = A12.
3. User 2 attempts to open INVOICE-AREA as EXCLUSIVE UPDATE but sees a DB-STATUS code of 1309400 and goes into a wait loop.
4. User 1 completes updating the INVOICE and issues a FINISH INVOICE-AREA command.
5. User 2's wait loop ends because the value of DB-STATUS is now zero.

Another way to control deadlock is through COMMIT and ROLLBACK. By testing DB-STATUS for the code XX01100, where XX denotes any valid statement code, a deadlock can be detected. At that time, the ROLLBACK command should be issued. When a transaction is completed, and no deadlock is indicated, the COMMIT command should be issued. Most DBMSs automatically issue a COMMIT when the run-unit finishes.

10.11   PRE-1981 CODASYL DML DIFFERENCES

The most important difference in the CODASYL DML prior to 1981 concerns the FIND option that is used to access records based on primary keys. Rather than using FIND ANY USING, the earlier models used FIND ANY. This was because there was only one primary key (remember that it was called a *CALC key*).

Also, the earlier models lacked the transaction processing commands—COMMIT and ROLLBACK—and the ability to retrieve records based on ORDER KEYs.

10.12   TAB: A MICROCOMPUTER IMPLEMENTATION OF IDMS

Online/Database Software, Inc., markets a product called The Application Builder (TAB), which supports almost all of Cullinet's release 10.0 of IDMS and runs on a microcomputer. In the episode that follows this chapter, you will see that IDMS, and hence TAB, is quite faithful to the CODASYL model.

A main menu provides access to the IDD (Integrated Data Dictionary), the application development system/on-line language (ADS/O), several utilities, including one for uploading and downloading to and from an IBM mainframe, and a COBOL development environment.

Development of a database proceeds in the same way as with IDMS. After entering the records, elements, and sets into the IDD, the schema and sub-schemas are written and stored in the IDD.

The differences are:

- Aliases can be assigned to elements and records.
- No support for COMP-1 or COMP-2 data elements is available in the current release (2.1).
- Areas cannot be split across external files.
- There are no unload-load utilities for database structure changes; two COBOL programs must be written.
- Cullinet has a utility for restructuring databases; TAB doesn't.
- The data dictionary is only menu driven; there is no equivalent to Cullinet's command-drive Data Dictionary Definition Language.
- There is no journal file.
- Records are automatically locked during an update and released if the update is successful. The next release supposedly will include exclusive and shared locks for LAN support.

However, none of these shortcomings have kept the product from offering companies the benefits of doing program development on a PC and gaining the kinds of efficiencies we discussed with relational database application development on microcomputers.

10.13   SUMMARY

The CODASYL DML contains a rich combination of procedural commands to add, maintain, and delete records. In addition, its FIND command enables us to process records randomly or sequentially. The DML also contains commands to assist with data integrity and concurrent processing.

After each DML statement is executed, we test one of the communications data items, DB-STATUS, for possible database exceptions. If a nonzero value is detected, we take appropriate action, which usually includes a display of the error code. If a DECLARATIVE is used, such error trapping can be done by the DBMS automatically.

The UWA is specified by coding the SUBSCHEMA SECTION. This is the area in which we build records to be inserted by the DBMS and records are placed by the DBMS after accessing them. It effectively replaces the COBOL FD for the database records.

New records are inserted with the STORE command. If the schema DDL specified that all sets use SET SELECTION . . . BY KEY, the run-unit has to MOVE values to all the primary key components for each owner. It then MOVEs values into the data items in the UWA for the record to be added and issues a STORE command.

The FIND command is the most flexible of the DML commands and hence the most complex. Records can be accessed sequentially within a set occurrence or by RECORD ORDER KEY. They can also be found randomly based on a primary or secondary key. Finally, owners of set occurrences can be found.

Modification and deletion of records are also quite easy. When using the ERASE command, however, we must always be aware of whether or not the record being deleted is the owner of a nonempty set. In that case, we may or may not elect to simultaneously delete all associated member occurrences as well.

Insertion data integrity and update integrity are guaranteed if SOURCE IS is used when defining foreign keys and SET SELECTION IS . . . THRU . . . KEY is specified for the set. These clauses are coded in the schema DDL. Deletion integrity is provided by a combination of the ERASE command and the RETEN-TION clause in the DDL.

REVIEW QUESTIONS

1. What kinds of activities are prohibited when an area is opened as PROTECTED? EXCLUSIVE?

2. Explain what a UWA is and how it is implemented in a COBOL application.

3. Which form of the FIND statement would you use to:
    a. Retrieve a specific ITEM?
    b. Retrieve all the DUE-DATE records?
    c. Access the INVOICEs due on a DUE-DATE that is current of run-unit?
    d. Find the first INVOICE due on a given DUE-DATE when the currency indicator points to the third INVOICE due on that date?

4. What is the difference in retrieval order for FIND NEXT DETAIL WITHIN CONTAINS and FIND NEXT DETAIL WITHIN AREA-1 if the current of run-unit is positioned at INVOICE A22?

5. In the example where we deleted item 10 from INVOICE A12, we mentioned that this deletion would also affect the IS-ORDERED set. Show the new occurrence using an occurrence diagram.

6. Explain the impact of ERASE DETAIL if the CONTAINS set uses:

   a. FIXED.

   b. MANDATORY.

   c. OPTIONAL.

7. In Figure 10.10, which record would be accessed if we issued a FIND FIRST DETAIL WITHIN CONTAINS statement, assuming the current of HAS-SENT = 47?

8. Give a general description of the steps involved in writing a load program. Assume no intersection record types or batch input files. Use the Microtech DSD as the basis for your answer.

9. Which DML commands work only with the current of run-unit?

10. Under what schema DDL conditions is the DISCONNECT prohibited?

11. Explain the potential problem(s) associated with changing a connection data item value.

12. What does the clause RETAINING CURRENCY do?

13. What is a DECLARATIVE?

14. Explain how ROLLBACK can remove incomplete transactions.

15. What role does COMMIT play in your answer to Question 14?

16. Compare the ability of the CODASYL model to enforce domain constraints and referential integrity with that of the relational model.

PROBLEMS

Provide the coding necessary for answering Problems 1 through 11. Assume the UWA uses the same data item names as in Figure 9.11. Don't include the READY statement, but do show FINISH. Use pseudocode for the moving of data to the print record and its subsequent printing. For example:

"move INVOICE data to PRINT-REC and print it"

1. Assuming there are 1,000 different items in inventory and 100 invoices, determine whether or not item 100 appears on invoice B77. Use the most efficient search path.

2. Redo your answer to Problem 1 assuming that INVOICE and ITEM have no primary keys. Use the most efficient coding methods.

3. List the INVOICEs and their supporting DETAIL, including item descriptions, for those INVOICEs sent by ACME during October.

4. What is the total amount due for December's INVOICEs? (The two due dates are 12/15/XX and 12/30/XX).

5. List all the INVOICEs, together with the associated VENDOR information, on which item 566 appears.

6. Delete VENDOR ACME. Be sure to include consideration of all INVOICES the vendor HAS-SENT. Assume CONTAINS used FIXED RETENTION.

7. INVOICE B789 was mistakenly connected to a vendor with code BKR. It should be associated with ACME. Show all the coding necessary for accomplishing this, assuming that HAS-SENT uses RETENTION IS OPTIONAL. Why was this assumption necessary?

8. List the INVOICE numbers of those items whose on-hand amount is less than 100.

9. Are there any invoices from ACME containing an item with the description, "11 × 15 paper"?

10. List all the DETAIL records in the database, together with their associated invoice numbers.

11. Assume you have just read a SALES-IN record with the following format:

```
01   DETAIL-IN.
       03 INV-NO-IN                    PIC X(5).
       03 ITEM-CODE-IN                 PIC X(7).
       03 UNITS-SOLD-IN                PIC 9(7).
       03 PRICE-PER-UNIT-SOLD-IN       PIC 9(7)V99.
```

Show the coding necessary for storing a DETAIL record assuming all owners were previously stored and all sets use SET SELECTION IS THRU . . . APPLICATION.

12. Assume that INVOICE has no primary key. List the DETAIL items for INVOICE A12.

13. Using the assumption from Problem 12, redo the affected portions of your answer to Problem 11.

14. Change the name of ACME to "The ACME Rental Co."

15. List the INVOICEs due to vendors in California (state code CA). How might the DBA have helped to make your solution easier?

▪▪ EPISODE 6

A Report Is Written Using IDMS/R

Barb assigned Alan Jones to write the receiving problems and Kevin to develop the billing programs. Exhibit 1 shows the conceptual subschema Alan used.

Exhibit 2 shows one of Alan's programs. It includes only the portion of his program that asks the receiving clerk for a purchase order number, then proceeds to show the items associated with that order. Missing from the program are the logic for asking whether or not the order is complete and the subsequent processing for complete orders.

We will first look at the general logic of the PROCEDURE DIVISION. Then we will listen in as Alan describes how his program differs from the one that would result if the classical CODASYL model had been used instead of IDMS/R.

The program assumes that the order is

EXHIBIT 1   **The RECEIVING Subschema Needed to Update the Amount on Hand**

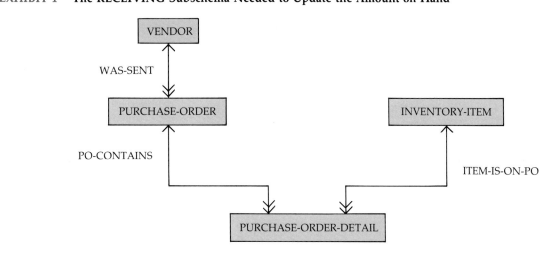

a partial one, so for every item on the purchase order, it asks the clerk how many of that item arrived, then updates the quantity of that item on hand.

Notice that in paragraph 150-WAIT in Exhibit 2, the program goes into a null loop if the READY command fails. The ON DB-OPEN-FAIL, explained later, is an error-trapping routine. It says that if IDMS/R returns an error code indicating that the area couldn't be opened, control is to again pass to the 150-WAIT paragraph. Use of this construct results in nonstructured coding.

The hospital realized that this could create a deadlock situation, but because there is only one terminal in the receiving area, it felt that the chances of such a deadlock were almost nil.

After asking for a purchase order number in paragraph 200-ASK-FOR-PO, the program checks for a value of zero, because that is the signal that the user is finished and the program should terminate. If this is indicated, the program executes paragraph 1000-WRAP-UP, which

FINISHes the database and closes any nondatabase files before terminating.

If the PO number isn't zero, the program attempts to use it as the basis for a hashed access (FIND ANY PURCHASE-ORDER), retrieves the purchase order record, and then displays it. Once this is done, the 300-F-DETAIL loop for each item on the purchase order is executed. It is within this loop that the user is prompted about the number of units of each item that arrived. The FIND OWNER is necessary because that is where the units on hand are kept.

When there are no more items for this purchase order, a flag is set and the clerk can request the next purchase order.

You might have noticed the error trapping is done differently than with the CODASYL model described in the chapter. The FIND ANY command also differs. Other changes were made to the ENVIRONMENT and DATA DIVISIONs as well.

As recently as one year prior to acquiring IDMS, the hospital wasn't certain that

EXHIBIT 2   **An IDMS/R Program that Updates the Purchase Orders by Requesting a PO Number, Then, for Each Item on the PO, Asks How Many Units Have Arrived, and Then Updates the INVENTORY Quantity on Hand**

```
IDENTIFICATION DIVISION.

PROGRAM-ID.                    MMPROG01.

        .

        .


        .

ENVIRONMENT DIVISION.
                       .
* set up CRT as a special name

 SPECIAL-NAMES.

 system-name IS CRT.

INPUT-OUTPUT SECTION.

FILE-CONTROL.

        .

        .

        .

IDMS-CONTROL SECTION.

PROTOCOL.

           MODE IS BATCH-AUTOSTATUS
```

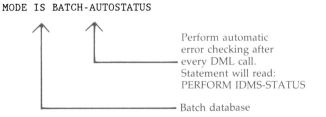

Perform automatic error checking after every DML call. Statement will read: PERFORM IDMS-STATUS

Batch database

EXHIBIT 2   **(continued)**

```
                    IDMS-RECORDS WITHIN WORKING-STORAGE SECTION.
```

Place source statements for all records, sets, and any necessary UWA communications into WORKING-STORAGE

```
            DATA DIVISION.

            SCHEMA SECTION.

            DB RECEIVING WITHIN PAT-CARE.
```

Schema name

Subschema name. Not shown in Episode 5

```
            FILE SECTION.

                    .

                    .

                    .

            WORKING-STORAGE SECTION.

            01   WS-PO-NO   PIC X(10).

            01   SWITCHES.

                    03 DETAIL-SW    PIC X.

                        88 NO-MORE-DETAIL    VALUE 'N'.

                    03 DB-SWITCH    PIC X    VALUE 'N'.

                        88 DB-OPEN          VALUE 'Y'

                        88 DB-NOT-OPEN      VALUE 'N'.

                    03 ACTION       PIC X    VALUE 'N'.

                        88 USER-WANTS-TO-QUIT  VALUE 'Y'.
```

EXHIBIT 2   **(continued)**

```
*    IDMS record and set descriptions would be

*      copied in here by precompiler because of the IDMS-RECORDS

*      clause above

* Next, the IDMS control register would be copied in here. We

*  show it for explanation purposes only. In reality it

*  wouldn't be inserted until precompile time

* COPY IDMS SUBSCHEMA-CTRL.


  01 SUBSCHEMA-CTRL.

        03 PROGRAM-NAME          PIC X(8).

        03 ERROR-STATUS          PIC X(4)

                                 VALUE '1400'.



        88 DB-STATUS-OK

           VALUE '0000'.

        88 ANY-STATUS

           VALUE '0000' THRU '9999'.

        88 ANY-ERROR-STATUS

           VALUE '0001' THRU '9999'.

        88 DB-END-OF-SET

            VALUE '0307'.

        88 DB-REC-NOT-FOUND

           VALUE '0326'.

        88 DB-OPEN-FAIL

           VALUE '0910'
```

EXHIBIT 2   (continued)

```
            03  DBKEY                   PIC S9(8) COMP SYNC.

            03  RECORD-NAME             PIC X(16) VALUE SPACES.

            03  AREA-NAME               PIC X(16).

            03  ERROR-SET               PIC...

            03  ERROR-RECORD            PIC...

            03  ERROR-AREA              PIC...

            03  ...



        PROCEDURE DIVISION.

    *  COPY IDMS SUBSCHEMA-BINDS

    *  COBOL code that binds run-unit/IDMS would be inserted here by

    *   the precompiler

                PERFORM 100-OPEN-DATA-BASE

                PERFORM 200-ASK-FOR-PO THRU 200-EXIT

                UNTIL USER-WANTS-TO-QUIT.

                PERFORM 1000-WRAP-UP.

        100-OPEN-DATA-BASE.

      * put pgm into loop until can open the areas

                    PERFORM 150-WAIT THRU 150-EXIT.

        100-EXIT.

                    EXIT.

        150-WAIT.

                    READY MATL-MGT-AREA USAGE MODE EXCLUSIVE UPDATE

                    ON DB-OPEN-FAIL
```

↑_____ Override execution of IDMS-STATUS
if get ERROR-STATUS value of 0910

EXHIBIT 2   (continued)

```
                GO TO 150-WAᴵᵀ.
    *
    * open OK... set switch
    *
                MOVE 'Y' TO DB-SWITCH.
      150-EXIT.
                EXIT.
      200-ASK-FOR-PO.
                DISPLAY 'Enter PO. #    (0 to quit)'
              UPON CRT.
                ACCEPT PO-NO FROM CRT.
                IF PO-NO = 0
              THEN
                  MOVE 'Y' TO ACTION
                      GO TO 200-EXIT.
                  MOVE WS-PO-NO TO PO-NO.

                FIND ANY PURCHASE-ORDER
    *                            ↑
    *                              ──── Note that there is no USING clause
    * or could use: OBTAIN ANY PURCHASE-ORDER, which eliminates
    *        the subsequent GET statement to actually
    *          transfer the PURCHASE-ORDER record to the UWA
    *

                ON DB-REC-NOT-FOUND
    * if hadn't used AUTOSTATUS, above line would have been:
    *    IF ERROR-STATUS = '0326'
    *
```

EXHIBIT 2   (continued)

```
            DISPLAY 'No such PO...try again'

            GO TO 200-EXIT.
```

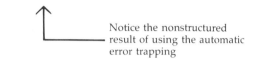

Notice the nonstructured result of using the automatic error trapping

```
            GET PURCHASE-ORDER

* Move and print the PO heading here

* next find all the detail items, after initializing loop

            MOVE 'Y' TO DETAIL-SW

        PERFORM 300-F-DETAIL THRU 300-EXIT UNTIL

            NO-MORE-DETAIL.

  200-EXIT.

            EXIT.

  300-F-DETAIL.

            FIND NEXT PURCHASE-ORDER-DETAIL WITHIN PO-CONTAINS

            ON DB-END-OF-SET

*

* if hadn't used AUTOSTATUS, above line would have read:

*   IF ERROR-STATUS = '0307'

*

            MOVE 'N' TO DETAIL-SW

            GO TO 300-EXIT.

            GET PURCHASE-ORDER-DETAIL

* move data and print it here

* assume the PO is a partial shipment, ask how many
```

EXHIBIT 2   (continued)

```
*  units arrived

             DISPLAY 'How many units ?'

             ACCEPT UNITS FROM CRT

* now find inventory and update on hand

             MOVE D-ITEM-CODE TO ITEM-CODE

             FIND OWNER WITHIN ITEM-IS-ON-PO

             GET INVENTORY-ITEM

             COMPUTE ON-HAND = ON-HAND + UNITS

             MODIFY INVENTORY-ITEM

*

* IDMS will invoke IDMS-STATUS if MODIFY returns non-zero

*   value for ERROR-STATUS

*

 300-EXIT.

             EXIT.

 1000-WRAP-UP.

             FINISH.

             CLOSE.

             GOBACK.
                ⬑─────── Return to IDMS control

 COPY IDMS-STATUS.

    (IDMS precompiler will copy IDMS-STATUS here)

* COPY IDMS IDMS-STATUS.
```

EXHIBIT 2   (concluded)

```
IDMS-STATUS SECTION.

    IF DB-STATUS-OK GO TO ISABEX.

    PERFORM IDMS-ABORT.

    DISPLAY '*************************'

                ' ABORTING - 'PROGRAM-NAME

            '  '               ERROR-STATUS

            '  '               ERROR-RECORD

        '  ****** RECOVER IDMS ****'

            UPON CONSOLE.

        DISPLAY 'PROGRAM NAME   -----   ' PROGRAM-NAME.

        DISPLAY 'ERROR STATUS   -----   ' ERROR-STATUS.

        DISPLAY 'ERROR RECORD   -----   ' ERROR-RECORD.

        .

        .

        .


ROLLBACK

ISABEX.

    EXIT.

IDMS-ABORT.

        DISPLAY 'PROGRAM ABENDED...DATABASE BEING ROLLED BACK'
```

that was going to be their DBMS. Consequently, it felt that many IS personnel should receive CODASYL training independently of any vendor's product. Alan, who attended these classes, was asked to make a presentation to the project team about how the IDMS/R DML differs from

CODASYL's. He would use the program listing from Exhibit 2 as a basis.

"I guess I'd better start with some of the mechanics for compiling a COBOL program," Alan began. "IDMS uses a precompiler that translates each DML statement into a COBOL CALL statement. For example, where I might code STORE VENDOR, the precompiler would substitute something like:

```
* STORE VENDOR
    CALL 'IDMS' USING
    SUBSCHEMA-CTRL,
    IDBMSCOM(42), SR508, VENDOR
```

"Notice that the actual DML is first converted into a comment. The SUB-SCHEMA-CTRL is a group data item used for communication with IDMS, IDBMSCOM(42) designates a STORE, and SR508 is the record ID for VENDOR that was assigned by the schema compiler.

"Next, I'm going to discuss the program changes I had to make by DIVISION. In the ENVIRONMENT DIVISION, I had to add a new SECTION: IDMS-CONTROL. Its purposes are to define the **operating mode** in which the run-unit is to execute, determine whether or not to invoke automatic error checking, and indicate where to allocate storage for the subschema records and the UWA.

"BATCH is the default. It means that the program will operate in a batch environment. Use of IDMS-DC instead of BATCH means an on-line, multiuser, centralized environment is required. When this is specified, the IDMS **central version (CV)** is automatically used.

"The PROTOCOL option, -AUTOSTA-TUS-, specifies that I want to have IDMS insert a source statement after each DML call, which automatically invokes the standard IDMS error-checking routine called IDMS-STATUS. The line will read: PERFORM IDMS-STATUS. I can override this automatic error checking any time I choose in the PROCEDURE DIVISION by using an ON statement. You can see several examples of this in my listing. Don't worry, I'll go over the ON statement later.

"The second line says that I want

IDMS to copy the subschema source definitions, records and sets, into the WORKING-STORAGE SECTION.

"Unless anyone has questions, I'll talk about the DATA DIVISION changes next."

No one did, so Alan continued.

"The first change is a new SECTION: SCHEMA SECTION, which serves the same purpose as the SUBSCHEMA SECTION did in the CODASYL model: It invokes the RECEIVING subschema and specifies the PAT-CARE schema name.

"Because I used the IDMS-RECORDS clause up in the PROTOCOL section, IDMS copied in the Data Dictionary definitions of all the records and sets as well as the other required UWA elements.

"The following structures are automatically inserted into WORKING-STORAGE: SUBSCHEMA-CTRL, SUBSCHEMA-SSNAME, SUBSCHEMA-RECNAMES, SUBSCHEMA SETNAMES, and the record definitions from the subschema. Collectively, these constitute the UWA. On your listing, I blocked off the actual entries for the SUBSCHEMA-CTRL structure, which is sometimes called the **IDMS Communications Block.** It is a 216-byte structure and immediately follows the record and set definitions. It represents the area where IDMS will communicate the equivalent of the CODASYL items DB-RECORD-NAME, DB-STATUS, etc.

"PROGRAM-NAME will contain the PROGRAM-ID of the program invoking IDMS, MMPROG01. Next comes ERROR-STATUS, which will contain a value indicating the status of my call to IDMS. It is a four-byte character item with a default value of 1400. Notice that there are some 88-level items associated with it. Two that I use a lot are DB-END-OF-SET and DB-REC-NOT-FOUND. As you can see, the corresponding values for ERROR-STA-TUS are 0307 and 0326, respectively.

"The ERROR-STATUS register, as well

as most of the others, takes its name from the 1971 DBTG. Also borrowed from this early report are many of its error codes. While different, IDMS's codes are used in the same ways as those we saw in our training class. Some of the relevant codes are on the handout I'm going to give to you now [see Exhibit 3].

"I'd like you to look at the handout. Like the CODASYL DB-STATUS values, each ERROR-STATUS code has two parts: a two-byte value indicating the kind of operation being performed when the error was detected and a two-byte code that specifies the nature of the error. For example, a value of 03 as the first two bytes indicates a FIND error, while 12 means a STORE error.

"For our purposes, the two most important values are 0307 and 0326. The first code indicates the end of set, while the second value designates that no record could be found that matches a given hashing value. Because IDMS/R automatically sets up some condition names within SUBSCHEMA-CTRL to specify these conditions, I don't have to code statements like 'IF ERROR-STATUS = '0307' . . . '. Instead I can code "IF END-OF-SET . . . ", etc.

"Look at the program again. The next SUBSCHEMA-CTRL element is DBKEY, which will contain the database key value of the current of run-unit. Following that are RECORD-NAME, the name of the most recently accessed record, and AREA-NAME, the name of the most recently accessed area. Many of the remaining items indicate which set, record, etc. were involved in an operation just prior to ERROR-STATUS becoming nonzero.

"That's all the preliminary stuff. I'll go over the PROCEDURE DIVISION changes next.

"In addition to expanding the DML call as I discussed earlier, the precompiler inserts source code as a result of two statements: COPY IDMS SUBSCHEMA-BINDS and COPY IDMS IDMS-STATUS.

"The first statement, COPY SUB-SCHEMA-BINDS, allows IDMS/R and the host program to share the SUBSCHEMA-CTRL communications block and also initializes many of its data elements. This must be the first logically executable DML statement within the PROCEDURE DIVISION.

"The other PROCEDURE DIVISION insertion is the optional error-handling routine. When using IDMS, instead of examining DB-STATUS as we saw in the CODASYL model, the run-unit checks ERROR-STATUS and, when it detects a nonzero value, PERFORMs an error routine. Rather than coding the error-handling routine, we can use IDMS/R's general-purpose one called *IDMS-STATUS*.

"You can see this routine at the end of my listing. It is a SECTION that first checks ERROR-STATUS for a value of zero. Notice that the condition name DB-STATUS-OK [see SUBSCHEMA-CTRL] has been used rather than "IF ERROR-STATUS = '0000' . . . '. If the status is zero, control passes to ISABEX, the exit paragraph, so the run-unit will continue

---

EXHIBIT 3   **The Handout Prepared by Alan Showing Some of the IDMS ERROR-STATUS Values**

0307	End of set or area
0326	Record not found
1205	Duplicate data item
1208	Record name not found
1225	One of the owner's set occurrences is NULL

with the statement after the one that called IDMS-STATUS. If the value of ERROR-STATUS is zero, control will return. But if the value is anything else, look what happens.

"A programmer-defined routine called IDMS-ABORT is executed, several messages describing the record, area, set, etc. that were current are displayed, the database is restored to the last quiet point (called a *checkpoint* by IDMS] through the ROLLBACK command, and the program is aborted. In my program, IDMS-ABORT simply displays a short message, but I could have made it as elaborate as needed.

"To actually use the IDMS-STATUS routine, after a DML statement just code: PERFORM IDMS-STATUS. It's even easier if AUTOSTATUS is used [and it was]. Now it isn't necessary to actually code the PERFORM, because IDMS inserts it automatically after each call.

"One thing I don't like about this feature is the fact that it sometimes forces me to use a nonstructured programming technique. Let me explain.

"To override the automatic invocation of IDMS-STATUS, I had to use the IDMS option 'ON condition-name imperative statement.' For example, if my program doesn't find the desired purchase order, note the lines that I coded:

```
ON DB-REC-NOT-FOUND
    DISPLAY 'No such PO . . . try again'
    GO TO 200-EXIT.
```

The GO TO is necessary because if I had left it out and placed a period after the display statement and the record wasn't found, the program would simply transfer control to the next line, where I GET the PO record. If the FIND fails, I

don't want to execute the FIND. To skip the GET, I therefore had to use the GO TO. It almost seems better to omit the AUTOSTATUS PROTOCOL. If I had, the coding would have been:

```
IF ERROR-STATUS = '0326'
    THEN
        DISPLAY 'No such PO . . . try
        again'
    ELSE
        GET . . .
```

"The other things I want to mention to you pertain to the FIND command. First, everywhere I coded the DML statement pair FIND/GET, I could have substituted OBTAIN, which executes both statements as one. The other thing I wanted to point out is the syntax for the hashed FIND statement.

"Instead of the 'FIND ANY record-name USING key-name' syntax that we saw in our classes, IDMS/R uses a syntax based on the 1971 DBTG, FIND CALC or FIND ANY. Although most IDMS/R programmers use FIND CALC or OBTAIN, I intentionally used the more CODASYL-like form FIND ANY. Notice that there isn't a USING clause, because there can be but one hash field defined in the schema.

"Sorry this took so long, everyone, but it was necessary to give you some guidance about the IDMS/CODASYL differences. Until each of you has actually written a host program, much of what I've said probably won't sink in. When you do write an application, I think the listing I gave you will be of considerable help.

"If anyone has questions, ask them now."

Fortunately, no one did!

V

The Hierarchical Data Model

Part V examines the most popular implementation of the hierarchical model: IBM's Information Management System (IMS). As recently as 1986, there were more IMS mainframe database installations than all other DMBS installations combined. Recently, however, IBM customers began switching to DB2. During 1988, the number of IMS installations grew by less than 1 percent to a little over 7,000, while the number of DB2 users doubled to about 3,500.

Chapter 11 reviews some hierarchical-model terminology. Then it discusses how to define the conceptual and external databases, which IMS calls *physical* and *logical databases*. Episode 7 of the Community Hospital continuing case follows Chapter 11. It provides a complete example of how conceptual and ex-

ternal databases are defined using IMS. One of the purposes of the episode is to extend the concept of logical relationships discussed in the chapter. Because this concept is difficult, you may want to just skim the episode. However, if you want to see just how complex IMS can be, the episode illustrates this quite well.

Chapter 12 is more applicable to the programmer/analyst, because it demonstrates how applications use Data Language I (DL/I), IMS's DML. It shows how to access records directly and sequentially, how to insert new records, and how to delete existing ones. Episode 8 of the Community Hospital case follows Chapter 12. There we will see an almost complete program that invokes DL/I to produce a report.

CHAPTER

11

The Hierarchical Data Model and IMS

Unlike the other two models we have discussed, the hierarchical data model has no standard. We will examine the most popular hierarchical implementation: IBM's Information Management System (IMS), which runs under its VSE (as DL/I) and MVS operating systems. Because the number of IMS acronyms is enormous, you may wish to refer to Table 11.2 at the end of the chapter frequently.

First, we will look at the hierarchical-model concepts and see how to define the conceptual and external databases. In the next chapter, we will learn how to manipulate an IMS database using its DML, Data Language I (DL/I).

At the conclusion of this chapter, you will be able to:

- Define the IMS terms *segment type, root, dependent segment, parent, child, hierarchical path, hierarchic order, hierarchic concatenated key, physical database, logical database, and logical relationship*.
- Define a conceptual database using the DBDGEN utility.
- Define an external database using the PSBGEN utility.

In Chapter 3, we saw that a hierarchical data structure is characterized as one in which no record type can be the destination of more than one relationship. We also saw that the hierarchical data structure can be called a *tree structure*, that the model substitutes the words *parent* and *child* for *origin* (*owner*) and *destination* (*member*), respectively, and that it uses the term *segment type*, or *segment*, instead of *conceptual file*, or *record type*.

One of the difficulties you will face in this chapter is the fact that IBM does not use the standard CODASYL/ANSI terminology to describe the architecture of a database. A conceptual database consists of one or more *physical databases* (*PDBs*), and is defined using a utility called the *data base description generator* (*DBDGEN*). The translated result is the *data base description* (*DBD*).

An external database, or user view, is known as a *logical database*. After translation by a program known as the *program specification generator* (*PSBGEN*), it results in a *program communication block* (*PCB*). The DBA can group several PCBs into a single unit, roughly equivalent to a CODASYL subschema, that is processed by an application. This unit is called the *program specification block* (*PSB*). The database is manipulated using the DML called *Data Language I* (*DL/I*).

Implementations of the hierarchical model are about as old as those of the network model, going back to the early 1960s and a joint effort between IBM and North American Aviation (Rockwell). The result of that collaboration was the creation of Information Management System (IMS).

Because a hierarchical data model limits the range of problems that can be modeled, many wonder why IBM developed and marketed such a product when the network model is so much more flexible. Another common question concerns the reason for IBM's choice of a sequential methodology for implementing the physical database. We can answer both questions by examining the origins of the package.

11.1 HISTORICAL PERSPECTIVE

The roots of IMS can be traced to the Apollo project of the 1960s. In 1961, Rockwell was selected as the prime contractor for that project. Getting a person to the moon resulted in the largest engineering feat ever undertaken. One of the most formidable aspects was the need to manage over 2 million parts, most of them related to one another in a hierarchical manner. The way in which objects are aggregated to form larger components that in turn are aggregated to form yet larger components is reminiscent of a hierarchical data structure and is the primary reason why such a data structure was chosen by the project team. You may have heard such an arrangement of parts called a *bill of materials*.

Rockwell began developing a database management system to manage the parts problem before IBM joined the project team in 1964. Because of a lack of sophisticated disk storage systems, Rockwell used magnetic tape as the storage medium, thus eliminating the possibility of using pointers to relate records. This forced Rockwell (and, later, IBM) to adopt a sequential-based strategy for implementing the physical database.

When Rockwell's database grew to 18 tape volumes and was found to contain over 60 percent redundancy, the company decided to alter its strategy. The next step was to convert the data to a disk-based system. Borrowing from the evolving database theory, Rockwell also decided to develop an access method that was independent of both medium and language and also controlled redundancy. The resulting software was called GUAM (Generalized Update Access Method). At about this time, IBM joined the project. Because GUAM was already being used, the companies decided to extend its capabilities to create a product that IBM could market and Rockwell could use to manage the Apollo project.

Most of the design work for IMS took place during 1966–67. The next year almost saw the demise of IMS. By 1967, manned Apollo flights were a reality, which reduced the importance of the IMS project to Rockwell. Also, the project was falling behind schedule, and each company was doing separate and unrelated things, none of them in keeping with the original objectives of the project. IBM was rewriting the existing code to make it more efficient so that the commercial product would be more marketable, and Rockwell was developing online interfaces and languages. Neither seemed interested in a methodical plan for testing the extremely large and complicated system. Both were neglecting the schedule and the objectives of the project.

In March 1968, most of the project team members quit. After examining the alternative of scrapping the entire project, a new team, headed by William Grafton, was formed. Grafton proved to be the correct choice, because by August of that year the first IMS application was released. When asked why he had used the hierarchical approach, Grafton gave two reasons: (1) GUAM, the predecessor of IMS, was hierarchical, and (2) such an approach conserved disk space, a scarce commodity in 1968. The team knew of Bachman's work at GE with networks but decided that that approach required too much disk storage.

When Rockwell ended the joint project, the team received an acknowledgment on the inside cover of the first release of the manuals, a waiver of license fees, and 10 free sets of manuals (for the first three releases). Because IMS is probably the most widely used mainframe database management system in the world, this deal must be considered one of the worst in information systems history!

IMS's place in today's IBM world is diminishing each month as more and more customers switch to DB2. However, for those organizations that maintain large transaction processing systems and require fast terminal response, IMS is still a substantial force and will likely continue to be so for the foreseeable future.

11.2 IMS CONCEPTS AND TERMINOLOGY

IMS records must be hierarchically related to one another in the manner shown in Figure 11.1. Although the form of the diagram differs somewhat from the conceptual databases we have seen, its components are the same: entities and relationships. There is one difference in the way the DSD is constructed: There are no heads on the arrows, which is in keeping with the IBM style. However, each line represents a 1:M relationship.

FIGURE 11.1   **A Typical Hierarchical Conceptual Database: No Child Has More than One Parent**

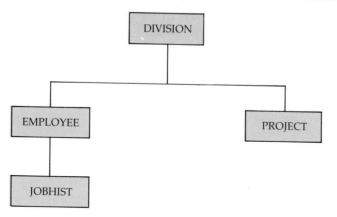

The name of the database is DIVDB. Later in the chapter you will see how this name is assigned.

Segments and Segment Occurrences

Instead of *entities,* we say that an IMS conceptual database consists of **segment types,** or simply **segments,** plus zero, one, or more 1:M relationships, each composed of a single parent (origin) segment type and one or more child (destination) segments. For example, Figure 11.1 shows four segment types, DIVISION, EMPLOYEE, JOBHIST, and PROJECT, and three relationships, DIVISION:EMPLOYEE, DIVISION:PROJECT, and EMPLOYEE:JOBHIST. Recall that the segment at the top is called the *root.*

In Figure 11.1, there are three levels. We sometimes refer to such a structure as a *three-level hierarchy,* or *tree.* IMS limits a database to 15 such levels. Because of performance considerations—and processing complications that grow at least proportionately to the number of levels—most installations limit the number of levels to four or fewer. Another restriction is that a database cannot contain more than 255 segment types. Like the limit on the number of levels, this constraint is probably never reached because of the complexity that would result.

In IMS, an occurrence of a segment is called a **segment occurrence.** Occurrences of the same segment type having the same parent are called **twins.** Using this definition, EMPLOYEEs working for the same DIVISION would be twins, while EMPLOYEEs working for different DIVISIONs would not.

Segment occurrences are the smallest unit of data that IMS can access from a database. Like CODASYL's record types, they contain fields. Besides the usual ways of classifying fields by type, by length, and so on IMS has two more: **key sequence** and **search.** When the physical database is defined, each segment can have an associated single field designated as its **key sequence field** (**KSF**). This field is a sort mechanism whereby child occurrences are sorted within their immediate parents. For the root segment, IMS can also use the KSF as a hash field or index, providing direct access to the root segment occurrences.

The other kind of field is a **search field.** Like COBOL, IMS gives the DBA the option to either explicitly name and define each field within a segment or use a mechanism like COBOL's FILLER to allocate space for a field without naming it. Only fields that have been explicitly named can be used by an application as the basis for a search.

Relationships

When we draw a DSD using the form shown in Figure 11.1, the relationships are indicated by the lines, also known as **branches,** or **paths. A hierarchical path** (see Section 3.8 in Chapter 3) is defined as a sequence of segments, one per level, that leads from a segment at one level to a segment immediately below it until the desired segment is reached. For example, the hierarchical path to JOBHIST would be DIVISION-EMPLOYEE-JOBHIST.

Earlier we said that the origin segment in each relationship is called the *parent* and the destination segment the *child*. This makes DIVISION the parent of EMPLOYEE and, simultaneously, EMPLOYEE the child of DIVISION. Every segment except the root must have one—and only one—parent. In Figure 11.1, DIVISION is the root. All the other segments are known as **dependent segments.** A child segment that is one level removed from its parent is called a **direct dependent.** This means that JOBHIST is a direct dependent of EMPLOYEE but not of DIVISION because it is two levels removed from DIVISION.

Hierarchic Sequence: Hierarchic Order Plus KSF

The physical representation of an IMS database is essentially a sequential one, in keeping with the use of tape as a storage medium when IMS was being developed. This ordering is used when IMS stores segments in the database and thus also affects the way segments can be retrieved. IBM calls this a **hierarchic ordering.** In Section 3.8, we called it a *left-list layout,* or *preorder traversal.*

When we retrieve segment occurrences from the database based on this ordering, the resulting sequence is called the **hierarchic sequence.** Two items completely determine the hierarchic sequence of a database:

- The hierarchic order of segment types
- The key sequence field for each segment type

The **hierarchic order** specifies the sequence of the segment *types;* the KSF determines the ordering of the *occurrences* within each type. In Section 3.8, we provided these rules for determining the hierarchic order:

1. Construct the conceptual database
2. Beginning at the root, descend the leftmost set of branches
3. As each segment type is visited, record it
4. When the bottom is reached, back up one level and descend any branches not yet visited, proceeding from left to right
5. Record any new segment types, but don't repeat any already recorded
6. Stop when all segment types have been visited

FIGURE 11.2   Alternative Hierarchical Designs that Result in Different Physical Databases

(a) A hierarchical design with ORDER segments on a hierarchi path along a left-brance of the root. The key sequence field is used to sort child occurrences

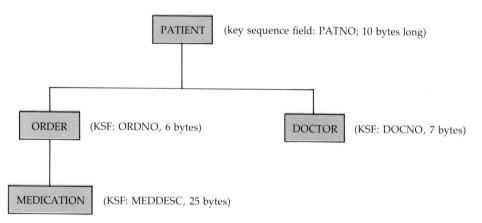

(b) An alternative design where ORDER segments are found on a hierarchical path that lies on a right-branch of the root. If ORDERs of a PATIENT are more frequently accessed than DOCTORs, this design will be seen to be less efficient than that shown in part (a)

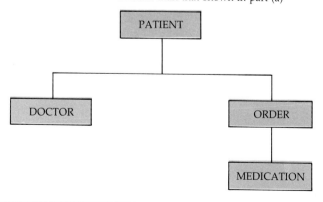

Once the ordering of the segment types is determined, the sequence of the occurrences of each type is determined by the KSF values. Let's look at some examples.

Figure 11.2 shows two DSDs. As you will see, the two data structures result in different physical databases, because they result in different hierarchic orders. Part (a) shows the key sequence field for each segment. Figure 11.3 shows the resulting hierarchic order for both parts of Figure 11.2.

Once the hierarchic order of the segment types is determined, IMS stores occurrences of each type according to its key sequence field values. Assume the sequence field for PATIENT, ORDER, MEDICATION, and DOCTOR are PATNO, ORDNO, MEDDESC, and DOCNO, respectively. This means that within a PATIENT all the related ORDERs will be sequenced on their numbers and within an ORDER all associated medications will be sorted by medication description.

We need some segment occurrences in order to be able to demonstrate the hierarchic order resulting from the two designs in Figure 11.2. Assume the patient with PATNO value P1 is treated by two doctors having DOCNO values D1 and D2. The patient has two drug orders: O1 and O2. Order number O1 is for two medications with descriptions M11 and M12. Order O2 is for a single medication: M21. Figure 11.4 shows the hierarchic sequence resulting from the conceptual design in Figure 11.2(b).

An occurrence of a root and all its dependent segments is called a **database record,** or **tree occurrence.** Thus, Figure 11.4 qualifies as a database record. If there were 200 Patients in the hospital, there would be 200 such database records in the database. The sequence numbers indicate the retrieval sequence IMS would follow in accessing the database record.

Figure 11.5 shows the database record resulting from the conceptual database in Figure 11.2(a). The resulting hierarchic sequence is P1, O1, M11, M12, O2, M21, D1, D2.

When this sequence is physically implemented, it is done so in a sequential manner. Although child/twin or hierarchical pointers (discussed in Section 5.3 and later in this chapter) can be used to implement the hierarchic order, the result will always be a sequential organization based on the hierarchic sequence. Figure 11.6 shows the implementation of Figure 11.5 as a physical sequential file.

The sequential nature of the hierarchic sequence can lead to processing inefficiencies, which can be alleviated to some degree by choosing a "better" conceptual and/or logical design. Assume an end user wants to access a particular DOCTOR occurrence for a given PATIENT. As Figures 11.5 and 11.6 show, the database resulting from the conceptual design in Figure 11.2(a) stores the DOCTOR occurrences at the end of each database record. Thus, to retrieve the DOCTOR records, all the ORDER and MEDICATION occurrences must be read first. Although IMS does this transparently, the process can be quite inefficient. Fortunately, IMS permits direct or indexed access to root segment

FIGURE 11.3   The Hierarchic Ordering of Segment Types Resulting from the Two Data Structures in Figure 11.2

(a) The hierarchic order resulting form Figure 11.2(a)

(b) The hierarchic order resulting from Figure 11.2(b)

FIGURE 11.4   The Hierarchic Sequence Resulting from Figure 11.2(b) and the Key Sequence Field Values

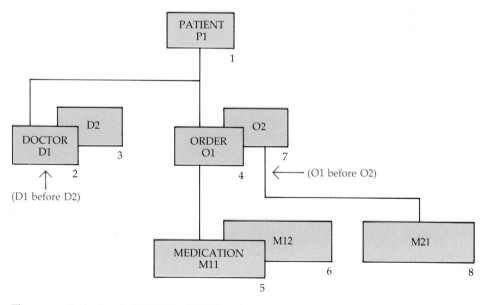

The sequence field values for DOCTOR, ORDER, and MEDICATION are shown. This figure also represents one physical database record (PDBR). Every PATIENT would be the root for a similar PDBR. The collection of all the PDBRs determines the physical database.

FIGURE 11.5   The Hierarchic Ordering of Segment Occurrences Based on Figure 11.2(a)

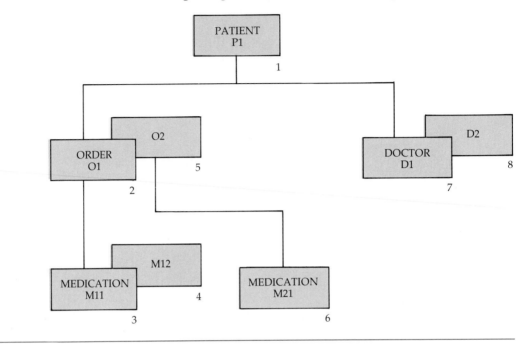

FIGURE 11.6   The Sequential Nature of the Hierarchic Sequence

P1	O1	M11	M12	O2	M21	D1	D1

The figure is based on Figures 11.5 and 11.3(a). It shows one PDBR (physical database record). In fact, it is a single record from the sequential file that IMS uses to store segment occurrences. Notice that a PDBR contains several segment occurrences of differing types.

occurrences. Consequently, the above search could begin at the desired PATIENT database record rather than at the initial PATIENT in the database.

Had the DBA chosen the design shown in Figure 11.2(b) the DOCTOR segments would precede the ORDER segments in the hierarchic order, as indicated in Figure 11.4 and hence could be retrieved more quickly than with the other design. The selection of one design over the other cannot be done without knowledge of the most common access path.

Physical and Logical Databases

Based on the conceptual database, the DBA defines two kinds of IMS databases: a *physical database* (*PDB*) and one or more *logical databases* (*LDBs*). Each consists of a set of database records. Each record is composed of a root occurrence and all the associated dependent segment occurrences.

The Physical Database (DBD). Functionally, the **physical database (PDB)** is the equivalent of CODASYL's schema plus its DMCL or DSDL. It is described using a utility known as the **data base description generator (DBDGEN)** and results in a **data base description (DBD)**, which is then stored in an IMS library. The DBD contains information about the segment and field names, the IMS access method to use, and the device on which to store the database.

Recall from our discussion of the "database approach" that ideally an organization strives to have a single conceptual database from which all external databases (user views) can be extracted. IMS views things a bit differently. Rather than a single physical, organizationwide database, IMS proponents often develop physical databases at the application level. In fact, several physical databases may be defined for a given application. IBM defines a physical database as the collection of all the physical database records. Thus, the physical database for Suburban Hospital would consist of a series of physical database records, each conceptually like that shown in Figure 11.5 and physically like that illustrated in Figure 11.6.

The Logical (External) Databases (PSB). Recall that the description of a **logical database (LDB)** (also called a *user view* or *external database*) is called a **program specification block (PSB)** and consists of one or more **program communication blocks (PCBs)** where each PCB is a subset of a physical database. Most of the time we will constrain a logical database to be a subset of a single physical one, much like the CODASYL subschema concept.

In constructing a PSB of this type, the DBA can select any subset of segments and fields from any single physical database.

Assume an end user requests an application that needs a subset of the DIVDB database from Figure 11.1 and that the external database looks like that in Figure 11.7. There are only two segments: DIVISION and EMPLOYEE. If a PSB is defined according to the figure, host programs using it will be able to access only those two segments.

Tree occurrences of a logical database are called **logical database records (LDBRs).** To an application processing the database in Figure 11.7, each database record would consist of a DIVISION and all the EMPLOYEEs working in that DIVISION.

Another kind of logical database is one that requires subsets of two physical databases. Assume that we have another database, TRAINDB, which is shown

FIGURE 11.7   A Conceptual Logical Database Derived from the Database in Figure 11.1

The database would be defined by the PSBGEN program.

FIGURE 11.8   The TRAINDB Physical Database

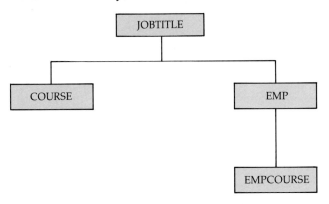

Like all PDBs, this database is defined through the DBDGEN process.

in Figure 11.8. Each root occurrence of TRAINDB is associated with a JOBTITLE within the organization. The COURSE segments refer to in-house training courses that teach one or more of the skills necessary for the JOBTITLE. The EMP segments are used to store data about employees having that JOBTITLE. The EMPCOURSE occurrences are used to store the courses that each EMPLOYEE has taken.

Figure 11.9 shows a user view (external database) derived from segments from Figures 11.1 (DIVDB) and 11.8 (TRAINDB). The user needs two segments from the DIVDB database and two from TRAINDB. Each view will result in a separate program communication block, which, through the program specification generator, will be combined into a single program specification block. Figure 11.10 illustrates this.

FIGURE 11.9   Two User Views, Each Based on a Different Physical Database (PDB)

The first user view is based on DIVDB (Figure 11.1) and the second on TRAINDB (Figure 11.8).

FIGURE 11.10   How a PSB Can Be Constructed from Two User Views, Each View Based on a Different Physical Database

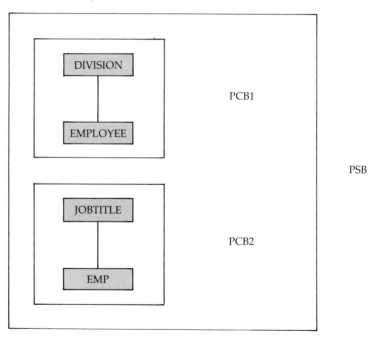

PCB1 is derived from DIVDB and PCB2 from TRAINDB.

There are two external (logical) databases in Figure 11.10: one that contains DIVISION and EMPLOYEE and another that contains JOBTITLE and EMP. Using the PSBGEN utility, the DBA would define a program communication block for each logical database, then combine them into a single program specification block and give it a name. The translated result then would be stored in an IMS library. Because they are combined into a single PSB, the two PCBs would be accessible as a unit to any application.

11.3   IMPLEMENTING RELATIONSHIPS USING POINTERS

Earlier we saw that one way to implement a tree occurrence is as a sequential file. Because of the inherent difficulties associated with maintaining such files, other, more efficient methods for implementing tree occurrences are usually used. In Section 5.3, we saw how we can alternatively use hierarchical and child/twin pointers to effect a much more responsive implementation. This section expands on these options.

There are three kinds of pointers we can use to implement an IMS database:

- Hierarchical pointers, which connect one segment to the next one in the hierarchic sequence.
- Physical child pointers, which connect a segment occurrence to its first and last child.
- Physical twin pointers, which connect twins.

Hierarchical Pointers

A *hierarchical (H) forward pointer* connects a segment to the one that follows it in the hierarchic sequence. Figure 11.11 shows the hierarchical forward pointer implementation of Figure 11.4. The nine segments shown could be anywhere on the disk.

However, like the physical sequential method, the hierarchical pointer implementation still requires that an application retrieve all segments in the hierarchic sequence prior to the desired one. For example, to access the MEDICATION with description M21, IMS could hash to segment number 1, then use the hierarchical pointers to sequentially access segments 2 through 7 before retrieving segment 8.

Hierarchical backward (HB) pointers connect the segments in reverse hierarchic order. As we have seen several times, we use such pointers when there are a lot of deletes, because they improve the performance when deleting from linked lists.

FIGURE 11.11   Hierarchical Forward Pointers Used to Implement Figure 11.4

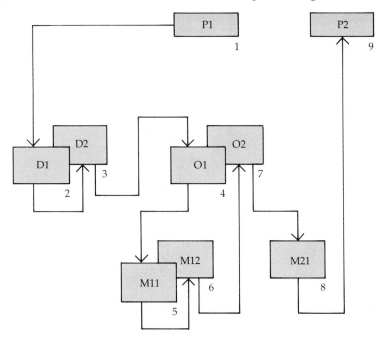

Each segment points to the one that follows it in the hierarchic sequence.

First-Child Pointers

First-child pointers are associated with a parent occurrence and connect the parent to the first occurrence of each child of a different type. As an example, each PATIENT occurrence is the parent of two child types: ORDER and DOCTOR. Thus, we can expect two first-child PATIENT pointers: one that points to the first ORDER for that PATIENT and one that points to the first DOCTOR. Figure 11.12 shows these pointers.

Let's assume a user wants the first MEDICATION (M11) for ORDER O1 associated with PATIENT P1. Using the hierarchical pointers from Figure 11.11, an almost complete scan of the physical database record will be necessary before the desired record is located. In fact, a total of five I/Os will be required. Using child pointers, IMS can go directly from P1 to O1, then to the desired MEDICATION occurrence, for a total of three I/Os. This shows the potential advantage of child pointers for random retrievals. We say *potential* because if we want to access MEDICATION M12, we have no first-child pointer to use. To access M12, we will need a twin pointer from M11.

FIGURE 11.12   Physical First-Child Pointers Used to Implement the Database Record in Figure 11.4

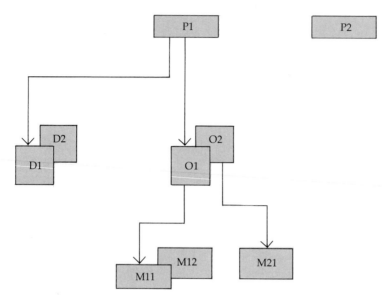

Each parent contains one or more pointers, which connect it to the first child occurrence associated with each of its direct-descendent segment types.

Twin Pointers

A *twin pointer* connects a segment to its twin in either the forward or the backward direction. Such pointers can be associated with any segment, including the root. A *twin forward pointer* (T or TF) connects segments in the forward direction, while a *twin backward pointer* (TB) does so in the opposite direction.

Summary

In summary, we use hierarchical pointers when we desire hierarchical (sequential) retrieval. We should use a combination of child and twin pointers if we make frequent "random" retrievals. IMS also permits the mixing of pointer types, where the types of pointers vary by segment type, thus offering the potential for both random and sequential access via pointers.

11.4 LOGICAL RELATIONSHIPS

A **logical relationship** is a mechanism for implementing some nonhierarchical data structures. Such a relationship can be established among segments within the same physical database or in different ones. It enables us to:

- Have two parents for a given segment (effectively allowing a limited network structure)
- Connect two physical databases
- Reduce redundancy
- Implement indexes

As an example of a need for such a relationship, let's look at a portion of the conceptual database for Microtech Luggage Company's accounts payable database, reproduced in Figure 11.13.

The DETAIL segments store the connection items—item code and invoice number—as well as description, units ordered, and price per unit. The ITEM segment also carries item code, plus item description, total units on order (for all INVOICEs), quantity on hand, and so on. A major problem is that DETAIL has two parents and hence cannot be directly implemented by IMS. Let's assume we don't want to use the technique from Chapter 5 for decomposing a network into a family of trees.

Another solution to the problem is to construct two physical databases (PDBs) and then connect them using a logical relationship. Figure 11.14 shows the two physical databases, INVDB and ITEMDB, and the logical relationship.

The segment that has two parents, DETAIL, is a **logical child.** The parent segment that is stored in the same database as its child is its **physical parent,**

FIGURE 11.13   A Segment Type with Two Parents

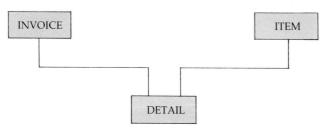

Through the use of a logical relationship, IMS can implement this limited network.

FIGURE 11.14   A Logical Relationship between Segment Types in a Single PDB

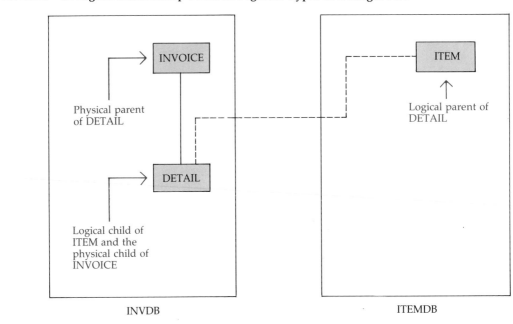

while the other parent is its **logical parent.** This makes INVOICE the physical parent and ITEM the logical one, because INVOICE and DETAIL are stored in the same database. To connect the logical child to its logical parent, we need to introduce a path (branch) that connects not only two segments but two PDBs. It is this new path that is the logical relationship. It is shown on a DSD by a dotted line as in Figure 11.14. The DETAIL occurrences will now be stored only in the INVDB database, reducing redundancy. Also, we have managed to implement a network data structure.

The occurrences of a logical child that have the same logical parent are called **logical twins.** Because it is likely that an ITEM in the ITEMDB would be related to many DETAIL occurrences in the other database, the DETAIL occurrences related to the same ITEM would be logical twins.

Logical relationships can be **unidirectional** (from the logical child to its logical parent) or **bidirectional** (from parent to child, or vice versa). Like physical parents and children, logical relationships are implemented by means of pointers, but we won't show how this is done.

11.5   IMS ACCESS METHODS

The method IMS uses to store the segments and any associated overhead depends on the **physical storage structure,** referred to by IBM as an *access method.* Let's look at the access methods presented in Table 11.1.

HSAM and HISAM, the first two access methods, physically store segments within each database record in the sequential, hierarchical, physically contiguous manner represented in Figure 11.6. The third and fourth access methods, HDAM and HIDAM, use pointers to maintain the hierarchic sequence. The next two, MSDB and DEDB, are used when the fastest possible access to a database is necessary. The last method, INDEX, stores secondary indexes or indexes created by the HIDAM access method.

HSAM

The *hierarchic sequential access method* (*HSAM*) employs the hierarchic sequence as shown in Figure 11.6. Because the segments are physically adjacent on the storage medium, such an access method can be implemented on either tape or disk. Using IMS, segments in an HSAM database cannot be deleted, nor can new segments be added, except when the database is initially loaded. Records can only be read. Applications must use conventional file processing techniques and languages to update the database. This access method should be chosen for those applications that require only sequential retrieval.

Loading such a database must be done such that the roots are stored in ascending order by their KSFs. If a KSF is not specified, this requirement is waived and the segments must be presented to IMS in the exact sequence desired for their access. Dependent segments must be stored in hierarchic sequence, but KSFs are optional. Notice the implications of this statement. To store the data in Figure 11.5, the input records *must* be in the order P1, O1, M11, M12, O2, and so on; that is, they must be in their hierarchic sequence.

TABLE 11.1   **IMS Access Methods**

Access Method	Description	Operating System Access Method
HSAM	Hierarchic sequential access method	BSAM or QSAM
HISAM	Hierarchic indexed sequential access method	ISAM or VSAM
HDAM	Hierarchic direct access method	VSAM
HIDAM	Hierarchic indexed direct access method	VSAM
MSDB	Main storage database	None
DEDB	Data entry database	VSAM
INDEX	Index database	VSAM

HISAM

A *hierarchic indexed sequential access method* (*HISAM*) database stores segments in the hierarchic sequence but provides the ability to index the root occurrences on their KSF values. This permits indexed access to PATIENTs (Figure 11.2) or to DIVISIONs (Figure 11.1), but not to any dependent segments. We use HISAM when we desire indexed access to roots and sequential access to dependent segments.

The segments are stored in the order presented during the initial load. The root segments must be presented in ascending KSF order, and all dependent segments must be in their hierarchic order. We saw an example of this sequence in the section on HSAM.

When a segment is deleted, HISAM sets a delete-byte in an overhead area associated with each segment called the **prefix area.** This means that the delete is a logical one. Dependent segments of the deleted segment are not marked, but because their parent is deleted, they cannot be accessed. All segments marked for deletion (or whose parents are) are physically removed when the database is reorganized.

The next two access methods preserve the hierarchic sequence by using three kinds of pointers discussed in Section 11.3.

HDAM

The *hierarchic direct access method* (*HDAM*) permits hashed access to root occurrences. Unfortunately, the roots cannot be accessed sequentially. HDAM is used when quick access to roots is required but when there is no need to sequentially process the database in sequential root order.

Pointers are used to relate the dependent segments to one another, allowing IMS to store the segments anywhere on the disk drive. However, the segments cannot be moved once stored.

Loading a HDAM database is a bit easier than we discussed previously, because the root records presented to the load program can be in any sequence. However, the dependent segments must be in their hierarchic sequence.

HIDAM

The *hierarchic indexed direct access method* (*HIDAM*) is almost the same as HDAM, but in addition to providing hashed (actually indexed) access to roots, it permits sequential access. For example, if used with Figure 11.2(b), we could randomly or sequentially access PATIENT occurrences.

Unlike HISAM, in which the index is transparent to the application, HIDAM requires a second database called an **index database.** The access method is slower than HDAM, because IMS must maintain this second database when a segment is added or deleted. The primary advantage of HIDAM over HDAM is that

HIDAM maintains the root segments in KSF order, permitting sequential access of the roots and their accompanying database records.

Initial loading of a HIDAM database is done in the same way as for most of the others: present the physical records to IMS in ascending order of root KSFs. The dependent segments must be inserted in their hierarchic sequence.

The next two access methods are used with an optional IMS feature called *Fast Path,* discussed later, which enables an organization to more quickly retrieve data from an exceptionally large database in an on-line environment. Although the Fast Path facility does greatly improve the performance of the database, the kinds of data structures that can be processed using this facility are limited.

MSDB

A *main storage database* (*MSDB*) access method can be used only with databases that contain fixed-length root segments. The DBA usually puts the most frequently accessed data into such a database. For example, a bank might store its checking account segments in an MSDB and then use another type of database (i.e., access method) for the customer segments. By keeping the complete database in memory (virtual), quick retrieval of segments is guaranteed.

DEDB

A *data entry database* (*DEDB*) is, in many ways, more general than an MSDB because it can contain up to 127 segment types and up to 15 levels. On the other hand, its segments are of a special type, called sequential dependent segments, which are stored in time sequence as they are inserted. Otherwise, it is similar to an MSDB except that segments are stored on a disk drive.

INDEX

Both HISAM and HIDAM, as well as segments that have a secondary index defined, require that a separate database, called an *index database,* be set up for storing the indexing data. While this database is automatically maintained by IMS, the DBA must define it. When defining this database, the access method specified must be INDEX.

11.6 DEFINING THE PHYSICAL DATABASE: THE DBDGEN UTILITY

Recall that the physical database is defined using the DBDGEN utility. This is where the access method is chosen, segments assigned names, field specifications provided, and the hierarchic order defined. In addition, this is where the DBA defines logical relationships and secondary indexes. The resulting object module is called the **data base description,** or **DBD.**

The following items are defined using this utility:

- The name of the physical database
- The access method
- The device on which the database is to be stored
- The names of the segments
- The names and specifications of the fields
- Identification of logical children and secondary index fields
- The hierarchic order

Restrictions include 255 segment names, 15 levels, and 255 fields per segment. Also, a maximum of 1,000 total field names per database are allowed. To save space, the DBA may elect not to define each field but to use the FILLER-like facility mentioned earlier. Finally, a field can be redefined, thus providing access to fields under different names and specifications.

Specifying the PDB Name

The name of the database is chosen first, and up to eight alphanumeric characters can be used. Both the name and the access method appear on a DBD macro statement of the type shown in line 1 of Figure 11.15. The figure shows most of the statements required for defining the HIDAM database in Figure 11.2(a). The line numbers in the figure are for explanation purposes only; they are not actually coded.

The DBD in line 1 identifies this statement as the data base description macro. The object form of the DBD is to be HOSP. This name will be referenced by the PSBGEN utility.

Line 1 also indicates that the DBA has chosen the HIDAM access method. Recall that this will permit both hashed and sequential access of the PATIENTs (the root).

This access method also requires an index. Line 8 specifies that the associated index is a logical child, can be found in another database called INDEXDB, and is to be stored in a segment within that database having the name INDEX. In effect, this defines a logical relationship.

Defining the Data Set

Line 2 of Figure 11.15 specifies the name of the underlying operating system data set (file) that is to be used to store the segment occurrences. In the example, the name of that data set is PRIMARY and the location is on a 3380 DASD. (See Appendix A for a review of IBM disk technology.)

The "BLOCK= . . . " clause specifies either a blocking factor, provided that the access method permits blocking—HSAM and HISAM—or, as in our case, the block size: 1,000. HDAM and HIDAM databases cannot be blocked.

FIGURE 11.15   **The HIDAM DBDGEN Statements to Define the Conceptual Database in Figure 11.2(a)**

```
1    DBD            NAME=HOSP,ACCESS=HIDAM

2    DATASET        DD1=PRIMARY,DEVICE=3380,BLOCK=1000

3    SEGM           NAME=PATIENT,BYTES=128,PTR=(H,HB,T),

                    FREQ=300

4    FIELD          NAME=(PATNO,SEQ,U),BYTES=10,START=1,TYPE=C

5    FIELD          NAME=PATNAME,BYTES=25,START=11,TYPE=C

6    FIELD          NAME=AMOUNT,BYTES=5,START=36,TYPE=P

7    ...  (other field definitions here)

8    LCHILD         NAME=(INDEX,INDEXDB),  PTR=INDX

9    SEGM           NAME=ORDER,BYTES=100,PTR=(H,HB,T),

                    PARENT=PATIENT

10   FIELD          NAME=(ORDNO,SEQ,U),BYTES=6,START=1,TYPE=C

11   FIELD          NAME=ORDPATNO,BYTES=11,START=7,TYPE=C
```

The connection field.
It relates an ORDER
to the PATIENT

```
12   FIELD          NAME=ORDATE,BYTES=8,START=18,TYPE=C

13   FIELD          NAME=RPHINIT,BYTES=3,START=26,TYPE=C

14   FIELD          NAME=ORDSTAT,BYTES=1,START=29,TYPE=C

15   FIELD          NAME=ORDCHRGE,BYTES=5,START=30,TYPE=P

16   ... (other ORDER field definitions would follow)

17   SEGM           NAME=MED,BYTES=50,PTR=(H,HB,T),

                    PARENT=ORDER
```

FIGURE 11.15   (concluded)

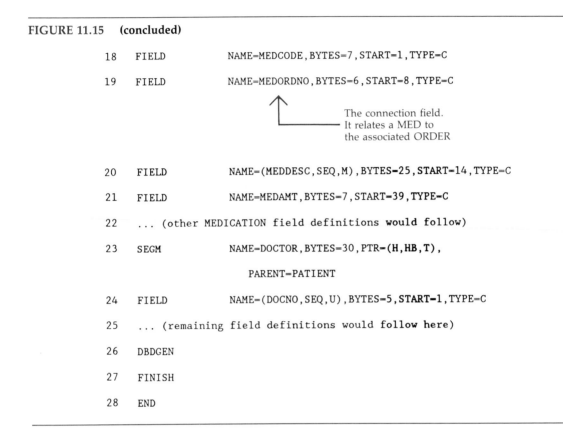

```
18    FIELD           NAME=MEDCODE,BYTES=7,START=1,TYPE=C

19    FIELD           NAME=MEDORDNO,BYTES=6,START=8,TYPE=C
```

        The connection field.
        It relates a MED to
        the associated ORDER

```
20    FIELD           NAME=(MEDDESC,SEQ,M),BYTES=25,START=14,TYPE=C

21    FIELD           NAME=MEDAMT,BYTES=7,START=39,TYPE=C

22    ... (other MEDICATION field definitions would follow)

23    SEGM            NAME=DOCTOR,BYTES=30,PTR=(H,HB,T),

                      PARENT=PATIENT

24    FIELD           NAME=(DOCNO,SEQ,U),BYTES=5,START=1,TYPE=C

25    ... (remaining field definitions would follow here)

26    DBDGEN

27    FINISH

28    END
```

Defining the Segments and Their Hierarchic Order

Following the DATASET statement, the DBA must define each segment in its hierarchic order. According to Figure 11.3(a), that order should be PATIENT, ORDER, MEDICATION, and DOCTOR.

Line 3 defines the first segment's name as PATIENT and, because it appears first, also establishes it as the root. The segment length is 128 bytes, and the segment is to contain three pointers: a hierarchical forward (H), a hierarchical backward (HB), and a forward twin (T).

The optional clause "FREQ= . . . " is the estimated number of times the segment will occur. If the clause appears on a child segment definition, it is the estimated number of occurrences of that segment within its parent. In our case, the DBA estimated there will be 300 PATIENTs.

Line 9 begins the definition of the next hierarchic segment: ORDER. Notice there is an explicit declaration of the immediate parent of ORDER:

PARENT = PATIENT. The PATIENT segment definition had no such clause, because it was the root.

Because a segment's name is limited to eight characters, we had to change MEDICATION to MED.

Defining the Fields

Line 4 of Figure 11.15 assigns the name PATNO to the first field, specifies that it is 10 bytes long, that it begins at byte 1 within the segment, and that it is a character field (TYPE = C). Names are limited to eight characters. Besides character data, the DBD can specify:

- Packed decimal (P)
- Hexadecimal (X)
- Binary full-word (F)
- Half-word (H)

Notice that when we defined the fields in Figure 11.15, we included connection data items per our design guideline from Chapter 4. For example, MEDORDNO relates a MED segment occurrence to its ORDER parent, and ORDPATNO relates an ORDER to its PATIENT parent.

Specifying the KSF. Look at the SEQ clause inside the parentheses that surround the PATNO field name in line 4. Notice that the next field, PATNAME, has no such clause or any parentheses. The SEQ clause specifies that this field is the KSF. Thus, PATIENTs will be sequenced by their patient numbers.

The optional parameter U means that the PATNO field is unique. Root segments *must* use this option. Use of the other option, M, means there can be multiple child occurrences having the same KSF value within a parent occurrence. For example, MEDICATION uses MEDDESC as its KSF, and the DBA used the M option. This means that within a given ORDER, it is acceptable for two MEDICATION segments to have the same description.

Although not required for all segments, we adopt the guideline that all segments will have a KSF, and hence we will always use the SEQ option for some field within each SEGM. Only one field can comprise the KSF; no concatenated KSFs are permitted.

Implicit Field Definitions. Line 3 of Figure 11.15 specifies that the PATIENT segment occurrences are 128 bytes each. Assume the only FIELD statement that followed line 3 was this one:

FIELD   NAME = (PATNO,SEQ,U), BYTES = 10, . . .

This would mean that the remaining 118 bytes were undefined and thus not usable as search fields. In effect, the other fields would be treated like FILLER fields in COBOL.

The remaining lines for the other segments are similar to those we have already discussed, except for the last three. Those lines do not pertain to a segment; rather, they are DBDGEN control statements. Line 26 specifies the name of the utility to use (DBDGEN), and lines 27 and 28 indicate that the DBD is complete (FINISH and END).

Defining a HIDAM Index Database

HIDAM databases require a separate database to store the index. Line 8 of Figure 11.15 shows the LCHILD macro. The HIDAM index database name is INDEXDB, and the associated index segment name is INDEX. Because only root segments can be indexed with HIDAM, this macro can appear only in the SEGM statement that defines the root—PATIENT in our example. Furthermore, IMS assumes the index is to be based on the KSF of the root—in our example, PATNO.

The PTR = INDX clause in line 8 is required. It establishes the fact that there is to be an index to connect the primary database to the index database.

In a separate DBD, the DBA must also code the index database. This is shown in Figure 11.16. The name of the index database is INDEXDB, and the database uses the INDEX access method (ACCESS = INDEX). It contains a single segment with the name INDEX (SEGM NAME = INDEX). This must be the name of the segment, because it has to match the name appearing as the first parameter inside the parentheses in line 8 of the HOSP primary database.

According to line 3, the length of each INDEX segment is 10 bytes, corre-

---

FIGURE 11.16   The Index Database Definition for the HIDAM Database in Figure 11.15

```
1   DBD         NAME=INDEXDB,ACCESS=INDEX

2   DATASET     DD1=INDXDB1,DEVICE=3380

3   SEGM        NAME=INDEX,BYTES=10,FREQ=500

4   LCHILD      NAME=(PATIENT,HOSP),INDEX=PATNO

5   FIELD       NAME=(INDXSEQ,SEQ,U),BYTES=10,START=1

6   DBDGEN

7   FINISH

8   END
```

sponding to the length of the PATNO field, the field being indexed. The fourth line in the INDEXDB database specifies a logical child: PATIENT in HOSP. It also specifies that PATNO is the name of the field in PATIENT that is to be used as the basis of the index.

The FIELD macro in line 5 contains only one field—INDXSEQ, which is where the PATNO values will be stored. It is within a prefix area of each segment occurrence of INDEX that the corresponding disk address of the PATIENT occurrences will be stored.

11.7 DEFINING THE IMS LOGICAL (EXTERNAL) DATABASES: THE PSBGEN UTILITY

In many ways, defining the logical database is easier than defining the physical database, because the PSB contains no field definitions. As we stated earlier, this utility will identify the accessible segments and fields and specify which processing options are permissible for each segment.

To define a program specification block (PSB), the DBA:

- Codes a program communication block (PCB) macro for each logical database
- Defines the accessible segments, called **sensitive segments**, for each PCB
- Defines the available (sensitive) fields for each sensitive segment
- Combines several PCBs into a single PSB, if necessary

Figure 11.17 shows a conceptual logical IMS database consisting of only three sensitive segment types: PATIENT, ORDER, and MEDICATION. They are all

---

FIGURE 11.17   **A Conceptual Logical Database Derived from Figure 11.2(a)**

Each segment is said to be sensitive.

found in a single database, HOSP, which was conceptually defined in Figure 11.2(a).

Figure 11.18 shows the PSB that would define that logical database. Look at the PCB statement. The TYPE = DB means that the database is to be a batch one. There are two other choices besides DB, but they are not shown. Next, the PCB statement identifies the underlying physical database DBD name as HOSP, the name assigned to the PDB in Figure 11.15. The PROCOPT = A means that all processing options (G,I,R,D, below) are permitted for the logical database. Other choices are:

- G for Get; provides read-only access to segments in the PCB
- I for Insert; permits the addition of new segments in the PCB
- R for Replace; permits segments to be modified or retrieved
- D for Delete; permits segments to be deleted or retrieved

The last clause, KEYLEN = 41, requires some explanation. The value that follows KEYLEN = is the longest **concatenated hierarchical path** in the hierarchy. When IMS retrieves a segment, it constructs a **hierarchic concatenated key (HCK)** consisting of all the KSF values for the sensitive segments accessed along the hierarchical path to the desired segment. In our logical database, there are three segments—PATIENT, ORDER, and MED—with key lengths of 10, 6, and 25, respectively. When a PATIENT is accessed, its concatenated key length will be 10 bytes, consisting only of a patient number. However, if an ORDER has

---

FIGURE 11.18   **A Program Specification Block Generation (PSBGEN) Corresponding to the Logical Database in Figure 11.17**

1	PCB	TYPE=DB,DBDNAME=HOSP,PROCOPT-A,
		KEYLEN=41
2	SENSEG	NAME=PATIENT,PARENT=0,PROCOPT-G
3	SENSEG	NAME=ORDER,PARENT=PATIENT,**PROCOPT-A**
4	SENFLD	NAME=ORDNO,START=1
5	SENFLD	NAME=RPHINIT,START=11
6	SENSEG	NAME=MED,PARENT=ORDER,PROCOPT-A
7	PSBGEN	LANG=COBOL,PSBNAME=PHARMPSB
8	END	

been accessed, the concatenated key will be 16 bytes long, consisting of the patient number concatenated with the order number. Finally, after retrieval of a MED segment, the length of the concatenated key will be 41 bytes: 10 for the patient number, 6 for the order number, and 25 for the medication description. The longest concatenated key length is 41; hence that is the value used in the clause.

The two remaining macros, SENSEG and SENFLD, specify which segments and fields are to be made available to an application. In the example, there are three sensitive segments: PATIENT, ORDER, and MED. As in the DBD, the hierarchic order must be preserved and the root of the PCB must correspond to the root of the underlying physical database.

The PROCOPT clause can also be used at the segment level, as shown by line 2. It says that PATIENT segment can only be retrieved (PROCOPT = G), while all processing options are permitted for the ORDER and MED segments (PROCOPT = A).

Other options are:

- G, I, R, and D, all of which have the same meaning as with the PROCOPT clause on the PCB statement in Figure 11.18
- A, which designates G, I, R, D (i.e., ALL)

FIGURE 11.19   A PSB Skeleton that Contains Segments from Two Physical Databases

```
PCB          TYPE=DB,DBDNAME=DIVDB,...

                          ↑_____ Define a PCB based
                                                     on DIVDB
SENSEG       NAME=DIVISION, ...
SENSEG       NAME=EMPLOYEE, ...

PCB          TYPE=DB,DBDNAME=TRAINDB, ...

                          ↑_____ Define a PCB on
                                            TRAINDB

SENSEG       NAME=JOBTITLE, ...
SENSEG       NAME=EMP, ...


PSBGEN       LANG=COBOL, PSBNAME=COMBDB

                          ↑_____ Give a single name to
                                            the resulting PSB
END
```

See also Figure 11.10.

Dependent segments must explicitly identify their parent. The parent of MED is ORDER, as indicated by the PARENT = ORDER clause in line 6.

Use of the SENFLD permits the DBA to change the ordering of fields or to limit the end user's ability to see particular fields. In Figure 11.18, the only ORDER fields that are made available are ORDNO and RPHINIT. This can be seen by examining lines 4 and 5. Omitting the SENFLD macro makes all fields in the segment sensitive.

The PSBGEN macro in line 7 specifies that the language that will be used to process the logical database is COBOL and that the PSB name to be assigned to this database is PHARMPSB. Besides COBOL, the DBA can specify ASSEM— for Assembler—or PL/1.

The final statement is END, which indicates the end of the PSBGEN macro.

If there is more than one PCB to be included, each must be defined in a similar way. The additional coding goes before the PSBGEN statement in line 7. Figure 11.19 shows a skeleton PSBGEN that would create the logical database for Figure 11.10. Recall that that database was composed of two PCBs, one each from the DIVDB and TRAINDB databases.

11.8 SECONDARY INDEXES

Normally, only the root segments can be accessed directly or through an index. Secondary indexing results in an inverted data structure that provides for (1) alternate search paths to root segments and (2) direct accessing of dependent (nonroot) segments.

Features of secondary indexes include the following:

- Up to five noncontiguous fields can be combined to form the index.
- When multiple fields make up the index, the primary one is called the **sequence field** and the others **subsequence fields**.
- More than one secondary index can be defined per segment type.
- Both root and dependent segments can be indexed, but usually only roots are.
- A second database, called an *index database*, is necessary for each indexed field.
- The data in the index database is automatically maintained by IMS.

As an example, assume the key sequence field for the DIVISION segment in the DIVDB database is DIVCODE. Depending on the access method specified, access to DIVISION segments could be indexed or hashed. Access to all dependent segments would be sequential only. If it is necessary to randomly retrieve EMPLOYEE segments (a dependent segment) by employee code, a secondary index could be created on the employee code. The segment the user wants to retrieve through use of the index is called the **target segment**. The segment that

FIGURE 11.20   **A Conceptualization of a Secondary Index**

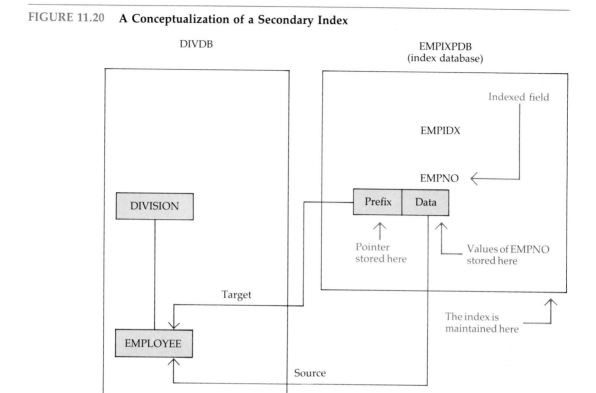

The index is based on EMPNO, a field in EMPLOYEE. Thus, EMPLOYEE is the source segment. *Because we want to use the index to retrieve EMPLOYEE segments, this makes EMPLOYEE the* target segment *also.*

The values of EMPNO are carried in the data area of the EMPIDX occurrences in the index database. The prefix area for each record carries a pointer to the corresponding EMPLOYEE.

contains the values to be indexed is called the **source segment**. Usually these two are the same, and we will refer to such segments as the *target*. These concepts are illustrated in Figure 11.20.

Because the coding necessary for defining a secondary index is quite involved, we will omit the details. For more information, consult the IBM IMS manuals cited in the bibliography in the text.

11.9   FAST PATH

When we need very rapid access to segments of large databases, we should at least consider Fast Path. Unfortunately, the kinds of databases to which Fast Path feature of IMS can be applied are limited. Fast Path is usable only under IMS's on-line version (IMS/DC) and cannot be used with its more popular teleprocessing (TP) monitor, Customer Information Control System (CICS). Also, the kinds of data structures Fast Path supports are limited to either root segments only (an option called *Main Storage Data Base*, or *MSDB*) or a root segment and a limited number of dependent segments (a *Data Entry Data Base*, or *DEDB*).

By making heavy use of main memory for storing and updating segments, Fast Path can more quickly access and modify segments, thus greatly improving its performance over the conventional IMS database.

The Main Storage Database

While more limiting than a Data Entry Database, a Main Storage Database is faster because all the segment updating is done in main (or virtual) memory. The amount of main memory available limits the size of an MSDB, however.

The Data Entry Database

A Data Entry Database is more flexible than the other Fast Path option, because in addition to the root, there can be up to 126 segment types and up to 15 levels. Much of its speed comes from the fact that each PDBR becomes a VSAM data set (file). Furthermore, each data set can be individually tuned for performance, varying the underlying VSAM Control Interval and Control Area parameters. IMS calls each of these data sets an *area*. (See Appendix B for a review of VSAM.)

Typically we use a DEDB when we need rapid access to both root occurrences and dependent segments.

11.10   SUMMARY

An IMS database consists of hierarchical relationships among segment types. If the conceptual database includes nonhierarchical structures, they must be eliminated. Much of its limited ability to handle network-type structures stems from its roots in the 1960s, when DASDs were either nonexistent or minimally available. In order to be able to use magnetic tape, Rockwell, and later IBM, developed a technique that allowed for a limited kind of network in which a member (child) had at most two owners (parents) and could use tape as a storage medium.

A data base description (DBD) is a file that contains both conceptual and physical definitions of the conceptual database. The program the DBA uses to define a DBD is the data base description generator (DBDGEN). Through a series of statements, or macros, the DBA defines the segments and the fields that are to be carried in the database. Resulting from this process is a database known as the *physical database* (PDB). This PDB is similar to CODASYL's schema concept, and the DBDGEN program is similar to the schema DDL.

Each PDB can be used as a basis for a *logical database,* which in its simplest form is a subset of the PDB. The DBA can define several user views on separate PDBs, then combine them into a unit called a program specification block (PSB). When a user view is defined, it results in a program communication block (PCB). Thus, we can say that a PSB consists of one or more PCBs. The PSB is conceptually close to the subschema concept we have been using in the text. Each PCB contains statements that identify which segments and fields are sensitive and which processing options are permitted for each segment.

Complicating an already complex situation are the facts that the DBA can construct a logical relationship between two PDBs and the resulting structure is also called a *logical database* even though it is defined using the DBDGEN

TABLE 11.2   An IMS Acronym Glossary

DBD (data base description)	An object file created by the DBDGEN utility to describe the conceptual and physical properties of a database
DBDGEN (data base description generator)	The utility that describes physical databases
DL/I (Data Language I)	The DML for IMS
ESDS (entry-sequenced data set)	A VSAM sequencing option that maintains records in the order in which they were entered; permits duplicate keys
IMS (Information Management System)	A comprehensive hierarchical-database package from IBM
KSF (key sequence field)	A single field used to sequence child occurrences
LDB (logical database)	A user view based on a single physical database, on two or more unconnected PDBs, or on a logical relationship
LDBR (logical database record)	An occurrence of an LDB
PCB (program control block)	The object form of a user view based on a single PDB
PDB physical (database)	The collection of all the PDBRs
PDBR (physical database record)	A tree occurrence of the physical database
PSB (program specification block)	The subschema; can consist of one or more PCBs
PSBGEN (program specification block generator)	A utility for defining the PSB
SENFLD (sensitive field)	A field made available to a user view (logical database)
SENSEG (sensitive segment)	A segment made available to a user view

program, which is usually used to define physical databases. These logical relationships can then be used to define the more usual kinds of logical databases.

Fortunately, defining an IMS database is the responsibility of the DBA. Only highly sophisticated IS shops use IMS. Luckily, the degree of sophistication required on the part of the programmer is not nearly as great as that for the DBA, as the next chapter will show.

REVIEW QUESTIONS

1. Define the following terms:
   a. Segment.
   b. Segment occurrence.
   c. Root segment.
   d. Dependent segment.
   e. Sensitive segment.
   f. Hierarchical path.
   g. Hierarchic order.
   h. Hierarchic concatenated key.

2. Explain the main difference between a key sequence field and a search field.

3. Explain how these terms differ: PDB, PDBR, DBD, DBDGEN.

4. Which items are defined in the DBD?

5. What is a logical relationship?

6. How are secondary indexes defined?

7. Give definitions for these secondary key terms:
   a. Index database.
   b. Source segment.
   c. Target segment.

8. Why should more frequently accessed segment types be on a left branch of the root?

9. Give the full name for each of the following access methods, and briefly state the kinds of situations where each might be considered:
   a. HSAM.
   b. HISAM.
   c. HDAM.
   d. HIDAM.

10. If HDAM and HIDAM both provide hashed access to root segments, what is the primary advantage of one over the other?

11. What is an index database? Under what circumstances is it needed?

12. What is an LCHILD macro? When is it used?

13. What is the chief disadvantage of not formally defining a field in the DBD?

14. What is a Fast Path database?

15. What is the major restriction of an MSDB database?

16. How does an MSDB database get its speed?

17. List and discuss three kinds of pointers used with the hierarchical access methods.

18. What are logical parents, logical children, and logical twins?

19. What is an SENSEG?

20. How can a DBA restrict user access to fields?

PROBLEMS

Use the following DSD and table for Problems 1–4.

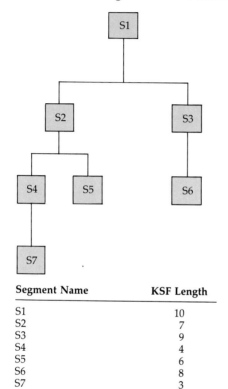

Segment Name	KSF Length
S1	10
S2	7
S3	9
S4	4
S5	6
S6	8
S7	3

1. Give the hierarchical path to S7.
2. What is the HCK length for the path to S6?
3. What is the longest HCK length?
4. Give the hierarchic order.
5. Assume an end user requires the following logical database (based on the HOSP PDB):

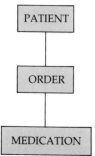

Also, assume that only the ORDER's number is to be made available to the logical database and that ORDERs cannot be deleted. All fields in the other two segments are sensitive, and all DL/I commands are also permitted for those other segments. Code the required PCB and PSB macros.

Use Figure 11.8 for Problems 6 through 10.

6. Give the hierarchic order.
   Assume the following fields, field-types, and lengths:

JOBTITLE	COURSE	EMP	EMPCOURSE
JCODE/C/7	CID/C/6	EID/N/10	CEMPID/N/10
JDESC/C/25	CDESC/C/25	ENAME/C/25	CCID/C/6
			CDATE/C/8

where C = character and N = numeric.

7. Code the DBD(s). Make any other assumptions that are needed. (However, the organization needs to be able to access JOBTITLE segments sequentially and randomly.)

8. Code a complete PSB assuming access to all segments and fields.

9. Based on the following records, show the HCK for the EMPCOURSE segment. Assume the segment occurrences provided all fall on the same hierarchical path (when appropriate).

JOBTITLE

P10	Programmer/Analyst 4

EMP

123451212	Puerer, I.M.

COURSE

CIS101	Assembly Language Coding I

EMPCOURSE

12341212	CIS101	12/15/XX

10. After much discussion with the training department employees, it was discovered that 75 percent of the time queries access the EMPLOYEE occurrences that are related to a given JOBTITLE versus 25 percent of the time in which queries access COURSES that support a title. Draw the DSD that would better support these needs. Base your design on efficiency.

▪▪ EPISODE 7

Defining the IMS Conceptual Database

*Note: Much of this episode presents informa-
tion not found in the chapter and also expands
on our discussion of logical relationships. It
can be skipped without causing problems in
the next episode, which discusses how a
COBOL program references the logical databases defined in this one.*

Barb realized that she couldn't directly
implement her schema (presented in Episode 3) because it contained several portions that included network structures.
Exhibit 1 shows how, for the pharmacy
portion of the conceptual schema from
Episode 3, she developed a hierarchical
logical model by establishing eight physical databases together with several logical
relationships. Barb called a meeting with
Kevin and Alan to discuss her overall design.

"Thank you all for coming," she began. "I know how busy you are, but I

need to explain the conceptual database
design before you begin defining it using
the DBDGEN and PSBGEN utilities.

"The first thing I want you to notice is
that there are eight physical databases.
Basically, I set up a database for each entity group. The dotted lines portray the
logical relationships that I added to handle the network relationships. Let me describe some of the databases for you.

"The FACILITY database contains segments pertaining to the nursing units
(NUs) and their associated ROOMs. The
PATIENT segment carries much of the
data in our original design. For example,
we store DRG (Diagnosis-Related Group)
and location data (nursing unit, room,
and bed) in the PATIENT segment to facilitate reporting. The PATIENT database
will also carry the intersection segment,
PATDOC, which will tell us which PHY-
SICIANs are treating that PATIENT. To

EXHIBIT 1   The Eight Physical Databases for Community Hospital's IMS Database

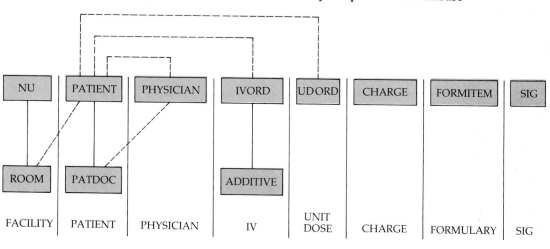

relate the PHYSICIAN to all the PA-TIENTs he or she treats, I set up a logical relationship, shown as the dotted line between PHYSICIAN and PATIENT.

"Because we need to be able to relate a ROOM to the PATIENTs in that ROOM, I also set up a logical relationship between those two segments.

"The fourth and fifth databases are for IV and UNITDOSE orders, respectively. PATIENT segments from the PATIENT database are logical parents of both kinds of orders, thus making those order segments logical children. I also wanted to create a logical relationship between FORMITEM in the FORMULARY database and the root for both databases. However, because IMS supports only one logical parent and one physical parent per segment, and since PATIENT is already the logical parent for both, this wasn't possible. Instead, when we need detailed information about a prescribed drug, we'll just use the drug code contained in the order segment and look up that drug in the FORMULARY database.

"The due times for any order will be determined by storing the SIG code in both IVORD and UDORD. Then, using this code as a key, we can perform a direct look-up of the times in the SIG database. Finally, both the IVORD and UDORD segments will supply data for the CHARGE database, which contains only a root segment. I've not shown a re-lationship between either kind of order and the CHARGE segment. Instead, when an order is filled, we'll update the CHARGE segment in the CHARGE database; there's no real need to relate the two segments using IMS.

"Are there any questions before I proceed?"

Alan spoke up. "Barb, I always have trouble differentiating logical children from their parents. Could you make us a list showing both of them for each of the logical relationships?"

"Sure," replied Barb. "Let me do that, right now." Exhibit 2 shows what she drew for her employees.

Barb explained, "I decided to make all the relationships bidirectional virtual so that we could relate segments in either direction and wouldn't increase redundancy."

Alan interrupted, "What did you say?"

"Sorry," Barb replied, "I guess bidirectional virtual must sound like real computerese. When a logical relationship is set up, it can be unidirectional or bidirectional. The former permits access of a logical parent from a logical child only. A bidirectional relationship is two-way, and that's what we need. The 'virtual' part means that the logical child won't actually be stored but will appear to be.

"Alan, I want you to present some of the conceptual databases our applications have to support."

EXHIBIT 2   The Logical Relationships from Exhibit 1

Logical Relationship	Type
PHYSICIAN:PATDOC	BV
PATIENT:IV	BV
PATIENT:UNITDOSE	BV

The first segment is the logical parent and the second the child. The second column describes whether the relationship is unidirectional (U) or bidirectional virtual (BV).

Alan began by showing three user views, which he called PSB1 through PSB3. These are shown in Exhibit 3.

"The first one permits us to prepare lists of PHYSICIANs, showing all the PA-TIENTs treated for each PHYSICIAN. As you both know, this is becoming more important because most of the hospital's payments are flat fees based on a patient's DRG, and so we have to know which PHYSICIANs require more dollars than we are allocated to treat the PA-TIENTs."

Alan continued, "The next PSB contains two PCBs, one from the IV database and the other from FORMULARY. The last PSB is similar to the second one, so unless there are any questions, I'll let Barb talk again."

Barb concluded the meeting, but only after scheduling another one in three weeks to describe how the coding for the

EXHIBIT 3   Three User Views Based on the Databases in Exhibit 2

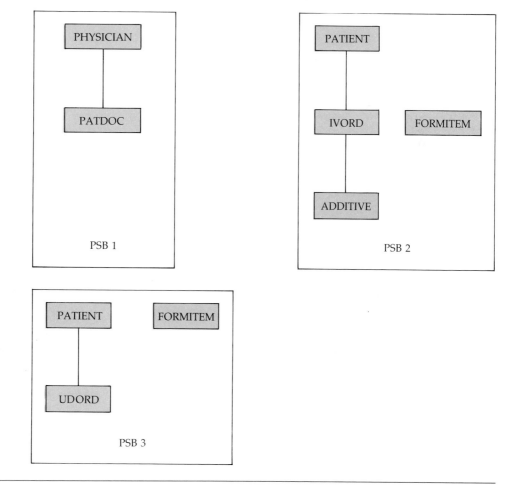

DBDs was progressing. Let's listen in on part of that subsequent meeting.

Barb began, "Kevin, you were assigned the responsibility of defining the PATIENT database [see Exhibit 4]. Could you please explain how you did this?"

Kevin replied, "The database is HIDAM, so we can produce a listing of all the PATIENTs by patient number, which is the key sequence field. Look at the PATIENT segment. The first LCHILD macro is for the index database. It shows that it

---

EXHIBIT 4   The DBDGEN for the PATIENT Database

```
DBD      NAME=PATIENT,ACCESS=HIDAM
DATASET...
SEGM     NAME=PATIENT,PARENT=0,BYTES=256,PTR=(T)
FIELD    NAME=(PATNO,SEQ,U),BYTES=11,START=1
FIELD    NAME=PATNAME,BYTES=25,START=12
FIELD    NAME=NU,BYTES=4,START=38
FIELD    NAME=ROOM,BYTES=4,START=43
FIELD    NAME=BED,BYTES=2,START=47
FIELD    NAME=DRG,BYTES=4,START=49
  .
  .
  .
LCHILD NAME=(PIDX,PATIDX),PTR=INDEX
LCHILD NAME=(UDORD,UNITDOSE),PAIR=PUD,PTR=SNGL
LCHILD NAME=(IVORD,IV),PAIR=PIV,PTR=SNGL
...
SEGM     NAME=PATDOC,PARENT=((PATIENT,DBLE),
         (PHYSICIAN,PHYSICIAN))
FIELD    NAME=(DOCNO,SEQ,U),BYTES=...
  .
  .
  .
SEGM     NAME=PIV,PTR=PAIRED,PARENT=PATIENT,
         SOURCE=((IVORD,IV))
* this PIV segment is for the bidirectional logical relationship
*  between PATIENT and IVORD in the IV database
FIELD    NAME=(PIVORD,SEQ,U), BYTES...
FIELD    NAME=PORDNO,...
  .
  .
  .
* unit dose virtual segment next
SEGM     NAME=PUD,PTR=PAIRED,PARENT=PATIENT,
         SOURCE=((UDORD,UNITDOSE))
FIELD    NAME=(...),...
  .
  .
  .
DBDGEN
FINISH
END
```

is called PATIDX and that the segment that will store the index entries in that database is PIDX.

"Next, I defined the two logical children [see Exhibit 1]: UDORD and IVORD, both of which appear in other databases. Because Barb decided on virtual pairing for the logical relationships, I set up two virtual segments: PIV and PUD. It will appear to the end users that the PIV and PUD segments are children of PATIENT, but they really won't be. This will enable us to handle PSB 2 and 3 that we saw in our previous meeting.

"The PAIR statement on the second LCHILD macro states that UDORD and PUD are really the same segment, and therefore when an application requests a PUD segment, DL/I should actually retrieve a UDORD one. The last parameter, PTR = SNGL, means that IMS is to maintain a logical first-child pointer in each occurrence of PATIENT that points to the initial unit dose order. I won't explain the next LCHILD, which is for the IVORD relationship, because it is similar to the previous one.

"The next interesting point is that PATDOC has two parents: one a physical one, PATIENT, and the other a logical one, PHYSICIAN, which is stored in the PHYSICIAN database. Look at the definition of PATDOC as I explain it. First, I coded the reference to the physical parent (PATIENT) and decided to use both a first- and last-child pointer for all of the physical parent [PATIENT] occurrences. This is specified by the DBLE clause inside the parentheses.

"The second set of PATDOC parentheses specifies that the logical parent is PHYSICIAN [the first parameter] and is found in the PHYSICIAN database [the second parameter].

Let me describe the virtual segments next. The first segment's name is PIV, which stands for PATIENT-IV. It is

PAIRED with IVORD, and the source for the paired segment is the IV database; the segment's name is IVORD, and its virtual parent is PATIENT. The remainder of the FIELD macros merely redefine the actual IV fields except for the virtual one. When we access a PIV segment, we'll actually be retrieving an IVORD segment.

"The other virtual segment is PUD (PATIENT-UNIT DOSE). This is also a virtual child of PATIENT. Because the PAIR statement in the LCHILD macro for UDORD used the value PUD as the PAIRED segment name, I had to use that same name in coding the PUD segment. Its parent is PATIENT, and the actual segments are called UDORD, which can be found in the UNITDOSE database.

"I think that about completes the PATIENT DBDGEN. Any questions?"

"I don't think so," Barb replied. "Alan, how about the IV database that you defined? Would you mind going over it for us?"

Alan began, "Well, the first tricky thing [see Exhibit 5] was how to specify the logical parent of the IVORD segment. I had to define the segment as a root, which I did by specifying the zero inside the first pair of parentheses. I could have omitted the zero clause, since it is optional, but I included it for the sake of clarity. Next, I defined the logical parent. The second set of parentheses indicates that its logical parent is a segment called PATIENT and is found in the PATIENT database. Kevin already discussed how the PATIENT segment used the LCHILD macro to tie this database to his, so hopefully I don't need to discuss this.

"The other thing I had some trouble with was deciding what kinds of pointers to use with the IVORD segments. I finally decided on a logical parent pointer (LP), which connects each IVORD occurrence back to its logical parent in the PA-

---

EXHIBIT 5   The DBDGEN for the IV Database

```
DBD      NAME=IV,...
DATASET...
SEGM    NAME=IVORD,PARENT=((0),(PATIENT,PATIENT)),
        BYTES=128,PTR=(LP,LT,TB)
* notice the two parents: one physical, one logical
*   the logical one is called PATIENT and is in the
*   PATIENT database
FIELD  NAME=(ORDNO,SEQ,U),BYTES=5,START=1
  .
  .

  .
* define the index next
LCHILD NAME=(IVIDX,IVXDB),PTR=INDEX
SEGM   NAME=ADDITIVE,PARENT=((IVORD),(FORMITEM,FORMULARY)),
       BYTES=100,PTR=(TB)
* the logical parent is FORMITEM and is in the
*   FORMULARY database
FIELD...
DBDGEN
FINISH
END
```

EXHIBIT 6   The DBDGEN for the FORMULARY Database

```
DBD  NAME=FORMULARY,...
DATASET...
SEGM   NAME=FORMITEM,PARENT=0,BYTES=128
FIELD  NAME=(ITEMCODE,SEQ,U),BYTES=7,START=1
  .
  .

  .
* define index location next
LCHILD NAME=(FORMIDX,FRMIDX),POINTER,INDX
DBDGEN
FINISH
END
```

TIENT database; a logical forward twin pointer (LT), which connects the IVORD occurrences for a given PATIENT; and [physical] twin backward pointers (TB), which connect one IVORD to the previous one.

"Since you also asked me to define the FORMULARY database, I might as well show it to you now [see Exhibit 6]. It's quite simple, because it contains only a root, but it does have a single logical child that is used for the index because it's a HIDAM database. I really wish we could make it a logical parent of both IVORD and UDORD, but we can't.

"Are there any questions?"

EXHIBIT 7   A PSB to Implement PSB Number 2 in Exhibit 3

```
PCB      TYPE=DB,DBDNAME=PATIENT
SENSEG   NAME=PATIENT,PARENT=0,PROCOPT=A
PCB      TYPE=DB,DBDNAME=IV
SENSEG   NAME=IVORD,PARENT=0,PROCOPT=A
SENSEG   NAME=ADDITIVE,PARENT=IV,PROCOPT=A
PCB      TYPE=DB,DBDNAME=FORMULARY
SENSEG   NAME=FORMITEM,PARENT=0,PROCOPT=A
PSBGEN   LANG=COBOL,PSBNAME=PSB001
```

No one had any, so the meeting concluded. Barb scheduled yet another one for the following week to discuss the PSBs.

"WOW!" exclaimed Kevin. "I didn't realize that defining an IMS database would be so complicated."

"Sorry, Kevin", Barb responded, "But since you were the first to speak up, why don't you begin by explaining how you coded the PSB for the IV processing? I guess that's the one we labeled PSB2."

Kevin replied, "As you can see from my figure [Exhibit 7], I actually had to pull segments from three databases: PATIENT from PATIENT, IVORD and ADDITIVE from IV, and FORMITEM from FORMULARY. Since we didn't want to create any logical databases, I left all the segments separate, each coded as a different PCB. The result is a collection of three user databases that can be used in a single application. The PSB name we will use in our applications in PSB001, and all processing options are OK."

The rest of the meeting concluded with the members of Barb's database team presenting their PSBs.

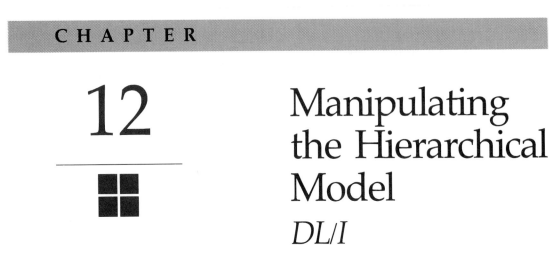

12

Manipulating the Hierarchical Model

DL/I

Of all the components of IMS, none is as important for our purposes as Data Language I (DL/I), the IMS component that an application calls to insert (ISRT), replace (REPL), or delete (DLET) segments. This chapter looks at the COBOL calls to DL/I and the four ways in which the application and DL/I communicate with each other.

At the conclusion of this chapter, you will be able to:

- Identify the four communication mechanisms that enable an application and DL/I to communicate with each other
- Describe the components of a DL/I call from COBOL
- Code a segment search argument (SSA)
- Discuss how to code, and the uses for, command codes
- Retrieve segments directly or sequentially
- Add new records to an existing database
- Delete and update existing segments

We will begin by examining how the host application and DL/I work together. For them to do so, a host program must establish four communication mechanisms:

- Passing of control to the application from IMS
- Communicating of processing requests to DL/I
- Exchanging of information with DL/I
- Termination of the communications with IMS

The relationship between an application and IMS is symbiotic; each depends on the other for success, and each benefits from the other's existence. Both typically share a single memory partition, with IMS viewing the application as a subtask of itself and the application treating IMS as a subprogram that is called like any subprogram using the COBOL CALL statement. Thus, each "thinks" it is in charge of the partition. The host program is responsible for four layers of communication between the two:

- ENTRY/GOBACK to initiate/cease communications
- CALL to designate which functions and segments are to be used
- The establishment of a shared communications region, called a program communication block mask
- The establishment of one or more I/O areas for transfer of segment contents

Using an ENTRY statement in the COBOL program, the application indicates where IMS is to give control to the application when it is ready to do so. This statement must be the first executable one in the PROCEDURE DIVISION. To cease communications with IMS, the program must issue a GOBACK statement rather than a STOP RUN.

The communication with DL/I about the kind of processing to be performed is achieved through CALL statements, which, like the DML statements we saw with the CODASYL network and relational models, are embedded within the COBOL program. Because the exact syntax is complicated, we will often substitute a shorthand coding scheme that omits many of the details. In the calls to DL/I, the application must share two kinds of information: the result (success or failure) of each call and the segment occurrences.

With the other two models, we saw there is a mechanism for the sharing of data between the DBMS and the host program: CODASYL uses special registers that the host program doesn't need to define, and DB2 uses SQLCA, a programmer-defined structure containing several data elements. When using IMS, the application sets up a comparable area called the **program communication block (PCB) mask**, which is coded in the LINKAGE SECTION and contains nine fields. The programmer must be careful in defining the PCB mask, because IMS expects eight of the fields to be of a predetermined length, and any deviation will result in an abnormal program ending (ABEND). Because of this problem, most organizations copy the PCB mask source code into the COBOL program from a source statement library, where the PCB mask was stored as a **library member.**

The segments that are accessed by DL/I and those to be stored by DL/I are passed back and forth between the application and IMS in an I/O area, which is simply a collection of record definitions in the WORKING-STORAGE SECTION. Each sensitive segment should have a corresponding I/O area.

The call statement contains four parameters:

- The function to be performed
- The PCB mask name
- The I/O area name in WORKING-STORAGE

■ Zero, one, or more **segment search arguments** (**SSAs**), parameters that qualify the segment to be retrieved

DL/I call statements can be embedded in either batch or on-line applications, but we will examine only the former. First, we will explore the four kinds of communications. Then we will look at the call statements in detail.

All the examples in this chapter are based on the three-level PHARMPSB from Chapter 11. Recall that the logical database (called the *external, subschema,* or *user view* by other models) contained three segments: PATIENT, ORDER, and MED (in Chapter 11, we changed the name from MEDICATION to MED). The program communication block (PCB) and program specification block (PSB) were defined in Figure 11.18.

Figure 12.1 shows a program skeleton that we will use for much of our discussion. The nine item numbers in the right margin are reference points for later discussion.

12.1   THE ENTRY AND GOBACK STATEMENTS: ESTABLISHING AND TERMINATING COMMUNICATIONS WITH IMS

The first executable statement of a batch IMS program in the PROCEDURE DIVISION must be an ENTRY statement of the form shown by item 7 in Figure 12.1:

ENTRY 'DLITCBL' USING PCB-MASK1, . . .

                ↑————————— Other PCB mask names
                                would be coded here

To execute an IMS program, the operating system passes control to IMS, which in turn gives control to the application at the above ENTRY point. The only requirement is to use all the PCB masks the program will be referencing—one in our example. If a PSB contains multiple PCBs (as in Figure 11.19), then all the PCBs must be listed in the same order as in the PSB. We discuss PCB masks in more detail in Section 12.2.

The GOBACK statement (item 9) returns control to IMS. An IMS application must use this statement rather than STOP RUN to terminate. If it fails to do so, control will return not to IMS but to the operating system, denying IMS a chance to perform some of its necessary housekeeping routines.

In addition to sharing the memory partition, IMS and the application must share PCBs. Only a portion of each PCB is actually available to the application: the portion specified by the PCB mask. IMS communicates with an application in

FIGURE 12.1   General Structure of an IMS Host Program

```
WORKING-STORAGE SECTION.
*
* set up a WORKING-STORAGE variable for each DL/I function
*
*       01 DLI-FUNCTIONS COPY DLI-FUNCTIONS
        01 DLI-FUNCTIONS.
*          COPY IMSFUNCT.
           03  GU                    PIC X(4) VALUE 'GU  '.
           03  GN                    PIC X(4) VALUE 'GN  '.
           03  GNP                   PIC X(4) VALUE 'GNP '.
           03  GHU                   PIC X(4) VALUE 'GHU '.
           03  GHNP                  PIC X(4) VALUE 'GHNP'.
           03  REPL                  PIC X(4) VALUE 'REPL'.      (1)
           03  DLET                  PIC X(4) VALUE 'DLET'.
           03  REPL                  PIC X(4) VALUE 'REPL'.
*
* UWAs for database segments next
*
        01 WS-PAT.
           03 WS-PAT-NO              PIC X(10).
           03 WS-PAT-NAME            PIC X(25).                  (2)
           03 WS-PAT-AMOUNT-BILLED   PIC 9(7)V99 COMP-3.

        01 WS-ORDER.
              03 WS-ORD-NO           PIC X(6).
              03 WS-ORD-PAT-NO       PIC X(11).
              03 WS-ORD-DATE         PIC X(8).                   (3)
              03 WS-RPH-INIT         PIC X(3).
              03 WS-ORDER-STATUS     PIC X.
              03 WS-ORD-CHARGE       PIC 9(7)V99 COMP-3.

        01 WS-MED.

              03 WS-MEDCOD           PIC X(7).
              03 WS-ORDERNO          PIC X(6).
              03 WS-MEDDESC          PIC X(25).                  (4)
              03 WS-MED-AMOUNT       PIC X(7).
*
* sample SSA next
*
*       01 PAT-SSA COPY PAT-SSA
        01 PAT-SSA.
           03 PAT-SSA-SEG-NAME       PIC X(8) VALUE 'PATIENT '.
           03 PAT-SSA-CMD-STAR       PIC X VALUE '*'
           03 PAT-SSA-CCDS.
              05 PAT-CC1             PIC X VALUE '-'.
              05 PAT-CC2             PIC X VALUE '-'.            (5)
           03 PAT-SSA-LEFTP          PIC X VALUE '('.
           03 PAT-SSA-FIELD-NAME     PIC X(8) VALUE 'PATCOD  '.
           03 PAT-SSA-REL-OP         PIC X(2) VALUE ' ='.
           03 PAT-SSA-FIELD-VALUE    PIC X(10).
           03 PAT-SSA-RIGHTP         PIC X VALUE ')'.
```

FIGURE 12.1   (concluded)

```
*
* rest of WORKING-STORAGE here
*
      .
      .
      .

 LINKAGE SECTION.
*
* define Program Communiction Block (PCB) masks next
*
       01   PHARM-PCB.
            03  PHARM-DBD-NAME          PIC X(8).
            03  PHARM-SEG-LEVEL         PIC X(2).
            03  PHARM-STATUS            PIC X(2).
            03  PHARM-PROCOPTS          PIC X(4).                (6)
            03  PHARM-RES-IMS           PIC S9(5) COMP.
            03  PHARM-SEG-NAME          PIC X(8).
            03  PHARM-KEY-FEEDBACK-LEN  PIC S9(5) COMP.
            03  PHARM-NO-SENSEGS        PIC S9(5) COMP.
            03  PHARM-KFBACK            PIC X(42).
PROCEDURE DIVISION.

       ENTRY 'DLITCBL' USING PHARM-PCB                          (7)
       .
       .
       .
       CALL 'CBLTDLI' USING FUNCTION,PHARM-PCB,UWA,SSA1,...      (8)
       .
       .
       .
       GOBACK                                                   (9)
       .
       .
       .
```

The numbers to the right are keyed to comments within the chapter; they are not part of the program.

---

essentially the same way that a COBOL program communicates with a subprogram: IMS is the main-line, and the application is the subprogram.

All parameters passed from a COBOL main-line to a subprogram must be defined in the LINKAGE SECTION. That's all a PCB mask is: a series of data elements used to communicate with a DL/I subprogram. A mask must be defined for each logical database (PCB) found in the PSB. For example, based on Figure 11.19, the ENTRY statement might look like this:

ENTRY 'DLITCBL' USING DIVPCB, TRAINPCB

TABLE 12.1   **The Nine Fields in a PCB Mask**

Field Name	Length (in Bytes)
Database name	8
Segment level number	2
Status code	2
Processing options	4
Reserved for IMS	4
Segment name	8
Length of key feedback area	4
Number of sensitive segments	4
Key feedback area value	Variable

where DIVPCB and TRAINPCB are defined like PHARM-PCB in Figure 12.1, but have different values for the lengths of their respective key feedback areas.

DL/I is called by an application through a COBOL CALL statement, performs the desired operation, and places information about the results (not the segment's field values) into the PCB mask indicated by one of the parameters in the CALL statement. It places the results (segment values) into the UWA.

All PCB masks contain nine fields, eight of which must be defined according to IMS standards. The names of the fields are immaterial, but their lengths are predetermined. Table 12.1 shows the nine fields together with their lengths.

Consider the PHARMPSB database. Because there is only one logical database (PCB), there need be only one PCB mask in the host programs that reference it. Item 6 in Figure 12.1 shows a suitable PCB mask.

Let's examine the nine fields in Figure 12.1 in order.

The DBD Name

After each CALL to DL/I, the DBD name field, PHARM-DBD-NAME, will contain the name of the database description (DBD) where IMS accessed or stored a segment. Because the PCB mask in Figure 12.1 was defined on the HOSP database (see Figure 11.18), this field will always contain the value HOSP.

The Segment Level Number

When a segment is retrieved, DL/I places its level number into the segment level number field. For example, if a MED occurrence is retrieved, PHARM-SEG-LEVEL will have a value of 3 because its hierarchical path is PATIENT, ORDER, MED.

If a call is unsuccessful, DL/I will put the level number of the last segment it was able to access into the field. For example, if an error occurred in moving from an ORDER occurrence to the desired MED, the field's value will be 2.

TABLE 12.2   Some IMS/VS Status Code Values

AK	An SSA contains an invalid field name.
AO	The access method (VSAM, QSAM, etc.) has reported a physical error.
DJ	The application tried to do a DLET or REPL without first issuing a "hold" command.
FC	An invalid CALL for the segment has been issued.
GA	DL/I crossed a hierarchical boundary from a segment at one level to one at a higher level.
GB	In trying to satisfy a GN command, the physical end of the database was reached.
GE	DL/I couldn't find the requested segment or couldn't find the parent of a segment being inserted.
GK	In retrieving a segment occurrence, DL/I crossed from one segment type to another segment type, but at the same level. Seen with unqualified GN or GNP calls.
GP	Although an application has issued a GNP call, no parentage was established.
II	The application tried to insert a segment that already exists.
LC	The key field of the segment being loaded is out of sequence.
LD	No parent exists for the segment being loaded.
bb	(Blanks) The call was successful.

The Status Code

PHARM-STATUS is the two-byte field the host program must check to determine the success or failure of all IMS calls. Table 12.2 shows the most important of the over 100 status codes that DL/I can return. Notice that if a call is successful, the status code will contain two blanks. Two commonly used nonblank codes are GK and GA.

When sequentially processing a database, segments from different levels will likely be retrieved. A code of GK means that the most recently accessed segment is of a different type than the previous one and is also at the same level. This is not a fatal error but an informational message. A code of GA is similar, but it means that a segment in a higher level than the previous one has been retrieved. In both cases, the desired segment was retrieved without a problem, but a level boundary was crossed and DL/I is indicating this.

Another commonly used value is GB, meaning that the end of the database has been reached. A value of GE means that the requested segment couldn't be found—usually the result of a "direct" access. (Recall that with few exceptions, IMS cannot perform a true direct access.)

The Processing Options

The four-byte field PHARM-PROCOPTS will contain the processing options that this program can issue. The value is the same as that found in the PROCOPT statement of the PSBGEN process, which we saw in the previous chapter.

The Reserved for IMS Field

IMS uses this field for internal linkage. We won't discuss it here.

The Segment Name

When a call is successful, the name of the lowest segment level that DL/I was able to access will be placed into PHARM-SEG-NAME. Usually it contains the name of the desired segment. When the call is unsuccessful, it will contain the name of the last segment that DL/I could process.

The Length of the Key Feedback Area

This is the length of the hierarchic concatenated key (HCK) that we discussed in the previous chapter. In Figure 12.1, PHARM-KEY-FEEDBACK-LEN will contain the size (in bytes) of the concatenated key resulting from the retrieval of a given segment.

For example, after retrieval of a PATIENT, which has a key sequence field length of 10 bytes, PHARM-KEY-FEEDBACK-LEN would be 10. However, if a MED occurrence were retrieved, the field's value would be 41, as explained in Chapter 11.

The Number of Sensitive Segments

DL/I will place the number of segments to which the application is sensitive into this field. Since PHARMPSB was sensitive to three segments, PHARM-NO-SENSEGS will always have a value of 3.

The Key Feedback Area

The key feedback area field contains the actual concatenated key value. For example, when a MED segment is retrieved, the 41 bytes of PHARM-KFBACK will consist of the PATNO value concatenated with ORDNO and then with MEDDESC (the KSFs for the segments on the hierarchical path—PATIENT, ORDER, MED). When a PATIENT segment is retrieved, PHARM-KFBACK's value will be the same as PATNO, the KSF for PATIENT.

This field, like the segment level number and name fields, is most useful when performing a sequential scan of the database or when a program ends abnormally. Unlike the other fields, its length is variable and should equal the KEYLEN value on the PSBGEN (see Figure 11.18).

12.3   THE I/O AREAS: RECORD DEFINITIONS (UWAs) FOR IMS SEGMENT TYPES

As part of the call's syntax, an I/O area must be specified indicating where DL/I is to place the retrieved segment occurrence or where to find the segment to be inserted into the database. Like a COBOL FD, and similar in function to the CODASYL subschema SECTION that defines the UWA, an IMS I/O area defines a segment, but it is coded in the WORKING-STORAGE SECTION. Each sensitive segment should have an I/O area defined in the WORKING-STORAGE SECTION.

In Figure 11.18, the DBA defined three sensitive segments for the PHARMPSB database: PATIENT, ORDER, and MED. This means that there should be three record definitions within the I/O area. These are indicated in Figure 12.1 as items 2 through 4.

Each of the three records corresponds to its definition in the DBD (see Figure 11.15), but the field names have been changed and those fields that were defined as Packed now use the COMP-3 specification. We took some liberties with the data elements in ORDER because, according to Figure 11.18, only three are sensitive; yet we defined six of them in Figure 12.1.

When we build a record prior to passing it to DL/I for storage, we will do so in one of these three areas. Also, when DL/I retrieves a segment, it will be placed into one of them depending on the syntax of the call to DL/I. Finally, before a segment can be deleted or replaced, it must be placed into its respective I/O area. To replace (update) a segment, we modify the field values in the I/O area rather than those in the DBD.

12.4   THE DL/I COBOL CALL

There are four components of a DL/I call from COBOL:

- The function name
- The PCB mask name
- The I/O area to use
- Zero, one, or more segment search arguments (SSAs)

A sample call is item 8 in Figure 12.1. In general, the COBOL CALL statement is coded as in Figure 12.2.

Function

Table 12.3 shows nine DL/I commands. The length of the command name that is passed to DL/I must be four bytes. For example, to use the GU function we might code: CALL 'CBLTDLI' USING 'GU   ', ...

Using this method of calling DL/I invites coding errors, however, so it is

FIGURE 12.2   **Components of a DL/I CALL Statement**

> CALL 'CBLTDLI' USING FUNCTION, PCB-MASK, WS-SEG-NAME, SSA1, SSA2, . . .

where:

FUNCTION is a four-byte function abbreviation chosen from Table 12.3.

PCB-MASK is the name of the PCB mask to be used by IMS to communicate the results of the CALL back to the application.

WS-SEG-NAME is the name of the record in WORKING-STORAGE that is to be used by both DL/I and the application to transfer segments back and forth.

SSA1, SSA2, . . . are segment search arguments used to qualify the function.

An SSA contains three optional parameters:

A segment name.
Zero, one, or more **command codes.**
A qualifying statement or statements.

TABLE 12.3   **Some DL/I Commands**

Command	Purpose
GU (Get Unique)	Direct retrieval
GN (Get Next)	Sequential segment retrieval
GNP (Get Next within Parent)	Sequential retrieval of dependent segments only
GHU (Get Hold Unique)	Like GU but used to retrieve a segment for subsequent deletion (DLET) or replacement (REPL)
GHN (Get Hold Next)	Like GN (see GHU for usage)
GHNP (Get Hold Next within Parent)	Like GNP (see GHU for usage)
ISRT (Insert)	Add a new segment to the database
REPL (Replace)	Modifies segment field values
DLET (Delete)	Deletes segments

customary for an IS department to establish a source statement library member that contains nine data elements, then COPY the member into the COBOL source program within the WORKING-STORAGE section. This was the method assumed in item 1 in Figure 12.1.

Once the COBOL source statements that define the function names are copied into a host program, as in Figure 12.1, the DL/I call might look like this:

CALL 'CBLTDLI' USING GU, . . .

where GU is one of the 03-level names in the DLI-FUNCTIONS structure in Figure 12.1.

PCB Mask Name

The PCB mask name is the name of the PCB mask DL/I will use to communicate with the host program. In our example, the name has to be PHARM-PCB. The call to DL/I can now be expanded to include the PCB mask name:

CALL 'CBLTDLI' USING GU, PHARM-PCB, . . .

I/O Name

When IMS accesses a segment, it places it into the I/O name specified in the CALL statement. Assuming that a PATIENT segment is to be retrieved, our evolving call now looks like this:

CALL 'CBLTDLI' USING GU, PHARM-PCB, WS-PAT, . . .

⌐I/O name (see item 2 in Figure 12.1)

    After the PATIENT segment occurrence is retrieved, the application uses the WS-PAT record and its associated COBOL data element names for any subsequent processing, not the names found in the DBD.

Segment Search Arguments (SSAs)

A **segment search argument** (**SSA**) is a mechanism used to qualify a call to DL/I. There are three possible elements to an SSA: a segment name, one or more command codes, and a qualifying statement. They are coded like this:

> segment-name cc (search-field-name ro value)
>
> where: cc indicates a command code.
>   ro indicates a relational operator
>   value is a search argument value for the search field

Unqualified SSAs. If a call to DL/I contains a segment name only, the SSA is said to be **unqualified.** An unqualified SSA example, using a shorthand coding scheme that omits the CALL, PCB-mask, and I/O area name, would be:

GU MED

This requests the first MED occurrence.

Qualified SSAs. If the SSA also contains a search field and one or more search values, the SSA is **qualified.** An example would be:

MED (MEDCODE = PCN).

MEDCODE is the search field, and the value after the equal sign is the search value.

Neither of the above examples uses a command code (discussed shortly).

Let's look at the SSA components in more detail.

The Segment Name. The segment name parameter tells DL/I which segment type to retrieve and must match the name used in the DBD. The application must be sensitive to the segment. A complicating factor is that SSAs can be concatenated, with several appearing in a CALL statement. In this case, unless a particular command code is used, the only segment that is retrieved will be the one whose name appears in the last SSA.

The Command Codes. The command codes specify an advanced function option. To inform DL/I that we will use a command code, we put an asterisk (∗) immediately after the segment name. We can also mix null codes—hyphens— with command codes to reserve positions for later use. To mark the end of a command code, we use either a blank (when the SSA is unqualified) or a left parenthesis (when the SSA is qualified).

Table 12.4 shows several of the available command codes that we will discuss later.

Qualifying Statements. To further qualify the call, we can tell IMS to search for a particular segment occurrence. Now the SSA must contain one or more **qualifying statements.** Each qualifying statement requires five elements:

- A left parenthesis
- A search field name
- A relational operator

TABLE 12.4   Some of the DL/I Command Codes

Command Code	Meaning
D	A path call meaning to retrieve, or insert, multiple segments with a single function call
F	Retrieve the first occurrence of the specified segment type
L	Retrieve the last occurrence of the specified segment type
Q	Lock the segment that is accessed
P	Set parentage at the accessed segment
-	A null command code, useful when using a data structure to define SSAs

- A search, or comparative, value
- A right parenthesis

For example, to search for a PATIENT whose last name is SMITH we might code the line shown in Figure 12.3. If compound operators are needed, we use * or & for AND and + or | for OR.

Let's complete the sample call we have been developing. Assume we want the PATIENT occurrence with a PATNO value of 111403789A. The complete qualified SSA call is:

```
CALL 'CBLTDLI' USING GU, PHARM-PCB, WS-PAT,
        'PATIENT (PATNO = 111403789A)'
```
↑
└─────────────── This complete literal is the SSA

Using our shorthand, the above call would be:

GU PATIENT (PATNO = 111403789A)

Instead of coding the SSA as a literal in the CALL statement, as above, most organizations use standard SSAs, which are defined and stored in a source statement library. Then they COPY the members into the application in WORK-ING-STORAGE, as we did in item 5 in Figure 12.1. If we looked at how PAT-SSA looks in memory, we would see this:

"PATIENTb*--(PATCOD = bbbbbbbbbb')"
↑
└─Represents blanks ⇒
PAT-SSA-FIELD-VALUE has no value yet

In effect, we have simply created the SSA in WORKING-STORAGE. The only thing missing is a value for PAT-SSA-FIELD-VALUE. To use PAT-SSA, we first MOVE a value to PAT-SSA-FIELD-VALUE, then use PAT-SSA in the call:

```
MOVE '111403789A' TO PAT-SSA-FIELD-VALUE
CALL 'CBLTDLI' USING GU, PHARM-PCB, WS-PAT, PAT-SSA
```

FIGURE 12.3   A Complete DL/I Call Using Command Codes and a Qualified SSA

```
CALL 'CBLTDLI' USING GU, PHARM-PCB, WS-PAT, 'PATIENT * - - (LNAME = SMITH)'
                                                          ΛΛΛ
                          A Command code sequence────────┘┘┘
                            " – " ⇒ null code

                          Relational operator ──────────────────┘
                          Search value ──────────────────────────────┘
```

If the organization adopts this principle (and most do), there will be several SSAs in the source statement library for each segment—one for each possible search field.

12.5 KINDS OF CALLS

There are two general kinds of calls to DL/I: unqualified and qualified. An unqualified call has no SSAs, while a qualified one does. To complicate things, as we discussed above, there are two kinds of qualified calls: those with qualified SSAs (these have a left parenthesis, a segment name, and a qualifying statement) and those without (an unqualified SSA call), which contain only a segment name.

Unqualified Calls

An unqualified call might look like this:

CALL 'CBLTDLI' USING GU, PHARM-PCB, WS-PAT

No SSA ⟶

Using our shorthand, it would be expressed this way:

GU

The example is unqualified because there is no SSA.

Qualified Calls

We have seen examples of both kinds of qualified calls: those with unqualified SSAs (have no qualification statements) and those with qualified SSAs (contain qualification statements). IMS looks for the left parenthesis to determine whether or not the SSA is qualified. An unqualified SSA call, using our shorthand, might be:

GU ORDER

⟶ Segment name only = unqualified SSA

It is unqualified because only a segment name is used. To qualify the SSA, we would add a qualification statement, for example:

GU ORDER (ORDNO = 100)

⟶ Segment name + search field + search value = a qualified SSA

The above is a qualified SSA call because it contains a search field in addition to a segment name.

We are now ready to look at the DL/I DML. First, we discuss direct retrieval, a misnomer for all but root segments, because of IMS's reliance on the hierarchic sequence of segment occurrences.

12.6 DIRECT RETRIEVAL: THE GET UNIQUE (GU) FUNCTION

Direct access is technically possible only for root (HDAM and HIDAM) segments. However, the GU function can be used on any segment. For dependent segments, the call results in IMS having to follow the hierarchic sequence of segment occurrences until it locates the desired occurrence. Using pointers can reduce this search time.

Direct Retrieval of the First Root: The Unqualified GU Call

Using the GU function without an SSA results in the program accessing the first root occurrence in the database. It is useful as a priming read when followed by one of the sequential (Get Next) calls.

As an example, let's retrieve the first PATIENT in the database. The full syntax would be

CALL 'CBLTDLI' USING GU, PHARM-PCB, WS-PAT

or, using our shorthand,

GU

The statement will place the initial PATIENT root segment into the WS-PAT structure (item 2 in Figure 12.1).

Direct Retrieval of the First Occurrence of Any Segment: An Unqualified SSA Call

When we need to access the first occurrence of a given segment type, we use an unqualified SSA call consisting of GU plus the segment name.

Problem 1. **Retrieve the first ORDER in the database using the shorthand call syntax.**

Solution. The answer is:

GU ORDER

The function is GU, and the SSA consists of merely a segment name. If we wanted to access the other ORDERs, we would follow this with a loop containing a GN function call, which we will discuss later.

Direct Retrieval of a Specified Occurrence: A Qualified SSA Call

To directly retrieve a given segment, we use the GU function with a qualified SSA. This function might be better thought of as "Find First," because if several segments satisfy the request, only the first one is retrieved.

Problem 2. **Retrieve the first PATIENT with last name SMITH.**

Solution.

```
GU PATIENT (LNAME = SMITH)
IF PHARM-STATUS = 'GE'
     THEN
          DISPLAY 'NO SUCH PATIENT'
     ELSE
          MOVE WS-PAT TO PRINT-LINE . . .
```

This problem shows not only the GU function but also one of the two possible status code values, discussed next.

GU Status Codes

The GU status codes are as follows:

bb The call was completely successful

GE DL/I could not find a segment that met the request

In Problem 2, if DL/I couldn't find a PATIENT with the name SMITH, the value of PHARM-STATUS would be GE. As we did with the CODASYL and relational models, we should check for possible errors and take appropriate action following every DML call.

GU with Multiple SSAs

Problem 3. **What is the first ORDER for PATIENT 123?**

Solution.

```
GU PATIENT (PATCOD = 123)
     ORDER
IF PHARM-STATUS = 'GE'
     THEN
          DISPLAY 'NO ORDERS FOR PATIENT', PATCOD
     ELSE
          MOVE WS-ORD TO PRINT-LINE . . .
```

In this example, two SSAs are specified. As previously mentioned, when two or more SSAs are used, only the segment at the lowest level is moved to the I/O area. This means that only the ORDER segment would be moved to WORK-ING-STORAGE and that in the complete syntax WS-ORDER would be specified as the I/O area.

Because the first level is qualified, the search for the ORDER is restricted to that PATIENT. Remember that GU always finds the first occurrence that matches the qualified SSA. Because the second SSA is unqualified, DL/I will retrieve the first ORDER for that PATIENT.

If you omit an SSA for any level, DL/I assumes one. Usually the assumption is that the SSA is unqualified. Let's look at an example.

Problem 4. **List the first ORDER in the database.**

Solution.

GU ORDER

Because we didn't specify a PATIENT, a level-1 segment, DL/I assumes we coded

GU PATIENT
    ORDER

that is, that the SSA for PATIENT was unqualified.

The above solution does not guarantee that the ORDER will be for the first PATIENT because the initial SSA is unqualified. Rather, it says to find the first ORDER regardless of with which PATIENT it is associated.

GU with Command codes

Problem 5. **What is the last ORDER for PATIENT 123?**

Solution.

GU PATIENT (PATCOD = 123)
    ORDER *L
IF PHARM-STATUS = 'GE'
    THEN
        DISPLAY 'NO ORDERS FOR PATIENT', PATCD.

The use of the L command code changes how GU works. Instead of the first ORDER, DL/I will retrieve the last one. This command code cannot be used with root segments. If it is, DL/I will ignore it.

Problem 6. **What is the name of the PATIENT assigned to the first ORDER?**

Solution.

GU PATIENT *D
    ORDER

When we use the D (*path*) command code, we are telling DL/I to retrieve not only the segment found in the last SSA but also the one containing the D code.

It might be helpful if we look at a more complete (yet still not complete) syntax:

GU, PHARM-PCB, WS-PAT, PATIENT *D, ORDER

This is more complete because we have indicated the I/O area. Because two segment types are retrieved, we should have expected two I/O areas. However, notice that only the WS-PAT area is specified. When using the D command code, the I/O areas must be defined in WORKING-STORAGE in their hierarchic order; that is, we must define WS-PAT, then WS-ORDER. DL/I will retrieve both the PATIENT and ORDER segment occurrences and will place the records into contiguous memory locations beginning at the location of the I/O area specified in the SSA. In our example, the two segments would be placed into memory beginning at the location of WS-PAT. Obviously this area is not large enough to hold both records, but the portion of the data that won't fit into WS-PAT will be placed into memory immediately following WS-PAT: WS-ORDER. (Also see items 2 and 3 in Figure 12.1)

12.7   SEQUENTIAL RETRIEVAL: THE GET NEXT (GN) FUNCTION

To retrieve the next segment satisfying an SSA, we use GN. To use GN, we must establish a current position for the desired segment type. If the call includes no SSAs, DL/I will retrieve the next segment in the hierarchic sequence regardless of type. This means segments of differing types can be accessed by this command.

Before you get the impression that GN is like FIND NEXT in the CODASYL model, note that this function does not consider parentage (ownership). Whereas FIND NEXT retrieves the NEXT member in a set, GN retrieves the next physical record. The GNP (Get Next within Parent) function corresponds more closely to FIND NEXT.

GN Status Codes

The GN status codes are as follows:

bb   When a GN causes DL/I to move to a segment at a lower level, or to access a segment of the same type as the previous one, the status code will be two blanks

GA   DL/I has retrieved a segment of a different type at a higher level than the previous one

GK   DL/I has accessed a segment of a different type but at the same level as the previous one

GB   DL/I has reached the physical end of the database

Unqualified Calls: Retrieval of Every Segment in a Database

Problem 7. **List every segment in the database.**

Solution. Figure 12.4 shows the solution. The first GU establishes currency at the first root segment, a term called **position** by IMS. Paragraph 100-LIST-AND-READ prints the segment just accessed (it must be a PATIENT the first time through, since that's the root), then uses GN to successively access the remaining segments in the database. As this occurs, DL/I will return segments of different types and status codes of different values.

Let's walk through the program using Figure 11.5, which showed the hierarchic order and is reproduced as Figure 12.5.

First, the GU call retrieves segment number 1, which is for PATIENT P1. The value of PHARM-STATUS would be bb. The first time the GN is executed in paragraph 100-LIST-AND READ, segment 2, an ORDER, would be accessed. What would be the value of PHARM-STATUS? Because the new segment is below the previous one, the value would again be bb. Table 12.5 shows the

---

FIGURE 12.4   A Program Segment to Satisfy Problem 7: List All the Segments in the Database

```
        GU

* GU establishes position at the first segment in the DB

        PERFORM 100-LIST-AND-READ

            UNTIL PHARM-STATUS = 'GB'

        GOBACK.

100-LIST-AND-READ.

        MOVE WS-DUMMY-SEG TO PRINT-LINE

        WRITE PRINT-LINE...

* printed this one, get next one

        GN.
```

FIGURE 12.5   **A Reproduction of Figure 11.5 Showing the Hierarchic Ordering of the Database Record for PATIENT P1**

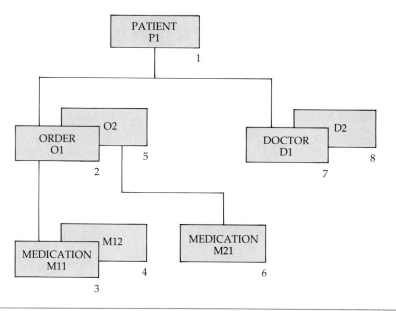

TABLE 12.5   **The Hierarchic Order and Status Values Obtained from Accessing the Occurrences shown in Figure 12.5**

Call	Segment Number	PHARM-STATUS
GU	1	bb
GN	2	bb
GN	3	bb
GN	4	bb
GN	5	GA
GN	6	bb
GN	7	GA
GN	8	bb
GN	8	GB

segment number and status values for all the other calls resulting from the execution of the program in Figure 12.4.

Notice that when DL/I retrieved ORDER O2, the status code was GA because an ORDER segment is at a higher level than a MED, which was the segment type retrieved by the previous GN call. Assume there are no MEDs for ORDER O2. Now, after retrieving ORDER O2, DL/I will retrieve DOCTOR D1. Because

DOCTOR is at the same level as an ORDER, the status code will be GK, indicating that a new segment type at the same level as the previous one has been accessed.

Had there been more than one PATIENT in the database, the last call would have returned a value of GA instead of GB (end of database), because DL/I would retrieve the next PATIENT after accessing the last DOCTOR for the current one and a PATIENT segment is at a higher level (1 versus 2) than DOCTOR.

Problem 8. **After the second GN in Problem 7, how could we determine which segment was retrieved?**

Solution. This can be done by examining the PHARM-SEG-NAME field within the PCB mask. It is important to realize that unqualified GN calls result in the retrieval of segments of different types and that identification of exactly which type was retrieved can be complicated.

Unqualified SSA Calls: Retrieving All the Segments of a Given Type

When we want all the occurrences of a given segment type, we use an unqualified SSA call inside a loop as shown in Figure 12.6.

FIGURE 12.6   **A Program that Will Access All the ORDER Segments**

```
* first establish position at the first ORDER
      GU ORDER
* now print it
      PERFORM 200-PRINT-IT.
* now loop through the other ORDER segments
      PERFORM 100-READ-AND-PRINT
        UNTIL PHARM-STATUS = 'GE'
      GOBACK.
   100-READ-AND-PRINT.
      GN ORDER
      IF PHARM-STATUS NOT = 'GE'
        PERFORM 200-PRINT-IT.
   200-PRINT-IT.
      MOVE WS-ORDER TO PRINT-LINE
      WRITE PRINT-LINE. . .
```

FIGURE 12.7   The Solution to Problem 9: Show All the MED Segments that Use PENICILLIN

```
       GU MED (MEDDESC=PENICILLIN)

       PERFORM 100-PRINT-AND-READ-REST

           UNTIL PHARM-STATUS = 'GE'

       GOBACK.

  100-PRINT-AND-READ-REST.

 *

 *    statements to move and print WS-MED fields would go here

 *

 * use qualified GN to retrieve the rest

 *

       GN MED (MEDDESC=PENICILLIN).
```

The initial GU call establishes position at the first ORDER. The GN ORDER inside the loop accesses each succeeding ORDER until a GE status code is returned by DL/I. When an SSA is used, the status code returned when there are no more segments satisfying the request is GE; when a call uses an unqualified SSA, DL/I returns GB.

Qualified SSA Calls: Accessing Specific Segment Occurrences for a Given Type

Problem 9. **Show all the MED segments that use PENICILLIN.**

Solution. Figure 12.7 shows the solution.

12.8   SEQUENTIAL RETRIEVAL OF CHILDREN: THE GET NEXT WITHIN PARENT (GNP) FUNCTION

GNP works just like GN except that the retrieval of segments is limited to the children of the parent. For example, suppose we want to print all the ORDERs for a given PATIENT or the MEDications for a given ORDER. In both situations, we need to restrict access to only the children of a given parent. One of the problems associated with this command is that it doesn't establish parentage. We will see how this problem affects us in a later example.

GNP Status Codes

The GNP status codes are as follows:

bb Two blanks, meaning the call was completely successful.

GA Same meaning as with GN: a segment at a higher level has been reached. However, because the segment is still below the established parent, IMS continues.

GE DL/I couldn't find the requested segment. The segment either doesn't exist or it exists but, because it is in front of the starting point of the GNP search, it couldn't be found. Like GN, GNP begins its accesses based on the current position in the database. If you begin searching at a segment that follows the desired one in the hierarchic sequence, DL/I won't find it because it searches only in the forward direction.

GK The segment retrieved is of a different type but at the same level as the previous one.

Establishing Parentage

Two ways to establish a segment occurrence as a parent are: (1) use GU or (2) use GN. After either call type, IMS establishes parentage at the lowest level specified by the call. A third way is to use the P command code in any of the three retrieval calls, including GNP, to force parentage at the segment that was retrieved using that command code. Notice that this means GNP does not establish parentage unless the call includes a P command code.

Unqualified Calls: Retrieval of All Children

Problem 10. **Retrieve all the ORDERs, MEDs, and DOCTORs for PATIENT P1.**

Solution. Figure 12.8 shows the solution. Using Figure 12.5, the first call would retrieve segment 1 and return a PHARM-STATUS code of bb. Each of the remaining calls and its associated segment number and status value is shown in Table 12.6.

Following the sequence of calls is reminiscent of Table 12.5, which showed the GN call results. The only differences are:

- DL/I won't go beyond the last child for PATIENT P1, because that's where parentage was established.
- A status code of GE is returned when there are no more segments satisfying the SSA.

Our solution isn't very elegant, because determining which of the three segment types was retrieved for each call would be difficult and time-consuming.

FIGURE 12.8   Solution to Problem 10: Retrieve All the ORDERs, MEDs, and DOCTORS for PATIENT P1

```
        GU PATIENT (PATNO = P1)

* GU establishes parentage at the desired PATIENT

* the CALL used an abbreviated form of the complete CALL format

        PERFORM 200-PRINT-AND-FIND-REST

            UNTIL PHARM-STATUS = 'GE'.

        GOBACK.

 200-PRINT-AND-FIND-REST.

* move the data from dummy I/O area to the print-line and

*    print

            GNP

* the unqualified call using GNP will retrieve every

*    child of the parent. In our case, this will include

*    segments of three different types: ORDER, MED and DOCTOR
```

TABLE 12.6   The Segment Number, Segment Type, and Status Code Values Returned by Successive GNP Calls after Establishing Parentage at PATIENT P1

Call Number	Segment Number	Segment Type	PHARM-STATUS
2	2	ORDER	bb
3	3	MED	bb
4	4	MED	bb
5	5	ORDER	GA
6	6	MED	bb
7	7	DOCTOR	GA
8	8	DOCTOR	bb
9	8	DOCTOR	GE

The segment numbers are from Figure 12.5.

FIGURE 12.9   The Solution to Problem 11: What MEDications Are Prescribed for ORDER O1?

```
        GU ORDER (ORDNO=O1)

*  the GU establishes parentage at ORDER O1

        PERFORM 200-PRINT-AND-FIND-MEDS

            UNTIL PHARM-STATUS = 'GE'

        GOBACK.

    200-PRINT-AND-FIND-MEDS.

        GNP

        IF PHARM-STATUS NOT = 'GE'

            THEN

*  move and print MED coding goes here.
```

Problem 11. What MEDications are prescribed for ORDER O1?

Solution. Figure 12.9 shows the solution. Because the first GU establishes parentage at ORDER O1, all subsequent GNP calls will be restricted to accessing segments that are children of that ORDER—MEDications identified with segment numbers 3 and 4 in Figure 12.5.

Unqualified SSA Calls: Retrieving All the Children of a Specific Type

When an SSA is present but contains no qualifying statement, DL/I will retrieve all the children of the type specified.

Problem 12. Print all the ORDERs for PATIENT P1.

Solution. Figure 12.10 shows the solution. Because parentage is established at PATIENT P1, GNP will access only its children. Furthermore, by using the unqualified SSA, only ORDER segments are retrieved. Note that if the call had been an unqualified call (GNP only), not only ORDERs but MEDication and DOCTOR segments would have been retrieved as well.

Problem 13. Print all the ORDERs and MEDs for PATIENT P1.

Solution. The solution shown in Figure 12.11 contains a mistake. The problem is one we mentioned earlier: GNP does not establish parentage. The GU at the

FIGURE 12.10   **A Program Segment to Determine All the ORDERs for PATIENT P1**

```
GU PATIENT (PATNO=P1)

* established parentage at the PATIENT segment

    PERFORM 200-FIND-ORDS

        UNTIL PHARM-STATUS = 'GE'

    GOBACK.

200-FIND-ORDS.

* use an unqualified SSA call

    GNP ORDER

    IF PHARM-STATUS NOT = 'GE'

        THEN

* move and print ORDER coding goes here.
```

beginning establishes parentage at PATIENT P1. Therefore, when paragraph 200-FIND-ORDS is repeatedly executed, parentage will remain with PATIENT. This means that the inner loop (paragraph 300-FIND-MEDS) will return all the MEDs for all the patient's ORDERs, not just for a single ORDER. For example, if 7 ORDERs were associated with PATIENT P1 and each ORDER was related to 5 MEDs, all 35 MED occurrences would be retrieved during the initial execution of the 300-FIND-MEDS paragraph loop. No more MEDs would be found for the other ORDERs.

We can see this by examining Figure 12.12. The first time through paragraph 200-FIND-ORDS, the first ORDER (segment 2) will be retrieved. However, because GNP does not establish parentage, parentage will still be at segment 1. Then the GNP MED in paragraph 300-FIND-MEDS will be executed until a status code of GE is returned. Because parentage is at PATIENT P1, all the MED children of P1 will be retrieved: 35 in all (segments 3–7, 9–13, etc.). MED position is now at the last MED record (segment 43). Now paragraph 200-FIND-ORDS will be executed again, resulting in the retrieval of a new ORDER (O2) but not the changing of parentage. Because the MED position is at 43, the last segment, and the parent is still segment 1, IMS thinks there are no more children and immediately returns a status code of GE. This pattern will be repeated for all the remaining ORDERs.

As each ORDER is retrieved, we need to make it a parent. Then, when we

---

FIGURE 12.11   A Program Intended to List All the ORDERs and MEDications for PATIENT P1

```
GU PATIENT (PATNO=P1)
```

Establishes parentage at
PATIENT P1

```
PERFORM 200-FIND-ORDS

    UNTIL PHARM-STATUS = 'GE'.

GOBACK.

200-FIND-ORDS.

    GNP ORDER

    IF PHARM-STATUS NOT = 'GE'

* move and print ORDER coding goes here

    THEN

        PERFORM 300-FIND-MEDS

            UNTIL PHARM-STATUS = 'GE'.

300-FIND-MEDS.

    GNP MED

    IF PHARM-STATUS NOT = 'GE'

        THEN

* move and print MED coding here
```

---

loop through paragraph 300-FIND-MEDS, only the MED children for that OR-DER (parent) will be accessed. To do so, we either follow the GNP ORDER call with a GU or use the P command code. We leave the first solution to you as a problem at the end of the chapter, but we will discuss the command code solution here.

To use the P command code, we include it in the GNP ORDER line in paragraph 200-FIND-ORDS so that it establishes parentage at that segment. The coding is:

GNP ORDER *P

FIGURE 12.12   A Physical Database Record in Which Parentage Is Established at the Root

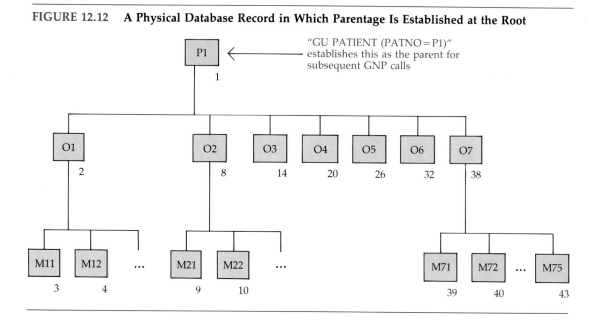

Now when DL/I accesses an ORDER, it will make that ORDER the parent, so subsequent GNP calls (like the one in paragraph 300-FIND-MEDS) will be limited to retrieval of children of that ORDER.

Qualified SSA Calls: Retrieval of Specified Child Occurrences

Problem 14. Retrieve all the ORDERs for PATIENT P178 that were entered by pharmacist Mary Jones (MAJ).

Solution. The solution is shown in Figure 12.13. The qualified SSA GU call will limit the retrieval of ORDERs to just those associated with PATIENT P178. The qualifying statement associated with the GNP ORDER call will limit retrieval of ORDERs to just those entered into the database by the designated pharmacist. When there are no more such ORDERs for the parent, DL/I will return a status of GE.

Problem 15. Print all the MEDs for all the ORDERs entered on 12/25/XX.

Solution. Figure 12.14 shows the solution. Notice that it contains a mixture of GU, GN, and GNP commands. The initial GU is needed to establish a starting point for the subsequent GN ORDER calls. It accesses the first ORDER on the specified date. Once that ORDER is retrieved, it is printed. Next the program

FIGURE 12.13   **A Program Segment that Solves Problem 14: Retrieve all the ORDERs for**
PATIENT P178 that Were Entered by Pharmacist Mary Jones

```
* first access the PATIENT segment parent

        GU PATIENT (PATNO=P178)

* loop thru ORDERs until status is GE

        PERFORM 200-FIND-ORDS

            UNTIL PHARM-STATUS = 'GE'

        GOBACK.

    200-FIND-ORDS.

* Use GNP to limit search to children of the parent only

        GNP ORDER (PHARM-INIT =  MAJ)

        IF PHARM-STATUS NOT = 'GE'

            THEN

* move and print ORDER coding goes here
```

loops through paragraph 300-FIND-THE-MEDs, which processes all the MEDs
for that ORDER. The paragraph uses an unqualified SSA with the GNP so that
only MEDs for the parent (the ORDER) are retrieved.

After control returns from paragraph 300-FIND-MEDS, we begin the loop at
paragraph 200-FIND-REMAINING-ORDS, which uses a GN to sequentially process the remaining ORDER segments entered on the designated date and all the
associated MEDs.

12.9   ADDING NEW SEGMENTS: THE INSERT (ISRT) FUNCTION

The Insert (ISRT) function is used when new segments are added or when the
database is initially loaded. The segment to be added is built in the WORKING-
STORAGE I/O area; then the ISRT command is given. When the segment being
added is a root, DL/I will insert it into its proper location in the hierarchic
sequence based on its key value. If the segment isn't a root, the child should
be stored using an unqualified SSA call, provided the parent already has been
stored. The segment being added *must* use an SSA (at least the segment name),
or else DL/I won't know what kind of segment to add.

FIGURE 12.14   A Program Segment that Solves Problem 15: Print All the MEDs for All the ORDERs Entered on 12/25/XX

```
        GU ORDER (ORDATE =  12/25/XX)

*

* coding for moving and printing the ORDER segment goes here

*

        PERFORM 300-FIND-THE-MEDS

            UNTIL PHARM-STATUS = 'GE'.

*

* the above will find all MEDS for the first order

*

        PERFORM 200-FIND-REMAINING-ORDS

            UNTIL PHARM-STATUS = 'GE'

        GOBACK.

 200-FIND-REMAINING-ORDS.

*

* retrieve the next ORDER, and make it the parent

*

        GN ORDER (ORDATE =  12/25/XX)

*

* was the retrieval successful

*

        IF PHARM-STATUS NOT = 'GE'

            THEN

*

* an ORDER was retrieved...PRINT then process MEDs

* coding for printing the ORDER goes here
```

FIGURE 12.14   (concluded)

```
*

            PERFORM 300-FIND-THE-MEDS

                UNTIL PHARM-STATUS = 'GE'.

   300-FIND-THE-MEDS.

*

* get the next MED for this ORDER

*

        GNP MED

*

* see if any more to retrieve

*

            IF PHARM-STATUS NOT = 'GE'

                THEN

*

* coding for moving and printing the MED segment goes here

*
```

ISRT Status Codes

The ISRT status codes are as follows:

bb   The call was successful

II   A attempt was made to insert a segment having the same KSF value as an existing segment

LC   The key field is out of sequence

LD   No parent exists for the segment being added

Inserting a Child for an Existing Parent

Problem 16. **Add another MED to ORDER O1.** It contains penicillin (code PCN) and is for 500mg.

Solution. First, we need to build the MED record by moving values to the fields in WORKING-STORAGE not in the MED segment in the database:

MOVE 'PCN' TO WS-MEDCODE
MOVE 'PENICILLIN' TO MEDDESC
MOVE '500MG' TO WS-MED-AMOUNT
MOVE 'O1' TO MEDORDNO

Now we issue the ISRT call:

ISRT ORDER (ORDNO = O1)
        MED
IF PHARM-STATUS = 'II'
    THEN
            DISPLAY 'ATTEMPT TO ADD DUPLICATE . . . '

Adding a Child When the Parent Hasn't Been Stored Yet: The Path Call

If the parent isn't stored yet, we can use the "path call" version of the ISRT command to store it at the same time as the child.

Problem 17. **Add a new PATIENT, with PATNO P34.** The patient's name is John Jones, and he is in nursing unit 1A, room 123. At present he has one ORDER, O45, entered by MAJ on 12/26/XX; it is for 200mg of Tagamet (code TAG) for which the PATIENT is charged $2.50.

Solution. We can store the PATIENT, the ORDER, and the MED segment using a single call. First, we build the three segments in WORKING-STORAGE. Then we issue this call:

ISRT PATIENT *D
        ORDER
        MED

Not only will the MED be added; so will the PATIENT and the ORDER. All of this is because of the use of the path call, indicated by the D command code. Notice that we used it only with the SSA on the first level; it isn't necessary to use it on subsequent levels.

12.10   UPDATING SEGMENTS: THE REPLACE (REPL) FUNCTION

Like CODASYL's MODIFY and DB2's UPDATE, the Replace (REPL) command is used to change field values for existing segments. To do so, we retrieve the desired segment using one of the "hold" retrievals—GHU (Get Hold Unique),

GHN (Get Hold Next), or GHNP (Get Hold Next within Parent)—and update the field names in the I/O area. Then we issue the REPL.

Use of the three hold calls is identical to that of the three retrieval calls discussed earlier. Once the segment is retrieved, the field names in WORKING-STORAGE (I/O area) are modified, not those in the DBD. There are two restrictions of which you must be aware. First, you cannot change the value of the KSF if the segment being changed has one. Second, you cannot use a qualified SSA with the REPL call; if you do so, the REPL will be unsuccessful.

REPL Status Codes

If you get any status code other than two blanks, the modification was unsuccessful. The REPL status codes are as follows:

AJ   A qualified SSA was used with the REPL command

DA   An attempt to modify the KSF was made

DJ   A REPL was issued without first issuing a hold command

Problem 18. **Change the ORDER status of ORDER number 123 to S.**

Solution.

```
    GHU ORDER (ORDNO = 123)
*
* always do all updating using the WS fields
*
    MOVE 'S' TO WS-ORDER-STATUS
    REPL
```
⟶ Cannot be a qualified SSA here

Problem 19. **A mistake has been made on ORDER 100 for PATIENT P12. The charge that was incorrectly entered as 10.00 should be 12.00. The ORDER has been filled three times. Because the ORDER would show a billing amount of $10.00, WS-ORD-CHARGE must be changed. Also, the PATIENT's total amount billed field, WS-PAT-AMOUNT-BILLED, which includes charges from several ORDERs, should be incremented by 3 × 2.00, or $6.00.**

Solution. We can use the path call in Figure 12.15 to make both changes at the same time.

When a command code of D is used, indicating a path call, and the REPL is preceded by a hold function, DL/I will update all segments in the entire path when the REPL is executed.

FIGURE 12.15   A Path Call that Updates Two Segment Occurrences at One Time Because the GHU Was a Path Call

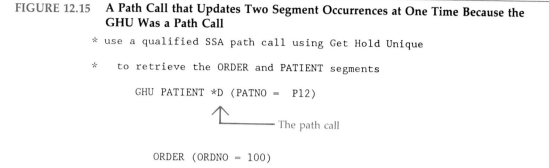

```
* use a qualified SSA path call using Get Hold Unique

*   to retrieve the ORDER and PATIENT segments

        GHU PATIENT *D (PATNO =  P12)
                                          ── The path call

            ORDER (ORDNO = 100)

        COMPUTE WS-PAT-AMOUNT-BILLED =

            WS-PAT-AMOUNT-BILLED + 6

        MOVE 12.00 TO WS-ORD-CHARGE

* use WS field names for updating

        REPL
```

12.11   DELETING SEGMENTS: THE DELETE (DLET) FUNCTION

We delete segments in the same way we modify them:

1. Retrieve the desired segment using a "hold" call.
2. Issue the DLET command.

The status codes that can result from a DLET are the same as those for REPL.

Problem 20. **Delete ORDER number 400.**

Solution.

GHU ORDER (ORDNO = 400)
DLET

When a segment is deleted, so are all its children. In this problem, any MEDs associated with ORDER 400 will also be deleted from the database.

12.12   DATA INTEGRITY: THE CHECKPOINT (CHKP) FUNCTION AND IMS LOGS

While log files can be used with both batch and on-line databases, we will examine only the batch form. When a program aborts prematurely, IMS automatically does some minimal housekeeping involving the underlying data sets (files) that store the database. But unless logs are used, transactions posted to the database cannot be removed.

Using either tape or DASDs, an IMS log file contains segment before and after images (see Chapter 1). These images restore the database to a state prior to the program's aborting.

By using what IMS calls **write-ahead logging,** we write segment updates to the log **before** they are posted to the database. That way the log is always ahead of the database. Fortunately, the logging activities are transparent to the application.

When a program aborts, the DBA uses an IMS utility to perform either a forward or backward recovery. A forward recovery is usually used when there is physical damage to the database. Here all the change data is applied to a complete version of the database that existed prior to the aborting. The complete copy of the database is made by operations using yet another utility, while the accumulated changes are provided by the log file.

A backward recovery removes transactions from a database. The transactions are those made since the program began or since a checkpoint was last issued. This is the more usual situation, because it is used when the application ended under its own control but there was a situation the application decided not to handle.

This purpose of the Checkpoint (CHKP) call is similar to that of the Commit function of the CODASYL and relational models: it physically posts all changes to the database. Until this call is issued, the changes are kept in buffers in main memory. In a batch program, this is automatically done at the beginning and end of the program. If more frequent checkpoints are needed, this function can be used.

12.13   ROLLING BACK UPDATES: THE ROLL AND ROLB FUNCTIONS

Both the ROLL and ROLB commands roll back any changes made to the database since the last checkpoint. However, ROLL causes the program to be terminated after the rollback, while ROLB returns control to the host program after the rollback is performed, thus leaving the application in control.

12.14   IMSVS86: IMS FOR THE MICROCOMPUTER

We conclude our discussion of IMS by describing a microcomputer implementation of the mainframe product. This section discusses a product by Stingray Software called IMSVS86.

IMSVS86 can be used with Micro Focus's COBOL compiler or in a standalone mode. It includes the following modules:

- DBDGEN
- PSBGEN
- Checkpoint-Restart
- Database load/unload utilities
- Database reorganization utilities
- COBOL TRACE facilities

Using this product together with the Micro Focus compiler, an organization can completely define an IMS database, write the COBOL applications, and debug the applications, all without touching a mainframe. Once the programs are debugged, they can be ported (moved) to the mainframe without changes. This is because both the COBOL compiler and IMSVS86 are almost 100 percent compatible with their mainframe counterparts.

IMSVS86 returns the same status codes as IMS, uses the same syntax for DBDs and PSBs, and supports all IMS access methods, including HISAM and secondary indexes. It can even be used to develop on-line systems, because it simulates IBM's 3270-type display terminals.

Organizations that use this product on microcomputers almost always have IMS on their mainframes. By using the better COBOL debugging tools and the shorter turnaround time on the micros, systems can be implemented much faster than they could if all development work were done on the mainframe.

12.15 SUMMARY

At the beginning of 1989, there were an estimated 7,000 IMS installations. The DML for those 7,000 installations was DL/I, the topic of this chapter.

To use DL/I, the portion of IMS that serves as its access method, an application must be responsible for four kinds of communications with DL/I: receiving control from DL/I, passing control to DL/I when the program finishes, telling DL/I which function to perform, and exchanging information with DL/I about the success or failure of the call, the segment name that was retrieved, and so on.

Control is passed from DL/I to the application through an ENTRY statement, and GOBACK terminates the relationship. The function that DL/I is to execute is specified by using a CALL statement containing several parameters. DL/I uses the PCB mask to communicate with the application.

A call to DL/I contains four elements: a function, a PCB mask name, an I/O area, and optional SSAs. We discussed nine batch and three transaction processing functions, all of which must be specified as four-byte fields. The PCB mask contains nine fields and, after the call is completed, will store information about the status of the call. When DL/I retrieves a segment, or is to store or modify a segment, the I/O area name provides a work area into which DL/I will place the segment or look for the new or updated segment field values. Usually the coding order of these segments in WORKING-STORAGE doesn't matter, but when a path call is going to be used, the I/O areas must be in their hierarchic order. The final element, the SSA, is used to qualify the call. There are three elements to an SSA: a segment name, one or more command names, and one or more qualifying statements.

After calling DL/I, the application should check the status field in the PCB mask. Unless two blanks are found, the call either failed or, although it completed, DL/I is sending along some additional information.

There are three retrieval calls: GU, GN, and GNP. GU accesses the first segment that satisfies the SSA request. GN finds the next segment satisfying an SSA. GNP retrieves the next child for the SSA specified. Use of GN without specifying a starting position, or of GNP without providing a parent, results in a fatal status.

New segments are added using ISRT. To delete or modify segments, we access the desired segment using a "hold" call, then issue the REPL or DLET command. The field names being modified are those of WORKING-STORAGE, not those in the DBD. Deleting a segment will also delete all of its dependents, so we must be careful when using this command.

REVIEW QUESTIONS

1. Describe four kinds of communications between an application and DL/I.
2. What must be the first statement in the PROCEDURE DIVISION? What is its purpose?
3. Is the order of the PCB masks in the LINKAGE SECTION important or not important? If it is important, explain the rules for determining the order.
4. Why would the length of the last item in the PCB mask differ in length from PCB to PCB?
5. How can an application determine if a DL/I call was successful?
6. When might an application use the key feedback area value?
7. Most of the time, the ordering of the I/O areas in WORKING STORAGE is unimportant. What is the exception to this rule?
8. Describe three kinds of DL/I calls.
9. What three items are necessary or useful to qualify an SSA?
10. What three items must be specified in the call to DL/I? Which item is optional?
11. Why do we sometimes use a dummy segment name when using unqualified GN or GNP calls?
12. What is a command code?
13. What status code is returned when:
    a. The physical end of database is encountered?
    b. No segment that satisfies the SSA?

    c. A hierarchical boundary is crossed, resulting in a segment of a different type at a higher level than the previous one?

14. List three ways to establish parentage.

15. What is a path call? When is it useful?

PROBLEMS

Use the IMS shorthand and COBOL to answer the following problems.

1. Print all the ORDERs for the PATIENT with last name SMITH.

2. Change your answer to Problem 1 to print the MEDications for all of SMITH's ORDERs.

3. Display the name of PATIENT 345's DOCTOR.

4. The auditing department has called and asked for a report that shows the total filling charge for all PATIENTs, but the report is to be programmed such that for each PATIENT all ORDERs are retrieved and the relevant field used to accumulate the sum. Show the COBOL code to produce the report.

5. Produce a detailed listing of all the PATIENTs and their associated ORDERs and MEDications.

6. Resolve Problem 13 from the chapter using GU instead of the P command code within paragraph 200-FIND-ORDS. (*Hint:* Use the connection data item and a qualified SSA.)

7. Display the patient numbers of all patients on penicillin (code PCN).

8. Display the medications that PATIENT P10 receives.

9. List all the items not used since January 1, 19XX.

10. ORDER number 056 has been canceled. Using a single call, delete it and all its MEDications.

11. A new ORDER, number 099, is to be entered for PATIENT P456123. Using a path call, show how to enter it and its MEDication. The PATIENT's name is Jackson, Thomas. The ORDER is for 500mg of aspirin (code ASP), and the charge per dose is $.50 Use 06/15/XX as the date of the ORDER, and assume MAJ are the pharmacist's initials.

12. Show the coding necessary to change the amount of Tagamet for ORDER 089 from 200mg to 500mg.

Use Figure 11.8 in Chapter 11 as the basis for Problems 13 through 15. Assume the following DBD segments and fields:

JOBTITLE (<u>TITLECOD</u>, TITLEDESC)
COURSE (<u>COURSNO</u>, COURSNAM, INSTRCTR, LASTDATE)
EMP (<u>EMPNO</u>, EMPNAME, EMPOFFICE, EMPHONE)
EMPCOURSE (<u>ECOURSE</u>, DATETKN, SCORE)

The KSF is underlined. The fields are obvious except for ECOURSE and INSTRCTR. The first field is a course identification number. INSTRCTR is a six-character code designating the instructor. Assume that all WORKING-STORAGE fields have the same name as their DL/I counterparts, but have a WS- prefix. Use STATUS as the status indicator.

13. Print all the COURSEs taught by Agnes Robertson. Her instructor code is R68790.

14. List the course code for all courses taken by employee SMITH, AGNES between January 1, 19XX, and June 15, 19XX.

15. Modify the answer to Problem 14 to include the name of each course.

▪▪ EPISODE 8

A Program that Uses DL/I to Print an IV Order Report

Because Barb realized that most of the applications that processed the pharmacy databases were going to be similar, she coded the first one. As usual, she called a meeting to review her coding so the others on her team could follow her standards and guidelines.

Barb opened the meeting: "Let's begin by looking at the copy book members that I added to our source library. These are the standard DL/I call elements that I want all of you to use [see Exhibit 1].

"Next, because the PSB for IV processing, which we labeled as PSB2, contained segments from three PCBs [see Episode 7], I had to set up three PCB masks in the source statement library [see Exhibit 2]. When a host program accesses the IVORD or ADDITIVE segments, which are both found in the IV database, the calls should use IV-PCB as the mask. When accessing the PATIENT or FORM-ITEM segments, use PAT-PCB and FORM-PCB, respectively.

I grouped all the SSAs we might need into a single structure called IV-SSAs, which I'm going to distribute now [see Exhibit 3]. Notice that the individual SSAs are set up as 03 levels within IV-SSAS. To use an SSA for the IVORD segments, you would specify IVORD-SSA.

Like the others, this SSA has space for two command codes and uses the left-parenthesis mechanism to specify whether or not the call is a qualified one. I only provided for a search on the key sequence field for each segment, so if any of your applications require a search on other fields, you'll have to set your own SSAs. But please add them to the source statement library; don't hard-core them into your applications.

"The fourth, and final, book member category is the collection of I/O areas to be used to receive the segments from IMS. I'll give them to you now [see Exhibit 4]. I don't think they require any explanation, because they mimic the actual segment definitions from the DBD.

"Now, I'm ready to describe the first program, which I've handed out to you [see Exhibit 5].

"In paragraph 300-GET-PAT-NO, it requests a patient's number from the end user, checks for a termination indicator value (SPACES), then uses paragraph 400-FIND-PAT to find the PATIENT occurrence. As I'll explain later in more detail, paragraph 500-FIND-ORDS uses a GNP with a P command code to sequentially retrieve all the IV orders and also loops through paragraph 900-GET-ADDI-

---

EXHIBIT 1   DL/I Function Calls Source Statement Library Member

(DL/I Function Calls)

```
01  DLI-FUNCTIONS.

    03 GU      PIC X(4) VALUE 'GU  '.

    03 GN      PIC X(4) VALUE 'GN  '.

    03 GNP     PIC X(4) VALUE 'GNP '.

    03 GHU     PIC X(4) VALUE 'GHU '.

    03 GHN     PIC X(4) VALUE 'GHN '.

    03 GHNP    PIC X(4) VALUE 'GHNP'.

    03 ISRT    PIC X(4) VALUE 'ISRT'.

    03 DLET    PIC X(4) VALUE 'DLET'.

    03 REPL    PIC X(4) VALUE 'REPL'.

    03 ROLL    PIC X(4) VALUE 'ROLL'.

    03 ROLB    PIC X(4) VALUE 'ROLB'.

    03 CHKP    PIC X(4) VALUE 'CHKP'.
```

TIVES to retrieve all the ADDITIVEs [drugs] associated with each IV order. Paragraph 900-GET-ADDITIVES also calls paragraph 600-FIND-FORM, which looks up the FORMITEM segment in the FORMULARY database so that each drug's description can be determined.

"That's enough of an overview. Let's take a five-minute break. When we return, I want to discuss some standards that I want all of you to follow. Then I'll go over the program I gave you."

After the break, the meeting resumed.

Barb began, "I want all of you to use the standards that I'm going to discuss for all applications that you, or any of the other application programmers, write.

First, use the COPY statement to load source statements into WORKING-STORAGE for the function calls, the I/O areas, and the SSAs. You can see how I accomplished this in my WORKING-STORAGE SECTION.

"Next, use condition names for all your program tests. I set up five of them in the SWITCHES structure in WORKING-STORAGE. PAT-FOUND-SW will tell me whether or not a PATIENT was found. FORM-FOUND-SW will do the same, but for FORMITEM items. The switch labeled ACTION tells the application whether or not the end user wants to quit. Two of the switches contain the word MORE. They indicate if the last

---

EXHIBIT 2   The Three PCB Masks, Shown as Members, Necessary for Processing PSB 2, which Was Coded Using the PSBGEN in Episode 7 (Exhibit 7)

```
01 PAT-PCB.
      03 PAT-DBD-NAME                 PIC X(8).
      03 PAT-SEG-LEVEL                PIC X(2).
      03 PAT-STATUS                   PIC X(2).
      03 PAT-PROCOPTS                 PIC X(4).
      03 PAT-RES-IMS                  PIC S9(5) COMP.
      03 PAT-SEG-NAME                 PIC X(8).
      03 PAT-KEY-FEEDBACK-LEN         PIC S9(5) COMP.
      03 PAT-NO-SENSEGS               PIC S9(5) COMP.
      03 PAT-KFBACK                   PIC X(24).


01 IV-PCB.
      03 IV-DBD-NAME                  PIC X(8).
      03 IV-SEG-LEVEL                 PIC X(2).
      03 IV-STATUS                    PIC X(2).
      03 IV-PROCOPTS                  PIC X(4).
      03 IV-RES-IMS                   PIC S9(5) COMP.
      03 IV-SEG-NAME                  PIC X(8).
      03 IV-KEY-FEEDBACK-LEN          PIC S9(5) COMP.
      03 IV-NO-SENSEGS                PIC S9(5) COMP.
      03 IV-KFBACK                    PIC X(24).


01 FORM-PCB.
      03 FORM-DBD-NAME                PIC X(8).
      03 FORM-SEG-LEVEL               PIC X(2).
      03 FORM-STATUS                  PIC X(2).
      03 FORM-PROCOPTS                PIC X(4).
      03 FORM-RES-IMS                 PIC S9(5) COMP.
      03 FORM-SEG-NAME                PIC X(8).
      03 FORM-KEY-FEEDBACK-LEN        PIC S9(5) COMP.
      03 FORM-NO-SENSEGS              PIC S9(5) COMP.
      03 FORM-KFBACK                  PIC X(24).
```

---

child segment of that type has been retrieved and will be used to end my GNP loops.

"The final standard to be followed is that you are to COPY the PCB masks into the LINKAGE SECTION, as I've done. Because there are three PCBs involved, I copied three masks into the program.

"Now let's look at the PROCEDURE DIVISION. Paragraph 100-OPEN-FILES opens the print file, and paragraph 200-OPEN-PCBS provides the ENTRY point for IMS. The PCB names in the ENTRY statement correspond to their order in the PSBGEN. Notice that I used all three PCB names in the ENTRY statement.

"The other short paragraph is 1000-WRAP-UP, which issues the GOBACK statement to return control to IMS after the program finishes. The only time this

EXHIBIT 3   SSA Members to Be Used to Process PSB 2 from Exhibit 7 in Episode 7

```
01  IV-SSAS.
    03 PAT-SSA.
       05 PAT-SSA-SEG-NAME        PIC X(8) VALUE 'PATIENT '.
       05 FILLER                  PIC X    VALUE '*'.
       05 PAT-CCS.
          07 PAT-CC1              PIC X    VALUE '-'.
          07 PAT-CC2              PIC X    VALUE '-'.
       05 PAT-SSA-QUAL            PIC X    VALUE '('.
       05 PAT-SSA-SFIELD          PIC X(8) VALUE 'PATNO   '.
       05 PAT-SSA-REL-OP          PIC X(2) VALUE ' ='.
       05 PAT-SSA-FVALUE          PIC X(11).
       05 FILLER                  PIC X    VALUE ')'.
    03 IVORD-SSA.
       05 IVORD-SSA-SEG-NAME      PIC X(8) VALUE 'IVORD '.
       05 FILLER                  PIC X    VALUE '*'.
       05 IVORD-CCS.
          07 IVORD-CC1            PIC X    VALUE '-'.
          07 IVORD-CC2            PIC X    VALUE '-'.
       05 IVORD-SSA-QUAL          PIC X    VALUE '('.
       05 IVORD-SSA-SFIELD        PIC X(8) VALUE 'ORDNO'.
       05 IVORD-SSA-REL-OP        PIC X(2) VALUE ' ='.
       05 IVORD-SSA-FVALUE        PIC X(11).
       05 FILLER                  PIC X    VALUE ')'.
    03 ADD-SSA.
       05 ADD-SSA-SEG-NAME        PIC X(8) VALUE 'ADDITIVE'.
       05 FILLER                  PIC X    VALUE '*'.
       05 ADD-CCS.
          07 ADD-CC1              PIC X    VALUE '-'.
          07 ADD-CC2              PIC X    VALUE '-'.
       05 ADD-SSA-QUAL            PIC X    VALUE '('.
       05 ADD-SSA-SFIELD          PIC X(8) VALUE 'ADRUG'.
       05 ADD-SSA-REL-OP          PIC X(2) VALUE ' ='.
       05 ADD-SSA-FVALUE          PIC X(11).
       05 FILLER                  PIC X    VALUE ')'.
    03 FORM-SSA.
       05 FORM-SSA-SEG-NAME       PIC X(8) VALUE 'FORMULARY'.
       05 FILLER                  PIC X    VALUE '*'.
       05 FORM-CCS.
          07 FORM-CC1             PIC X    VALUE '-'.
          07 FORM-CC2             PIC X    VALUE '-'.
       05 FORM-SSA-QUAL           PIC X    VALUE '('.
       05 FORM-SSA-SFIELD         PIC X(8) VALUE 'FORMITEM'.
       05 FORM-SSA-REL-OP         PIC X(2) VALUE ' ='.
       05 FORM-SSA-FVALUE         PIC X(11).
       05 FILLER                  PIC X    VALUE ')'.
```

EXHIBIT 4   Segment Members to Be Used as I/O Areas in WORKING-STORAGE

```
01   WS-PAT.
        03 PAT-NO                    PIC X(11).
        03 PAT-NAME                  PIC X(25).
        03 PAT-LOC.
           05 PAT-NU                 PIC X(4).
           05 PAT-ROOM               PIC X(4).
           05 PAT-BED                PIC X(2).
        03 PAT-DRG                   PIC X(4).
        .
        .
        .

   (PAT-SEG member)

01   WS-IV.
        03 IV-NO                     PIC X(5).
        03 IV-DRUG-CODE              PIC X(7).
        03 IV-CHARGE                 PIC S9(7)V99 COMP-3.
        03 IV-RPH                    PIC X(3).
        .
        .
        .

    (IV-SEG member)

01   WS-ADDITIVE.
        03 ADDITIVE-DRUG-CODE        PIC X(7).
        03 AMOUNT-TO-ADD             PIC X(7).

   (ADD-SEG member)

01   WS-FORM.
        03   ITEM-CODE               PIC X(7).
        03   ITEM-DESC               PIC X(25).
        03   ITEM-COST               PIC S9(7)V99 COMP-3.
        03   ITEM-CHARGE             PIC S9(7)V99 COMP-3.
        .
        .
        .

   (FORM-SEG member)
```

---

occurs is when the user enters spaces for the desired patient number. You can see this in paragraph 300-GET-PAT-NO.

"Paragraph 300-GET-PAT-NO is repeatedly executed by my main-line routine until the user indicates a desire to quit by entering the spaces I just mentioned. It first requests a value for PATIENT-NO. If the user enters blanks, after moving Y to ACTION, the program

EXHIBIT 5   **A program to Accept a Patient Number, Then Print All the IV Orders, Their Additives, and Related Drug Information.**

```
        IDENTIFICATION DIVISION.
        PROGRAM-ID...
        ENVIRONMENT DIVISION.
   *  set up CRT as a special name
        SPECIAL-NAMES.
        system-name IS CRT..
        .
        .
        .

        DATA DIVISION.
        FILE SECTION.
        FD   PRINT-FILE
             RECORD CONTAINS 133 CHARACTERS
             BLOCK CONTAINS 0 RECORDS
             RECORDING MODE IS F
             LABEL RECORDS ARE OMITTED.
        01   PRINT-REC       PIC X(133).
        WORKING-STORAGE SECTION.
        01   DLI-FUNCTIONS COPY DLI-FUNCTIONS.
        01   WS-PAT          COPY WS-PAT.
        01   WS-IV           COPY WS-IV.
        01   WS-ADDITIVE     COPY WS-ADDITIVE.
        01   WS-FORM         COPY WS-FORM.
        01   IV-SSA          COPY IV-SSAS.
        01   SWITCHES.
             03   PAT-FOUND-SW              PIC X.
                  88 PAT-FOUND                 VALUE 'Y'.
                  88 PAT-NOT-FOUND             VALUE 'N'.
             03   MORE-ORDS-THIS-PAT-SW     PIC X.
                  88  MORE-ORDS                VALUE 'Y'.
                  88  NO-MORE-ORDS             VALUE 'N'.
             03   MORE-ADDITIVES-THIS-ORD-SW PIC X.
                  88 MORE-ADDS                 VALUE 'Y'.
                  88 NO-MORE-ADDS-THIS-ORD     VALUE 'N'.
             03   FORM-FOUND-SW             PIC X.
                  88 FOUND-FORM                VALUE 'Y'.
                  88 FORM-NOT-FOUND            VALUE 'N'.
             03   ACTION                    PIC X    VALUE 'N'.
                  88 USER-WANTS-TO-QUIT  VALUE 'Y'.
        01 PATIENT-NO        PIC X(11).
        .
        .
        .

        LINKAGE SECTION.
        01   PAT-PCB         COPY PAT-PCB.
        01   IV-PCB          COPY IV-PCB.
        01   FORM-PCB        COPY FORM-PCB.
        PROCEDURE DIVISION.
           PERFORM 100-OPEN-FILES.
           PERFORM 200-OPEN-PCBS
           PERFORM 300-GET-PAT-NO UNTIL USER-WANTS-TO-QUIT
           PERFORM 1000-WRAP-UP.
        100-OPEN-FILES.
               OPEN OUTPUT PRINT-FILE.
```

EXHIBIT 5 (continued)

```
200-OPEN-PCBS.
        ENTRY 'DLITCBL' USING PAT-PCB,IV-PCB,FORM-PCB.
300-GET-PAT-NO.
    ACCEPT PATIENT-NO FROM CRT.
    IF PATIENT-NO = SPACES
        MOVE 'Y' TO ACTION
    ELSE
        PERFORM 400-FIND-PAT
        IF PAT-FOUND
            MOVE 'Y' TO MORE-ORDS-THIS-PAT-SW
            PERFORM 500-FIND-ORDS THRU 500-EXIT
                UNTIL NO-MORE-ORDS.
        ELSE
            DISPLAY 'NO SUCH PATIENT...TRY AGAIN'.
400-FIND-PAT.
* move input value to PATIENT SSA field value
    MOVE PATIENT-NO TO PAT-SSA-FVALUE.
* try to find this PATIENT
    CALL 'CBLTDLI' USING GU,PAT-PCB,WS-PAT,PAT-SSA
    IF PAT-STATUS = 'GE'
        MOVE 'N' TO PAT-FOUND-SW
    ELSE
        MOVE 'Y' TO PAT-FOUND-SW.
500-FIND-ORDS.
* when GNP the order, use P command code
* to establish parentage at the IV order segment
    MOVE 'P' TO IVORD-CC1.
    MOVE SPACES TO IVORD-SSA-QUAL
    CALL 'CBLTDLI' USING GNP,IV-PCB,WS-IV,PAT-SSA,IVORD-SSA
    IF IV-STATUS = 'GE'
        MOVE 'N' TO MORE-ORDS-THIS-PAT-SW
        GOTO 500-EXIT.
* found one...print it after looking up the FORMITEM
* item
    MOVE IV-DRUG-CODE TO FORM-SSA-FVALUE
    PERFORM 600-FIND-FORM.
    PERFORM 700-MOVE-AND-PRINT-ORD-DATA.
* now loop through the ADDITIVES
    MOVE 'Y' TO MORE-ADDITIVES-THIS-ORD-SW.
    PERFORM 900-GET-ADDITIVES THRU 900-EXIT
        UNTIL NO-MORE-ADDS-THIS-ORD.
500-EXIT.
    EXIT.
600-FIND-FORM.
    CALL 'CBLTDLI' USING GU,FORM-PCB,WS-FORM,FORM-SSA
* don't bother to check status code,
* the drug code was checked when the order
* was first inserted
    MOVE ITEM-DESC TO PRINT-IV-DESC.
700-MOVE-AND-PRINT-ORD-DATA.
    MOVE IV-NO TO PRINT-IV-NO.
    MOVE IV-DRUG-CODE TO PRINT-IV-DRUG-CODE.
        .
        .
```

EXHIBIT 5   (concluded)

```
        WRITE PRINT-FILE FROM PRINT-LINE.
    900-GET-ADDITIVES.
        CALL 'CBLTDLI' USING GNP,IV-PCB,WS-ADDITIVE,ADD-SSA
        IF IV-STATUS = 'GE'
            MOVE 'N' TO MORE-ADDITIVES-THIS-ORD-SW.
            GOTO 900-EXIT.
*   look up the FORMITEM item.
        MOVE ADDITIVE-DRUG-CODE TO FORM-SSA-FVALUE
        PERFORM 600-FIND-FORM.
        MOVE ITEM-DESC TO...
*   move all relevant data to print items in print
*   records and print them
        .
        .
        .
    900-EXIT.
        EXIT.
    1000-WRAP-UP.
        CLOSE PRINT-FILE.
        GOBACK.
```

This program requires accessing data from three PCBs.

will end. Otherwise, paragraph 400-FIND-PAT, which attempts to find the PATIENT in the PATIENT database, is executed.

In that paragraph, I first MOVE PATIENT-NO to the SSA search field (PAT-SSA-FVALUE) that I defined in the SSA for PATIENT. Next, I issue the GU call to try to access the PATIENT. If the PATIENT isn't found, I set my PAT-FOUND-SW switch accordingly. Regardless of whether or not the segment is found, control returns to paragraph 300-GET-PAT-NO immediately after the PERFORM 400-FIND-PAT line.

"Notice the IF PAT-FOUND clause in paragraph 300. I'm checking the switch to see if DL/I found the PATIENT. If it didn't, I print a message.

"If a PATIENT was found, I next execute a double GNP loop: one to retrieve all the IV orders (IVORD) for this PA-

TIENT (PERFORM 500-FIND-ORDS) and an inner one inside paragraph 500, which sequentially retrieves all the ADDITIVEs for each order (900-GET-ADDITIVES).

"In paragraph 500-FIND-ORDS, I needed to make the IVORD segment the parent so that my subsequent GNP ADDITIVE would limit itself to a single order. I did this by using a P command code, which you can see as the first executable line in paragraph 500-FIND-ORDS. As I'm sure you all expected, the actual CALL used the IV-PCB mask, the WS-IV I/O area, and the GNP function. The two SSAs used in the CALL in effect make the CALL look like this:

GNP PATIENT(PATNO = PATIENT-
            NUMBER)
    IVORD

"Because I wanted an unqualified GNP call in paragraph 500-FIND-ORDS, I moved SPACES to the left-parenthesis byte within the IVORD-SSA. Following the GNP call, the program checks IV-STATUS to determine if DL/I found another order (IVORD). If not, the appropriate switch is set.

"On the other hand, if an order was retrieved, I look up the drug in the FORMULARY database by PERFORMing paragraph 600-FIND-FORM. Notice that in that paragraph, I used the FORM-PCB mask rather than IV-PCB, which the CALL in paragraph 500-FIND-ORDS used.

"I didn't bother to check for an item that wasn't in the FORMULARY database, because there is no way for an order to be stored without the drug being in the FORMULARY database.

"Once the drug is looked up, control returns to paragraph 500-FIND-ORDS. Here I print what I have so far by calling paragraph 700-MOVE-AND-PRINT-ORD-DATA. Then, I begin the inner loop that uses GNP to cycle through the ADDITIVEs for this IV by initializing the loop control switch, MORE-ADDITIVES-THIS-ORD-SW, then PERFORMing 900-GET-ADDITIVES within a loop construct.

"Paragraph 900-GET-ADDITIVES, which performs a GNP call to retrieve the next ADDITIVE segment, also looks up the FORMITEM item by also PERFORMing paragraph 600-FIND-FORM.

"I guess that's all I have to say. If there aren't any questions, I'd like all of you to begin writing the programs I assigned you. We'll have monthly review meetings to discuss your progress. Good luck."

VI

Database Management

Part VI looks at some issues not specifically related to the data models: database administration, distributed databases, database machines, and 4GLs. Chapter 13 focuses on database administration. Like the other organizational resources, the enterprise's data must be assigned to a custodian. This person carries out a fairly well-defined set of duties, which the chapter describes. It also discusses a technique for selecting the DBMS best suited for a given organization.

Chapter 14 deals with three topics concerned with how to disseminate data more quickly and efficiently. All of these topics use SQL. The first topic is the distributed database, an environment in which portions of the database reside on different computers, usually at different sites, and users need to share this data. We assume that all sites use SQL, making the task of communicating among the nodes a bit easier. Next, the chapter looks at back-end computers, specially designed devices that usually carry out SQL orders. This product represents a small but important market, especially for those organizations desiring better performance from their DBMSs. Next the chapter examines the role of the microcomputer in today's distributed DBMS environment. Finally, the chapter discuss two excellent 4GL products, both of which use SQL as their DBMSs. The intent is not to teach you how to use a 4GL but to help you appreciate its features and ease of use.

13 Database Administration

MINICASE Telecorp

Telecorp had been evaluating IDMS/R for about eight months. Because of the firm's small size, the chief information officer (CIO) felt that a full-time database administrator wasn't justified. As a result, Mary Rodgers, the systems analyst most experienced with IDMS/R, had been serving as an interim DBA. However, all was not going as well as she would have liked.

Last week Mary told Adam Keefe, manager of application programming, to instruct all of his programmers who were developing new systems or doing maintenance on existing ones to meet with her. She explained that she had a long-term plan for implementing the DBMS and wanted to check all programming efforts for possible data inclusion under the three databases currently in operation.

The day before yesterday, Mary discovered that three programmers had been assigned to work on the revised general ledger system, and several more of Adam's employees had been assigned to the new payroll system. None had called her for the required meetings. When she confronted one of them, she was told, "I just don't have time to meet with you. Adam said that my work was important and that we don't have time to meet with

you and still get the projects done on time. Besides, I'm paid by Adam, and he's the one who evaluates me. If I spend time with you in meetings, I'll just get further behind. Nothing personal, but I just can't be bothered to take the extra time. Maybe next time.

"Besides, Adam said that you're always in meetings, so we can't ever get to see your data dictionary listings if we want to. In order for this to work, you'd have to be available 24 hours a day. Sorry, Mary, but we just don't think your idea is gong to work."

Adam had his own troubles. Rob Smith, manager of the human resource management (HRM) department, called twice to complain about some improperly altered data. Apparently some non-HRM employees had changed data in three of his database files, and he wanted Adam to "do something about it."

Then last Friday (these things always seem to happen on Friday!), Tom Roberts, manager of purchasing, called to complain. Twice he had lost data. Once the computer system had crashed and his inventory master file had been destroyed. Luckily there was a three-week-old backup, but the activity data in the file was all wrong, as were the quantities on hand. After 24 hours of overtime, his employees were reasonably sure that they had reapplied all the transactions since the backup had been made, but he wanted insurance that this wouldn't happen again .

The second time, the purchasing system was running and the PC master file had just been updated, indicating that several items were ordered, when lightning struck. Thus, the UNITS-ON-ORDER fields in the inventory file weren't updated, and the data was out of sync. Like Rob, Tom wanted to know what could be done to prevent this from happening again.

Discussion

1. List five of Telecorp's data management problems.

2. Even if the programmer who met with Mary was correct, what could Telecorp's management do to help her enforce her standards?

3. Which IDMS/R and DB2 command would have prevented the second problem with the purchasing system?

4. What could Mary do to make her data dictionary more readily available?

5. What kinds of recovery techniques could help with the first purchasing problem? (You may need to reread Chapter 1.)

6. Who should be responsible for backing up files in individual systems? Defend your answer.

Five resources flow through an organization: manpower, machines, money, materials, and data. Except for data, the organization will always assign one or more individuals as custodians of the resource. Often it isn't until the organization realizes the importance of data, or decides to begin using the database approach, that it appoints someone as custodian of the data. This chapter concerns that individual.

At the conclusion of this chapter, you will be able to:

- Discuss the administrative and technical duties of the DBA
- Use the scoring model approach to select a DBMS
- Explain when rollforward and rollback are useful and how each works
- State the different categories of end user tools and representative commercial products from each
- Describe problems associated with concurrent processing and some strategies for solving them
- Discuss the alternative ways to organize the DBA function

Data is an organizational asset; in fact, many experts contend that it is the most important asset an organization has. The larger the enterprise, the heavier its dependence on data. In a small organization, the owner can see personally how each employee and department is performing, but as the firm grows, data becomes a surrogate for personal observation.

The other organizational resources—money, machines, manpower, and materials—are assigned to one or more individuals for their management. In the case of data, that responsibility falls on either the database administrator (DBA) or a database administration department.

Section 13.1 looks closely at the responsibilities of this function. Section 13.2 examines in detail one of the technical responsibilities of database administration: concurrency control. Section 13.3 looks at some alternative ways to organize the DBA function, ranging from diffused responsibility—with no one person being in charge—to a complete functional organization in which the DBA has a complete staff of subordinates.

13.1 DATABASE ADMINISTRATION FUNCTIONS

There is no one "right" way to depict database administration duties, but Figure 13.1 illustrates a commonly used taxonomy. The four-way breakdown divides the duties into two types of responsibilities, administrative and technical. Then it breaks down each of these into the two object areas that database administration controls: applications or end users and the DBMS-related software.

FIGURE 13.1   **A Taxonomy of Database Administration Functions**

Type of Object of Responsibility	Application/End User	Software Systems
Administration	Conceptual database management Establishment of goals and policies in: 　DBMS acquisition 　DBMS implementation 　DBMS performance 　Data dictionary 　Auditing 　Security 　Backup and recovery User documentation	Acquisition of DBMS Acquisition of data dictionary Provision of access tools, such as 4GLs Training of users in use of DBMS and 4GLs
Technical	Conceptual database generation External database maintenance DD implementation and maintenance Implementation of database audits	Performance monitoring/tuning Backup and recovery implementation Database reorganization Installation of DBMS DBMS update maintenance

---

Administrative Responsibilities

The administrative tasks are usually management oriented. The application/end-user-related duties include:

- Management of the conceptual database
- Creation of database goals and policies related to DBMS and data dictionary (DD) acquisition, DBMS implementation and performance, auditing, security, standards, and backup and recovery
- Creation of end user documentation

The administrative software duties relate to:

- Acquisition of the DBMS
- Acquisition of the data dictionary
- Provision of data access tools for end users
- Training of users in accessing data in the DBMS and using 4GLs

Conceptual Database Management. Conceptual database management is probably the most important DBA duty. Without an accurate conceptual database, the resulting applications are doomed to failure. In Chapter 5, we saw that such a design should be independent of applications, hardware, and the DBMS, yet must be able to support the transactions required of both existing and future applications. One way to verify the accuracy of the design is to ensure that it can supply the data necessary to satisfy the business's rules. Recall that this task usually culminates in a model, which is built using either an entity-relationship or data structure diagramming technique.

It is wrong to assume that the resulting design is a static one; rather, changes will occur as new applications are developed and existing ones evolve or are retired. Remember, the conceptual database is designed to fit the needs of the organization; as the organization changes, so must the conceptual database.

Some aids for facilitating this maintenance problem are available. Some promising work is being done in the area of computer-aided software engineering (CASE). For example, Index Technologies markets a widely used, PC-based product called Excelerator. Among its many components are modules for drawing data structure and entity-relationship diagrams, integration of a data dictionary with the diagrams, determination of foreign keys, and checking of the conceptual design for third normal form. Most CASE products are "front-end" products, meaning they are most useful during the development of a system. In reality, up to 90 percent of an IS department's time is devoted to maintaining existing systems. There is at least one commercial package that addresses the data needs of this type of IS project.

Charles Bachman markets a reverse-engineering CASE product that can read DB2, IMS, IDMS, and other DBMS and non-DBMS files and construct the underlying conceptual data models. Such products are expected to proliferate, because maintaining the conceptual data model by hand is an arduous, time-consuming, often mundane task. Reverse-engineering products can automate this task allowing more time for activities such as championing the database approach.

Recall from Chapter 1 that the database approach embodies the spirit of cooperation and sharing. While the conceptual database is being designed—and on a continuing basis thereafter—the DBA must take steps to foster this spirit. When conflicts arise, the DBA must be able to do whatever is in the best interests of the organization.

We can expect many politically based objections from users who are reluctant to give up portions of their data empire, whether that empire is based on data acquisition, stewardship, or distribution. A common trait among many users is the desire for more power. One way to measure power is by the amount of control one has over resources, and we saw at the beginning of this chapter that data is an organizational resource. We are advocating that almost all of the power associated with data be centralized in a single department or under one individual. This will require that others (both in and out of the IS department) relinquish their control over the asset, with an apparent corresponding reduction in power. Convincing former holders of the power of the benefits of such a plan can be a political nightmare.

Goal and Policy Establishment. Ideally, goals of all kinds originate at the top of the organization and are passed down the managerial hierarchy. Each subordinate unit in the hierarchy then develops its own goals designed to support those received from the higher levels and formulates plans to implement both sets of goals.

Policies are plans or methods of action that provide guidance in accomplishing the goals. Database goals and policies must support those of the organization, not conflict with them.

The goals and policies the DBA formulates relate to:

- Acquisition of the DBMS
- DBMS implementation
- DBMS performance
- The data dictionary
- Auditing of data
- Data security
- Backup and recovery

DBMS Acquisition. Selecting the "best" data model is becoming easier, because it is an almost foregone conclusion that the organization will select a relational package. The only decision remaining is which one? In the next section, we will look at a technique for assisting with this decision. One of the administrative tasks necessitated by the technique is the establishment of criteria for evaluating the vendors of the DBMSs being considered. Two categories of criteria to consider are non-performance- and performance-related criteria.

Among the non-performance-related criteria that should be considered are total cost; the underlying data model; the ability to perform transaction and concurrent processing management; availability of end user tools, such as 4GLs; ease of installation; degree of data independence; procedural language interfaces; number and sophistication of end user tools; database limits (table sizes, row sizes, field types, etc.); degree of compliance with industry standards; level of security; and distributed and teleprocessing support.

When deciding how to measure DBMS costs, it is wrong to focus exclusively on the initial cost of the software. Other one-time charges include:

- The data dictionary, if not included with the package
- End user tools, such as 4GLs
- Teleprocessing (TP) monitors if the database is to be on-line and the organization doesn't already have a TP monitor
- Training costs for both IS and end user employees
- Installation of the DBMS
- Development of a pilot project
- Additional main memory, terminals, and disk drives

Continuing costs include:

- DBMS maintenance or lease costs
- Vendors' manual updates
- Database administration staff increases
- Utilities to help tune and audit the databases

DBMS Implementation. Implementation policies for the DBMS will include the dates associated with milestones like delivery, initial installation of the package, testing and debugging, and development of a pilot system that uses the DBMS. If the organization wants the database approach to succeed, the project it chooses for the pilot should have high visibility, have a high probability of success, and be led by someone who will champion the database approach.

DBMS Performance. Other DBMS goals relate to performance once the DBMS is installed: What should be the average response time? What is an acceptable response time for on-line applications? How many transactions per second should the DBMS applications be able to process?

Several standard benchmarks are currently used to compare the performances of relational DBMSs. One such benchmark is the Wisconsin Benchmark, first developed in 1983 by Dr. D. Bitton. Her algorithm evaluated the built-in optimizers of the relational products and contained 32 SQL queries whose performances were measured in a stand-alone environment with five megabytes of data. The benchmark didn't test indexing speed or the effects of locking and buffer sizes. Vendors began tuning their products specifically to the Wisconsin Benchmark by gearing their optimizers to the 32 queries and varying buffer sizes to the point where complete tables were in memory. In effect, the benchmark became meaningless.

In 1988, Dr. Bitton developed a new methodology called the ANSI SQL Standard Scalable and Portable Benchmark. It contains three modules. The first is for single-user environments and tests database utilities (e.g., indexing and loading) as well as specific queries. It also measures the speed of backup and recovery and the degree of referential integrity present in the DBMS.

The second and third modules are for multiuser environments. They test the speed of the RDBMS with respect to on-line transactions (OLTP) per second, as well as the speed under varying workload conditions, such as multiuser retrievals concurrent with OLTP. Her set of three modules is more versatile than her first benchmark and attempts to prevent vendors from designing their products to simply perform well on the benchmark.

Other benchmarks are used to compare performances of RDBMSs, including TP1, a banking-oriented benchmark, which IBM uses frequently. The DBA should select a benchmark, then establish performance goals consistent with the criteria results the benchmark reports. For example, if the benchmark reports transactions per second (TPS), the DBA might establish the goal of 75 TPS.

Data Dictionary Objectives. Many experts believe that the acquisition of the data dictionary (DD) should precede that of the DBMS, because without a data dictionary the database approach cannot be implemented. There are two kinds of data dictionaries: active and passive.

An **active data dictionary** is one that forces programmers to use it to write the applications. The only source of data about the data (recall the term *metadata*) is the data dictionary. This approach results in the greatest data control. The DB2 data dictionary is an example of an active DD.

A **passive data dictionary** is largely for people; the applications don't directly interact with such a dictionary. Many vendors offer add-on dictionaries for IMS and IDMS/R. If acquired, these products will be accessed not by applications using the DBMS but by programmers and end users who need to query the databases.

The DD that accompanies a DBMS is usually an active one, but it provides facilities for managing data for objects pertaining only to that product. For example, DB2's DD includes recordkeeping for tables, columns, users, views, indexes, and so on. If the organization needs a complete repository for all of its IS needs, an external, passive DD is also necessary. For example, Excelerator stores data about the following items:

- Data entities
- Data flows
- Data N-ary relationships (the term used to describe the relationship in an E-R diagram)
- Data relationships (the relationship on a DSD)
- Data stores
- Elements
- External entities
- Functions (procedures on a structure chart)
- Modules
- Presentation graphs
- Processes
- Reports
- Records
- Screens
- Users
- Tables of codes used for program edits

Many of these objects are not used in a database setting; rather, they are used by systems analysts who employ the structured approach to IS design. The point is that the active data dictionary that accompanies the DBMS will be insufficient for general use by all IS employees. A passive DD that stores data about all the system-related objects will probably be required as well. We should point out that keeping the data in both dictionaries in sync is difficult. The work of Bachman and others who are pursuing reverse-engineering tools should help alleviate this problem.

Once the decision about which data dictionary to use is made, the DBA should begin collecting the data that will be entered. He or she must identify the data elements the organization currently uses, as well as those that aren't currently used but are required to meet some business rule identified during the conceptual design of the database.

As part of this data dictionary task, the DBA must also decide on naming conventions and the types of values to be associated with particular elements. For example, will military time be used or the more familiar 12-hour clock with A.M. and P.M. indicators? What will be the standard date format? What abbreviations will be used to designate weight, sex, height, and so on?

Next, the DBA should establish domain constraints for each data item. Remember that we can use implicit or explicit domains. Implicit domains consist of a type and a range, while explicit domains enumerate each possible value. Even if the DBMS doesn't support domain enforcement, the applications must, so the domains must be determined.

Finally, there should be a check for redundancy. Because this may require time-consuming searches through the list of data elements, this task might be better left until the dictionary is actually implemented. When redundant items are found, the DBA must decide which definition to use as the primary one and which to convert into synonyms.

Another issue is the method of data dictionary accessibility. Data dictionaries can be on-line or off-line. As Mary found out in the minicase, if the data dictionary is off-line, access by users becomes difficult. If it's on-line, on the other hand, what happens if a programmer is called in at 3:00 A.M. and the dictionary is inaccessible? Perhaps a hard copy of it also should be made available.

Auditing. Also essential is the need to establish audit goals for the database applications. One of these goals is frequently imposed by the organization's internal audit staff: the guarantee that there are no orphaned record occurrences—records that cannot be accessed by following pointers.

With pointer-related systems, such as network and hierarchical DBMSs, hardware or software failures can result in broken chains. This can lead to records being inaccessible via pointers.

The DBA must establish a procedure for physically dumping every record, without following the pointers. Then the DBA must be able to show that all active records appearing on the dump can be accessed via pointers. This can be a manual or computerized procedure. Finally, the DBA must develop a procedure for repairing broken chains. Repairing of chains can be accomplished by using a DBMS utility or by running an operating system utility that permits the direct changing of bytes of any file on a disk drive. Fixing broken chains is tedious, error-prone work, but its value cannot be overestimated, because without this ability data will be lost and incorrect decisions made.

Another audit issue is to decide whether or not an audit trail of user activity against the database or any of its components is desirable. For example, the internal audit staff might want to know about all invalid attempts to log on to a given database or efforts to alter a table's data that fail because that user lacked the proper rights. Both of these examples indicate potential security breaches. This could help with Rob Smith's problems in the Telecorp example. The fact that unauthorized users were able to change data in some files indicates that the organization needs to impose some additional security measures. Passwords plus an audit file of accesses should resolve Rob's complaints.

The ORACLE package includes an AUDIT command that can track attempts to access or change tables, audit SQL statements against tables, and monitor both successful and unsuccessful attempts to log on to ORACLE. For example, the statement

AUDIT ALTER, INSERT, SELECT, UPDATE ON ORDERS WHENEVER
SUCCESSFUL

will cause a row to be stored in the table called AUDIT_TRAIL any time a user changes the structure or adds, retrieves, or changes a row in the ORDERS table.

While most DBMS vendors have optional audit facilities like those found in ORACLE, the DBA must evaluate the performance trade-off that results from using the feature versus the desire to provide data security and integrity. In most cases, the DBMS must maintain not only this table but also a transaction log table plus the base tables. Users might notice a drop-off in performance when such additional tables are maintained.

To help the DBA choose the proper audit features, the American Institute of Certified Public Accountants (AICPA) has identified three database audit areas:

- Access control
- Coordination of shared resources
- Security of data

Regarding the first area, the AICPA states that users should be able to see only the data they are entitled to see and shouldn't have to worry about problems associated with concurrent updating. We have seen how implementations of the CODASYL models use LOCKS and how the relational model uses the GRANT facility for limiting access to record types and tables. IMS has no inherent techniques for limiting access to its segments by unauthorized users. Furthermore, all three models have built-in facilities for handling concurrent processing. Access control strategies are highly integrated into today's DBMSs.

The next area addresses the fact that data is a shared resource. The DBMS (and the DBA) must guarantee that all users who share data can understand its descriptions and that any replicated (duplicated) data be consistent.

It is common for an organization to extract data from its transaction database and store it in separate files in formats specific to end-user-related packages, such as 4GLs and report writers. This is done because of worries about possible security breaches from allowing end users direct access of database records, because in many DBMSs, especially CODASYL and hierarchical ones, accessing data can be too complicated for most end users and because the 4GLs and report writers are more flexible than the DBMS-specific utilities that have similar purposes but either come with the DBMS or are extra-cost options.

Another trend today is for end users to download such extracted data to their microcomputers so that they can manipulate it using more user-friendly and familiar software such as dBASE IV, Paradox, R:BASE, and so on. The result is that data can be replicated even with a database approach. Imagine the problems when the DBA discovers that the data in the transaction database is wrong! In such environments, it is incumbent on the DBA to ensure that the host programs that update the transaction database have adequate edit facilities to guarantee the data's integrity.

Another situation in which replicated data can occur is in the are of *distributed databases,* in which shared data is stored in several locations and often intentionally duplicated. This topic is covered in the next chapter.

Data is a shared resource. The DBA must take steps to ensure that this sharing is properly coordinated. The results of all users of shared data must be considered; everyone using shared data has to see the same data values, even if the data is replicated; and everyone using the data must understand its semantics.

Finally, the AICPA recognizes the importance of data security, a subject that we discuss in the next section.

Security. Among the methods for ensuring a secure data environment are:

- Passwords
- Establishment of user rights (access tables)
- User views (external databases)
- Encryption

Passwords. We have discussed passwords throughout the text. For instance, with a RDBMS, passwords can be required for logging on at the database, table, column, or view level. One aspect of passwords that we haven't mentioned is that passwords should be changed periodically and when an employee leaves the organization. If passwords aren't changed, unauthorized employees will eventually learn them. A familiar story concerns the employee who wrote his password on a piece of paper, then stuck it to his terminal for easy reference—and for easy viewing by unauthorized employees. If passwords are changed regularly, the consequences of such actions will be short-lived.

Establishment of User Rights. The DBA can extend the password concept by associating rights with each password. Among the commonly used rights are read-only, read/write, open, and delete. One way to represent and plan for access rights is to use an *access table.* Such tables include *rights*—sometimes called *actions*—*subjects,* and *objects.* The *subject* is the user of the database. Examples of subjects would be a group of users—pharmacists, for instance—or people who perform the same tasks, such as vice presidents. *Objects* are the units that are to be made secure and can range from the entire databases down to a single data element. The size of the secure object determines its *granularity.* Security at the database level is considered to be of large granularity, while data element security is said to be of low granularity.

Figure 13.2 illustrates a portion of an access table that might be used for Suburban Hospital. Here the security granularity level is at the table level. Two tables (objects) are listed: ORDERS and a management table called MANAGEMENT, which might have columns for the date, the number of new patient orders entered, the number changed, and the number deleted. One row would be added to the table per day.

FIGURE 13.2   Example of an Access Table

Subjects	Objects	
	ORDERS	MANAGEMENT
Directors	READ	ALL
Pharmacists	ALL	READ__WRITE
Technicians	READ	WRITE

There are three subjects in Figure 13.2: directors of the hospital, pharmacists, and pharmacy technicians. Directors are permitted to only read the ORDERS rows, while pharmacists can perform all ORDERS functions. Directors have all MANAGEMENT privileges, while technicians may only write to the MANAGEMENT table. This privilege is necessary because as a technician enters or changes an order, an update of the MANAGEMENT table will be required. Because Suburban does not want technicians to be able to view this table, it has not given them read rights.

Determining the access rights of all potential users isn't an easy task. As we mentioned above, some DBMSs permit the assignment of rights to groups of subjects, thus reducing the amount of work considerably. For example, all vice presidents might be given all rights to all files, while clerical employees might be assigned read-only privileges.

Once group rights are assigned, the individual rights are examined. When an individual right exists, the DBMS will usually use it even if a group right conflicts with it.

User Views. User views, also called *external databases* or *subschemas*, should be familiar to you. The ability of a single user to view or alter data can be made different from that of all other users, permitting the DBA to provide a view commensurate with that employee's place in the organizational hierarchy. For example, in the Suburban Hospital pharmacy, a technician who works in an IV area might be precluded from viewing ORDERs of types other than Intravenous. To establish this using SQL, the DBA might code:

```
DEFINE VIEW IV__ORDERS
    AS SELECT * FROM ORDERS
        WHERE ORDER__TYPE = 'IV';
```

Now when a technician SELECTs from IV__ORDERS, only IV orders will be displayed. If IMS is used instead of a SQL product, the DBA must define a suitable PCB. If the organizational DBMS follows the CODASYL model, a subschema will accomplish the same thing as a VIEW in SQL or a new PCB in IMS.

Encryption. Another type of security is that produced by **encryption,** a process that transforms stored data values into an unrecognizable form. Of particular use are characters that cannot be printed or displayed. In EBCDIC, for example, a code of 01110000 is not associated with any printable character. Thus, if we map the letter *a* onto this bit pattern, no one can display it without first going through a **decryption process,** a technique that converts the data into its original form.

These tools are becoming popular with microcomputers in which the encryption/decryption programs remain in memory even while another application is running (called a *terminate and stay resident,* or *TSR,* program). This way, the data can be transparently encrypted and decrypted without the user having to run special programs.

Backup and Recovery. The next area of goal setting involves backup and recovery. The backup policy is a key component in guaranteeing data integrity. Remember Murphy's law: "Whatever can go wrong will." In the Telecorp mini-case, Tom Roberts had some difficulties because of an inadequate backup policy. A backup had been made, but it was quite old, and the transactions applied to the master files subsequent to the backup apparently had not been saved. In a conventional IS system, backups can be made by the operations department, thereby relying on their complete backup of all DASD files, or as a module within the individual information system. The latter provides for more control at the system level but may be difficult for an analyst to implement because of the need for access to system utilities. In a database environment, the database administration function should be responsible for backups of the databases.

A policy concerning the maximum length of time that a backup and/or recovery can take should be established. Is six hours acceptable, or must the backup and recovery processes be done in less than an hour? One of the considerations made in setting these goals is whether or not the DBMS must be shut down (locked) while the backup is being performed. Such schemes are called **quiescent backups.** For organizations that must run 24 hours a day, a policy that requires all users to log off the database while the potentially long backup procedure is executed will not work. The other backup option is a **synchronic backup,** meaning that backup can take place without locking everyone out of the DBMS and that applications can continue to run while the database is being backed up.

Other backup/recovery objectives should include cost, the ability to restore a portion of the database, and the availability of utilities for things such as printing directories of the backup and doing partial backups (perhaps backing up all changes since the last complete backup) and restores. A related policy concerns when to perform the backup and who should be responsible for it.

Still other considerations involve the log, or journal, file. Questions to be resolved include whether or not a log file is to be maintained, what its contents should be, and what medium should be used. It is doubtful that any DBA would choose not to use a log file, so we can skip further discussion of this issue.

Let's look briefly at the content question. Remember that a log file can contain before images, after images, and transactions. The DBA must weigh the benefits and problems associated with each category of data. While logging all three kinds of data would result in the most secure data backup, because of the need to save all the data, the resulting performance level of applications might be unacceptable.

The answer to the medium question also is unclear. If the log file is on tape, it slows down the system. But if a disk drive is used, a controller or channel failure might result in the inability to subsequently access the log file for recovery purposes as well as the database.

This completes our discussion of goal and policy setting. We will return to many of these topics as we discuss the software systems duties, as they are largely concerned with the implementation of these goals. The next section discusses the last of the administrative application duties: end user documentation.

End User Documentation. When data dictionaries are not on-line, the database administration function must provide a way to inform IS employees and end users of items such as the names of databases, tables, and fields. Without this knowledge, they cannot access the database. Thus, the production of user documentation is essential.

End users aren't technical experts, so this documentation should be free from jargon and should emphasize how to access the data, not how to manage it. Among the procedures and documentation that should be specified are how to log on to the operating system, how to log on to the database, a summary of database access commands, a listing of error codes and their meanings and how to correct the problem causing the errors, and how to produce a hard-copy listing of queries.

This concludes our discussion of the administrative application/end user responsibilities. The next section looks at the software/systems duties, most of which concern the implementation of the goals developed in the previous section. First, let's see how the DBMS comparison criteria we discussed earlier can be used to help select a DBMS or DD.

DBMS and Data Dictionary Acquisition. This section develops a technique that can be applied equally to the acquisition of either the DBMS or the data dictionary. It is often referred to as a *scoring model*. Although we emphasize how the technique can be applied to acquiring a DBMS, it can easily be transferred to that of selecting a DD.

Assuming the relational model was selected and a RDBMS is needed, the DBA should send all relevant vendors a **request for proposal** (**RFP**), a document that describes the needs of the organization and requests the vendor to respond to questions and provide an actual price quotation. Once the organization receives the proposals, it must evaluate them and select the best DBMS.

Probably the most widely used technique for evaluating DBMS packages is the **scoring model.** This is a step-by-step procedure for comparing alternatives when several criteria are used to evaluate them. The steps are as follows:

1. Choose several independent criteria.
2. Collect the data about each criterion from each vendor.
3. Develop "relative importance" weights for each criterion.
4. Develop a scoring table for each criterion based on the data.
5. Determine the vendor's score for each criterion using the tables.
   a. For each criterion, multiply the score by the weight, yielding a weighted score.
   b. Add up the weighted scores for each vendor.
6. Choose the vendor with the highest score.

Choose Several Independent Criteria. The word *independent* in this context means that none of the criteria "overlap." For example, if one criterion is total cost and another installation cost, the effect of the second cost will be double-counted because presumably we included installation cost as a component in the total cost. A commonly asked question is: How many criteria are needed? Research suggests that as few as 7 to 10 can result in the same decision as scores of criteria. In practice, most organizations use from 20 to 100 criteria.

Figure 13.3 shows five assumed criteria that we will use to illustrate the technique. Notice that total discounted cost, amount of memory required, and number of transactions processed per second are *quantitative* (that is, numeric values can be used to measure them). The others—ease of installation and availability of 4GLs—are *qualitative* (i.e., numeric measures can't be used).

Collect Data from Vendors. Among the questions the DBA should ask in the RFP are the values for the quantitative criteria. Developing data about the qualitative criteria is more difficult.

FIGURE 13.3   **Five Independent Criteria to Use in Choosing a DBMS**

Criterion
Total discounted cost
Ease of installation
Amount of money
Availability of 4GLs
Number of transactions processed per second

Another question usually asked in an RFP is "List names, addresses, and phone numbers for users of your product." A good starting point for determining values for the qualitative criteria is to phone users on the list supplied by the vendor. Another source is to use a consulting service such as *Data Pro 70*, an invaluable product from Data Pro that compares all products of a given type. Its hardware comparisons include mainframes, mini- and small computers, microcomputers, printers, terminals, and controllers. On the software side, *Data Pro 70* compares and evaluates database management software, application software, and teleprocessing monitors. Included in its comparisons are a technical analysis of each product, a management summary, and end user surveys. Included in the surveys are summaries of ratings (usually 1 to 4) for each vendor for items such as ease of use, ease of installation, satisfaction with service, and so on—all qualitative criteria that might be used as part of the scoring model.

Develop Relative Importance Weights. The next step involves the assignment of relative importance weights to each criterion. Most organizations assign these weights prior to collecting data from the vendors. Strictly speaking, the weights should be determined after the data is collected, because they must reflect the data. Because the technique for developing these weights based on the actual data is complicated and beyond the scope of this text, we will assume that the weights are determined as above—in advance.

We usually assign weights of 1 to 10 to each criterion. These weights assume a ratio scale, meaning that a weight of 10 is twice as important as a weight of 5. Because acquisition of a DBMS influences the entire organization, the weights often represent the perceptions of a group of decision makers, including managers from systems programming, applications programming, operations, the chief information officer, and the DBA. As you might expect, getting everyone to agree on a weight can be frustrating. However, this step must be completed for the method to work.

Figure 13.4 shows the assumed weights for our example.

FIGURE 13.4   **Importance Weights Associated with Each Criterion**

Criterion	Weight
Total discounted cost	7
Ease of installation	4
Amount of memory	4
Availability of 4GLs	6
Number of transactions processed per second	10

FIGURE 13.5   Example of a Scoring Table for a Quantitative Criterion

Amount of Memory Required

Interval	Score
50–90K	5
91–130K	4
131–170K	3
171–210K	2
211–250K	1

Develop Scoring Tables for Each Criterion. It is important that these tables be developed only after the data is collected. The scoring tables look like that in Figure 13.5.

Each table must have the same number of scores, five in the example. The range for each *quantitative* criterion is calculated this way:

1. Determine the largest value.
2. Determine the smallest value.
3. Subtract the smallest value from the largest value, giving a criterion range difference.
4. Divide the range by the number of intervals (five in our example), giving an interval size.
5. Add this number to the smallest value, which gives the first interval.
6. Continue adding until there are no more intervals.

Let's look at the "total discounted cost" criterion. Assume that three vendors, A, B, and C, have provided quotations and that the total discounted cost for each is calculated as $75,000, $90,000, and $60,000, respectively. The largest value is $90,000, the smallest $60,000, and the difference $30,000. This means that the size of each interval will be $30,000/5, or $6,000. The resulting table will therefore be:

Interval	Score
$60,000–66,000	5
$66,001–72,000	4
$72,001–78,000	3
$78,001–84,000	2
$84,001–90,000	1

Many make the mistake of assuming that a low criterion value is always associated with a high score, as was the case with the discounted-cost example. However, consider the criterion "transactions processed per second (TPS)." Here, because more TPS are preferred to fewer, a low value should be associated with a low score and a high value with a high score. The point is: Think about which criterion values are "better," low ones or high ones. Always associate the higher scores with the better criterion values.

For *qualitative* criteria, we use a table like this:

Value	Score
Inferior	1
Below average	2
Average	3
Above average	4
Superior	5

Again, be sure that each qualitative table has the same number of values—five in our example.

Calculate the Total Weighted Score for Each Vendor. Based on actual values found in the vendor's proposal, we next determine a **raw criterion score** for each criterion for each vendor. For example, based on our "total discounted cost" scoring table above, vendor A would receive a raw score of 3, because its cost is $75,000, placing the vendor into the third interval, which has a score of 3. This procedure is repeated for every criterion.

Next, we multiply the raw score by the criterion's weight, yielding a **weighted criterion score.** For the cost attribute, vendor A would thus receive a weighted criterion score of 21 (3 × 7). Now we add the weighted scores across all criteria for each vendor, yielding a **total weighted score** for each. A table such as that in Figure 13.6 is useful for recording our work.

Choose the Vendor with the Highest Score. Largely a mechanical step, all we need to do is scan across the "Totals" row in Figure 13.6 and find the largest total weighted score. In this case, it is 111 and belongs to vendor A. Thus, we select vendor A's product.

FIGURE 13.6   The Completed Scoring Model

Criterion	Score	Vendor A Score	Vendor A WS	Vendor B Score	Vendor B WS	Vendor C Score	Vendor C WS
Total cost	7	3	21	1	7	5	35
Installation	4	3	12	2	8	1	4
Amount of memory	4	5	20	4	16	3	12
Availability of 4GLs	6	3	18	3	18	2	12
Transactions per second	10	4	40	3	30	3	30
Totals			111		79		93

WS indicates the weighted score and equals the product of score and weight.

Provide Data Access Tools. One way to encourage end user access of data is to acquire a 4GL. There are several categories of 4GLs, including query generators, report writers, and application generators. One thing is common to all three: They contain a nonprocedural language and thus appeal to end users.

Query generators usually provide an easy way to define screen layouts and to indicate which fields should be displayed at various points on the screen, a facility sometimes referred to as *screen painting*. These packages make it very easy to retrieve data from a single table or file within an existing database and display it at predetermined locations on screen. However, using them with multiple tables becomes difficult to accomplish for most end users, and they usually do not provide for updating data or producing sophisticated reports. Two exceptions are QBE and SQL; these query languages can perform updating tasks, but they lack sophisticated report capabilities. Figure 13.7 lists some of the popular query languages.

While such packages usually can route a query to a hard-copy device, applications that require sophisticated report formatting capabilities may need a **report writer.** When a column-oriented report with relatively simple control-break and subtotaling requirements is necessary, a query language will suffice. But for applications demanding noncolumnar formatting or linking of several files, a report writer should be considered. Figure 13.8 shows some of the popular report-writer packages.

The final category of 4GL is the **application generator.** Figure 13.9 lists the most popular ones. Whereas programs from the other two categories can produce reports and screens, packages in this group can produce complete applications. Most of them force the end users to use files created by the 4GL, but

---

FIGURE 13.7   **Popular Query Languages**

Package	Vendor
INTELLECT	Artificial Intelligence Corporation
On-Line English	Cullinet
QBE	IBM
SQL/DS	IBM

FIGURE 13.8   **Popular Report Writers**

Package	Vendor
Easytrieve Plus	Pansophic
GIS	IBM
Mark IV	Informatics
NOMAD	NCSS

FIGURE 13.9   **Popular Application Generators**

Package	Vendor
FOCUS	Information Builders
INFORMIX-4GL	INFORMIX
MANTIS	CINCOM
NATURAL	Software AG
ORACLE	Oracle Corporation
RAMIS	Mathematica Inc.

this software is increasingly permitting users to access DB2 files or use their own SQL implementation. An example of such a package was illustrated in Chapter 6, and we will see another in the next chapter.

Once such packages are procured, users must be trained in their use. The ease-of-use characteristic of such packages can actually become a liability, however. For example, a user in a large public utility had just taken a class in SQL and returned to his desk. Out of curiosity, he attempted to perform a join on the organization's IBM 3090 600E (a very large mainframe). After two days (it was a weekend), the join was still being performed when an operator noticed the problem and canceled the job!

The point is that end user tools can be inefficient and misused. The DBA must decide which applications are to programmed by IS professionals using 3GLs like COBOL, which can be programmed by IS employees using 4GLs, and which can be programmed by end users using 4GLs.

Technical Responsibilities

Many of the technical responsibilities parallel the administrative tasks. However, the latter focus on planning and goal setting, while the former are more technical or operational in nature.

The first five technical responsibilities apply to the application/end user category:

- Conceptual database generation and maintenance
- External database maintenance
- Data dictionary implementation and maintenance
- Performing database audits
- Establishment and maintenance of a test database

Conceptual Database Generation and Maintenance. Once the conceptual database is developed, the DBA must translate it into a physical reality through the DDL. With IDMS and IMS, separate modules must be used. However, with DB2, the SQL language is used to CREATE TABLEs and databases.

External Database Maintenance. As each application is developed, the DBA must ensure that its business rules can be met. Remember that an external database maps a specific user's data needs onto the conceptual database. After designing the external databases, the DBA must transform them into physical representations using software such as CODASYL's subschema DDL, IMS's DBDGEN, or SQL's CREAT VIEW.

In addition to the data requirements for end users, the DBA must weigh their rights to access the data. Through a combination of techniques discussed earlier in this chapter, the DBA must now implement the access rights plans and views.

Data Dictionary Implementation and Maintenance. As we have seen, the contents of data dictionaries vary. Among their database-related components are:

- Field names
- Field specifications
- Field synonyms
- Field rights
- File (table) names
- File contents
- File "owners" (who created them)
- File rights
- Conceptual database definitions
- External database definitions

The technical tasks refer to the actual implementation of the data dictionary, from its initial loading of data to its maintenance as new items are added and its presentation to all users.

Performing Database Audits. Earlier we saw that the DBA sets up audit goals and policies. The technical responsibilities concern implementing those policies. Assuming that the DBA is interested in security, he or she should occasionally dump the audit file (if one exists) and, in cooperation with the EDP audit staff, examine the dump to ensure that only authorized employees are altering or viewing data. If the access rights software does its job, this task should result in no observed difficulties.

Maintenance of a Test Database. One way to test nondatabase applications is to construct test files. Once the applications are debugged and installed, they becomes part of the **production environment.** This approach is also followed in a database environment except that instead of test files we use a test database, which is generated and maintained by the DBA.

With conventional applications, files are "owned" by that application; thus debugging runs for existing programs and for new ones can affect only those files. In a shared environment, a bug in one program can bring down the entire database and all the production applications that use it. This means that a separate **test environment** should be made available. That way, when a program under development fails, only the test database will be affected. Only when applications have successfully completed a test plan developed by the DBA can the new applications (or changed ones) be added to the production environment.

The remainder of the technical responsibilities concern the DBMS and the database rather than the end user or applications. We will discuss the four responsibilities listed in Figure 13.1:

- Performance monitoring and tuning
- Backup and recovery implementation
- Database reorganization
- DBMS installation and update maintenance

Performance Monitoring and Tuning. It is the DBA's responsibility to guarantee that the necessary response times are met. By using special performance monitors, the DBA can collect data about the following:

- Number of disk I/Os for a given run-unit
- Average seek time for each access
- Applications responsible for the accesses
- User responsible for each access
- Number of simultaneous users
- CPU time associated with a particular job
- Number of transactions processed per unit of time
- Number of accesses to a particular table or record type
- Response time

For the quantitative data, both averages and peak values can be determined. Based on these values the DBA decides if the database is meeting its performance goals and, if it isn't, takes steps to see that it does. This process of database performance improvement is sometimes called **tuning** the database.

There is no accepted method for using this data to decide if the database's performance is unacceptable or using it to make database performance changes. Suffice it to say that the DBA considers all of this data for determining the current performance level and for deciding what action to take.

Another input into the evaluation of the current level of performance is the opinions of end users. Through complaints, follow-up memos, meetings, and observation of end users, the DBA collects opinions concerning the level of satisfaction with applications that retrieve data from the database. This does not mean that every complaint results in a new index, a restructuring of the schema, and so on. The DBA's responsibility is to ensure that the actual performance of the database meets the objectives set forth. As long as the overall performance goals are being met and the goals are still viable, no adjustment may be necessary.

When performance is below expectations, the DBA can make many adjustments. One technique is **clustering,** which places frequently accessed data physically near one another. For example, if a patient and his or her orders are often accessed together, it makes sense to place these records near each other. Another performance enhancer is the use of pointers to facilitate the clustering; that is, there would be a pointer from a patient to the first related order, much like that used with network systems, and pointers from one order to the next.

Other options include placing particular record types at certain physical locations on the disk, perhaps to take advantage of a fixed head (see Appendix A); complete restructuring of the database; addition of new access paths (indexes); acquisition of faster disk drives or a faster CPU; procurement of a database machine (discussed in the next chapter); and reprogramming of applications.

Backup and Recovery Implementation.   As an administrative task, the DBA chooses the appropriate strategy for backing up the system and for recovering from crashes. The technical aspect of this concerns the actual carrying out of the processes. Failure to do so will eventually result in a catastrophe. Inevitably the hardware will, at some time, fail. Equally certain is that the application software will fail. In either case, if the installation doesn't have a recent backup, there may be no easy way to recover. This may require the DBA, together with all end users, to reenter all data since the last backup. If the last backup occurred a long time ago, this may not even be possible, forcing the DBA to rebuild all files from scratch.

In Chapter 1, we first introduced the recovery concepts of rollback and rollforward. When the integrity of the database is threatened because of incorrect posting of transactions, a rollback is necessary to remove the incorrect changes. Here the DBA begins with the current database and applies the before images of any changed records, in effect undoing any changes and restoring the database to its state just prior to the erroneous transactions.

As an example of this, look at Figure 13.10. The JOURNAL file contains before and after images of all records affected by transactions posted to the database, as well as the time the record was created. Two ORDER occurrences are shown: a before image record indicating 45 units of penicillin (code PCN) have been given and an after image showing 50 units. These are the result of an application that updated patient P1's ORDER record to reflect the fact that five additional units of penicillin were dispensed. You can see that the database has been updated to account for the new units, because the ORDER table also contains the 50 units.

FIGURE 13.10   **Using Rollback to Remove a Transaction.**

JOURNAL

RECORD NAME	RECORD CONTENTS	TIME	TYPE
.			
.			
.			
ORDER	P1 PCN 500mg 45	0902	B
ORDER	P1 PCN 500mg 50	0903	A
.			
.			
.			

ORDER row before change
ORDER row after change

Note: A = after image
      B = before image

ORDER

PATIENT NUMBER	DRUG CODE	DOSAGE	UNITS USED
.			
.			
.			
P1	PCN	500 mg	50
.			
.			
.			

This row was changed from 45 units to 50; using the before image from the JOURNAL file, the value can be restored

INVENTORY

DRUG CODE	DRUG DESCRIPTION	ONHAND
.		
.		
.		
PCN	PENICILLIN	700

AS DBMS attempts to update ONHAND value, program aborts

The ORDER table has been updated to reflect an increase of five units of Penicillin used. As the INVENTORY table is about to be updated, the program aborts. The DBA wants to remove the effects of the last transaction from the ORDER table. This is done by selecting the before image record from the effects of JOURNAL file.

Assume that as the program tries to access the appropriate INVENTORY record to reduce the amount of penicillin ONHAND from 700 to 695, the transaction aborts because of a program error. Ignoring the potential use of the COMMIT command that we have seen several times, the DBA must restore the ORDER table to its state prior to the problem. To do so, the DBA uses the current database (containing the incorrect changes) and simply reapplies the before image of the changed ORDER record, restoring the database to its original value.

Rollforward is used when it is necessary to restore the database to some point in time with new changes applied. Typically used when the database is physically damaged, this procedure begins with the most recent backup of the database that does not contain the damaged portion. Next, the after images are applied to update the database.

Probably the simplest procedure is to merely copy each after image on top of its exiting record in chronological order. However, this can be inefficient if the same record has been changed several times.

Consider the example in Figure 13.11. At noon, the DBA made a complete backup of the INVENTORY table. Since that time, the penicillin INVENTORY row has been changed several times and the aspirin row once. Due to a head crash, the DBMS cannot presently access the INVENTORY table. Now assume the DBA decides to first use the INVENTORY copy, then successively apply the after images. Notice that there were penicillin updates at the following times; 1201, 1211, 1237, 1416, and 1434. This procedure will result in successively writing over the penicillin row four unnecessary times; only the after image at time 1434 is relevant. The conclusion is that only the last after image should be applied in a rollforward.

Database Reorganization. Most DBMSs logically delete records. One of the tasks of reorganization is the physical deletion of records that had been logically deleted. It also includes the job of adapting the conceptual database to changing environments. Objectives change, and when they do, the database's structure may need to be changed as well.

Modification of a database's physical structure is difficult to perform with network or hierarchical packages and less so with relational ones. In Chapter 1, we said that the ability to restructure the data without affecting existing applications is one aspect of data independence. Unfortunately, this data independence refers only to data usage, not management. As a result, reorganization can be a major chore for the DBA.

One frequently used method is the **unload/reload** procedure. First, the data from each file or table is copied to a work file. Note that we said "data only"; the structure (pointers) isn't copied. This is the unloading step, and its purpose is to free the data from its structure and to make an external copy of the data in this unstructured form.

Next, a new database structure is defined. Of course, the starting point for this new structure is the old one. Next, the old data is read from the work files

FIGURE 13.11   Use of Rollforward

INVENTORY

DRUG CODE	DRUG DESCRIPTION	ONHAND
.		
.		
.		
PCN	PENICILLIN	672

←── Current value for PCN row

JOURNAL

RECORD NAME	RECORD CONTENT				TIME	TYPE
INVENTORY	PCN	PENICILLIN		700	1201	B
INVENTORY	PCN	PENICILLIN		696	1201	A
INVENTORY	PCN	PENICILLIN		696	1210	B
INVENTORY	PCN	PENICILLIN		688	1211	A
ORDER	P1	PCN	500mg	75	1234	B
ORDER	P1	PCN	500mg	83	1234	A
.						
.						
INVENTORY	PCN	PENICILLIN		688	1235	B
INVENTORY	PCN	PENICILLIN		680	1237	A
ORDER	P10	ASP	800mg	80	1332	B
ORDER	P10	ASP	800mg	88	1333	A
INVENTORY	ASP	ASPIRIN		1510	1341	A
INVENTORY	ASP	ASPIRIN		1502	1341	A
INVENTORY	PCN	PENICILLIN		680	1415	B
INVENTORY	PCN	PENICILLIN		676	1416	A
INVENTORY	PCN	PENICILLIN		676	1434	B
INVENTORY	PCN	PENICILLIN		672	1434	A

←─USED 8 units

←─ONHAND PCN reduced by 8

INVENTORY (Backup from 1200 hours)

DRUG CODE	DRUG DESCRIPTION	ONHAND
.		
PCN	PENICILLIN	700

←── Matches the starting value in the JOURNAL table

A backup of the INVENTORY table was made at noon. Since then, the PCN row has been updated several times. Presently, a hardware failure has made it impossible to read the INVENTORY table. The DBA has decided to use the backup, then reapply the after image.

into the new structure. This is the reloading step. Finally, the old structure is deleted.

Naturally, the new definitions of the data in the new structure should be as close as possible to that of the data in the work files. If a character item is stored in the work file, the DBA cannot define the item as COMP-3 in the new structure. Also, the new structure won't conform exactly to the data in the work files, so some customization of that data may be necessary before performing the reload operation.

DBMS Installation and Update Maintenance. Figure 13.1 lists two other technical responsibilities: implementation of the DBMS and management of its updates. Initial installation is usually a straightforward activity, done with the help of systems programmers and several calls to the vendor. If the installation fails or requires more time than planned, there is no harm done to existing applications. However, with DBMS updates, this isn't the case.

As vendors improve their products or fix bugs in them, new releases are issued to the database administration department. Presumably the organization by now has a large installed base of programs using the DBMS. It is therefore very important that the new release be thoroughly tested against the test database before it is installed for use by the production database. Failure to do so could bring the entire organization to a halt while the problems are being resolved.

13.2   CONCURRENCY CONTROL

Concurrency control could be considered a technical/software or technical/end user responsibility, but because of its importance, we include it in a separate section. We introduced this concept in Chapter 1 and addressed it several times as we discussed the different data models. Each of the three models has facilities for preventing of lost data, locking, and deadlock prevention, all features designed to assist with the multiuser access of databases. Let's begin by reviewing the major problem associated with such processing: interleaved updating.

Assume two users access the same INVENTORY item at the same time. Assume user 1 reduces the amount on hand by five units, changes the description, and rewrites the record to the database. User 2 reduces the amount on hand by seven units, then rewrites the record. Because user 2 retrieved the record prior to the changes made by user 1, the final version of the INVENTORY record will not reflect the changes made by user 1. The result will be a *lost update*. A similar problem is *incorrect data*, which can occur this way. User 1 is computing the average value of the inventory, while user 2 is simultaneously changing the amount on hand to reflect the arrival of a new shipment of items. Some of the on-hand amounts retrieved by the averaging program will be the updated ones, but some will be the old values. The result will be an incorrect average.

The solution is to use a locking facility, often called the **lock manager,** to lock a portion of the database. Locking can be at the byte, sector, page, physical record, or file level. The level of the lock is its granularity. The finer the granularity, the higher the overhead, but the better the control.

When we discussed the CODASYL model, we saw that two kinds of locks are permissible: *shared* and *exclusive.* These two kinds of locks are available for most DBMSs. A shared lock permits simultaneous access of the locked unit but prevents other users from updating it. On the other hand, an exclusive lock prevents other users from even accessing the locked unit. This type of lock is usually applied to an update operation.

Usually we use an exclusive lock, update the row (record), then unlock it. Some DBMSs automatically unlock after the record is written; others force the programmer to issue an unlock command. The longer the lock is held, the more likely the chance for a deadlock. Recall that this occurs when each application holds a lock on a resource that another resource needs. Thus, all must wait. One way to prevent this is to force all applications to lock in the same sequence, a technique sometimes called **scheduled locking.** For example, an application that used three tables, T1, T2, and T3, will always have to acquire locks in that sequence. If another user already has locked one of the tables, the application will abort because the schedule of locks cannot be met. This is a poor solution, because the granularity is too coarse.

A better solution is the **two-phase locking protocol.** During phase 1, an application acquires locks as it needs them; during phase 2, it releases them. The effect is that no locks are released until the transaction is committed. For example, suppose a user needs to update the ONHAND amount for an IN-VENTORY file and the STATUS of a related PURCHASE__ORDER record. User A reads the INVENTORY record, locks it, changes the balance to 255 units, writes it back, then unlocks the record because there is no longer a need to process it. The application then reads, locks, updates, and unlocks the required PURCHASE__ORDER record. While the PURCHASE__ORDER record is being updated, user B's program, which has been waiting for the same INVENTORY record that user A has been using, reads the record and then updates the ONHAND amount to reflect the fact that four units were returned by a dissatisfied customer. Now user A's program aborts and calls for a rollback. This restores the INVENTORY record to its original state, eliminating the transaction posted by user B. Even though locking was used, a lost update has occurred. The solution is to release no locks until the transaction is completed and committed.

An alternative to orchestrated lock management is to simply lock any needed resources and, if a deadlock occurs, break it. Unless applications are carefully written, however, the only way to accomplish this may be to cancel one of the applications. When a deadlock is detected, the application should take an appropriate action, such as informing the end user, then presenting the option to try again later or attempt a new transaction. While some DBMSs have a status code indicating deadlock, others do not. This complicates the problem, but we won't discuss it here.

13.3   ORGANIZING THE DATABASE ADMINISTRATION FUNCTION

We begin this topic of organizing the database administration function by looking at IS department organization in general. Figure 13.12 shows one of the many ways to accomplish this.

Three managers report to the chief information officer (CIO):

- The manager of applications
- The manager of operations
- The manager of technical services

The applications manager is responsible for developing new systems and maintaining existing ones. Several applications programmers, systems analysts, and/or programmer/analysts report to this manager.

The operations manager is usually responsible for running applications, installing new hardware, troubleshooting hardware problems, backing up and recovering files, assisting users with hardware-related questions and problems, and perhaps maintaining the operating system, including the installation of new system utilities. Employees typically include systems programmers, computer operators, tape librarians, and data entry clerks. Other organizations may merge operating system responsibilities with those of technical services.

The technical services manager heads the department that typically provides much of the IS planning, is responsible for the development of standards and their enforcement, and trains other IS employees. This department may also act as a consultant to other IS users, answering questions about Job Control Language (JCL), the location and access of program libraries, and other system-

FIGURE 13.12   **One Way to Organize an Information Systems Department**

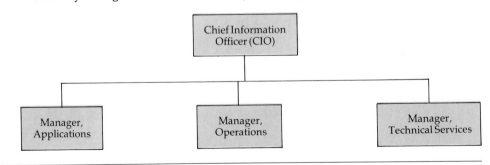

related questions. As we discussed above, this department may also be responsible for maintenance of the operating system.

Once the organization has made a commitment to the database approach—the philosophy that data is a corporate resource—it must decide how to organize management of this function. Several organizational approaches have been used:

- Diffused responsibility
- Staff organization
- Functional organization
- Line organization

Diffused Responsibility

With diffused responsibility, no one individual or department is responsible for all the data management functions. Particularly popular in small IS departments, responsibility is diffused among the other departments. Operations may be responsible for backup and recovery as well as installation and maintenance of the DBMS. The applications department may be responsible for preparing the conceptual and external databases and establishing most of the user data usage policies and procedures. Technical services may be responsible for maintaining the physical database. (In some instances, operations performs this function.)

Unfortunately, no one individual is responsible for data management so there is no real data control. Disputes over data ownership, usage, and security will arise and, because of the lack of a definitive authority, probably won't be resolved.

Staff Organization

Figure 13.13 shows how the organization can create a new advisory database administration function that reports to the CIO. Here the DBA probably is responsible only for planning and policy formulations. The other data management tasks are decentralized among the other departments. Again there is a lack of control and authority.

Functional Organization

In the functional form of organization, database administration has operational and functional as well as advisory responsibilities but as Figure 13.14 shows, reports to the manager of technical services. While the database administration function has a wider range of responsibilities, serving as a project team member on large projects, it still lacks sufficient authority to act as an organizational decision maker. Because of the location of the function, the DBA may have less authority than many of his or her fellow project team members. For example, consider a project to implement a new payroll system. Because of its importance,

FIGURE 13.13   An Organization in Which the DBA Function Is a Staff One Reporting to the CIO

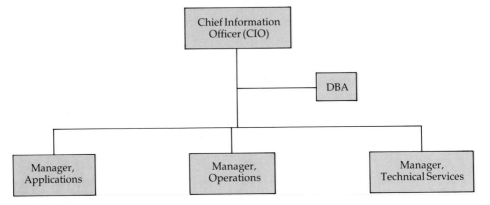

In this form of organization, the DBA lacks the authority to carry out his or her own policies.

FIGURE 13.14   A Functional Organization, with the DBA Reporting to the Technical Services Manager

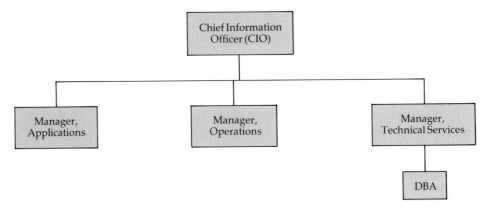

Now the DBA can carry out policies but does not have sufficient authority to always act in the best interests of the organization.

the organization's payroll manager will probably be on the project team. Imagine his or her reaction if a "mere" employee of technical services (the DBA) spoke up about an issue that seemingly was not in the best interests of the payroll department or if a new policy was imposed by the DBA with which the payroll manager disagreed. It would be much better if the DBA function had an organ-

FIGURE 13.15   A Line Organization

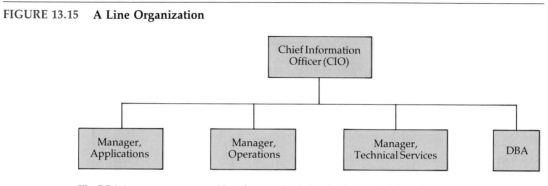

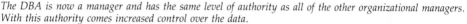

The DBA is now a manager and has the same level of authority as all of the other organizational managers. With this authority comes increased control over the data.

izational level at least equal to that of the project team members and of the employees for whom the DBA established policies, procedures, and standards.

This is the situation Mary faced in the Telecorp minicase at the beginning of this chapter. Her attempt to impose standards on Adam Keefe and his employees created a situation where a subordinate was establishing standards for a superior and other subordinates. As Mary discovered, unless authority is present it is difficult, if not impossible, to carry out one's responsibilities successfully.

Line Organization

Under a line organization, shown in Figure 13.15, the DBA can not only make policies but enforce them. By reporting directly to the CIO, the DBA has equal authority with the other IS managers and, in most cases, at least equal with that of all the other project members. This is the preferred organizational placement for the database administration function.

13.4 SUMMARY

This chapter first reviewed the role of the database administrator. The tasks assigned to this individual can be divided into four categories: administrative/application, administrative/system, technical/application, and technical/system.

Broadly speaking, administrative tasks are managerial, while technical tasks are operational in nature. Among the administrative functions are the establishment of goals, objectives, and policies, the development of end user documentation, and the acquisition of the DBMS and data dictionary. A commonly used approach for choosing the best DBMS is the scoring model, a six-step procedure that enables the DBA to choose the best alternative when faced with multiple evaluation criteria.

Many of the DBA's technical tasks are maintenance in nature: maintaining the physical database, the data dictionary, the DBMS (evaluating and then implementing DBMS software updates), the conceptual schema, and the external databases.

Other technical tasks include regular backup of the databases, assistance with their recovery, helping EDP auditors with audits, monitoring database performance, and reorganizing and tuning the database.

REVIEW QUESTIONS

1. What is meant by *conceptual schema management*?
2. List the steps to be followed in implementing a scoring model.
3. What are independent criteria?
4. What is the difference between an active and a passive data dictionary?
5. Explain the term *quiescent backup*.
6. What is the primary advantage of a synchronic backup?
7. What are the advantages and disadvantages of using audit tables?
8. Discuss the kinds of documentation the DBA might prepare for end users.
9. Why is it important for the database goals to be developed in light of the organizational ones?
10. What are some of the database adjustments the DBA can use to improve database performance?
11. Describe four technical DBA functions.
12. Discuss three data security protection techniques.
13. List four administrative DBA tasks.
14. Why should a test database environment be maintained?
15. List five pieces of data the DBA can examine to evaluate the level of database performance.
16. What is meant by *unload* and *reload*? What are their purposes?
17. Explain the differences between rollforward and rollback.
18. Suggest situations where rollback and rollforward should be used.
19. What are the disadvantages of each of these DBA organizations?
    a. Diffused responsibility.
    b. Staff organization.
    c. Functional organization.

14

Database Efficiencies

Data Organization and Access

MINICASE Tri-State Gas and Electric

Tri-State Gas and Electric (TSG&E) has just hired John Shaver as a consultant to develop a plan to help it implement a complex IS philosophy. The utility serves 500,000 customers in Pennsylvania, Maryland, and West Virginia. Twenty-five district offices handle customer requests at the community level.

TSG&E has three operating companies (subsidiaries) that provide the actual service for a designated area: West Virginia Power and Light, Pennsylvania Power, and Potomac Power. Each operating company has a large degree of autonomy, including its own purchasing, inventory control, accounts receivable, and accounts payable departments.

The central IS department uses an IBM 3090 600E with several 3380 disk drives and uses IBM's Customer Information Control System (CICS) Tele-Processing (TP) monitor. Each operating company has a minicomputer

with sufficient disk capacity to meet its needs for the next five years and a small staff to handle remote job entry (RJE) functions and act as an information center to support the recent proliferation of personal computers.

Although TSG&E has attempted to standardize the IBM PS2 as the only supported product line, many end users have acquired their own non-IBM machines. Typical uses of the microcomputer are Lotus 1-2-3 analyses, microcomputer-based database management applications, downloading of selected data from central files, and word processing.

After several months of analysis, John Shaver has developed two alternatives for integrating data among all the sites:

- Establishment of a central database function at the corporate headquarters
- Development of a distributed environment,

with each site having its own data and the ability to share data whenever necessary

The centralization plan includes acquisition of IBM's DB2, installation of several high-speed lines to each operating company, equipping of each micro that needs access to data with a micro-mainframe link, and training of the local staffs in the use of SQL within an information center. Under this plan, all data will reside at the corporate site only.

The second plan is more ambitious. It calls for local data to be distributed to each of the three operating companies and, when necessary, at departmental sites within each company. If required, the distributed data can be aggregated at the central site for dissemination and analysis. At this time, John has found no package that can handle this, but he has heard that within 18 months at least two vendors will offer such products.

Discussion

1. List problems with each of the two approaches.
2. What are some advantages of each approach?
3. Assuming the Lotus 1-2-3 spreadsheet models use both central and local data of some sort, what database features do you think TSG&E users would like?
4. Assuming the second alternative is accepted, what problems would be encountered if:
   a. The mainframe, mini, and personal computers had different operating systems?
   b. There was a need for the same data at both the operating company and the central site?
   c. Portions of a single file were distributed to several sites, for example, if data about purchase orders for each company were stored locally?

The main purposes of this chapter are to illustrate how enterprises organize their data to match their organizational structure and to show two techniques for making databases more productive: database machines and 4GLs. Both techniques use SQL. In many ways, this chapter expands on our discussion of the relational model.

We begin with *distributed databases* and their management. The TSG&E mini-case described situations where such systems are desirable. In this chapter, we will see what they are and how to manage them and discuss their advantages, disadvantages, and objectives. We will also see how the microcomputer is playing an increasingly important role in a distributed environment.

Next, we will see what a *database machine* is and its use in a distributed environment. While this may not appear to be a very quickly growing market, such a product is essential for certain kinds of database needs.

Finally, we will examine the role SQL-based 4GLs play in today's DBMS environment. We will use INFORMIX-4GL for most of the examples.

At the conclusion of this chapter, you will be able to:

- Describe the two ways in which data is distributed
- Discuss the problems associated with partitioning and replication
- Discuss the purpose of the two-phase commit and how it is implemented
- Define the two strategies for the distribution of data
- Discuss the advantages and disadvantages of distributed databases
- Describe a database server and when one might be used
- List the objectives of a distributed database environment
- Describe what a database machine is and its advantages and disadvantages
- Describe the features of a 4GL and its use in database applications

14.1   OVERVIEW OF DISTRIBUTED DATABASES

A **distributed database (DDB)** is a collection of data stored on different computers at sites connected by a communications network, in which each site needs to share data with or examine data at other sites.

Users of distributed databases shouldn't need to be aware of the physical location of the data as they construct queries against the database, a characteristic called **location transparency.** A database management system that supports such an environment is called a **distributed database management system (DDBMS).** Figure 14.1 shows a conceptual model of a DDBMS environment.

Although this book is not about data communications, we will give you an overview so that you can appreciate the complexity of the distributed database environment. A **network** is a group of interconnected *nodes,* also called *sites* or *workstations.* A node can be a microcomputer, a minicomputer, a terminal, or one of several other computer devices. The nodes may be in close proximity, in which case we call the network a **local area network (LAN).** Most such networks connect users within a single department, but they are capable of connecting workstations a mile or more apart. When the nodes are geographically diverse, we call the result a **wide area network (WAN).**

Designers of LANs and WANs can choose among several topologies. The **topology** of a network refers to the physical arrangement of nodes. Connecting one node to another is a **link,** or **line.** For our purposes, the most frequently used topologies are the ring and the bus. In a **ring,** each site is connected to the next, with the last site connected back to the first one. A **bus** or **multi-drop line,** is a single line with nodes connected to it. In both cases, two or more nodes will likely want to use the network at the same time. This invites a collision, so some sort of **link control,** or **access method,** is needed. The first two link controls we will discuss are typically used in a LAN, while the third is used with IBM's mainframe network.

The most common link control method for the ring is the **token,** usually a

FIGURE 14.1   The DDBMS Environment

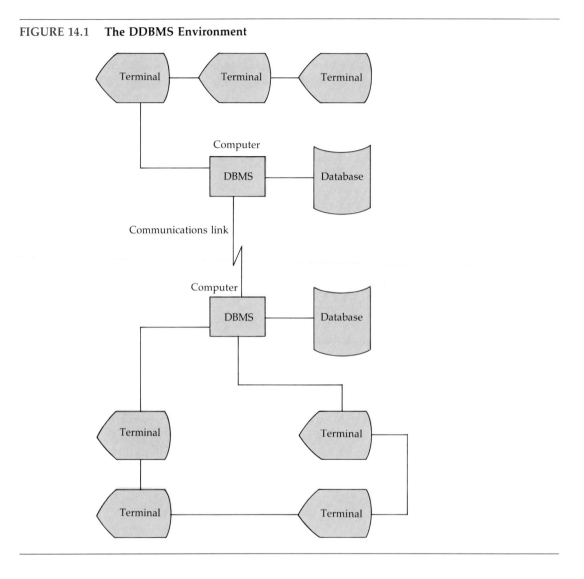

sequence of 24 bits that circulate among the nodes in one direction. To use the network, a node must capture the token. Only the node that possesses the token can use the network. When that node is finished sending messages, the token is circulated again. Thus, only one user at a time can use the network, and collisions are avoided. IBM promotes use of its token ring solution for implementing LANs that must be connected to an IBM mainframe.

The second type of link control is called **carrier sense multiple access/collision detect,** or **CSMA/CD.** Usually used with a bus, the node "listens" to the link to detect a carrier—a signal indicating that the link is idle (*carrier sense*). Because all the nodes can do the same thing, multiple workstations will likely perform the same procedure (*multiple access*). When a carrier is detected, the workstation begins to send its message. If two workstations send messages at the same time, a collision will occur. If the network determines that a collision has occurred (*collision detect*), both workstations must wait a certain amount of time (determined by a random number), then retransmit their messages. Probably the most widely used implementation of this type of link control is found in ETHERNET, a bus solution developed by XEROX and widely used by both Digital Equipment Corporation (DEC) and Apple computer users.

The third form of link control, **synchronous data link control (SDLC),** is used with IBM mainframes. SDLC is part of IBM's data communications architecture, known as Systems Network Architecture (SNA), and was first implemented in 1972. The basic unit of SDLC transmission is the **frame,** a variable-length packet of data that contains 48 bits of overhead and the message to be transmitted.

Connecting the sites are links that carry data (messages) from one site to another. The medium is often twisted-pair phone lines but can also be coaxial cable (like that used by cable television companies), twin-axial cable, fiber optic cabling, microwave, and so on.

In addition to the medium, a *terminal manager,* or *teleprocessing (TP) monitor,* is needed to manage the terminals and, in the case of mainframes, main memory. In an IBM-based LAN, each node must run two operating systems: the usual MS-DOS/PC-DOS or OS/2 and a **network operating system (NOS).** The NOS performs most of the functions of the mainframe's TP monitor. Available from third-party companies like Novell and 3-COM and from IBM and Microsoft, a NOS manages node addressing, locks resources, including records and files, and routes messages, sometimes called **packets.** A complicating factor is the fact that each workstation (PC) must contain a **network interface card (NIC),** which contains the necessary hardware and software, embedded in ROMs (read-only memory), to carry out the instructions of the NOS and manage the link control overhead.

When all sites use the same version of a resource, a **homogeneous environment** occurs. When different resources are used by two or more sites, the result is a **heterogeneous environment.** Heterogeneous networks are the more common, with differing topologies and link controls, one or more LANs and a WAN, and many different media, all separated by hundreds or even thousands of miles.

Separate networks are connected by bridges and gateways. A **bridge** connects networks (usually LANs) of differing technologies (see Figure 14.2). A bridge is a combination of hardware and software (firmware) inserted into a node to enable sites with similar architectures, such as two LANs, to share data and messages. The LANs may also be connected to the organization's WAN by a **gateway,** a similar device that lets users of two different technologies (such as SDLC and token ring) communicate. In our context, a gateway would permit users on the

---

FIGURE 14.2   A Bridge that Connects Two LANs with Different Architectures

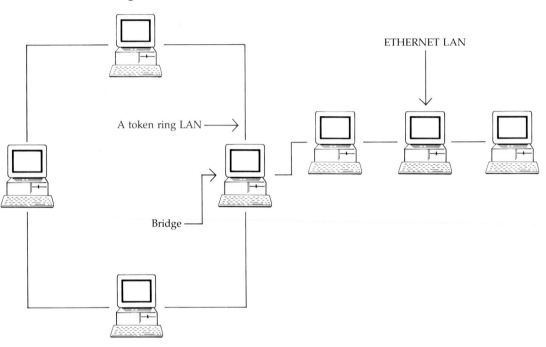

One of the microcomputers contains a special device that converts data between the two architectures. Each micro contains a network interface card (NIC), its own DOS, and a network operating system (NOS).

LAN to access the mainframe as though they were a node on the mainframe's network. Figure 14.3 illustrates a gateway. With a bridge, data might be stored and retrieved from one of several LANS, while a gateway offers the potential for distributing data to local microcomputers on a LAN or on a stand-alone basis.

Figure 14.1 shows two connected networks, one a token ring and the other an ETHERNET bus. Both contain storage capabilities. Sometimes the data is **partitioned,** meaning either that some of the database tables are stored at one location and some at another or that individual tables have been split, along either the row or column dimension, and the resulting tables dispersed to the different locations. An alternative is to **replicate** the data, that is, copy tables and then disperse them to the other locations.

The various sites can also have a disparate collection of processing equipment: a mini at one site, a mainframe at another, and a LAN or individual microcomputers at still another. As you might expect, each site would therefore use a

---

FIGURE 14.3   A Gateway

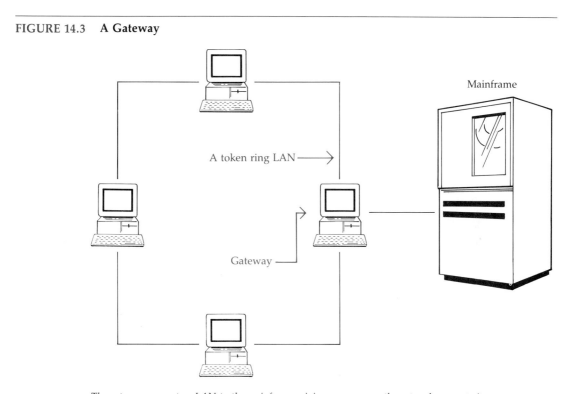

The gateway connects a LAN to the mainframe, giving everyone on the network access to it.

---

different operating system and even use different database management systems representing different data models.

In an effort to reduce the possibilities for a heterogeneous database environment, most vendors of DDBMSs advocate use of SQL-based products. That way, even if one site is running ORACLE, INGRES, or INFORMIX (all of which have distributed capabilities) on a PS/2 and another is executing DB2 on a mainframe, the sites can communicate with each other using the common language.

We have seen that in a distributed environment data can be replicated or partitioned to sites that have processors and operating systems from different vendors, use differing topologies and media to connect the sites, use different link control methodologies to manage the network, and use different types of DBMSs, with data stored on microcomputers at a distant site or on the central mainframe. Such an environment is complicated to manage, but the IS field is complex and most IS professionals expect this. On the other hand, users of the data must be shielded from having to know about these complexities.

14.2   DISTRIBUTED DATABASE GOALS

Chris Date, executive vice president of Codd & Date Consulting Group, has established 12 DDBMS goals:

1. *Local autonomy.* In many cases, users won't commit themselves to a sharing environment unless they are sure that the data is secure. With local autonomy, the users at a particular site are responsible for guaranteeing their own data security and (unfortunately) for doing their own backup.

2. *No reliance on a central site.* Each site should be able to function on its own. Thus, if the central site is down, the local site can continue to operate. Also, the data dictionary, or catalog, has to be distributed as well as the data.

3. *Continuous operation.* In some systems, adding a new site means bringing down the database. With continuous operation, this is not necessary. This feature also permits updating local software without having to take down the database.

4. *Location independence.* Users shouldn't need to be aware of the physical location of the requested data. Through the data dictionary, the DDBMS should be able to determine the location of all requested data.

5. *Fragmentation independence.* When required for performance reasons, the DDBMS or DBA should partition the database, and users should be unaware of this process.

6. *Replication independence.* When data is replicated, the DDBMS has several sites from which to retrieve. Replication independence means that the DDBMS should use the closest site to minimize communication costs and should do so transparently.

7. *Distributed query optimization.* With a distributed database, the requirement for a query optimizer is even more important than with a purely centralized one. Some data is local and some is distant. The algorithm should determine the lowest-cost query resolution.

8. *Distributed transaction management.* With a distributed database, concurrency control, consistency, and transaction posting using the COMMIT command all become much more difficult to manage. The *two-phase commit process,* discussed later, was developed to accomplish this objective.

9. *Hardware independence.* The DDBMS should support multivendor, heterogeneous configurations.

10. *Operating system independence.* As with hardware, organizations often use different operating systems at different sites. With operating system independence, this will not create a problem for the DDBMS.

11. *Network independence.* As we have seen, there are many networking architectures for connecting remote devices into a network. The DDBMS should not be affected if, for example, a LAN uses ETHERNET or a token ring and the mainframe uses SDLC.

12. *DBMS independence.* In a heterogeneous database environment, several sites use different DBMSs, each of which may employ a different data model. One site might use IMS (the hierarchical model), another IDMS/R (the network model), and another DB2 or ORACLE (the relational model). One way to solve this problem is to use a **metaschema,** which acts as a "black box" front end to the DBMS, making the adjustments necessary for responding to user requests. While users could still communicate using SQL, the metaschema would attempt to map the DML statements into ones appropriate for the local database management system. Such a scheme is often implemented through a **back-end database machine,** a device that acts as a "slave" to the main CPU, carrying out the actual database requests and thereby freeing the "master" CPU to perform other tasks.

As we said earlier, there are two techniques for distributing the database: partitioning (fragmentation) and replication. The next two sections discuss these techniques in more detail.

14.3 PARTITIONING A DATABASE

The term **fragmentation** means that portions of a single database reside at different nodes. Typically, each node contains the data necessary to support processing only at that site. After the DBA partitions the database, the DDBMS must know the physical location of each partition and, when the data is not at the site where it is to be used, provide the communication facilities necessary for transferring the data from its storage location to the site that made the request. The entire process must be transparent to the end user; that is, the end user should perceive the database as being a central one. Although partitioning is possible with any of the three data models, we will use the relational model for our discussion.

There are several possibilities for implementing the partitioning. First, we might store complete tables from a single database at different sites. For example, as Figure 14.4 illustrates, we could store an INVENTORY table at a warehouse site, a VENDOR table at the accounts payable site, and so on.

An alternative would be to split individual tables into multiple parts, storing the various portions at different sites. This splitting can be done horizontally—placing sets of rows at each of several locations—or vertically—extracting different columns for each site.

Horizontal Partitioning

To illustrate *horizontal partitioning,* let's continue with the INVENTORY table example. Assume there are three warehouses, each at different locations, and that WAREHOUSE is an attribute of the table. This suggests a horizontal partitioning so that we can store data associated with a given warehouse at that

FIGURE 14.4   A Partitioned Database with Individual Tables Distributed to the Nodes

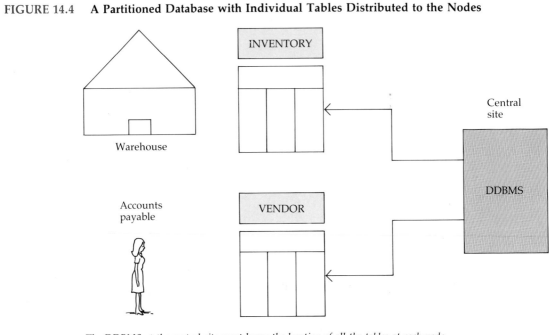

The DDBMS at the central site must know the location of all the tables at each node.

site. In this way, data needed by a warehouse is available without having to transfer the rows using costly communications facilities. We would classify this as a horizontal partitioning because we are selecting a subset of rows, with each row containing all the attributes of the original table. If a subsequent need for centralized reporting arises, we can combine the separate databases (using the UNION operator).

Let's look at an example. Figure 14.5 shows the INVENTORY table before it is distributed. Assume that three warehouses need to have their own versions of the INVENTORY table but the local tables should contain only data pertinent to each warehouse. We need to extract three sets of rows, one set for each warehouse, with each row having all the INVENTORY columns. The result is shown in Figure 14.6.

In each case, a new table is created from the original one and contains all the attributes of INVENTORY, but only the rows that pertain to that warehouse. To show you how easy this can be if we use SQL to populate the table for the warehouse at site 1, assuming the table has been defined, we just code the following:

FIGURE 14.5   **An INVENTORY Table Before It Is Distributed**

INVENTORY

ITEMCODE	VENDOR	WAREHOUSE	COST	ONHAND
A1	10	W1	10.00	100
A1	20	W2	10.50	200
A2	10	W3	15.75	200
A1	20	W3	10.00	50
A2	33	W2	16.00	100

FIGURE 14.6   **The Horizontally Partitioned INVENTORY Table, One Distributed Table per Site**

INVENTORY1

ITEMCODE	VENDOR	WAREHOUSE	COST	ONHAND
A1	10	W1	10.00	100

INVENTORY2

ITEMCODE	VENDOR	WAREHOUSE	COST	ONHAND
A1	20	W2	10.50	200
A2	33	W2	16.00	100

INVENTORY3

ITEMCODE	VENDOR	WAREHOUSE	COST	ONHAND
A2	10	W3	15.75	200
A1	20	W3	10.00	50

```
INSERT INTO INVENTORY1
    SELECT * FROM INVENTORY
        WHERE WAREHOUSE = 'W1';
```

Horizontal partitioning is used whenever there is a need to store data as close to the intended user as possible. Its two primary advantages are a reduction in the costs associated with transmitting the data from a central site and better data security, because only data relevant to a node is made available to it.

The major disadvantage is that each local site is responsible for backup. Instead of a centralized staff of well-trained computer operators, a functional manager or clerk may be responsible for this very important task. If this is the case, it is quite likely that backups won't be done on a regular basis, because the employees have other job-related tasks that are usually deemed more important than backing up the database.

Vertical Partitioning

Vertical partitioning is usually done when there is a need to divide a table by organizational function rather than by geographical considerations. As an example, assume we begin with the original INVENTORY table but we partition it over the ITEMCODE, VENDOR, and COST columns, storing the resulting table in a computer at the accounting department site. Figure 14.7 shows the result.

Vertical partitioning has the same advantages and disadvantages as horizontal partitioning.

FIGURE 14.7   Result of a Vertical Partitioning of the INVENTORY Table

INVENTORY

ITEMCODE	VENDOR	WAREHOUSE	COST	ONHAND
A1	10	W1	10.00	100
A1	20	W2	10.50	200
A2	10	W3	15.75	200
A1	20	W3	10.00	50
A2	33	W2	16.00	100

A vertical partition with ITEMCODE, VENDOR, and COST in one table and ITEMCODE, WAREHOUSE, and ONHAND in another.

ITEMCOST

ITEMCODE	VENDOR	COST
A1	10	10.00
A1	20	10.50
A2	10	15.75
A1	20	10.00
A2	33	16.00

NEW_INVENTORY

ITEMCODE	WAREHOUSE	ONHAND
A1	W1	100
A1	W2	200
A1	W3	200
A1	W3	50
A1	W2	100

The ITEMCOST table might be stored on a computer in the accounting department.

14.4   REPLICATING A DATABASE

Sometimes data is intentionally replicated at multiple sites, usually for performance reasons. If someone at a central site has the same need to routinely examine the same data as does someone at a remote site, it may be beneficial to replicate the data at both locations. When a user requests data that has been replicated, the built-in query optimizer should take into account all the locations of that data and select the site that will minimize communication costs and response time. Replication, however, can lead to inconsistencies.

In Chapter 1 we discussed the concept "multiple versions of truth" in the context of looking at problems associated with traditional IS processing methods. The same potential problem exists with replicated data within a database.

What happens if a transaction has been processed by a local site and the data is updated at that site but not at the other(s)? The ability of the database to maintain this consistency without the user realizing it is called **consistency,** or **replication, transparency,** another objective of a DDBMS. There are two approaches for implementing replication transparency: using a master/slave technique and using a two-phase commit.

The Master/Slave Technique

With the **master/slave technique,** one of the databases is designated as the **master,** or **primary, database** and the others as **slave databases.** The DDBMS at the primary site is responsible for maintaining the integrity at the slave sites. As long as the master is updated successfully, the data at the slave sites can be assumed to be in synchronization with the master, because that's the responsibility of the master DDBMS. If one of the remote sites is unavailable to the master DDBMS when it attempts to update the replicated data, it will keep trying until it completes the task.

The Two-Phase Commit

The **two-phase commit** is becoming quite popular. One approach designates the master site as the **coordinator.** When an application wants to commit replicated data, it makes the request to the coordinator, which then sends a request to each affected site to prepare to locally commit the transactions. Then each site sends one of two messages back to the coordinator: Either it is ready for the commit or it isn't. It is important that all sites respond to the request for commit preparation, or the technique will fail.

If all sites specify that they are ready, the coordinator sends back the message that the commit should be made and writes an entry to its log specifying that this was its action. Then the local nodes commit the transaction, write a message to their logs, and send an acknowledgment back to the coordinator, which in turn indicates on its log that the transaction is completed.

On the other hand, if *any* site is unavailable for the commit, the transaction is aborted, the commit fails, and local rollbacks are executed. Again the coordinator records its decision in the log.

Thus, there are two possible scenarios: prepare-commit or prepare-rollback. Regardless of the outcome, you should be able to see that this technique can result in many messages transmitted over the network, which is one of its disadvantages.

Thus far, we have seen what a distributed database environment is, what its objectives are, and how to accomplish them. The next two sections look at its advantages and disadvantages.

14.5   ADVANTAGES OF A DISTRIBUTED DATABASE

There are many reasons for using a distributed database:

- More efficient processing
- Improved accessibility
- Local control of data
- Improved system reliability

More Efficient Processing

When we distribute data, we intend that it be as close as possible to the destined user. This leads to improved efficiencies, since we minimize the costs and response times associated with data communications. Instead of having to send a request message (a SQL SELECT command) to the central site, wait for the central DDBMS to locate the records and then wait for the results to be sent back over a transmission line; the DDBMS hopefully will find the requested data at the local site. If it doesn't find the data there, the DDBMS should automatically search other locations in increasing order of cost.

Improved Accessibility

With improved accessibility, users in, say, New York can access data in San Francisco, or vice versa. It thus permits distributed access to data regardless of its physical location. Ideally the DDBMS finds the data without user intervention—the concept of location transparency, which we explored earlier.

Local Control of Data

When each site is responsible for maintaining its own data, worries about security are alleviated and users can retain a sense of ownership at the local sites. In Chapter 1, we said that we wanted to eliminate the "my-file" syndrome, but with a distributed database users can still retain some control over "their" data while relinquishing other controls so that the data can be shared whenever needed. This control brings with it the responsibilities of managing it: deleting unneeded data, backing it up, and so on.

Improved System Reliability

With a completely centralized database, if the disk drive on which the database resides fails, or the CPU that executes the central DBMS fails, the entire network goes down, leaving users without access to their data. With a DDBMS, however, if one node fails, the remaining ones remain operative, which should result in a greater availability of resources.

14.6   DISADVANTAGES OF A DISTRIBUTED DATABASE

The DDB approach is not without its faults. Among the disadvantages are:

- Updating problems
- More difficulty query resolutions
- More complex recovery procedures
- A possible degradation in performance

Updating Problems

As we have seen, a distributed database can result in replication of data. This leads to potential updating problems where one site is updated but another isn't. The solutions to this problem were discussed in the section on replication transparency.

Query Resolution

Suppose a user in the purchasing department has entered the following SQL statement:

```
SELECT ITEM_CODE, ITEM_DESC
    FROM INVENTORY, PO_DETAIL
    WHERE PO_NO = 10
        AND INVENTORY.ITEM_CODE = PO_DETAIL.ITEM_CODE;
```

There are many considerations for the DDBMS as it resolves the query: Where are the INVENTORY rows stored? Which rows are replicated? When there are several locations for the same row, which location results in the lowest cost? The fastest response time?

Questions about the sequence of the SELECT and PROJECT operators also arise. Let's expand on the details of the situation. Assume the INVENTORY table contains 10,000 rows and is stored on computer A. The PO__DETAIL table contains 500 rows and is stored on computer B at the purchasing department site. Only five PO__DETAIL rows pertain to PO__NO 10.

One way to satisfy the query is to transmit all 500 PO__DETAIL rows from computer B to computer A and have the DDBMS perform the join and select there. The resulting five rows will then be sent back to computer B, the requesting site, resulting in a total of 505 messages.

A second solution is to transmit the 10,000 rows of the INVENTORY table from computer A to computer B, which is where the request was made and where the query will be resolved. This will require sending 10,000 messages. We don't have to transmit the five resulting rows, because the work will be done by the DDBMS at the purchasing department site.

The third alternative is to extract the five rows that pertain to PO__NO 10 from computer B and send them to computer A for processing. The result—five rows—will need to be sent back to computer B, the local site. This will require a total transmission of only 10 messages.

Obviously, each of the above alternatives will work, but each will take significantly different amounts of time to implement.

This example, together with the questions we posed earlier, should lead you to conclude that a DDBMS requires a sophisticated query optimizer that can resolve these kinds of issues quickly and without user intervention.

More Complex Recovery Procedures

Assume a row is replicated at two sites. Consider the problems if one site issues a rollback without the other doing so. The site that did not execute the rollback will have the most recent transactions posted to it, including the incorrect data that presumably caused the rollback, while the other will have been rolled back to a previous state.

The two-phase commit process can help resolve this problem. The controller issues a "prepare-rollback" command to all sites, waits for confirmation, and issues the actual rollback command to each site.

Performance Degradation

Depending on the number of steps the DDBMS requires to maintain concurrency control and the locations of the data to be transmitted to the user, the performance of a distributed database can be inferior to that of a centralized one. As you might expect, performance related to updating the database is inversely proportional to the amount of replication: The more the data is replicated, the greater the effort and the slower the response time needed to maintain the multiple copies and enforce concurrency.

14.7 THE ROLE OF MICROCOMPUTERS IN A DISTRIBUTED ENVIRONMENT

There are two DDB situations that involve a microcomputer: those where a local area network (LAN) consisting only of microcomputers is used and those where a micro plays the role of a "dumb" or "intelligent" terminal in a mainframe or minicomputer network.

LAN DDBMSs

At the time of this writing, several vendors, including Ashton-Tate, ORACLE, INGRES, and INFORMIX, use a **database,** or **SQL, server approach** like that shown in Figure 14.8. The **server** is a dedicated microcomputer that runs a single copy of the DDBMS. ORACLE calls its product LANServer. LANServer runs only under a multiuser operating system called Unix (or Xenix) and must be installed on a micro that can support it. All database requests are routed to the server for resolution, which means that the server must be capable of processing requests from several nodes simultaneously. Assuming the request contained a SELECT, the appropriate rows are then sent back to the local site. In all cases, a status code is also returned, indicating the success or failure of the command.

Use of the server approach versus an environment in which each site runs its own DDBMS leads to a reduction in network traffic and improves concurrency control and data integrity. Consider a simple request to compute the average salary:

SELECT AVG(SALARY)
    FROM SALTABLE
    WHERE SALARY> 1000;

Even though this results in a single data item (the average), its computation requires access to the entire SALTABLE table. If the database is stored at a central site—or at any site other than the local one—and the request is processed by a DBMS at the local site, the entire file will have to be transmitted to that site—an expensive undertaking. With a SQL server, however, the central DDBMS will access the database, perform the calculations, and transfer only the result— a substantial savings in messages being transmitted.

In January 1988, Ashton-Tate and Microsoft announced a similar product called SQL Server. This product is also a database server, acquired from Sybase Inc., which runs under OS/2 and allows end users to use dBASE III or IV commands or use SQL to make requests against a database. Microsoft calls the product a *work-group program,* which functions as a "back-end" product (a subject we discuss later) responding to "front-end" requests from PCs on a LAN. Because OS/2's NOS (LAN Manager) is a multiuser, multitasking program that can "simultaneously" respond to SQL requests from multiple sites, this approach enables all sites to share data among users within a work group.

FIGURE 14.8   **A SQL (Database) Server that Handles All SQL Requests**

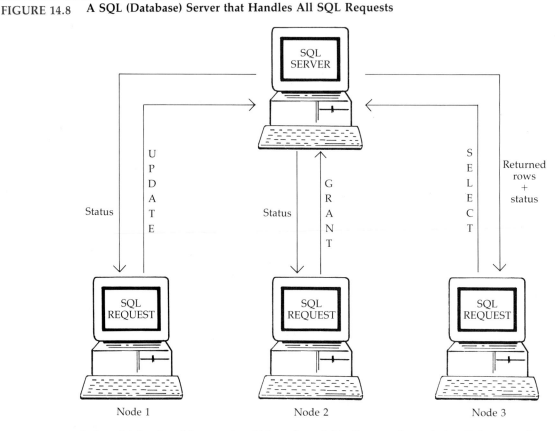

Each workstation formulates requests, which are forwarded to the server for resolution. If the request is a SELECT, the results (rows) plus the status are returned; otherwise only a status indicator is returned.

The Microcomputer as a Terminal

In this distributed database environment, the microcomputer acts as a "dumb" terminal, or plays the role of a **client** or **requestor,** in an environment that is sometimes called **client/server.** A dumb terminal is connected to the mainframe but does not perform any front-end computing, such as editing or validation; rather, it transmits and receives messages. In this case, the microcomputer's role is like that of any other terminal.

In a client role, the microcomputer might perform data edits, handle screen management, input data into a local application, and perform other front-end steps that prepare the data for transmission to the central database. This requires a gateway or a micro-mainframe link to permit access to the mainframe from the micro. A common scenario is one in which an end user downloads data from the mainframe to a user-friendly, microcomputer-based file or database manager, manipulates it on the micro, then uploads the data back to the mainframe. In the Tri-State Gas and Electric minicase at the beginning of the chapter, we saw an occasion of this: End users needed the ability to download data from the mainframe into a Lotus 1-2-3 spreadsheet. Let's look at the practicality of such procedures.

Microcomputer DBMSs and spreadsheet programs typically include windows, sophisticated screen-handling facilities, including the ability for the end user to easily "paint" the screen to be used, graphics, and an interactive interface. It is no wonder that end users prefer this to the mainframe environment. Unfortunately, implementation of this environment can be difficult, and users can experience long delays while the data is being transmitted.

Assume a user has used a 9,600-baud modem to access an IBM mainframe and wishes to download a 2MB file into a popular microcomputer database manager. The modem converts the computer's digital signal into an analog one (sound), and vice versa. A 9,600-baud modem transmits approximately 960 characters per second. However, before this can be done, the data on the mainframe must be converted from IBM's EBCDIC (Extended Binary Coded Decimal Interchange Code) into the micro's ASCII (American Standard for Information Interchange). Let's ignore the time this takes. Now the data can be transmitted. This will require about one-half hour. Once it arrives the data must be stored, so 2MB of disk space is necessary. Now the data must be converted into the format required by the microcomputer package.

Most packages can import ASCII files, but they require that specific delimiters be used, such as quotation marks around the character strings, commas between fields, a specific end-of-record indicator, and so on. If the incoming file doesn't conform to the package's specifications, a program must be written and then executed. Assume the 2MB represents 200,000 records and that it takes 0.1 second per record to convert. This adds 5.5 hours to the process and another 2MB to store the converted file. Now the 200,000 records must be actually imported into the local database package. Based on published benchmarks, the average number of records imported by such packages per minute is about 1,000. For 200,000 records, this adds another 3.3 hours.

Now the data can be manipulated and reports printed. If the data is changed, it must then be uploaded to the mainframe. If the entire file needs to be transferred, another half hour elapses. As you can see, downloading data from a mainframe to a micro can be a lengthy procedure, and at the time of this writing many large corporations have begun to shy away from such procedures whenever large files are involved.

In either a stand-alone or distributed database environment, a host program forwards requests to a DBMS, which carries out those requests by first sending a program to the access method, which in turn sends a program to a channel. The channel then sends signals to a controller, instructing the disk drive where to find the table's row. When the data has been located, the controller sends it back to the channel. The channel then interrupts the CPU, and the operating system resumes control briefly but quickly returns to the DBMS for further instructions. The DBMS takes the data from the channel, puts it into the buffer area of the host program, indicates any errors, then returns control to the host program. (See Appendix A for a review of this process.) In an on-line environment, there might be hundreds or even thousands of users making similar requests. The effects can be a mainframe that is spending too much time accessing data and too little time processing it. One solution is to use a database machine—the topic of the next section.

14.8   DATABASE MACHINES

Figure 14.9 shows what a **database machine** environment might look like. The application runs in the host CPU and makes a database request. The request is forwarded to the database machine, which is logically located between the host CPU and the disk drive where the database is stored. Due to its logical relationship to the host CPU, the database machine is sometimes called a **back-end computer.**

The database machine then translates the database request (SQL) into a series of channel commands and forwards them to the channel, which in turn sends them to the disk controller. When the controller signals that the data has been accessed, the channel so informs the database machine. This interrupts the host CPU, and processing by the host can proceed.

Use of such devices usually leads to improved performance. Because we are offloading the host CPU, it is free to process other programs while the database machine is carrying out the request. In this sense, a database machine can be considered a special-purpose channel.

Another contribution to performance is the fact that database machines are designed with a single purpose: to interpret and carry out database requests. This means that the designers of such machines can construct hardware components that perform a single, predetermined task rather than components that perform many tasks. A report out of the Department of Pediatrics at the University of Minnesota has stated that to do the work of its database machine on a mainframe, the department would have had to spend 45 times what they did.

On the other side of the performance issue, each host request results in a transmission to the database machine. Consider use of such an environment in an IMS environment, where each record must be requested individually. In an earlier example, we assumed that an INVENTORY table contained 10,000 items. If we used IMS to request all the INVENTORY segments, 10,000 communications between the host and back-end computer would result. On the other hand, a SQL (set-at-a-time) command would result only in one transmission. This means

FIGURE 14.9   A Database Machine Configuration

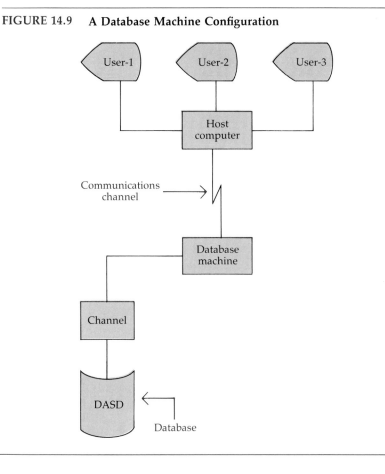

that record-at-a-time-oriented databases don't lend themselves well to this concept.

Another performance factor of the database machine is that all of its memory can be used to hold the DBMS and associated indexes. Because it doesn't have to store an application, any memory left over after loading the DBMS can be devoted to storing indexes. It should be clear that searching a memory-based index is several times faster than searching a disk-based one.

The downside of this performance potential is that unless the applications heavily utilize a database, the database machine may be achieving a low utilization. When an organization invests in any product, it must get a high utilization for the acquisition to be profitable.

Teradata and Britton Lee are the two primary vendors of database machines. As of the end of 1988, Teradata's product (DBC/1012) was in about 100 installations. It can support a heterogeneous hardware environment with up to 64 different hosts, mainframes, minis, and micros. Using a Teradata product containing 128 parallel processors along with an Amdahl 5840 as the host, Citibank was able to process 130 transactions per second. A similar configuration at K mart has 260 parallel CPUs, with a long-range goal of 500. One benchmark running DB2 resulted in 450 transactions per second (tps) on an IBM 3090 600E. The same benchmark on a Teradata cost 40 percent less and resulted in 1,100 tps. Britton Lee claims over 850 installations, but the machines installed are less powerful.

14.9   THE 4GL ENVIRONMENT: INFORMIX-4GL AND ORACLE

In an effort to reduce the information systems backlog of work and be able to respond more quickly to end user requests, organizations are turning to 4GLs. These are packages typically containing the following elements:

- A nonprocedural report writer
- A screen-handling facility
- Built-in menuing capabilities
- Data validation built in to the data dictionary
- An integrated help facility
- Use of SQL as the DBMS

One trend that began in the late 1980s is the proliferation of microcomputer 4GLs that are identical to their mini and mainframe counterparts. This enables organizations to develop applications on the micro, making full use of its friendlier nature, then porting them to larger computers for actual operation. This section looks at two representative packages: INFORMIX-4GL from Informix and ORACLE from ORACLE.

INFORMIX-4GL

Informix's product contains several modules. Its first module, INFORMIX-SQL, is an almost complete implementation of IBM's SQL. It contains three main parts: an interactive SQL processor, an application development system, and a report writer. The other modules include INFORMIX-4GL, an interactive debugger for the 4GL, and a database server called INFORMIX-TURBO.

The Informix solution loads the DBMS into the normal 640K or into extended memory, if available. The advantage of the latter is that the lower 640K is left for application development.

Informix provides an excellent application programming interface (API) that makes it unnecessary to know SQL in order to use the product. In Chapter 7, we defined a hospital database and, in Figure 7.7, several tables within the database, all of which used DB2. Let's do some of the same steps using IN-FORMIX-SQL.

To create the database, we select the Database option from the main menu, which is shown as screen 1 in Figure 14.10. Next, the DATABASE menu is presented. We selected the Create choice on the menu, as shown in screen 2. The next screen shows that we entered the name HOSPRX as the database's name. INFORMIX-SQL then creates a directory named HOSPRX.DBS.

Now we need to define the tables. Instead of successively entering the SQL statement CREATE TABLE, as we did in Figure 7.7, followed by the column specifications, we can use a series of menus and prompts to effect the same operations but without having to know SQL. For example, the steps shown in Figure 14.11 indicate how to define the PATIENT table.

First, we select the Table function from the main menu, then highlight the Create option on the TABLE menu. In response to the prompt requesting a name, we enter PATIENT. INFORMIX-SQL then displays the first screen in Figure 14.12. We enter the value "pid" as the first column's name. INFORMIX-SQL then displays screen 2, asking us to enter the column's type. We are presented with a menu of the valid column types, and we chose Char. The next screen asks us to specify the length of the column, and we respond with a 10. In screens 4 and 5, we specify a unique index (primary key) on the patient number column. Finally, screen 6 indicates that we have specified that NULL values are not to be allowed. Figure 14.13 shows the completed table definition.

Another ease-of-use feature of INFORMIX's interactive SQL is that a default screen can be generated for inputting data and for doing a QBE search. Instead of having to repetitively construct and then execute the SQL statement

INSERT INTO PATIENT
    VALUES (value-list);

the INFORMIX end user is presented with a blank screen containing default captions that match the column names. After entering the data, a "save" key is struck, causing the SQL INSERT statement to be automatically generated, the data written to the PATIENT table, and the screen cleared in preparation for input of the next patient. Even though INFORMIX executes a SQL INSERT statement, the end user never sees it. Rather than having to repetitively use an editor and enter an INSERT statement over and over, the user utilizes a fill-in-the-blank form on a display screen and hits a "save" key several times.

Figure 14.14 shows the default screen for our PATIENT table. The top portion shows that the user can Query the table (using a variation of IBM's QBE), find the Next row that matches the query's criteria, find the Previous row, Add a new row, Remove (delete) a row, and so on.

In all cases, even though Informix is executing SQL statements, the end user is shielded from having to know how to formulate the SQL commands. Instead, he or she merely uses a series of menus to accomplish the desired task. In

FIGURE 14.10   Using INFORMIX-SQL to Create the Database

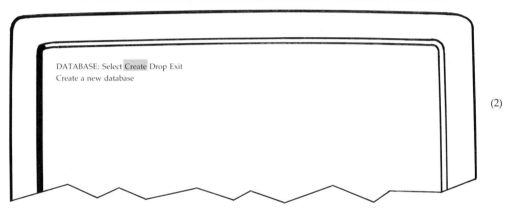

INFORMIX-SQL: Form Report Query-Language User- menu Database Table Exit
Create, Alter, or Drop a database

(1)

Select Database from main menu

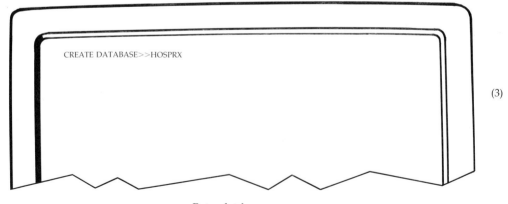

DATABASE: Select Create Drop Exit
Create a new database

(2)

Select Create from DATABASE menu

CREATE DATABASE>>HOSPRX

(3)

Enter database name

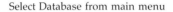

FIGURE 14.11   Creating the PATIENT Table

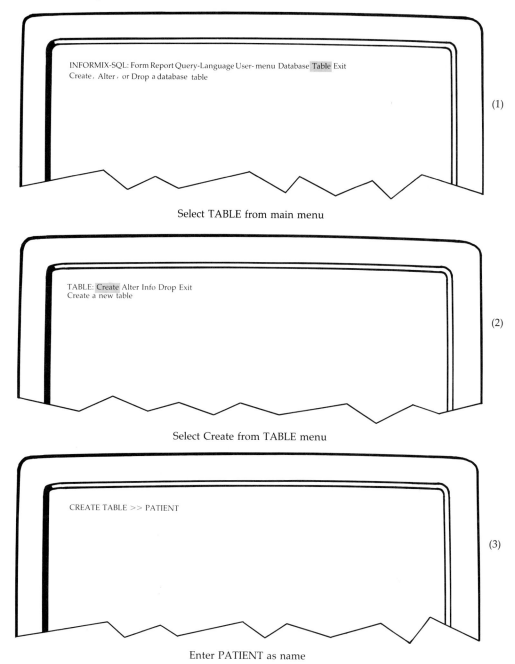

INFORMIX-SQL: Form Report Query-Language User- menu Database Table Exit
Create, Alter, or Drop a database table

(1)

Select TABLE from main menu

TABLE: Create Alter Info Drop Exit
Create a new table

(2)

Select Create from TABLE menu

CREATE TABLE >> PATIENT

(3)

Enter PATIENT as name

FIGURE 14.12   Six Screens Showing How to Define the PID Column

```
ADD NAME >> PID
Enter column name, RETURN add it, INTERRUPT returns to CREATE/ALTER menu

Column Name    Type    Length    Index    Nulls
pid
```
(1)

Enter the column's name

```
ADD TYPE PATIENT :  Char  Numeric  Serial  Date  Money

Permits any combination of letters, numbers, and symbols

Column Name    Type    Length    Index    Nulls
pid
```
(2)

Choose Char for pid

```
ADD LENGTH >>10
Enter column length. RETURN adds it

Column Name    Type    Length    Index    Nulls
pid            Char       10
```
(3)

Choose a length

FIGURE 14.12   Concluded

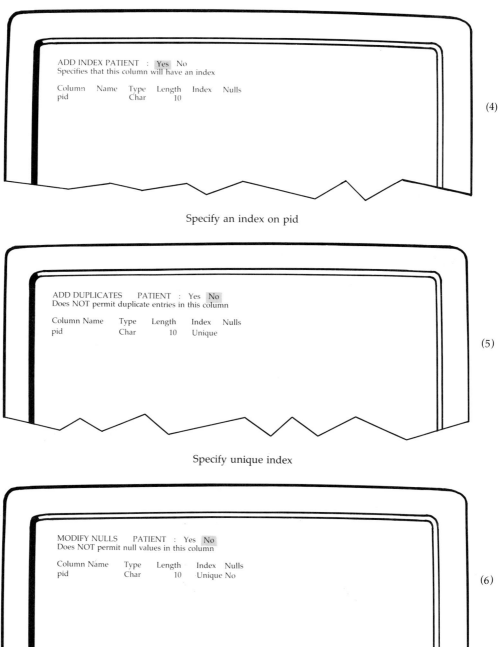

Specify an index on pid

Specify unique index

FIGURE 14.13   The Completed PATIENT Definition

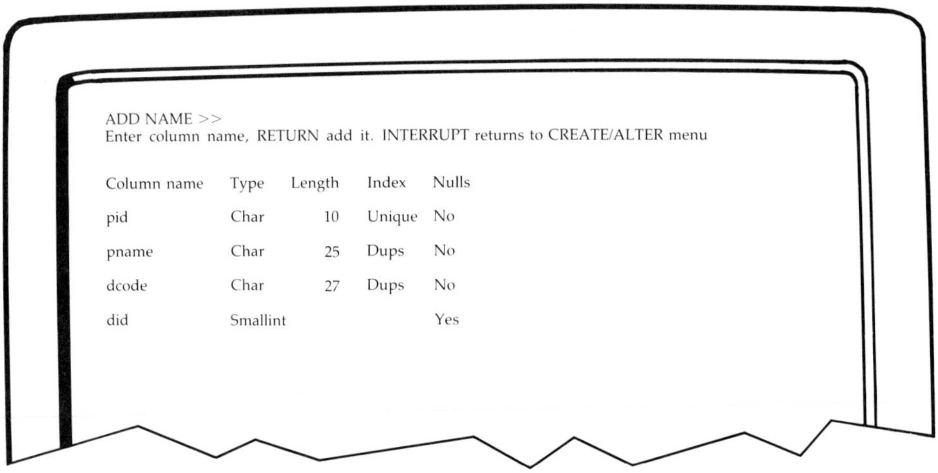

```
ADD NAME >>
Enter column name, RETURN add it. INTERRUPT returns to CREATE/ALTER menu

Column name    Type      Length    Index     Nulls

pid            Char        10      Unique    No

pname          Char        25      Dups      No

dcode          Char        27      Dups      No

did            Smallint                      Yes
```

FIGURE 14.14   The Default Screen for the PATIENT Table in Figure 14.13

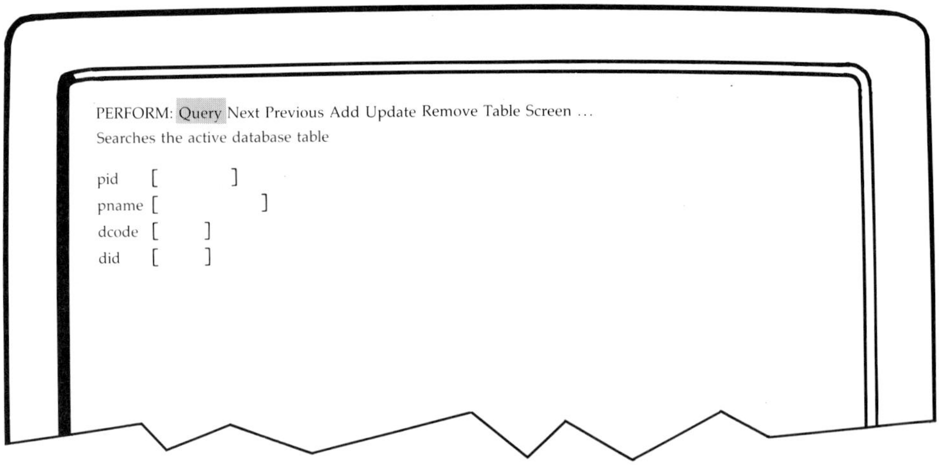

```
PERFORM: Query Next Previous Add Update Remove Table Screen ...
Searches the active database table

pid    [        ]
pname  [            ]
dcode  [    ]
did    [    ]
```

addition to the menu-driven SQL module, INFORMIX includes the ability to execute SQL commands interactively.

A particularly appealing feature of INFORMIX is that a program written using its 4GL doesn't have to be recompiled to be run on another hardware platform. For example, a developer can create an INFORMIX application on a PC, then port it to a DEC/VAX or Data General minicomputer without having to make any changes or recompile the application. Let's look at two of INFORMIX's 4GL components: the report writer and the screen handler.

Report Writer. One key feature of any 4GL is the ability to quickly produce complicated reports using a nonprocedural language. INFORMIX's report writer is no exception. Assume we want to produce an accounts payable report (ar__ report) from a STORES database containing three tables: ORDERS, ITEMS, and CUSTOMERS. Figure 14.15 shows the columns in each table.

Figure 14.16 shows the desired report and Figure 14.17 the 4GL program.

With INFORMIX, table data isn't written directly to a screen, report, or program. Instead, a suitable record must be defined within a program to accept or build the rows. The first part of Figure 14.17 defines a program record called "r." It consists of nine fields, each defined to be LIKE columns found in several of the base tables. Using LIKE, we can change the specification of a column and

---

FIGURE 14.15   Three Tables in a STORES Database

ITEMS (ITEM__NUM, ORDER__NUM, STOCK__NUM, MANU__CODE, QUANTITY,
    TOTAL__PRICE)

ORDERS (ORDER__NUM, ORDER__DATE, CUSTOMER__NUM, SHIP__INSTRUCT, BACKLOG,
    PRO__NUM, SHIP__DATE, SHIP__WEIGHT, SHIP__CHARGE, PAID__DATE)

CUSTOMER (CUSTOMER__NUM, FNAME, LNAME, COMPANY, ADDRESS1, ADDRESS2,
    CITY, STATE, ZIPCODE, PHONE)

FIGURE 14.16   A Portion of an Accounts Payable Report

East Coast Wholesalers, Inc.
Statement of ACCOUNTS RECEIVABLE, Jan 01, 1991
Owner Name/Company Name

Order Date	Order Number	Ship Date	Amount
03/25/1991	1007	04/25/1991	$1,696.00
06/05/1991	1012	06/09/1991	$1,040.00
			$2,736.00

Each time the customer number changes, the report writer prints a summary of all the amounts, then produces a new page heading. The order number, order date, and ship date are carried in the ORDERS table, and the amount is determined through the TOTAL__PRICE column in the ITEMS table. Several ITEMS rows may be associated with a given ORDER__NUM value.

FIGURE 14.17   The INFORMIX Program to Produce the Report in Figure 14.16

```
DATABASE stores

MAIN

    DEFINE r RECORD

        customer_num LIKE customer.customer_num,

        fname LIKE customer.fname,

        lname LIKE customer.lname,

        company LIKE customer.company,

        order_num LIKE orders.order_num,

        order_date LIKE orders.order_date,

        ship_date LIKE orders.ship_date,

        paid_date LIKE orders.paid_date,

        total_price LIKE items.total_price
```

↑ ———— Define program variables to be LIKE columns in existing tables

```
        END RECORD,

    DECLARE ar_list CURSOR FOR

    SELECT customer.customer_num,fname,lname,company,

        orders.order_num,order_date,ship_date,paid_date,

                total_price

        FROM customer,orders,items

            WHERE customer.customer_num=orders.customer_num AND

                    paid_date IS NULL AND

                    orders.order_num=items.order_num

                ORDER BY 1,5
```

↑ ———————————— Define a cursor, like DB2 and COBOL

```
    START REPORT ar_report TO PRINTER
```
← ——— Send to printer

FIGURE 14.17   (continued)

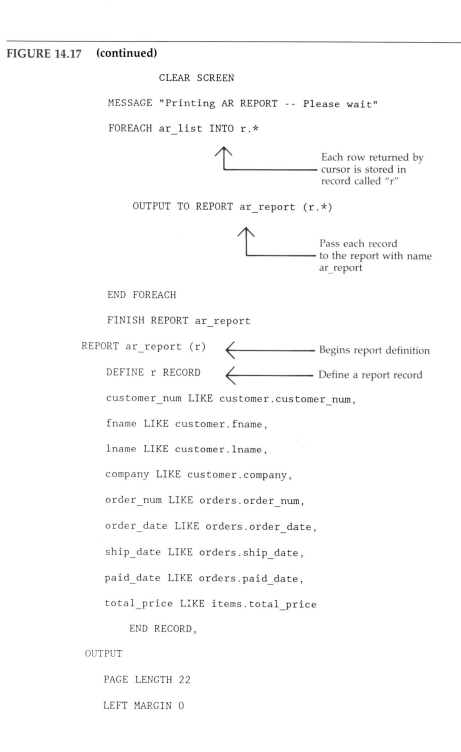

```
            CLEAR SCREEN

        MESSAGE "Printing AR REPORT -- Please wait"

        FOREACH ar_list INTO r.*
```
Each row returned by cursor is stored in record called "r"

```
            OUTPUT TO REPORT ar_report (r.*)
```
Pass each record to the report with name ar_report

```
        END FOREACH

        FINISH REPORT ar_report

    REPORT ar_report (r)
```
Begins report definition

```
        DEFINE r RECORD
```
Define a report record

```
        customer_num LIKE customer.customer_num,

        fname LIKE customer.fname,

        lname LIKE customer.lname,

        company LIKE customer.company,

        order_num LIKE orders.order_num,

        order_date LIKE orders.order_date,

        ship_date LIKE orders.ship_date,

        paid_date LIKE orders.paid_date,

        total_price LIKE items.total_price

            END RECORD,

    OUTPUT

        PAGE LENGTH 22

        LEFT MARGIN 0
```

FIGURE 14.17 **(continued)**

```
FORMAT
```

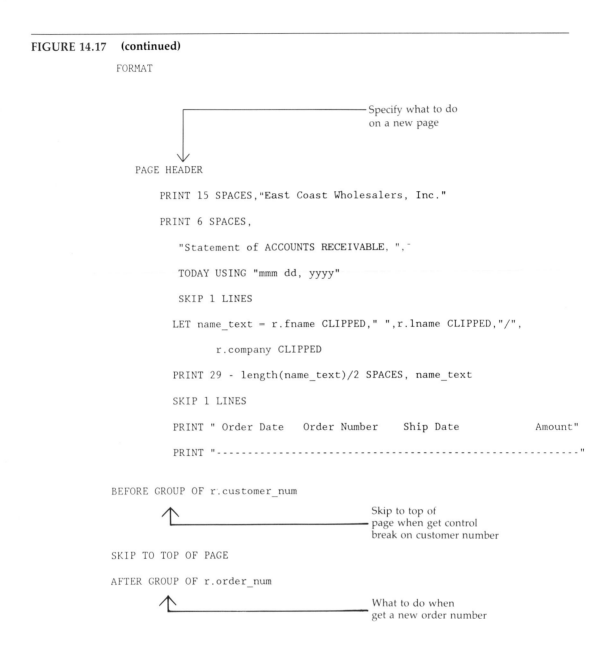

```
PAGE HEADER

    PRINT 15 SPACES,"East Coast Wholesalers, Inc."

    PRINT 6 SPACES,

        "Statement of ACCOUNTS RECEIVABLE, ",

        TODAY USING "mmm dd, yyyy"

        SKIP 1 LINES

    LET name_text = r.fname CLIPPED," ",r.lname CLIPPED,"/",

            r.company CLIPPED

        PRINT 29 - length(name_text)/2 SPACES, name_text

        SKIP 1 LINES

        PRINT " Order Date    Order Number     Ship Date                Amount"

        PRINT "----------------------------------------------------------------"

BEFORE GROUP OF r.customer_num

SKIP TO TOP OF PAGE

AFTER GROUP OF r.order_num
```

FIGURE 14.17   (concluded)

```
NEED 3 LINES

PRINT " ",r.order_date,7 SPACES,r.order_num USING "###&",8 SPACES,

      r.ship_date," ",

      GROUP SUM(r.total_price) USING "$$$$,$$$,$$$.&&"
                ↑_____ A group calculation


AFTER GROUP OF r.customer_num

PRINT 42 SPACES,"----------------"

PRINT 42 SPACES,GROUP SUM(r.total_price) USING "$$$$,$$$,$$$.&&"

END REPORT
```

not have to change the program, because the report writer will make the record's column components match the new definition whenever the report is run.

Next, a cursor—a topic we discussed in Chapter 8—is defined. It will be used to SELECT the specified columns from the three tables after performing a join and to restrict the search to those ORDERS.PAID_DATE rows that have a NULL value, which indicates they haven't been paid yet. To actually produce the report, we send data to it from a MAIN 4GL routine or a function. Three statements are used:

START REPORT report-name
OUTPUT TO REPORT report-name (argument list)
FINISH REPORT report-name

The START REPORT is coded prior to the report and initiates the report's production. The next command, OUTPUT TO REPORT, is coded within a loop and, through arguments, specifies which variables are to be printed. In the example, we used INFORMIX's FOREACH construct, which specifies that something is to be done for every row returned by the cursor. After the loop, a FINISH REPORT is required.

The actual report definition for ar_report is coded next. After defining report variables to be LIKE their table counterparts, the program specifies some page formatting instructions, setting the page length and left margin.

The FORMAT portion of the report first defines the header (PAGE HEADER). There you can see a reference to TODAY, which is a function that returns the current date. Use of CLIPPED results in the removal of trailing blanks. Next come three sections that contain instructions for control-break processing.

Through the "BEFORE GROUP r.customer__num" clause, the program specifies that when a new customer number is passed to the report definition, the program is to force a page break. A similar clause, AFTER GROUP, tells IN-FORMIX what to do after a control break. There are two such clauses in Figure 14.17.

When a new order number is passed to the report, the "AFTER GROUP OF r.order__num" section says to first be sure that at least three lines remain on the page and, if so, to print the order's date, number, and shipping date. The GROUP SUM clause says to total the price for the group (the group of rows having the same order number) just printed. The other AFTER GROUP section specifies that the program should print an underline, then total all the amounts, when a new customer is passed to the report.

This is a fairly typical report specification. Notice there were no procedural statements to count lines, check for control breaks through a series of IF statements, accumulate totals, and so on. Instead, we can spend more time designing the report, worrying little about users changing their minds because of the ease with which we can add new reports or change existing ones.

In this section, we briefly looked at some of INFORMIX's nonprocedural reporting capabilities. In the next one, we will see how easy it is to develop screen forms.

Screen Forms and Windows. Figure 14.18 shows a 4GL program that includes a screen form. Look at the OPEN FORM cust__form "customer" statement. This associates a logical form name (cust__form) with the physical form (customer), which is a specification file stored on a disk. Figure 14.19 shows its specifications.

After specifying the database name, we state that a screen form is being defined (SCREEN). Next comes the screen layout, which we have "painted." Instead of coding statements like AT ROW 10,COLUMN 15 DISPLAY "Number," we use a word processor or text editor to construct a visual representation of the form and INFORMIX will translate this image into specific row-column coordinates to be used when displaying the data.

The layout includes spaces for nine fields, each containing a caption, an identifier, called a *field tag* by INFORMIX, and two field length delimiters. The identifier is a cross-reference mechanism to the ATTRIBUTES section that appears after the screen is defined. For example, f001 refers to the CUSTOMER.FNAME column. The f001 entry in the ATTRIBUTES section includes a color change (COLOR=1), the conversion of all lowercase letters to uppercase (UPSHIFT), and the displaying of a comment on line 25 (COMMENTS = . . .), all of which occur whenever the cursor is in the fname field on the screen. Table 14.1 lists most of the available ATTRIBUTES from which we can choose.

The END statement specifies that we are finished specifying the screen's visual image. Next comes the TABLES section, where we identify the tables to be used.

FIGURE 14.18   A Portion of a 4GL Program that Contains a Screen Form

```
DATABASE stores

MAIN

    DEFINE p_customer RECORD LIKE customer.*,
        answer CHAR(1),
        found SMALLINT
```
⬆_____ Defines a program record
                      and two variables

```
    OPEN FORM cust_form FROM "customer"

    DISPLAY FORM cust_form
```
⬆_____ Display a blank form

```
    MESSAGE "Selecting all rows from the customer table . . ."

    SLEEP 3
```
⬆_____ Wait 3 seconds
```
    MESSAGE ""
```
⬆_____ Clear message line

```
    DECLARE q_curs CURSOR FOR

      SELECT * FROM customer
```
⬆_____ Define cursor for retrieval

```
    LET found = FALSE

    FOREACH q_curs INTO p_customer.*

      LET found = TRUE

      DISPLAY BY NAME p_customer.*
```
⬆_____ Show the current row of
             the cursor using the
             custom form

```
      PROMPT "Do you want to see the ",
      "next customer row (y/n) ? "  FOR answer
```

FIGURE 14.18   (concluded)

```
      IF answer = "n" or answer ="N" THEN

      EXIT FOREACH
```

—— Exit FOREACH loop

```
         END IF

      END FOREACH


      IF found = FALSE THEN

         MESSAGE "No rows found.   End program."

      ELSE
         IF answer = "y" THEN

         MESSAGE "No more rows.   End program."

         ELSE

         MESSAGE "End program."

         END IF

      END IF

      SLEEP 3

      CLEAR SCREEN

   END MAIN
```

Then we code the ATTRIBUTES section, discussed earlier. After that comes the INSTRUCTIONS section, where a screen record consisting of the CUSTOMER's first name through the phone number columns is defined. The entire record will be passed to the program in Figure 14.18 for displaying.

The program in Figure 14.18 first displays a blank form using the screen we defined in Figure 14.19. Then it displays a message, waits three seconds, and clears the message. Next, it establishes a cursor to be used to select all the CUSTOMER rows and columns.

A FOREACH statement automatically processes a cursor, handling the OPEN, FETCH, and CLOSE statements without having to code them. Within the FOREACH loop in Figure 14.18, the program uses the cursor to sequentially

FIGURE 14.19   **The Form Used for the 4GL Program in Figure 14.18**

```
DATABASE stores

SCREEN

                          CUSTOMER   FORM

                                      ———————— Called a field tag


          Number:     f000

       First Name:    f001              Last Name:    f002

          Company:    f003

          Address:    f004
                      f005

             City:    f006

            State:    a0    Zipcode:    f007

        Telephone:    f008

END

TABLES
customer

ATTRIBUTES
f000 = customer.customer_num;

                                       Associates a column from table
                                       with field tag f000

f001 = customer.fname,
   COLOR=1, UPSHIFT,
   COMMENTS ="You must enter a name";
   .
   .
   .

                          (see Table 14.1 for attribute options)

END

INSTRUCTIONS
SCREEN RECORD sc_cust (customer.fname THRU customer.phone)

                                       Defines a record to be used for screen
                                       form. It includes every CUSTOMER column
                                       from fname to phone
END
```

The pid column is 10 characters long and cannot have NULL values. INFORMIX is to set up a unique index on the column.

TABLE 14.1   Some Attributes that Can Be Associated with a Screen Field

AUTONEXT	Program automatically skips to the next field when current field is full
COLOR	One of eight colors can be selected
COMMENTS	Causes a message to be displayed on the Comment Line at the bottom of the screen when the cursor moves into this field
DEFAULT	Specifies a default value for the field
DOWNSHIFT	Converts to lowercase
FORMAT	Controls format of display
INCLUDE	Specifies acceptable values for field
NOENTRY	Specifies as being display only
PICTURE	Like PIC clause with COBOL—specifies character fill pattern
REQUIRED	Forces data entry for specified field
REVERSE	Specifies reverse video
UPSHIFT	Converts all letters to uppercase
VERIFY	Forces user to enter data twice

retrieve each row and uses the screen form to show it. The program pauses after each row is displayed to ask us if we want another row.

If a program needs to read data from a screen rather than display on it, we use the INPUT statement instead of DISPLAY. This command is very powerful, as it can specify what processing to perform BEFORE or AFTER the cursor enters a particular screen field, what to do if a particular key is struck (ON KEY), provide automatic context-sensitive help messages, and so on. In addition, all the editing keys (delete, insert, cursor movement, etc.) are automatically used without our having to program for them.

INFORMIX also includes windowing capabilities. For example, if we can't remember a particular item code, we can pop up a window that shows all of the item codes and descriptions from an INVENTORY table and allows us to pick a row from the window using the cursor keys, then clear the window and "paste" the results onto the underlying screen. All of this can be done with just 10 to 15 lines of code.

Use of windows allows us to work with detailed information without the applications developer having to clutter up the screen. The windows can be defined once, then used repeatedly whenever needed.

This section has given you just a taste of how a 4GL can be used to define a screen. You should remember that instead of the programmer having to develop code to display data on the screen at specific locations, check for function keys being struck, handle editing chores, constantly check the cursor's location, and so on, a quick prototype can be designed, placing the focus on processing rather than screen handling.

Other 4GL Statements.   We cannot do justice to the complete 4GL in one section of a text on database management. There are over 125 commands in the IN-FORMIX language. It supports such programming structures as CASE, IF, FOR,

CONTINUE, and FOREACH. It contains 18 screen-related commands and 18 SQL-based data definition commands, such as CREATE TABLE, CREATE VIEW, and so on. Of particular benefit in a multiuser, transaction processing environment are its nine data integrity statements. Among them are BEGIN WORK, ROLLBACK WORK, RECOVER TABLE, and CREATE AUDIT. The AUDIT statement generates an audit trail—a complete history of all additions, deletions, and updates—on a table-by-table basis. The RECOVER TABLE statement allows the DBA to completely restore a database after a failure provided a backup was made when the AUDIT was begun. It also provides for dynamic SQL, in which the end user enters his or her SQL command and the INFORMIX 4GL PREPARES, then EXECUTES it.

ORACLE

This section briefly discusses the most popular of the SQL-based 4GLs: ORACLE. Because its 4GL is nonprocedural, most developers use its report writer and screen-handling facility but frequently must resort to COBOL or C to do most of the transaction processing.

ORACLE sells Professional ORACLE, which is the same as its minicomputer and mainframe versions but runs on a microcomputer with 640K of normal memory, plus at least 876MB of extended memory and an 80286- or 80386-based microprocessor unit.

ORACLE's components are exactly the same as those of the mini and mainframe versions:

- SQL
- SQL*Plus
- SQL*Forms
- SQL*Reports
- Pro*C
- SQL*Calc

The version of SQL provided by ORACLE is a superset of IBM's SQL/DS and DB2. While it contains several commands and operators not found in the IBM packages, it includes almost all of IBM's SQL commands. There are some minor incompatibilities: Catalog names differ, and some of the DB2 data types are not supported. Also, at the time of this writing, the program does not support DB2's referential integrity facility, although version 7.0 is supposed to, when released.

Besides offering a superset of SQL, Professional ORACLE includes an interactive programming environment: SQL*Plus. SQL*Plus provides access to any text editor, a help facility, and the ability to save and run SQL statements.

ORACLE's nonprocedural report writer is called SQL*Report. SQL*Report can be used to produce a tabular report from a single table or a complicated one with various levels of control breaks, totals, and subtotals. It includes the ability to write procedural macros for even more complex reporting needs.

Much of the ability to produce ORACLE applications comes from its fourth-generation, forms-oriented language: SQL*Forms. SQL*Forms is used to create and modify end user screens and to describe the data to be entered, including its edit rules—even referential integrity—and for querying the database.

A unique feature is its **trigger** facility. A **trigger** is a procedure that is executed whenever a predetermined event occurs. Among these events are the cursor entering a field on the screen, its leaving a field, the user pressing a "help" key, and so on. For example, we might program a trigger for the patient number field on a patient entry screen. Whenever the cursor leaves its assigned location on the screen, SQL*Forms will automatically look up the patient in the PATIENT table and, if it finds it, display the name, age, sex, and so on of that patient.

Besides referential integrity checking, SQL*Forms can perform domain checks, control the displayed format of the data, and display help text. Being nonprocedural, this language can be used to quickly develop applications. For those applications too complex for SQL*Forms, or for those portions of the application that the language can't address, ORACLE provides the ability to use embedded SQL in either COBOL (only REALIA COBOL is supported on the microcomputer) or C (either Microsoft or Lattice C can be used on micros).

ORACLE's implementation of embedded SQL within COBOL programs (an extra-cost option) is almost identical to that we saw earlier in the text. There are a few differences, such as the use of a different value for SQLCODE when a row can't be found, but the compatibility level is at least 95 percent. In fact, one study found that writing DB2 applications using ORACLE and REALIA COBOL on a PC, then porting the result to the mainframe, takes 1/20 of the time it takes when all the work is done on the mainframe using IBM's VS COBOL II and DB2.

SQL*Calc is a Lotus 1-2-3 look-alike with the ability to code SQL statements in a cell. By using SQL statements, we can SELECT data from an ORACLE database, manipulate it using the spreadsheet, then UPDATE the tables. In addition, the spreadsheet program can ROLLBACK, DELETE rows, LOCK rows, INSERT new rows, or even CREATE new tables. For example, if we coded "$SELECT * FROM ORDERS" into a spreadsheet cell, ORACLE would go to the database, retrieve the field names as well as the associated rows from the ORDERS table, and insert them into the worksheet at the cell in which we entered the command. We could then change the associated cell values and enter a SQL UPDATE command into another cell, which would update the original ORACLE table.

The reason ORACLE requires extended memory (over 640K) is that it loads itself into the higher memory addresses, leaving the lower memory for applications that can call ORACLE. For example, a COBOL program might run in conventional memory and be able to call ORACLE, just as is done on a mainframe.

In summary, ORACLE is a complete RDBMS, comparable to IBM's DB2 or SQL/DS. Not only can it be used as a stand-alone package; the SQL calls can be embedded in COBOL or C programs. Optional features include a multiuser version for running on a LAN and a data communications module that permits micro-based applications to be part of a distributed database system.

This concludes our brief discussion of 4GLs. Using INFORMIX and ORACLE as a reference, we have seen that the typical 4GL environment includes:

- An integrated development environment
- A nonprocedural report-writer
- A Query-By-Example facility
- A screen-handling facility
- Window control
- Data validation that can be verified by the DBMS without us having to do any programming
- Help facilities that are automatically invoked
- Assess to SQL

It wasn't until the 4GLs were developed that all of the above features were combined into a single language. While the features were available in the 3GL environments, each typically came from a different source, making program development difficult and program testing even more so. Because of their almost universal standardization on SQL and their ease-of-use features for screen and report design, application developers can quickly prototype new systems, showing end users what the screens and reports will look like, in a very short period of time.

14.10 SUMMARY

The pressure to distribute data in today's information processing environment is increasing. One cause of this pressure is the increasingly widespread use of personal computers and the trend for organizations to become larger, bringing with it wide geographical dispersion of employees.

Each site typically has local computing power at the microcomputer level and perhaps mini and mainframe power as well. Certainly each site has local data that might need to be shared with others in the organization.

One way to distribute data is to partition it, placing selected data at each site. Such partitioning can be horizontal—rows are distributed—or vertical—complete columns are stored at different sites. Once data is partitioned, the actual location of each fragment should be transparent to all end users.

Another approach is to replicate the data, knowingly duplicating strategic data in an effort to get it as close to the end user as possible, yet retaining additional copies wherever necessary, often at the central site. In this case, the DDBMS must be able to choose the closest data storage site whenever a request is made. Because of the possibility for inconsistencies, it is preferred that DDBMSs possess replication transparency—the ability to automatically enforce consistency without end user involvement.

Depending on need, both partitioning and replication can be done functionally or geographically. In many instances, both replication and partitioning may be necessary along functional and/or geographical lines.

The distributed environment brings the need for more sophisticated query optimization, concurrency control, replication control, and recovery procedures and the potential for performance degradation. These problems hopefully are offset by the ability to have data closer to its users, more efficient processing, and improved reliability.

The role played by micros is twofold: that of a participant in a LAN and that of either a "dumb" terminal or a client in a WAN involving mini- or mainframe computers. A recent LAN development is the database server, where a single image of the DDBMS is run in a database server.

With heterogeneous hardware or DBMS environments, or where there is a high volume of database activity, an increasingly popular approach is the use of a second CPU to carry out all database requests. The requests are handled and the results (data plus status) are sent back to the host. Such a device is called a *database machine*, a *database computer*, or a *back-end computer*. While database machines have their pros and cons, the consensus seems to be that if there is a large volume of requests against a database and those requests are based on SQL, these devices can be cost-justified.

In an effort to eliminate the IS backlog of work and to help end users develop many of their own reports, 4GLs that combine SQL with features such as report writing, screen handling, and a nonprocedural language have been developed. We looked at INFORMIX-4GL and ORACLE, two of the major vendors of such products. Both run on the complete spectrum of computers: micro, mini, and mainframe. This flexibility means that applications can be developed on the more "friendly" micros, then ported to the larger platforms after they are debugged.

REVIEW QUESTIONS

1. Define the following:
   a. DDB
   b. DDBMS
   c. NIC
   d. NOS
   e. Database server

   f.   Location transparency

   g.   Replication transparency

   h.   Metaschema

   i.   Back-end computer

2. Describe the difference between horizontal and vertical partitioning.

3. Show an example of the two kinds of partitioning mentioned in Problem 2.

4. How can location transparency be implemented?

5. Describe a gateway.

6. When is replication justified?

7. What are the problems associated with replication?

8. Assuming that data is both partitioned and replicated, what must a query optimizer consider before responding to a request?

9. Describe the two-phase commit process, including its purpose and disadvantage.

10. Discuss the advantages and disadvantages of distributing databases.

11. What is meant by the term *client*?

12. What is the advantage of a database server versus each node having its own DBMS?

13. Define these independence qualities: location, fragmentation, hardware, operating system, and DBMS.

14. What features of a database machine enable it to increase the performance of a database system?

15. What are the potential problems associated with a database machine?

16. What is the advantage in a database machine of having all requests formulated in SQL?

17. Describe the two-phase rollback.

18. Why is concurrency control made more difficult with DDBs?

19. What are some of the costs associated with the distributed environment?

20. Why might a location directory be necessary with a DDB?

A

Disk-Based Input/Output

This appendix discusses how data are stored. Specifically, it examines the **input/output system** as it relates to disk drives, which are also known as **direct access storage devices (DASDs).** Like any system, the I/O system has inputs, outputs, and processing.

Figure A.1 shows that the input to the I/O system is the request by an application to read or write a record. The output of the system is the record that is returned to the application or written to the disk. The processing component is quite complex, requiring the interaction of both software and hardware. Necessary software includes the application, the operating system, and the access methods. The required hardware components are the CPU, main memory, channels, controllers, and the disk drives themselves.

The purpose of this appendix is to provide the technical background necessary to understand how these components interact to allow an application to store or retrieve data from disk drives. Much of the appendix discusses disk drives and formulas for calculating storage capacity and timing. Table A.3 at the end of the appendix alphabetizes the parameters used in the equations. It also cross-references each parameter with the equation numbers using it. Another useful reference at the end of the appendix is Table A.4, which summarizes most of the IBM disk hardware discussed.

Although the roles played by hardware and software in the management of input and output are intertwined, we will try whenever possible to discuss them separately. At times that may be impossible, but we will minimize our discussion of one when discussing the other. We begin our study of input/output management by briefly discussing central processing unit (CPU) concepts.

FIGURE A.1   The Disk System

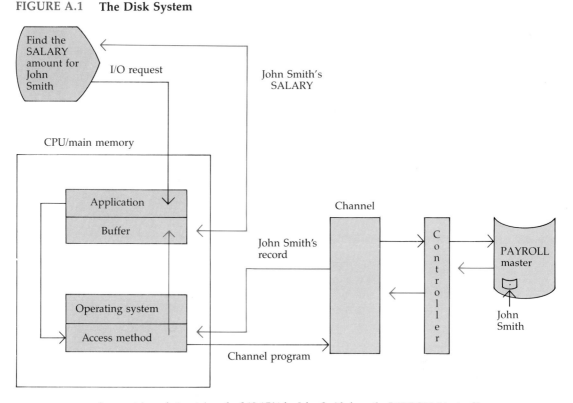

A request is made to retrieve the SALARY for John Smith from the PAYROLL Master file.

A.1   THE CPU

The **central processing unit (CPU)** is the engine that drives the entire input/output (I/O) process. It sequentially retrieves one instruction at a time from a host program (an application that calls a DBMS) that has been compiled, link-edited, and loaded into main memory. Representative IBM mainframe CPUs include the 3090 and 43XX families. At the top of the product line is the IBM 3090 model 600 E; the smaller mainframe computers are the 4361 and 4381. The 3090 series machines are much faster, are more flexible, and can handle more users, but they cost more than the 43XX machines.

FIGURE A.2   Three Jobs in Memory at One Time, Each Being Concurrently Executed by the Operating System

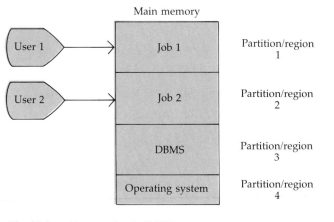

Main memory

Job 1	Partition/region 1
Job 2	Partition/region 2
DBMS	Partition/region 3
Operating system	Partition/region 4

The third partition contains the DBMS.

A.2   THE OPERATING SYSTEM

The operating system acts as an administrator, delegating tasks to specific software and hardware components. For our purposes, its role begins with the sequential loading of each program into a particular area of memory, called a **partition,** or **region,** as illustrated in Figure A.2.

A *memory partition* is an area in memory created by the operating system. Each partition has a beginning and ending address that a program cannot cross, thus isolating it from all others that may be executing concurrently. In the figure are four partitions. In a database setting, the DBMS resides in one partition and the host programs reside in the others.

The operating system directs the hardware and other software components in the managing of system resources, scheduling and supervising of jobs, and interfacing with peripheral devices such as DASDs and printers. Examples of IBM operating systems used in the text are:

- DOS/VSE (Disk Operating System/Virtual Storage Extended)
- MVS/ESA (Multiple Virtual Storages/Enterprise Systems Architecture)
- VM/370 (Virtual Machine Facility/370)

Figure A.2 shows several programs in memory at once. If each is run concurrently (alternating from one to another), the environment is called a **multiprogramming** one.

A.3   CHANNELS

The most critical devices for the implementation of multiprogramming and for efficient I/O processing are **channels,** or **I/O processors**—devices that carry out I/O instructions sent to them by the access method, thereby freeing the CPU to continue processing even while the channels are carrying out their programs simultaneously. We could say that a channel is a computer within a computer that has a single task: to relieve the CPU from the burden of performing I/O instructions.

While an I/O device is responding to an application's request to read or write data, the CPU can perform many calculations. Unfortunately, it cannot perform these calculations for the requesting program, because it is waiting for the I/O device and channel to complete their work. The only way to have the CPU continue processing is to have another program in memory along with the first one. This is the essence of multiprogramming, and the illustration of memory in Figure A.2 depicts this kind of processing. In the figure, main memory is divided into several partitions, with one partition storing the operating system and the others storing application load modules. As one program is suspended pending completion of its I/O request, the operating system can switch to another program and begin processing it.

A.4   ACCESS METHODS

The access methods remove the hardware-specific I/O handling from the programmer's responsibility and transfers it to the operating system. As Figure A.1 suggests, when a program requests a record, the access method takes over, locating the proper peripheral device and then passing a small program to the channel. The channel executes this program and instructs yet another hardware component, called a **controller,** on how to find the record and physically read it or how to find some unused space on the device so that a new record can be stored. When the channel and controller have completed their duties, the channel interrupts the CPU, signaling that the record has been processed.

There are three categories of IBM access methods:

- Basic
- Queued
- Virtual

IBM's mainframe operating systems support **four basic access methods:**

- Sequential
- Direct
- Partitioned
- Indexed sequential

A *queued access method* is used when grouping several records into a unit called a *block*. It offers more data-handling capabilities than do any of the basic access methods. Finally, IBM uses a combination of the modified queued and basic access methods for its *virtual storage access method (VSAM)*.

Selecting the proper access method is based on the desired organization of the data on the device and the specific accessing required by the application programs. Access methods play a very important role in managing input and output. Specifically, they:

- Provide a degree of device independence
- Provide control over creation, maintenance, and deletion of stored data
- Forward the channel programs to the appropriate controller
- Protect data against unauthorized access
- Provide a common method of communicating to all devices through JCL statements

Basic Access Methods

Basic access methods are just that: they provide a minimum of help for the programmer. As the basic access method reads a record from the input device, it places it in an input buffer area within the application's memory partition. When used in this context, the term **buffers** means locations in main memory where records are placed after being physically read or prior to being physically written to the I/O device. The records that are placed in the buffers are called **physical records,** or **blocks.** The basic access methods read and write physical records only. This means that the logical and physical records must be the same. A **logical record** is the record from the application or user view. When an application requests a logical record, the access method first checks the buffer area. If it finds the record there, it passes it to the record definition area (the FD's 01 level in a COBOL program) in the program. This transferring of a record from the buffer to the program's record area is a **logical read,** or **logical I/O,** meaning that despite the fact that a read was requested, the disk drive was not used. Because this logical I/O uses a memory-to-memory transfer, it occurs very quickly.

Queued Access Methods: Blocking and Buffering

Queued access methods handle the tasks of *blocking* and *unblocking* and provide for *anticipatory buffering*.

First, we will discuss **blocking** in general terms. To better utilize disk space, we usually store several logical records together as a block, which is the unit that is transferred to and from the disk; the device knows nothing about the individual records comprising the physical record. The number of logical records in the physical record is its **blocking factor.** In Figure A.3 there are three logical records in a block, so the blocking factor is 3.

A queued access method automatically performs the tasks of blocking the logical records into physical ones and unblocking the physical records into logical records that are compatible with the records described in the FD portion of COBOL applications.

Anticipatory buffering means that the access method "guesses" which record will be needed next and reads that record into a second buffer.

Figure A.4 shows a file with the COBOL default value of two buffers. Using this default value permits the queued access method to perform its anticipatory buffering. More or fewer than two buffers can be assigned by using the "RE-SERVE integer AREAS" clause in the SELECT statement for the file.

FIGURE A.3   **Two Physical Records, or Blocks, Stored on a Disk**

Each block contains three logical records; therefore the blocking factor is 3.

FIGURE A.4   **An Example of Anticipatory Buffering**

(a) A record has been requested by an application. Because both buffers are empty, a physical I/O has been executed, transferring the first block (physical record) into buffer area 1

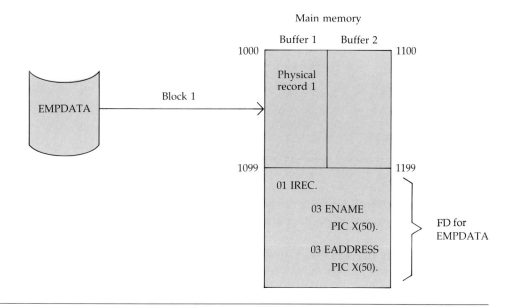

FIGURE A.4   **(concluded)**

(b) The first logical record is moved to the record definition in the FD area, and the second block is transferred into the second buffer — The first buffer is now "empty," and the third block could be transferred

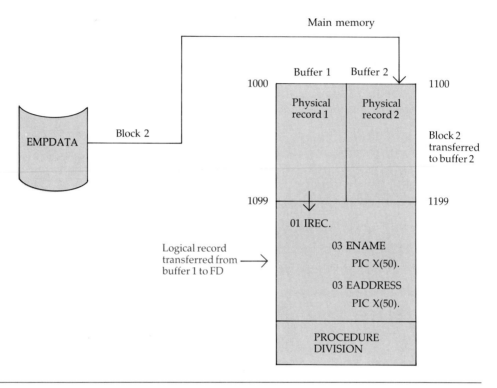

not as confusing as it sounds: be patient!) The initial physical record is read into buffer 1.

In Figure A.4(b), the first record is being transferred from the buffer into the record description area in the program so that it can be processed. At this point, that buffer is empty and ready to accept the third record.

While the application is processing the record in buffer 1, the second (physical) record is being anticipated by the queued access method and transferred into buffer 2 by the channel. Anticipating the next record is easy for sequential files, since the application must process the records in the physical order in which they are stored. For direct files this is not true, and thus we do not use a queued access method for such files.

Virtual Storage Access Method

IBM's **virtual storage access method (VSAM)** uses modified versions of both the queued and basic access methods to provide an environment where records can be accessed sequentially or directly. In addition, it provides:

- A way to store records independently of the DASD on which they are stored
- Routines for accessing records sequentially, by key, or by their relative positions in the file
- High performance due to its internal method for quickly locating records, the manner in which records are added and deleted, and its ability to minimize mechanical disk movements

We will look at VSAM and the other access methods in Appendix B.

A.5 INTERFACE EQUIPMENT: GETTING DATA FROM HERE TO THERE

Transferring data between a peripheral device and main memory is a complicated affair requiring not only the efforts of the operating system, the access method, the application system, and the I/O device but also the efforts of two types of interface equipment: *channels* and *controllers*.

Channels

Every I/O device is slow when compared to the speed of the CPU. Consequently, mainframes and minicomputers have **channels,** also called **input/output processors,** that carry out the actual I/O operation. While the channel is carrying out its orders, the CPU can process another program. When the channel is finished, it interrupts the CPU. Channels are special-purpose computers that run a **channel program,** which is sent to the channel by the access method. These programs are unique to each device. Thus, a disk channel program is vastly different from a tape channel program. It is important to realize that it is because of the channel that the computer can appear to do several things at a time, and it is the use of channels that permits multiprogramming.

Controllers

Channels forward their instructions to **controllers,** which are required for every input/output device. Disk controllers perform the following tasks:

- Carry out the access commands issued by the channel.
- Convert data codes from disk format to CPU format, and vice versa.

- Check for and, if possible, correct device errors.
- Send status information to the channel.

Carrying out access commands for a disk drive might include switching on the correct read/write head, spinning the disk pack, searching for a particular data key, and so on.

Data stored on I/O devices is physically stored in a manner incompatible with the requirements of the CPU. The controller does the necessary conversions so that the CPU and I/O device can effectively communicate. The controller also checks for and tries to correct certain types of errors.

Two common error-checking methods are **parity checking** and **cyclic checking.** Both techniques require that additional bits or bytes be attached to the data block when the block is initially written. As a block is read, the extra bits or bytes are compared to an expected pattern, and a deviation will or will not be detected. If the extra characters do not match the expected sequence, an error is reported. The controller checks for the deviation and, if detected, tries reading the record several times. It also must remove these extra characters before sending the data to the channel.

IBM has recently begun using **cache control units** in an effort to speed up the processing of disk data. This technique is also becoming prevalent with microcomputer disks. One of IBM's controllers, the 3880 model 23, adds some high-speed cache memory (up to 16 megabytes) to the controller. By using a **least recent used (LRU) algorithm,** blocks that have recently been accessed are kept in the cache memory rather than on the disk. Using the cache to handle I/O requests results in transmission of the data to the buffer area in nanoseconds rather than in milliseconds.

The Role of the Interface Equipment: Putting It All Together

The following scenario depicts a fairly typical set of events that would occur following a COBOL READ request for a disk record. It may be helpful if you look at Figure A.1 after reading these steps.

1. The application program issues the READ request.
2. The access method determines that the desired record is not in any input buffer.
3. The access method sends the channel its channel program.
4. The channel runs its disk channel program.
5. The application program may be stopped pending completion of the channel program.
6. The channel forwards relevant commands to the DASD controller.
7. The controller performs the actual data read.
8. The controller signals the channel that it has successfully completed its job.

9. The channel interrupts the CPU, signaling the end of its tasks.
10. The access method accepts the physical record from the channel and puts it into the buffer area of the application program.
11. The access method moves the logical record from the buffer to the FD area.

Hopefully the steps involved in the processing and management of input and output are clear to you. The interrelationships of both hardware and software components, and their respective roles, is quite complex. This section has tried to demonstrate these relationships for you. The next section discusses the role the disk drive plays in the input/output process.

A.6   THE DISK SYSTEM

Disk systems are considered direct access storage devices (DASDs), because records can be accessed directly versus only sequentially as with tape systems. To access a record directly means to go directly to the location where the desired record is stored and retrieve just that record. For instance, to retrieve the 10th record on a tape device, the tape system must begin reading at the beginning of the tape and read 9 records before getting to the desired one. Contrast this with a disk system that could go directly to the 10th record and retrieve it.

Devices other than disks can be classified as DASDs, including data cells and drums. However, those devices are seldom used and DASD has come to mean a disk system. Throughout the appendix, we will use the two terms interchangeably.

A disk system has three subsystems:

- A spindle or drive
- A pack
- An access mechanism

The Disk Drive or Spindle: The Device

The disk drive is the **device** to which data is written or from which it is read. Some drives have removable packs, while others require permanently mounted packs. The drives with the removable packs are mounted on a *spindle* like that found on a turntable. The drive spins the disk pack at a constant speed and never stops except to switch packs or because the power has been turned off.

The Disk Pack: The Medium

Disk packs, also called **volumes,** usually consist of a stacked series of aluminum **platters,** or **disks,** each coated with an iron oxide substance, much like the coating on an audio- or videotape. The pack is the **medium** that actually stores the records. A disk stores data on a series of concentric circles called **tracks.**

Usually the tracks are numbered on a surface from zero to n − 1, where n is the number of tracks per surface. Track 0 is the outermost track.

Because the platters are stacked on top of each other, track 0 on surface 1 is directly above track 0 on surface 2, and so on. This concept defines a **cylinder,** the same track number on every surface. In the example, we have described cylinder 0.

Tracks. Tracks are placed on both sides of a platter when the disk is formatted. Although the track circumferences get smaller as they get closer to the center, every track stores the same amount of data. This is called the track **capacity,** which we denote by the letter *S*.

If there are p platters per pack, and t tracks per surface, there are a maximum of 2tp total tracks on a disk pack. The 2 is needed because each side of a platter can be used. By multiplying this figure by the track capacity, we can readily compute the volume capacity. It would be:

$$V = 2tpS. \tag{1}$$

These equations, as well as some others, are summarized in Figure A.5.

We used the word *maximum* above because not every surface may be usable by a program; knowing the actual number of surfaces is not always relevant.

FIGURE A.5   Some Track and Volume Storage Calculations

If:

t = tracks/surface
p = platters/pack
S = track capacity in bytes
T = total tracks per pack
U = surface capacity

then

$U = St$ $\qquad\qquad$ (2)
$T = 2tp$ (when every surface is usable)
V = volume capacity in bytes = ST

But substituting for T,

$V = S (2tp)$

$\quad = S2tp$

$\quad = St (2p)$

$\quad = U2p$

$\quad = 2Up$ $\qquad\qquad$ (3)

For example, several IBM drives are incapable of using the top of the first platter or the bottom of the last one.

Problem 1. **Each track on a pack with 10 platters and 200 tracks per surface has a capacity of 13,030 bytes. What is the capacity of each surface?**

Solution. Using equation 2, from Figure A.5,

$$U = St = 13{,}030 \times 200 = 2{,}606{,}000 \text{ bytes/surface.}$$

Problem 2. **What is the volume's capacity?**

Solution. Assuming every surface is usable, ————————————— Track capacity

$$V = \frac{\text{tracks}}{\text{surface}} \times \frac{\text{usable surfaces}}{\text{volume}} \times \frac{\text{bytes}}{\text{track}} \qquad (4)$$

$$= 200 \times 20 \times 13{,}030 = 52{,}120{,}000 \text{ bytes/volume.}$$

Fixed-Block Architecture. Some disk models divide their tracks into units called **sectors.** Each sector is a fixed number of bytes, such as 512, 1,024, and so on. Figure A.6 shows that unless record lengths are close to the sector size, there can be much wasted space within each sector. The figure shows an example where 412 bytes per sector are unused because the logical record size is only 100 bytes while the sector size is 512.

When records are read or written, they are done so in units of sectors rather than as programmer-defined blocks. This allows the disk system to always read

---

FIGURE A.6   **The Potential Waste that Results When a Block Size Is Not Close to a Multiple of the Sector Size When Fixed-Block Architecture Is Used**

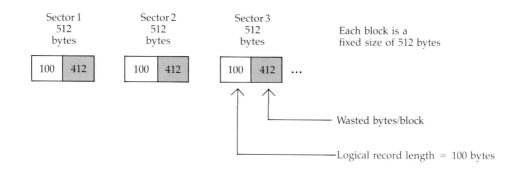

IBM's 3310 and 3370 series employ this kind of disk architecture.

---

the same number of bytes regardless of the actual record size. The earlier architecture will now be called **conventional architecture.**

IBM examples include the IBM 3310 and 3370 disk systems, which use 33 sectors per track and 600 bytes per sector. Only 32 of the sectors are usable for data storage and of the 600 bytes per sector, only 512 can be used by applications; the remainder of each track is used for overhead.

Cylinders. As we saw earlier, a cylinder is the same track number on all surfaces. For the disk in Problem 1, there are 200 tracks per surface; this means there are 200 cylinders. The number of cylinders is always equal to the number of tracks per surface. These relationships are shown in Figure A.7.

***Problem 3.* How many cylinders does a disk pack have if there are 8 platters with 300 tracks each?**

Solution. Since the number of cylinders equals the number of tracks per surface, there are 300 cylinders.

Table A.1 shows track and cylinder information about several of IBM's disk systems. It also shows data concerning the speeds of the various IBM disk drives.

***Problem 4.* Using the data from Table A.1, what is the capacity of an IBM 3350 surface?**

Solution. Recall that there are as many cylinders on a pack as there are tracks per surface, so there must be 555 tracks per surface on a 3350. Each track can hold 19,254 bytes, so a surface can store 19,254 bytes/track × 555 tracks/surface = 10,685,970 bytes/surface.

FIGURE A.7   The Cylinder Concept

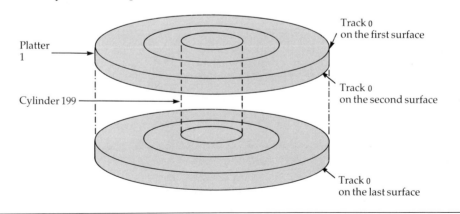

TABLE A.1   IBM Disk Drive Track and Cylinder Statistics

	IBM DASD Model Number				
	3310	3340	3350	3370	3380
Platter size	8″	14″	14″	14″	14″
Tracks/cylinder	11	12	30	12	15
Cylinders	358	348	555	750*	885*
Nominal track capacity	32 600 byte blocks	8355	19254	62 600 byte blocks	47968
Maximum track capacity**	32 512 byte blocks	8368	19069	62 512 byte blocks	47476
Data transfer rate (KB/sec)	1031	885	1198	1859	3000
Seek times (ms.)					
Minimum	9	10	10	5	3
Average	27	25	25	20	16
Maximum	46	50	50	40	30
Rotational delay (ms.)					
Average	9.6	10.1	8.4	10.1	8.3
Maximum	19.1	20.2	16.8	20.2	16.7

*Has two actuators, so multiply by 2 for totals.

**Maximum capacity is that usable by programmers. It is the nominal capacity less the space required for the track descriptor record (R0, used by the disk system), the home address, the address marker, and so on.

The Access Mechanism

The access mechanism is responsible for positioning a read/write head at the correct cylinder, switching on the read/write head corresponding to the track within the cylinder where the record is found or is to be written, and transferring the data to the controller.

We usually see conventional access mechanisms where a single mechanism serves the entire pack. Alternative architectures are **fixed-head architectures,** where the heads do not move, and **dual-access mechanisms,** like the 3370 mentioned earlier, where each mechanism serves one-half of the stack of platters.

Conventional Access Mechanisms. Most disk drives have one **access assembly** with one access arm per platter, as shown in Figure A.8. Notice that each arm in the figure has *two* read/write heads—one reads the underside of a surface, while the other reads the top surface of the next platter. Because all the heads are attached to their respective arms and all the arms connect to a common mechanism, when the access mechanism is positioned at a track on one surface it can read every track in that cylinder without moving. This is the most efficient way to store and retrieve data. That is, given a file that takes multiple tracks to

---

FIGURE A.8   **An Access Assembly**

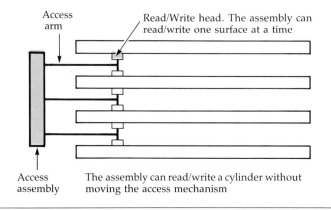

Access
arm

Read/Write head. The assembly can
read/write one surface at a time

Access
assembly

The assembly can read/write a cylinder without
moving the access mechanism

---

store, the controller should store the data on a cylinder basis, since *that* will minimize the mechanical access assembly movement.

It should be pointed out, however, that the access assembly can read from only one surface at a time. This is illustrated in the figure by the shaded read/write head.

Problem 5. **A file requires 120 tracks. How many cylinders are needed to store the data on a 3380 drive?**

Solution. There are 15 tracks per cylinder, so the file will occupy 120/15 = 8 cylinders. In this example, the answer is an integer. Because the controller does not use part of a cylinder for one file and another part for another file, we always take fractional answers to the next higher integer. The rule is:

$$c = \text{cylinders required} = \text{ceil}\left(\frac{\text{tracks required}}{\text{tracks/cylinder}}\right) \qquad \textbf{(5)}$$

where ceil means *ceiling.*

Problem 6. **A file requires 45 tracks on a 3350. How many cylinders are needed?**

Solution.

$$c = \text{ceil}\,(45/30) = \text{ceil}\,(1.5) = 2.$$

Dual-Actuator Mechanisms. IBM's 3370 uses two actuators per drive. Each **actuator** consists of a lightweight swing arm and read head combination with fewer parts and a smaller motor than with conventional access mechanisms. A servo track in the 3370 provides coarse movement of the access arm. Then the read/write head itself fine-tunes until it is positioned at the precise location. Each actuator has its own address and accesses one-half of the surfaces on the 3370. This means that while one actuator is reading, or moving (called **seeking**), the other one can be writing at the same time.

Fixed-Head Architecture: No Seeks. This type of drive has one read/write head per track. Such a disk pack with 80 tracks/surface would have 80 heads per surface—an expensive but fast design. The time necessary to move the access mechanism to the desired cylinder, then switch on the desired read/write head, is called the **seek time.** Because seek time is a result of mechanical motion, it accounts for most of the time spent by the I/O system in writing or reading records to or from the disk. By using fixed heads, we eliminate the need for mechanical motion, thus speeding up the I/O processing.

Combination Architectures: Fixed and Movable Heads. The third and final drive design uses a combination of some fixed heads with a conventional access assembly. Records that are frequently accessed should be put in the fixed-head area and less frequently accessed records in the conventional area. An example of such a drive is the IBM 3340. It has one 5-cylinder section in which each of its 12 tracks is served via 60 fixed heads. The remainder of the drive uses a conventional access assembly.

The IBM 3340 is also an example of the **Winchester** technology, in which the access assembly and platters are sealed together, thus eliminating the potential problem of contaminates causing head crashes, permitting vendors to pack the data more densely and reducing the distance the head floats above the surface.

Disk Addresses. To directly access a record on a DASD, the address of the desired record must be specified. There are four ways to specify a record's address on an IBM DASD:

1. Physical location
2. Relative record number
3. Relative track number
4. Relative track number plus key value

The first method, called **physical location addressing,** provides the controller with an eight-byte field containing three components: (1) the cylinder number; (2) the track number within the cylinder (the head number); and (3) the block number on the track relative to the first one. The first block on a track has a value of 1.

The second way to specify a record's location is to provide its **relative record (block) number (RRN)** through a three-byte binary field. A record's relative record number is its record displacement from the beginning of the file. The first record has a relative record number of 0. This means that if we had a 10 record file, its records would be assigned RRNs 0–9.

The third address specification scheme, **relative track addressing,** requires the specification of the record's relative track number, a three-byte field of the form TTR, where:

- TT is the **relative track number (RTN)** of the desired record, with the first track having a RTN value of 0.
- R is the block number on the track relative to the beginning of the track. The first block has a relative number of 1, because the first block (called R0) is used for system information.

The final address specification method is **relative track and key.** Here the controller is given a two-byte binary field containing the relative track address plus the value of the key value of the desired record. The controller searches the given track until it finds a matching key.

Figure A.9 shows a track containing three records. Beside each record is its address as it would be specified for each of the four addressing methods. In the example, we assume the file begins on cylinder 10, track 4.

First, consider the physical addressing method that requires the cylinder number, the track number, and the record number of the desired record. The cylinder and track number for all three records are the same: cylinder 10, track 4. The final component of the physical address is the relative record number, beginning with 1 on each track. Notice that the first record on the track has been assigned record number 1 in accordance with the rule; the next record has record number 2, and so on. The three X characters indicate that the values are no longer used by IBM.

Next, look at the relative record method. With this technique, the first record in the file is assigned RRN 000, the second RRN 001, and so on. Thus, in Figure A.9, the first record (key 1222) has been given address RRN 000 and the third one RRN 002.

With the relative track addressing method, the first two digits represent the RTN while the last digit depicts the relative record number for the record relative to the records on that track. Because all records on the same track have the same relative track number, every record in the example has the same first two digits (00). The digits are 00 because the given track is assumed to be the first one in the file.

The fourth technique, the relative track plus key method, is also shown in the figure. Here we attached the record's key value to the RTN rather than attaching the relative record number as in the previous method. The key appears after the colon.

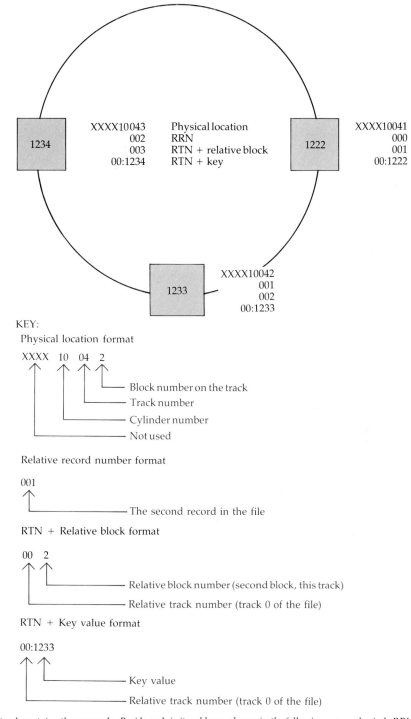

The track contains three records. Beside each is its address, shown in the following ways: physical, RRN, RTN + relative block, and RTN + key value. In reality, only one would be selected. The format of addressing methods follows. The sample values in the key are for the record with key value 1233.

Accessing a Record. To directly access a record using conventional architecture disk systems, the access mechanism goes through these four steps:

1. The access assembly is moved to the correct cylinder.
2. The read/write head corresponding to the track within the cylinder is switched on.
3. The desired record spins beneath the read/write head.
4. The block (record) is transferred.

Steps 1 and 2 combined are called a **seek,** or **access.** A seek from one cylinder to the next is called a **minimum seek,** a seek from the first cylinder to the last is a **maximum seek,** and a seek that moves the access mechanism over one-half of the total number of cylinders is called an **average seek.** The third step in the I/O transfer is called **disk rotation** and the last one **data transfer.**

Disk Timing: Seek, Rotate, and Transfer. There are three important time segments that determine how long it will take to transfer a record or file:

- Seek time
- Disk rotation time
- Block transfer time

Seek Time. The amount of time it takes to perform a seek is the **seek,** or **access time.** The vendor of the disk drive usually provides three seek times: minimum, maximum, and average seek times, corresponding to the three types of seeks described earlier. When calculating the time to transfer a directly accessed record we use average seek time, because there is no way of knowing exactly how many cylinders the access mechanism must traverse.

Average seek times range from 110ms (milliseconds) for a disk on an IBM XT (a microcomputer) to 16ms for the IBM 3380. The minimum seek time is important when calculating how long it takes to transfer a complete sequential file. The maximum seek time will not be used in this text.

Rotational Delay. The time it takes to complete a disk rotation or a portion of a rotation is the disk's **rotational delay,** or **latency.** There are three measures of rotational delay: minimum, average, and maximum. Minimum rotational delay, always equal to zero, is used when the disk did not have to spin; the desired record was beneath the read/write head when it was switched on. The maximum time is used if the disk must make a complete revolution. The average time is used if the portion of a revolution the disk must make is unknown. We will always use the average rotational delay figure, because we cannot predict with certainty where the desired block is on the track relative to the read/write head. Refer to Figure A.8 for the three rotational delay times for the IBM drives.

Transfer Time. The last time component is called **block transfer time (BTT)**. The amount of time depends on the size of the record and the **data transfer rate (DTR)** of the drive. Data transfer rates range from 5 million bits per second on the IBM XT to 3 million bytes (24 million bits) per second for the IBM 3380 drive.

Putting It All Together. The three times can be combined to develop an equation for the block transfer time. It is shown in Figure A.10.

Problem 7. **How long will it take to randomly find, wait for disk rotation, and then transfer a 3,000-byte record if it is stored on an IBM 3380 disk drive? Express your answer in milliseconds (ms).**

Solution. From equation 6 in Figure A.10,

$$BTT = 16ms + 8.3ms + \left(\frac{3,000 \text{ bytes}}{3,000,000 \text{ bytes/sec.}} \right)$$

$$= 24.3ms + .001 \text{ sec.}$$

$$= 24.3ms + .001 \text{ sec} \times \frac{1,000 \text{ ms.}}{\text{sec.}}$$

$$= 24.3ms + 1ms \qquad \text{Convert seconds to ms}$$

$$= 25.3 \text{ ms.}$$

When working with sequential files, we are usually concerned with how long it takes to transfer the entire file to or from the disk rather than a single record. The expression for the file transfer time (FTT) is shown as equation 7 in Figure A.11.

First, the access assembly moves to the beginning of the file. The time required to accomplish this is the average seek time. The access assembly is now sitting on the first cylinder.

Next, we account for the movements of the access mechanism from cylinder to cylinder. If there are c cylinders required, the access assembly must be moved a total of $(c - 1)$ times to read the remainder of the file. The amount of time it takes to move the assembly one cylinder is the minimum seek time = m. Thus, to move $(c - 1)$ cylinders, it takes $m(c - 1)$ units of time.

FIGURE A.10   The Equation for Determining the Time Required to Transfer a Block

$$\text{block transfer time (BTT)} = r + a + D/R \qquad (6)$$

where
r = average seek time
a = average rotational delay
R = data transfer rate (bytes/second)
D = data subblock size (equals the block size for now)

FIGURE A.11   The Equation for Determining the Amount of Time Necessary to Transfer a Complete Sequential File

$$FTT = r + m(c - 1) + B (BTT) + T \qquad (7)$$

where

r = average seek time
m = minimum seek time
c = total number of cylinders required to store the file
B = total blocks to transfer
BTT = block transfer time
T = total rotational delay

The third component in equation 7 accounts for the time needed to transfer all blocks. To transfer a block would take D/R units of time. This means:

$$BTT = D/R.$$

After transferring a block, the disk will spin, on average, one-half of a revolution before it is positioned for the next read operation. Thus, the total rotational delay (T) to transfer B blocks will be B times the average rotational delay, and

$$T = B \times a. \qquad (8)$$

Putting it all together gives equation 9:

$$FTT = r + m(c - 1) + B (D/R + a) \qquad (9)$$

Problem 8. How many seconds will it take to transfer a sequential file containing 10,000 blocks if each block is 1,000 bytes long? Assume the file is stored on an IBM 3340 and 10 blocks are stored per track.

Solution. Table A.1 showed that there are 12 tracks per cylinder on a 3340 data module. This means the total number of cylinders required is:

$$c = \text{ceil} \left[10,000 \text{ blocks} \left(\frac{1 \text{ track}}{10 \text{ blocks}} \right) \left(\frac{1 \text{ cylinder}}{12 \text{ tracks}} \right) \right]$$

$$= \text{ceil} (83.3 \text{ cylinders})$$

$$= 84 \text{ cylinders}.$$

Using equation 9,

$$FTT = 25\text{ms} + 10\text{ms}(84 - 1) + 10,000 \left(\frac{1,000 \text{ bytes}}{85,000 \text{ bytes/sec.}} + 10.1 \text{ ms} \right)$$

$$= 855\text{ms} + 10,000 \left[\left(.0011 \text{ sec.} \right) \left(\frac{1,000 \text{ ms.}}{\text{sec.}} \right) + 10.1 \text{ ms.} \right]$$

$$= 855ms + 10,000(11.2ms)$$
$$= 12,055ms.$$

Now we convert the answer to seconds:

$$= 12,055ms \left(\frac{1 \text{ sec.}}{1,000ms} \right)$$
$$= 12.055 \text{ sec.}$$

Data Storage

Data is stored on an IBM drive in one of two formats: **count-data** or **count-key-data.** Before we look at these two formats, we need to look in detail at blocking, the method for conserving disk space and for increasing the speed of our applications.

Blocking. There are two reasons to block logical records into physical ones:

- To save space
- To increase processing speed

Space is saved because associated with each physical record is an overhead of up to several hundred bytes (this overhead is described in the next section). By blocking records, we can reduce the number of physical records and thus reduce the percentage of space used to store the overhead, giving us more room for the logical data records.

The other reason for blocking is to reduce the total access time of a record. Through blocking, only one rotational delay per block is required, which means that all records in the block are transferred at once. Unfortunately, unless the records are physically stored in sequential order within the block, the time required to access and transfer records will actually increase. Because it takes more time to transfer a longer block than a shorter one, unless the next logical record is in the same block as the one just read, the disk will have to perform another seek and transfer a very large block. In this case, we are actually better off not blocking. This is the reason we usually do not block direct access files.

Let's review blocking. Consider a COBOL program with the following record description:

```
01 IREC.
     03 ENAME     PIC X(50).
     03 EADDRESS PIC X(50).
```

To the COBOL processing programs, this record consists of two 50-byte fields; hence **its logical record length (LRECL)** is 100 bytes.

Blocking means storing two or more logical records into a physical unit called the **data subblock, block,** or **physical record.** Recall that the number of logical records in a block is its blocking factor. Block sizes can be controlled through the application, through JCL statements, or by the operating system.

The number of bytes in a block (D) is normally its **physical record length (PRECL)** and can be calculated for sequential files as the LRECL times the blocking factor (represented by b). For keyed files, the expression for D becomes more complicated:

$$D = b \times LRECL = \text{(for sequential files)} \tag{10}$$

Problem 9. **A file consists of 10,000 employee records. If the file is blocked by 5, how many blocks are required to store the file?**

Solution. Since the block contains 5 logical records, there would be 10,000/5 = 2,000 data blocks. Figure A.12 shows this problem pictorially.

Problem 10. **If the LRECL in Problem 9 is 150 bytes and the file is sequentially organized, what is its block size?**

Solution.

$$D = PRECL = LRECL \times \text{blocking factor}$$
$$150 \times 5 = 750 \text{ bytes.}$$

Equation 10 can be rearranged to derive a mathematical expression for the blocking factor:

$$b = \text{blocking factor} = D/LRECL. \tag{11}$$

Problem 11. **A sequential file has a block size of 1,125 bytes. Its COBOL record description is shown below. What is the blocking factor?**

```
01 DREC.
      03 PART-NO      PIC X(10).
      03 PNAME        PIC X(25).
      03 PRICE        PIC 9(5)V99.
      03 TYPE         PIC X(3).
```

Solution. The LRECL is 10 + 25 + 7 + 3 = 45 bytes. Therefore, the blocking factor = block size/LRECL = 1,125/45 = 25.

The **optimal blocking factor** is the most efficient way to process a disk-based file. It is the block size that results in a physical record size that is as close to the track capacity as possible without exceeding it. That way, each physical I/O reads one complete track. The blocking factor that gives this number is the optimal one. This concept is also called **full track blocking.**

FIGURE A.12   **Blocking a File by 5**

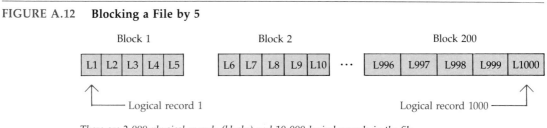

There are 2,000 physical records (blocks) and 10,000 logical records in the file.

Track Format. You may be surprised at the amount of overhead that is stored in addition to our data. The overhead is necessary so that the disk system can quickly locate a record. Figure A.13 shows the IBM track format used with its conventional disk systems. As you can see, each track has:

- One index point
- One home address
- One address marker per block
- One count area per block
- Zero or one key areas per block (depending on access method)
- Several data subblocks

Index Point. The *index point* is a special sequence of bits that mark the beginning of each track.

Home Address. The track's *home address,* used by the controller to determine that the access arm is positioned at the correct location, is a seven-byte field containing the following data:

- A flag indicating whether or not the track is usable (one byte)
- The cylinder number (two bytes)
- The track number within the cylinder, i.e., the head number (two bytes)
- A cyclic check field (two bytes)

The *cyclic check field* consists of several characters that are calculated and stored by the controller as the track is written. By recalculating the cyclic character when data is transferred and then comparing that value to the stored value, errors hopefully can be detected.

There is one index point and one home address point per track. The other items found on a track appear together for each block, although the key area is used with only some access methods.

FIGURE A.13   An IBM track format

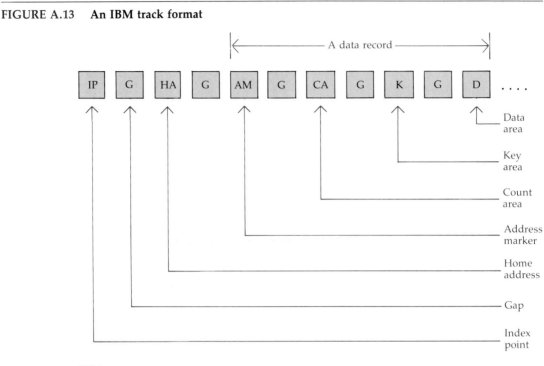

KEY:

IP = Index Point,   1 / track
HA = Home Address,   1 / track (7 bytes)
AM = Address Marker,   1 / block, which marks the beginning of the block
CA = Count Area,   1 / block (11 bytes)
K   = Key Area,   1 / block...optional with variable size
D   = Data Area (subblock)

The size of the data record = AM + CA + K + D + gaps

Address Marker. The *address marker* represents a few bytes written by the controller to designate the beginning of the block that follows. It is usually a relative block number, relative to the beginning of the track. This means that the first block would be designated as block 0, the next as block 1, and so on.

Count Area. The *count area* is an 11-byte overhead that is included with each block. Its contents are shown in Figure A.14.

Count areas are not used with FBA disks, because every data sector is the same size and keys are included with the data record.

FIGURE A.14   The Contents of the Count Area for an IBM Disk

- A flag indicating whether or not the track is usable (one byte).
- The cylinder number (two bytes).
- The head number (two bytes).
- The record number that follows relative to the beginning of the track (one byte).
- The key length—equals zero if record does not use keys (one byte).
- The length of the data block that is to follow (two bytes).
- A cyclic check field (two bytes).

Key Area. Although any file can use the *key area,* it is normally used only with COBOL Indexed and DIRECT files, a subcategory of direct access. In both cases, the access method requires a key value external to the key that may or may not be included in the actual data record. The key area is sometimes called the *key subblock.*

Gaps. *Gaps* separate the track components from one another. The gaps vary in size according to the area they follow on the track. Gaps on FBA drives are of fixed size and are usually shorter than those found on conventional drives.

Data Area or Data Subblock. The *data area,* or *data subblock,* is where the actual records are stored. For sequentially organized files, the size of the data subblock is the PRECL. For keyed files that contain fixed-length, unblocked records, equation 12 shows how to calculate the data subblock size:

$$D = K + L, \tag{12}$$

where K is the key length in bytes and L is the LRECL.

Data Record. A *data record* consists of an address marker, up to three gaps, a count area, the optional key area, and the data subblock area. When a record is transferred, only the data subblock area is actually moved to the CPU for storage in the buffer area of our programs. The controller removes the extra bytes before transferring the block. The *data record length* is the sum of the number of bytes in the key, count, gaps, and data subblock areas.

Count-Data versus Count-Key-Data Storage. Every block is stored with a count area and a data area. If there is no separate key area, the records are in the *count-data* format. The *count-key-data* format uses a separate key area in addition to the above. A record containing keys may or may not be in count-key-data format. It is wrong to assume that because a record has a key, its blocks have an external key area. Choosing to have or not have such an area is up to the programmer. The key area is specified through JCL.

Extents. When records are physically stored on a disk, they are stored in contiguous areas called *extents*. Usually records are stored in one extent, but when sufficient space cannot be found in one area of the disk, additional extents are necessary. The number of extents and how the operating system manages them are transparent to the user and will not be discussed further.

Data Storage Formats. On IBM drives, there are five possible storage formats:

- Fixed-length, unblocked
- Fixed-length, blocked
- Variable-length, unblocked
- Variable-length, blocked
- Undefined

The fixed-length, unblocked format results from unblocked files, where each record is the same size. When the records are blocked, the format is called fixed-length, blocked. Sequential files that are blocked fall into this category.

When a COBOL record description contains an OCCURS DEPENDING clause, the resulting file contains variable-length records and, if the blocking factor is 1, results in an unblocked, variable-length format. If the blocking factor is greater than 1, the file is blocked. An undefined format is for circumstances where a programmer cannot use any of the other three formats.

A.7 Track Capacities

We can determine the number of blocks that will fit on a track by using equation 13:

$$n = \frac{S}{C + K + D} \tag{13}$$

where

C = a constant that varies according to disk drive model and whether keys are used

TABLE A.2   Overhead (C) Associated with IBM 3350 and 3380 DASDs

	IBM 3350	IBM 3380
Without keys	185	480
With keys	267	704

The value of C is used when calculating track capacities.

K = size of the key field, in bytes
D = data subblock size

Table A.2 shows the values for C for two IBM DASDs.

Problem 12. How many unblocked keyed records can fit on a 3350 track if the file uses 10 byte keys and the LRECL is 200 bytes?

Solution. First, we calculate D. For keyed, unblocked records, D is determined by equation 12 as K + L = 10 + 200, or 210 bytes. Now we use equation 13:

$$n = \frac{19,254}{267 + 10 + 210}$$

$$= \frac{19,254}{487}$$

$$= 39.53.$$

However, we must truncate any remainders, so the final answer is 39 blocks.

Problem 13. How many 200-byte records can be stored on a 3350 track if the file is unkeyed and blocked by 10?

Solution.

$$D = 10 \times 200 = 2,000.$$

$$n = \frac{19,254}{185 + 0 + 2,000}$$

$$= \frac{19,254}{2185}$$

$$= 8.81$$

$$= 8.$$

The number of logical records = $10 \times 8 = 80$, because each block contains 10 records.

A.8 SUMMARY

This appendix presented the management of input and output. The operating system component that performs I/O management is the access method. We saw that there are three types of access methods: basic, queued, and virtual.

To make the CPU more efficient, channels, or I/O processors, perform the actual I/O operations. While the channel is waiting for the controller to read or write the record, the CPU may switch to another application in memory, a concept known as *multiprogramming*.

Usually we store database data on a disk, a device that permits locating the records via three addressing methods: by disk address, by relative record number, or by relative track number. The data that is stored on the disks is done so in areas called *data subblocks*. Accompanying each data subblock is a count area, an optional key area, and many overhead areas. To reduce the amount of overhead, we usually block several logical records into one physical record, also called a *block*.

TABLE A.3   Summary of the Important Disk Parameters

This table sumarizes the parameters used in the appendix. The numbers in parentheses are the equation numbers that use the parameters.

a	=	average seek time (6, 8, 9)
B	=	number of blocks to be stored (7, 8, 9)
b	=	blocking factor (10, 11)
BTT	=	block transfer time (6, 7)
C	=	track overhead, accounting for gaps, a count area, and an address marker (13)
c	=	number of cylinders needed to store a file (5, 7, 9)
D	=	size of the data subblock (6, 9, 10, 12, 13)
FTT	=	file transfer time (7, 9)
K	=	size of a key field (12, 13)
L	=	LRECL (10, 11, 12)
m	=	minimum seek time (7, 9)
N	=	PRECL
n	=	number of blocks stored per track (13)
p	=	number of platters per volume (1)
R	=	data transfer rate of the drive (6)
r	=	average seek time (6, 7, 9)
S	=	track capacity (1, 4)
T	=	total rotational delay to read entire file (7, 8)
t	=	number of tracks per surface (1)
U	=	capacity of a DASD surface (2, 3)
V	=	capacity of a volume (1, 3, 4)

TABLE A.4   A Partial List of the Characteristics of Some IBM Disk Drives

Product Code	Characteristics
Drives:	
3310	FBA
3340	Winchester, removable packs, combination architecture
3350	Nonremovable packs
3370	FBA, 2 actuators
3380	High-capacity, nonremovable, costs to $120,000
Controllers:	
3880	(model 23) Cache controller

The last sections examined how long it takes to read a sequential file or a direct access record and how to calculate how many records fit on a track.

Table A.3 summarizes the parameters in the equations presented in the appendix. Table A.4 summarizes the IBM disk hardware discussed.

REVIEW QUESTIONS

1. Explain how multiprogramming works. Describe the roles of buffers, the operating system, the access method, and the channels.
2. When blocks are read by the operating system, where are they stored?
3. What is a disadvantage of blocking?
4. Explain anticipatory buffering.
5. What is the main difference between a basic access method and a queued access method?
6. Describe the three basic access methods.
7. What is the relationship between the logical record length and the physical record length?
8. List the steps and the hardware required to retrieve a record from a disk drive.
9. Where does the channel get its program?
10. List three things a disk controller might do.
11. What is a cache controller?
12. Explain fixed-block architecture and fixed-head architecture.
13. What is the advantage of a fixed-head DASD?
14. List the primary advantage and disadvantage of fixed-block architecture disks.
15. Describe the three quantities we must calculate to determine how much time is required to read a record directly.
16. Explain the differences among minimum, average, and maximum seek times.
17. When using conventional architecture drives, what are the three components of a physical disk address?
18. List four items, other than a data subblock, together with their purposes, that are found on an IBM disk track.
19. List the four ways to specify a disk address.
20. Why would the value of C in equation 13 be larger for keyed files than for nonkeyed fields?

PROBLEMS

1. A file is double-buffered with a logical record length of 128 bytes (including a 10-byte key) and a blocking factor of 10. There are 1,000 records to store.

   a. How many bytes are required for the buffer area?

    b. How many physical I/Os are needed to read 20 records? If the file was sequential, blocked by 10, how would your answer change?

    c. How many logical I/Os? If the file was sequential, blocked by 10, how would your answer change?

    d. What is the PRECL?

2. How long will it take to transfer a sequential file stored on a 3380 if there are 1,000 physical records to be read and 10 blocks per track. The PRECL is 10,000.

3. Use the data in Problem 2, but assume a random access file. Find the block transfer time. The extra key portion of the data subblock isn't transferred.

Use the following data to solve Problems 4 through 10. Assume that a file containing 1,000 employees has been stored on a 3350 using the count-data format without being blocked. The LRECL is 100 bytes long.

4. What is the data subblock size?

5. How many blocks can fit on a 3350 track?

6. How many logical records?

7. How many tracks are necessary to store the complete file?

8. How many cylinders?

9. How many bytes on a track are dedicated to storing data?

10. How many bytes per track would be allocated for overhead?

11–17. Resolve Problems 4 through 10 assuming a blocking factor of 20. (Let t = tracks/surface.) What conclusions do you draw about the benefits of blocking?

B

File Organization and Access

Traditional Storage and Retrieval of Data

This appendix essentially is a continuation of Appendix A. There we saw how data is physically stored on disks, or DASDs. Here we discuss the different ways to organize and access stored data.

B.1 FILE CHARACTERISTICS

As we discuss the ways to organize and access files, we will have occasion to refer to a file's percentage of activity, the ability of the file to provide a desired response time, the volatility of the file, and the file's packing factor, or density.

A file's **percentage of activity** refers to the fraction of records in the file that are accessed for a given processing run. Mathematically we can state this as:

Percentage of activity = [(records added + records deleted + records changed)/(total records)] × 100

Problem 1. **A file contains 10,000 records. On an average updating run, 10 new records are added, 3 are deleted, and 17 are updated. What is the file's percentage of activity?**

Solution.

$$\text{percentage of activity} = [(\text{records added} + \text{records deleted}$$
$$+ \text{records changed})/(\text{total records})] \times 100$$
$$= [(10 + 3 + 17)/(10,000)] \times 100$$
$$= (30/10000) \times 100$$
$$= .003 \times 100$$
$$= .3\%.$$

The **response time** is the time elapsed between the request for information by a user and the receipt of that information. The response time for a sequentially accessed file is much longer than that for a directly accessed one. In fact, while the former's response time might be measured in minutes, the latter's time is probably in milliseconds. Response times are usually a systems design criterion set by an end user. For example, an accounts payable manager might set a response time of less than 10 seconds for the retrieval of an invoice, while the human resource management supervisor might set a response time of a week or more for a report on employee absenteeism.

Volatility refers to the attempt to measure the growth or shrinkage of a file in terms of how many records are typically added to or deleted from it. Mathematically volatility can be defined as:

$$\text{Volatility} = (\text{records added} + \text{records deleted})/(\text{total records}).$$

A **static** file has low volatility, and a **dynamic** file has a high rate of additions and deletions.

To compute a file's **packing factor,** or **density,** we divide the number of records stored by the number allocated. Problem 2 gives an example.

Problem 2. **A file that was allocated for 10,000 records presently has 500 records stored. What is its packing factor?**

Solution.

$$\text{packing factor} = \text{number of actual records/total number of records allocated}$$
$$= 500/10,000$$
$$= .05, \text{ or } 5\%.$$

Problem 3. **A file contains 8,000 records. How many locations must be reserved if a packing factor of .70 is required?**

Solution.

$$\text{locations reserved} = 8,000/.70 = 11,428.6 = 11429.$$

Now that we have defined these terms let's see how we apply them.

B.2 FILE ORGANIZATION VERSUS FILE ACCESS: AN INTRODUCTION

When a database management system isn't used to store and retrieve data, we must resort to conventional file processing techniques. Figure B.1 shows that there are five ways to organize data but only two ways to process it.

Despite the fact that many programmers and analysts discuss organization and access as if they were one concept, there is a fundamental difference between the two terms. *Organization* refers to the way the data is physically stored on the I/O device and how the records are logically related to one another. *Access* refers to how the data is retrieved or processed.

Access

We begin our discussion by describing the two kinds of access: direct and sequential.

Direct Access. *Direct access* means that any record can be retrieved independently based on a predictable relationship between the primary key value of the desired record and the location of that record on the disk. *Independent* means that the ability to retrieve subsequent records is in no way dependent on the record previously retrieved.

FIGURE B.1   **File Organization versus Access**

Organization	Access	
	Sequential	**Direct**
Sequential	X	*
Partitioned	X	X
Indexed	X	X
Direct:		
Direct access	X	
Hashed access		X
Virtual	X	X

*Only with difficulty.

The choice of organization can affect the ability of the information system to retrieve the data stored there.

Suppose an organization has four vendors to store in a VENDOR master file. Assume the vendor's code is unique, is used as the primary key, and the records have been stored. As an example of direct retrieval, assume an end user has processed VENDOR records with codes 100, 105, 107, and 103, in that order. The records were not processed in a logical sequence (that is, the numerical ordering was random, rather than sorted), and only the desired records were accessed.

We use direct access for situations where there is a low percentage of activity (less than 10 percent), high volatility, and/or a need for the shortest possible response time. These situations are most often found with on-line systems, which explains why these kinds of systems make heavy use of direct access. Contrast these characteristics with those of sequential access.

Sequential access. *Sequential access* means that records can be processed only in their key sequence (logical order of the records' sort keys). When a file is sequentially processed, each record is read in succession based on the sort key of the file. If the end user retrieved the vendors sequentially, the only sequence possible would be 100, 103, 105, and 107. Furthermore, if vendor 103's record has just been accessed, the only record that can be processed next is that belonging to vendor 105; we can read only the next logical (and usually physical) record. Or, we can say that the ability to process a "next" record depends on which record was previously processed. This is not true with direct processing, in which we can process records in any sequence regardless of which record was previously retrieved.

We use sequential access when there is a high percentage of activity (over 10 percent), low volatility, and a long response time. These situations are often encountered in batch processing; hence we frequently use sequential access for master files for those types of systems.

We have alluded to the terms *logical* and *physical* orderings on several occasions. Let's see what these terms mean.

Physical sequential organization and processing means that the records are physically stored in sequence according to their key values and that to produce the records in key sequence, a program must physically read each record in succession.

Figure B.2 shows a VENDOR file that is physically organized in key sequence according to the keys discussed earlier. Notice that vendor 100 physically precedes vendor 103, which physically precedes vendor 105, and so on. If each record is consecutively read in succession, the logical order of the vendor codes will be preserved and the keys will be presented in sequential order.

Logical sequential organization and processing means that while the records are not physically stored in key sequence, the logical order is preserved by other means. Look at Figure B.3. The records are not physically organized by key values, but each record has a *pointer* attached to it, a field that leads from one

FIGURE B.2   A File in Logical and Physical Order

This file is in logical sequential order because the output would be in order numerically. It's in physical sequential order because the physical order of the records matches the desired logical one.

FIGURE B.3   A Logical Sequential File

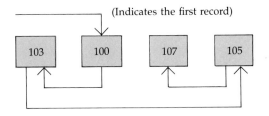

(Indicates the first record)

Even though the records are not physically in sequential order, by following the pointers, indicated by arrows, the logical order is preserved.

related record to the next. The arrow attached to each record represents the pointer and indicates the record that logically follows the current one. Thus, while the physical order is vendor 103, then 100, followed by 107, and, finally, 105, the pointers can be followed to logically process the records in key sequence.

Beginning with the second record, the arrow pointer leads to the first record where vendor number 103 is stored. Next, we follow the pointer from vendor 103's record to that of vendor 105, which in turn points to vendor 107. Thus, the user's perceived order is 100, 103, 105, and 107, which is logically correct despite the fact that the records were not physically in order by their keys. Two of the organizations discussed next—indexed and virtual—provide the ability to do logical sequential processing even though the records are not physically in key sequence order.

Organization

There are five ways to organize IBM-based DASD data:

- Sequential
- Partitioned
- Indexed sequential

- Direct
- Virtual

With sequential organization, this section will introduce you to the five organizations and give you insight into how you can process such files. The remainder of the appendix discusses the individual organizations in depth.

The records are almost always physically stored in sequence based on the file's **sort key** (also called a **control key**). Before the records are stored, they must be sorted. If this isn't done, there will be no inherent order to the records.

Because adding, deleting, or changing sequential records requires rewriting the entire file, we generally use sequential organization only if we anticipate a high percentage of activity.

Partitioned files (data sets) are divided into small units called **members.** Each member has a unique name that is used to directly access it. Within a member, individual records are organized sequentially. Typically, this organization is used for storing sequential data like programs, subprograms, and table files. For example, we might store all the subprograms for a given system as a partitioned data set, where each member is one subprogram. Then, when the system is run, the access method can load each subprogram as the main program requires it. Because partitioned data sets play only a minor role in database systems, we won't discuss them further.

We use direct organization when we must access a record in the shortest possible time or when the percentage of activity is low. Direct organization means that there is a predictable relationship between a primary key value and the location of the corresponding record on the disk. The disk location can be specified in any of the four ways discussed in Appendix A. There are two categories of direct organization: directly addressable and hashed. **Directly addressable** means that the primary key value of a record directly provides the corresponding disk address of the record. For example, if an employee's number is always six digits long, it could be used as a relative record number (RRN) and the employee records would be stored at the record number corresponding to the employee's number. Consequently, the employees would end up being stored sequentially by their key values; that is, employee number 3 would be at record 3, employee number 5 at record 5, and so on. This is quite flexible, because records can be accessed sequentially (since the records will physically be in employee sequence) or directly.

The other category of direct organization is called **hashed,** or **indirect.** Here the programmer codes an algorithm that transforms the primary key into the disk address of the record. Using hashed addressing precludes accessing the records sequentially, but it is used more often because we cannot usually use the primary key directly as a disk address.

Unfortunately, while hashed organization is quite flexible, IBM has left implementation of the routine that converts data keys into disk addresses to the programmer, and such routines are not easy to write. Another problem is that it cannot be used in high-percentage-of-activity situations, where it is necessary to print or update an entire file.

We use indexed sequential organization in situations where records must be accessed sequentially and directly. It is suitable for situations where the percentage of activity is high or low. With indexed sequential organization, records are stored in a sequential-like order that permits sequential retrieval, but several indexes are maintained to permit direct retrieval of individual records. While processing the records sequentially is no slower than when using conventional sequential or queued access methods, direct retrieval times may be considerably longer than those found when using direct organization and access.

Recall that adding records to a sequential file requires a complete rewrite of the file (unless the record is added at the end of the file). To eliminate this problem, indexed sequential files have two overflow areas specifically designed to store additions to the file. Unfortunately, as these areas fill up, the performance of the file declines. Also, indexed organization is highly hardware dependent; if we change the disk drive characteristics, we will have to perform a major reorganization of the file.

Virtual organization (called *Virtual Storage Access Method,* or *VSAM,* by IBM), like the indexed form, permits both sequential and direct access of records. Unlike indexed organization, however, virtual organization offers hardware independence and does not suffer performance problems as records are added to a file. Hardware independence is possible because the records are organized on the DASD by their **relative byte displacement** from the beginning of the file. Changing disk drive models will in no way alter a record's byte displacement from the beginning of the file. Because of VSAM's flexibility and speed, IS departments that use IBM computer systems tend to use it for most of their file processing needs.

B.3   SEQUENTIAL ORGANIZATION AND ACCESS: KEY SEQUENCE STORAGE

Sequentially stored records are characterized by several features. These are summarized in Table B.1.

Sequential files are generally used to store table data or as temporary work files. Database management systems use sequential organization to store journal files. We do not usually use sequential organization for master files unless we are processing a very high percentage of the records on any given run, such as we do with batch systems like payroll. It is inappropriate to use sequential organization for on-line applications, because the response time is unacceptable. With sequential access, the elapsed time might be in terms of hours or even days, since such files are often off-line and may need to be retrieved from secure areas where the off-line media are kept.

TABLE B.1   Characteristics of Sequential Organization and Access

Characteristics	Advantages	Disadvantages
The physical order is the same as the logical order	Records can be blocked to save storage requirements	Slow to update with low file activity
The records are usually in key sequence order based on a sort key field	Little disk space is wasted (no holes)	Adding/deleting records requires complete file rewrite
When stored on a DASD, the records are usually stored "without keys," i.e., count-data format	Rapid access to next record	Slow retrieval
To retrieve the nth record, the previous n − 1 records must be processed	Relative ease of programming	Transactions must be batched and stored

Sequential Organization

Sequentially organized files can be fixed or variable in length and are formatted without keys. When the file is created, sufficient room on the disk must be allocated to store the maximum number of records that the file will ever contain. Once this maximum number is determined, we calculate the number of cylinders necessary to store the records. In Appendix A, we saw how this can be done. Overestimation of cylinder requirements results in wasted disk space, but underestimation can result in abnormal endings from which it may be difficult to recover.

Problem 4. **A PURCHASE-ORDER master file will have a maximum of 10,000 records, each 512 bytes long. It is to be blocked by 10. Assuming 3350 disk drives, how many cylinders are required for the file?**

Solution. Since this topic was discussed in detail in Appendix A, we won't go into the theory behind the solution.
We can store:

$$\text{int } (19{,}254)/(185 + 5120) = 3 \text{ blocks per track.}$$

This represents 30 logical records per track, so 30×30, or 900, logical records can be stored per cylinder (there are 30 tracks per 3350 cylinder). Thus, we need a total of ceil $(10{,}000/900) = 12$ cylinders.

As the first item shown in Table B.1 suggests, the sequence of the records on the disk must match the desired order of the user of the sequential file. Unless pointers are used, the physical order will match the logical one. One implication

---

FIGURE B.4   A Partial Conceptualization of a PURCHASE-ORDER Master File

Record Number	Purchase Order Number	Date of Issue	Vendor Code
1	1	01/04/XX	103
2	4	01/04/XX	123
3	7	01/09/XX	103
4	9	01/10/XX	133

FIGURE B.5   Sequential Organization of the PURCHASE-ORDER Master File from Figure B.4

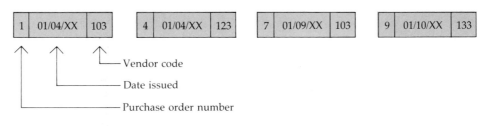

The file is both physically and logically sorted on purchase order number.

---

of this is that each sequence forces a complete sorting of the file, resulting in a new file, which subsequently will be used to produce the report.

Figure B.4 shows a portion of the PURCHASE-ORDER master file as a director of purchasing might envision it. The logical sequence is by purchase order number. Figure B.5 shows how that file might be sequentially organized on a 3350 disk drive. Notice that the order of the records on the disk is in purchase order number sequence; the physical order matches the logical one.

If the purchasing director wants a report in a sequence other than by purchase order number, we will have to resort the file to a temporary file, then read the temporary file to produce the report.

Processing Sequential Files

A sequentially organized file is almost always processed in a sequential manner—reading one record after another in key sequence order. Because a sequential file can be physically sequenced in only one way, difficulties arise when users request a sequence other than the physical one. The usual solution is to create a new, temporary file that is sorted in the desired sequence.

B.4   INDEXED SEQUENTIAL ORGANIZATION AND ACCESS: FLEXIBILITY WITH A PRICE

When all or most of the records in a file are processed, we choose sequential organization. Organized this way, however, individual records cannot be accessed should the need arise. If selected records must be accessed in the shortest possible time, we use direct access. Unfortunately, this decision means that records cannot be processed sequentially. If both sequential and direct capabilities are necessary, and if it is acceptable that the system run a bit slower when directly accessing records, indexed sequential is a better choice. A file organized in this way is initially stored in physical key sequence to allow sequential access, but it also has two kinds of indexes (actually three, but we won't discuss the third) that permit direct access.

To use an indexed organization, the access method organizes the file with a **prime data area** and several indexes. The data records are initially stored sequentially, are formatted with keys, may or may not be blocked, and can be fixed or variable length. If the records are blocked, each logical record must contain a key. When records are stored, each track is completely filled before the next one is used. This means that additions to the file will cause problems, since there is no room on the tracks to accommodate the additions. Because of

---

FIGURE B.6   An Indexed Sequential File Format

Track	Cylinder 2	Cylinder 3	Cylinder 4	Cylinder 5	Cylinder 6
0		Track index	Track index		
1	Cylinder index				
2					
3		Prime data area		General overflow area	
4					
5					
6					
7					
8					
9		Cylinder overflow area			

One track per cylinder has been allocated for a cylinder overflow area. Two cylinders are reserved for a general overflow area, which is used when one of the cylinder overflow areas is full.

the way the indexed sequential method handles additions, the organization results in a logical sequential order, not a physical one. As Figure B.6 shows, storage of the actual data records is done in an area designated as the primary data area.

Additions to the file go in one of three places: on the track where they belong, in a **cylinder overflow area,** or in the **independent (or general) overflow area.** Records that end up in either of the overflow areas cannot be blocked. IBM's Indexed Sequential Access Method (ISAM) automatically handles the tasks involved in placing records in these areas. Although once a record has been placed into an overflow area the file is no longer physically in key sequence, by using a **link field,** which is automatically attached to each overflow record as it is stored, a logical sequencing of the records can be maintained.

The two index types, *track* and *cylinder,* are updated by ISAM as records are added to the file and are used only when the application accesses records directly. Whereas there is only one cylinder index per file, there are several track indexes, one per cylinder. One way to address a record discussed in Appendix A is to provide the disk controller with the physical address of the record. This address consists of a cylinder number, a head number, and a record number or key value. ISAM uses the cylinder index and track indexes to determine the first two components of a record's address. Let's look at the prime data area, the cylinder index, the track indexes, and the overflow areas and see how they function together.

Prime Data Area

The records are initially stored in key sequence within the prime data area using the count-key-data format. As records are stored, each track is completely filled before the next one is used. As you can see in Figure B.6, the primary data area begins at the first complete cylinder following the cylinder index and extends over several cylinders, but it excludes some tracks within each cylinder, which are designated as the **cylinder overflow area.** A default value of 10 percent of the total tracks within a cylinder is reserved for this area, which is where new or existing records will be stored as records are added. Since the sample cylinders in the figure contain 10 tracks each, 1 track (10 percent of 10) from each is reserved for this purpose.

The Cylinder Index

The cylinder index is actually a small file that is stored on the cylinder prior to the primary data area and uses the count-key-data format. Each index entry, or record, is a pair of numbers; (K,A), where A represents a cylinder address and K the highest-valued key at that address. There are as many cylinder index entries as there are cylinders necessary to store the file.

This index is used in conjunction with the track indexes only when directly accessing an ISAM record. It provides the access method with the cylinder number portion of the desired record's address.

Figure B.7 shows a portion of our conceptual VENDOR file. Figure B.8 shows how that file would be organized using ISAM. In Figure B.8, it is assumed that the file was stored on cylinders 7 and 8. Notice that the records are stored in key sequence according to vendor code: track 1 of cylinder 7 contains the values 100, 103, and 105, while the next track stores vendors 107, 110, and 115.

Because the file requires two cylinders, there are two records in the cylinder index. The first entry contains the pair of numbers (126,0703) and the next one (140,0802). These mean that the highest-valued vendor code on cylinder 7 is 126, while 140 is the highest one on cylinder 8 (the 03 and 02 that follow the cylinder numbers—07 and 08, respectively—refer to the track number within the cylinder where the highest-valued key can be found).

Assume we are trying to directly access vendor number 123. The first component of its physical disk address is the cylinder number where the record can be found. To determine this, we serially compare the value found in the key area component for each cylinder entry against the desired key value. When a key area value that contains a value greater than or equal to the desired key is found, the process is finished and the accompanying data area value will be the desired cylinder number. In our example, the first key value encountered is 126. Since this is greater than 123, the process is terminated and cylinder 7 is used as the cylinder number component of vendor 123's record. Next, the access method needs the correct track within the cylinder. This is found by searching the other index: the track index.

FIGURE B.7   A Portion of a Conceptual Representation of a VENDOR Master File

Vendor Code	Vendor Name
100	Camus, Inc.
103	Abrams Corp.
105	Davis Brothers
107	Consolidated Coal
110	Babcock and Williams
115	Xerox Corp.
120	IBM
123	Baker and Sons
126	Lewis, Inc.
128	Acme Uniforms
129	Brown Fabricating
136	Kern Supplies, Inc.
137	Kolinski Plumbing
140	Consolidated Supplies Co.

FIGURE B.8   An Indexed Sequential VENDOR File

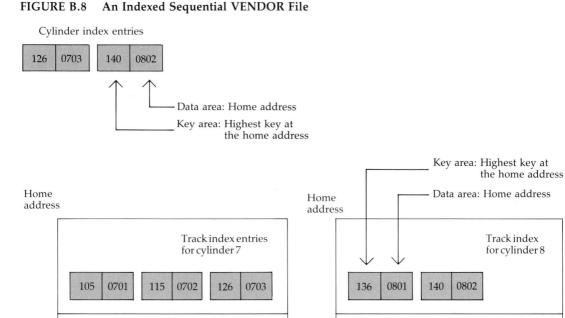

The cylinder entries would be located in the first cylinder of the file (see Figure B.7). Notice that the last record in the first cylinder has key value 126, which matches the entry in the cylinder index for location 0703. This is also the value for the last track entry for cylinder 7.

Track Indexes

Each indexed file has one track index per cylinder, which is physically located beginning with the first track of each cylinder. There are as many track indexes as there are cylinders necessary to store the file—two in our example. Each record in the index is again stored using the count-key-data format, with each key area storing the highest key value on the track whose value is carried as the data area of the index entry. There as many records for each index as there are usable primary data area tracks on that cylinder. For example, cylinder 7 uses three tracks, thus, there are three records in the track index for that cylinder.

Look at the three index records in Figure B.8. The first pair of (key, data area) values is (105,0701), meaning that vendor number 105 is the highest-valued key on track 1 of cylinder 7. Similarly, the pair of numbers (115,0702) found as the next entry means that the highest-valued key on track 2 of the cylinder is 115.

Let's continue the quest to directly find vendor 123. Recall that we have already determined the correct cylinder (cylinder 7) by searching the cylinder index. Now the track number (head) within cylinder 7 is required. ISAM will order the disk controller to execute a seek to cylinder 7, where a sequential search of the track index records found there will begin. This search will compare the key area values against the desired value (123) until a greater-than or equal-to condition is detected. In our example, the search begins by first comparing the key area value of 105 to 123. Since 105 is less than 123, the search continues to the next record in the index. This time, the key area contains 115; the value is still less than 123. The third entry has a key value of 126. Because this value is greater than 123, the search stops. The data area value is 0703, indicating that the desired record (if it exists) should be on track 3 of cylinder 7.

The access mechanism will then be ordered to switch on the third read/write head within cylinder 7, and the controller will wait until a key area on the track comes around that has a value greater than or equal to the desired vendor code, 123.

Overflow Areas

New records are placed in one of three locations: in the prime data area on the track where they belong, in the cylinder overflow area for that cylinder, or in the independent overflow area. Records stored in the prime data area are said to be at their **home address.** Deciding where the new record goes depends on which of three rules applies:

1. If the new record has a key value greater than that of the last record on a track but less than the last one on the next track, it will be assigned to the prime data area of the next track, bumping the last record on the track to the cylinder overflow area.

2. If the new record has a key value less than that of the last record on a track but greater than that of the first record on the same track, it is placed in the prime data area. Again, this causes the former "last" record on the track to be bumped to the cylinder overflow area.

3. If the record key is greater than that of the last record on a track but less than some previous overflow record from that track, the record is assigned to the cylinder overflow area, and appropriate pointers are adjusted to maintain a logical key sequencing.

Any attempt to store a record in the cylinder overflow area that does not fit because the area is full will result in the record being stored in the independent overflow area at the end of the file. Because of the need to sequentially process an ISAM file, all records in the overflow areas contain pointers that logically connect the records in order.

Let's see what these rules mean by looking at some examples. Note that the discussion is simplified; the actual processing steps are much more involved than our discussion will indicate.

First, let's see what will happen if we add a vendor with a key value of 106. Look at Figure B.9. Because the new value is greater than that of the last key on track 1 of cylinder 7 (105) but less than that of the last record on track 2 (115), it will be stored on track 2 of cylinder 7, causing vendor 115 to be bumped to the cylinder overflow area (COA). Vendor 110 is now the highest-valued vendor

---

FIGURE B.9   The ISAM VENDOR File after Adding Vendor 106

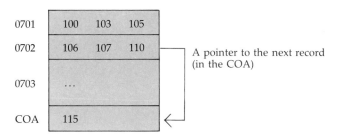

This is an example of using ISAM addition rule 1.

on track 2, and a pointer has been added to it; it points to the record that was bumped, vendor 115. At this time, the second record in the track index for cylinder 7 will have to be updated, because the last record on track 2 now contains a key value of 110.

A situation illustrating the second rule is the addition of vendor 108, which is shown in Figure B.10. Its vendor code is less than 110 but greater than 107, so according to rule 2 it should be stored on track 2, causing vendor 110 to be bumped. The new record will be the last one on track 2 and must point to vendor 110, which is now in the COA. Notice that 110 still points to vendor 115 even though 110 is now in the COA.

FIGURE B.10   The ISAM File after Adding Vendor 108

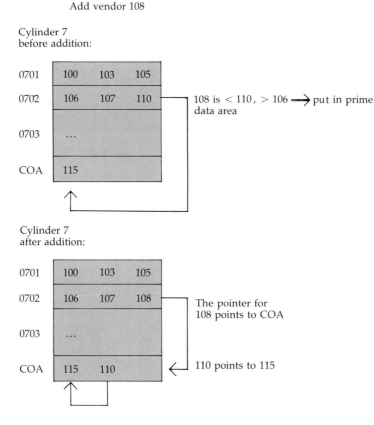

This is an example of using ISAM addition rule 2.

FIGURE B.11   The ISAM File after Adding Vendor 112

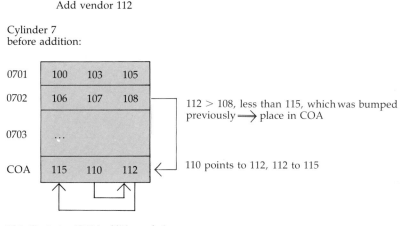

This illustrates ISAM addition rule 3.

The third situation can be demonstrated by next adding vendor 112, a record with a key value between the two already stored in the cylinder overflow area: 110 and 115. Look at Figure B.11. The link field for 110 now points to 112 and 112's to 115.

When a record cannot fit in the cylinder overflow area because it is full, it is stored in the independent overflow area. This results in a deterioration of the performance of the system, because finding records in the independent overflow area requires a seek over a substantial number of cylinders, while records in the cylinder overflow area can be found merely by switching on a different head.

B.5   DIRECT ORGANIZATION

As we have seen, direct organization means that there is a predictable relationship between a primary key value and the location of that record on the disk. When a hashing routine is used, the physical ordering of records on the disk appears random, which helps explain why the word *random* is sometimes used when describing direct organization.

If the key values are directly usable as disk addresses, the data records will be sequentially stored according to their key values. This is called **direct addressing** and, if this is the case, records can be accessed sequentially or directly and will not appear to be in random order. Unfortunately, this is not the normal situation. Usually we discover that the primary key values are spread out over

TABLE B.2   **Direct File Organization Characteristics**

Characteristics	Advantages	Disadvantages
The physical order differs from the logical one	Quick updating for low-activity files	Records usually not blocked
Retrieval of the nth record can be done immediately	Transactions entered as they occur and without sorting	Many holes
The records have a primary key	Adding/deleting involves writing only one record	No sequential access
The records are usually stored "with keys"	Fast response time	Handling synonyms
		Performance may slow down with a volatile file and many synonyms

too large a range, that they are nonnumeric, or that some other problem prevents us from using the primary key value as a disk address. In this case, a **hashing routine** that transforms the record's primary key value into a suitable disk address must be written. This is the situation that leads to an apparent random distribution of records.

We use a direct organization when the fastest access to a particular record is necessary, a situation encountered with on-line applications. It is also appropriate to use direct organization and access when the percentage of activity is low. Recall that direct processing means that any "next" record can be processed rather than always having to retrieve the next physical record, as with sequential access. When the activity percentage is low, it is quite likely that the distribution of record access will be randomly spread out over the entire data space. Thus, we can't predict which record will be next, and direct organization is appropriate.

Direct organization can be compared along the same lines as those for sequential files. This is shown in Table B.2. As we discuss direct organization and access, we will occasionally refer to these characteristics.

Physical Organization

Direct records are formatted with keys and, unless we can use direct addressing, cannot be blocked. Figure B.12 shows what the file organization for our VENDOR file might look like if we use direct organization. Each vendor's disk address is a RRN equal to its vendor code value.

As you can see, the records are physically stored in key sequence, although there are some gaps (holes) indicating unassigned numbers. Contrast this organization with that shown in Figure B.13, where vendor key values were transformed by means of a hashing routine, which we will examine later. Now records seem to be randomly distributed all over the storage space.

FIGURE B.12   **A Direct Organization of a VENDOR File (see Figure B.7) Using Direct Addressing**

Record Number	Vendor Code	Record Number	Vendor Code
100	100		
101		121	
102		122	
103	103	123	123
104		124	
105	105	125	
106		126	126
107	107	127	
108		128	128
109		129	129
110	110	130	
111		131	
112		132	132
113		133	
114		134	
115	115	135	
116		136	136
117		137	137
118		138	
119		139	
120	120	140	140

Only the vendor codes are shown with each record.

FIGURE B.13   **A Direct Organization of a VENDOR File Using a Hypothetical Hashed Addressing Scheme**

Record Number	Vendor Code
1	133
18	100
76	103
93	105
107	128
110	107
117	140
122	133
130	110
136	135
138	115
150	132
158	123
200	126

Direct Addressing and Processing

Occasionally we encounter situations where the primary keys for a file are numeric, unique, without gaps, and fairly uniformly distributed. Under this circumstances, direct addressing and access are possible. This is the situation illustrated in Figure B.12.

Indirect Addressing and Processing

More often than not, direct addressing is not possible and **indirect addressing** is needed. If the keys have many gaps, are alphanumeric, or are in some other way incompatible with the addressing schemes presented in Appendix A, a complicated hashing technique is required.

Hashing Routines. A **hashing routine** is a procedure for converting a data key into a disk address based on a mathematical transformation of the key value. Sometimes the routine is called a **randomizing routine.** Figure B.14 shows a conceptualization of this routine, which must be coded by the programmer when using IBM mainframes.

Hash functions should possess these characteristics:

- They should be simple to use.
- They should waste as little disk space as possible.
- Synonyms should be minimized.
- The average number of disk I/Os should be minimized.

First, hashed routines should be easy to program. There is no point in using a sophisticated routine if there is a simpler one that will work. If the vendor numbers are unique and there aren't many unused numbers, we use those digits as a relative record number, as we did earlier, and will not even need a hashing routine.

Next, we do not want the records to be spread out on the disk with many gaps or holes. If eventually there was going to be 10,000 VENDOR records, we would have to plan for this by allocating room for all 10,000. If we currently stored only 100 of them, there would be 100 VENDOR records spread out over 10,000 locations; the packing factor would be only 10 percent.

FIGURE B.14   A Conceptual Model of a Hashing Routine

Synonyms are records whose key values generate the same disk address. When this happens, we must develop ways to handle the synonyms. As we shall see, this can be quite complex, so it is advantageous to avoid synonyms.

Finally, we do not want to make the access mechanism perform a physical seek unless it is absolutely necessary. If the disk must make several seeks to find the desired record, the time required to retrieve the record will be excessive.

Hashing Methods. For any of the four addressing methods of Appendix A, the disk address can be generated by using one of two popular hashing routines: **prime division/remainder** or **folding.**

The **prime division/remainder** method, sometimes called the **modulus** method, is the more common technique. For the relative record number addressing scheme, the algorithm can be represented as: "Divide the data key by the closest prime number $>=$ the total number of records. Use the remainder as the RRN."

Problem 5. **A hashing routine is to be written to load 1,000 512-byte purchase order records to a 3350 disk drive. Each record has a nine-byte key and is to use the relative record addressing technique. Assume an 80 percent packing factor. Determine a suitable divisor for the hashing routine.**

Solution. When we allow for the packing factor in determining the total number of tracks, we modify the algorithm to read" . . . $<=$ the number of records . . . ." With an 80 percent packing factor, we must determine the closest prime number less than 1,250, because 1,000/.8 = 1,250. This number is 1.249.

Problem 6. **Using the answer to Problem 5, what relative record number would be assigned to purchase order 31406?**

Solution.

$$
\begin{array}{r}
25 \\
1249\,\overline{)31406} \\
2498 \\
\overline{6426} \\
6245 \\
\overline{181}\ \ \text{(remainder)}
\end{array}
$$

The record will be found (or stored) at relative record 181.

If using the relative track number (RTN) plus key addressing scheme, a common rule for generating the disk address is again modified: "Divide the key by the closest prime $>=$ the required number of tracks. The remainder will be the RTN. Use the record's key as the second component of the address." We leave an example of this as Problem 8 at the end of the appendix.

The other hashing technique is called **folding**—a process in which the primary key is split into two parts, the parts added, and the result, or a portion of the result, used as the address. Alternatively, the results can be combined with the modulus method to generate the final address.

As an example of folding, suppose purchase order number 1234567 is to be transformed into a four-digit relative record address. We could add the first four digits to the last three to arrive at the desired RRN: $1234 + 567 = 1801$.

Regardless of which method is used, synonyms occur, which results in **collisions**—duplicate disk addresses. Consider the example in Figure B.15. Employees are being stored in an unblocked direct file, and the RRN method is to be used. The primary key is a 5-byte employee number, and there are 100 employees to store. The first employee (Figure B.15(a)) is number 207.

The closest prime number greater than or equal to 100 is 101; hence it is used as the denominator. The hashing routine results in an RRN of 5. Figure B.15(a) shows the record in its home address, the address generated by the hashing routine. The next employee is employee 108. That key hashes to an RRN of 7, and the record is stored there. (See Figure B.15(b)). When the address for the third employee, employee 308, is determined, it turns out to be the same as for employee 207: RRN 5.

The fact that employee number 308 results in the same disk address as employee 207 means their keys are synonyms and the records are said to be **in collision.** Because two records cannot occupy the same RRN location, one record must be left in its home address and the other moved to an **overflow address.**

FIGURE B.15   An Example of Hashed Addressing

(a) An example of a prime division remainder hashing algorithm where the primary key value is divided by 101, and the remainder used as the RRN

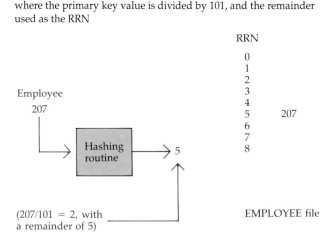

FIGURE B.15   (concluded)

(b) Adding another record to the EMPLOYEE file. Now add number
108. The remainder is now 7, so the employee is stored at RRN 8

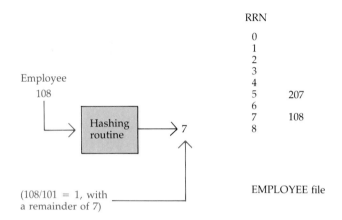

(108/101 = 1, with
a remainder of 7)

(c) An example of a collision. Now try to add employee number 308.
The remainder is again 5, but there is already an EMPLOYEE record
at that location. Keys 308 and 207 are synonyms, and their addresses
are in collision with each other

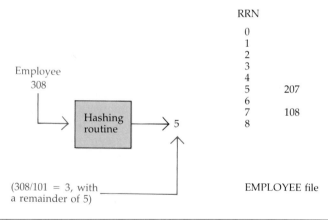

(308/101 = 3, with
a remainder of 5)

Handling Synonyms. It is up to the programmer to devise schemes that will
properly store and then retrieve the synonyms. There are three ways to process
synonyms:

- Use a progressive overflow methodology

- Use a separate overflow area
- Use buckets

One frequently used method is **the progressive overflow** (sometimes called **open addressing**) technique. When this is used, the synonym record is placed into the next available position. In our example, the next available position is RRN 6, so employee 308 would be stored there.

If we perform the hashing routine for employee 409, we will find that it too generates RRN 5. However, location 5, the home address, is already used, so we next try RRN 6. Employee 308 is stored there. The next RRN is 7, but employee 108 is already occupying that address. It isn't until RRN 8 that we reach an available address.

Records should always be stored in their home addresses whenever possible. Employee 311, when stored, results in an RRN of 8. The record that is already there (employee 409) resulted from a collision at location 5. Because employee 311's home address is 8, it "deserves" to be stored there. The record already at RRN 8 should be moved to the next available location: location 9. This is starting to be difficult to visualize, let alone process!

A better way to handle overflow records is to use pointers to a separate overflow area on the disk, a technique called the **overflow area method.** As we saw with indexed organization, a pointer is a field in the data record that indicates the location of a related record. In this case, a pointer would be stored in the record at its home address and would point to the location of the record that also belongs there but was stored elsewhere because of a collision.

Figure B.16 shows that each employee record has now expanded to include such a pointer field. In the previous example, three employee values hashed to RRN 5: 207, 308, and 409. We will use the overflow area method to handle these collisions.

Each record now includes a pointer that associates a synonym record to the next related one. Sometimes the pointer is from a record in the EMPLOYEE file to one in the OVERFLOW file and at other times points from one OVERFLOW record to another. The result is a simple list structure of the type discussed in Chapter 3, with the "first" pointer being carried in the EMPLOYEE file and "next" pointers carried in records in the OVERFLOW file. For example, employee 207 has a pointer value of 1, indicating that there is a synonym, and it can be found at RRN 1 in the OVERFLOW file. RRN 1 in the OVERFLOW file is employee 308, the first synonym. The pointer value associated with that employee is RRN 2, which is the RRN for employee 409, the last synonym.

Using pointers to a separate file, or to a separate area of the same file, is much more efficient than the progressive overflow method and is the one most often used.

The final way to handle synonyms is to use buckets. A **bucket** can be considered a data subblock where the block contains several logical records— in

FIGURE B.16   Using Pointers to Connect Synonyms

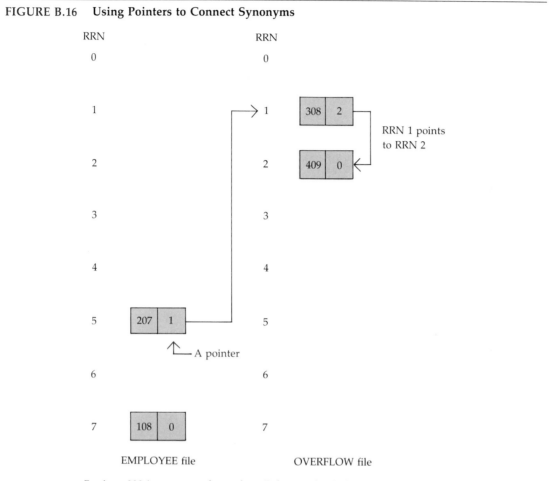

Employee 308 is a synonym for employee 5, because they both result in RRN 5. RRN 5 in the employee file contains a pointer to RRN 1 in the overflow file. Similarly, 409 results in yet another collision, so it too is placed in the overflow file, and a pointer form 308 to 409 is used to physically connect the synonyms. A pointer value of 0 indicates that there are no more pointers to be followed.

effect, a blocking mechanism. Instead of storing single records at a given RRN, we take advantage of the blocking concept and establish fixed-sized buckets at each RRN location, each of which can hold several logical records. If several records can be stored in a bucket, several synonyms can fit into a single subblock. This can result in a lot of wasted space, because room will be left at each disk address for several synonyms. Since synonyms seldom occur, there will be many buckets only partially filled. On the other hand, the use of buckets makes the distribution of free space more uniform and decreases the likelihood of collisions.

Reducing Collisions. There are two ways to reduce collisions:

- Reduce the packing factor
- Improve the hashing routine

Recall that the ratio of records stored to the maximum number of records allowed is the file's packing factor. By artificially making the total number of records allowed quite high when the file is initially created, the packing factor is made smaller and the probability of a collision is reduced. The hashing routine used in the example divided the primary key by 101, the closest prime to the number of records. When a number is divided by n, the range of remainders (the RRNs) will be 0 through n − 1. We divide a number by 2, and the remainders will always be 0 or 1. If the key is divided by a larger number, the range of remainders will be greater and the chances of a collision therefore reduced.

In the example, the chances of a collision would decrease if the denominator were made larger than 101—503, for example. Of course, this would artificially increase the size of the file and might generate quite a large amount of reserved but unused disk space. We must consider both the advantages and the disadvantages of reducing the packing factor.

The other way to reduce collisions is to use "better" hashing routines. By trying different prime numbers as divisors and dividing each into a sample of, say, 1,000 employee keys and then plotting the resulting RRNs looking for collisions, we might be able to come across a more suitable divisor. This technique can be formalized and is called a **digit analysis.**

Random Access: An Analysis. As stated in the beginning of this section, random access is not very efficient when there is a high activity ratio. A typical application that has such a ratio is one that simply prints a detailed listing of the complete file in key order. To print all the employees in our hashed file in employee order would be very difficult, because we access records sequentially only by their disk address—RRN 1, RRN 2, and so on—or we can use a hashing routine on the keys. Following the RRN addresses will result in a truly random sequence of employees, so this is not a particularly effective approach unless we want to sort the resulting data.

The other way is equally disheartening, since each employee's number must be known in advance. Here each number is passed, in sequence, to the hashing routine, which then waits for the access method to retrieve the record corresponding to the result of the routine.

Random access is an excellent choice for low-activity updating but a poor choice for sequential applications. Why can't we have an access method that has good updating characteristics but also provides sequential processing capabilities? Earlier we discussed the indexed organization, but while it offers these qualities, it suffers from efficiency problems as its overflow areas fill up and is highly dependent on the actual disk drive model used. The Virtual Storage Access Method (VSAM) eliminates the performance problem while retaining the other desired qualities.

B.6   VIRTUAL STORAGE ACCESS METHOD

IBM's Virtual Storage Access Method (VSAM) was introduced in 1972 as a re-placement for its Indexed Sequential Access Method (ISAM). Whereas ISAM did not meet the ANSI COBOL-74 standards, VSAM did. ISAM has virtually disappeared, since IBM no longer supports it.

VSAM uses a structure called a *B-tree*. First developed by Bayer and McCreight in 1972, the structure has a very attractive property: The number of disk accesses to find a record grows slowly as new records are added. In many cases, the number does not change at all. This is important because as records are added, the processing efficiency will not decline as with ISAM but will remain constant.

VSAM, like ISAM, uses indexes to enable both random and sequential ac-cessing of records. Through job control language (JCL) statements invoked when the VSAM file is first created, the programmer specifies:

- The size of control intervals
- The location and size of each record's key field
- The record minimum and maximum lengths
- Free-space allocation

Records are stored in **control intervals (CI's)** that may or may not correspond to a track's size. They store the actual records as well as some control information: namely the record size of each record in the CI and the location of free space. **Free space** refers to unused areas that can be used as additions are made to the file.

Control intervals are grouped into units called **control areas,** which are similar in concept to cylinders. Just as tracks make up cylinders, control intervals are aggregated to comprise control areas. Figure B.17 shows both concepts as they apply to our familiar VENDOR file.

The shaded area in each CI in Figure B.17 is used for the control interval overhead mentioned earlier. Control interval 1 contains three vendors: 100, 103, and 105. This is the same number of records that we assumed fit on track 1 of cylinder 7 in Figure B.8 and shows the similarity of control intervals to tracks. This assumption, however, is not always valid. We made them the same only so that you could see the similarity between control intervals and tracks. Control intervals not only are similar to tracks; they may even be called **logical tracks.** Similarly, because control intervals make up control areas, we sometimes refer to control areas as **logical cylinders.**

FIGURE B.17   **The VENDOR File Using VSAM's Key-Sequenced Data Set (KSDS) Organization**

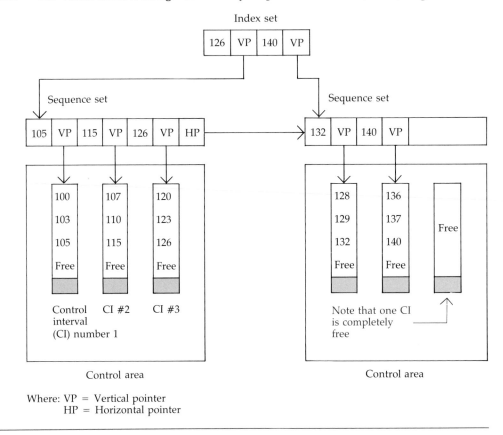

As records are stored, they are assigned a **relative byte address (RBA),** the displacement of the first byte in the record from the beginning of the file. For instance, if each VENDOR record is 100 bytes long, the first record will begin at RBA 0 and end at 99; the second record therefore will begin at RBA 100; and so on.

Each record must have a unique primary key and can also have a secondary key, called an **alternate key.** The VENDOR file would probably use VENDOR-CODE as the primary key and possibly VENDOR-NAME as its secondary key. Because several vendors could have the same name, the field is not unique—one of the characteristics of secondary keys. To process duplicates, there is a READ NEXT statement that sequentially processes records having similar secondary key values.

Adding records to a VSAM file is easily done because of **distributed free space. Distributed free space** means that there is room left within each CI to add new records, a concept similar to the bucket technique we saw in the section on reducing collisions. In addition, complete CIs within a control area are left vacant when the file is initially loaded. Again refer to Figure B.17. Notice that each control interval has some free space and that the second control area has one control interval that is completely free.

VSAM Organizations

There are three ways to organize VSAM records:

- Key-sequenced data sets (KSDSs)
- Entry-sequenced data sets (ESDSs)
- Relative record data sets (RRDSs)

A **key-sequenced data set (KSDS)** permits both sequential and random access and is the only one discussed here in detail. As its name implies, a KSDS organizes a data set (file) into key sequence just as ISAM does. By using its accompanying indexes, both sequential and random accessing of the records are possible. An **entry-sequenced data set (ESDS)** stores records in chronological order and does not use indexes. A **relative record data set (RRDS)** is like random access in that each record has an RRN that is used to store and locate records in the VSAM data set.

Key-Sequenced Data Sets. To permit both direct and sequential processing, VSAM uses a hierarchical collection of indexes grouped into two categories: a **sequence set** and an **index set.** While there may be several indexes making up the index set, there is only one index in the sequence set.

The Sequence Set. There is one **sequence set** record per control area. This index is used to sequentially process the file. We will demonstrate this later. In Figure B.17, there are two control areas and therefore two sequence set records, each containing a series of pairs of data. The first element is used to store the highest-valued key in a control interval. The second element stores a **vertical pointer (VP)** to the actual control interval. Note the similarity to ISAM's track index. At the end of each sequence set record is a **horizontal pointer (HP)** that points to the next sequence set record. Remember, a vertical pointer points to data, but a horizontal one points to the next sequence record. In Figure B.17, we illustrated these pointers as arrows.

In Figure B.17, the first sequence set record has three pairs of entries, one for each control interval. The first pair illustrates the fact that the highest-valued VENDOR-CODE in CI number 1 of the first control interval is 105. The next (value, pointer) pair shows that the second CI's highest VENDOR-CODE is 115. The horizontal pointer at the end of the first sequence set points to the next sequence set record number.

The Index Set. The **index set** is used to randomly access records. While only one index in the set has been shown in Figure B.17, there can be several, depending on the size of the actual data set.

As usual, each index record has two parts: a key and a vertical pointer. The key portion is the primary key value for the last record of the sequence set entry pointed to by the vertical pointer. Notice we said "last record in the sequence set."

In Figure B.17, the highest-valued vendor in the first sequence set record is 126, while that in the second is 140. These two numbers are the values of the key entries in the index set.

Figure B.18 is a more accurate example of a KSDS, because it shows actual

FIGURE B.18   A KSDS with Relative Byte Addresses

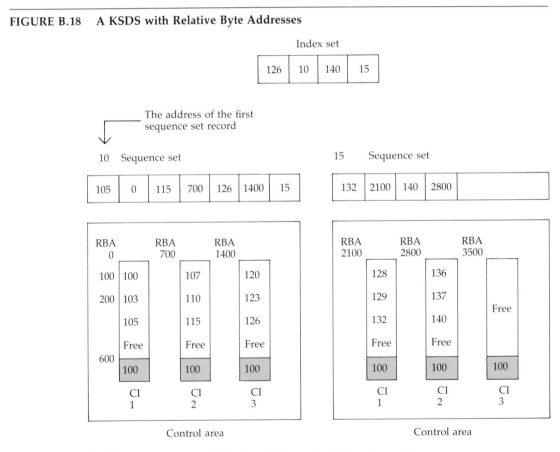

The file represents a more actual portrayal of the vendor file from Figure B.17.

RBAs and pointers. The vertical pointers in the index set and the horizontal pointers in the sequence set, which were indicated by arrows in Figure B.17, have now been replaced with record numbers. The vertical pointers appearing in the sequence set are now RBAs.

The Data Area. In Figure B.18, each logical vendor record is 100 bytes long (we are assuming a blocking factor of 1). The first control interval begins at RBA 0 and goes through RBA 699. Three 100-byte records are stored there, representing vendors 100, 103, and 105. The control information at the end of the CI (the number 100) means that each record is 100 bytes long. If variable-length records consisting of record lengths 100, 250, and 75 had been stored, the control information would consist of those three integers. It is this overhead that the shading in Figures B.17 and B.18 represents.

Notice that 300 bytes of each CI are unused, as are some complete control intervals. These areas will be used to add new vendors and represent the biggest organization change from ISAM.

Accessing a VSAM KSDS: A Theoretical Approach

First, we will look at direct retrieval.

Direct Access. To directly retrieve vendor 129, VSAM would perform the following steps:

1. Search the index set for the first key value greater than or equal to the desired key. The key value meeting this criterion is 140. The associated vertical pointer value is 15. The number 15 is the record number of the correct sequence set entry.

2. Search the sequence set record found at location 15 until a greater-than or equal key value is found. The first key value at record 15 is 132. This value is greater than 129, so the key-matching process stops. The vertical pointer associated with key value 132 indicates that the associated CI begins at RBA 2100. Search the CI beginning at RBA 2100 until a greater-than or equal-to-match is determined. The search ends at RBA 2200.

Sequential Access. Sequential retrieval is performed by using only the sequence set. The sequence set indicates that we should begin sequentially reading the file at the CI beginning at RBA 0. After reading all records found in that CI, vendors 100, 103, and 105, we proceed to the CIs beginning at RBA 700, then 1400. Next, we go to the sequence record entry specified by the horizontal pointer: record 15. This record indicates that the next vendor in key sequence begins at the CI at RBA 2100, followed by those in the CI that starts at RBA 2800.

FIGURE B.19   The Steps Necessary to Add Two New Vendors to the VSAM Data Set in Figure B.18

1. Add vendor number 130

Store in the CI at RBA 2100
The CI now looks like this:

| 128 |
| 129 |
| 130 |
| 132 |

Because the last record's key value hasn't
changed, no update to the indexes is necessary

2. Add vendor number 135

Also stored in CI at RBA 2100
The new CI:

| 128 |
| 129 |
| 130 |
| 132 |
| 135 |

Because the highest-key value is 135, update the indexes.

The new sequence set record associated with
the second CA will look like this:

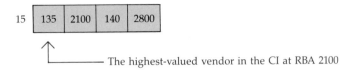

15 | 135 | 2100 | 140 | 2800

⬆
└────── The highest-valued vendor in the CI at RBA 2100

Adding Records to a KSDS

When records are added to a VSAM data set, the records in the appropriate CI are moved to make room for them. If there is insufficient room in the CI, the CI is *split*, with about half the original CI's records being left in the CI and the second half moved to one of the unused intervals. Should there not be enough room in the control area to accommodate the new interval, the area is split into two, with the new half being moved to a new, and previously unused, control

FIGURE B.20   **The VSAM File Data Set after Adding Vendors: 130, 133, and 135**

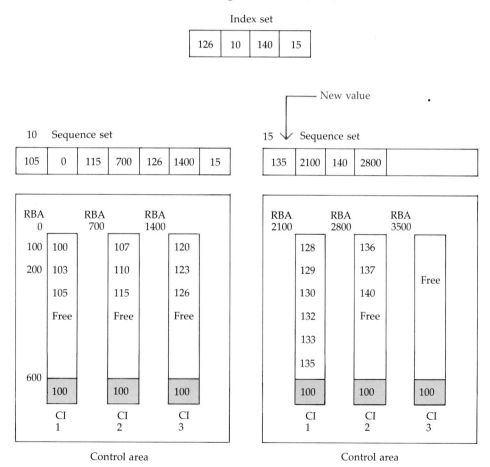

The first control interval in Control area 2 is now full. Also, the second sequence set entry has been updated, so that the key value associated with RBA 2100 is now 135.

area. The latter process is known as a **control area split.** As records are added to a CI, it may become necessary to change one or more of the indexes.

Assume there is room for six VENDOR records in each CI in Figure B.18. If we add vendor 130, the record should go into the CI beginning at RBA 2100. Vendor 132 must be moved. Since the last vendor record key in the CI is still 132, no index adjustment is necessary. If we next insert vendor 135, it will be stored at the end of the CI beginning at RBA 2100, and the key value for the second sequence set index record will change from 132 to 135, the new highest-valued key in the CI at RBA 2100. There are now five records in the CI. All of these steps and changes are summarized in Figure B.19.

FIGURE B.21.   The KSDS after Adding Vendor 134, Which Causes an Interval to Split

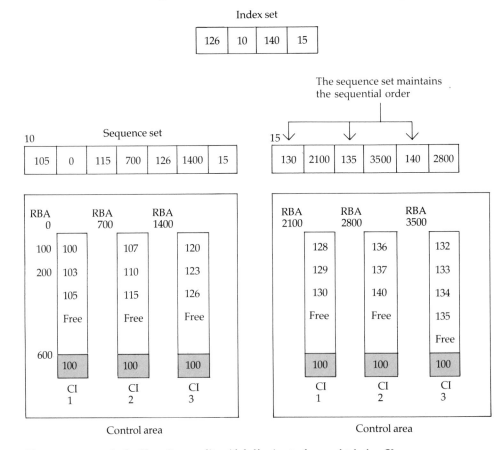

There was no room in the CI, so it was split, with half going to the completely free CI.

Now we add vendor 133. Figure B.20 shows the result. Notice the CI is filled; there is no more room for additions.

Finally, we add vendor 134. The access method finds that there is no more room in the CI. Figure B.21 shows what happens. Vendors 128, 129, and 130 are left in the original CI, but vendors 132, 133, 134, and 135 are moved to the free CI beginning at RBA 3500, a previously unused CI. Despite the fact that the CIs are no longer physically in key sequence order, changing the sequence set values can give us the proper **logical sequential sequence.**

While the records within each CI are physically in sequential order, the same is not true across CIs. For example, the vendors in the third CI of control area 2 logically belong before those of the second. However, by following the sequence set entries, the proper logical sequencing can be obtained. Let's see how.

We begin at RBA 2100 and read records with keys 128 through 130. The next sequence set entry has a vertical pointer value of 3500, so VSAM will instruct the controller to go to that location next. Records with vendor keys 132 through 135 will therefore be transferred. The last pointer leads the controller to a lower RBA value, 2800. At the CI beginning there, the records for vendors 138 through 140 are found. The sequential ordering is thus preserved.

Advantages of VSAM

There are four major advantages of using VSAM. First, due to the splitting technique, files can expand in size without creating performance problems. Second, VSAM files can be moved from one DASD type to another without altering the file, a concept called *device independence*. This is so because relative bytes will be the same regardless of the device used. Third, VSAM offer· benefits of both sequential and random processing without the corres· problems. Finally, it allows secondary key processing.

B.7   SUMMARY

Choosing the correct file organization can have a large impact on our ability to subsequently retrieve records. There are five file organizations to choose among, of which we discussed four. Sequential organization should be used sparingly for batch systems, because it limits us to sequential access. Indexed organization is no longer supported, so we needn't consider it anymore. Direct organization offers the best performance but, unless we can take advantage of direct addressing, presents almost insurmountable problems with synonyms. IBM's VSAM seems to offer a satisfactory compromise and is in fact the most widely used file organization in use today.

Accessing records can be done sequentially or directly (or randomly). We use sequential access when we need to process a high percentage of the records in a file. We use random retrieval when very fast access is necessary for any record regardless of which record was just processed.

REVIEW QUESTIONS

1. Define *response time*.
2. Define *packing factor*.
3. Define *percentage of activity*.
4. Distinguish between file organization and access.
5. What is direct access?
6. Contrast direct access with sequential access. What are the merits and disadvantages of each? When should we use them?
7. What is the difference between physical and logical sequential processing?
8. List the five file organizations.
9. What are the advantages of ISAM over sequential organization?
10. What are the potential problems in using ISAM?
11. Explain how ISAM determines whether to put a new record in the prime area, the cylinder overflow area, or the independent overflow area.
12. Why can't ISAM ever put a new record into the prime data area without causing another record to be bumped?
13. Describe the contents of the key area and data area for the cylinder index entries.
14. Records that are at their expected location are said to be where?
15. Explain the difference between direct and hashed addressing.
16. Why wouldn't an employee's social security number be a good choice for a direct addressing key?
17. Describe three objectives of a hashing routine.
18. Explain the difficulty in implementing a synonym-handling routine using the progressive overflow method.
19. What are the three possible VSAM organizations? How do they differ?
20. Explain how VSAM accesses a record randomly.

PROBLEMS

1. A file has been allocated room for 20,000 records. At the present time, only 2,000 records are stored in the file. What is its packing factor?
2. On a typical updating run, the file in Problem 1 has 10 adds, 5 deletes, and 20 updates. What is its typical percentage of activity? Its volatility?
3. Using arrows for pointers, show how the following file can be logically accessed in key sequence:

4. Add vendor numbers 121 and 108 to Figure B.8. Show the new track index, the resulting prime data area, and the cylinder overflow area.

5. Add vendors 124 and 127 to Figure B.8. Show the new cylinder index entries, the track index entries (normal and overflow), the prime data area, and the cylinder overflow areas.

6. Using the same hashing routine as that shown in Figure B.15, what addresses would the following records have: 7, 107, 207, 100, and 17? Which would result in collisions either with records already stored in Figure 15(c) or with the new records?

7. Show where the new records would go on Figure 15(c). Draw all necessary pointers.

8. We need to store 8,000 450-byte vendor records on a 3350. The records have four byte keys, and the addresses are to be converted to relative track plus record disk addresses. Assuming an 80 percent packing factor and the following prime numbers— 29, 307, 311, 1199, 7999, 8001, 9973, and 10001—give the disk address for vendors with the following keys:

   a. 368041.

   b. 853351.

9. Describe the sequence of events needed to randomly retrieve vendor 126 in Figure B.18.

10. Add vendors 142, 145, 147, and 149 to Figure B.20. Redraw the data set. You will need a new control area. Assume that when an area is split, one CI is left blank in the original one.

ANNOTATED BIBLIOGRAPHY

ACM. *ACM Computing Surveys*. Association for Computing Machinery 8, no. 1, March 1976. This 150-page document serves as an excellent introduction to the network and hierarchical models. Because of it age, its relevance to the relational model is somewhat limited, but it has many theoretical discussions about different languages that were being proposed at that time.

AGELHOF, R. *A Primer on SQL*. Homewood, Ill., Times Mirror/Mosby, 1988. An excellent tutorial on how to use SQL. Examples are solved using the ORACLE implementation.

ANSI X3H2. *Proposed American National Standard for a Data Definition Language for Network Structured Databases*. American National Standards Institute, 1981.

APPLETON, D. "Business Rules: The Missing Link." *Datamation,* October 15, 1984. Focuses on the importance of formulating business rules and the roles they play in data modeling.

APPLETON, D. "Rule-Based Data Resource Management." *Datamation* 32, no. 9, May 1, 1986. Discusses the concept of how to develop the organization's rules that a database must support.

ATRE, S. *Data Base: Structured Techniques for Design, Performance, and Management*. New York, Wiley-Interscience, 1980.

BABCOCK, C. "4GL-DB2 Link Shaky." *Computerworld,* April 6, 1987.

BABCOCK, C. "ANSI's SQL Standard Differs from IBM's, Other Versions." *Computerworld,* January 19, 1987.

BABCOCK, C. "Referential Integrity Eludes DB2." *Computerworld,* February 2, 1987.

BOHL, M. *Introduction to IBM Direct Access Storage Devices*. Chicago, Science Research Associates, 1981.

BRADLEY, J. *Introduction to Data Base Management in Business*. New York, Holt, Rinehart & Winston, 1987. A technical database treatment, told mainly from the IBM mainframe perspective.

BROWN, R. "Data Integrity and SQL." *Database Programming & Design* 1, no. 3, March 1988. Discusses how to use SQL to enforce referential integrity constraints when the SQL implementation does not do so automatically.

BROWNING, D., and H. BLASDEL. "Managing Databases, Mainframe Style." *PC Tech Journal* 5, no. 12, December 1987. Discusses the implementation of ORACLE on the PC.

CARDENAS, A. F. *Data Base Management Systems*. Boston, Mass., Allyn & Bacon, 1979.

CARLYLE, R. E. "DB2: Dressed for Success." *Datamation,* March 1, 1987. Describes the overwhelming success of DB2 in the marketplace and how it turned around IBM's declining DBMS market share.

CERI, S., and G. PELAGATTI. *Distributed Databases Principals and Systems*. New York, McGraw-Hill, 1984.

CHAMBERLIN, D. D., et al. "SEQUEL 2: A Unified Approach to Data Definition, Manipulation and Control." *IBM Journal of Research and Development* 20, no. 6, November 1976.

CHEN, P. "The Entity-Relationship Model: Toward a Unified View of Data." *ACM Transactions on Database Systems* 1, no. 1, March 1976.

CHEN, P. *Entity-Relationship Approach to Information Modeling*. E-R Institute, 1981.

CODASYL *Data Base Task Group Report, 1971*. Association for Computing Machinery, 1975.

CODASYL. Data Description Language Committee. *DDL Journal of Development*, 1978.

CODASYL. Data Description Language Committee. *DDL Journal of Development*, 1981.

CODASYL COBOL Committee. *COBOL Journal of Development*, 1978.

CODD, E. F. "A Relational Model of Data for Large Shared Databanks." *Communications of the ACM* 13, no. 6, June 1970. The genesis of the relational approach.

CODD, E. F. "Extending the Relational Model to Capture More Meaning." *ACM Transactions on Database Systems* 4, no. 4, December 1979.

CODD, E. F. "Fatal Flaws in SQL, Part 1." *Datamation* 34, no. 16, August 15, 1988. Dr. Codd writes about imperfections in IBM's RDBMS products.

CODD, E. F. "Is Your DBMS Really Relational?" *Computerworld,* October 14, 1985. A classic article spelling out 12 rules with which a DBMS should comply in order to be classified as relational.

CULLINET SOFTWARE CORPORATION. *IDMS-DB/DC Programmer's Guide.* Westwood, Mass., Cullinet, 1986.

CULLINET SOFTWARE CORPORATION. *IDMS-DB/DC DML Reference—COBOL.* Westwood, Mass., Cullinet, 1985.

DATE, C. J. *A Guide to DB2.* Reading, Mass., Addison-Wesley, 1985. Although the embedded examples use PL/1, the book is a complete treatment of IBM's DB2 package and a worthy possession for any IS professional.

DATE, C. J. *An Introduction to Database Systems, Volume 1,* 4th ed. Reading, Mass., Addison-Wesley, 1986.

DATE, C. J. *Relational Database Selected Writings.* Reading, Mass., Addison-Wesley, 1986.

DATE, C. J. "Where SQL Falls Short." *Datamation,* May 1, 1987. Describes the faults with the SQL language regardless of vendor.

EPSTEIN, R. "Why Database Machines?" *Datamation,* July 1983. One of Britton-Lee's designers discusses what database machines are and how they function.

FAGIN, R. "Multivalued Dependencies and a New Normal Form for Relational Databases." *Transactions on Database Systems* 21, no. 3, September 1977.

FAGIN, R. "A Normal Form that Is Based on Domains and Keys." *Transactions on Database Systems* 6, no. 3, September 1981.

FINKLESTEIN, R. "Judge SQL via Standards." *Computerworld,* April 20, 1987. Discusses DB2 and ANSI SQL differences.

FINKLESTEIN, R. "Lingua Franca for Databases." *PC Tech Journal* 5, no. 12, December 1987. A general introduction to SQL.

FINKLESTEIN, R., and F. PASCAL. "SQL Database Management Systems." *BYTE* 13, no. 1, January 1988.

FRANKLIN, C. "SQL-Based Database Managers." *BYTE* 13, no. 1, January 1988. A brief review of users' comments about microcomputer versions of INFORMIX-SQL, ORACLE, and INGRES.

GARDE, S. H. "The Enterprise and Information Model." *Database Programming & Design* 1, no. 1, January 1988.

GORDON, J. "Save Time and Debug on a PC." *Database Programming and Design* 1, no. 2, February 1988. A description of the PC version of ORACLE and how organizations can save time by using it to develop mainframe DB2 applications.

HAWRYSZKIEWYCZ, I. T. *Database Analysis and Design.* Chicago, Science Research Associates, 1984.

HORWITT, E., and C. BABCOCK. "Data Base Makers Rush to Distribute." *Computerworld* 21, no. 9, March 1987.

HORWITT, E. "Redefining the Information Center." *Business Computer Systems,* September 1985.

HOWE, D. R. *Data Analysis for Data Base Design.* London, England, Edward Arnold, 1983.

IBM CORPORATION. *Business Systems Planning, Information Systems Planning Guide,* 2d ed. IBM Corporation, 1978.

IBM CORPORATION. *Data Language/I Disk Operating System/Virtual Storage General Information.* IBM Document GH20–1246–9, 1983.

IBM CORPORATION. *DB2, QMF and DXT Presentation Guide.* IBM Document GG24–1586–00, 1983.

IBM CORPORATION. *DB2 Interactive (DB2I) Demonstration Guide*. IBM Document GG24–1587–00, 1983.

IBM CORPORATION. *IBM Database 2 Advanced Application Programming Guide*. IBM Document SC26–4292–0, 1983. An excellent reference for dynamic SQL.

IBM CORPORATION. *IBM Database 2 Application Programming Guide*. IBM Document SC26–4293–0, 1983. A good reference for embedded SQL in COBOL applications.

IBM CORPORATION. *IBM Database 2 Concepts and Facilities Guide*. IBM Document GG24–1582–00, 1983.

IBM CORPORATION. *IBM Database 2 Relational Concepts*. IBM Document GG24–1581, 1983.

IBM CORPORATION. *IBM Database 2 SQL Usage Guide*. IBM Document GG24–1583–00, 1983.

IBM CORPORATION. *IBM Database 2 V1 R2 Release Guide*. IBM Document GG24–1583, 1983.

IBM CORPORATION. *IMS/VS Version 1 Application Programming*. IBM Document SH20–9026–9, 1984.

IBM CORPORATION. *IMS/VS Version 1 Data Base Administration Guide*. IBM Document SH20–9025–9, 1984.

IBM CORPORATION. *IMS/VS Version 1 Fast Path Feature General Information Manual*. IBM Document GH20–9069–2, 1978.

IBM CORPORATION. *IMS/VS Version 1 General Information Manual*. IBM Document GH20–1260–12, 1984.

IBM CORPORATION. *IMS/VS Version 1 Master Index and Glossary*. IBM Document SH20–9085–5, 1984.

IBM CORPORATION. *IMS/VS Version 1 System Administration Guide*. IBM Document SH20–9178–2, 1984.

IBM CORPORATION. *IMS/VS Version 1 Utilities Reference Manual*. IBM Document SH20–9029–9, 1986.

IBM CORPORATION. *Information Management System/Virtual Storage/Multiple Virtual Storage Performance and Tuning Guide*. IBM Document G320–6004–03, 1986.

IBM CORPORATION. *Query Management Facility: Reference*. IBM Document SC26–4344–0.

IBM CORPORATION. *SQL/Data System for VM/SP*. IBM Document G320–0094–0.

IBM CORPORATION. *SQL/Data System Release 2 Guide*. IBM Document GH24–5042–0, 1983.

IBM CORPORATION. *SQL/DS Release 3 Guide*. IBM Document GG24–1689–0, 1985.

IBM CORPORATION. *Systems Application Architecture: Common Programming Interface Database Reference*. IBM Document SC26–4348–0, 1987.

IMSVS86 DB/DC for the PC. Stingray Software Co. The manual for the microcomputer version of IMS.

JOHNSON, J. "Enterprise Analysis." *Datamation*, December 15, 1984.

KAPP, D., and J. F. LEBEN. *IMS Programming Techniques: A Guide to Using DL/I*. New York, Van Nostrand Reinhold, 1978. A good introduction to IMS; not as detailed or complete as the Lee text.

KERR, J. "Corporate Data Models Flourish from the Bottom Up." *Computerworld*, May 11, 1987. Discusses the benefits of developing a complete data model for the organization using a bottom-up (versus a top-down) approach.

KROENKE, D. M., and K. DOLAN. *Database Processing Fundamentals, Design, Implementation*. Chicago, Science Research Associates, 1988.

LEAVITT, D. "Fourth-Generation Programming: The End-User Environment." *Software News*, April 1985.

LEE, D. *IMS/VS DL/I Programming with COBOL Examples*. New York, CCD Online Systems, 1985.

LOOMIS, M. E. S. *The Database Book*. New York, Macmillan, 1987. A good book for implementing the conceptual and logical databases and how to map one to the other.

MARTIN, J. *Fourth-Generation Languages, Volume I: Principles*. Englewood Cliffs, N.J., Prentice-Hall, 1985.

MARTIN, J. *Fourth-Generation Languages, Volume II: Representative 4GLs*. Englewood Cliffs, N.J., Prentice-Hall, 1986.

MARTIN, J. "Supra Gets High Relational Grades." *Computerworld*, May 11, 1987. Another discussion about Supra's RDBMS qualities and its data integrity features.

MARTIN, J. *Managing the Database Environment.* Englewood Cliffs, N.J., Prentice-Hall, 1983.

MCFADDEN, F. R., and J. A. HOFFER. *Data Base Management.* Benjamin Cummings, 1988.

PASCAL, F. "Relational Power, PC Ease." *PC Tech Journal* 5, no. 12, December 1987. A discussion of the PC version of INGRES.

PERCY, T. "The Importance of Good Relations." *Datamation* 30, no. 21, December 15, 1984. The benefits of modeling data relationships are discussed, as well as the tools that modelers use.

PETRELEY, N., R. KHALOGHLI, and D. CHALMERS. "Gang of 4 Multiuser Databases." *Infoworld* 11, no. 15, April 10, 1989. A review of Advanced Revelation, INFORMIX SQL, dBASE IV, and Paradox 3. All of these are multiuser, microcomputer-based database managers. The review contains some useful benchmarks.

PORTER, K. "The PC Holds Its Own." *Database Programming & Design* 1, no. 8, August 1988. A good article extolling the virtues of using a PC to develop mainframe applications on a PC.

PUGLIA, V. "Ingres: Too Much Power for One PC?" *PC Week*, July 28, 1987.

RAPAPORT, M. "Interview with E. F. Codd." *Database Programing & Design* 1, no. 2, February 1988. A general critique of commercial implementations of Codd's relational model.

ROWE, L. A. "Tools for Developing OLTP Applications." *Datamation*, August 1, 1985.

SEIGLER, L. "Relating to Database Machines." *Datamation* 32, no. 7, April 1, 1986.

STONEBRAKER, M. R., et al. "The Design and Implementation of INGRES." *Transactions on Database Systems* 1, no. 3, September 1976.

"Supra Declared Most Relational." *Software News*, February 1987. A review of statements made by E. F. Codd proclaiming Cincom's product as the one that comes closest to his definition of a relational DBMS.

SWEET, F. "What, If Anything, is a Relational Database?" *Datamation* 30, no. 11, July 15, 1984.

TOPPER, A. "The PC/IDMS Alliance." *PC Tech Journal* 6, no. 3, March 1988. Discusses TAB, a PC-based version of IDMS.

VENKATAKRISHNAN, V. "IMS: Past, Present, Future." *Datamation* 29, no. 9, September 1983.

ZLOOF, M. M. "Query By Example." *Proceedings of the National Computer Conference, AFIPS* 44, May 1975.

GLOSSARY

ABEND Abnormal ending. What occurs when a program ends in other than the expected manner; usually caused by a program or data error.

Abort To end a program due to an error, or to remove the set of updates related to a transaction.

Anomaly An undesirable update characteristic, due to a faulty database design.

Arity *See* **Degree.**

Association Entity/Record Type The entity that results from the decomposing of a complex network data structure. It relates the original entity occurrences to each other.

Atomic Attribute A single characteristic of an entity.

Attribute A characteristic of an entity.

Bachman Diagram *See* **Data Structure Diagram.**

Back-End Computer *See* **Database Computer.**

Backup A complete copy of a database.

Base Table A table whose values are stored on a disk drive.

Branch The 1:M relationship between two nodes in a hierarchical data structure.

Candidate Key A set of attributes that could be chosen as a primary key.

Cardinality The nature of a relationship between entities. It can be one-to-one, one-to-many, or many-to-many. In a table, it refers to the number of rows.

Cartesian Product *See* **Product.**

Chain *See* **List.**

Checkpoint A time at which the results of all transactions are physically written to the database.

Child A hierarchical term meaning that the node is the direct descendent of another; the destination node in a 1:M relationship.

Clustering A way to optimize database performance by placing records that are frequently accessed together near each other on the disk.

CODASYL Committee on Data Systems Languages. The group that developed COBOL and the CODASYL implementation of the network model.

Commit To make the results of all transactions permanent. *See* **Checkpoint.**

Complex Network A data structure that contains at least one many-to-many relationship.

Composite Attribute A characteristic of an entity that consists of two or more attributes, and which is often given a single name. For example, NAME might consist of LAST__NAME + FIRST__NAME.

Conceptual Database The organizational view of the entities and their relationships, expressed graphically using a DSD or E-R diagram.

Concurrent Processing The result of having two or more users concurrently updating the same record. The possibility of a lost update exists due to one user overwriting a record previously retrieved, changed, and written back by the other user.

Connection Data Item *See* **Foreign Key.**

Constraint A rule whose validity can be determined.

Currency Indicator In a CODASYL DBMS, the disk address of the most recently accessed record. There is a current of run-unit, as well as one for each record and set type.

Cursor A mechanism used by third-generation programs to sequentially process a set of records returned via a SQL statement.

Database A collection of related records stored with a minimum of redundancy.

Database Administrator The person that is responsible for managing the organization's data.

Database Computer A computer that acts as a slave to the main computer, executing database DML commands.

Data Dictionary A catalog or repository of data about records, fields, and relationships. It can be active (required by the DBMS) or passive (used only by humans).

Data Model A data structure plus a set of tools and techniques for operating on the data. There are three dominant models: the relational, the hierarchical, and the network.

Data Structure Diagram A graphical tool for depicting entities and their relationships. Used especially by advocates of the network model.

DASD Direct Access Storage Device. An I/O device that enables us to retrieve a record directly. Usually used as a synonym for a disk drive.

DB2 IBM's relational DBMS for its MVS mainframe users.

DBKEY Database key. The value of a currency indicator in the CODASYL network model; usually a Relative Record Number (RRN).

DBMS Database Management System. A collection of programs that is used to define records, fields, and their relationships, and that can be called by a host program to update data in a database.

DBTG Database Task Group. A committee of CODASYL that released the first network specification in April 1971.

DDBMS Distributed Database Management System. A DBMS that can manage a database that is stored on multiple computers at multiple sites.

DDL Data Description Language. The portion of DBMS that defines entities, fields, and, for the network and hierarchical models, relationships between entities.

Deadlock A situation where the computer can freeze, or lock up, due to two or more users attempting to lock the same resources.

Deadly Embrace *See* **Deadlock.**

Degree The number of columns (attributes) in a table (relation).

Destination The entity on the many side in a 1:M relationship.

Determinant One or more attributes, the values of which determine the value of another attribute. Social security number is a determinant of an employee's name.

Difference A relational operator that compares two union-compatible tables. The result is the set of rows that are in the first table but not the second.

Distributed Database A database where parts of it are stored on different computers at different sites.

Distributed Database Management System *See* **DDBMS.**

DL/I Data Language/I The DML portion of IBM's hierarchical DBMS, IMS.

DMCL Device Media Control Language. The portion of a CODASYL DBMS that is used to define the physical characteristics of the database.

DML Data Manipulation Language. The portion of a DBMS used by a host program to update data in the database.

Domain The set of allowable attribute values.

Download To copy data from one computer (usually a mainframe) to another (usually a personal computer).

DSD *See* **Structure Diagram.**

Entity A thing, event, or person in the organization's environment about which someone wants to collect data.

Entity Integrity A rule that asserts that no part of a primary key can be null.

E-R Diagram Entity-relationship diagram. A graphical technique for representing conceptual, logical, and external databases. It focuses on relationships and requires that they be given names.

Equijoin A join based on an equality operator, where both joining columns are carried in the resulting table.

External Database *See* **View.**

Foreign Key A secondary key, the values of which must be null or must match the primary key value for some occurrence of the file to which it refers.

Form A VDT screen used for displaying and inputting data.

Functional Dependency Attribute B is functionally dependent on attribute A if the same value of attribute B is always associated with the same value for attribute A.

Granularity The level of locking. Locking at the database level is coarse, while field locking is fine.

Hierarchical Data Model A model where all relationships are trees, or hierarchies.

Hierarchical Order A sequential-like representation of a tree structure. It is called a preorder traversal or left-list layout.

Hierarchical Sequence The sequence of node occurrences that results from the structure's hierarchical order plus the key sequence field values.

Host Program *See* **Run-Unit.**

IDMS/R Cullinet's network and relational DBMS.

Input *See* **Download.**

IMS Information Management System. IBM's hierarchical DBMS.

Information-Bearing Set In a CODASYL DBMS, where foreign keys are not carried in the member records. Relationships are represented only by pointers.

Interleaved Updating A condition that can occur when two or more users concurrently attempt to update the same record. The user saving last will overwrite the record saved by the other users.

Intersection A relational operator that operates on two union-compatible tables. The result is a third table that has the rows that are in common between the two tables.

Intersection Entity/Record Type *See* **Association Entity.**

I/O Input/output. The process of reading or writing to a secondary storage device.

Join A relational operator that matches rows of tables based on a joining condition involving one or more common columns.

Journal File *See* **Log File.**

Key Sequence Field A hierarchical term for a segment data item that is used to sequence child occurrences within a parent.

LAN Local area network. A collection of connected computers, usually personal computers, in a small geographic area, oftentimes within a single department or work group.

List A data structure where records are related to each other in a single direction using pointers.

Log File A file that contains before-images and after-images of updated database records, and optionally, transactions. It is used for recovery of databases.

Logical Access Map (LAM) A graphical representation that shows the path through a DSD necessary to respond to a given query.

Logical Data Independence The ability to add or delete fields, or rearrange the sequence of fields, without affecting existing programs.

Logical Database The result of adapting the conceptual database to the specific requirements of one of the three data models. Also an IMS user view.

Logical Unit of Work *See* **Transaction.**

Lock A restriction of access to a computer resource to one user at a time. Typically used by a DBMS to prevent concurrent updating problems.

Member In a CODASYL DBMS, the record that is the destination (the many side) of a one-to-many relationship.

Meta-data *See* **Data Dictionary.**

Multivalued Dependency Attribute A multidetermines attribute B if the same value of attribute A is always associated with the same set of values for attribute B. If A also multidetermines attribute C but there is no relationship between B and C, we have an independent multivalued dependency, and anomalies can occur.

Natural Join A join of two tables such that all duplicate columns are eliminated; that is, the joining column is carried once in the result.

Network A data structure where any entity can be the destination of an unlimited number of 1:M relationships.

Network Data Model A data model that supports the network data structure. The CODASYL implementation is the most popular one.

Node A site in a local area network. A record in a tree or hierarchical data structure.

Normal Form The results of applying a set of rules to eliminate anomalies. These normal forms have been defined: first, second, third, Boyce-Codd, fourth, fifth, and domain-key. We didn't discuss fifth normal form because of its complexity.

Normalization The process of organizing attributes in a relation in order to minimize anomalies.

Null An attribute value that means *unknown*. It is different than zero or blank.

Origin The entity on the one side in a 1:M relationship.

Outer Join A join where the result contains all the rows from the first table, even those that don't match the joining condition.

Owner In a CODASYL network, the origin of a 1:M relationship.

Panel *See* **Form.**

Parent In a hierarchical data structure, the origin of a 1:M relationship; the record on the one side.

Partitioning The separation of a table (file) along either its vertical or horizontal dimension. The result is two or more tables (files), often stored at different locations in a distributed database.

Physical Database The database as it is stored on a disk drive. It may be called the internal database.

Pointer A field attached to a record that contains the location of the next related record.

Preorder Traversal *See* **Hierarchical Order.**

Precompiler A program that reads in a source program containing DML calls and substitutes valid source statements, usually CALL statements.

Primary Key A field whose values uniquely differentiate one record from all the others. A field whose value isn't repeated within the file.

Product A relational operator that concatenates each row of table 1 with every row of table 2.

Project A relational operator that vertically parses a table along its column dimension, yielding a table that has all the rows of the original table but only the columns specified.

QBE Query-By-Example. A graphical approach for extracting data from tables, first suggested by Zloof.

Quiet Point *See* **Checkpoint.**

Referential Integrity Enforcement of a foreign key constraint.

Relation A data structure that contains rows and columns, with no repeating columns.

Relationship An association between entities or attributes. There are three kinds of relationships: one-to-one (1:1), one-to-many (1:M), and many-to-many (M:N).

Ring A data structure where the last record in a list points to the first one.

Rollback A database recovery procedure where transactions are removed.

Rollforward A database recovery procedure that reapplies transactions to a backup of the database.

Root The only node in a hierarchical data structure that has no parent.

Run-Unit A program that calls a DBMS.

Secondary Key A field that can have duplicate values, and that can be used as a search path by end users.

Schema The CODASYL term that refers to the organizational view of its data and relationships among the data.

Segment *See* **Node.**

Segment Occurrence A specific instance of a segment.

Select A relational operator that parses a table along its row dimension by specifying search criteria. Also known as restriction or restrict. The SELECT command within SQL parses a table along its column dimension.

Set Occurrence An occurrence of the owner of a set together with its related member records.

Set Type A CODASYL term for a named M relationship between two or more record types.

Simple Network A data structure where at least one record type is the destination of two or more 1:M relationships. In CODASYL terms, a record type is a member of two or more sets.

SQL Structured Query Language. The ANSI standard language for manipulating relational databases.

Subkey One of the components of a composite primary key.

Subschema The CODASYL term for the external

database (user view). It consists of the record types, fields, and sets that an application can access.

Transaction An event within the organization's environment that generates data to be used to update the database.

Tree A data structure where every node except the first one has a maximum of one child. No node is the destination of more than one 1:M relationship.

Tuple A row in a table occurrence.

Two-Phase Commit A two-step process used in a distributed database environment. The slave DBMSs are told to prepare to commit; then, if all slaves respond that they are ready, a master DBMS issues the command to do so.

Two-Phase Lock A process where locks are acquired (grown) for all tables relevant to a transaction. The locked resources are unlocked only when all the tables affected by the transaction have been updated.

User View *See* **View.**

Union A relational operator that combines two union-compatible tables into a third, such that the resulting table has all the columns from table 1 (or table 2) and the rows that were found in table 1 or table 2.

Union-Compatible Two or more tables that have the same degree, and whose respective columns come from the same domain.

Uploading The process of copying data from one computer to another, usually from a personal computer to a mainframe or minicomputer.

Value-Based Set A CODASYL set where foreign key values are carried in the member record.

View The collection of records, fields, and relationships that an application can process.

Virtual Field A field whose values are computed at run-time.

INDEX